Directory of the World's

CAPITAL SHIPS

Directory of the World's
CAPITAL SHIPS

Paul H. Silverstone

LONDON
IAN ALLAN LTD

First published 1984

ISBN 0 7110 1222 9

Published by Ian Allan Ltd, Shepperton, Surrey; and printed by Ian Allan Printing Ltd at their works at Coombelands in Runnymede, England.

It has been a conscious decision to include in this volume photographs of historic interest which might, in other conditions, have been excluded on grounds of quality. It is hoped that the reader will accept the consequent reduction in the production standards of some plates.

Cover:
***New Jersey* — 'Iowa' class battleship as recommissioned in 1982.** *US Navy*

Below:
USS *Dunderberg* — At Brooklyn incomplete c1866. Notice casemate superstructure and ram bow.
J. Fred Rodriguez collection

Contents

Introduction

The spectacle of large and powerful warships at sea creates a thrilling picture. These ships had a mystique about them whether a line of dreadnoughts in World War 1, a fast carrier task force in World War 2 or the small and ugly but deadly monitors of the American Civil War.

These ships are grouped under the loose overall term 'capital ships' to which I have given a wide definition, including not only battleships and battlecruisers, but also all old armoured vessels, monitors, coast defence ships and armoured cruisers, and in addition, aircraft carriers.

It was the conception of this book that one volume was needed to bring together in a concise style basic information about the major fighting ships of the world's navies from the beginning of the age of armour to the present. Although some of this information is not difficult to obtain, it is found in diverse references with differing formats. Other information is to be found, if at all, in obscure places in difficult languages.

Many fine and detailed books have been published on individual ships or classes of ships. It is my intention to give the researcher a single source with which to begin, giving the basic characteristics of each ship, changes which took place during its career and a general description of its career and final disposition. For further and more detailed information on any particular ship the reader is referred to these other works.

Particulars published in different reference works official or otherwise often disagree. Many books included details of contemporary vessels which were incorrect for reasons of security or lack of information; sometimes false details were given out purposely to mislead.

To find much of the information in this book a large number of reference books and private sources was consulted. Principal reference works consulted include:

Aguilera y Elias: *Buques de Guerra Españoles 1885-1971*
Aichelburg: *Die 'Tegetthoff' Klasse* (1979)
Battenberg; *Men-of-War Names* (1897)
Bauer; *Ships of the (US) Navy 1775-1969*
Bennett; *Steam Navy of the United States* (1896)
Breyer; *Battleships and Battlecruisers 1905-1970*
Buxton; *Big Gun Monitors* (1978)
Couhat; *French Warships of World War 1* (1974); *French Warships of World War 2* (1971)
Cracknell; *USS Tennessee (BB-43)* (1972); *US Navy Monitors in the Civil War* (1973)
Destefani; *Manual de Historia Naval Argentina* (1970)
Dousset; *Les Porte-Avions Français* (1978)
Dumas & Guiglini; *Les Cuirassés Français de 23500 Tonnes* (1980)
Fraccaroli; *Italian Warships of World War 1* (1970); *Italian Warships of World War 2* (1968)
Gogg; *Osterreiche Kriegsmarine 1848-1918* (1967)
Greger; *Austro-Hungarian Warships* (1976)
Groner; *Die Deutsche Krieggschiffe* (1966)
Jenkins; *HMS Furious* (1972)
Jentschura; *Warships of the Imperial Japanese Navy 1869-1945* (1977)
King; *Warships & Navies of the World* (1880)
Kronenfels; *Das Schwimmende Flottenmaterial der Seemächte* (1881)
LeMasson; *The French Navy* (1969)
Lautenschlager; *USS Mississippi* (BB 23) (1973)
Lenton; *American Battleships & Carriers* (1968); *British Battleships & Carriers* (1972); *German Surface Vessels* (1966); *Royal Netherlands Navy* (1968)
Lenton & Colledge; *(British) Warships of World War 2* (1973)
Meister; *The Soviet Navy* (1972)
Moiseev; *Spisok Korabley Russkogo Parovogo i Bronenosnogo Flota 1861-1917* (1948)
Northcott; *Renown & Repulse* (1978)
Parkes; *British Battleships* (1966)
Philbin; *SMS Konig* (1973)
Preston; *Battleships of World War 1* (1972)
Raven; *King George V Class Battleships* (1972)
Raven & Roberts; *Queen Elizabeth Class Battleships* (1975)
Reilly & Scheina; *American Battleships 1886-1923* (1981)
Rohwer & Hummelchen; *Chronology of the War at Sea 1939-1945* (1972)
Ruge; *SMS Seydlitz* (1972)
Smith; *British Battle Cruisers* (1972)
Steensen; *Vore Panserskibe 1863-1943* (Danish) (1968)
Terzibaschitsch; *Schlachtschiffe der US Navy im 2.Weltkrieg* (1976); *Flugzeugtrager der US Navy* (1978)
Tomitch; *Warships of the Imperial Russian Navy, vol 1* (1968)
Vichot; *Repertoire des Navires de Guerre Francais* (1967)
Watts; *Japanese Warships of World War 2* (1966)
Watts & Gordon; *The Imperial Japanese Navy* (1971)
Orizzonte Mare; *Navi Italiane nella 2a Guerra Mondiale, 1-3* (1973); *La Navi di Linea Italiana* (1962)
Conway's All the World's Fighting Ships 1860-1905 (1979)
Dictionary of American Naval Fighting Ships, vol 1-8

Annuals
Brassey's Naval Annual
Combat Fleets of the World
Jane's Fighting Ships
Ships & Aircraft of the US Fleet
Ships' Data US Naval Vessels
The Naval Pocket Book

Periodicals
Marine News
The Belgian Shiplover
US Naval Institute Proceedings
Warships
Warship International

Acknowledgements

The author wishes to extend his thanks to the following for their assistance with information and photographs: Richard M. Anderson, Siegfried Breyer, Christian de Saint Hubert, Martin Holbrook, J. J. Colledge, E. Lacroix, Jacques Cornic, L. L. von Munching, Isik Erim, Lt Col K. S. Yamashita USA (ret), Giuliano Franceschini and C. R. Haberlein of the US Naval Historical Centre. Also Mr Phateev, Chief of the Central Navy Museum of the USSR, and the naval attaches in Washington of Norway, Capt Per Haugstad; Denmark, Capt Helge Nielsen; Sweden, Capt Ake Johnson and Brazil, Capt Carlos Oliveira Froes, and Anita Zabotin for help with translations.

Paul H. Silverstone

How to use this book

To reduce unnecessary duplication of material all the entries in this book have been abbreviated to their essentials and each entry presents standard information in a standard form. The book contains details of the capital ships of 22 navies, each national section being divided into two parts: the first lists classes of ships in chronological order, the second lists individual ships in alphabetical order.

Below are reproduced standard entries for both alphabetical and class listings with an explanation of the information they contain.

It should be noted that there were detail variations within the classes. These variations, and any changes made to ships during their lifetime, are indicated with the entry preceded by the ship's name and/or date of change in italics; eg Armament: 12×305mm/45 (*Courbet*: 10) would indicate that *Courbet* had only 10×305mm/45 guns compared to the 12 of the rest of the class.

The reader is referred also to the additional information about shipyards and builders, actions and operations of the US Civil War and of World Wars 1 and 2, and to the list of abbreviations that follows.

Class Details

1. Name of class.
2. Date of programme under which first ship of class was built or date for order of construction of ship.
3. Type of ship.
4. Name(s) of ship(s) in class; those indicated by square brackets were not completed.
5. 'See later photo' refers the reader to a photo of the ship in alphabetical listing.
6. Displacement measured as standard (and fully laden when information available) tonnages:
   Standard = fully manned and stored but without fuel and reserve feed water (defined in the Washington Naval Treaty of 1922).
   Full load = fully manned, stored and with fuel and ammunition.
7. Dimensions are given in feet'inches with metric equivalents in square brackets: length (oa, pp, wl) × beam × mean draught at standard displacement.
   overall (oa) = length between extremities,
   perpendicular (pp) = length between foreside of stem and aftside of rudder post,
   waterline (wl) = length between waterline extremities.
   Other dimensions may be stated in the text.
8. Number of screws.
9. Type of engines/prime mover.
10. Constructor of engines; the term 'builder(s)' indicates that the engines were built by the hull constructors.
11. Number and type of boilers.
12. Horsepower and maximum speed (as designed, at standard displacement and mean draught):
    brake (BHP) = power available at crankshaft,
    indicated (IHP) = power produced by expansion of gases in cylinder of reciprocating steam engines,
    shaft (SHP) = power delivered to propeller shaft.
13. Endurance in nautical miles at constant speed in knots (as designed).
14. Number of guns, calibre (1) of projectile/calibre (2) of barrel, type of weapon.
    calibre (1) = diameter of projectile or barrel,
    calibre (2) = length of barrel in projectile calibres;
    eg, a 305mm/45 gun has a projectile calibre of 305mm, the length of the barrrel is 45 calibres, and so the barrel has a length of (305×45) 13,275mm or 13.275m.
    The calibre is measured in millimetres except for warships of the USA and UK for which it is given in inches.

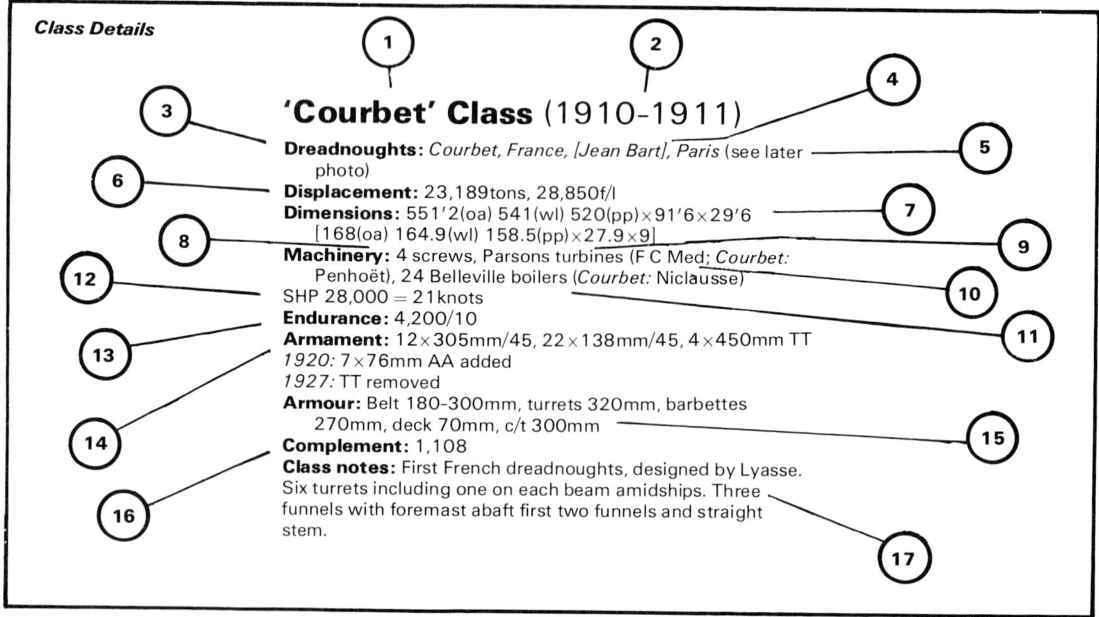

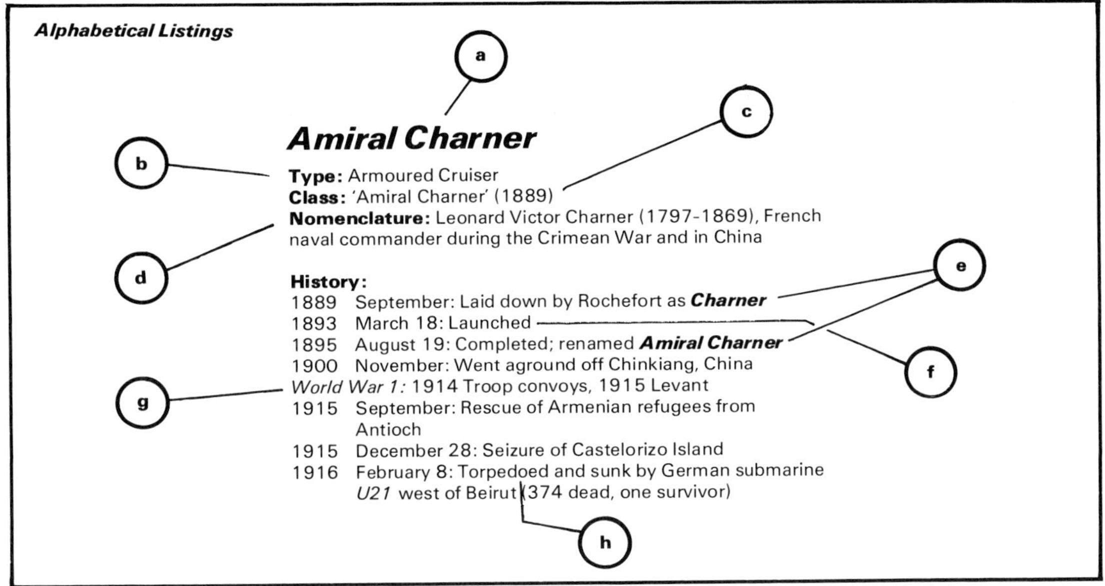

15. Armour is given as a maximum-minimum range or maximum thickness only.
16. Complement: normal peacetime figures are indicated; wartime establishments would vary within the class.
17. Class notes provide additional information on design, performance and alterations in layout of the vessels.

Alphabetical Listings

a. Name of ship.
b. Type of ship.
c. Class of ship (as reference to chronological class section).
d. Nomenclature: meaning or derivation of ship's name.
e. First use of name or renaming of individual ship given in bold italic print.
f. Details of construction, etc.
g. War service given in the form of battle honours and other significant events in a ship's history.
h. Ultimate fate.

Operations of the US Civil War

N Atlantic BS North Atlantic Blockading Squadron, 1863-65 (off mid-Atlantic states)
S Atlantic BS South Atlantic Blockading Squadron, 1863-65 (off Southern Atlantic states)
Charleston Attacks and occupation of Charleston, SC, 1863-64
Fort Fisher Attacks and occupation of Fort Fisher, NC, 1863-64
James River Operations on James River, Va, 1863-65
Mobile Bay Battle of Mobile Bay, August 5 1864
Red River Operations on Red River, Ar, 1864

Operations of World War 1

Adriatic Operations in the Adriatic Sea 1915-18
Baltic German operations in the Baltic Sea against Russia 1917
Coronel Battle of Coronel, November 1 1914
Dardanelles Operations in the Dardanelles and landings at Gallipoli, 1915
Doggerbank Battle of the Doggerbank, January 24 1915
Dover patrol Operations in the English Channel, 1914-18
Falklands Battle of the Falklands, December 8 1914
Goeben operations Search for German battlecruiser *Goeben*, Mediterranean, August 1914
Grand Fleet British Grand Fleet 1914-18
Gulf of Riga Operations in the Gulf of Riga, 1916-18
Heligoland Battle of Heligoland Bight, August 28 1914
High Seas Fleet German High Seas Fleet, 1914-18
Jutland Battle of Jutland, May 31 1916
North Russia Allied intervention in North Russia, 1918-19
North Sea Operations in the North Sea 1914-18
Spee squadron Search for von Spee's squadron, South Pacific, 1914
Suez Canal defence Defence of the Suez Canal against Turkey, 1915-16
Tsingtao Capture of German colony of Tsingtao, August 1914
Zeebrugge British raid on Zeebrugge, April 23 1918

Operations of World War 2

Aleutians Japanese attack on the Aleutian islands, June 1942
Arctic 1942-43 Arctic Ocean convoy operations to Russia, 1942-43
Atlantic convoys North Atlantic convoy operations 1940-43
Attu US landings on Attu island, Aleutians, May 11 1943
Bismarck operations Search for and destruction of German battleship *Bismarck* North Atlantic, May 1941
Cape Spartivento Battle of Cape Spartivento
Ceylon Japanese carrier raids on Ceylon and India, April 1942
Channel dash Movement of German ships from Brest to Germany, February 12 1942
China Japanese operations in China, 1937-40
Coral Sea Battle of the Coral Sea, May 4-7 1942
Crete German landings in Crete, May 1941
Dakar British attack on French forces at Dakar, September 23-25 1940 (Operation 'Menace')
Darwin Japanese carrier raid on Darwin, Australia, February 19 1942

Diego Suarez Landings at Diego Suarez, Madagascar, May 5 1942 (Operation 'Ironclad')
Dutch Harbor Japanese carrier raid on Dutch Harbor, Alaska, June 3 1942
East Indies Operations against the Japanese, Dutch East Indies, January-March 1942
Eastern Solomons Battle of the Eastern Solomons, August 23-25 1942
Eniwetok Landings on Eniwetok, Marshall Islands, February 181944 (Operation 'Catchpole')
Force 'H' British squadron in Western Mediterranean, 1940-42
Gilbert islands Landings on Makin and Tarawa, November 20 1943 (Operation 'Galvanic')
Guadalcanal battle Naval battle of Guadalcanal, November 12-15 1942
Guadalcanal-Tulagi Landings on Guadalcanal and Tulagi, August 7-9 1942
Guam Landings on Guam, July 21 1944
Hollandia Landings at Hollandia, Tanahmerah Bay and Aitape, New Guinea, April 21 1944
Home Fleet British Home Fleet, 1940-44
Iwo Jima Landings on Iwo Jima, February 19 1945 (Operation 'Detachment')
Java Japanese operations around Java, February 1942
Kwajalein Landings on Kwajalein, Roi and Namur, January 31 1944 (Operation 'Flintlock')
Leyte Landings on Leyte, October 20 1944
Lingayen Landings at Lingayen, Luzon, January 9 1945
Malaya Japanese operations against Malaya, December 1941
Matapan Battle of Cape Matapan, March 28 1941
Malta convoys Convoys in Mediterranean to relieve Malta, 1941-42
Midway Battle of Midway, June 3-6 1942
Morotai Landings on Morotai islands, September 15 1944
Narvik Battle of Narvik, April 1940
Normandy Landings in Normandy, June 6 1944 (Operation 'Overlord')
North Africa Landings in Morocco and Algeria, November 8 1942 (Operation 'Torch')
North Cape Battle of North Cape, December 26 1943
Norwegian campaign German invasion of Norway, April 10 1940
Okinawa .ndings and capture of Okinawa, April-June 1945
Oran British attack on French fleet at Mers-el-Kebir, Oran, July 3 1940 (Operation 'Catapult')
Pacific raids Carrier raids on various targets in the Pacific area, 1943-45
Palau Landings on Peleliu and Angaur, Palau, September 15 1944
Pearl Harbor Japanese attack on Pearl Harbor, Hawaii, December 7 1941
Philippine Sea Battle of the Philippine Sea, June 19-20 1944
Rabaul Japanese landings at Rabaul and Kavieng, January 20-23 1942
Raids (see Pacific raids)
Sabang British carrier raids on Sabang and Palembang, Sumatra, 1944
Saipan Landings on Saipan, June 15 1944 (Operations 'Forager')
Salerno Landings at Salerno, Italy, September 9 1943 (Operation 'Avalanche')
Santa Cruz Battle of Santa Cruz islands, October 26 1942
Sicily Landings in Sicily, July 10 1943 (Operation 'Husky')
Southern France Landings in Southern France, August 15 1944 (Operation 'Anvil')
Surigao Strait Battle of Surigao Strait, Leyte Gulf, October 25 1944
Taranto British carrier raid on Taranto, Italy, November 1940
Tinian Landings on Tinian, July 24 1944
Walcheren British landings on Walcheren, Netherlands, December 1944

Abbreviations

AA anti-aircraft
AB crane ship
AC collier
AG auxiliary (miscellaneous)
AGMR communications relay ship
Al Alabama
ASW anti-submarine warfare
AV seaplane tender
AVT aviation transport/pilot trainer

B&W Babcock and Wilcox
BB battleship
BHP brake horsepower
BL(R) breech loading (rifle)
BM monitor
BS blockading squadron

Cal California
CA cruiser, heavy
CB cruiser, large
CBC command ship, large
CC battlecruiser
CL cruiser, light
c/t conning tower
CV aircraft carrier (multi-mission)
CVA(N) aircraft carrier, attack (nuclear powered)
CVB aircraft carrier, large
CVL aircraft carrier, light
CVS ASW carrier

d/e double-ended
De Delaware
DP dual purpose

fd full draught
f/l full load/fully laden
FRAM Fleet rehabilitation and modernisation (US programme)

Ga Georgia

HSE horizontal single-expansion
HTE horizontal triple-expansion

IHP indicated horsepower
ITE inverted triple-expansion
IX unclassified vessel

LPH amphibious assault ship

Md Maryland
MG machine gun
ML(R) muzzle loading (rifle)
mm millimetres

NC North Carolina
NJ New Jersey
NY New York
NYd Navy Yard

oa overall
Or Oregon

Pa Pennsylvania
pdr pounder
pp perpendicular

QE quadruple-expansion
QF quick firing

RNR Royal Naval Reserve

SAM surface-to-air missile
SB smooth bore
SC South Carolina
s/e single-ended
SHP shaft horsepower
SSM ship-to-ship missile

TE triple-expansion
Tn Tennessee
TT torpedo tubes

Va Virginia
VQE vertical quadruple-expansion
VTE vertical triple-expansion
VTOL vertical take-off and landing

wl waterline

Shipbuilders

Admiralty Admiralty Dockyard, St Petersburg (Russia)
Adriatico Cantieri Riuniti dell'Adriatico, Trieste (Italy)
Allaire Allaire Iron Works, New York, NY (USA)
Amsterdam *Amsterdam Dockyard, Amsterdam (Netherlands)
Ansaldo Gio Ansaldo & Co, Sestri Ponente, Genoa (Italy)
Arman L'Arman Frères (Chantiers & Ateliers de l'Océan), Bordeaux (France)
Armstrong Sir W. G. Armstrong, Whitworth & Co Ltd, Elswick & High Walker, Newcastle-on-Tyne (UK) (later Vickers)
Asano Asano Shipbuilding Co Ltd, Tsurumi (Japan)
Atlantic Atlantic Iron Works, Boston, Ma (USA)
Atlantique Chantiers de l'Atlantique (Penhoët), St Nazaire (France)

Baird C. Baird, St Petersburg (Russia) (later Franco-Russian)
Baltic Baltic Shipyard & Engineering Works, St Petersburg (Russia) (later Ordzhonikidze)
Bath Bath Iron Works, Bath, Maine (USA)
Beardmore Wm Beardmore & Co Ltd, Dalmuir (UK)
Bergsunds Bergsunds Mekaniska Verkstads Akt, Stockholm (Sweden)
Bilbao SA de los Astilleros del Nervion, Bilbao (Spain)
Blohm & Voss Blohm & Voss, Hamburg (Germany)
Boston *Boston Navy Yard, Charlestown, Massachusetts (USA)
Bremerton *Puget Sound Navy Yard, Bremerton, Washington (USA)
Brest *Arsenal de Brest (France)
Brooklyn *New York Navy Yard, Brooklyn, NY (USA)
Burmeister Burmeister & Wain, Copenhagen (Denmark)

Cadiz Vea Murguia Noriega & Cia, Cadiz (Spain)
Cammell Laird Cammell Laird & Co Ltd, Birkenhead (UK)
Carr & McPherson Carr & McPherson, St Petersburg (Russia)
Carraca *La Carraca Dockyard, Cadiz (Spain)
Cartagena *Cartagena Dockyard, Cartagena (Spain)
Castellammare *Cantiere di Castellammare di Stabia, Castellammare (Italy)
Chatham *Chatham Dockyard, Chatham (UK)
Cherbourg *Arsenal de Cherbourg (France)
Cockerill John Cockerill SA, Antwerp (Belgium)
Constantinople *Constantinople Dockyard, Constantinople (Turkey)
Continental Continental Iron Works, Greenpoint, NY (USA)
Continental Continental Iron Works, Secor & Co, Vallejo, Ca (USA)
Copenhagen *Copenhagen Dockyard, Copenhagen (Denmark)
Cramp Wm Cramp & Sons Ship & Engine Building Co, Philadelphia, Pennsylvania (USA)
Creusot (see Schneider)

Danubius Ganz & Co, Danubius M. W. & Schiffbau AG, Fiume (Hungary)
Danzig *Kaiserliche Werft, Danzig (Germany)
Delamater C. H. Delamater Iron Works, New York, NY (USA)
Deutsche Deutsche Werke Kiel AG, Kiel (Germany)
Devonport *Devonport Dockyard, Devonport (UK)
Dudgeon J. & W. Dudgeon, Millwall (UK)

Earle Earle's Shipbuilding & Engineering Co Ltd, Hull (UK)
Egells F. A. Egells, Berlin (Germany) (later Markisch)
Elder John Elder & Co, Govan (UK) (later Fairfield)
Etna Etna Iron Works, New York, NY (USA)

F C Med Forges et Chantiers de la Mediteranée (see La Seyne)
Fairfield Fairfield Shipbuilding & Engineering Co Ltd, Govan (UK)
Ferrol *Sociedad Española de Construccion Naval, Ferrol (Spain)
Fijenoord NV Mij Fijenoord, Rotterdam (Netherlands)
Finnboda Finnboda, Stockholm (Sweden)
Flushing *Flushing Dockyard, Flushing (Netherlands)
Foce Cantiere della Foce, Genoa (Italy) (later Ansaldo)
Fore River Fore River Shipbuilding Co, Quincy, Massachusetts (USA) (later Quincy)
Franco-Russian Franco-Russian Works, St Petersburg (Russia)
Fulton Fulton Iron Works, New York, NY (USA)

GE General Electric Co, Schenectady, NY (USA)
Galernii *Galernii Island Yard, St Petersburg (Russia) (later Admiralty)
Germania Fried Krupp AG Germaniawerft, Kiel (Germany)
Gironde Chantiers et Ateliers de la Gironde, Bordeaux (France)
Gotaverken A/B Gotaverken, Goteborg (Sweden)
Gouin Gouin, Nantes (France)
Graville Forges et Chantiers de la Mediteranée, Le Havre (France)
Greenock Foundry Greenock Foundry Co, Greenock (UK)
Greenwood Miles Greenwood, Cincinnati, Ohio (USA)

Hamilton Wm Hamilton & Co Ltd, Port Glasgow (UK)
Harlan & Hollingsworth Harlan & Hollingsworth Co, Wilmington, Delaware (USA)
Harland & Wolff Harland & Wolff Ltd, Belfast (UK)
Harland & Wolff, Govan Harland & Wolff Ltd, Govan, Glasgow (UK)
Harrison I. Harrison, Millwall (UK)
Harrison Loring Harrison Loring, Boston, Massachusetts (USA)
Hawthorn Leslie R. & W. Hawthorn, Leslie & Co Ltd, Hebburn, Newcastle-upon-Tyne (UK)
Horten *Horten Dockyard, Horten (Norway)
Howaldt Howaldtswerke AG, Kiel (Germany)
Humphrys Humphrys Tennant & Co Ltd, Deptford (UK)

Indret Establissement d'Indret, Nantes (France)

John Brown John Brown & Co Ltd, Clydebank, Glasgow (UK)
John Roach John Roach & Co, Chester, Pennsylvania (USA)

Karlskrona *Karlskrona Dockyard, Karlskrona (Sweden)
Kawasaki Kawasaki Dockyard Co, Kobe (Japan)
Kiel *Kaiserliche Werft, Kiel (Germany) (later Deutsche Werke)
Kockums Kockums Mekaniska Verkstads A/B, Malmo (Sweden)

Kronstadt *Kronstadt Dockyard, Kronstadt (USSR)
Kure *Kure Dockyard, Kure (Japan)

La Seyne Forges et Chantiers de la Mediteranee, La Seyne, Toulon (France)
La Spezia *Arsenale di La Spezia (Italy)
Laird Laird Bros Ltd, Birkenhead (UK) (later Cammell Laird)
Lewis Nixon Lewis Nixon Co, Elizabethport, New Jersey (USA)
Lindholmens Lindholmens Verkstads A/B, Goteborg (Sweden)
Loire Ateliers et Chantiers de la Loire, St Nazaire (France)
Loire-St Denis Ateliers et Chantiers de la Loire, St Denis (France)
London & Glasgow London & Glasgow Engine & Iron Shipbuilding Co Ltd, Govan, Glasgow (UK) (later Harland & Wolff)
Lorient *Arsenal de Lorient (France)

McKie & Baxter McKie & Baxter Ltd, Paisley, Glasgow (UK)
Mare Mare & Co, Blackwall, London (UK) (later Thames Iron Works)
Mare Island *Mare Island Navy Yard, Vallejo, California (USA)
Markisch Markisch-Schlesischer Maschinenbau und Hutten AG, Berlin (Germany)

Marti *Marti Yard, Leningrad (USSR)
Marti North *Marti North Yard, Nikolaiev (USSR)
Marti South *Marti South Yard, Nikolaiev (USSR)
Maudslay Maudslay Sons & Field (UK)
Mazeline Mazeline Engine Works, Le Havre (France) (later F C Med)
Merrick Merrick & Sons, Philadelphia, Pa (USA)
Milford Haven Milford Haven Shipbuilding & Engineering Co, Pembroke (UK)
Mitchell Mitchell & Co, St Petersburg (Russia) (later Baltic Works)
Mitsubishi Mitsubishi Zosen Kaisha, Nagasaki (Japan)
Molotovsk *402 Yard, Molotovsk (USSR)
Moran Moran Bros & Co, Seattle, Washington (USA)
Morgan Morgan Iron Works, New York, NY (USA)
Morris J. P. Morris & Co, Philadelphia, Pa (USA)
Motala Motala Mekaniska Verkstads A/B, Goteborg (Sweden)

NSM Nederlandsche Stoomboot Mij Rotterdam (Netherlands) (later Fijenoord)
Napier R. Napier & Sons Ltd, Dalmuir, Glasgow (UK) (later Beardmore)
Nevski Nevski Works, St Petersburg (Russia)
New Admiralty *New Admiralty Yard, St Petersburg (Russia)
New York (see Brooklyn)
New York Sbdg New York Shipbuilding Co, Camden, New Jersey (USA)
Newport News Newport News Shipbuilding & Dry Dock Co, Newport News, Virginia (USA)
Nikolaiev Admy Nikolaiev Admiralty Yard, Nikolaiev (Russia)
Nikolaiev Nikolaiev Factories Co, Nikolaiev (Russia) (later Marti North)
Norfolk *Norfolk Navy Yard, Portsmouth, Virginia (USA)
Novelty Novelty Iron Works, New York, NY (USA)

Odero Cantieri Navali Odero SA, Sestri Ponente, Genoa (Italy)
Ordzhonikidze *Ordzhonikidze Yard, Leningrad (USSR)
Orlando Fratelli Orlando & Co, Livorno (Italy)

Palmers Palmer's Shipbuilding & Engineering Co, Hebburn (UK)
Parsons Parson's Marine Steam Turbine Co, Wallsend (UK)
Pembroke *Pembroke Dockyard, Pembroke (UK)
Penhoët Chantiers et Ateliers de St Nazaire (Penhoët), St Nazaire (France)
Penn John Penn & Sons, Greenwich (UK)
Philadelphia *Philadelphia Navy Yard, Philadelphia, Pennsylvania (USA)
Pola *Pola Dockyard, Pola (Austria)
Poletika Semyannikov & Poletika, St Petersburg (Russia)
Portsmouth *Portsmouth Dockyard, Portsmouth (UK)
Portsmouth NYd *Portsmouth Navy Yard, Kittery, Maine (USA)
Pusey & Jones Pusey & Jones Co, Wilmington, De (USA)

Quincy Bethlehem Steel Co, Quincy, Massachusetts (USA)
Quintard Quintard Iron Works, New York, NY (USA)

Ravenhill Ravenhill & Co (UK)
Reaney Reaney, Son & Archbold, Chester, Pennsylvania (USA)
Rennie G. Rennie & Co, Greenwich (UK)
Rochefort *Arsenal de Rochefort (France)
Ropit, Sevastopol Ropit & Co, Sevastopol (Russia)
Russian Russian Shipbuilding Co, Nikolaiev (Russia) (later Marti South)

Samuda Samuda Bros Ltd, Poplar, London (UK)
San Francisco San Francisco Navy Yard, San Francisco, California (USA)
San Rocco Cantiere San Rocco, Livorno (Italy)
Sasebo *Sasebo Dockyard, Sasebo (Japan)
Schichau F. Schichau GmbH, Danzig (Germany)
Schifter Schifter, Nyholm (Denmark)
Schneider Schneider & Cie, Le Creusot (France)
Scotts Scotts' Shipbuilding & Engineering Co Ltd, Greenock (UK)
Secor Secor & Co, Jersey City, New Jersey (USA)
Sevastopol Sevastopol Dockyard, Sevastopol (Russia)
Sheerness *Sheerness Dockyard, Sheerness (UK)
Snowden & Mason Snowden & Mason, Pittsburgh, Pennsylvania (USA)
Stab Tecnico Stabilimento Tecnico Triestino, San Rocco & San Marco, Trieste (Italy) (later Adriatico)
Stephen A. Stephen & Sons Ltd, Govan (UK)
Swan Hunter Swan, Hunter & Wigham Richardson Ltd, Wallsend-on-Tyne (UK)
Swift Evans Swift Evans & Co, Cincinnati, Ohio (USA)

Terrestre Maquinista Terrestre y Maritima, Barcelona (Spain)
Thames Thames Iron Works & Shipbuilding Co Ltd, Blackwall (UK)
Thomson J. & G. Thomson Ltd, Clydebank, Glasgow (UK) (later John Brown)
Tirreno Cantieri del Tirreno, Riva Trigoso, Genoa (Italy)
Toulon Arsenal de Toulon (France)

Union Union Iron Works, San Francisco, California (USA)

Venice *Arsenale di Venezia, Venice (Italy)
Vickers Vickers Ltd, Barrow-in-Furness (UK) (formerly Naval Construction & Armaments Co Ltd & Vickers Sons & Maxim Ltd)
Vickers, Tyne Vickers Ltd, Newcastle-upon-Tyne (UK)
Vulcan, Hamburg AG 'Vulcan', Hamburg (Germany)
Vulcan, Stettin AG 'Vulcan', Stettin (Germany)

Wallsend Wallsend Slipway & Engineering Co, Wallsend-on-Tyne (UK)
Webb William H. Webb, New York, NY (USA)
Weser AG 'Weser', Bremen (Germany)
Westinghouse Westinghouse Machine Co, Pittsburgh, Pennsylvania (USA)
Westwood Baillie Westwood, Baillie & Co, Poplar, London (UK)
White J. Samuel White & Co Ltd, Cowes (UK)
Wilhelmshaven *Kaiserliche Werft, Wilhelmshaven (Germany)
Woolwich *Woolwich Dockyard, Woolwich (UK)

Yokohama Yokohama Dock Co Ltd, Yokohama (Japan)
Yokosuka *Yokosuka Dockyard, Yokosuka (Japan)

* Government dockyard.

Argentina

A permanent Argentine navy was established only in 1872 when a number of vessels including two armoured monitors was ordered. The small battleship *Almirante Brown* was built in the 1880s and the smaller 'Independencia' class at the end of the decade.

A border dispute with Chile in the 1890s led to a naval race and four armoured cruisers were purchased from Italy. The dispute was settled in 1902 and two larger cruisers under construction were sold to Japan. However, the rapid build-up of the fleet had threatened Brazil's position and a new naval race occurred which led to construction of Argentina's only two Dreadnoughts. These vessels remained the largest and most prominent units of the fleet until the 1950s. Argentina was neutral during both world wars.

In 1958 Argentina acquired a small aircraft carrier which was replaced by another vessel purchased from the Netherlands in 1968.

Class Details

'El Plata' Class (1873)

Monitors: *El Plata, Los Andes*
Displacement: 1,535tons
Dimensions: 186(oa) 179.8(pp)×44'3×9'6 [56.7(oa) 54.8(pp)×13.5×2.9]
Machinery: 2 screws, compound engines (Laird)
IHP 750 = 9knots
Endurance: 2,880/10
Armament: 2×230mm ML
1901: 2×203mm BL, 2×114mm
Armour: Belt 90-152mm, turret 203-254mm, deck 25mm
Complement: 120
Class notes: Single turret monitors with no rigging and single funnel. The superstructure forward of the turret was narrow enough to permit firing forward. Rearmed in 1901

'Almirante Brown' (1878)

Central Battery Ship: *Almirante Brown*
Displacement: 4,200tons
Dimensions: 249(oa) 240(pp)×50×20'6 [75.9(oa) 73.2(pp)×15.2×6.2]
Machinery: 2 screws, vertical compound engines (Maudslay), 8 cylindrical boilers
IHP 4,500 = 14knots
Endurance: 4,300/10
Armament: 8×203mm BLR, 6×114mm BLR
1898: 10×150mm/50, 4×119mm, 8×3pdr, 2 TT
Armour: Belt 140-230mm, battery 203mm, bulkheads 178mm, deck 38mm
Complement: 520, *1898:* 380
Class notes: Coast defence battleship with main armament in armoured redoubt. Single funnel and two military masts. Rearmed in 1898

'Independencia' Class (1889)

Coast Defence Ships: *Independencia, Libertad*
Displacement: 2,300tons
Dimensions: 240(oa) 230(wl)×44'5×13 [73.2(oa) 70.1(wl)×13.6×4]
Machinery: 2 screws, vertical compound engines (Laird), 4 cylindrical boilers
IHP 2,780 = 14.25knots
Endurance: 4,500/10
Armament: 2×240mm/35, 4×119mm/40, 4×3pdr, 2×457mm TT
Armour: Belt 203mm, bulkheads 152-203mm, barbettes 127-203mm, deck 25-50mm, c/t 102mm
Complement: 230
Class notes: Small armoured vessels with two single turrets fore and aft and single military mast. Refitted 1927, converted to oil fuel, reclassified gunboats

'Garibaldi' Class (1895)

Armoured Cruisers: *Garibaldi, General Belgrano, Pueyrredon, San Martin*
Displacement: 6,822tons; *Belgrano:* 7,282tons
Dimensions: 328(oa)×59'8×23'3 [100(oa)×18.2×7.1]; *Belgrano:* beam 61'10 [18.8]
Machinery: 2 screws, VTE engines (Ansaldo; *Belgrano* and *San Martin*: Hawthorn Guppy), 8 cylindrical boilers (*Pueyrredon:* 16 Belleville); *Belgrano* and *Pueyrredon, 1926-28:* 8 Yarrow
IHP 13,000 = 20knots
Endurance: 6,000/10
Armament: 2×254mm/40, 10×152mm/40 (*Belgrano:* 14), 6×120mm/44 (*Belgrano:* none), 10×6pdr, 4×457mm TT
San Martin: 4×203mm/45, 10×152mm/44, 6×120mm/40, 12×6pdr, 4×457mmTT
Armour: Belt 75-152mm, barbettes 152mm, protective deck 25-50mm, c/t 152mm
Complement: 425
Class notes: All purchased from Italy prior to completion. Main armament in turrets fore and aft, remainder in casemates. Two widely spaced funnels and single military mast amidships. *Belgrano* and *Pueyrredon* refitted 1926-34, reboilered, main deck battery removed, tripod mast fitted. All reclassified coast defence ships 1932

'Moreno' Class (1901)

Armoured Cruisers: *[Moreno, Rivadavia]*
Displacement: 7,600tons
Dimensions: 366'6(oa) 344(pp)×61'4×25'3 [111.7(oa) 104.9(pp)×18.7×7.7]
Machinery: 2 screws, VTE engines (Ansaldo), 8 boilers
IHP 14,800 = 20knots
Armament: 4×203mm/45, 14×152mm/45, 10×76mm/40, 4×457mmTT
Armour: Belt 150mm, barbettes 150mm, deck 113mm, c/t 150mm
Complement: 560
Class notes: Designed by Masdea. Modified 'Garibaldi' class ordered in Italy and sold to Japan prior to completion 1904

'Rivadavia' Class (1908)

Dreadnoughts: *Moreno* (see also later photo), *Rivadavia*
Displacement: 28,000tons, 30,600f/l

Dimensions: 604(oa) 557'9(pp)×95'6×27'9 [184.1(oa) 170(pp)×29.1×8.5]
Machinery: 3 screws, Curtis turbines (Fore River), 18 B&W boilers
SHP 39,500 = 22.5knots; *1925:* SHP 45,000
Endurance: 11,000/11
Armament: 12×305mm/50, 12×152mm/50, 12×102mm/50, 2×533mmTT
1925: 102mm replaced by 4×76mmAA
Armour: Belt 203-279mm, turrets 229-305mm, deck 76mm c/t 305mm
Complement: 1,080
Class notes: Built in US. Main armament in six turrets including two diagonally placed wing turrets. Two widely spaced funnels and distinctive derrick posts between. Cage foremast and pole mainmast. Had trouble on trials. Refitted 1925, converted to oil fuel, tripod replaced pole mainmast, AA guns fitted, new boilers and engines

'Independencia' (1958)

Light Aircraft Carrier: *Independencia*
Displacement: 18,400tons, 19,540f/l
Dimensions: 695(oa) 630(pp)×80×23'6; 118(oa beam) [211.8(oa) 192(pp)×24.4×7.2; 36(oa beam)]
Machinery: 2 screws, Parsons geared turbines (Harland), 4 Admiralty 3-drum boilers
SHP 42,000 = 25knots
Endurance: 12,000/14
Aircraft: 21
Armament: 8×40mm AA
Complement: 1,076
Class notes: Former British *Warrior* purchased 1958

'25 de Mayo' (1968)

Light Aircraft Carrier: *Veinticinco de Mayo*
Displacement: 15,892tons, 19,896f/l
Dimensions: 697'9(oa) 630(pp)×80'4×24'6; 133'6(oa beam) [212.7(oa) 192(pp)×24.5×7.5; 40.7(oa beam)]
Machinery: 2 screws, Parsons geared turbines (Cammell Laird), 4 Admiralty 3-drum boilers
SHP 40,000 = 24.5knots
Endurance: 12,000/14
Aircraft: 14
Armament: 10×40mm AA
Complement: 1,509
Class notes: Former Dutch *Karel Doorman* purchased 1968. Refitted 1968, new turbines from incomplete British carrier *Leviathan* installed

Top left:
***El Plata* — Monitor of 1873.** *Naval Historical Centre*

Centre left:
***Almirante Brown* — Central battery ship of 1878.** *Marius Bar*

Bottom left:
***Pueyrredon* — Armoured cruiser of 1895, 'Garibaldi' class.** *Marius Bar*

Individual Ships

Almirante Brown

Type: Central Battery Ship
Class: 'Almirante Brown' (1878)
Nomenclature: Guillermo Brown (1777-1857), commander of the Argentine fleet during the War of Independence

History:
—— Laid down by Samuda
1880 October 6: Launched
—— Completed
1897-98 Refit at La Seyne, rearmed
1927 Hulked
1932 Broken up

Los Andes

Type: Monitor
Class: 'El Plata' (1873)
Nomenclature: Andes mountains

History:
—— Laid down by Laird
1874 October 29: Launched
1875 Completed
1878 Expedition to Santa Cruz
1893 September 27: Damaged by gunfire of government vessels in the Parana River off Rosario during civil disturbance
1901 Refit, rearmed
1927 Stricken

Garibaldi

Type: Armoured cruiser
Class: 'Garibaldi' (1895)
Nomenclature: Giuseppe Garibaldi (1807-1882), Italian patriot and soldier

History:
—— Laid down by Ansaldo for Italy as ***Giuseppe Garibaldi***
1895 May 27: Launched
1895 July 14: Sold to Argentina, renamed ***Garibaldi***
1896 December 10: Arrived at Buenos Aires
1900 Refit at Genoa
1921 Artillery school ship
1932 Reclassified coast defence ship
1936 November 5: Sold and broken up

General Belgrano

Type: Armoured Cruiser
Class: 'Garibaldi' (1895)
Nomenclature: Manuel Belgrano (1770-1820), Argentine patriot and general of the Argentine War of Independence

History:
1896 June: Laid down by Orlando for Italy as ***Varese***
1897 Sold to Argentina, renamed ***General Belgrano***
1897 July 25: Launched
1898 October 8: Completed
1928 Refit; reboilered, converted to oil fuel, tripod mast fitted
1932 Reclassified coast defence ship
1933 Submarine tender, at Mar del Plata

1947 May 8: Stricken
1953 April: Broken up at Buenos Aires

Independencia

Type: Coast Defence Ship
Class: 'Independencia' (1889)
Nomenclature: Independence

History:
1890 Laid down by Laird
1891 February 26: Launched
1892 Completed
1893 September: In action with rebel-held monitor *Los Andes* in Parana River
1925-27 Refit; converted to oil fuel, reclassified gunboat
1946 Stricken

Independencia

Type: Light Aircraft Carrier
Class: 'Independencia' (1958)
Nomenclature: Independence

History:
1942 December 12: Laid down by Harland & Wolff as British ***Warrior***
1944 May 20: Launched
1946 January 24: Completed
1958 October 4: Sold to Argentina, renamed ***Independencia***
1971 January: Stricken

Libertad

Type: Coast Defence Ship
Class: 'Independencia' (1889)
Nomenclature: Liberty

History:
—— Laid down by Laird as ***Nueve de Julio***
1890 December 11: Launched
1891 Completed
1892 Renamed ***Libertad***
1925-27 Refit; converted to oil fuel, reclassified gunboat
1946 Stricken, stationary cadet training ship

Moreno

Type: Armoured Cruiser
Class: 'Moreno' (1901)
Nomenclature: Mariano Moreno (1778-1811), leader of the Argentine Revolution

History:
1902 March 29: Laid down by Ansaldo as ***Roca***
1902 Renamed ***Moreno***
1903 February 9: Launched
1903 December 29: Sold to Japan incomplete, renamed ***Nisshin***

Moreno

Type: Dreadnought
Class: 'Rivadavia' (1908)

History:
1910 July 9: Laid down by New York Sbdg
1911 September 23: Launched
1915 March: Completed
1924-25 Refit in US
1937 Cruise to Europe
1950 Depot ship
1955 Prison ship
1957 February 8: Sold and broken up in Japan

El Plata

Type: Monitor
Class: 'El Plata' (1873)
Nomenclature: River Plata (Rio de la Plata)

History:
—— Laid down by Laird
1874 August 29: Launched
1875 Completed
1901 Refit, rearmed
1927 Stricken

Pueyrredon

Type: Armoured Cruiser
Class: 'Garibaldi' (1895)
Nomenclature: Juan Martin de Pueyrredon (1776-1850), Argentine general, first Supreme Director of the United Provinces of Rio de la Plata

History:
—— Laid down by Ansaldo for Italy as ***Giuseppe Garibaldi***
1897 Sold to Argentina, renamed ***Pueyrredon***
1897 September 25: Launched
1898 August: Completed
1926-34 Refit
1932 Reclassified coast defence ship
1941 Training ship
1954 August 2: Stricken
1957 June: Broken up at Savona, Italy

Rivadavia

Type: Armoured Cruiser
Class: 'Moreno' (1901)
Nomenclature: Bernardino Rivadavia (1780-1845), Argentine statesman and leader in the Argentine War of Independence

History:
1902 March 10: Laid down by Ansaldo as ***Mitra,*** renamed ***Rivadavia***
1902 October 22: Launched
1903 December 29: Sold to Japan before completion, renamed ***Kasuga***

Rivadavia

Type: Dreadnought
Class: 'Rivadavia' (1908)

Top right:
***Moreno* — Battleship of 1908 as completed with pole mainmast, 1915.**

Bottom right:
***Moreno* — Battleship, after reconstruction, May 1937.**
Wright & Logan

History:
1910 May 25: Laid down by Fore River
1911 August 26: Launched
1914 December: Completed
1924-25 Refit in US
1937 Cruise to Europe
1952 Decommissioned
1957 February 8: Sold and broken up at Genoa

San Martin

Type: Armoured Cruiser
Class: 'Garibaldi' (1895)
Nomenclature: Jose de San Martin (1778-1850), Latin American revolutionary general

History:
—— Laid down by Orlando for Italy as ***Varese***
1896 May 25: Launched
1896 October: Sold to Argentina, renamed ***San Martin***
1898 April 25: Completed
1832 Reclassified coast defence ship
1935 December 18: Stricken, hulk at Rio Santiago
1947 Broken up

Veinticinco de Mayo

Type: Light Aircraft Carrier
Class: '25 de Mayo' (1968)
Nomenclature: 25 May 1810, independent government of Rio de la Plata established

History:
1942 December 3: Laid down by Cammell Laird as British ***Venerable***
1943 December 30: Launched
1945 January 17: Completed
1948 Transferred to Netherlands, renamed ***Karel Doorman***
1968 October 15: Sold to Argentina, renamed ***Veinticinco de Mayo***
1968 Refit by Wilton-Fijenoord, re-engined with turbines from incomplete carrier *Leviathan*
1980 Refit, flightdeck enlarged

***25 de Mayo* — Light aircraft carrier, September 1969, formerly the Dutch *Karel Doorman*.** *P. A. Vicary*

Austria

Austria was primarily a land power with only a short coastline along the Adriatic with the result that the navy was subordinated to the army. Always short of money, the navy was forced to rely on less powerful ships than its neighbours which were only completed when already obsolescent.

The early Austrian ironclads engaged the Italian navy at the Battle of Lissa in 1866 and scored a signal success. At that time the navy was fortunate in having two leaders of importance, Archduke Ferdinand Max and Adm Tegetthoff, whose influence promoted the interests of the navy and inspired its personnel. After the early loss of these men the navy once again declined as a result of disinterest and lack of funds. New ships were not authorised but were built under the guise of repairing old vessels, and other obsolete ships were reconstructed.

The construction of the 'Monarch' class in 1893 initiated a new stage and six years later the 'Habsburg' class was laid down. New ships were built more frequently but lack of funds continued to hinder development. Once again, during the period before World War 1, the navy had two able supporters, the heir to the throne, Archduke Franz Ferdinand, and the navy commander, Adm Montecuccoli. The 'Radetzky' class of obsolescent pre-dreadnoughts was authorised only after completion of the *Dreadnought*. In 1911 the first and only class of dreadnoughts was ordered with Montecuccoli authorising the start of construction before the government actually approved the ships. As a political measure, the *Szent Istvan* was built by an inexperienced yard at Fiume, then in Hungary, which resulted in an inferior vessel.

During World War 1 the large vessels of the Austrian navy remained in port as a 'fleet in being' which tied up considerable enemy naval strength. Two of the dreadnoughts were sunk, the *Viribus Unitis* having been previously turned over to the Yugoslavs. The remainder of the fleet was scrapped after being turned over to the victorious Allies.

Class Details

'Drache' Class (1861)

Broadside Ships: *Drache* (see also later photo), *Salamander*
Displacement: 2,824tons, 3,110f/l
Dimensions: 230(pp)×45'10×22'3 [70.1(pp)×14×6.8]
Machinery: 1 screw, HSE engines, 4 boilers
IHP 2,060 = 10.5knots
Armament: 10×48pdr SB, 18×24pdr
1867: 10×178mm ML, 2×51mm bronze ML
Armour: Belt 115mm
Complement: 343
Class notes: Wood hull armoured corvettes with bark rig and ram bow. Refitted and rearmed 1869-72. Built as a response to Sardinian 'Formidabile' class

'Kaiser Max' Class (1861)

Broadside Ships: *Juan de Austria, Kaiser Max, Prinz Eugen*
Displacement: 3,588tons
Dimensions: 230(pp)×44'3×23'4 [70.1(pp)×13.5×7.1]
Machinery: 1 screw, HSE engines
IHP 2,600 = 11knots
Endurance: 2,000/10
Armament: 16×48pdr SB, 14×24 pdr
1867: 12×178mm ML, 2×75mm
Armour: Belt 110mm
Complement: 386
Class notes: Designed by Romako. Enlarged 'Drache' type, wood hull armoured frigates. Poor sea boats. *Juan de Austria* served at Lissa with its armour incomplete. Equipment from these vessels placed in new hulls with same names 1875

'Habsburg' Class (1863)

Broadside Ships: *Erzherzog Ferdinand Max, Habsburg*
Displacement: 5,140tons
Dimensions: 262'5(pp)×52'6×25'7 [80(pp)×16×7.8]
Machinery: 1 screw, HSE engines, box boilers
IHP 3,150 = 12knots
Armament: *Designed:* 32×48pdr SB
Completed: 16×48pdr SB, 2×4pdr
1867: 14×178mm ML, 6×89mm, 2×70mm
Armour: Belt 87-123mm
Complement: 489
Class notes: Designed by Romako. Armoured frigates with wood hulls and bark rig. Delivery of German-made guns held up because of 1866 war and these ships served at Lissa with temporary armament and rigging. Modernised 1880

'Lissa' (1865)

Central Battery Ship: *Lissa*
Displacement: 6,680tons
Dimensions: 284'9(pp)×56'9×28'6 [86.8(pp)×17.3×8.7]
Machinery: 1 screw, HSE engines (Stab Tecnico), 4 boilers
IHP 4,200 = 13.3knots
Endurance: 2,480/10
Armament: 12×240mm, 6×47mm
Armour: Belt 152mm, battery 127mm, bulkheads 114mm
Complement: 582
Class notes: Designed by Romako. Wood hull with guns in armoured redoubt, ship rig and large draft

'Erzherzog Albrecht' (1867)

Central Battery Ship: *Erzherzog Albrecht*
Displacement: 5,994 tons
Dimensions: 300'9(oa) 285'2(pp)×56'2×24'3 [91.7(oa) 86.9(pp)×17.1×7.4]
Machinery: 1 screw, horizontal return connecting-rod engines (Stab Tecnico), 6 box boilers
IHP 3,600 = 13knots
Endurance: 2,320/10
Armament: 8×240mm/22, 8×89mm/24, 2×70mm, 4×350mm TT
Armour: Belt 203mm, casemates 177mm, bulkheads 152mm, deck 38mm
Complement: 550
Class notes: Iron hull, similar to *Lissa* with less draft. Central battery designed to permit axial fire for guns. Single funnel with full ship rig

345

'Kaiser' (1868)

Central Battery Ship: *Kaiser*
Displacement: 5,810tons
Dimensions: 265'9(oa) 254'3(pp)×58'5×25 [81(oa) 77.5(pp)×17.8×7.6]
Machinery: 1 screw, horizontal return connecting-rod engines (Stab Tecnico), box boilers
IHP 3,200 = 13knots
Endurance: 1,500/10
Armament: 10×230mm MLR, 6×89mm BLR
1885: 3×350mm TT added
Armour: Belt 102-152mm, casemates 127mm, bulkheads 127mm
Complement: 560
Class notes: Wood hull with iron upperworks. Built 1858 as wood line-of-battle ship, converted to ironclad 1869-74. Barkentine rig, no ram bow

'Custoza' (1868)

Central Battery Ship: *Custoza*
Displacement: 7,100tons, 7,730f/l
Dimensions: 311'8(oa) 302'2(pp)×57'9×26'8 [95(oa) 92.1(pp)×17.6×8.2]
Machinery: 1 screw, horizontal return connecting-rod engines (Stab Tecnico), 8 rectangular boilers
IHP 4,400 = 14knots
Endurance: 1,620/10
Armament: 8×260mm/22, 8×89mm, 2×70mm, 4×350mm TT
Armour: Belt 114-229mm, battery 127-178mm, bulkheads 152mm, deck 38mm
Complement: 548
Class notes: Designed by Romako. Englarged 'Erzherzog Albrecht' type with casemate set in hull so that guns could fire forward by shifting them within the casemate

'Kaiser Max' Class (1874)

Central Battery Ships: *Don Juan d'Austria, Kaiser Max, Prinz Eugen*
Displacement: 3,548tons
Dimensions: 249(oa) 240'3(wl) 229'8(pp)×48'2×19'4 [75.9(oa) 73.2(wl) 70(pp)×14.7×5.9]
Machinery: 1 screw, horizontal return connecting-rod engines, box boilers
IHP 2,700 = 12.7knots
Endurance: 2,000/10
Armament: 8×210mm, 4×89mm, 12×47mm, 4×350mm TT
Armour: Belt 102-203mm, casemates 127-152mm, bulkheads 115mm, deck 25mm
Complement: 431
Class notes: Old wood hull ships of 1860 rebuilt with new hulls of iron and steel using some previous armour and machinery. Bark rig. Modernised 1896, rigging removed and two military masts fitted

Top left:
***Drache* — Armoured corvette of 1861, after refit 1868.**

Centre left:
***Habsburg* — Armoured frigate, in late 1870s.**

Bottom left:
***Erzherzog Albrecht* — Central battery ship of 1867, in 1889 prior to reconstruction.**

'Tegetthoff' (1875)

Central Battery Ship: *Tegetthoff* (see also later photo)
Displacement: 7,390tons
Dimensions: 303'1(oa) 293(wl) 286'9(pp)×62'8×24'10 [92.4(oa) 89.3(wl) 87.4(pp)×19.1×7.6]
Machinery: 1 screw, horizontal compound engines (Stab Tecnico) 8 boilers; *1892:* 2 screws, VTE engines (Schichau), 8 cylindrical boilers
IHP 8,800 = 16knots
Endurance: 3,300/10
Armament: 6×280mm, 6×89mm, 2×67mm
1893: 6×240mm/35, 5×150mm/35, 9×3pdr/44, 6×3pdr/33, 4TT
Armour: Belt 230-356mm, battery 127-305mm, bulkheads 254-300mm, deck 76mm, c/t 178mm
Complement: 550
Class notes: Designed by Romako. Two funnels and barkentine rig. As in *Custoza* casemate guns could fire forward but without necessity of shifting them. Machinery not successful and was replaced during reconstruction of 1891-93 when it was converted to two shafts and rigging was replaced by two military masts

'Kronprinz Rudolf' (1883)

Barbette Ship: *Kronprinz Erzherzog Rudolf*
Displacement: 6,940tons, 7,432f/l
Dimensions: 320'6(oa) 314'8(wl) 295'10(pp)×63×24'3 [97.7(oa) 95.9(wl) 90.2(pp)×19.2×7.4]
Machinery: 2 screws, vertical compound engines (Stab Tecnico), 10 cylindrical boilers
IHP 7,500 = 16knots
Armament: 3×305mm/35, 6×120mm/35, 9×47mm, 2×37mm, 4×400mm TT
Armour: Belt 62-305mm, barbettes 254mm, bulkheads 203-242mm, deck 70mm
Complement: 550
Class notes: Guns arranged in three single open barbettes, two side by side forward and one aft. Two funnels and single mast. Too small for effective use

'Kronprinzessin Stephanie' (1884)

Barbette Ship: *Kronprinzessin Erzherzogin Stephanie*
Displacement: 5,130tons, 5,631f/l
Dimensions: 286(wl) 279'10(pp)×55'9×21'8 [87.2(wl) 85.3(pp)×17×6.6]
Machinery: 2 screws, vertical compound engines (Maudslay), 10 cylindrical boilers
IHP 8,300 = 17knots
Armament: 2×305mm/35, 6×150mm/35, 9×47mm, 2×37mm, 4×400mm TT
Armour: Belt 102-229mm, barbettes 283mm, deck 22mm, c/t 50mm
Complement: 470
Class notes: Second barbette ship with smaller hull and only two single barbettes side by side forward

'Maria Theresia' (1890)

Armoured Cruiser: *Kaiserin und Königin Maria Theresia*
Displacement: 5,270tons, 6,122f/l
Dimensions: 373(oa) 366'6(wl) 351'(pp)×53'4×22'5 [113.7(oa) 111.7(wl) 107(pp)×16.3×6.8]
Machinery: 2 screws, HTE engines (Stab Tecnico), 10 cylindrical boilers
IHP 7,000 = 19.3knots

Endurance: 3,500/10
Armament: 2×240mm/35, 8×150mm/35, 18×47mm, 4×450mm TT
1907: 240mm replaced by 2×194mm/42
Armour: Belt 100mm, turrets 100mm, casemates 80mm, deck 57mm, c/t 50mm
Complement: 475
Class notes: Two single barbettes fore and aft, two funnels and two heavy military masts. Armament was increased during construction. Two pole masts fitted 1903, 150mm guns resited 1910

'Monarch' Class (1892)

Second Class Battleships: *Budapest, Monarch* (see later photo), *Wien*
Displacement: 5,600tons, 5,800f/l
Dimensions: 325'6(oa) 320'6(wl) 306'2(pp)×55'9×21 [99.2(oa) 97.7(wl) 93.3(pp)×17×6.4]
Machinery: 2 screws, VTE engines (Stab Tecnico; *Monarch:* Pola), 8 cylindrical boilers (*Budapest:* Belleville)
IPH 8,500 = 17knots
Endurance: 3,000/10
Armament: 4×240mm/40, 6×150mm/40, 14×47mm, 2×450mm TT
Armour: Belt 220-270mm, citadel 80mm, turrets 250mm, casemates 80mm, barbettes 160mm, deck 60mm, bulkheads 200mm, c/t 220mm
Complement: 450
Class notes: Small compared to foreign contemporaries, designed by Popper. Two twin turrets fore and aft, single funnel and military foremast

'Kaiser Karl VI' (1895)

Armoured Cruiser: *Kaiser Karl VI* (see later photo)
Displacement: 6,250tons
Dimensions: 390'3(oa) 386'10(wl) 367'5(pp)×56'10×22'2 [119(oa) 117.9(wl) 112(pp)×17.3×6.8]
Machinery: 2 screws, VTE engines (Stab Tecnico), 18 Belleville boilers
IHP 12,300 = 20knots
Endurance: 3,500/10
Armament: 2×240mm/40, 8×150mm/40, 16×47mm, 2×450mm TT
Armour: Belt 170-220mm, turrets 200mm, casemates 80mm, bulkheads 200mm, deck 60mm, c/t 200mm
Complement: 535
Class notes: Modified 'Maria Theresia' type with two single turrets and secondary armament in casemates. Three tall funnels and two pole masts

'Habsburg' Class (1898-1899)

Pre-Dreadnoughts: *Arpád, Babenberg, Habsburg*
Displacement: 8,300tons, 8,876f/l
Dimensions: 375'8(oa) 371(wl) 353(pp)×65×23'3 [114.5(oa) 113.1(wl) 107.6(pp)×19.8×7.1]
Machinery: 2 screws, VTE engines (Stab Tecnico), 16 Belleville boilers
IHP 15,000 = 20knots
Endurance: 3,600/10
Armament: 3×240mm/40, 12×150mm/40, 10×66mm, 12×37mm, 2×450mm TT
1916: 1×66mm AA added
Armour: Belt 180-220mm, turrets 210-280mm, casemates 135mm, deck 40mm, c/t 200mm
Complement: 630
Class notes: Designed by Popper; again too small but successful for their size. Twin turret forward and single turret aft. Secondary battery in three double casemates. Modernised 1910-11

'Sankt Georg' (1900)

Armoured Cruiser: *Sankt Georg*
Displacement: 7,300tons, 8,070f/l
Dimensions: 407'9(oa) 404'3(wl) 383'10(pp)×62'5×22'5 [124.3(oa) 123.2(wl) 117(pp)×19×6.8]
Machinery: 2 screws, VTE engines (Stab Tecnico), 12 Yarrow boilers
IHP 13,000 = 21knots
Endurance: 4,500/10
Armament: 2×240mm/40, 5×194mm/42, 4×150mm/40, 9×66mm, 10×47mm, 2×450mm TT
Armour: Belt 165-210mm, turrets 210mm, deck 50mm, bulkheads 190mm, c/t 200mm
Complement: 628
Class notes: Improved 'Kaiser Karl VI' of similar appearance

'Erzherzog Karl' Class (1901-1903)

Pre-Dreadnoughts: *Erzherzog Ferdinand Max, Erzherzog Friedrich* (see later photo), *Erzherzog Karl*
Displacement: 10,600tons, 11,500f/l
Dimensions: 414(oa) 407'10(wl) 388'9(pp)×71'2×24.8 [126.2(oa) 124.3(wl) 118.5(pp)×21.7×7.5]
Machinery: 2 screws, VTE engines (Stab Tecnico), 12 Yarrow boilers
IHP 18,000 = 20.5knots
Endurance: 4,000/10
Armament: 4×240mm/40, 12×194mm/42, 12×66mm, 6×47mm, 4×37mm, 2×450mm TT
1916: 1×66mm AA added
Armour: Belt 120-210mm, turrets 240mm, casemates 170mm, secondary turrets 120-150mm, bulkheads 200mm, deck 55mm, c/t 220mm
Complement: 748
Class notes: Good for their size but obsolescent when completed. Secondary armament in four single turrets and casemates. Three funnels and two pole masts

'Radetzky' Class (1907)

Pre-Dreadnoughts: *Erzherzog Franz Ferdinand, Radetzky* (see later photo), *Zrinyi* (see later photo)
Displacement: 14,500tons, 15,665f/l
Dimensions: 455'4(oa) 450'9(wl) 430'2(pp)×80'9×26'6 [138.8(oa) 137.4(wl) 131.1(pp)×24.6×8.1]
Machinery: 2 screws, VTE engines (Stab Tecnico), 12 Yarrow boilers
IHP 20,000 = 20.5knots
Endurance: 5,000/10
Armament: 4×305/45, 8×240mm/50, 20×100mm/50, 6×66mm, 2×47mm, 3×450mm TT
1916: 2×66mm replaced by 2×66mm AA
Armour: Belt 60-230mm, turrets 150-250mm, barbettes 250mm, secondary turrets 200mm, casemates 120mm, deck 48mm, c/t 250mm

Top right:

***Kaiser* — Central battery ship, converted to ironclad 1872.**

Bottom right:

***Custoza* — Central battery ship 1889 following modernisation. Notice forward firing casemate forward of boats.**

Top:
***Prinz Eugen* — Central battery ship as it appeared in 1894, with new masts after modernisation.**

Above:
***Tegetthoff* — Central battery ship of 1875 as completed.**

Top right:
***Kronprinzessin Erzherzogin Stephanie* — Barbette ship of 1884. Notice prominent barbette below bridge.**

Centre right:
***Kaiserin und Königin Maria Theresia* — Armoured cruiser of 1890, shown in 1900. Note distinctive masts which were later replaced.**

Bottom right:
***Budapest* — Second class battleship, 1906.**

Complement: 830
Class notes: Again small compared to foreign contemporaries. Secondary armament in four twin turrets and smaller guns in casemates. Two funnels and two pole masts

'Tegetthoff' Class (1911)

Dreadnoughts: *Prinz Eugen, Szent István* (see later photo), *Tegetthoff, Viribus Unitis*
Displacement: 20,000tons, 21,595f/l
Dimensions: 499'4(oa) 496'9(wl) 469'2(pp) ×89'6×26'11 [152.2(oa) 151.4(wl) 143(pp)×27.3×8.2]
Machinery: 4 screws (*Szent István:* 2), Parsons turbines (Stab Tecnico; *Szent István:* AEG), 12 Yarrow boilers (*Szent Istvan:* B&W)
SHP 25,000 = 20knots
Endurance: 4,200/10
Armament: 12×305mm/45, 12×150mm/50, 18×66mm/50, 2×47mm, 4×533mm TT
1916: 6×66mm replaced by 2×76mm AA
Armour: Belt 280mm, turrets 150-280mm, barbettes 160-280mm, citadel and casemates 180mm, deck 36mm, c/t 280mm
Complement: 1,046
Class notes: Designed by Popper. First Austrian dreadnoughts with main guns in four triple superfiring turrets all on centreline. Weak protection against torpedoes and low speed, but compared favourably with Italian contemporaries. Original proposed names were *Tegetthoff, Prinz Eugen, Don Juan* and *Hunyadi. Szent István* had a searchlight platform built around the forward funnel

'Ersatz Monarch' Class (1914)

Dreadnoughts: 4 unnamed
Displacement: 24,560tons, 25,600f/l
Dimensions: 574'10(oa) 564'4(wl)×93'6×27'6 [175.2(oa) 172(wl)×28.5×8.4]
Machinery: 4 screws, turbines, 15 Yarrow boilers
SHP 31,000 = 21knots
Armament: 10×350mm/45, 14×150mm/50, 8×90mm, 12×90mm AA, 5×530mm TT
Armour: Belt 140-310mm, barbettes 320mm, casemates 150mm, c/t 320mm
Class notes: Designed by F. Pitzinger. Improved 'Tegetthoff' type having heavier armament, with two triple turrets superimposed over two twin turrets. None was ever laid down

Individual Ships

Arpád

Type: Pre-Dreadnought
Class: 'Habsburg' (1898)
Nomenclature: Arpád (d907), Chief of the Magyars, national hero of Hungary

Top left:
***Árpad* — Second class battleship, 1900, secondary battery in double casemates.**

Centre left:
***Tegetthoff* — Dreadnought 1914.** *Conway Photo Library*

Bottom left:
***Drache* — Armoured corvette, about 1866, prior to refit.**

History:
1899 June 10: Laid down by Stab Tecnico
1901 September 11: Launched
1903 June 15: Completed
1911-12 Refit
1918 Training ship
1918 November: Interned at Pola
1920 Broken up in Italy

Babenberg

Type: Pre-Dreadnought
Class: 'Habsburg' (1898)
Nomenclature: Franconian family, ruling dynasty of Austria 976-1246

History:
1901 January 19: Laid down by Stab Tecnico
1902 October 4: Launched
1904 May 24: Completed
1918 Accommodation ship
1918 November: Interned at Pola
1920 Broken up in Italy

Budapest

Type: Second Class Battleship
Class: 'Monarch' (1892)
Nomenclature: Capital of Hungary

History:
1893 February 16: Laid down by Stab Tecnico
1896 April 27: Launched
1898 May 12: Completed
1913-14 Training ship
1918 Accommodation ship for Naval Academy, Fiume
1918 November: Conversion and rearmament incomplete, interned at Pola
1920 Broken up in Italy

Custoza

Type: Central Battery Ship
Class: 'Custoza' (1868)
Nomenclature: Austrian victories over Sardinia 1848 and Italy 1866

History:
1869 November 17: Laid down by Stab Tecnico, San Rocco
1872 August 20: Launched
1875 February: Completed for trials
1877 Refit, rerigged
1882 Modernised
1894-95 Reconstructed
1902 Cadet training ship
1914 Accommodation ship, Pola
1920 Ceded to Italy and broken up

Don Juan d'Austria

Type: Central Battery Ship
Class: 'Kaiser Max' (1874)
Nomenclature: (see *Juan de Austria*)

History:
1874 February 14: Laid down by Stab Tecnico, San Rocco
1875 October 25: Launched
1876 June 26: Completed
1904 June 29: Stricken; accommodation ship, Pola

1919 Sank at anchor at Pola

Drache

Type: Broadside ship
Class: 'Drache' (1861)
Nomenclature: Dragon

History:
1861 February 18: Laid down by Stab Tecnico
1861 September 9: Launched
1862 November: Completed
1866 July 20: Battle of Lissa, damaged
1867-68 Refit, rearmed
1875 January 13: Stricken
1883 Broken up

Erzherzog Albrecht

Type: Central Battery Ship
Class: 'Erzherzog Albrecht' (1867)
Nomenclature: Archduke Albert, Duke of Teschen (1817-1895), field marshal and commander of the Austrian army at Custoza

History:
1870 June 1: Laid down by Stab Tecnico
1872 April 24: Launched
1874 June: Completed at Pola
1877 Refit
1892 Reconstructed
1908 Gunnery school training ship, renamed ***Feuerspeier***
1915 Accommodation ship for German U-boat crews
1920 Ceded to Italy, renamed ***Buttafuoco***
1946 Broken up

Erzherzog Ferdinand Max

Type: Broadside Ship
Class: 'Habsburg' (1863)
Nomenclature: Archduke Ferdinand Maximilian (1832-1867), later Emperor of Mexico, promoted development of the Austrian navy

History:
1863 May 6: Laid down by Stab Tecnico
1865 May 24: Launched
1866 Completed
1866 July 20: Battle of Lissa, flagship of Admiral Tegetthoff, rammed and sank Italian flagship *Re d'Italia*
1880 Refit
1886 May 19: Stricken
1889 Hulk, gunnery training ship
1916 Broken up

Erzherzog Ferdinand Max

Type: Pre-dreadnought
Class: 'Erzherzog Karl' (1901)

History:
1904 March 9: Laid down by Stab Tecnico
1905 May 21: Launched
1907 December 21: Completed
1918 November: Interned at Cattaro
1920 Ceded to Britain and broken up

Erzherzog Franz Ferdinand

Type: Pre-dreadnought
Class: 'Radetzky' (1907)
Nomenclature: Archduke Franz Ferdinand (1863-1914), heir to the Austrian throne, assassinated at Sarajevo

History:
1907 September 12: Laid down by Stab Tecnico
1908 September 30: Launched
1910 June 15: Completed
1918 November: Interned at Pola, later moved to Venice
1920 Broken up in Italy

Erzherzog Friedrich

Type: Pre-dreadnought
Class: 'Erzherzog Karl' (1901)
Nomenclature: Archduke Frederick (1812-1847), commander-in-chief of the Austrian navy 1844-47

History:
1902 October 4: Laid down by Stab Tecnico
1904 April 30: Launched
1907 January 31: Completed
1918 November: Interned at Cattaro
1920 Ceded to France and broken up

Erzherzog Karl

Type: Pre-dreadnought
Class: 'Erzherzog Karl' (1901)
Nomenclature: Archduke Charles, Duke of Teschen (1771-1847), field marshal and commander of the Austrian forces against Napoleon

History:
1902 July 24: Laid down by Stab Tecnico
1903 October 4: Launched
1906 June 17: Completed
1918 November: Interned at Cattaro
1920 Ceded to France
1920 Went aground near Bizerte while in tow to Toulon
—— Broken up

Habsburg

Type: Broadside Ship
Class: 'Habsburg' (1863)
Nomenclature: Ruling dynasty of Austria-Hungary 1282-1918

History:
1863 June: Laid down by Stab Tecnico, San Rocco
1865 June 25: Launched
1866 Completed
1866 July 20: Battle of Lissa
1877 Refit
1886 Harbour depot ship and accommodation ship, Pola
1898 October 22: Stricken and broken up 1900

Habsburg

Type: Pre-dreadnought
Class: 'Habsburg' (1898)

History:
1899 March 13: Laid down by Stab Tecnico, San Rocco
1900 September 9: Launched

Above:
***Erzherzog Friedrich* — Battleship of 1901.**

Below:
***Kaiser Karl VI* — Armoured cruiser of 1895.**

1902 December 31: Completed
1910-11 Refit
1918 Training ship
1918 November: Interned at Pola
1920 Broken up in Italy

Juan de Austria

Type: Broadside Ship
Class: 'Kaiser Max' (1861)
Nomenclature: Don Juan of Austria (1545-1578), Spanish general, victor of Lepanto, natural son of Emperor Charles V

History:
1861 October: Laid down by Stab Tecnico
1862 July 26: Launched
1863 Completed
1864 Served in North Sea during war with Denmark
1866 July 20: Battle of Lissa
1867 Refit
1873 December: At Trieste for 'rebuilding'
1886 Broken up

Kaiser

Type: Central Battery Ship
Class: 'Kaiser' (1868)
Nomenclature: Emperor

History:
1855 March 25: Laid down at Pola as 91-gun wood screw ship-of-the-line
1858 October 5: Launched
1864 Served in North Sea during war with Denmark
1866 July 20: Severely damaged at Battle of Lissa (24 dead)
1869 February 2: Conversion to ironclad begun
1871 December 20: Launched
1874 Conversion completed
1877 Refit
1901 Hulk, accommodation ship, Pola, renamed ***Bellona***
1920 Broken up in Italy

Kaiser Karl VI

Type: Armoured Cruiser
Class: 'Kaiser Karl VI' (1895)
Nomenclature: Charles VI, Holy Roman Emperor (1685-1740), last of the Habsburg Emperors in the direct male line

History:
1896 June 1: Laid down by Stab Tecnico
1898 October 4: Launched
1900 May 23: Completed
1902-03 Served in East Asia
1918 November 1: Interned at Sebenico
1920 Broken up in Italy

Kaiser Max

Type: Broadside Ship
Class: 'Kaiser Max' (1861)
Nomenclature: Maximilian I, Holy Roman Emperor (1459-1519)

History:
1861 October: Laid down by Stab Tecnico, San Rocco
1862 March 14: Launched
1863 Completed
1864 Served in North Sea during war with Denmark
1866 July 20: Battle of Lissa
1867 Refit
1873 December: 'Rebuilt'

Kaiser Max

Type: Central Battery Ship
Class: 'Kaiser Max' (1874)

History:
1874 February 14: Laid down by Stab Tecnico
1875 December 28: Launched
1876 October 26: Completed
1904 December 30: Stricken; accommodation ship, Cattaro
1920 To Yugoslavia, renamed ***Tivat***, later renamed ***Neretva***
1941 April: At Sibenik, fate unknown

Kaiserin und Königin Maria Theresia

Type: Armoured Cruiser
Class: 'Maria Theresia' (1890)
Nomenclature: Empress and Queen Maria Theresa (1717-1780), whose succession to the throne led to the War of the Austrian Succession

History:
1891 October 6: Laid down by Stab Tecnico
1893 April 29: Launched
1895 March 24: Completed
1900-02 Served in China
1903 Refit
1909 Reconstructed
World War 1: Guardship at Sibenik
1917 Accommodation ship for U-boat crews at Pola
1920 Broken up

Kronprinz Erzherzog Rudolf

Type: Barbette Ship
Class: 'Kronprinz Rudolf' (1883)
Nomenclature: Archduke Rudolf, Crown Prince of Austria (1858-1889), only son of Emperor Francis Joseph I

History:
1884 January 25: Laid down at Pola
1887 July 6: Launched
1889 September 20: Completed for trials
1890 Served abroad
1893 Modernised
1906 Stricken, station ship
World War 1: Harbour defence, Cattaro
1919 To Yugoslavia, renamed ***Kumbor***
1922 Sold and broken up

Kronprinzessin Erzherzogin Stephanie

Type: Barbette Ship
Class: 'Kronprinzessin Stephanie' (1884)

Top left:
***Monarch* — Second class battleship of 1892, stern view showing aft turret and casemate guns.**

Bottom left:
***Radetzky* — Pre-dreadnought, 1914. Forward turret trained to port.**

***Szent István* — Dreadnought of 1911.**

Nomenclature: Archduchess Stephanie (1864-1945), wife of Crown Prince Archduke Rudolf

History:
1884 November 12: Laid down by Stab Tecnico as ***Erzherzog Ferdinand Max;*** renamed ***Kronprinzessin Erzherzogin Stephanie***
1887 April 14: Launched
1889 July 11: Completed for trials
1898-1906 In reserve
1906 Stricken, accommodation and station ship, Cattaro
1910 Hulk
World War 1: Accommodation ship for mine school, Pola
1914 August 7: Renamed ***Gamma***
1919 Ceded to Italy
1926 Broken up

Lissa

Type: Central Battery Ship
Class: 'Lissa' (1865)
Nomenclature: Austrian naval victory over Italy, 20 July 1866, off Lissa (now Vis)

History:
1867 June 20: Laid down by Stab Tecnico
1869 February 25: Launched
1871 May: Completed
1875-77 Refit
1892 November 13: Stricken and broken up 1893

Monarch

Type: Second Class Battleship
Class: 'Monarch' (1892)
Nomenclature: Monarch

History:
1893 July 31: Laid down at Pola
1895 May 9: Launched
1898 May 11: Completed
1898 July 22: In collision with torpedo boat *Bussard* off Dalmatian coast
1913-14 Training ship
1918 Accommodation ship
1918 November: Interned at Cattaro
1920 Broken up in Italy

Prinz Eugen

Type: Broadside Ship
Class: 'Kaiser Max' (1861)
Nomenclature: Prince Eugene of Savoy (1663-1736), brilliant Austrian general and Imperial field marshal gaining victories against the Turks and French

History:
1861 October: Laid down by Stab Tecnico
1862 June 14: Launched
1863 March: Completed
1866 July 20: Battle of Lissa
1867 Modernised
1873 Hulk
1876 Gunnery training ship, renamed ***Feuerspeier***
1886 Stricken and broken up

Prinz Eugen

Type: Central Battery Ship
Class: 'Kaiser Max' (1874)

History:
1874 October: Laid down at Pola
1877 September 7: Launched
1878 November: Completed
1891-92 Modernised
1904 December 30: Stricken
1906-08 Converted to repair ship, renamed ***Vulkan***
1920 Ceded to Italy and sold to Yugoslavia, never handed over

Prinz Eugen

Type: Dreadnought
Class: 'Tegetthoff' (1911)

***Tegetthoff*— Central battery ship of 1875 as reconstructed in 1893. Notice hull indented to permit axial fire of guns.**

History:
1912 January 16: Laid down by Stab Tecnico
1912 November 30: Launched
1914 July 8: Completed
1915 May 24: Bombarded Ancona
1918 November: Interned at Cattaro
1920 Allocated to France
1922 June 28: Sunk as a target off Toulon by French battleships *France* and *Bretagne*

Radetzky

Type: Pre-dreadnought
Class: 'Radetzky' (1907)
Nomenclature: Count Joseph Wenzel Radetzky von Radetz (1766-1858), field marshal, victor of Custoza and Novara

History:
1907 November 26: Laid down by Stab Tecnico
1909 July 3: Launched
1911 January 15: Completed
World War 1
1914 October 21: Bombarded Mount Lovcen at Cattaro
1918 November: Sailed to Split under Yugoslav flag
1922 Broken up in Italy

Salamander

Type: Broadside Ship
Class: 'Drache' (1861)
Nomenclature: Salamander

History:
1861 February: Laid down by Stab Tecnico
1861 August 20: Launched
1862 May: Completed
1866 July 20: Battle of Lissa
1867-68 Refit, rearmed
1883 March 18: Stricken, mine depot ship
1896 Broken up

Sankt Georg

Type: Armoured Cruiser
Class: 'Sankt Georg' (1900)
Nomenclature: St George, patron saint of soldiers

History:
1903 March 11: Laid down at Pola
1903 December 8: Launched
1905 July 21: Completed
1907 Visited North America
1918 November: Interned at Cattaro
1920 Broken up

Szent István

Type: Dreadnought
Class: 'Tegetthoff' (1911)
Nomenclature: Stephen I (975-1038), King and patron saint of Hungary

History:
1912 January 29: Laid down by Danubius
1914 January 17: Launched
1915 November 17: Completed at Pola for reasons of security
1918 June 10: Torpedoed and sunk by Italian MTB *MAS15* off Premuda Island (89 dead)

Tegetthoff

Type: Central Battery Ship
Class: 'Tegetthoff' (1875)
Nomenclature: Wilhelm von Tegetthoff (1827-1871), admiral, victor of Lissa

History:
1876 April 1: Laid down by Stab Tecnico, San Rocco
1878 October 18: Launched
1882 August 5: Completed for trials
1891-93 Modernised, re-engined
1906 Stricken, harbour guardship
1912 Renamed ***Mars***
1914 Guardship, Pola

1917 Training ship
1920 Broken up in Italy

Tegetthoff

Type: Dreadnought
Class: 'Tegetthoff' (1911)

History:
1910 September 24: Laid down by Stab Tecnico
1912 March 31: Launched
1913 July 14: Completed
1914 May: Visited Malta
1915 May 24: Bombarded Ancona
1918 November: Interned at Venice
1920 Allocated to Italy
1924 Broken up at La Spezia

Viribus Unitis

Type: Dreadnought
Class: 'Tegetthoff' (1911)
Nomenclature: With United Effort, motto of the Austrian Emperor

History:
1910 July 24: Laid down by Stab Tecnico
1911 June 24: Launched
1912 October 6: Completed
1914 May: Visited Malta
World War 1: Fleet flagship
1914 July: Carried body of Archduke Franz Ferdinand to Trieste
1915 May 24: Bombarded Ancona
1918 October 31: Became flagship of new Yugoslav navy
1918 November 1: Sunk by Italian frogmen at Pola (400 dead)

Wien

Type: Second Class Battleship
Class: 'Monarch' (1892)
Nomenclature: Vienna, capital of Austria

History:
1893 February 16: Laid down by Stab Tecnico
1895 July 7: Launched
1897 May 13: Completed
1913-14 Gunnery training ship
1917 December 10: Torpedoed and sunk by Italian MTB *MAS9* in Trieste harbour

Zrinyi

Type: Pre-dreadnought
Class: 'Radetzky' (1907)
Nomenclature: Count Miklos von Zrinyi (1508-1566), Ban of Croatia, hero of the siege of Szigetvar

History:
1909 January 20: Laid down by Stab Tecnico
1910 April 12: Launched
1911 September 15: Completed
1918 November: Sailed to Split under Yugoslav flag
1922 Broken up in Italy

***Zrinyi* — Pre-dreadnought of 'Radetzky' class.**

Brazil

As a country with a long coastline, Brazil has always maintained a substantial navy. During the war with Paraguay in the 1860s, Brazil acquired a fleet of small armoured monitors which carried out a riverine campaign in the interior of the South American continent.

Two modern turret ships were built in the 1880s; these remained the backbone of the fleet for several decades. A major civil war occurred in 1893 and the fleet was divided between the contending factions, sustaining losses including the turret ships *Aquidaban* and *Javary*.

The increased size of the Argentine navy as a result of a dispute with Chile led Brazil to start construction of two dreadnoughts in Britain in 1907. As a result, Brazil had dreadnoughts in commission before such larger powers as France, Italy and Russia. During the naval race that followed Brazil ordered the huge *Rio de Janeiro* and the even larger *Riachuelo* but the resulting financial crisis caused the sale of the first and cancellation of the second. During World War 1 Brazil offered to send its dreadnoughts to join the British Grand Fleet but the offer was refused.

Between the wars the *Minas Gerais* was modernised but its sister-ship was not and during World War 2 both were inactive.

In 1956 Brazil acquired its only aircraft carrier, *Minas Gerais*, but no aircraft were acquired for several years as a result of a dispute with the air force.

Class Details

'Brasil' (1863)

Central Battery Ship: *Brasil*
Displacement: 1,520tons
Dimensions: 208(oa) 197'3(pp)×35'2×12'2 [63.4(oa) 60.1(pp)×10.7×3.7]
Machinery: 1 screw, single expansion engine (F C Med)
IHP 1,500 = 11.25knots
Armament: 4×180mm MLR, 4×68pdr SB
Armour: Belt 114mm, battery 114mm
Complement: 180
Class notes: Iron hull coast defence ship with armoured redoubt. Single funnel forward of the battery and three masts. First Brazilian armoured vessel, paid for by popular subscription

'Bahia' (1864)

Monitor: *Bahia*
Displacement: 928tons
Dimensions: 175'8(pp)×35'2×7'9 [53.5(pp)×10.7×2.4]
Machinery: 2 screws, horizontal trunk engines (Laird), 2 boilers
IHP 1,640 = 10knots
Armament: 2×180mm 150pdr MLR
Armour: Belt 76-114mm, turret 140mm
Complement: 120
Class notes: Iron hull monitor with single turret and bark rig. Originally ordered by Paraguay and purchased by Brazil before completion

'Mariz e Barros' (1864)

Coast Defence Ship: *Mariz e Barros*
Displacement: 1,197tons
Dimensions: 193×37'6×9'9 [58.8×11.4×3]
Machinery: 2 screws, single expansion engines
IHP 600 = 9knots
Armament: 2×180mm MLR, 2×68pdr
Armour: Belt 115mm, battery 121mm
Complement: 110
Class notes: Wood hull central battery ship classified as armoured corvette. Ordered by Paraguay and purchased 1865

'Lima Barros' (1864)

Coast Defence Ship: *Lima Barros*
Displacement: 1,705tons
Dimensions: 200'2(pp)×38'2×12'8 [61(pp)×11.6×3.9]
Machinery: 2 screws, single expansion engines (Ravenhill)
IHP 600 = 11knots
Armament: 4×150mm
Armour: Belt 115mm, turrets 115mm
Complement: 170
Class notes: Small ironclad with two turrets classified as armoured frigate. Iron hull, bark rig

'Silvado' (1864)

Coast Defence Ship: *Silvado*
Displacement: 1,350tons
Dimensions: 216'6×45'10×7'6 [66×14×2.3]
Machinery: 2 screws, single expansion engines (Mazeline)
IHP 950 = 10knots
Armament: 4×150mm MLR
Armour: Belt 115mm, turrets 115mm
Complement: 170
Class notes: Similar to *Lima Barros*, iron hull with two turrets and bark rig

'Herval' (1864)

Coast Defence Ship: *Herval*
Displacement: 1,440tons
Dimensions: 190(pp)×36×19 [57.9(pp)×10.9×5.8]
Machinery: 2 screws, single expansion engine
IHP 950 = 9knots
Armament: 2×120mm, 2×68pdr
Armour: Belt 115mm, battery 121mm
Complement: 110
Class notes: Wood hull central battery ship originally ordered by Paraguay

'Independencia' (1872)

Turret Ship: *[Independencia]*
Displacement: 9,310tons
Dimensions: 300(pp)×63×25 [91.4(pp)×19.2×7.6]
Machinery: 1 screw, horizontal trunk engines (Penn), 8 rectangular boilers
IHP 8,500 = 14.2knots

Endurance: 1,480/10
Armament: 4×305mm MLR, 2×203mm MLR
Armour: Belt 229-305mm, redoubt 203-254mm, turrets 279-330mm, bulkheads 152-203mm, decks 51-76mm, c/t 152-203mm
Complement: 540
Class notes: Similar to British *Devastation* with bark rig, superstructure for which deprived the two turrets of axial fire. Hull had to be rebuilt after suffering damage during launching. Purchased by Britain after launching 1878 and renamed *Neptune*

'Solimões' Class (1874)

Turret Ships: *Javary, Solimões*
Displacement: 3,641tons
Dimensions: 240(pp)×58×11'5 [73.1(pp)×17.7×3.5]
Machinery: 2 screws, compound back-acting engines (F C Med), 8 cylindrical boilers
IHP 2,200 = 11.2knots
Endurance: 680/10
Armament: 4×250mm MLR
Armour: Belt 152-305mm, turrets 279-330mm, deck 76mm
Complement: 135
Class notes: Iron hull ships with low freeboard, two twin turrets, single funnel and single mast

'Riachuelo' (1881)

Turret Ship: *Riachuelo*
Displacement: 5,700tons, 6,100f/l
Dimensions: 320'6(oa) 305(pp)×52×19'6 [97.7(oa) 93(pp)×15.8×5.9]
Machinery: 2 screws, vertical compound engines (Humphrys), 10 cylindrical boilers
IHP 6,000 = 15knots
Endurance: 6,000/10
Armament: 4×229mm BLR, 6×140mm, 5×355mm TT
1895: 4×240mm/40 BL, 6×120mm/45, 6×47mm
Armour: Belt 178-280mm, turrets 255mm, bulkheads 255mm, deck 50mm, c/t 255mm
Complement: 390
Class notes: Steel hull with two twin turrets mounted en echelon amidships and two funnels. Designed with bark rig but completed with two masts. Reconstructed 1895 when two heavy military masts were fitted. These were removed 1904

'Aquidaban' (1882)

Turret Ship: *Aquidaban*
Displacement: 4,950tons
Dimensions: 280(pp)×52×18'8 [85.3(pp)×15.8×5.7]
Machinery: 2 screws, vertical compound engines, 8 cylindrical boilers
IHP 5,000 = 15knots
Endurance: 5,500/10
Armament: 4×234mm BLR, 4×140mm, 5×355mm TT
1898: 4×240mm/40, 4×120mm/45, 2×47mm, 5 TT
Armour: Belt 150-280mm, turrets 255mm, bulkheads 255mm, deck 50mm, c/t 255mm
Complement: 388
Class notes: Similar to *Riachuelo* but somewhat smaller with single funnel. Reconstructed 1898, fitted with two heavy military masts and rearmed. Military masts removed 1904

'Deodoro' Class (1896)

Coast Defence Ships: *Marescìallo Deodoro, Maresciallo Floriano* (see later photo)
Displacement: 3,162tons
Dimensions: 267'6(wl)×47'11×22 [81.5(wl)×14.6×6.8]
Machinery: 2 screws, VTE engines (F C Med), 8 Lagrafel-d'Allest boilers; *1912:* B&W boilers
IHP 3,400 = 14knots
Endurance: 2,500/10
Armament: 2×234mm/45, 4×120mm/50, 2×12pdr, 4×6pdr, 2×457mm TT
Armour: Belt 150-350mm, turrets 220mm, casemates 75mm, c/t 125mm
Complement: 200
Class notes: Small armoured vessels with low freeboard and two single turrets fore and aft, single funnel and two masts. Fighting tops removed from masts 1916

'São Paulo' Class (1906)

Dreadnoughts: *Minas Gerais, São Paulo* (see also later photo)
Displacement: 19,280tons, 21,200f/l
Dimensions: 543(oa) 532'9(wl) 500(pp)×83×25 [165.5(oa) 162.4(wl) 152.4(pp)×25.3×7.6]
Machinery: 2 screws, VTE engines (Vickers), 18 B&W boilers; *Minas Gerais, 1938:* 6 Thornycroft boilers
IHP 23,500 = 21knots; *Minas Gerais, 1938:* IHP 30,000 = 22knots
Endurance: 8,000/10
Armament: 12×305mm/45, 22×120mm/50
1919: 2×76mm AA added
Minas Gerais, 1938: 8×120mm removed, 4×40mm AA added
Armour: Belt 102-230mm, turrets 203-230mm, battery 230mm, bulkheads 75mm and 230mm, c/t 305mm
Complement: 850
Class notes: Enlarged 'Dreadnought' type with superfiring turrets. Six twin turrets with two on beam amidships. Tripod mast abaft forward funnel. Offer for them to serve with Grand Fleet in 1917 not accepted because of difficulties with fuel. Secondary armament reduced 1917-20. *Minas Gerais* reconstructed 1934-37, reboilered and forward funnel removed. Reconstruction of *São Paulo* in 1939 cancelled

'Rio de Janeiro' (1910)

Dreadnought: *[Rio de Janeiro]*
Displacement: 27,500tons, 30,250f/l
Dimensions: 671'6(oa) 632(pp)×89×27 [204.7(oa) 192.6(pp)×27.1×8.2]
Machinery: 4 screws, Parsons turbines (Vickers), 22 B&W boilers
SHP 34,000 = 22knots
Armament: 14×305mm/45, 20×152mm/50, 10×76mm, 3×533mm TT
Armour: Belt 102-229mm, barbettes 76-229mm, turrets 203-305mm, bulkheads 76-152mm, c/t 305mm
Complement: 1,115
Class notes: Ordered to ensure Brazilian superiority in Latin American waters but sold to Turkey before completion. Eventually completed as British *Agincourt*

Top right:
***Solimoes* — Turret ship of 1874, wrecked 1892.**
Marius Bar

Centre right:
***Riachuelo* — Turret ship as reconstructed in 1895 with heavy military masts.** *Marius Bar*

Bottom right:
***Maresciallo Deodoro* — Coast defence ship of 1896.**
Marius Bar

A11

'Riachuelo' (1914)

Dreadnought: *[Riachuelo]*
Displacement: 30,500 tons
Dimensions: 670(oa) 620(pp)×94×28 [204.2(oa) 189(pp)×28.7×8.5]
Machinery: 4 screws, Parsons turbines, B&W boilers
SHP 40,500 = 22.5knots
Armament: 8×381mm/42, 14×152mm/50, 10×102mm/50, 4×76mm AA, 2×533mm TT
Armour: Belt 102-343mm, barbettes 330mm, c/t 330mm
Class notes: Similar to contemporary British battleships of 'Queen Elizabeth' class. Little work was done before the war; the keel was never laid

'Minas Gerais' (1956)

Light Aircraft Carrier: *Minas Gerais*
Displacement: 15,890tons, 19,890f/l
Dimensions: 693'4(oa) 630(pp)×80'3×21'4 [211.3(oa) 192(pp)×24.5×6.5]
Machinery: 2 screws, Parsons geared turbines (Wallsend), 4 Admiralty 3-drum boilers
SHP 42,000 = 25knots
Endurance: 12,000/14
Aircraft: 35
Armament: 10×40mm AA
Complement: 1,300
Class notes: Former British *Vengeance* purchased 1956. Reconstructed 1960; angled flightdeck, steam catapults, rearmed, new fire control and radar

Individual Ships

Aquidaban

Type: Turret Ship
Class: 'Aquidaban' (1882)
Nomenclature: Battle which ended the war with Paraguay, 1870

History:
1883 June 18: Laid down by Samuda
1885 January 17: Launched
1885 June 16: Completed for trials
1887 Completed
1893 September 7: Seized by rebels at Rio de Janeiro
1894 April 16: Torpedoed and sunk in shallow water at Santa Catarina by government torpedo boats during Civil War
1894 June: Salved and refitted
1894 July: Renamed ***Vinte Quatro de Maio***
1897-98 Reconstructed by Vulcan, Stettin
1900 Renamed ***Aquidaban***
1906 January 21: Blew up and sank near Rio de Janeiro (212 dead, including Rear Admirals Rodrigues da Rocha, Candido Brasil and Calheiros da Graça)

Top left:
***Sao Paulo* — Dreadnought, as completed at Barrow, 1910.**

Centre left:
***Minas Gerais* — Light aircraft carrier purchased 1956.**

Bottom left:
***Maresciallo Floriano* — Coast defence ship of 1896 as completed. Note fighting tops which were later removed.** *Marius Bar*

Bahia

Type: Monitor
Class: 'Bahia' (1864)
Nomenclature: A state of Brazil, now Baia

History:
1864 Laid down for Paraguay by Laird as ***Minerva***
1865 June 11: Launched as ***Bahia***
1866 January 22: Completed
1866-68 Paraguayan War operations
1873 Refit
1893 Civil War
1894 Stricken

Brasil

Type: Central Battery Ship
Class: 'Brasil' (1863)
Nomenclature: Brazil

History:
1864 Laid down at La Seyne
1864 December 2: Launched
1865 July: Completed; left Toulon for trials and did not return in order to escape embargo
1865 August 23: Arrived at Rio de Janeiro
1866-68 Paraguayan War operations
1879 Floating battery
1905 Broken up

Herval

Type: Coast Defence Ship
Class: 'Herval' (1864)
Nomenclature: Manoel Luis Osorio, Marques do Herval (1808-1879), an army commander during the Paraguayan War

History:
1864 Laid down for Paraguay by Rennie as ***Medusa***
1865 Launched as ***Herval***
1866 June 14: Completed
1866-68 Paraguayan War operations
1885 Stricken

Independencia

Type: Turret Ship
Class: 'Independencia' (1872)
Nomenclature: Independence

History:
1873 Laid down by Dudgeon
1874 July 30: Launch incomplete, stuck on the ways
1874 September 10: Launched successfully
1878 March: Sold to Great Britain, renamed ***Neptune***

Javary

Type: Turret Ship
Class: 'Solimoes' (1874)
Nomenclature: River on the upper Amazon

History:
1874 January: Laid down at Graville
1875 Launched
1875 March 10: Completed for trials

1893 September 7: Seized by rebels at Rio de Janeiro; engines disabled
1893 November 22: Capsized and sank after engaging government coastal batteries in Rio de Janeiro harbour during Civil War

Lima Barros

Type: Coast Defence Ship
Class: 'Lima Barros' (1864)
Nomenclature: Francisco Jose de Lima Barros (1847-1865), a midshipman killed in action at the Battie of Riachuelo, 11 June 1865

History:
1864 Laid down by Laird as ***Belona***
1865 December 21: Launched as ***Lima Barros***
1866 April 3: Completed
1866-68 Paraguayan War operations
1883 May 8: Stricken
1905 Broken up

Maresciallo Deodoro

Type: Coast Defence Ship
Class: 'Deodoro' (1896)
Nomenclature: Manuel Deodoro da Fonseca (1827-1892), prominent general in the Paraguayan War and a leader in the overthrow of Dom Pedro

History:
1896 December: Laid down at La Seyne as ***Ypiranga***
1896 Renamed ***Maresciallo Deodoro***
1898 June 20: Launched
1900 Completed
1924 April 24: Sold to Mexico, renamed ***Anahuac***
c1940 Discarded

Maresciallo Floriano

Type: Coast Defence Ship
Class: 'Deodoro' (1896)
Nomenclature: Floriano Vieira Peixoto (1842-1895), a leader on the overthrow of Dom Pedro, later President of Brazil

History:
1897 March: Laid down at La Seyne
1899 June 6: Launched
1900 December 31: Completed
1924-25 Refit
1934 April 25: Stricken
1936 June 6: Sold and broken up

Mariz e Barros

Type: Coast Defence Ship
Class: 'Mariz e Barros' (1864)
Nomenclature: Antonio Carlos de Mariz e Barros (1835-1866), commanding officer of the *Tamandaré,* killed in action at Paso de la Patria, Paraguay, 28 March 1866

History:
1864 Laid down for Paraguay by Rennie as ***Triton***
1865 Launched as ***Mariz e Barros***
1866 July 23: Completed
1866-68 Paraguayan War operations
1879 July 1: Reclassified floating battery
—— Rearmed
1897 June 23: Stricken

Minas Gerais

Type: Dreadnought
Class: 'Sao Paulo' (1906)
Nomenclature: A state of Brazil

History:
1907 April 17: Laid down by Armstrong
1908 September 10: Launched
1910 January 5: Completed
1910 November 22: In revolt against government and shelled Rio de Janeiro
1910 December 10: Helped quell rebellion by marines on Cobras island
World War 1: South Atlantic 1917-18, offer to serve in British Grand Fleet not accepted
1920-21 Refit at New York
1924 July: Helped quell rebellion at Santos
1934-37 Reconstructed at Rio de Janeiro
World War 2: Floating battery at Salvador, Bahia
1954 Sold and broken up at Genoa

Minas Gerais

Type: Light Aircraft Carrier
Class: 'Minas Gerais' (1956)

History:
1942 November 16: Laid down by Swan Hunter as British ***Vengeance***
1944 February 23: Launched
1945 January 15: Completed
1956 December 13: Sold to Brazil, renamed ***Minas Gerais***
1957-60 Reconstructed by Verolme Dock, Rotterdam
1961 January: Completed
1976-81 Refit

Riachuelo

Type: Turret Ship
Class: 'Riachuelo' (1881)
Nomenclature: Battle of the war with Paraguay, 11 June 1865

History:
—— Laid down by Samuda
1883 June 7: Launched
1884 July 15: Completed
1893-95 Reconstructed at La Seyne
1904 Refit
1910 Sold
1911 Foundered in tow en route to Europe for breaking up

Riachuelo

Type: Dreadnought
Class: 'Riachuelo' (1914)

History:
1914 Ordered from Vickers but never laid down

Rio de Janeiro

Type: Dreadnought
Class: 'Rio de Janeiro' (1910)
Nomenclature: Capital of Brazil

History:
1911 September 14: Laid down by Armstrong

1913 January 22: Launched
1914 January 9: Sold incomplete to Turkey, renamed ***Sultan Osman I***

São Paulo

Type: Dreadnought
Class: 'São Paulo' (1906)
Nomenclature: A state of Brazil

History:
1907 Laid down by Vickers
1909 April 19: Launched
1910 September 19: Completed
1910 November 22: In revolt against government and shelled Rio de Janeiro
1910 December 10: Helped quell rebellion by marines on Cobras island
1917 Refit at New York
World War 1: South Atlantic 1917-18; offer to serve in Grand Fleet not accepted
1921 December: Carried remains of Emperor Pedro II back to Brazil
1922 July 7: Helped quell rebellion at Fort Copacabana
1939 Reconstruction cancelled
World War 2: Floating battery at Recife
1946 Stricken
1951 August: Sold
1951 November 4: Foundered off the Azores while in tow to breaking up

Silvado

Type: Coast Defence Ship
Class: 'Silvado' (1864)
Nomenclature: Americo Brasilio Silvado, commanding officer of the *Rio de Janeiro* killed when his ship was sunk at Curuzu, Paraguay, 2 September 1866

History:
1864 Laid down by Arman as ***Nemesis***
1865 Launched as ***Silvado***
1866 September 15: Completed
1866-68 Paraguayan War operations
1880 June 3: Stricken

Solimões

Type: Turret Ship
Class: 'Solimoes' (1874)
Nomenclature: River on the upper Amazon

History:
1874 January: Laid down at La Seyne
1875 January 2: Launched
1875 April 23: Completed
1892 May 21: Wrecked off Cape Polonio, Uruguay while en route to assist in suppressing insurrection in Mato Grosso (125 dead)

Vinte Quatro de Maio, see *Aquidaban*

Nomenclature: 24th of May, anniversary of the Battle of Tuiuti

***Sao Paulo* — Dreadnought of 1906, as completed.**

Chile

Several years after a Spanish squadron bombarded the Chilean port of Valparaiso, two modern ironclad warships were built for the Chilean navy. In 1879 Bolivia and Peru declared war on Chile. The Chilean navy with its ironclads was superior at sea and in several engagements the Peruvian navy was annihilated. The ironclad *Huascar* was captured in a bitter fight and added to the navy.

Civil war broke out in 1891 in which several naval actions occurred and the ironclad *Blanco Encalada* was sunk by government vessels. A border dispute with Argentina in the 1890s led to a naval race and Chile built two armoured cruisers and ordered two battleships in Britain. The financial costs of the dispute caused its settlement and the battleships were sold to Britain. After Brazil and Argentina started adding dreadnoughts to their fleets, Chile ordered two in 1912 which were still under construction when World War 1 started. They were purchased by Britain and the *Almirante Latorre* was commissioned in the Royal Navy. Less progress had been made on the *Almirante Cochrane* and it was completed after the war as the aircraft carrier *Eagle*.

In 1920 the *Almirante Latorre* and other vessels were purchased back by Chile and it remained the flagship of the fleet until 1958.

Class Details

'Almirante Cochrane' Class (1872)

Central Battery Ships: *Almirante Cochrane, Blanco Encalada*
Displacement: 3,480tons
Dimensions: 210(oa) 204(pp)×46'9×19'8 [64(oa) 62.2(pp)×14.2×6]
Machinery: 2 screws, horizontal compound engines (Penn), 6 cylindrical boilers
IHP 3,000 = 12knots
Endurance: 1,200/10
Armament: 6×229 MLR, 1×20pdr, 1×9pdr, 1×7pdr
1890: 6×203mm/30, 1×13pdr, 4×6pdr, 3 TT
Armour: Belt 114-229mm, battery 152-203mm, bulkheads 152mm, deck 50-75mm, c/t 114mm
Complement: 300
Class notes: Designed by Reed. Iron hull with armoured redoubt and bark rig. Rearmed 1885-89. *Cochrane* re-engined and reboilered 1889, and reconstructed 1897-1900, sail rig replaced by single military mast

'Huascar' (1879)

Turret Ship: *Huascar*
Displacement: 1,870tons
Dimensions: 190(oa)×35'6×16 [57.9(oa)×10.8×4.9]
Machinery: 1 screw, horizontal return connecting-rod engines (Laird), 4 box boilers
IHP 1,100 = 9knots
Armament: 2×203mm BLR, 2×40pdr
Later: 2×120mm added
Armour: Belt 63-114mm, turret 140-190mm, deck 51mm, bulkhead 152mm, c/t 76mm
Complement: 135
Class notes: Small iron hull vessel with single turret amidships and brig rig. Captured in action with Peru 1879. Rearmed and commissioned

'Capitan Prat' (1887)

Barbette Ship: *Capitan Prat*
Displacement: 6,900tons
Dimensions: 364'2(oa) 328(pp)×60'8×26.4 [111(oa) 100(pp)×18.5×8]
Machinery: 2 screws, HTE engines (F C Med), 5 cylindrical boilers; *1909:* 12 B&W boilers
IHP 12,000 = 18.25knots
Endurance: 4,650/10
Armament: 4×240mm/36, 8×120mm/45, 8×57mm, 4×47mm, 4×450mm TT
Armour: Belt 200-300mm, citadel 80mm, barbettes 200-275mm, c/t 267mm
Complement: 480
Class notes: Steel hull small battleship with four single turrets, one each fore and aft and one on each beam. Two funnels and two military masts. Reconstructed 1910; new boilers, funnels raised

'Esmeralda' (1894)

Armoured Cruiser: *Esmeralda*
Displacement: 7,000tons
Dimensions: 468'3(oa) 436(pp)×53'2×20'2 [142.7(oa) 132.9(pp)×16.2×6.2]
Machinery: 2 screws, VTE engines (Humphrys), double-ended cylindrical boilers
IHP 16,000 = 23knots
Endurance: 4,650/10
Armament: 2×203mm/40, 16×152mm/40, 8×76mm, 9×57mm, 3×457mm TT
1910: 4×152mm removed
Armour: Belt 150mm, shields 115mm, bulkheads 150mm, deck 50mm, c/t 200mm
Complement: 500
Class notes: Designed by Watts. First armoured cruiser built by Armstrong, actually a 'belted' cruiser with two single mounts fore and aft, two funnels and two military masts

'General O'Higgins' (1895)

Armoured Cruiser: *General O'Higgins*
Displacement: 8,500tons
Dimensions: 412(oa) 407(pp)×62'9×22 [125.6(oa) 124.1(pp)×19.1×6.7]
Machinery: 2 screws, VTE engines (Humphrys), 30 Belleville boilers
IHP 16,500 = 21.25knots

Top right:
***Almirante Cochrane* — Central battery ship of 1872, as it appeared in 1888. Notice indentation in hull to permit axial fire of guns in the battery.** *Marius Bar*

Bottom right:
***Huascar* — Turret ship captured from Peru in 1879.**

Endurance: 6,000/10
Armament: 4×203mm/45, 10×152mm/40, 4×120mm/45, 10×76mm, 10×57mm, 3×457mm TT
Armour: Belt 127-178mm, turrets 127-178mm, deck 51mm, c/t 229mm
Complement: 500
Class notes: Designed by Watts. All main and secondary guns mounted in turrets or casemates. Three tall funnels and two military masts

'Constitucion' Class (1901)

Pre-dreadnoughts: *[Constitucion, Libertad]*
Displacement: 11,800tons
Dimensions: 479'9(oa) 458(wl) 436(pp)×71×25'4 [146.2(oa) 139.6(wl) 132.9(pp)×21.6×7.7]
Machinery: 2 screws, VTE engines (*Constitucion*: Humphrys; *Libertad*: Vickers), 12 Yarrow boilers
IHP 12,500 = 19knots
Endurance: 6,250/10
Armament: 4×254mm/45, 14×190mm/50, 14×14pdr, 2×12pdr, 4×6pdr, 2×457mm TT
Armour: Belt 76-178mm, barbettes 76-254mm, battery 178mm, casemates 178mm, c/t 279mm
Complement: 802
Class notes: Designed by Reed. Purchased by Britain before completion. Ordered as response to Argentine cruisers of 1900 which were later sold to Japan

'Almirante Latorre' Class (1911)

Dreadnoughts: *[Almirante Cochrane], Almirante Latorre* (see also later photo)
Displacement: 28,950tons, 32,000 f/l
Dimensions: 661(oa) 625(pp)×92'6×32 [201.5(oa) 190.5(pp)×28.2×9.8]. *1931:* Beam 103 [31.4]
Machinery: 4 screws, Brown-Curtis & Parsons turbines (*Latorre:* John Brown; *Cochrane:* Vickers) 21 Yarrow boilers; *Latorre, 1929:* Parsons geared turbines (Vickers)
SHP 37,000 = 23knots
Endurance: 4,400/10
Armament: 10×356mm/45, 16×152mm/50, 2×76mm, 4×3pdr, 4×533mm TT
1925: 2×152mm removed, 2×76mm AA added
1930: 4×102mm AA added, TT removed
1945: 18×20mm AA added

Above:
***Capitan Prat* — Barbette ship as completed in 1891.**
Marius Bar

Top right:
***General O'Higgins* — Armoured cruiser as completed 1898.**

Bottom right:
***Almirante Latorre* — Dreadnought, which served in Royal Navy during World War 1 as *Canada*, seen from the air c1935 with the crew dressing ship.**
US Naval Historical Centre

Armour: Belt 100-230mm, barbettes 100-255mm, turrets 255mm, bulkheads 75-115mm, decks 25-100mm, c/t 280mm
Complement: 1,075
Class notes: Designed as response to battleship plans of Argentina and Brazil. Five twin turrets all on centreline. *Latorre* taken over by Britain 1914 as *Canada*, repurchased and renamed *Latorre* 1920. Refit 1930-31, new engines, bulges fitted, converted to oil fuel. *Cochrane* became British carrier *Eagle*

Individual Ships

Almirante Cochrane

Type: Central Battery Ship
Class: 'Almirante Cochrane' (1872)
Nomenclature: Thomas, Lord Cochrane (1775-1860), Earl of Dundonald, British naval officer, commander of the Chilean navy in the war for independence
1873 Laid down by Earle
1874 January 23: Launched
1874 December: Completed
1879 Refit, sail rig removed
1879 Blockade of Iquique
1879 October 8: Damaged in action with Peruvian ironclad *Huascar* off Angamos
1880 Blockade and bombardment of Callao
1880 June 6: Damaged by Peruvian shore battery off Callao (seven dead)
1889 Refit; rearmed, re-engined and reboilered

1891 On Congressional side during civil war
1898 Torpedo and gunnery school ship
1908 Hulked
1934 Broken up

Almirante Cochrane

Type: Dreadnought
Class: 'Almirante Latorre' (1911)

History:
1913 January 22: Laid down by Armstrong as ***Constitucion***
1913 Renamed ***Santiago***; again renamed ***Almirante Cochrane***
1914 Taken over on the stocks by British government, projected name *India*
1917 Purchased by Great Britain for conversion to aircraft carrier; see ***Eagle***

Almirante Latorre

Type: Dreadnought
Class: 'Almirante Latorre' (1911)
Nomenclature: Juan Jose Latorre, commander of the *Almirante Cochrane* at the Battle of Angamos, 1879

History:
1911 November 27: Laid down by Armstrong as ***Libertad***
1912 Renamed ***Valparaiso***; later renamed ***Almirante Latorre***
1913 November 27: Launched
1914 September 9: Taken over by British government, renamed ***Canada***
1920 August 1: Returned to Chile, renamed ***Almirante Latorre***
1929-31 Refit at Devonport
1931 August 31: Seized by mutineers at Coquimbo, surrendered 9 September
attacked by Air Force without damage 6 September,
1948-49 Refit
1958 October: Stricken
1959 Sold and broken up at Yokohama

Blanco Encalada

Type: Central Battery Ship
Class: 'Almirante Cochrane' (1872)
Nomenclature: Manuel Blanco Encalada (1790-1876), first commander of the navy of Chile and later President of Chile

History:
1873 Laid down as ***Valparaiso*** by Earle
1875 May 8: Launched
—— Renamed ***Blanco Encalada***
—— Completed
1879 Blockade of Iquique
1879 October 8: Action off Angamos with Peruvian ironclad *Huascar*
1880 Blockade and bombardment of Callao
1885-86 Refit, rearmed
1891 On Congressional side during civil war
1891 January 16: Damaged by shore guns at Valparaiso (nine dead)
1891 April 23: Torpedoed and sunk by government gunboat *Almirante Lynch* in Caldera Bay during civil war (182 dead). First ironclad vessel sunk by a Whitehead torpedo

***Almirante Latorre* — Dreadnought, which served in Royal Navy during World War 1, virtually unchanged after the war.**

Capitan Prat

Type: Barbette Ship
Class: 'Capitan Prat' (1887)
Nomenclature: Arturo Prat (1848-1879), naval officer who was killed in action when his ship, *Esmeralda*, was sunk by Peruvian ironclad *Huascar*

History:
—— Laid down by La Seyne
1890 December 20: Launched
1891 Completed
1909-10 Reconstructed; reboilered, funnels raised
—— Submarine depot ship
1935 Stricken

Constitucion

Type: Pre-dreadnought
Class: 'Constitucion' (1901)
Nomenclature: Constitution

History:
1902 March 13: Laid down by Armstrong
1903 January 12: Launched
1903 December 3: Sold to British government, renamed ***Swiftsure***

Constitucion, see *Almirante Cochrane*

Esmeralda

Type: Armoured Cruiser
Class: 'Esmeralda' (1894)
Nomenclature: Emerald; a Spanish prize taken in 1818

History:
1895 July 4: Laid down by Armstrong
1896 April 14: Launched
1896 September 4: Completed for trials
1910 Refit, rearmed
1929 Stricken

General O'Higgins

Type: Armoured Cruiser
Class: 'General O'Higgins' (1895)
Nomenclature: Bernardo O'Higgins (1778-1842), revolutionary leader, victor of the Battle of Chacabuco

History:
1896 April 4: Laid down by Armstrong
1897 May 17: Launched
1898 April 2: Completed
1919-20 Refit
1928-29 Refit
1946 Stricken and broken up

Huascar

Type: Turret Ship
Class: 'Huascar' (1879)
Nomenclature: Previous name retained

History:
—— Laid down by Laird for Peru
1865 October 6: Launched
—— Completed
1879 October 8: Captured by Chilean warships in action off Angamos
1879 November 15: Commissioned by Chilean navy after repairs at Valparaiso
1891 Refit, rearmed
1891 On Congressional side during civil war
1960 Museum at Valparaiso

Libertad

Type: Pre-dreadnought
Class: 'Constitucion' (1901)
Nomenclature: Liberty

History:
1902 March 13: Laid down by Vickers
1903 December 3: Sold to British government, renamed ***Triumph***

Libertad, see ***Almirante Latorre***

Santiago, see ***Almirante Cochrane***

Valparaiso, see ***Almirante Cochrane***

Valparaiso, see ***Almirante Latorre***

China

Until 1895 the Chinese navy was actually a collection of four autonomous navies based at Canton, Foochow, Shanghai and in the Yellow Sea.

The Foochow navy was destroyed by the French in 1884. China's only capital ships were built as part of an ambitious programme to modernise the fleet in the 1880s. They were lost in the war with Japan in 1894-95 when the Yellow Sea navy was destroyed.

Class Details

'Ting Yuen' Class (1880)

Barbette Ships: *Chen Yuen, Ting Yuen*
Displacement: 7,220tons, 7,670f/l
Dimensions: 308′5(oa) 298′6(wl)×59×20 [94(oa) 91(wl)×18×6.1]
Machinery: 2 screws, horizontal compound engines (Vulcan), 8 cylindrical boilers
IHP 6,200 = 14.5knots
Endurance: 4,500/10
Armament: 4×305mm/20, 2×150mm/20, 2×4pdr, 3×356mm TT
1895: 2×150mm replaced by 2×57mm, 8×47mm added
Armour: Belt 305-355mm, barbettes 305mm, protective deck 76mm, bulkheads 355mm, c/t 203mm
Complement: 250
Class notes: The largest ships of the Chinese navy built in Germany on the style of the British *Ajax* with two twin barbettes arranged en echelon amidships. The echelon arrangement was reversed in the second vessel so as to permit a heavier weight of fire as the ships operated together. *Chen Yuen* was recommissioned by the Japanese in 1895

Individual Ships

Chen Yuen

Type: Barbette Ship
Class: 'Ting Yuen' (1880)
Nomenclature: Striking from afar

History:
1881 Laid down by Vulcan, Stettin
1882 November 28: Launched
1884 April: Completed
1885 July 3: Sailed to China under German mercantile ensign
1891 July: Visited Japan
1894 September 17: Severely damaged at Battle of the Yalu, later went aground en route to Wei Hai Wei
1895 February 9: Damaged by Japanese batteries at Wei Hai Wei and foundered
1895 February 13: Captured by Japan at capture of Wei Hai Wei; refloated and commissioned in Imperial Japanese Navy as ***Chin Yen***

Ting Yuen

Type: Barbette Ship
Class: 'Ting Yuen' (1880)
Nomenclature: Eternal peace

History:
1881 March 31: Laid down by Vulcan, Stettin
1881 December 28: Launched
1883 May: Completed
1885 July 3: Sailed to China under German mercantile ensign
1891 July: Visited Japan
1894 September 17: Flagship of Adm Ting Ju-Chang at Battle of the Yalu, damaged and set afire
1895 February 6: Torpedoed and sunk by Japanese torpedo boat *No 23* at Wei Hai Wei

***Chen Yuen* — Barbette ship with masts modified.**
P. A. Vicary

Confederate States

The Confederate States of America came into existence on 21 February 1861. One third of the officers of the United States Navy resigned to serve the Confederacy but, aside from the materiel captured at Norfolk Va, there was no naval force. Construction of warships and weapons was virtually impossible. The screw frigate *Merrimack* was raised at Norfolk and converted to a casemate ironclad ram with spectacular results. This success blinded the Confederates to any type of warship other than the casemate ironclad and many ships of similar design were built.

All these ironclads were built or converted at southern ports where they remained isolated. The Confederate navy was never able to join its forces together and gain command of the seas. In the end all were sunk or captured individually by Federal forces or scuttled by their own crews. The ironclads were armoured rams with guns low down and low freeboard, slow and non-seagoing. Many were never completed and others lacked armour or were built with inefficient engines.

Commerce raiders were commissioned abroad and orders were given for construction of modern ocean-going ironclad warships. The famous 'Laird rams' were seized by Britain prior to completion and only the *Stonewall*, built in France, actually went to sea under the Confederate flag.

Note: Details of Confederate vessels are in many cases conflicting or non-existent. Official records were destroyed or never made.

Class Details

'Virginia' (1861)

Casemate Ironclad: *Virginia*
Displacement: 3,200tons
Dimensions: 263(pp)×51′4×22 [80.1(pp)×15.7×6.7]
Machinery: 1 screw, horizontal back-acting engines, 4 boilers
IHP 1,200 = 9knots
Armament: 2×7″ MLR, 6×9″ SB, 2×6″ 32pdr MLR
Armour: 2″+24″ wood
Complement: 320
Class notes: Rebuilt from the hulk of the US screw frigate *Merrimack*. Cut down to the waterline and reconstructed with sloping armoured sides pierced for guns and a 4′ ram bow. Designed by Cdr John M. Brooke. Ship's activities limited by its excessive draft

'Arkansas' Class (1861)

Ironclad Rams: *Arkansas, [Tennessee]*
Dimensions: 165(pp)×35×11′6 [50.3(pp)×10.7×3.5]
Machinery: 2 screws, low-pressure engines
IHP 900 = 8mph
Armament: 2×9″ SB, 2×8″ 64pdr, 2×9″ shell guns, 2×6″ MLR, 2×32pdr SB
Armour: 18″ iron and wood
Complement: 200
Class notes: *Arkansas* hurriedly built at Memphis with poor engines. Casemate with sloped sides built on long flat hull with ram bow. *Tennessee* never completed.

'Atlanta' (1862)

Ironclad Ram: *Atlanta*
Displacement: 1,006tons
Dimensions: 204(pp)×41×15′9 [62.2(pp)×12.5×4.8]
Machinery: 3 screws
IHP —— = 8knots
Armament: 2×7″ MLR, 2×6.4″ MLR, spar torpedo
Armour: Casemate 4″, deck $\frac{1}{2}$″
Complement: 145
Class notes: Converted from British blockade runner *Fingal* in 1862 at Savannah. Captured by US monitors in 1863 and later served in US Navy until the end of the war

'Albemarle' Class (1862)

Ironclad Rams: *Albemarle, Neuse,* one unnamed. Also *[Jackson, Huntsville, Tuscaloosa]*
Dimensions: 152(oa) 139(pp)×34×9 [46.3(oa) 42.4(pp)×10.4×2.7]
Machinery: 2 screws, horizontal non-condensing engines, 2 boilers
IHP 400 = 4knots
Armament: 2×6.4″ 100pdr MLR
Huntsville: 4×32pdr
Tuscaloosa: 1×6.4″ MLR, 3×32pdr
Armour: 4″ (*Tuscaloosa*)
Class notes: *Albemarle* built by Cdr James W. Cooke with an octagonal casemate on a flat hull. *Neuse* was similar; both had short careers. A third vessel was started in North Carolina. *Jackson* (also known as *Muscogee*) originally begun as a centre wheel ironclad but drew too much water and was rebuilt as a modified 'Albemarle' type. *Huntsville* and *Tuscaloosa* were modified also but saw no active service because of defective engines and lack of armour

'Richmond' Class (1862)

Ironclad Rams: *Chicora, North Carolina, Palmetto State, Raleigh, Richmond, Savannah*
Dimensions: 172′6(oa) 150(pp)×34×12; [52.6(oa) 45.7(pp)×10.4×3.7]; *Chicora:* beam 35 [10.6]
Machinery: 1 screw
IHP —— = 6knots
Armament: *Chicora:* 2×9″ SB, 4×6″ 32pdr MLR
North Carolina: 4 guns
Palmetto State: 10×7″ MLR
Releigh: 4×6″ MLR
Richmond: 4 MLR, 2 shell guns, spar torpedo
Savannah: 2×7″ MLR, 2×6.4″ MLR
Armour: 4″+22″ wood
Complement: 180
Class notes: Similar ships built at different locations to basic design of John L. Porter. *Chicora* and *Palmetto State* operated out of Charleston, South Carolina. *North Carolina* and *Raleigh* operated at Wilmington, North Carolina, completion being delayed by strikes and lack of equipment and crew. Both were poorly built. *Richmond* built at Norfolk and remained blocked in the James River. Sometimes referred to as *Virginia II* or *Young Virginia. Savannah* built in Georgia

'Charleston' (1862)

Ironclad Ram: *Charleston*
Dimensions: 189(oa) 167(pp)×34 [57.6(oa) 50.9(pp)×10.4]
Machinery: IHP —— = 6knots
Armament: 2×9" SB, 4 MLR
Complement: 150
Class notes: Built in South Carolina

'Milledgeville' Class (1862)

Ironclad Rams: *[Milledgeville]*, 3 unnamed
Dimensions: 175(pp)×35'3×9 [53.3(pp)×10.7×2.7]
Armament: 6 guns
Class notes: Two were building at Savannah and two at Charleston but none completed

'North Carolina' Class (1862)

Turret Ships: *[Mississippi, North Carolina]*
Displacement: 2,750tons
Dimensions: 224'6(pp)×42'6×17 [68.4(pp)×12.9×5.2]
Machinery: 1 screw, horizontal direct-acting engines (Laird), 4 boilers
IHP 1,450 = 10knots
Armament: 4×9" MLR
Armour: Turrets 5", sides 4.5"
Complement: 153
Class notes: Seagoing warships superior to any Federal vessel. The famous 'Laird rams' built secretly for the Confederate government and seized by the British government in October 1863. Completed for the British Navy as *Wivern* and *Scorpion*

'Columbia' Class (1862)

Ironclad Rams: *Columbia, [Texas]*
Dimensions: *Columbia:* 216(oa) 189(pp)×51'4×13'6 [65.8(oa) 57.6(pp)×15.6×4.1]
Texas: 217(oa)×48'6 [66.1(oa)×14.8]
Machinery: 1 screw (*Columbia*), 2 screws (*Texas*), horizontal direct-acting non-condensing engines, 5 boilers
Armament: 6 guns
Armour: 6"
Complement: 50
Class notes: Similar vessels built to same basic design. *Columbia* operated at Charleston, SC. *Texas* built at Richmond and captured incomplete

Above left:
Virginia* — Casemate ironclad, the former Federal steam frigate *Merrimack. An official drawing published 1921.

Left:
***Arkansas* — Ironclad ram built at Memphis 1862.**

Below:
***Atlanta* — Ironclad ram, 1864, in the James River after being recommissioned by US Navy.** *US Navy*

'Tennessee II' (1862)

Ironclad Ram: *Tennessee*
Displacement: 1,273tons
Dimensions: 209(oa) 189(pp)×48×14 [63.7(oa) 57.6(pp)×14.6×4.3]
Machinery: 2 screws and sidewheels, non-condensing engines, 4 boilers
IHP —— = 6knots
Armament: 2×7" MLR, 4×6.4" MLR
Armour: 6"
Complement: 133
Class notes: Modified 'Columbia' type, operated in Mobile Bay. Briefly commissioned in US Navy. Engines taken from steamer *Alonzo Child*

'Fredericksburg' (1863)

Ironclad Ram: *Fredericksburg*
Dimensions: 188(oa) 170(pp)×40'3×9'6 [57.3(oa) 51.8(pp)×12.3×2.9]
Machinery: 2 screws
Armament: 1×11" SB, 1×8" MLR, 2×6.4" MLR
Complement: 150
Class notes: Enlarged 'Albemarle' type, built at Richmond, but remained blocked in the James River

'Virginia II' (1863)

Ironclad Ram: *Virginia II*
Dimensions: 197(oa) 180(pp)×47'6×14 [60(oa) 54.9(pp)×14.5×4.3]
Machinery: 1 screw
IHP —— = 10knots
Armament: 1×11" SB, 1×8" MLR, 2×6.4" MLR
Armour: Sides 5", forward 6"
Complement: 150
Class notes: Built at Richmond with shortened casemate. Remained blocked in the James River

'Stonewall' Class (1863)

Ironclad Rams: *Stonewall* (see also later photo), 1 unnamed
Displacement: 1,390tons
Dimensions: 186'9(oa) 165'9(wl) 157'6 (pp)×32'6×14'3 [56.9(oa) 50.5(wl) 48(pp)×9.9×4.2]
Machinery: 2 screws, horizontal direct-acting engines (Mazeline), 2 boilers
IHP 1,200 = 10.8knots
Armament: 1×11" 300pdr MLR, 2×5" 70pdr MLR
Armour: Belt 4.5", c/t 5.5"
Complement: 135
Class notes: Built in France under code names *Sphinx* and *Cheops* but embargoed by the French government. *Sphinx* sold to Denmark but later completed and commissioned for the Confederate navy as *Stonewall*. At Havana when the war ended it was turned over to the US Navy and sold to Japan as *Azuma*. *Cheops* became the Prussian *Prinz Adalbert*. Twin coupled rudders and twin keels

***Chicora* — A rare photograph of the ironclad ram at Charleston, South Carolina.**
Old Court House Museum, Vicksburg

1865 April 27: Arrived at Norfolk NYd after being refloated by Federal forces
1867 October 15: Sold

'Santa Maria' (1863)

Broadside ship: Unnamed
Displacement: 3,200tons
Dimensions: 270'8(pp)×49'6×18'4 [82.5(pp)×15.1×5.6]
Machinery: 1 screw, horizontal direct-acting engines, 4 boilers
IHP 1,000 = 8.5knots
Armament: 20×60pdr MLR, 8×18pdr
Armour: Belt 4.5"
Complement: 500
Class notes: Known variously as *Frigate No 61*, *Santa Maria* and *Glasgow*, this vessel was cancelled by order of the British government. Sold to Denmark and renamed *Danmark* but delivery held up because of the war with Prussia

Individual Ships

Albemarle

Type: Ironclad Ram
Class: 'Albemarle' (1862)
Nomenclature: Inlet in North Carolina

History:
1863 April: Laid down by Gilbert Elliot at Edwards Ferry, NC
1863 November: Launched
1864 April 17: Completed at Halifax, NC
1864 April 19: Rammed and sank USS *Southfield* in action at Plymouth, NC
1864 May 5: Damaged during attack on Federal ships in Roanoke River
1864 October 28: Sunk in Roanoke River by spar torpedo boat under Lt W. B. Cushing

Arkansas

Type: Ironclad Ram
Class: 'Arkansas' (1861)
Nomenclature: A state of the Confederacy

History:
1861 October: Laid down by J. T. Shirley at Memphis, Tn
1862 April: Launched
1862 May 26: Completed at Yazoo City
1862 July 15: Damaged during engagement with Federal ships in Yazoo River
1862 August 6: Sunk to prevent capture following engagement with Federal ships at Baton Rouge

Atlanta

Type: Ironclad Ram
Class: 'Atlanta' (1862)
Nomenclature: City in Georgia

History:
1861 Launched by Thompson at Glasgow as merchant ship ***Fingal***
1862 September: Converted to ironclad ram at Savannah and renamed ***Atlanta*** after running Federal blockade
1863 June 17: Captured in Wassaw Sound, Ga by US monitors *Nahant* and *Weehawken* after being damaged by gunfire and run aground
1864 Commissioned in US Navy
1864-65 Served in S and N Atlantic BS
1865 Laid up
1869 May 4: Sold

Charleston

Type: Ironclad Ram
Class: 'Charleston' (1862)
Nomenclature: Principal city of South Carolina

History:
1862 December: Laid down by James M. Eason at Charleston, SC
1863 Launched
1864 Completed
1865 February 18: Destroyed to prevent capture at Charleston

Chicora

Type: Ironclad Ram
Class: 'Richmond' (1862)

History:
1862 April 25: Laid down by James M. Eason at Charleston, SC
1862 August 23: Launched
1862 November: Completed
1863 January 31: Engaged Federal vessels at Charleston
1863-64: Defence of Charleston
1865 February 18: Sunk to prevent capture prior to fall of Charleston

Columbia

Type: Ironclad Ram
Class: 'Columbia' (1862)
Nomenclature: City in South Carolina

History:
1864 March 10: Launched by J. M. Eason at Charleston, SC
1865 January 12: Damaged by running on to sunken wreck near Fort Moultrie
1865 April 26: Salvaged by US Navy and towed to Norfolk NYd
1865 May 25: Arrived at Norfolk
1867 October 10: Sold by US Navy

Fredericksburg

Type: Ironclad Ram
Class: 'Fredericksburg' (1863)
Nomenclature: City in Virginia

History:
1863 Launched at Richmond NYd, Va
1863 November 30: Completed unarmed
1864 March: Received armament
1864 Engaged Federal ships in James River on several occasions
1865 April 4: Sunk in James River to prevent capture after fall of Richmond

Huntsville

Type: Ironclad Ram
Class: 'Albemarle' (1862)
Nomenclature: City in Alabama

History:
1862 Laid down by Henry D. Basset at Selma, Al
1863 February 7: Launched; taken to Mobile for completion
1865 April 12: Sunk as blockship in Spanish River, near Mobile with *Tuscaloosa*

Jackson

Type: Ironclad Ram
Class: 'Albemarle' (1862)
Nomenclature: City in Mississippi

History:
1862 Laid down at Navy Yard, Colombus, Ga; also known as ***Muscogee***
1864 Launched but hauled out for redesign
1864 December 22: Launched again
1865 April: Destroyed by Federal forces prior to completion

Milledgeville

Type: Ironclad Ram
Class: Milledgeville (1862)
Nomenclature: City in Georgia

History:
1863 February: Laid down by Henry F. Willink at Savannah
1864 October: Launched
1864 December: Destroyed to prevent capture

Mississippi

Type: Turret Ship
Class: 'North Carolina' (1862)
Nomenclature: A state of the Confederacy

History:
1862 April: Laid down by Laird under cover name *El Monassir*
1863 August 29: Launched
1863 October: Seized by British government
1865 October 10: Completed for Royal Navy as ***Wivern***

Muscogee, see *Jackson*

Neuse

Type: Ironclad Ram
Class: 'Albemarle' (1862)
Nomenclature: River in North Carolina

History:
1862 Laid down at Whitehall, NC
1863 November: Launched
1864 April: Completed at Kinston, NC
1864 Went aground off Kinston
1865 March: Burned to prevent capture while still aground
1961 Wreck raised and placed on exhibit at Kinston, NC

North Carolina

Type: Turret Ship
Class: 'North Carolina' (1862)
Nomenclature: A state of the Confederacy

History:
1862 April: Laid down by Laird under cover name *El Tousson*
1863 July 4: Launched
1863 October: Seized by British government
1865 October 10: Completed for Royal Navy as ***Scorpion***

***Tennessee* — Ironclad ram 1865, after capture by USN.** *US Navy*

North Carolina

Type: Ironclad Ram
Class: 'Richmond' (1862)

History:
1862 Laid down by Berry & Bros at Wilmington, NC
1863 Launched
1863 December: Completed; guardship in Cape Fear River
1864 September 27: Foundered at Smithville, NC

Palmetto State

Type: Ironclad Ram
Class: 'Richmond' (1862)
Nomenclature: Nickname of South Carolina

History:
1862 January: Laid down by Cameron & Co at Charleston, SC
1862 October 11: Launched
1862 September: Completed
1863 January 31: Engaged Federal vessels off Charleston causing withdrawal of the inshore blockade
1863-64 Defence of Charleston
1865 February 18: Burned to prevent capture prior to fall of Charleston

Raleigh

Type: Ironclad Ram
Class: 'Richmond' (1862)
Nomenclature: City in North Carolina

History:
1864 Launched by J. L. Cassidy at Wilmington, NC
1864 April 30: Completed
1864 May 7: Went aground and was wrecked on Wilmington Bar following engagement with Federal vessels

Richmond

Type: Ironclad Ram
Class: 'Richmond' (1862)
Nomenclature: City in Virginia, capital of the Confederacy

History:
1862 March: Laid down at Norfolk
1862 May 6: Launched and towed to Richmond to avoid Federal forces
1862 July: Completed at Richmond
1864-65 Engaged Federal vessels in James River
1865 April 3: Sunk in James River to prevent capture prior to fall of Richmond

Savannah

Type: Ironclad Ram
Class: 'Richmond' (1862)
Nomenclature: City in Georgia

History:
1862 April: Laid down by Henry F. Willink at Savannah, Ga
1863 February 4: Launched
1863 June 30: Completed
1863-64 Guardship at Savannah
1864 December 21: Burned to prevent capture at Savannah

Stonewall

Type: Ironclad Ram
Class: 'Stonewall' (1863)
Nomenclature: Nickname of General Thomas Jonathan Jackson (1824-1863), died at Battle of Chancellorsville

History:
1863 Laid down by Arman under code name *Sphinx*
1864 March 31: Sold to Denmark by French government order, named ***Staerkodder***
1864 June 21: Launched
1864 October: Arrived in Copenhagen, Danish government refused delivery, and departed as ***Olinde***
1865 January: Commissioned at sea, named ***Stonewall***
1865 March 24: Left Ferrol, Spain when Federal warships declined battle
1865 May: At Havana at the end of the war
1865 July: Turned over to US by Spanish authorities
1867 Sold to Shogunate government of Japan; see ***Azuma***

Tennessee

Type: Ironclad Ram
Class: 'Arkansas' (1861)
Nomenclature: A state of the Confederacy

History:
1861 October: Laid down by John T. Shirley at Memphis, Tn
1862 June 5: Destroyed on stocks when Memphis was captured by Federal troops

Tennessee

Type: Ironclad Ram
Class: 'Tennessee II' (1862)

History:
1862 October: Laid down by Henry D. Basset at Selma, Al
1863 February: Launched
1864 February 16: Completed
1864 August 5: Surrendered to Federal vessels after being damaged at Battle of Mobile Bay
1864 August 9: Commissioned in US Navy
1865 August 19: Decommissioned
1867 November 27: Sold and broken up

Texas

Type: Ironclad Ram
Class: 'Columbia' (1862)
Nomenclature: A state of the Confederacy

History:
1863 Laid down at Navy Yard, Richmond, Va
1865 January: Launched
1865 April 3: Seized incomplete by US, taken to Norfolk
1867 October 15: Sold

Tuscaloosa

Type: Ironclad Ram
Class: 'Albemarle' (1862)
Nomenclature: City in Alabama

History:
1862 Laid down by Henry D. Basset at Selma, Al
1863 February 7: Launched; taken to Mobile for completion
1865 April 12: Sunk with *Huntsville* as blockship in Spanish River near Mobile

Virginia

Type: Casemate Ironclad
Class: 'Virginia' (1861)
Nomenclature: A state of the Confederacy

History
1855 June 14: Launched as US screw frigate ***Merrimack*** at Boston
1856 February 20: Completed
1861 April 20: Burned to prevent capture at Norfolk
1861 June: Refloated by Confederate navy and rebuilt as ironclad, renamed ***Virginia***
1862 February 17: Completed

***Stonewall* — Ironclad ram 1866; notice ram bow. Later became the Japanese *Azuma*.**

1862 March 8: Sank US sail frigates *Cumberland* and *Congress* in Hampton Roads
1862 March 9: Engaged US monitor *Monitor* at Battle of Hampton Roads, first engagement between ironclad warships
1862 May 11: Run ashore and burned by crew to prevent capture near Craney Island in James River

Virginia II

Type: Ironclad Ram
Class: 'Virginia II' (1863)

History:
1863 Launched at Richmond NYd
1864 June: Completed
1864 Engaged Federal forces in James River on several occasions
1865 April 3: Sunk to prevent capture in James River prior to fall of Richmond

Unnamed

Type: Ironclad Ram

***Stonewall* — Ironclad ram 1865 at Washington Navy Yard.** *US Navy*

Class: 'Albemarle' (1862)

History:
1864 Laid down by Gilbert Elliot at Edwards Ferry, NC
1865 April: Destroyed incomplete to prevent capture

Unnamed

Type: Ironclad Ram
Class: 'Stonewall' (1863)

History:
1863 Laid down by Arman under cover name *Cheops*
1864 June: Launched
1865 October 29: Sold to Prussia, renamed ***Prinz Adalbert***

Unnamed

Type: Broadside Ship
Class: 'Santa Maria' (1863)

History:
1863 Laid down by Thompson under cover name *Santa Maria*
1863 December: Sold to Denmark by order of British government
1864 February 23: Launched as ***Danmark***

Denmark

Although a small country with a small navy, Denmark had the honour of possessing one of the first ironclads in the world, *Rolf Krake*. This was the only ironclad in service at the time of the war with Prussia and Austria in 1864. A number of ironclad warships were built for coast defence and two vessels were purchased which had been intended for the Confederate navy. One of these was refused and became the Confederate *Stonewall*, the other was embargoed because of the war.

Denmark maintained a fleet of small coast defence ships and also maintained its neutrality throughout later European conflicts, until 1940 when the country was occupied by German troops. The two remaining coast defence ships were immobilised by this action until they, with the entire fleet, were scuttled in August 1943.

Class Details

'Dannebrog' (1862)

Broadside Ship: *Dannebrog*
Displacement: 3,057tons
Dimensions: 214'10(pp)×50'10×23'3 [65.5(pp)×15.5×7.1]
Machinery: 1-screw engines (Baumgarten & Burmeister)
IHP 1,150 = 8.7knots
Armament: 16×60pdr
Later: 6×203mm MLR, 10×152mm MLR
Armour: Belt and battery 114mm
Complement: 350
Class notes: Built as 72-gun sail ship-of-the-line and converted to ironclad frigate 1862. Bark rig

'Rolf Krake' (1862)

Monitor: *Rolfe Krake*
Displacement: 1,360tons
Dimensions: 191'3(oa) 185(pp)×38'3×10'5 [58.3(oa) 56.4(pp)×11.6×3.2]
Machinery: 1 screw, —— (Napier), 2 boilers
IHP 700 = 8knots
Endurance: 1,150/8
Armament: 4×60pdr SB
1868: 2×203mm MLR, 2×87mm
Armour: Belt and turret 114mm
Complement: 140
Class notes: First ironclad in Scandinavia with two Coles type turrets. Iron hull with schooner rig. Rearmed in 1868 with one gun in each turret

'Peder Skram' (1862)

Broadside Ship: *Peder Skram*
Displacement: 3,373tons
Dimensions: 226'3(pp)×49'6×21'8 [69(pp)×15.1×6.6]
Machinery: 1-screw single expansion engines (Baumgarten & Burmeister), 4 boilers
IHP 1,680 = 11.7knots
Endurance: 1,500/10
Armament: 6×203mm MLR, 12×26pdr
Later: 8×203mm MLR, 8×152mm 26pdr
Armour: Belt 127mm, battery 114mm
Complement: 450
Class notes: Laid down as wood screw frigate and converted to ironclad frigate before completion. Full ship rig

'Danmark' (1863)

Broadside Ship: *Danmark*
Displacement: 4,747tons
Dimensions: 270'8(pp)×49'6×19'4 [82.5(pp)×15.1×5.9]
Machinery: 1-screw, horizontal direct-acting engines, 4 boilers
IHP 1,000 = 8.5knots
Armament: 12×203mm, 12×152mm 26pdr
Armour: Belt 89-114mm, battery 89-114mm
Complement: 530
Class notes: Laid down for the Confederate navy and sold to Denmark prior to launching. Delivery held up during war with Prussia 1864. One funnel between main and mizzen masts and full ship rig. Reconstructed 1868. Poor sea boat and was little used

'Staerkodder' (1863)

Ironclad Ram: *Staerkodder*
Displacement: 1,300tons
Dimensions: 186'9(oa) 165'9(wl) 157'6(pp)×32'6×16'6 [56.9(oa) 50.5(wl) 48(pp)×9.9×5]
Machinery: 2 screws, horizontal direct-acting engines (Mazeline), 2 boilers
IHP 1,200 = 9knots
Armament: 1×11" MLR, 4×5"
Later: 1×279mm 300pdr MLR, 2×127mm 70pdr MLR
Armour: Belt 90mm, turret 38mm
Class notes: Built for the Confederate navy as *Stonewall* and purchased by Denmark after France embargoed delivery. Delivery finally refused by Denmark and resold to Confederate States. Later became Japanese *Azuma* 1869

'Lindormen' (1865)

Turret Ship: *Lindormen*
Displacement: 2,080tons
Dimensions: 215'9(pp)×39×13'9 [65.8(pp)×11.9×4.2]
Machinery: 2 screws, —— (Burmeister & Wain)
IHP 1,560 = 12.5knots
Endurance: 1,400/8.5
Armament: 2×229mm MLR
1875: 2×76mm MLR added
1879: 2×87mm BLR added
1885: 4×87mm BLR added, 76mm removed
Armour: Belt 127mm, turret 104mm, c/t 127mm
Complement: 140
Class notes: Iron hulled single turret monitor. Performed poorly on trials

'Gorm' (1866)

Turret Ship: *Gorm*
Displacement: 2,350tons

Dimensions: 235′8(pp)×40×14′5 [71.8(pp)×12.2×4.4]
Machinery: 2 screws, —— (Penn)
IHP 1,670 = 12.5knots
Armament: 2×254mm MLR
1875: 2×76mm ML added
1879: 2×87mm BL added
1889: 4×87mm BL added
1891: 4×57mm QF added
Armour: Belt 178mm, turret 203mm
Complement: 160
Class notes: Iron hull. Similar to *Lindormen* with heavier armament. Armoured conning tower added 1875

'Odin' (1870)

Central Battery Ship: *Odin*
Displacement: 3,090 tons; *1898:* 3,232tons
Dimensions: 240′2(pp)×48′3×15′9 [73.2(pp)×14.7×4.8]
Machinery: 1 screw, horizontal trunk engines (Burmeister & Wain)
IHP 2,300 = 12.4knots
Endurance: 1,200/9
Armament: 4×254mm MLR, 6×76mm
1883: 4×87mm BLR added, 76mm removed
Armour: Belt 102-303mm, casemate 178mm, deck 26mm
1898: c/t 142mm
Complement: 200
Class notes: Guns located in central armoured redoubt. Iron hull, ram bow with single funnel and two masts. Reconstructed 1898 with redoubt modified to permit greater arc of fire and armoured conning tower added

'Helgoland' (1875)

Coast Defence Torpedo Ram: *Helgoland* (see later photo)
Displacement: 5,370tons
Dimensions: 258′9(pp)×59×18′4 [78.9(pp)×18×5.6]
Machinery: 2 screws, horizontal compound engines (Burmeister & Wain), 8 cylindrical boilers
IHP 4,500 = 13.4knots
Endurance: 1,400/9
Armament: 1×305mm/20 BLR, 4×260mm/16 BLR, 5×120/27 BLR, 2×57mm, 2×380mm TT
1887: 1×120mm removed
1888: 2×350mm TT added
Armour: Belt 152-315mm, casemate 260mm, barbette 260mm, deck 52mm, c/t 33mm
Complement: 350
Class notes: The largest warship in Scandinavia with a single barbette forward and other guns in armoured casemate. Iron hull with ram bow, one funnel and single mast. Conning tower improved 1879. Refit 1896 with new boilers and two masts fitted

'Tordenskjold' (1878)

Coast Defence Ship: *Tordenskjold*
Displacement: 2,430tons
Dimensions: 221′6(pp)×43′3×15′5 [67.5(pp)×13.2×4.7]
Machinery: 2 screws, horizontal compound engines (Burmeister & Wain), 8 cylindrical boilers
IHP 2,600 = 13.3knots
Endurance: 1,500/9
Armament: 1×355mm BLR, 4×120mm BLR, 4×37mm, 1×380mm TT, 3×350mm TT
Armour: Belt none, barbette 203mm, deck 95mm, c/t 31mm (*1890:* 114mm)
Complement: 220
Class notes: Classified as torpedo ship until 1885. Steel hull with ram bow. Single barbette forward and two thin funnels with military mast between

'Iver Hvitfeldt' (1883)

Coast Defence Ship: *Iver Hvitfeldt*
Displacement: 3,290tons
Dimensions: 242′6(pp)×49′3×18′4 [73.9(pp)×15×5.6]
Machinery: 2 screws, horizontal compound engines (Burmeister & Wain), 8 cylindrical boilers
IHP 5,100 = 15.6knots
Endurance: 1,600/9
Armament: 2×260mm/35, 4×120mm/40, 2×57mm, 1×380mm TT, 2×350mm TT
1907: 8×57mm added, 4×120mm removed
Armour: Belt 178-292mm, barbettes 216mm, deck 53mm, c/t 115mm
Complement: 265
Class notes: Last barbette ship of the Danish navy with a single gun in each barbette fore and aft. Reconstructed 1898-99

'Skjold' (1893)

Monitor: *Skjold*
Displacement: 2,200tons
Dimensions: 242′9(oa) 227′8(pp)×38×13′6 [74(oa) 69.4(pp)×11.6×4.1]
Machinery: 2 screws, VTE engines (Burmeister & Wain), 4 Thornycroft cylindrical boilers
IHP 2,400 = 13.4knots
Endurance: 2,400/9
Armament: 1×240mm/40, 3×120mm/40, 4×47mm, 4 TT
Armour: Belt 178-229mm, turret 254mm, deck 50mm, c/t 200mm
Complement: 137
Class notes: Small monitor built for defence of Copenhagen. Single big gun in forward turret. Single funnel and mast

'Herluf Trolle' Class (1896)

Coast Defence Ships: *Herluf Trolle, Olfert Fischer* (see later photo)
Displacement: 3,470tons
Dimensions: 283′9(oa) 272(pp)×49′6×16′6 [86.5(oa) 82.9(pp)×15.1×5]
Machinery: 2 screws, VTE engines (*Herluf Trolle*: Burmeister & Wain; *Olfert Fischer*: builder), 6 Thornycroft boilers
Herluf Trolle: IHP 4,400 = 15.6knots; *Olfert Fischer*: IHP 4,600 = 15.8knots
Endurance: 2,500/9
Armament: 2×240mm/43, 4×150mm/43, 10×57mm, 3×450mm TT
Herluf Trolle, 1916: 6×37mm removed, 2×57mm AA added
Herluf Trolle, 1920: 6×75mm added
Armour: *Herluf Trolle:* Belt 178-205mm, turrets 152-178mm, casemates 140mm, deck 57mm

Top right:
***Lindormen* — Turret ship of 1865.**
US Naval Historical Centre

Centre right:
***Tordenskjold* — Coast defence ship, classified as torpedo ship until 1885.** *P. A. Vicary*

Bottom right:
***Herluf Trolle* — Coast defence ship of 1896, seen before World War 1.** *Imperial War Museum*

Olfert Fischer: Belt 152-190mm, turrets 165-190mm, casemates 150mm, deck 57mm
Complement: 255
Class notes: Small battleships with two single turrets fore and aft and secondary guns in casemates. Single funnel and two military masts

'Peder Skram' (1904)

Coast Defence Ship: *Peder Skram*
Displacement: 3,735tons
Dimensions: 286'9(oa) 275'7(pp)×51'6×16 [87.4(oa) 84(pp)×15.7×4.9]
Machinery: 2 screws, VTE engines (builder), 6 Thornycroft boilers
IHP 5,400 = 16knots
Endurance: 2,620/9
Armament: 2×240mm/43, 4×150mm/50, 10×75mm, 4×450mm TT
1914: 2×57mm AA added
1934: 8×75mm and 2×37mm added
1940: 2×40mm AA added
Armour: Belt 152-195mm, turrets 165-190mm, casemates 150mm, deck 57mm
Complement: 255
Class notes: Improved 'Herluf Trolle' type. Extensively refitted and rearmed 1934

'Niels Iuel' (1913)

Coast Defence Ship: *Niels Iuel*
Displacement: 3,800 tons, 4,320f/l
Dimensions: 295'3(oa) 285'6(pp)×53'6×16'6 [90(oa) 87(pp)×16.3×5]
Machinery: 2 screws, VTE engines (builder), 4 Yarrow boilers
IHP 6,000 = 16knots
Endurance: 5,000/10
Armament: *Designed:* 2×305mm, 8×119mm, 2×—, 4×450mm TT
Completed: 10×149mm/45, 4×57mm, 2×450mm TT
1936: 2×57mm added
1940: 2×40mm AA added
Armour: Belt 152-195mm, gunshields 45mm, deck 57mm, bulkheads 170mm, c/t 170mm
Complement: 310
Class notes: Designed as a modified 'Peder Skram' type with 2×305mm guns in two single turrets. Completion delayed and armament changed while under construction. Single funnel and tripod mast. Modernised 1935-36, AA guns added and tripod replaced by tower foremast

Individual Ships

Danmark

Type: Broadside Ship
Class: 'Danmark' (1863)
Nomenclature: Denmark

History:
1863 Laid down by Thomson for Confederate navy, known as *Santa Maria*
1863 December: Sold to Denmark, named ***Danmark***
1864 February 23: Launched
1867-68 Reconstructed prior to completion
1869 June 1: Commissioned
1876-77 Refit
1893 May 3: Accommodation ship
1900 November 22: Stricken
1907 June 29: Sold and broken up at Harburg

Dannebrog

Type: Broadside Ship
Class: 'Dannebrog' (1862)
Nomenclature: The name of the Danish national flag

History:
—— Laid down by Schifter, Nyholm, as sailing ship-of-the-line, 72 guns
1850 July 25: Launched
—— Completed
1862 May 21: Conversion to ironclad commenced
1864 March 30: Completed
1875 Accommodation ship
1875 February 15: Stricken
1896 May 30: Stricken, used as target
1897 Broken up

Gorm

Type: Turret Ship
Class: 'Gorm' (1866)
Nomenclature: First king of united Denmark (c883-936)

History:
1867 November 18: Laid down at Copenhagen
1870 May 17: Launched

Above left:
***Niels Iuel* — Coast defence ship of 1913 as it appeared in May 1937 following modernisation.**

Above:
***Helgoland* — Coast defence ship after refit, 1897.** *IWM*

1870 June 23: Completed
1875 Refit, armoured conning tower added
1912 June 12: Stricken and broken up at Stettin

Helgoland

Type: Coast Defence Torpedo Ram
Class: 'Helgoland' (1875)
Nomenclature: Danish naval victory over Prussia and Austria, 9 May 1864 off Heligoland

History:
1876 May 20: Laid down at Copenhagen
1878 May 9: Launched
1879 August 20: Completed
1884 Refit
1896 Refit, reboilered
1907 January 29: Stricken and broken up at Dordrecht

Herluf Trolle

Type: Coast Defence Ship
Class: 'Herluf Trolle' (1896)
Nomenclature: Herluf Trolle (1516-1565), Danish admiral, mortally wounded in action off Fehmarn

History:
1897 July 20: Laid down at Copenhagen
1899 September 2: Launched
1901 June 7: Completed
1932 April 30: Stricken and broken up

Iver Hvitfeldt

Type: Coast Defence Ship
Class: 'Iver Hvitfeldt' (1883)
Nomenclature: Iver Hvitfeldt (d1710), Danish naval officer and hero

History:
1884 April 9: Laid down at Copenhagen
1886 April 14: Launched
1887 June 1: Completed
1898-99 Reconstructed
1903 December 18: Severely damaged by fire
1907 In reserve
1919 February 26: Stricken and broken up 1920 in Holland

Lindormen

Type: Turret Ship
Class: 'Lindormen' (1865)
Nomenclature: Norse myth: a serpent

History:
1866 July 20: Laid down at Copenhagen
1868 August 8: Launched
1869 August 15: Completed
1885 Rearmed
1907 June 29: Stricken and broken up in Holland

Niels Iuel

Type: Coast Defence Ship
Class: 'Niels Iuel' (1913)
Nomenclature: Niels Juel (1629-1697), Danish admiral and victor over the Swedes at Kjoge Bay 1677

History:
1914 September 21: Laid down at Copenhagen
1918 July 3: Launched
1923 May 25: Completed
1935-36 Reconstructed
1943 August 29: Damaged by German aircraft and run aground at Isefjorden
1944 April 1: Refloated by Germans and repaired in Germany as training ship, renamed ***Nordland***
1945 May 3: Sunk by aircraft in Eckernforde Bay

Odin

Type: Central Battery Ship
Class: 'Odin' (1870)
Nomenclature: Norse myth: King of the gods

History:
1871 April 13: Laid down at Copenhagen
1872 December 12: Launched
1874 September 7: Completed
1898 Reconstructed
1912 June 12: Stricken and broken up in Holland

Olfert Fischer

Type: Coast Defence Ship
Class: 'Herluf Trolle' (1896)
Nomenclature: Olfert Fischer (1747-1829), Danish admiral, in command at the Battle of Copenhagen against Nelson, 2 April 1801

History:
1900 October 20: Laid down at Copenhagen
1903 May 9: Launched
1905 May 31: Completed
1917 Refit, new armament
1936 Stricken, used as aircraft bombing target and broken up at Copenhagen

Peder Skram

Type: Broadside Ship
Class: 'Peder Skram' (1862)
Nomenclature: Peder Skram (c1500-1581), Danish naval hero

History:
1859 May 19: Laid down as steam frigate by Suenson at Nyholm
—— Converted to ironclad
1864 October 18: Launched
1866 August 15: Completed
1876-78 Refit
1885 December 7: Accommodation ship
1897 Broken up

Peder Skram

Type: Coast Defence Ship
Class: 'Peder Skram' (1904)

History:
1905 April 25: Laid down at Copenhagen
1908 May 2: Launched
1909 Autumn: Completed
1934 Refit, new light armament added
1943 August 29: Scuttled at Copenhagen
1944 Refloated by Germans and repaired in Germany as cadet training ship, Kiel, renamed ***Adler***
1945 Sunk by Allied aircraft at Kiel
1945 Refloated, towed to Copenhagen
1949 Hulk broken up at Odense

Rolf Krake

Type: Monitor
Class: 'Rolf Krake' (1862)
Nomenclature: Legendary Viking king, cAD600

History:
1862 Laid down by Napier
1863 May 6: Launched
1864 February 11: Completed
1864 Action with Prussian shore batteries at Egernsund
1868 Refit, rearmed
1893 May 3: Gunnery training ship
1907 June 27: Sold and broken up at Dordrecht, Holland

Skjold

Type: Monitor
Class: 'Skjold' (1893)
Nomenclature: Legendary Danish Viking king (Shield)

History:
1894 January 18: Laid down at Copenhagen
1896 May 8: Launched
1897 May 25: Completed
1929 May 21: Stricken and broken up in Denmark

Staerkodder

Type: Ironclad Ram
Class: 'Staerkodder' (1863)
Nomenclature: Strong otter

History:
1863 Laid down by Arman for Confederate navy under code name *Sphinx*
1864 March 31: Purchased by Denmark, named ***Staerkodder***
1864 June 21: Launched
1864 Arrived in Copenhagen
1865 February 3: Sold back to Confederate navy, named ***Stonewall***

Tordenskjold

Type: Coast Defence Ship
Class: 'Tordenskjold' (1878)
Nomenclature: Peder Wessel Tordenskjold (Thundershield) (1691-1720), Danish admiral, hero of the Great Northern War

History:
1879 June 5: Laid down at Copenhagen
1880 September 30: Launched
1882 September 29: Completed as torpedo ship
1885 Reclassified coast defence ship
1908 March 13: Stricken and broken up at Stettin

***Olfert Fischer* — Coast defence ship of 1896.** *IWM*

France

France, England's greatest rival at sea for over a century, scored a significant advance in 1859 with the launching of the *Gloire*, the world's first ironclad warship. The British responded to this threat with the iron hulled *Warrior* and a naval race ensued. British superiority at sea had been temporarily threatened with both countries starting even with a new type, but British industrial strength enabled Britain to retain her mastery of the sea.

Interest in new types caused France to purchase two American vessels, *Dunderberg* and *Onondaga*, in 1867. The Franco-Prussian War of 1870 resulted in no significant naval actions but the French fleet blockaded Prussian ports in the North Sea. Defeat and its costs caused reductions in French naval budgets in the 1870s. This, combined with the leadership of the *jeune école*, a group of officers who believed in a defensive navy, led to emphasis on torpedo boats for defence and cruisers for attacking enemy trade. Nevertheless, the Minister of Marine, Pothuau, continued construction of smaller battleships during this period. When Adm Aube, leader of the *jeune école*, became Minister in 1884 he suspended battleship construction. French naval policy at this time was a series of changing policies as minister succeeded minister.

French battleships of this period were characterised by a heavy squat look with built up superstructure and a pronounced tumblehome which permitted an increased arc of fire for the guns in citadels and sponsons. Many innovations adopted by other navies appeared first in French ships such as the *Amiral Duperré, Hoche* and *Brennus*.

By 1909 the French navy had declined to fifth rank and the government made a determined effort to rebuild the fleet. The Anglo-French Entente of 1904 relieved France from competing with England and of responsibility for defending the Channel, so that France could concentrate its efforts in the Mediterranean against the combination of Italy and Austria. But French naval construction was slow and pre-dreadnoughts were still being completed as late as 1910. Between 1909 and 1913 16 dreadnoughts were authorised, a well-balanced navy being planned for completion by 1920, but World War 1 intervened. Nine battleships remained unfinished including four 'Normandie' class units already launched. Four battleships were among the numerous ships lost during the war. The French navy units were active principally in the Mediterranean where Austria was the only enemy.

Under the Washington Treaty of 1922, France accepted parity with Italy in battleships and carriers. The dreadnoughts received some modernisation and an unfinished battleship, *Béarn*, was completed as France's lone aircraft carrier. The *Dunkerque* and *Strasbourg* were built in the 1930s under the treaty, but it was denounced in 1935 in order to authorise construction of the 'Richelieu' class.

World War 2 was a disaster for the French navy. Divided by the armistice of June 1940 the French battleships remained widely scattered. The incomplete *Richelieu* and *Jean Bart* were removed from German-threatened ports to North Africa. The attacks by the British on the French ships at Oran and Dakar caused heavy damage. On 27 November 1942, the entire fleet at Toulon was scuttled as the Germans occupied the naval base. The remaining units located outside France then joined the Allies and took part in operations against the Germans and Japanese.

These vessels made up the nucleus of the postwar fleet. The battleship *Jean Bart* was only completed in 1949, the last battleship in the world to be commissioned.

For many years the *Béarn* was the only French aircraft carrier. Two vessels ordered in 1937 were never completed as a result of the debacle of 1940. In 1946 the *Arromanches* was acquired from Britain and two more light carriers were obtained from the United States. In the 1950s the first original French-built carriers of the 'Clémenceau' class were built.

Class Details

'Gloire' Class (1858)

Broadside Ships: *Gloire, Invincible, Normandie* (see later photo)
Displacement: 5,650tons
Dimensions: *Gloire:* 263'9(oa) 255'6(wl) 252'3(pp)×55'9×27'10 [80.4(oa) 77.9(wl) 76.9(pp)×17×8.5]
Invincible and *Normandie:* 253'3(pp)×53'2×25'7 [77.2(pp)×16.2×7.8]
Machinery: 1 screw, return connecting-rod engines (*Gloire* and *Invincible:* F C Med; *Normandie:* Mazeline), 8 oval boilers
IHP 2,500 = 13knots
Endurance: 4,000/8
Armament: 36×164mm MLR
Gloire, 1869: 6×240mm MLR, 2×194mm MLR
Invincible and *Normandie, 1869:* 8×240mm MLR, 6×194mm MLR
Armour: Battery 110-120mm
Complement: 572
Class notes: Designed by Dupuy de Lôme. *Gloire* was the first armoured ship-of-the-line in the world. Wood hull with armour plating to the upper deck because French industry was unable to provide sufficient plating and armour quickly for iron hulls. Design based on the steam frigate *Napoleon* with full-length battery along the hull. Barkentine rig later changed to full ship rig, and later bark rig

'Couronne' (1858)

Broadside Ship: *Couronne*
Displacement: 6,429tons
Dimensions: 268'5(pp)×54'9×25'10 [81.8(pp)×16.7×7.9]
Machinery: 1 screw, return connecting-rod engines (Mazeline), 8 oval boilers
IHP 2,000 = 12knots
Endurance: 2,410/10
Armament: 10×194mm 55pdr SB, 30×164mm BLR
1864: 4×164mm replaced by 4×225mm ML howitzers
1868: 16×194mm, 4×164mm
1878: 8×240mm, 4×194mm, 2×47mm
1881: 3×164mm, 15×138mm, 8×100mm, 1×90mm, 14×65mm, 2×47mm, 5×37mm
Armour: Belt 120-140mm
Complement: 615
Class notes: Designed by Audenet as a fourth unit of 1858 programme. Similar to *Gloire* but with iron hull

'Magenta' Class (1859)

Broadside Ships: *Magenta, Solférino* (see later photo)

Displacement: *Magenta:* 6,596tons, 6,985f/l; *Solférino:* 7,129tons
Dimensions: 301'10(oa) 283'9(pp)×56'9×28'3 [92(oa) 86.5(pp)×17.3×8.6]
Machinery: 1 screw, return connecting-rod engines (Mazeline), 8 cylindrical boilers
IHP 3,500 = 13knots
Endurance: 1,840/10
Armament: 16×194mm 55pdr SB, 34×164mm BL, 2×225mm ML howitzers
Magenta, 1868: 24×164mm replaced by 4×240mm and 8×194mm
Magenta, 1869: 10×240mm, 4×194mm
Solférino, 1869: 14×240mm
Armour: Belt 120mm, battery 109-120mm
Complement: 706
Class notes: Designed by Dupuy de Lôme. The only two-deck broadside ironclads built. Wood hulls with full ship rig. Good sea boats. First warships with ram bows. The armour covered the whole battery amidships but forward and aft the batteries were unprotected in order to save weight. *Solférino* was the only French ironclad with a figurehead, a golden eagle

'Flandre' Class (1860-1861)

Broadside Ships: *Flandre, Gauloise, Guyenne, Heroïne, Magnanime* (see later photo), *Provence, Revanche, Savoie, Surveillante, Valeureuse*
Displacement: 5,900tons
Dimensions: 272(oa) 258'10(pp)×55'9×27'6 [82.9(oa) 78.9(pp)×17×8.4]
Machinery: 1 screw, horizontal return connecting-rod engines (*Flandre, Gauloise, Heroïne* and *Magnanime:* Mazeline; *Guyenne, Surveillante* and *Valeureuse:* Indret; *Provence, Savoie* and *Revanche:* F C Med), 9 oval boilers (*Revanche:* 8)
Endurance: 2,410/10 (vary)
Armament: *Designed:* 30×164 BLR
1865: 11×194mm 55pdr SB
1869: 8×240mm, 4×194mm
1885: 8×240mm, 3×194mm, 2×138mm
Surveillante, 1885: 4×194mm, 4×138mm
Valeureuse, 1885: 1×194mm, 6×164mm, 1×120mm
Armour: Belt 109-152mm, c/t 102mm
Complement: 594
Class notes: Designed by Dupuy de Lôme. Improved 'Gloire' type with bark rig. Wood hulls except *Heroïne* which was built of iron

'Belliqueuse' Class (1863)

Armoured Corvettes: *Alma, Armide, Atalante, Belliqueuse* (see later photo), *Jeanne d'Arc, Montcalm, Reine Blanche, Thétis*
Displacement: 3,770tons
Dimensions: 229'8(oa) 225'9(wl)×46'3×24 [70(oa) 68.8(wl)×14.1×7.3]
Machinery: 1 screw, compound engines (F C Med; *Alma:* Mazeline; *Armide:* Schneider); 8 boilers
IHP 1,700 = 11.8knots
Endurance: 1,460/10
Armament: *Belliqueuse:* 14×164mm
Belliqueuse, later: 4×194mm, 6×164mm, 4×138mm
'Alma' class: 6×194mm, 4×120mm
Armour: Belt 150mm, battery 120mm
Complement: 329; *Belliqueuse:* 451
Class notes: Designed by Dupuy de Lôme. *Belliqueuse* was actually a separate class of broadside ironclad. *Alma* and others had two guns in barbette on the upper deck and four in battery. They were the first ironclads with guns in barbettes. *Jeanne d'Arc* and *Thétis* had two funnels abreast, others a single funnel. All bark rigged

'Taureau' (1863)

Coast Defence Ram: *Taureau*
Displacement: 2,456tons, 2,718f/l
Dimensions: 196'10(wl)×47'6×17'9 [60(wl)×14.5×5.4]
Machinery: 2 screws, horizontal return connecting-rod engines (Indret), 8 oval boilers
IHP 1,500 = 12knots
Endurance: 700/8.5
Armament: 1×240mm
Armour: Belt 150mm, barbette 120mm
Complement: 135
Class notes: Designed by Dupuy de Lôme. Wood hull with iron ram and upperworks. A development of the monitor type; a ram with a single revolving turret. Primarily a coast defence vessel with wood hull

'Océan' Class (1865)

Central Battery Ships: *Marengo, Océan, Suffren* (see later photo)
Displacement: *Marengo:* 7,860tons; *Océan:* 7,810tons; *Suffren:* 7,800tons
Dimensions: 308(oa) 282'10(pp)×57'5×27'6 [93.9(oa) 86.2(pp)×17.5×8.4]
Machinery: 2 screws (*Suffren:* 1 screw), compound engines (*Marengo* and *Suffren:* Indret; *Océan:* Schneider), 8 oval boilers
IHP 3,600 = 13.5knots; *Suffren:* IHP 4,100 = 14.3knots
Endurance: 3,000/10 (vary)
Armament: *Océan:* 4×240mm, 4×194mm, 4×164mm
Océan, 1869: 4×274mm, 8×240mm
Others: 4×274mm, 4×240mm, 7×138mm (*Suffren:* 6 and 1×120mm)
Others, 1885: 4×274mm (*Marengo:* 6), 4×240mm, 4×120mm (*Suffren:* 6)
Armour: Belt 178-203mm, battery 160mm, barbettes 150mm
Complement: 660
Class notes: Designed by Dupuy de Lôme. Wood hulls with ram bow and full ship rig, later changed to bark. Armour protection as in *Magenta* with watertight bulkheads. Main guns mounted on four platforms at corners of the central battery

'Friedland' (1865)

Central Battery Ship: *Friedland*
Displacement: 8,916tons
Dimensions: 331'8(oa) 317'2(wl) 307'4(pp)×58×28'3 [101.1(oa) 96.7(wl) 93.7(pp)×17.7×8.6]
Machinery: 1 screw, compound engines (Indret), 8 oval boilers
IHP 4,500 = 13.5knots
Endurance: 2,666/10
Armament: 8×274mm, 8×138mm
Later: 4×355mm TT added
Armour: Belt 178-203mm, battery 160mm
Complement: 688
Class notes: Designed by Sabattier as a fourth unit of 'Océan'

Top right:
***Couronne* — Broadside ship of 1858, in 1865.**
Marius Bar

Centre right:
***Magenta* — Broadside ship, 1861.** *Marius Bar*

Bottom right:
A 'Flandre' class broadside ship at Brest.
Naval Historical Foundation

Alma

class but with iron hull. Completion delayed by modifications during construction

'Bélier' Class (1865)

Coast Defence Turret Rams: *Bélier, Bouledogue, Cerbère, Tigre*
Displacement: 3,600tons
Dimensions: 233(oa) 216'6(wl)×52'10×19'4 [71(oa) 66(wl)×16.1×5.9]
Machinery: 2 screws, horizontal return connecting-rod engines (*Bélier:* F C Med; *Cerbère:* Schneider; *Bouledogue* and *Tigre:* Indret), 8 oval boilers
IHP 1,800 = 12knots
Armament: 2×240mm, 4×37mm
Armour: Belt 178-220mm, turret 178mm
Complement: 161
Class notes: Enlarged 'Taureau' type. Wood hull with one turret and two funnels abreast. Brig rig as designed but this discarded after completion of *Cerbère.* Remained in or near port during entire careers

'Rochambeau' (1867)

Casemate Ironclad: *Rochambeau* (see also later photo)
Displacement: 7,112tons
Dimensions: 380'3(oa) 352'4(pp)×76'6×32'5 [115.9(oa) 107.4(pp)×23.3×9.9]
Machinery: 1 screw, horizontal inverted compound engines, 6 boilers
IHP 5,000 = 12.5knots
Armament: 4×270mm BLR, 10×240mm BLR
Armour: Sides 89mm, casemates 114mm
Complement: 600
Class notes: Built in US as *Dunderberg* and purchased in 1867. Modified upon arrival in France without armament, bow rebuilt, new rudder fitted, armed and engines improved. Wood hull. Saw little service

'Onondaga' (1867)

Monitor: *Onondaga*
Displacement: 2,930tons
Dimensions: 228'8(pp)×51'2×12'6 [69.7(pp)×15.6×3.8]
Machinery: 2 screws, horizontal back-acting engines (Morgan), 4 boilers
IHP 640 = 7knots
Armament: 4×240mm
Armour: Belt 140mm, turrets 300mm, deck 25mm
Complement: 108
Class notes: Purchased from US in 1867. Iron hull and two turrets

'La Galissonnière' (1867)

Armoured Corvette: *La Galissonnière*
Displacement: 4,720tons
Dimensions: 260'6(wl)×48'10×24 [79.4(wl)×14.9×7.3]
Machinery: 2 screws, vertical compound engines (Indret), 4 oval boilers
IHP 2,400 = 13.75knots
Armament: 6×240mm, 4×120mm
Armour: Belt 152mm, battery and barbettes 120mm
Complement: 344
Class notes: Designed by Dupuy de Lôme. Wood hull with four guns in central battery and two in barbettes

'Richelieu' (1867)

Central Battery Ship: *Richelieu*
Displacement: 9,130tons
Dimensions: 333'8(oa) 321'10(pp)×57×27'10 [101.7(oa) 98.1(pp)×17.4×8.5]
Machinery: 2 screws, compound engines (Indret), 8 oval boilers
IHP 4,240 = 13.25 knots
Endurance: 3,300/10
Armament: 6×274mm, 5×240mm, 10×120mm
Later: 120mm replaced by 8×140mm, 4×355mm TT added
Armour: Belt 180-220mm, barbettes 160mm, bulkhead 160mm
Complement: 750
Class notes: Designed by Dupuy de Lôme. Modified 'Océan' type with larger central battery. Wood hull. Main battery mounted in a central battery and the secondary battery in barbettes at the corners of the deck above. Rebuilt after a fire in 1880

'Victorieuse' Class (1868)

Armoured Corvettes: *Triomphante, Victorieuse*
Displacement: 4,760 tons
Dimensions: 257'10(wl) 252(pp)×48'10×20'8 [78.6(wl) 76.8(pp)×14.9×6.3]
Machinery: 1 screw, vertical compound engines (Indret), 4 oval boilers
IHP 2,400 = 13knots
Endurance: 2,740/10
Armament: 6×240mm, 1×190mm (*Triomphante:* 3), 6×140mm
Armour: Belt 150mm, battery and barbettes 120mm, bulkheads 120mm
Complement: 393
Class notes: Designed by Sabattier and Dupuy de Lôme. Wood hulls. Similar to *La Galissonnière* with two guns in fixed armoured turrets in barbettes and four in a central battery

'Colbert' Class (1869)

Central Battery Ships: *Colbert, Trident*
Displacement: *Colbert:* 8,617tons; *Trident:* 8,857tons
Dimensions: 331'8(oa) 307'5(pp)×57×27'10 [101.1(oa) 93.7(pp)×17.4×8.5]
Trident: 335(oa)×58'9×28'3 [102.1(oa)×17.9×8.6]
Machinery: 1 screw, compound engines (Indret), 8 oval boilers
IHP 4,400 = 15.5knots
Endurance: 3,300/10
Armament: 8×274mm, 2×240mm, 6×140mm, 2×47mm
Later: 6 TT added (*Colbert:* 4)
Armour: Belt 178-225mm, battery 160mm, bulkheads 120mm
Complement: 774
Class notes: Designed by Sabattier. Wood hulls. Improved 'Richelieu' type without barbettes, substituting armoured towers at either end. *Trident* had a slightly different arrangement allowing for greater fire ahead and astern

Above left:
***Alma* — Armoured corvette of 1863.**
Naval Historical Foundation

Below left:
***Friedland* — Central battery ship of 1865.** *Marius Bar*

'Redoutable' (1872)

Central Battery and Barbette Ship: *Redoutable* (see later photo)
Displacement: 9,300tons
Dimensions: 330'4(oa) 318'6(wl) 311'8(pp)×64'8×25'6 [100.7(oa) 97.1(wl) 95(pp)×19.7×7.8]
Machinery: 2 screws, horizontal compound engines (Schneider), 8 oval boilers; *1894:* 1 screw, VTE engines, 8 cylindrical boilers
IHP 5,900 = 14 knots
Endurance: 2,800/10
Armament: 8×274mm, 6×140mm
1898: 4×240mm replaced 4×274mm in battery, 6×100mm, 2×47mm, 2×355mm TT
Armour: Belt 240-350mm, casemates 300mm, bulkheads 240mm, deck 65mm
Complement: 705
Class notes: Designed by de Bussy. Outer hull of iron with remainder of construction of steel. Four guns of main armament in central battery and four in barbettes. Originally fully rigged, later barkentine rig; large funnel. Reconstructed 1894, re-engined and reboilered, rigging and bowsprit replaced by two military masts

'Tonnerre' Class (1872)

Coast Defence Turret Ships: *Fulminant, Tonnerre*
Displacement: 5,820tons
Dimensions: 257'10(oa) 248(wl) 241'6(pp)×57'9×21'6 [78.6(oa) 75.6(wl) 73.6(pp)×17.6×6.5]
Machinery: 1 screw, *Tonnerre:* direct induction engines (F C Med), 8 cylindrical boilers; *Fulminant:* compound engines (Schneider), 8 cylindrical boilers
IHP 4,300 = 15knots
Endurance: 1,680/8
Armament: 2×274mm
Later: 4×47mm and 2 TT added
Armour: Belt 250-330mm, redoubt 300mm, turret 300mm, deck 50mm, bulkhead 300mm
Complement: 259
Class notes: Designed by de Bussy. Steel hull with iron armour. A monitor type without sails with an armoured redoubt and turret. *Tonnerre's* engines were removed from ironclad *Normandie*

'Tempête' (1872)

Coast Defence Turret Ship: *Tempête*
Displacement: 4,900tons
Dimensions: 257'10(oa) 248(wl) 241'4(pp)×57'9×19 [78.6(oa) 75.6(wl) 73.6(pp)×17.6×5.8]
Machinery: 1 screw, horizontal compound engines (Indret), 4 cylindrical boilers
IHP 2,000 = 11knots
Endurance: 527/10
Armament: 2×274mm, 4×47mm
Later: 2 TT added
Armour: Belt 250-330mm, redoubt 270-330mm, turret 305-360mm, deck 50mm, c/t 250mm
Complement: 174
Class notes: Designed by de Bussy. Similar to 'Tonnerre' class with smaller funnel

'Vengeur' (1873)

Coast Defence Breastwork Monitor: *Vengeur*
Displacement: 4,700tons
Dimensions: 260'2(oa) 241'6(pp)×57'9×17'9 [79.3(oa) 73.6(pp)×17.6×5.4]
Machinery: 2 screws, compound engines (Indret), 4 cylindrical boilers
IHP 2,000 = 10.7knots
Endurance: 825/10
Armament: 2×340mm, 6×47mm, 2×355mm TT
Armour: Belt 254-330mm, redoubt 270-330mm, turret 305-360mm, deck 60mm
Complement: 185
Class notes: Designed by de Bussy. Generally similar to *Tempête*

'Tonnant' (1873)

Coast Defence Barbette Ship: *Tonnant*
Displacement: 5,090tons
Dimensions: 248'8(wl) 242'2(pp)×58'4×17'3 [75.8(wl) 73.8(pp)×17.8×5.3]
Machinery: 1 screw, compound engines (Indret), 4 cylindrical boilers
IHP 2,000 = 11knots
Endurance: 825/10
Armament: 2×340mm
Armour: Belt 340-450mm, barbettes 338mm, deck 79mm
Complement: 185
Class notes: Improved 'Tonnerre' type with turtleback forecastle and single barbettes fore and aft and very low freeboard. Single military mast

'Furieux' (1874)

Coast Defence Barbette Ship: *Furieux*
Displacement: 6,020tons
Dimensions: 246'3(wl) 238(pp)×58'5×23'3 [75.1(wl) 72.5(pp)×17.8×7.1]
Machinery: 2 screws, compound engines, 8 cylindrical boilers; *1897:* VTE engines, 8 Belleville boilers
IHP 4,900 = 13.5knots; *1897:* IHP 5,000 = 13.5knots
Endurance: 1,500/10
Armament: 2×340mm/21, 4×47mm
1897: 2×240mm/40, 4×100mm, 12×47mm, 2×355mm TT
Armour: Belt 340-500mm, barbettes 450mm, deck 89mm
1897: Turrets 230mm, c/t 250mm
Complement: 259
Class notes: Improved 'Tonnerre' type with larger guns in barbettes fore and aft, heavier armour and turtleback forecastle. Design modified after keel was laid down. Reconstructed 1896, new engines and boilers fitted and new armament, two funnels forward of single military mast, and conning tower added

'Dévastation' Class (1874)

Central Battery and Barbette Ships: *Courbet, Dévastation*
Displacement: *Dévastation:* 10,704tons; *Courbet:* 10,520tons
Dimensions: *Dévastation:* 311'7(wl)×69'8×26'6 [95(wl)×21.3×8.1]
Courbet: 316'3(wl)×69'8×27'10 [96.4(wl)×21.3×8.5]

Top right:
***Cerbère* and *Bélier* — c1880. Coast defence rams in port with earlier *Taureau* at right.** *Photomatic*

Centre right:
***Rochambeau* — A rare drawing of the former American ironclad at sea.**

Bottom right:
***La Galissonnière* — Armoured corvette in 1883.** *Marius Bar*

43. LE COLBERT

Machinery: 2 screws, vertical compound engines (*Dévastation:* Indret; *Courbet:* Schneider), 12 cylindrical boilers; *Dévastation, 1898:* Belleville boilers
IHP 8,100 = 15knots
Endurance: 2,800/10
Armament: 4×340mm, 4×274mm, 6×138mm, 5×355mm TT
Courbet, 1900: 4×274mm, 3×240mm, 1×164mm, 10×100mm, 14×47mm, 5 TT
Dévastation, 1900: 340mm replaced by 274mm
Dévastation, 1902: 4×274mm, 2×240mm, 14×100mm, 14×47mm, 4 TT
Armour: Belt 225-380mm, battery 240mm, c/t 76mm
Complement: 733
Class notes: Designed by de Bussy. Improved 'Redoutable' type with heavier guns and believed superior to contemporary British vessels. Hull of steel and iron with double bottom. Four guns in the central battery, two mounted in barbettes and the remainder on deck. Lightly rigged, had two funnels abreast. Reconstructed 1898

'Turenne' Class (1875)

Second Class Battleships: *Bayard* (see later photo), *Turenne*
Displacement: 6,400tons
Dimensions: 266'6(wl)×57'5×26'3 [81.2(wl)×17.5×8]
Machinery: 2 screws, compound engines (*Bayard:* Schneider), 8 cylindrical boilers
IHP 4,000 = 14.25knots
Armament: 4×240mm, 2×194mm, 6×138mm, 2×65mm
Later: 2×355mm TT added
Armour: Belt 165-230mm, barbettes 200mm, deck 50mm, c/t 50mm
Complement: 450
Class notes: Designed by Sabattier for foreign service. Wood hulls with main guns in barbettes. *Bayard* had two funnels and *Turenne* only one. Reclassified armoured cruisers 1885

'Vauban' Class (1875)

Second Class Battleships: *Duguesclin, Vauban*
Displacement: 6,150tons
Dimensions: 269(wl)×57'6×27 [82(wl)×17.5×8.2]
Machinery: 2 screws, vertical compound engines (Indret), 8 cylindrical boilers
IHP 4,000 = 14knots
Armament: 4×240mm, 1×194mm, 6×138mm, 12×37mm, 2×355mm TT
Armour: Belt 165-250mm, barbettes 203mm, deck 50mm, c/t 50mm
Complement: 474
Class notes: Designed by Lebelin de Dionne. Similar to 'Turenne' type with steel hulls and guns in barbettes. Brig rig, single funnel and long ram bow. Rig changed later to two military masts

'Amiral Duperré' (1876)

Barbette Ship: *Amiral Duperré*
Displacement: 10,487tons
Dimensions: 318'3(oa)×65'8×27'10 [97(oa)×20×8.5]

Above left:
***Richelieu* — Central battery ship, after reconstruction.** *Marius Bar*

Below left:
***Colbert* — Central battery ship of 1869, as completed with bark rig.** *Naval Historical Foundation*

Machinery: 2 screws, compound engines (F C Med), 12 cylindrical boilers
IHP 7,400 = 14.2knots
Endurance: 2,850/10
Armament: 4×340mm, 1×160mm, 14×138mm, 2×65mm, 18×47mm, 4×355mm TT
Armour: Belt 260-548mm, barbettes 300mm, deck 58mm, c/t 38mm
Complement: 712
Class notes: New design by Sabattier with complete waterline armour belt but no main deck battery, guns being mounted in four barbettes. High freeboard and bark rig with two funnels abreast. First French armoured vessel built at a private yard

'Terrible' Class (1876)

Coast Defence Barbette Ships: *Caïman, Indomptable, Requin, Terrible*
Displacement: 7,197tons
Dimensions: *Terrible* and *Indomptable:* 287'9(oa)×58'4×24 [87.7(oa)×17.8×7.3]
Caïman and *Requin:* 273'3(oa)×59×24'7 [83.3(oa)×18×7.5]
Machinery: 2 screws, vertical compound engines (*Indomptable* and *Terrible:* Schneider; *Requin:* F C Med), 12 cylindrical boilers (*Requin:* 10); *Requin, 1896:* 8 Niclausse boilers
IHP 6,000 = 14knots
Endurance: 1,750/10
Armament: 2×420mm/19, 4×100mm, 4×355mm TT
Terrible, 1898-99: 2×340mm
Others, 1898: 2×274mm/45, 6×100mm, 10×37mm, 2×355mm TT (*Requin:* none)
Armour: Belt 300-500mm, barbettes 450mm, deck 100mm, c/t 300mm
Complement: 381
Class notes: Designed by Sabattier. Large coast defence ships with main guns in two barbettes and four funnels in pairs abreast. All except *Terrible* reconstructed between 1895 and 1901 with new boilers and new armament. *Requin*, rebuilt with two funnels on centreline and military masts, survived to serve in World War 1

'Baudin' Class (1878)

Barbette Ships: *Amiral Baudin, Formidable*
Displacement: 11,910tons
Dimensions: 347'9(oa) 343'2(wl) 321'6(pp)×69'6×27'3 [106(oa) 104.6(wl) 98(pp)×21.2×8.3]
Machinery: 2 screws, compound engines (*Amiral Baudin:* Indret; *Formidable:* Schneider), 12 cylindrical boilers
IHP 9,000 = 16knots
Endurance: 3,000/10
Armament: 3×370mm/28, 4×164mm, 8×138mm, 18×47mm, 6×355mm TT
1898: 1×370mm replaced by 4×164mm, 2×138mm
Armour: Belt 355-550mm, barbettes 450mm, deck 100mm, c/t 420mm
Complement: 649
Class notes: Designed by Godron. Improved 'Duperré' type with three barbettes on the centreline, single funnel and two military masts. Reconstructed 1897-98 when amidships barbette was removed and replaced by casemate, mainmast altered and new boilers fitted

'Hoche' (1880)

Barbette Ship: *Hoche*
Displacement: 11,052tons

Top left:
***Fulminant* — Coast defence ship of 1872.** *Marius Bar*

Top right:
***Furieux* — Coast defence ship of 1874 before reconstruction of 1896.** *Photomatic*

Centre left:
***Dévastation* — Central battery and barbette ship of 1874.** *Marius Bar*

Centre right:
***Duguesclin* — Armoured cruiser of 'Vauban' class, with military masts.**

Far left:
***Turenne* — Second class battleship of 1875, probably taken at Hong Kong 1895.**

Left:
***Amiral Duperré* — Barbette ship of 1876, a completely new type when built.** *Marius Bar*

Top:
***Indomptable* — Coast defence ship of 1876, 'Terrible' class. The two pairs of funnels have been cased together during reconstruction.**

Above:
***Formidable* — Barbette ship of 1878, after reconstruction of 1897. Notice heavy foremast and obviously slanted sides.** *Marius Bar*

Top right:
***Hoche* — Barbette ship of 1880. Notice low freeboard and built up superstructure.** *Photomatic*

Centre right:
***Magenta* — Barbette ship of 1880.** *Marius Bar*

Bottom right:
***Dupuy de Lôme* — Armoured cruiser of 1888, prior to 1905 reconstruction.** *IWM*

Dimensions: 346'6(oa) 336'7(wl)×65×27'10 [105.6(oa) 102.6(wl)×19.8×8.5]
Machinery: 2 screws, vertical compound engines (Indret), 8 cylindrical boilers; *1900:* VTE engines, 16 Belleville boilers
IHP 11,300 = 16.25knots
Endurance: 4,700/10
Armament: 2×340mm/26, 2×274mm/28, 18×138mm/30, 10×47mm
1900: 138mm replaced by 12×138mm QF and 4×65mm, 5×450mm TT added
Armour: Belt 350-450mm, barbettes and turrets 400mm, deck 90mm, c/t 65mm
Complement: 714
Class notes: Designed by Huin. Armament in two 340mm turrets fore and aft and one 274mm barbette on each beam amidships. Low freeboard and greatly built up superstructure between the barbettes. Reconstructed 1898 with new engines and boilers

'Neptune' Class (1880)

Barbette Ships: *Magenta, Marceau,* (see later photo), *Neptune*
Displacement: 10,600tons
Dimensions: 341'3(oa) 323'6(pp)×66'3×27'10 [104(oa) 98.6(pp)×20.2×8.5]
Machinery: 2 screws, vertical compound engines (*Magenta:* Schneider; *Marceau:* F C Med; *Neptune:* Indret), 8 cylindrical boilers (*Neptune:* 12); *1901:* Belleville boilers (*Marceau:* Niclausse)
IHP 12,000 = 16knots
Endurance: 4,000/10
Armament: 4×340mm/30, 16×138mm/45 (*Magenta:* 14; *Marceau:* 18), 6×65mm, 12×47mm, 5×450mm TT
Armour: Belt 230-450mm, barbettes 450mm, deck 80mm, c/t 120mm
Complement: 660
Class notes: Designed by Huin & Bertin. Similar ships with differing characteristics, improved 'Hoche' type with main armament in four barbettes fore and aft and one on each beam. Reconstructed 1901-03

'Brennus' (1888)

Barbette Ship: *Brennus*
Displacement: 11,550tons
Dimensions: 375'8(oa) 361(wl) 344'6(pp)×67'6×27'10 [114.5(oa) 110(wl) 105(pp)×20.6×8.5]
Machinery: 2 screws, VTE engines (Indret), 32 Belleville boilers
IHP 13,000 = 18knots
Endurance: 2,710/10
Armament: 3×340mm/42, 10×164mm/45, 4×65mm, 14×47mm, 4×450mm TT
Armour: Belt 350-450mm, battery 102mm, turrets 450mm and 400mm, deck 80mm, c/t 150mm
Complement: 696
Class notes: Designed by Huin. First French battleship with watertube boilers and without a ram bow. Had a light armour belt above the main belt which set a standard for all navies for 20 years. Originally started in 1882 but redesigned and reordered in 1888. Last French warship with a figurehead. Mainmast removed after completion to save weight

Top left:
***Chanzy* — Armoured cruiser of 'Amiral Charner' class, wrecked 1907.** *Marius Bar*

Centre left:
***Bouvet* — Pre-dreadnought of 1891.** *Marius Bar*

Bottom left:
***Masséna* — Battleship of 1891, in 1911.**

'Dupuy de Lôme' (1888)

Armoured Cruiser: *Dupuy de Lôme* (see also later photo)
Displacement: 6,300tons
Dimensions: 373'8(wl) 364'2(pp)×51'6×25'11 [114(wl) 111(pp)×15.7×7.9]
Machinery: 3 screws, HTE and VTE (Loire-St Denis), 13 cylindrical boilers; *1904:* 18 Normand-Sigaudy boilers
IHP 14,000 = 20knots
Endurance: 4,000/12.5
Armament: 2×194mm/40, 6×164mm, 4×65mm, 8×47mm, 2×450mm TT
Armour: Belt 120mm, turrets 102mm, deck 37mm, c/t 125mm
Complement: 544
Class notes: An innovative design by De Bussy with all guns and turrets having a wide arc of fire and a complete belt over the hull. The long bow was not a ram but secured buoyancy without a forecastle exposed to gun blast. Two uneven funnels and two military masts. Difficulty with engines and boilers necessitated long period of trials. Reconstructed 1905, reboilered and third funnel added, mainmast removed. 'Sold' to Peru 1914 but sale not completed. Converted to merchant ship 1920.

'Bouvines' Class (1889)

Coast Defence Ships: *Amiral Tréhouart* (see later photo), *Bouvines, Jemmapes* (see later photo), *Valmy*
Displacement: 6,610tons; *Jemmapes* and *Valmy:* 6,590tons
Dimensions: 293'3(wl)×58'9×24'8 [89.4(wl)×17.9×7.5]
Jemmapes and *Valmy:* 283'9(wl)×57'4×24'6 [86.5(wl)×17.5×7.5]
Machinery: 2 screws, HTE engines (Loire-St Denis; *Bouvines:* F C Med; *Amiral Tréhouart:* Indret), 16 Lagrafel-d'Allest boilers (*Amiral Tréhouart:* 12 Belleville)
IHP 8,400 = 17knots
Endurance: 3,900/8
Armament: 2×305mm/35, 8×100mm/45, 8×47mm, 2×450mm TT
Jemmapes and *Valmy:* 2×340mm/40, 4×100mm/45, 4×47mm, 2×450mm TT
All, 1906: TT removed
Armour: Belt 250-464mm, turrets 320-370mm, deck 92mm, c/t 100mm
Complement: 363
Class notes: Designed by De Bussy & Opin. Last in series of coast defence ships. *Jemmapes* and *Valmy* had turtleback bows, others a built up forecastle. Two single turrets fore and aft, two funnels and military foremast. *Tréhouart* had a single funnel

'Amiral Charner' Class (1889)

Armoured Cruisers: *Amiral Charner, Bruix, Chanzy, Latouche-Tréville*
Displacement: 4,750tons, 4,990f/l
Dimensions: 374(wl) 363'6(pp)×47'3×20'4 [114(wl) 110.8(pp)×14.4×6.2]
Bruix and *Chanzy:* 359'3(pp)×45'10 [109.5(pp)×14]
Machinery: 2 screws, HTE engines (*Chanzy:* Schneider; *Latouche-Tréville:* F C Med), 16 Belleville boilers
IHP 8,300 = 19knots
Endurance: 3,460/10
Armament: 2×194mm/45, 6×138mm/45, 4×65mm, 8×47mm, 4×450mm TT
1906: TT removed

Armour: Belt 76-108mm, turrets 108mm, deck 50mm, c/t 108mm
Complement: 516
Class notes: Designed by Thibaudier. Smaller cruisers with two funnels and two military masts. The 138mm guns were in turrets low down on main deck level. Pole mast fitted later

'Charles Martel' (1890)

Pre-dreadnought: *Charles Martel*
Displacement: 11,882tons
Dimensions: 398'8(oa) 380'6(pp)×71.8×27'6 [121.5(oa) 116(pp)×21.7×8.4]
Machinery: 2 screws, VTE engines (Schneider), 24 Lagrafel-d'Allest boilers
IHP 14,500 = 18knots
Endurance: 3,250/10
Armament: 2×305mm/45, 2×274mm/45, 8×138mm/45, 4×65mm, 20×47mm, 6×450mm TT
Armour: Belt 275-450mm, turrets 400mm, secondary turrets 225mm, deck 78mm, c/t 228mm
Complement: 562
Class notes: Designed by Huin. First of a new series with single 305mm turrets fore and aft and 274mm turrets on each beam. Two funnels and two military masts and hull with great tumblehome

'Carnot' (1890)

Pre-dreadnought: *Carnot*
Displacement: 12,273tons
Dimensions: 380'6(wl) 374(pp)×72.2×28'10 [116(wl) 114(pp)×22×8.8]
Machinery: 2 screws, VTE engines (Indret), 24 Lagrafel-d'Allest boilers
IHP 15,000 = 18knots
Endurance: 3,000/10
Armament: 2×305mm/45, 2×274/45, 8×138mm/45, 4×65mm, 18×47mm, 4×450mm TT
Armour: Belt 275-450mm, turrets 370mm, secondary turrets 100mm, deck 68mm, c/t 150mm
Complement: 625
Class notes: Similar to *Charles Martel* but differed in appearance with less cluttered deck and pole mainmast

'Jauréguiberry' (1891)

Pre-dreadnought: *Jauréguiberry* (see later photo)
Displacement: 11,899tons, 12,229f/l
Dimensions: 367'2(wl) 360(pp)×72'6×27'9 [111.9(wl) 109.7(pp)×22.1×8.5]
Machinery: 2 screws, VTE engines (F C Med), 24 Lagrafel-d'Allest boilers
IHP 14,200 = 17knots
Endurance: 4,000/10
Armament: 2×305mm/45, 2×274mm/45, 8×138mm/45, 4×65mm, 14×47mm, 6×450mm TT
1906: 4 TT removed
Armour: Belt 275-450mm, turrets 370mm, secondary turrets 100mm, deck 70mm, c/t 230mm
Complement: 640
Class notes: Similar in details to *Charles Martel* but no flying deck and larger funnels.

'Bouvet' (1891)

Pre-dreadnought: *Bouvet* (see also later photo)
Displacement: 12,205tons
Dimensions: 402'3(oa) 397(wl) 386'6(pp)×70'3×27'7 [122.6(oa) 121(wl) 117.8(pp)×21.4×8.4]
Machinery: 3 screws, VTE engines (Indret), 24 Belleville boilers
IHP 14,000 = 18knots
Endurance: 4,000/10
Armament: 2×305mm/45, 2×274mm/45, 8×138mm/45, 8×100mm, 14×47mm, 4×450mm TT
1907: 2 TT removed
Armour: Belt 200-400mm, turrets 370mm, deck 88mm, c/t 300-320mm
Complement: 698
Class notes: Similar in details to *Charles Martel* with lighter military masts. Good sea boat

'Masséna' (1891)

Pre-dreadnought: *Masséna*
Displacement: 12,355tons
Dimensions: 384'2(oa) 380'6(wl) 369'7(pp)×66'8×26'11 [117.1(oa) 116(wl) 112.7(pp)×20.3×8.2]
Machinery: 3 screws, VTE engines (Loire-St Denis), 24 Lagrafel-d'Allest boilers
IHP 13,500 = 18knots
Endurance: 4,600/10
Armament: 2×305mm/40, 2×274mm/45, 8×138mm/45, 8×100mm, 14×47mm, 4×450mm TT
1906: 2 TT removed
Armour: Belt 246-450mm, turrets 347-398mm, secondary turrets 100mm, deck 68mm, c/t 350mm
Complement: 641
Class notes: Similar to *Charles Martel* with widely spaced funnels, little superstructure and shorter mainmast. Failed to attain contract speed on trials

'Pothuau' (1892)

Armoured Cruiser: *Pothuau*
Displacement: 5,460tons
Dimensions: 371(oa) 360'10(pp)×50'6×21'4 [113.1(oa) 110(pp)×15.4×6.5]
Machinery: 2 screws, HTE engines (F C Med), 18 Belleville boilers
IHP 10,000 = 19knots
Endurance: 4,500/10
Armament: 2×194mm/40mm, 10×138mm/45, 10×47mm, 5×450mm TT
1919: 194mm removed
Armour: Belt 50-100mm, turrets 240mm, deck 88mm, c/t 240mm
Complement: 461
Class notes: Designed by Thibaudier. Two single turrets fore and aft and secondary armament in casemates. Thin armour belt, three low funnels and projecting bow. Good sea boat

Top right:
***Pothuau* — Armoured cruiser 1898.** *Marius Bar*

Centre right:
***Jeanne d'Arc* — Armoured cruiser of 1895, unsuccessful with too light an armament for its size.**

Bottom right:
***Dupetit-Thouars* — Armoured cruiser, 'Gueydon' class.** *Marius Bar*

JEAN D' ARCQ

'Charlemagne' Class (1893)

Pre-dreadnoughts: *Charlemagne, Gaulois* (see later photo), *Saint Louis*
Displacement: 11,284tons
Dimensions: 386'2(oa) 380'9(wl) 374(pp)×66'8×27'6 [117.7(oa) 116(wl) 114(pp)×20.3×8.4]
Machinery: 3 screws, VTE engines (*Charlemagne:* Schneider; *Gaulois:* Loire-St Denis; *Saint Louis:* Indret), 20 Belleville boilers
IHP 14,500 = 18knots
Endurance: 4,200/10
Armament: 4×305mm/40, 10×138mm/45, 8×100mm/45, 20×47mm, 4×450mm TT
1904: 2 TT removed
Armour: Belt 200-368mm, turrets 380mm, battery 75mm, deck 90mm, c/t 330mm
Complement: 727
Class notes: Designed by Thibaudier. First French battleships with twin turrets fore and aft. Secondary armament in casemates. Were top heavy after 1913 refit and during World War 1 *Charlemagne* and *St Louis* had their superstructure and masts lightened

'Jeanne d'Arc' (1895)

Armoured Cruiser: *Jeanne d'Arc*
Displacement: 11,270tons
Dimensions: 477(pp)×63'8×26'8 [145.4(pp)×19.4×8.1]
Machinery: 3 screws, VTE engines, 36 Guyot-du Temple boilers; *later:* 48 Normand-Sigaudy boilers
IHP 28,000 = 23knots
Endurance: 13,500/10
Armament: 2×194mm/45, 14×138mm/45, 16×47mm, 2×450mm TT
Armour: Belt 75-150mm, barbettes 120-160mm, casemates 127mm, deck 55mm, c/t 150mm
Complement: 652
Class notes: Designed by Bertin. Innovative design but unsuccessful; armament too light for its size. Never reached contract speed. Six funnels in two groups of three

'Henri IV' (1896)

Second Class Battleship: *Henri IV*
Displacement: 8,800tons
Dimensions: 354'6(oa) 325(pp)×72'10×23 [108(oa) 99(pp)×22.2×7]
Machinery: 3 screws, VTE engines (Indret), 16 Niclausse boilers
IHP 11,345 = 17knots
Endurance: 6,000/10
Armament: 2×274mm/40, 7×138mm/45, 12×47mm, 2×450mm TT
Armour: Belt 75-280mm, turrets 305mm, deck 90mm, c/t 240mm
Complement: 460
Class notes: Designed by Bertin as a new type of seagoing monitor with two single turrets fore and aft on a small hull with low freeboard. Two square funnels and two heavy military masts. First appearance of a superfiring turret. Pole mainmast fitted later

Top left:
***Suffren* — Pre-dreadnought of 1898.** *Marius Bar*

Centre left:
***Gloire* — Armoured cruiser of 1898.**

Bottom left:
***République* — Pre-dreadnought of 1900.**

'Iéna' (1897)

Pre-dreadnought: *Iéna* (see later photo)
Displacement: 12,052tons
Dimensions: 400'10(oa) 396'4(wl)×68'3×27'10 [122.2(oa) 120.8(wl)×20.8×8.5]
Machinery: 3 screws, VTE engines (F C Med), 20 Belleville boilers
IHP 16,500 = 18knots
Endurance: 7,000/10
Armament: 4×305mm/45, 8×164mm/45, 8×100mm/55, 16×47mm, 4×450mm TT
Armour: Belt 230-320mm, turrets 320mm, battery 150mm, deck 80mm, c/t 300mm
Complement: 705
Class notes: Designed by Thibaudier. Modified 'Charlemagne' type with two twin turrets, two funnels and two military masts

'Gueydon' Class (1897)

Armoured Cruisers: *Dupetit-Thouars, Gueydon, Montcalm*
Displacement: 9,516tons
Dimensions: 459(oa) 452'9(wl)×64×24'8 [139.9(oa) 138(wl)×19.5×7.5]
Machinery: 3 screws, VTE engines (*Dupetit-Thouars:* Schneider; *Gueydon:* Loire-St Denis; *Montcalm:* F C Med, *Dupetit-Thouars:* 28 Belleville; *Gueydon:* Niclausse; *Montcalm:* 20 Normand boilers
IHP 20,000 = 21knots
Endurance: 8,500/10
Armament: 2×194mm/40, 8×164mm/45, 4×100mm/45, 16×47mm×2×450mm TT
Armour: Belt 80-150mm, turrets 160-176mm, casemates 120mm, deck 30-55mm, c/t 160mm
Complement: 615
Class notes: Designed by Bertin. Smaller 'Jeanne d'Arc' type with two separate pairs of funnels, military foremasts and pole mainmast. Too lightly armed

'Kléber' Class (1897)

Armoured Cruisers: *Desaix, Dupleix, Kléber*
Displacement: 7,735tons
Dimensions: 433'4(oa) 426'9(pp)×58'4×24'4 [132.1(oa) 130.1(pp)×17.9×7.4]
Machinery: 3 screws, VTE engines (*Desaix;* Loire-St Denis; *Dupleix;* F C Med; *Kléber:* Schneider), 24 Belleville boilers (*Kléber:* 20 Niclausse)
IHP 17,800 = 21knots
Endurance: 7,600/10
Armament: 8×164mm/45, 4×100mm/45, 10×47mm, 2×450mm TT
Kléber, 1897: 100mm removed, 2×47 AA added
All, 1908: TT removed
Armour: Belt 85-100mm, turrets 100mm, deck 40-65mm, c/t 150mm
Complement: 580
Class notes: Designed by Bertin. Small armoured cruisers with weaker armament and protection. Two pairs of funnels and two pole masts

'Suffren' (1898)

Pre-dreadnought: *Suffren*
Displacement: 12,750tons
Dimensions: 422'6(oa) 413(wl)×70'3×27'6 [128.8(oa) 125.9(wl)×21.4×8.4]
Machinery: 3 screws, VTE engines (Indret), 24 Niclausse boilers
IHP 15,980 = 18knots

Endurance: 5,100/10
Armament: 4×305mm/40, 10×164/45, 8×100mm/45, 22×47mm, 4×450mm TT
Armour: Belt 230-300mm, turrets 200-320mm, casemates 130mm, deck 70mm, c/t 250-300mm
Complement: 730
Class notes: Adaptation of previous designs with less tumblehome and more orthodox arrangement of armament. Two funnels and two heavy military masts

'Amiral Aube' Class (1898-1899)

Armoured Cruisers: *Amiral Aube, Condé* (see later photo), *Gloire, Marseillaise, Sully*
Displacement: 10,400tons
Dimensions: 458'8(oa) 452'9(wl)×66'3×25'3 [139.8(oa) 138.9(wl)×20.2×7.7]
Machinery: 3 screws, VTE engines (F C Med; *Amiral Aube* and *Marseillaise:* Loire-St Denis; *Gloire:* Schneider), 24 Belleville boilers, (*Condé* and *Gloire:* 28 Niclausse)
IHP 20,500 = 21.5knots
Endurance: 12,000/10
Armament: 2×194mm/45, 8×164mm/45, 6×100mm/45, 18×47mm 5×450mm TT
Marseillaise, 1925: 194mm replaced by 164mm
Armour: Belt 106-170mm, turrets 173mm, secondary turrets 100mm, deck 45mm, c/t 150mm
Complement: 612
Class notes: Designed by Bertin. Improved 'Gueydon' class with similar armament and rig

'République' Class (1900)

Pre-dreadnoughts: *Patrie* (see later photo), *République*
Displacement: 14,865tons
Dimensions: 452'6(oa) 442'3(wl)×80×27'10 [137'9(oa) 134.8(wl)×24.4×8.5]
Machinery: 3 screws, VTE engines (*Patrie:* F C Med; *République:* Indret), 24 Niclausse boilers
IHP 17,500 = 18knots
Endurance: 8,100/10
Armament: 4×305mm/45, 18×164/45, 13×65mm, 10×47mm, 5×450mm TT
Armour: Belt 80-280mm, turrets 280-355mm, casemates 150mm, deck 60mm, c/t 305mm
Complement: 794
Class notes: This class ended the succession of individual types built in previous years. A good design but obsolete when completed because of long construction time. Two twin turrets fore and aft and six twin turrets for secondary guns with balance in casemates. Three funnels, two forward and one aft

'Gambetta' Class (1900-1901)

Armoured Cruisers: *Jules Ferry, Léon Gambetta, Victor Hugo*
Displacement: 12,550tons
Dimensions: 489'2(oa) 480'8(wl)×73'9×27 [149.1(oa) 146.5(wl)×22.5×8.2]
Machinery: 3 screws, VTE engines (Indret; *Léon Gambetta:* Penhoet), 28 Guyot-du Temple boilers (*Léon Gambetta:* Niclausse; *Victor Hugo:* Belleville)
IHP 27,500 = 22knots; *Léon Gambetta:* IHP 29,000 = 23knots
Endurance: 12,000/10
Armament: 4×194mm/45, 16×164mm/45, 24×47mm, 4×450mm TT
c1916: 2×164mm and 2TT removed, 4×47mm AA added
1918: 12×47mm removed
Armour: Belt 70-150mm, turrets 200mm, barbettes 100-183mm, secondary turrets 130-165mm, c/t 200mm
Complement: 734
Class notes: Larger than previous classes but weak in main armament carried in two turrets fore and aft. Two pairs of two funnels, military foremast and pole mainmast

'Jules Michelet' (1901)

Armoured Cruiser: *Jules Michelet*
Displacement: 12,600tons 13,370f/l
Dimensions: 493(oa) 485(pp)×69'10×27 [150.3(oa) 147.8(pp)×21.3×8.2]
Machinery: 3 screws, VTE engines (Indret), 28 Guyot-du Temple boilers
SHP 29,000 = 22knots
Endurance: 12,000/10
Armament: 4×194mm/45, 12×164mm/45, 24×47mm, 4×450mm TT
Later: 18×47mm and 2 TT removed, 4×47mm AA added
Armour: Belt 70-150mm, turrets 200mm, barbettes 100-183mm, secondary turrets 130-165mm, c/t 200mm
Complement: 724
Class notes: Similar to 'Gambetta' class with fewer secondary guns to save weight

'Justice' Class (1902-1903)

Pre-dreadnoughts: *Démocratie, Justice, Liberté, Verité*
Displacement: 14,900tons, 15,800f/l
Dimensions: 443'9(oa) 429'9(wl)×79'4×27'6 [135.3(oa) 131(wl)×24.2×8.4]
Machinery: 3 screws, VTE engines (F C Med: *Verité:* Indret; *Liberté:* Loire), 22 Belleville boilers (*Justice:* Niclausse)
IHP 17,500 = 18knots
Endurance: 8,400/10
Armament: 4×305mm/45, 10×194mm/50, 13×65mm, 10×47mm, 10×450mm TT
Armour: Belt 80-280mm, turrets 280-355mm, secondary turrets 140mm, deck 60mm, c/t 305mm
Complement: 742
Class notes: Similar to 'République' class with more powerful secondary armament. Good steamers and well armed, but obsolete when completed

'Ernest Renan' (1903)

Armoured Cruiser: *Ernest Renan*
Displacement: 13,644tons
Dimensions: 521'8(oa) 515(pp)×70'1×26'10 [159(oa) 157(pp)×21.4×8.2]
Machinery: 3 screws, VTE engines (Penhoët), 42 Niclausse boilers
IHP 37,000 = 23knots
Endurance: 5,100/10

Top right:
***Jules Ferry* — Armoured cruiser of 'Gambetta' class.** *Marius Bar*

Centre right:
***Liberté* — Pre-dreadnought of 'Justice' class, destroyed by explosion 1911.** *Marius Bar*

Bottom right:
***Ernest Renan* — Armoured cruiser, prior to World War 1.**

Armament: 4×194mm/50, 12×164mm/45, 16×65mm, 8×47mm, 2×450mm TT
Armour: Belt 90-170mm, turrets 170mm, barbettes 100-180mm, secondary turrets 165mm, deck 45-66mm, c/t 200mm
Complement: 750
Class notes: Designed by Bertin. Intended as unit of 'Gambetta' type but modified prior to construction. Longer, with two groups of three funnels, military foremast and pole mainmast. Mainmast removed 1918, but replaced 1927

'Edgar Quinet' Class (1904-1905)

Armoured Cruisers: *Edgar Quinet, Waldeck-Rousseau* (see later photo)
Displacement: 14,000 tons
Dimensions: 521′4(oa) 515′2(pp)×70′6×27′6 [159(oa) 157(pp)×21.5×8.4]
Machinery: 3 screws, VTE engines (Indret), *Edgar Quinet:* 40 Belleville; *Waldeck-Rousseau:* 42 Niclausse boilers
IHP 37,000 = 23knots
Endurance: 5,100/10
Armament: 14×194mm/45, 20×65mm, 2×450mm TT
1918: 2×75mm AA and 2×65mm AA replaced 12×65mm
Armour: Belt 90-170mm, turrets 150mm, casemates 120mm, deck 45-65mm, c/t 200mm
Complement: 843
Class notes: Similar to *Ernest Renan* but main armament now of a single calibre in two twin turrets fore and aft and three single turrets on each beam. *Edgar Quinet* had first and sixth funnels removed 1928 on becoming training ship

'Danton' Class (1906)

Pre-dreadnoughts: *Condorcet (*see later photo), *Danton, Diderot, Mirabeau, Vergniaud, Voltaire*
Displacement: 18,318tons, 19,450f/l
Dimensions: 480′11(oa) 475′5(pp)×84′8×30′2 [146.6(oa) 144.9(pp)×25.8×9.2]
Machinery: 4 screws, Parsons turbines (F C Med; *Condorcet, Diderot* and *Mirabeau:* Penhoët), 26 Belleville boilers (*Condorcet, Diderot* and *Vergniaud:* Niclausse)
SHP 22,500 = 19knots
Endurance: 3,370/10
Armament: 4×305mm/45, 12×240mm/45, 16×75mm/65, 10×47mm, 2×450 TT
1918: 4×75mm replaced by 2×47mm AA

***Edgar Quinet* — Armoured cruiser of 1904, seen as a training ship in 1929 with two funnels removed.**
Marius Bar

Armour: Belt 200-255mm, turrets 320mm, barbettes 280mm, secondary turrets 225mm, deck 75mm, c/t 300mm
Complement: 921
Class notes: First large French warships with turbines designed by L'Homme. Not too successful, obsolescent when laid down. *Condorcet, Vergniaud* and *Voltaire* had mainmast cut down in 1918 and range of main battery increased. *Condorcet* demilitarised 1931 and converted to training ship

'Courbet' Class (1910-1911)

Dreadnoughts: *Courbet, France, Jean Bart, Paris* (see later photo)
Displacement: 23,189tons, 28,850f/l
Dimensions: 551′2(oa) 541(wl) 520(pp)×91′6×29′6 [168(oa) 164.9(wl) 158.5(pp)×27.9×9]
Machinery: 4 screws, Parsons turbines (F C Med; *Courbet:* Penhoët), 24 Belleville boilers (*Courbet:* Niclausse)
SHP 28,000 = 21knots
Endurance: 4,200/10
Armament: 12×305mm/45, 22×138mm/45, 4×450mm TT
1920: 7×76mm AA added
1927: TT removed
Armour: Belt 180-300mm, turrets 320mm, barbettes 270mm, deck 70mm, c/t 300mm
Complement: 1,108
Class notes: First French dreadnoughts, designed by Lyasse. Six turrets including one on each beam amidships. Three funnels with foremast abaft first two funnels and straight stem. *Courbet* and *Jean Bart* reconstructed 1926-29 when two forward funnels were trunked into one, tripod foremast replaced pole and stepped forward of the fore funnel; range of main battery increased. *Paris* retained three funnels although forward pair were close together appearing as one

'Bretagne' Class (1912)

Dreadnoughts: *Bretagne, Lorraine* (see later photo), *Provence*
Displacement: 23,320tons, 28,500f/l
Dimensions: 544′8(oa) 541(pp)×88′6×32′2 [166(oa) 164.9(pp)×27×9.8]
Machinery: 4 screws, Parsons turbines (F C Med; *Lorraine:* Penhoët), 24 boilers (*Bretagne:* Niclausse; *Lorraine:*

Vergniaud **— Pre-dreadnought of 'Danton' class, before 1914.** *Marius Bar*

Belleville; *Provence:* 8 Guyot-du Temple); *All, 1932:* 6 Indret
SHP 29,000 = 20knots; *1932:* SHP 43,000
Endurance: 4,700/10
Armament: 10×340mm/45, 22×138mm/55, 4×47mm, 4×450mm TT
1921: 4×138mm removed, 8×76mm AA added
1932: 4×138mm removed
Lorraine, 1935: 2×340mm removed
Armour: Belt 180-270mm, turrets 250-430mm, barbettes 270mm, deck 50mm, c/t 320mm
Complement: 1,113
Class notes: Similar to 'Courbet' class with heavier armament and single turret amidships replacing previous deck edge turrets. *Bretagne* fitted with tripod foremast in 1918, elevation of main battery increased and fore funnel raised. These modifications made on other units 1919-20. In 1932-35, *Bretagne* and *Provence* were provided with new main battery from guns originally intended for 'Normandie' class, reboilered and converted to oil fuel. *Lorraine* in addition had amidships turret replaced by hangar and catapult

'Normandie' Class (1912-1913)

Dreadnoughts: *[Béarn, Flandre, Gascogne, Languedoc, Normandie]*
Displacement: 25,230tons
Dimensions: 578'9(oa) 576'2(wl) 559'9(pp)×88'6×28'10 [176.6(oa) 175.6(wl) 170.6(pp)×27×8.8]
Machinery: 4 screws, VTE engines and turbines (Turbines: *Normandie* and *Flandre:* Parsons; *Gascogne:* Rateau; *Languedoc:* Zoelly; *Béarn:* Parsons turbines only. Built: *Béarn:* F C Med; *Flandre:* Penhoët; *Gascogne:* Bretagne and Indret; *Languedoc:* Schneider; *Normandie:* Loire) Boilers: *Normandie* and *Gascogne:* 21 Guyot-du Temple; *Languedoc* and *Flandre:* 28 Belleville; *Béarn:* 21 Niclausse
SHP 32,000 = 21knots
Endurance: 1,800/21
Armament: 12×340mm/45, 24×138mm/45, 4×47mm 6×450mm TT
Armour: Belt 120-300mm, turrets 100-340mm, deck 70mm, c/t 300mm
Complement: 1,200
Class notes: Designed by Doyère. Introduction of quadruple turret allowed additional guns to be mounted on proportionately less weight. Three quadruple turrets all on centreline and single pole mast. Machinery returned to earlier type to conserve fuel. *Béarn* was to have turbines so as to form a homogenous squadron with 'Bretagne' class. Construction suspended at the outbreak of World War 1 and they were not completed. *Béarn* was completed as aircraft carrier

'Lyon' Class (1913)

Dreadnoughts: *[Duquesne, Lille, Lyon, Tourville]*
Displacement: 29,500tons
Dimensions: 638'2(oa) 623'4(pp)×95'2×30 [194.5(oa) 190(pp)×29×9.1]
Machinery: 4 screws, VTE engines and geared turbines
SHP 44,000 = 23knots
Armament: 16×340mm/45, 24×138mm/45, 7×40mm, 6×450mm TT
Armour: Never final, similar to 'Normandie' class
Class notes: Designed by Doyère. Enlargement of 'Normandie' class with an additional turret. Design had not been made final and none was ever laid down

'Béarn' (1922)

Aircraft Carrier: *Béarn* (see also later photo)
Displacement: 22,146tons, 25,000f/l; *1944:* 28,400 f/l
Dimensions: 599(oa) 559'9(pp)×101'9×30'6 [182.6(oa)170.6(pp)×31×9.3]
Machinery: 4 screws, Parsons geared turbines and VTE engines (Loire), 12 du Temple-Normand boilers
SHP 22,200+IHP 15,000 = 21.5knots
Endurance: 6,000/10
Aircraft: 40
Armament: 8×155mm/55, 6×75mm AA, 4×550mm TT
1943: 4×127mm/38 AA, 24×40mm AA
Armour: Belt 83mm, deck 70mm, casemates 70mm
Complement: 865; *1943:* 652
Class notes: Converted from incomplete hull of 'Normandie' class battleship. Original turbine propulsion replaced by combined system designed for *Normandie*. Immobilised at Martinique 1940-43. Too slow for combat in World War 2 and relegated to transport duties

'Dunkerque' Class (1931-1934)

Battleships: *Dunkerque* (see later photo), *Strasbourg*
Displacement: 26,500tons, 35,500f/l
Dimensions: 703'9(oa), 686(pp)×102×31'6 [214.5(oa) 209.1(pp)×31.1×9.6]
Machinery: 4 screws, Rateau (*Dunkerque*) Parsons (*Strasbourg*) geared turbines (*Dunkerque:* Loire; *Strasbourg*; Penhoet), 6 Indret boilers
IHP 100,000 = 29.5knots
Endurance: 7,500/15

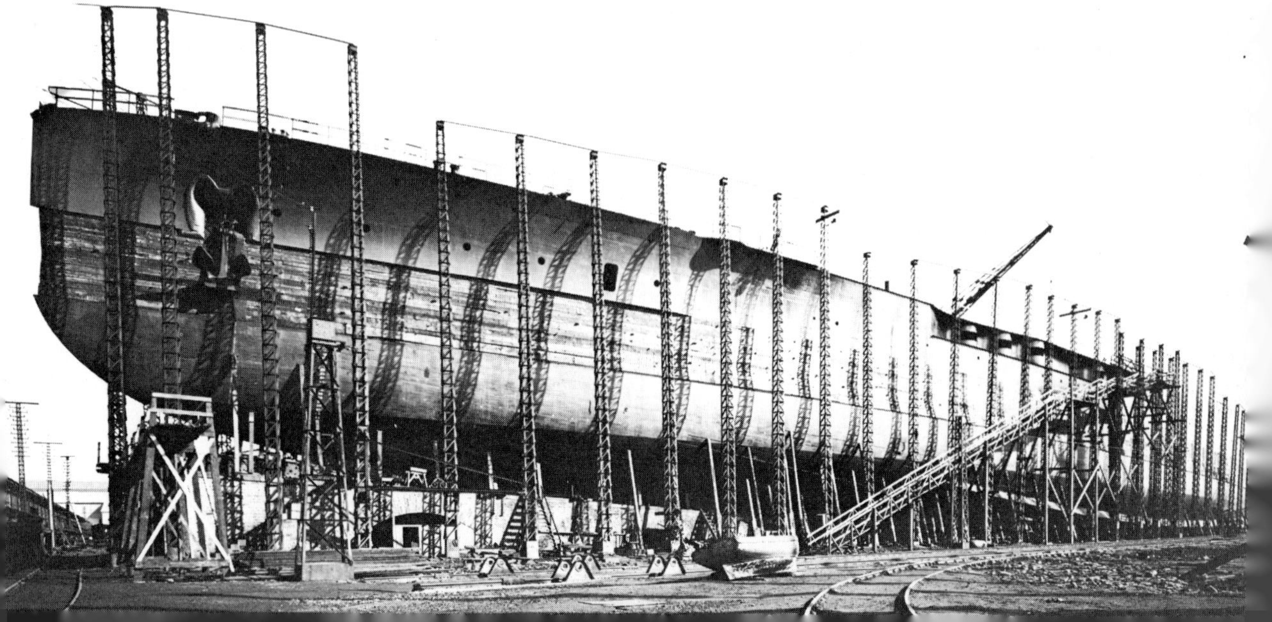

Armament: 8×330mm/52, 16×130mm/45 AA, 4×47mm, 8×37mm AA
1941: 4×90mm replaced 47mm
Armour: Belt 125-225mm, turrets 330-345mm (*Strasbourg:* 355-360mm), secondary turrets 80-90mm, bulkheads 98-228mm, deck 130-140mm, c/t 270mm
Complement: 1,431
Class notes: Fast battleships with the main battery forward in two quadruple turrets, an arrangement inspired by the British 'Nelson' class. A high percentage of displacement was allocated to protection. They differed in details of the bridge

'Richelieu' Class (1935-1938)

Battleships: *[Clemenceau], Jean Bart, Richelieu* (see also later photo)
Displacement: 38,500tons, 47,500f/l
Dimensions: 813(oa) 794'4(pp)×108'7×35 [247.8(oa) 242.1(pp)×33.1×10.7]
Machinery: 4 screws, Parsons geared turbines (*Richelieu:* Loire; *Jean Bart:* Penhoet), 6 Indret-Sural boilers
SHP 155,000 = 30knots
Endurance: 8,500/14
Armament: 8×380mm/45, 9×152mm/55 (*Clemenceau:* 12), 12×100mm/45, 16×37mm AA (*Clemenceau:* 8)
Richelieu, 1943: 37mm removed, 57×40mm AA added
Armour: Belt 327mm, bulkheads 251-383mm, turrets 170-430mm, barbettes 405mm, secondary turrets 130mm, deck 150-170mm, c/t 340mm
Complement: 1,550

***Jean Bart* as completed:**
Displacement: 42,806tons, 49,850f/l
Dimensions: Beam 116'3 [35.5]
Armament: 8×380mm, 9×152mm, 24×100mm, 28×57mm
Class notes: Expansion of 'Dunkerque' class with heavier guns and greater protection. Main armament in two quadruple turrets forward. Funnel trunked into mainmast structure. Six 152mm guns not fitted to provide more AA armament. In 1940 *Richelieu* proceeded to Dakar almost complete and was refitted 1943 when the catapults were removed and AA armament increased. *Jean Bart* escaped to Casablanca still incomplete with only half the machinery operating. As completed in 1949 the ship had new armament, modern radar and beam increased to reduce draft. *Clemenceau* was launched by the Germans but never progressed further

'Joffre' Class (1937-1938)

Aircraft Carriers: *[Joffre, Painlevé]*
Displacement: 18,000tons
Dimensions: 774'4(oa) 748(pp)×80'9×21'9; 113'5 (extreme beam) [236(oa) 228(pp)×24.6×6.6; 34.5 (extreme beam)]
Machinery: 2 screws, Parsons geared turbines, 8 Indret boilers
SHP 120,000 = 33knots

Top left:
***France* — Dreadnought of 1910, after the war. Note directors for fire control.** *Marius Bar*

Centre left:
***Provence* — Battleship, after postwar modification, with tripod foremast. Sunk at Mers-el-Kebir 1940.** *Marius Bar*

Bottom left:
***Normandie* — 'Normandie' class dreadnought on stocks prior to launching 1914, never completed.**

Endurance: 7,800/20
Aircraft: 40
Armament: 8×130mm AA, 8×37mm AA
Armour: Belt 105mm, deck 40-70mm
Complement: 1,251
Class notes: Flightdeck was incorporated into the hull and was angled to bypass the island. Neither was launched or completed

'Gascogne' Class (1938)

Battleships: *[Gascogne]*, 2 unnamed
Displacement: 40,000tons
Dimensions: 813(oa) 794'4(pp)×108'8×35 [247.8(oa) 242.1(pp)×33.1×10.7]
Machinery: 4 screws, Parsons geared turbines
Armament: 8×380mm/45, 9×152mm/55; 16×100mm/45, 20×37mm
Complement: 1,670
Class notes: Two additional units approved April 1940 but not ordered. Similar to 'Richelieu' class but arrangement of armament differed with main turrets carried fore and aft and secondary turrets all on centreline

'Arromanches' (1946)

Light Aircraft Carrier: *Arromanches*
Displacement: 13,190tons, 18,040f/l
Dimensions: 695(oa) 630(pp)×80'3×21'4; 112'6 (extreme beam) [211.8(oa) 192(pp)×24.5×6.5; 34.3 (extreme beam)]; *1958:* 725'9 (oa) [22.2 (oa)]
Machinery: 2 screws, Parsons geared turbines (Parsons), 4 Admiralty boilers
SHP 42,000 = 25knots
Endurance: 12,000/14
Aircraft: 43
Armament: 43×40mm AA
1957: 24×2pdr, 19×40mm AA (all removed 1960)
Complement: 1,620
Class notes: Former British *Colossus* transferred 1946. Reconstructed 1957-58 with angled flightdeck

'La Fayette' Class (1951)

Light Aircraft Carriers: *Bois Belleau, La Fayette* (see later photo)
Displacement: 11,000tons, 15,800f/l
Dimensions: 622'6(oa) 600(wl)×71'6×26; 109 (extreme beam) [189.7(oa) 182.9 (wl)×21.8×7.9; 33.2 (extreme beam)]
Machinery: 4 screws, GE geared turbines, 4 B&W boilers
SHP 100,000 = 31.6knots
Endurance: 11,000/15
Aircraft: 26
Armament: 26×40mm AA
Armour: Belt 50-127mm
Complement: 1,569
Class notes: Former US carriers *Belleau Wood* and *Langley*, transferred 1953 and 1951 respectively

'Clemenceau' Class (1954)

Aircraft Carriers: *Clemenceau, Foch* (see later photo)
Displacement: 22,000tons, 31,000f/l
Dimensions: 869'4(oa) 833'6(pp) 781(wl)×104×24'8 [265(oa) 254(pp) 238(wl)×31.7×7.5]
Machinery: 2 screws, Parsons geared turbines (Atlantique), 6 boilers
SHP 126,000 = 32knots

Endurance: 7,500/18
Aircraft: 60
Armament: 8×100mm/60 AA
Complement: 2,700
Class notes: Armament revised while under construction. Angled flightdeck, two steam catapults. *Foch* completed with bulges, added later to *Clemenceau*

Individual Ships

Alma

Type: Armoured Corvette
Class: 'Belliqueuse' (1863)
Nomenclature: Allied victory during the Crimean War, 20 September 1854

History:
1865 October 1: Laid down by Lorient
1867 November 25: Launched
1870 March 31: Completed
1870 Far East
1881 Operations off Sfax
1886 March 12: Discarded, harbour service
1893 May: Broken up

Amiral Aube

Type: Armoured Cruiser
Class: 'Amiral Aube' (1898)
Nomenclature: Hyacinthe Laurent Théophile Aube (1826-1890), admiral and navy minister; leader of the *jeune école* which advocated basing the fleet on cruisers and torpedo boats rather than battleships

History:
1899 August 9: Laid down by Loire
1902 May 9: Launched
1904 April 17: Completed
World War 1: 1914 English Channel, 1915-16 Eastern Mediterranean, 1918 North Russia
1916 Reserve
1922 April 4: Discarded
1922 September 15: Sold and broken up

Amiral Baudin

Type: Barbette Ship
Class: 'Baudin' (1878)
Nomenclature: Charles Baudin (1784-1854), admiral, commanded a French expedition to Mexico in 1838

History:
1879 February 1: Laid down by Brest as ***Infernal***

Top left:
***Béarn* — Aircraft carrier on trials after 1935 refit.**

Centre:
***Strasbourg* — Battleship, leaving Toulon 23 May 1942, the only French battleship in commission at the time.**
Marius Bar

Bottom:
***Richelieu* — Battleship c1946.** *Marius Bar*

Top right:
***Clémenceau* — Aircraft carrier 1962.** *Marius Bar*

—— Renamed ***Amiral Baudin***
1883 June 5: Launched
1889 January 21: Completed
1895 November 12: Went aground in Hyères Islands during manoeuvres, refloated 19 November
1897-98 Reconstructed, reboilered and rearmed
1900 November 23: In collision with cruiser *D'Estaing* off Brest
1902 In reserve
1909 Discarded, accommodation ship, Toulon
1911 August: Sold and broken up

Amiral Charner

Type: Armoured Cruiser
Class: 'Amiral Charner' (1889)
Nomenclature: Leonard Victor Charner (1797-1869), French naval commander during the Crimean War and in China

History:
1889 September: Laid down by Rochefort as ***Charner***
1893 March 18: Launched
1895 August 19: Completed; renamed ***Amiral Charner***
1900 November: Went aground off Chinkiang, China
World War 1: 1914 Troop convoys, 1915 Levant
1915 September: Rescue of Armenian refugees from Antioch
1915 December 28: Seizure of Castelorizo Island
1916 February 8: Torpedoed and sunk by German submarine *U21* west of Beirut (374 dead, one survivor)

Amiral Duperré

Type: Barbette Ship
Class: 'Amiral Duperré (1876)
Nomenclature: Baron Victor Guy Duperré (1775-1846), admiral and navy minister

History:
1877 January 1: Laid down by La Seyne
1879 September 11: Launched
1884 January 1: Completed
1888 December 12: Damaged by 340mm gun explosion off Toulon
1906 Discarded
1908 Used as a target and broken up

Amiral Tréhouart

Type: Coast Defence Ship
Class: 'Bouvines' (1889)
Nomenclature: François Thomas Tréhouart (1798-1873), admiral, commanded French fleet during the intervention in Argentina, 1845

History:
1889 October 20: Laid down at Lorient as ***Tréhouart***
1893 May 16: Launched
1895 March 25: Renamed ***Amiral Tréhouart***
1896 June 29: Completed
1914 Submarine depot ship
1920 July 4: Sold and broken up 1922

Armide

Type: Armoured Corvette
Class: 'Belliqueuse' (1863)
Nomenclature: Armida, a character in Tasso's 'Jerusalem Delivered'

History:
1865 October 6: Laid down at Rochefort
1867 April 12: Launched
1870 July 20: Completed
1870 North Sea and Baltic, blockade of Prussia
1873 Blockade of Cartagena, Spain
1882 October 25: Discarded
1887 Broken up

Arromanches

Type: Light Aircraft Carrier
Class: 'Arromanches' (1946)
Nomenclature: Site of American and British landings in Normandy, 6 June 1944

History:
1942 June 1: Laid down as British ***Colossus*** by Vickers, Tyne
1943 September 30: Launched
1944 December 14: Completed
1946 August 6: Transferred to France, renamed ***Arromanches***
1948-49 Indochina
1950-51 Refit
1951-54 Indochina
1956 Suez
1957-58 Refit
1978 Broken up

Atalante

Type: Armoured Corvette
Class: 'Belliqueuse' (1863)
Nomenclature: Greek myth: Atalanta, a virgin huntress

History:
1865 October 1: Laid down at Cherbourg
1868 April 9: Launched
1869 June 14: Completed
1870 North Sea
1884 Far East
1887 Hulk at Saigon
1890 Discarded, sank at moorings at Saigon

Bayard

Type: Second Class Battleship
Class: 'Turenne' (1875)
Nomenclature: Pierre du Terrail, Seigneur de Bayard (1473-1574), military hero, called 'Chevalier sans peur et sans reproche'

History:
1876 September 19: Laid down at Brest (projected name was *Condé*)
1880 March 27: Launched
1883 Completed
1883-85 Pacific and Far East
1885 Reclassified armoured cruiser
1894-98 Far East
1899 April 26: Discarded, hulk at Saigon
1904 Broken up at Saigon

Béarn

Type: 1) Dreadnought, 2) Aircraft Carrier
Class: 1) 'Normandie' (1913), 2) 'Béarn' (1922)
Nomenclature: A province of southwest France

Above:
***Amiral Tréhouart* — Coast defence ship of 1889, c1900, the only vessel of its class with a single funnel.**
Photomatic

Below:
***Bayard* — Armoured cruiser, 1898 at the end of its career. Notice two funnels.** *IWM*

History:
1914 January 10: Laid down at La Seyne as ***Vendée***
1914 Renamed ***Béarn***
1914 August: Construction suspended when 25% complete
1920 April 15: Launched to clear slip
1923 August 4: Conversion to aircraft carrier started at La Seyne
1926 September 1: Completed
1927 May: Commissioned
1935 Refit; flightdeck widened and straightened forward
1939-40 Inactive
1940 June 27: Demilitarised at Martinique
1943 May 19: Went aground at Martinique
1943 September 8: Refloated, towed to Puerto Rico
1943-44 Refit at New Orleans; rearmed, flightdeck shortened, reclassified as aircraft transport
1945 March: In collision with US transport *J. W. McAndrew* in North Atlantic
1945-46 Far East
1946 Training ship
1952 Reserve
1967 March 30: Condemned as *Q419;* sold and broken up at La Spezia

Bélier

Type: Coast Defence Turret Ram
Class: 'Bélier' (1865)
Nomenclature: Ram

History:
1865 August 1: Laid down at Cherbourg
1870 August 29: Launched
1874 January 28: Completed
1896 July 8: Discarded and broken up

Belliqueuse

Type: Armoured Corvette
Class: 'Belliqueuse' (1863)
Nomenclature: Bellicose

History:
1863 September 14: Laid down at Toulon
1865 September 6: Launched
1965 December: Completed
1866-69 Round-the-world cruise
1870 Levant
1886 May 3: Discarded
1888 Sunk as a target

Bois Belleau

Type: Light Aircraft Carrier
Class: 'La Fayette' (1951)
Nomenclature: Former name retained

History:
1941 August 11: Laid down by New York Sbdg

Top left:
***Béarn* — Aircraft carrier, camouflaged, c1945.**
Marius Bar

Centre left:
***Belliqueuse* — Armoured corvette of 1863. A single unit similar to later 'Alma' class.** *Marius Bar*

Bottom left:
***Bouvet* — Battleship of 1891.**

1942 December 6: Launched
1943 March 31: Completed as US ***Belleau Wood***
1953 September 5: Transferred to France, renamed ***Bois Belleau***
1960 September 12: Returned to US and broken up

Bouledogue

Type: Coast Defence Turret Ram
Class: 'Bélier' (1865)
Nomenclature: Bulldog

History:
1865 February 3: Laid down at Lorient
1872 March 26: Launched
1873 October 1: Completed
1895 July 31: Sank torpedo boat *No 69* in collision at Lorient
1896 Discarded and broken up

Bouvet

Type: Pre-dreadnought
Class: 'Bouvet' (1891)
Nomenclature: Pierre François Henri Bouvet (1775-1860), admiral, commanded French naval forces during the Napoleonic Wars

History:
1893 January 16: Laid down at Lorient
1896 April 27: Launched
1898 October 8: Completed
1903 January 29: In collision with battleship *Gaulois* in Mediterranean
1913 Refit
World War 1: 1914 Mediterranean convoys; 1915 Dardanelles
1915 March 18: Blew up and sank after being damaged by a mine in the Dardanelles (643 dead)

Bouvines

Type: Coast Defence Ship
Class: 'Bouvines' (1889)
Nomenclature: Battle in Flanders in 1214 in which King Philip II of France defeated the English and Imperial armies

History:
1890 September 30: Laid down at La Seyne
1892 March 29: Launched
1895 July 23: 47mm gun explosion
1895 December 1: Completed
1910 September 13: In collision with destroyer *Escopette* in English Channel
1914 Depot ship, Cherbourg
1918 June 8: Discarded
1920 June 19: Sold and broken up

Brennus

Type: Barbette Ship
Class: 'Brennus' (1888)
Nomenclature: Brennus (4th century BC), Gallic leader against the Romans

History:
1882 Laid down but construction suspended; design changed and reordered 1889
1889 January 2: Laid down at Lorient

1891 October 17: Launched
1893 December 16: Had trouble on trials, modified
1895 December 25: Completed
1900 August 11: Sank destroyer *Framée* in collision off Cape St Vincent
1914 Disarmed, accommodation ship
1919 October 30: Discarded
1922 Sold and broken up

Bretagne

Type: Dreadnought
Class: 'Bretagne' (1912)
Nomenclature: Brittany, a province of northwest France

History:
1912 July 22: Laid down at Brest
1913 April 21: Launched
1915 November 29: Completed
World War 1: 1916-18 Corfu
1919-20 Refit; tripod foremast and fire directors installed, fore funnel raised
1924-25 Refit
1932-34 Refit; new 340mm guns fitted, reboilered, converted to oil fuel
1937 Naval patrol, Spain
World War 2: 1939-40 Atlantic convoys
1940 July 3: Damaged by British gunfire at Mers-el-Kebir and blew up and capsized (1,012 dead)

Bruix

Type: Armoured Cruiser
Class: 'Amiral Charner' (1889)
Nomenclature: Etienne Eustache Bruix (1759-1805), admiral and navy minister, commander at sea against the British

History:
1891 November 9: Laid down at Rochefort
1894 August 2: Launched
1896 December 1: Completed
1898 September: Damaged in collision with pier at Dunkirk
World War 1: 1914 Troop convoys, 1915 Red Sea, 1916-18 Aegean
1920 July 9: Sold and broken up

Caïman

Type: Coast Defence Barbette Ship
Class: 'Terrible' (1876)
Nomenclature: Cayman, a type of crocodile

History:
1878 August 16: Laid down at Toulon
1885 May 21: Launched
1888 August 21: Completed
1901 Reconstructed
1910 Discarded; hulk at Rochefort
1927 Broken up

Carnot

Type: Pre-dreadnought
Class: 'Carnot' (1890)
Nomenclature: Lazare Nicolas Marguerite Carnot (1753-1823), statesman and general of the French Revolution; *also* Marie François Sadi Carnot (1837-1894), President of France, assassinated 24 June 1894

History:
1891 August 8: Laid down at Toulon as ***Lazare Carnot***
1894 July 7: Renamed ***Carnot***
1894 July 12: Launched
1897 June 25: Completed
1919 Discarded
1922 Broken up

Cerbère

Type: Coast Defence Turret Ram
Class: 'Bélier' (1865)
Nomenclature: Greek myth: Cerberus, a three-headed dog guarding the entrance to Hades

History:
1865 September 14: Laid down at Brest
1868 April 23: Launched
1868 September 20: Completed
1886 Discarded and broken up

Chanzy

Type: Armoured Cruiser
Class: 'Amiral Charner' (1889)
Nomenclature: Antoine Eugène Alfred Chanzy (1823-1883), general, commander during the Franco-Prussian War, Governor of Algeria

History:
1889 December 18: Laid down by Gironde
1894 January 24: Launched
1895 May 1: Completed
1900 February 20: Damaged by boiler explosion while leaving Toulon harbour
1907 May 20: Wrecked off China in the Chusan Archipelago
1907 June 12: Wreck destroyed

Charlemagne

Type: Pre-dreadnought
Class: 'Charlemagne' (1893)
Nomenclature: Charles the Great (742-814), King of the Franks and Emperor of the West 800-814

History:
1894 August 2: Laid down at Brest
1895 October 17: Launched
1899 September 12: Completed
1903 March 2: In collision with battleship *Gaulois*, not damaged
World War 1: 1914 Mediterranean convoys, 1915 Dardanelles, 1916-18 Salonika
1915 March 18: Damaged by shore batteries at the Dardanelles
1915 Refit
1920 June 21: Discarded
1923 Sold and broken up

Top right:
***Charles Martel* — Pre-dreadnought of 1890, first of new design.** *Marius Bar*

Centre right:
***Condé* — Armoured cruiser of 1898.**

Bottom right:
***Condorcet* — Pre-dreadnought of 'Danton' class, after 1919 with mainmast removed.** *Marius Bar*

Charles Martel

Type: Pre-dreadnought
Class: 'Charles Martel' (1890)
Nomenclature: Charles Martel ('the Hammer') (689-741), Frankish ruler who halted the Moorish invasion of Europe at Tours in 732

History:
1891 August 1: Laid down at Brest
1893 August 29: Launched
1897 March 8: Completed
1915 August: Discarded
1922 December 23: Sold and broken up

Clemenceau

Type: Battleship
Class: 'Richelieu' (1935)
Nomenclature: Georges Clemenceau (1841-1929), statesman, Premier of France during World War 1

History:
1939 January 17: Laid down at Brest
1940 June: 10% completed when Germans occupied Brest, incompleted hull designated R
1942 Hull section 130m long floated out
1944 August 27: Hull sunk by British aircraft at Brest

Clemenceau

Type: Aircraft Carrier
Class: 'Clemenceau' (1954)

History:
1955 November: Laid down at Brest
1957 December 21: Launched
1961 November 22: Completed
1977-78 Refit

Colbert

Type: Central Battery Ship
Class: 'Colbert' (1869)
Nomenclature: Jean Baptiste Colbert, Marquis de Seigneley (1619-1683), statesman who started construction of a large French navy

History:
1870 July 4: Laid down at Brest
1875 September 15: Launched
1877 June 6: Completed
1881 Operations at Sfax
1900 August 11: Discarded
1909 Sold and broken up

Condé, see *Bayard*

Condé

Type: Armoured Cruiser
Class: 'Amiral Aube' (1898)
Nomenclature: Louis II de Bourbon, Prince de Condé (1621-1686), noted general, called The Great Condé

History:
1901 March 20: Laid down at Lorient
1902 March 12: Launched
1904 August 12: Completed
World War 1: 1914 West Indies, 1918 Atlantic convoys
1919 North Russia
1933 Accommodation ship, Lorient
1940 Captured by Germans, used as submarine depot ship
1944 Sunk by aircraft bombs at Bordeaux

Condorcet

Type: Pre-dreadnought
Class: 'Danton' (1906)
Nomenclature: Marie Jean Antoine Nicolas de Caritat, Marquis de Condorcet (1743-1794), a leader of the French Revolution

History:
1907 August 23: Laid down by Loire
1909 April 20: Launched
1911 July 25: Completed
World War 1: 1914 Mediterranean convoys, 1915 Adriatic, 1918 Aegean
1923-24 Refit
1931 Converted to training ship
1942 November 27: Damaged by explosions at Toulon but not sunk; used by Germans as accommodation ship
1944 August: Severely damaged in Allied bombing raid
1945 December 14: Salved
1947 Discarded
1959 Broken up

Courbet

Type: Central Battery and Barbette Ship
Class: 'Devastation' (1874)
Nomenclature: Amedée Anatole Prosper Courbet (1827-1885), admiral prominent in the French occupation of Indochina who died during the war with China

History:
1875 July 19: Laid down at Toulon as ***Foudroyant***
1882 April 27: Launched
1885 June 25: Renamed ***Courbet***
1885 October 20: Completed
1895 November 12: Went aground in Hyeres islands during manoeuvres
1898 August: Holed by anchor at Cadiz
1898 Reconstructed
1909 February 5: Discarded
1910 August 25: Sold and broken up

Courbet

Type: Dreadnought
Class: 'Courbet' (1910)

History:
1910 September 1: Laid down at Lorient
1911 September 23: Launched
1913 October 8: Completed
World War 1: 1914 Mediterranean Fleet (flagship)
1914 August 16: Action off Albania, sank Austrian cruiser *Zenta*
1915 In reserve
1923 June 6: Damaged by boiler room fire
1923-24 Refit
1924 August 1: Damaged by boiler room fire
1927-31 Reconstructed
1931 Training ship
1937-38 Refit

World War 2: 1939 Channel, 1940 British (later Free French)
1940 June: Fire support at Cherbourg
1940 July 3: Seized by British at Portsmouth
1940 July 11: Returned to Free French
1940 Anti-aircraft and radar training ship
1941 April: Decommissioned
1944 June 9: Sunk as blockship at Normandy

Couronne

Type: Broadside Ship
Class: 'Couronne' (1858)
Nomenclature: Crown

History:
1859 February 14: Laid down at Lorient
1861 March 28: Launched
1862 February 2: Completed
1870 North Sea
1881 Gunnery training ship, converted at Toulon
1895 Refit, reboilered
1906 April: Gun explosion on board
1910 Discarded; hulk at Toulon
1934 Broken up

Danton

Type: Pre-dreadnought
Class: 'Danton' (1906)
Nomenclature: Georges Jacques Danton (1759-1794), a leader of the French Revolution

History:
1908 February 3: Laid down at Brest
1909 July 4: Launched
1911 June 1: Completed
World War 1: 1914 Mediterranean convoys, 1915 Adriatic, 1916 Aegean
1917 March 19: Twice torpedoed by German submarine *U64* and sank southwest of Sardinia (296 dead)

Démocratie

Type: Pre-dreadnought
Class: 'Justice' (1902)
Nomenclature: Democracy

History:
1903 May 1: Laid down at Brest
1904 April 2: Launched
1907 July: Completed
1913 December 20: In collision with battleship *Justice* off Hyeres
1914 August 17: In collision with battleship *Justice* off Corfu
World War 1: 1916-17 Aegean
1921 Discarded

Desaix

Type: Armoured Cruiser
Class: 'Kléber' (1897)
Nomenclature: Louis Charles Antoine Desaix (1768-1800), general under Napoleon, killed at Marengo

History:
1899 January 18: Laid down by Loire
1901 March 21: Launched
1904 April 5: Completed
World War 1: 1914 English Channel, 1915 Suez Canal, Levant, 1916 South Atlantic, 1918 West Indies, 1919 Far East
1915 September: Rescue of Armenian refugees from Antioch
1917 Refit
1921 June 30: Discarded
1927 Sold and broken up

Dévastation

Type: Central Battery and Barbette Ship
Class: 'Dévastation' (1874)
Nomenclature: Devastation

History:
1875 December 20: Laid down at Lorient
1879 August 19: Launched
1881 March 25: Completed
1898 Reconstructed
1909 Discarded
1922 May 8: Went aground en route to breaking up
1927 September 16: Refloated and broken up

Diderot

Type: Pre-dreadnought
Class: 'Danton' (1906)
Nomenclature: Denis Diderot (1713-1784), encyclopaedist

History:
1907 October 20: Laid down by Penhoet
1909 April 19: Launched
1911 August 1: Completed
World War 1: 1914 Mediterranean convoys, 1915 Adriatic, 1918 Aegean
1925 Refit
1936 Discarded and broken up

Duguesclin

Type: Second Class Battleship
Class: 'Vauban' (1875)
Nomenclature: Bertrand du Guesclin, Count de Longueville, (1320-1380), constable of France, great military commander

History:
1877 March 1: Laid down at Rochefort
1883 April 7: Launched
1884 Completed
1885 Reclassified armoured cruiser
1904 Discarded and broken up

Dunkerque

Type: Battleship
Class: 'Dunkerque' (1931)
Nomenclature: Dunkirk, city and port in northern France

History:
1932 December 26: Laid down at Brest
1935 October 2: Launched
1937 May 1: Completed
World War 2: 1930-40 Atlantic convoys, Mediterranean
1940 July 3: Severely damaged by British warships at Mers-el-Kebir; again damaged by torpedo attack three days later (210 dead)
1942 February 20: Sailed to Toulon after being refloated
1942 November 27: Blown up in drydock at Toulon
1945 August: Undocked, not repaired, hulk as *Q56*
1958 Hulk broken up

***Dunkerque* — Battleship as completed c1938.** *R. Perkins*

Dupetit-Thouars

Type: Armoured Cruiser
Class: 'Gueydon' (1897)
Nomenclature: Aristide Aubert Dupetit-Thouars (1760-1798), captain of the *Tonnant,* killed in action at the Battle of the Nile

History:
1899 April 17: Laid down at Toulon
1901 July 5: Launched
1905 August 28: Completed
World War 1: 1914-15 English Channel, 1918 North Atlantic convoys
1918 August 7: Torpedoed twice by German submarine *U62* and sank 400 miles west of Brest while escorting convoy (13 dead)

Dupleix

Type: Armoured Cruiser
Class: 'Kleber' (1897)
Nomenclature: Joseph François, Marquis Dupleix (1697-1763), Governor-General of French India

History:
1899 January 18: Laid down at Rochefort
1900 April 28: Launched
1903 September 15: Completed
World War 1: 1914, Far East, 1915 Levant, 1917 Suez Canal
1919 Discarded
1922 Broken up

Dupuy de Lôme

Type: Armoured Cruiser
Class: 'Dupuy de Lôme' (1888)
Nomenclature: Stanislas Charles Henri Laurent Dupuy de Lôme (1816-1885), naval engineer, designer of the first screw warship, *Napoleon,* and the first French armoured battleship, *Gloire*

History:
1888 July 1: Laid down at Brest
1890 October 27: Launched
1893 Modified prior to final completion after trials
1895 May 8: Completed
1901 January: Damaged in gale in English Channel
1905 Reconstructed; reboilered, military mainmast removed, two funnels
1911 August 29: Sold to Peru, renamed ***Commandante Elias Aguirre***
1912 September 12: Commissioned in Peruvian Navy, remained at Lorient
1919 Sold and converted to merchant ship under Belgian flag and renamed *Peruvier;* damaged by fire on maiden voyage and laid up
1923 Broken up at Flushing

Duquesne

Type: Dreadnought
Class: 'Lyon' (1913)
Nomenclature: Abraham, Marquis Duquesne (1610-1688), distinguished French admiral

History:
1914 Ordered from Brest; never laid down
1915 Contract cancelled

Edgar Quinet

Type: Armoured Cruiser
Class: 'Edgar Quinet' (1904)
Nomenclature: Edgar Quinet (1803-1875), writer and historian

History:
1905 November 6: Laid down at Brest
1907 Sepember 21: Launched
1910 Completed
World War 1: Adriatic and Eastern Mediterranean
1925-27 Converted to training ship; two funnels removed, 4×194mm guns removed

Dupuy de Lôme — **Armoured cruiser, after reconstruction of 1905.** *Foto Druppel*

1930 January 4: Went aground off Cap Blanc, Algeria, west of Oran and sank five days later

Ernest Renan

Type: Armoured Cruiser
Class: 'Ernest Renan' (1903)
Nomenclature: Joseph Ernest Renan (1823-1892), historian and philologist

History:
1903 October 1: Laid down by Penhoët
1906 March 9: Launched
1908 Completed
World War 1: Adriatic and Mediterranean
1918 Kite balloon ship; mainmast removed, AA guns added
1927-28 Gunnery school ship
1936 Discarded, sunk as target 1939

Flandre

Type: Broadside Ship
Class: 'Flandre' (1860)
Nomenclature: Flanders, a former province of France

History:
1861 January 28: Laid down at Cherbourg
1864 June 21: Launched
1865 February 20: Completed
1870 North Sea and Baltic, blockade of Prussia
1883 Discarded
1887 Sold

Flandre

Type: Dreadnought
Class: 'Normandie' (1912)

History:
1913 October 9: Laid down at Brest
1914 October 20: Launched
1915 Construction suspended when 65% complete
1924 Broken up incomplete at Toulon

Foch

Type: Aircraft Carrier
Class: 'Clemenceau' (1954)
Nomenclature: Ferdinand Foch (1851-1929), Marshal of France, Supreme Allied Commander during World War 1

History:
1957 February 17: Laid down by Penhoët
1959 July 18: Launched and towed to Brest for docking
1960 July 28: Launched at Brest
1963 July 15: Completed
1965-66 Refit
1980-81 Refit

Formidable

Type: Barbette Ship
Class: 'Baudin' (1878)
Nomenclature: Formidable

History:
1879 January 10: Laid down at Lorient
1885 April 16: Launched
1888 December 29: Completed
1895 November 12: Went aground in Hyeres islands during manoeuvres
1896-97 Reconstructed
1903 In reserve
1909 February 9: Discarded, base ship, Landevennec
1911 July: Sold and broken up

Foudroyant, see *Courbet*

France

Type: Dreadnought
Class: 'Courbet' (1910)

R99

History:
1911 November 30: Laid down by Loire
1912 November 7: Launched
1914 July 1: Completed
World War 1: 1914-18 Adriatic, Malta, Corfu
1919 Black Sea
1919 April 19: Crew mutinied and ship returned to Toulon
1922 August 24: Struck submerged rock and foundered in Quiberon Bay (one dead)

Friedland

Type: Central Battery Ship
Class: 'Friedland' (1865)
Nomenclature: Victory of Napoleon over the Russians, 14 June 1807

History:
1865 December 1: Laid down at Lorient; design modified prior to launching
1873 October 25: Launched
1877 June 20: Completed
1881 Operations at Sfax
1904 Discarded and broken up

Fulminant

Type: Coast Defence Turret Ship
Class: 'Tonnerre' (1872)
Nomenclature: Fulminant, explode violently

History:
1874 February 26: Laid down at Cherbourg
1877 August 20: Launched
1880 August 12: Completed
1885 Commissioned, delay caused by poor showing on trials
1893 Reboilered
1908 Discarded
1912 Broken up

Furieux

Type: Coast Defence Barbette Ship
Class: 'Furieux' (1874)
Nomenclature: Furious

History:
1875 January 1: Laid down at Cherbourg
1883 July 20: Launched
1887 March 1: Completed
1896-97 Reconstructed; re-engined and reboilered, rearmed
1910 Submarine tender
1913 Discarded
1922 Sold and broken up

Gascogne

Type: Dreadnought
Class: 'Normandie' (1912)
Nomenclature: Gascony, a province of southwest France

History:
1913 October 1: Laid down at Lorient
1914 September 20: Launched
1915 Construction suspended when 60% complete
1923 Broken up incomplete at Lorient

Top left:
***Foch* — Aircraft carrier.**

Centre left:
***Gaulois* — Battleship of 'Charlemagne' class.** *Marius Bar*

Bottom left:
***Iéna* — Battleship of 1897, destroyed by explosion 1907.**

Gascogne

Type: Battleship
Class: 'Gascogne' (1938)

History:
1938 Ordered from Loire, never laid down
1940 Designated *S* by Germans following occupation of St Nazaire

Gaulois

Type: Pre-dreadnought
Class: 'Charlemagne' (1893)
Nomenclature: An inhabitant of Gaul

History:
1896 January 8: Laid down at Brest
1896 October 6: Launched
1899 October 18: Completed
1900 February 22: In collision with destroyer *Hallebarde* off Toulon
1903 January 29: In collision with battleship *Bouvet* in Mediterranean
World War 1: 1914 Mediterranean convoys, 1915 Dardanelles
1915 March 18: Severely damaged by shell hit below waterline in Dardanelles and beached near Drapano
1915 October 27: Torpedoed and sunk by German submarine *UB47* off Cerigo Island (four dead)

Gauloise

Type: Broadside Ship
Class: 'Flandre' (1860)
Nomenclature: An inhabitant of Gaul

History:
1861 January 21: Laid down at Brest
1865 April 26: Launched
1867 April 12: Completed
1870 North Sea and Baltic, blockade of Prussia
1883 Discarded
1886 Broken up

Gloire

Type: Broadside Ship
Class: 'Gloire' (1858)
Nomenclature: Glory

History:
1858 May 1: Laid down at Toulon
1859 November 24: Launched
1860 July: Completed
1869 Refit, rearmed
1879 Discarded
1883 Broken up

Gloire

Type: Armoured Cruiser
Class: 'Amiral Aube' (1898)

History:
1900 January 10: Laid down at Lorient
1900 June 27: Launched
1904 April 28: Completed
World War 1: 1914-15 English Channel, 1916-18 South Atlantic, 1918 Atlantic convoys
1918 May: Damaged in collision with US liner *City of Athens*
1928 Discarded

Gueydon

Type: Armoured Cruiser
Class: 'Gueydon' (1897)
Nomenclature: Louis Henri, Comte de Gueydon (1809-1886), admiral, naval commander during the Franco-Prussian War

History:
1898 August 2: Laid down at Lorient
1899 September 20: Launched
1903 September 1: Completed
1903-06 Far East
World War 1: 1914 English Channel, 1915 Western Atlantic, 1916 South Atlantic, 1917 West Indies, 1918 North Russia, 1919 Baltic
1923 Refit
1928 Gunnery training ship, only 9×138mm and 4×75mm guns
1935 July 24: Accommodation ship, Brest
1944 August 27: Sunk by aircraft bombs at Brest to prevent use by Germans as a blockship

Guyenne

Type: Broadside Ship
Class: 'Flandre' (1860)
Nomenclature: Guienne or Aquitaine, a province of southwest France

History:
1862 March: Laid down at Rochefort
1865 September 6: Launched
1867 April 15: Completed
1870 North Sea and Baltic, blockade of Prussia
1882 Discarded
1887 Broken up

Henri IV

Type: Second Class Battleship
Class: Henri IV (1896)
Nomenclature: Henry, King of Navarre (1553-1610), later King Henry IV of France

History:
1897 July 15: Laid down at Cherbourg
1899 August 23: Launched
1903 September 21: Completed
1907 November: In collision with destroyer *Dard,* which lost bow, off Algiers
World War 1: 1915 Dardanelles
1917 In reserve
1920 July 9: Sold and broken up

Heroïne

Type: Broadside Ship
Class: 'Flandre' (1860)
Nomenclature: Heroine

History:
1861 June 10: Laid down at Lorient
1863 December 10: Launched
1865 June 7: Completed
1870 North Sea
1879 In reserve
1893 Floating workshop, Dakar
1901 Sunk by sloop *Ardent* off Dakar following yellow fever epidemic

Hoche

Type: Barbette Ship
Class: 'Hoche' (1880)
Nomenclature: Louis Lazare Hoche (1768-1797), general of the French Revolution

History:
1880 December 1: Laid down at Lorient
1886 September 29: Launched
1891 January 15: Completed
1892 July 7: Sank steamer *Marechal Canrobert* in collision off Marseille
1897 March 2: Damaged in collision with drydock
1898 May 13: Damaged by hitting submerged rock in Quiberon Bay
1898-1900 Reconstructed at Cherbourg; reboilered, new secondary armament
1911 May 23: Converted to target ship
1913 December 2: Sunk as target off Ile d'Hyères

Iéna

Type: Pre-dreadnought
Class: 'Iéna' (1897)
Nomenclature: Jena, victory of Napoleon over Prussia, 14 October 1806

History:
1897 April: Laid down at Brest
1898 September 1: Launched
1902 April 19: Completed
1907 March 12: Destroyed by internal explosion in after magazine while in drydock at Toulon (118 dead)
1909 December 2: Refloated but hulk capsized and sank at Porquerolles
1912 Hulk sold

Indienne, see **Montcalm**

Indomptable

Type: Coast Defence Barbette Ship
Class: 'Terrible' (1876)
Nomenclature: Indomitable

History:
1877 December 5: Laid down at Lorient
1883 September 18: Launched
1886 January 15: Completed
1896-97 Reconstructed, rearmed
1910 Discarded
1929 Broken up

Infernal, see *Amiral Baudin*

Invincible

Type: Broadside Ship
Class: 'Gloire' (1858)
Nomenclature: Invincible

History:
1858 May 1: Laid down at Toulon
1861 April 4: Launched
1862 March: Completed
1868 Rearmed
1870 North Sea, blockade of Prussia
1872 Discarded
1877 Broken up

Jauréguiberry

Type: Pre-dreadnought
Class: 'Jauréguiberry' (1891)
Nomenclature: Jean Bernard Jauréguiberry (1815-1887), admiral and navy minister

History:
1891 April 23: Laid down at La Seyne
1893 October 27: Launched
1897 February 16: Completed
1904 July 18: Struck rocks off Brest
1905 May 18: Damaged by torpedo fired in error by destroyer *Sagaie*
World War 1: 1915 Syria, Dardanelles, 1916 Suez Canal defence
1919 Accommodation ship for mechanics' school, Toulon
1920 June 20: Discarded
1934 July: Sold and broken up

Jean Bart

Type: Dreadnought
Class: 'Courbet' (1910)
Nomenclature: Jean Bart (1651-1702), naval commander and privateer

History:
1910 November 15: Laid down at Brest
1911 September 22: Launched
1913 September 2: Completed
1914 July: Carried President Poincaré on visit to St Petersburg
World War 1: 1914-1915 Adriatic
1914 August 16: Sank Austrian cruiser *Zenta* in action off Albania
1914 December 21: Torpedoed by Austrian submarine *U12* in Strait of Otranto
1919 Black Sea
1919 April 16: Bombarded Odessa
1923-25 Refit
1929-31 Reconstructed
1934 Training ship
1937 January 1: Renamed ***Océan***
1942 November 26: At Toulon, not scuttled; used as target ship by Germans
1945 December: Broken up

Jean Bart

Type: Battleship
Class: 'Richelieu' (1935)

History:
1937 January 1: Laid down by Loire and Penhoët at St Nazaire
1940 March 6: Launched
1940 June 19: When 77% complete sailed for Casablanca with only half machinery in use, one 380mm turret and 4×90mm guns fitted
1940 Main turret made fit for use for coast defence and 10×100mm and 5×37mm AA guns fitted
1942 November 8-10: Damaged by gunfire of US battleship *Massachusetts* and aircraft bomb at Casablanca
1945 Towed to Cherbourg and completed at Brest
1949 January: Completed for trials
1956 Suez
1961 Gunnery training ship
1970 July: Broken up at La Seyne

Jeanne d'Arc

Type: Armoured Corvette
Class: 'Belliqueuse' (1863)
Nomenclature: Joan of Arc (1412-1431), French saint and national heroine

History:
1865 May 1: Laid down at Cherbourg
1867 September 28: Launched
1870 April 12: Completed
1870 North Sea and Baltic, blockade of Prussia
1873 Blockade of Cartagena, Spain
1875 July 21: Rammed and sank despatch vessel *Forfait* in collision
1883 August 28: Discarded
1885 Broken up

Jeanne d'Arc

Type: Armoured Cruiser
Class: 'Jeanne d'Arc' (1895)

History:
1896 October 24: Laid down at Toulon
1899 June 8: Launched
1901 March: Did not reach contract speed on trials
1903 Completed
1912 Training ship
World War 1: 1914 English Channel; 1915-17 Levant, 1915 Dardanelles, 1918 North Atlantic convoys
1915 September: Rescue of Armenian refugees from Antioch
1915 December 28: Seizure of Castelorizo Island
1919-28 Training ship
1928 Reserve, renamed ***Jeanne d'Arc II***
1933 February 2: Discarded
1940 June: Moored at Brest and fell into German hands

Jemmapes

Type: Coast Defence Ship
Class: 'Bouvines' (1889)
Nomenclature: Victory of Dumouriez over Austria, 6 November 1792

History:
1890 Laid down by Loire
1892 April 27: Launched
1896 Completed
1910 Discarded
1927 Sold

Joffre

Type: Aircraft Carrier
Class: 'Joffre' (1937)
Nomenclature: Joseph Jacques Cesaire Joffre (1852-1931), Marshal of France, C-in-C during World War 1

History:
1938 November 26: Laid down by Penhoet
1940 May: Construction suspended when 28% complete, machinery well advanced

Jules Ferry

Type: Armoured Cruiser
Class: 'Gambetta' (1900)
Nomenclature: Jules François Camille Ferry (1832-1893), statesman, Premier of France

History:
1901 October: Laid down at Cherbourg
1903 August 23: Launched
1905 September: Completed
World War 1: Adriatic
1927 Discarded

Jules Michelet

Type: Armoured Cruiser
Class: 'Jules Michelet' (1900)
Nomenclature: Jules Michelet (1798-1874), historian

History:
1904 June 1: Laid down at Lorient
1905 August 31: Launched
1906 Armament modified
1908 Completed
World War 1: Adriatic and Mediterranean
1931 Discarded; artificers' training ship
1937 May 8: Sunk as a target by submarine *Thétis* off Toulon

Justice

Type: Pre-dreadnought
Class: 'Justice' (1902)
Nomenclature: Justice

History:
1902 May: Laid down at La Seyne
1904 September 27: Launched
1908 April 15: Completed
1913 December 20: Slightly damaged in collision with battleship *Démocratie* off Hyères
1914 August 17: Damaged in collision with battleship *Démocratie* off Corfu
World War 1: 1914-15 Adriatic, 1916-17 Aegean
1919 Black Sea
1919 May: Towed disabled battleship *Mirabeau* from Sevastopol to Toulon
1921 November 29: Discarded
1922 Broken up

Top left:
***Jauréguiberry* — Battleship of 1891, taken 1905. Notice forward 12" guns extend to bow.** *IWM*

Centre left:
***Jemmapes* — Coast defence ship of 1889.** *Photomatic*

Bottom left:
***La Fayette* — Light aircraft carrier at Malta, October 1955.** *A. & J. Pavia*

Kléber

Type: Armoured Cruiser
Class: 'Kléber' (1897)
Nomenclature: Jean Baptiste Kléber (1753-1800), a general of the French Revolution, assassinated in Egypt

History:
1898 April: Laid down at Gironde
1902 September 20: Launched complete, damaged bottom
1904 July 4: Completed
1907 March 7: Sank American freighter *Hugomak* in collision at Veracruz
1911-13 Far East
1912 July 12: Struck reef in Japanese Inland Sea
World War 1: 1914 English Channel, 1915 Dardanelles, Aegean, 1917 South Atlantic
1915 May 29: Went aground in Dardanelles under enemy fire
1915 July 7: Damaged in collision with British freighter at Mudros
1917 June 27: Sunk by mine off Cap St Mathieu (42 dead)

La Fayette

Type: Light Aircraft Carrier
Class: 'La Fayette' (1951)
Nomenclature: Marie Joseph Paul Yves Roch Gilbert du Motier, Marquis de La Fayette (1757-1834), French general and statesman

History:
1942 April 11: Laid down by New York Sbdg
1943 May 22: Launched
1943 August 31: Completed as US ***Langley***
1951 June 6: Transferred to France, renamed ***La Fayette***
1956 Suez
1963 March 20: Returned to US and broken up

La Galissonnière

Type: Armoured Corvette
Class: 'La Galissonnière' (1867)
Nomenclature: Roland Michel Barrin, Marquis de La Galissonnière (1693-1756), French naval commander

History:
1868 June 22: Laid down at Brest
1872 May 7: Launched
1874 October: Trials
1881 February 15: Completed
1881 Operations at Sfax
1884 Far East
1889 Far East
1894 December 24: Discarded, hulk at Cherbourg
1902 Sold and broken up

Languedoc

Type: Dreadnought
Class: 'Normandie' (1912)
Nomenclature: A province of south France

History:
1913 April 28: Laid down by Gironde
1915 May 1: Launched
1915 Construction suspended when 49% complete
1925 May: Sank while being broken up at Port de Bouc
1929 June: Refloated and broken up

Latouche-Tréville

Type: Armoured Cruiser
Class: 'Amiral Charner' (1889)
Nomenclature: Louis René, Count de Latouche-Tréville (1745-1804), admiral, prominent during the Napoleonic Wars

History:
1890 April 25: Laid down at Graville
1892 November 5: Launched
1895 May 6: Completed
1902 December 18: In collision with merchant vessel *Médoc* in Toulon harbour
1907 Gunnery school ship
1908 September 22: Turret explosion
1913 Refit, recommissioned
World War 1: 1914 Troop convoys, 1915 Levant, Dardanelles, 1916-17 Aegean, 1918 Corfu
1915 June 4: Damaged by gunfire at Gallipoli
1920 June 21: Discarded
1926 Broken up

Lazare Carnot, see *Carnot*

Léon Gambetta

Type: Armoured Cruiser
Class: 'Gambetta' (1900)
Nomenclature: Léon Gambetta (1838-1882), statesman, made a spectacular escape from Paris by balloon during the siege, 1870

History:
1901 January 15: Laid down at Brest
1902 October 26: Launched
1903 December: Ran aground in fog on trials
1905 July: Completed
World War 1: Adriatic
1915 April 24: Torpedoed and sunk by Austrian submarine *U5* in the Gulf of Otranto. Flagship of Rear-Adm Sénès who was lost (684 dead)

Liberté

Type: Pre-dreadnought
Class: 'Justice' (1902)
Nomenclature: Liberty

History:
1902 November: Laid down by Loire
1905 April 19: Launched
1907 February: Completed
1911 September 25: Destroyed by explosion in forward magazine at Toulon (204 dead)

Lille

Type: Dreadnought
Class: 'Lyon' (1913)
Nomenclature: City and commercial centre of northern France

History:
1914 Ordered from La Seyne, never laid down
1915 Contract cancelled

Lorraine

Type: Dreadnought
Class: 'Bretagne' (1912)
Nomenclature: A province of northeastern France

History:
1912 November 7: Laid down by Penhoët
1913 September 30: Launched
1916 July 1: Completed
World War 1: 1916-18 Corfu
1920-21 Constantinople
1921-22 Refit
1924-26 Refit
1929-31 Refit
1934-35 Reconstructed
1936 June 11: In collision with destroyer *Foudroyant* in English Channel
1937 Naval patrol, Spain
World War 2: 1939-40 Atlantic convoys, Mediterranean, Southern France, 1944-45 Bay of Biscay
1940 July 3: Disarmed at Alexandria
1943 May 30: Returned to French control
1944 Refit at Oran; catapult removed, AA guns increased, radar fitted
1945 Gunnery training ship
1947 Hulked
1953 February 17: Discarded
1953 November 27: Sold and broken up

Lyon

Type: Dreadnought
Class: 'Lyon' (1913)
Nomenclature: City and commercial centre of southeast France

History:
1914 Ordered from Penhoët, never laid down
1915 Contract cancelled

Magenta

Type: Broadside Ship
Class: 'Magenta' (1859)
Nomenclature: French and Sardinian victory over Austria, 24 June 1859

History:
1859 June 22: Laid down at Brest
1861 June 22: Launched
1862 May 22: Completed
1875 October 31: Caught fire and blew up in harbour of Toulon (3 dead)

Magenta

Type: Barbette Ship
Class: 'Neptune' (1880)

History:
1883 January 18: Laid down at Toulon
1890 April 19: Launched
1893 June 20: Completed
1902-03 Refit, reboilered

1909 Discarded
1911 August: Sold and broken up

Magnanime

Type: Broadside Ship
Class: 'Flandre' (1860)
Nomenclature: Magnanimous

History:
1861 February 27: Laid down at Brest
1864 August 19: Launched
1865 November 1: Completed
1870 North Sea
1882 Discarded
1885 Broken up

Marceau

Type: Barbette Ship
Class: 'Neptune' (1880)
Nomenclature: François Severin Marceau (1769-1796), general of the French Revolution, died of wounds

History:
1882 January 27: Laid down at La Seyne
1887 May 24: Launched
1891 March 14: Completed
1901-02 Reconstructed; reboilered, engines modernised
1917 Submarine depot ship
1920 October 1: Discarded
1923 Broken up

Marengo

Type: Central Battery Ship
Class: 'Océan' (1865)
Nomenclature: Victory of Napoleon over Austria, 14 June 1800

History:
1865 July: Laid down at Toulon
1869 December 4: Launched
1870 July 1: Completed
1881 Operations at Sfax
1894 Discarded

Marseillaise

Type: Armoured Cruiser
Class: 'Amiral Aube' (1898)
Nomenclature: The French national anthem

History:
1900 Laid down at Brest
1900 July 14: Launched
1903 Completed
World War 1: 1914-15 English Channel, 1916-17 West Indies, 1918 Atlantic convoys
1925-29 Gunnery school ship
1929 Discarded
1933 Broken up

Masséna

Type: Pre-dreadnought
Class: 'Masséna' (1891)
Nomenclature: André Masséna, Duc de Rivoli (1758-1817), Marshal of France under Napoleon

History:
1892 September: Laid down by Loire
1895 July 24: Launched
1898 May 25: Completed
1913 January 6: Damaged by boiler explosion
1913 March 1: Reduced to a hulk
1915 November 9: Sunk as breakwater at Seddulbahir in the Dardanelles

Mirabeau

Type: Pre-dreadnought
Class: 'Danton' (1906)
Nomenclature: Honoré Gabriel Victor Riqueti, Comte de Mirabeau (1749-1791), a leader of the French Revolution

History:
1908 May 4: Laid down at Lorient
1909 October 28: Launched
1911 August 1: Completed
World War 1: 1914 Mediterranean convoys, 1915 Adriatic, 1916-18 Aegean
1919 Black Sea
1919 February 8: Went aground during a snowstorm near Sevastopol
1919 April 6: Refloated following removal of forward turret and side armour and towed to Toulon by battleship *Justice*
1921 October 27: Discarded
1928 Broken up

Montcalm

Type: Armoured Corvette
Class: 'Belliqueuse' (1863)
Nomenclature: Louis Joseph, Marquis de Montcalm (1712-1759), French military leader killed at Quebec

History:
1865 October 26: Laid down at Rochefort as ***Indienne***
1867 March 25: Renamed ***Montcalm***
1868 October 16: Launched
1869 December 15: Completed
1870 Mediterranean
1891 April 2: Discarded

Montcalm

Type: Armoured Cruiser
Class: 'Gueydon' (1897)

History:
1898 September 27: Laid down at La Seyne
1900 March 27: Launched
1902 March 24: Completed
1902 Carried President Loubet to visit Russia
1903-06 Far East
1912-14 Far East
World War 1: 1914 South Pacific, 1915 Suez Canal, 1917 West Indies, 1918 North Atlantic convoys, North Russia
1923 Refit
1926 October 28: Discarded, accommodation ship, Brest
1934 September 26: Renamed ***Tremintin***
1944 August 16: Sunk by aircraft bombs at Brest

Neptune

Type: Barbette Ship
Class: 'Neptune' (1880)
Nomenclature: Roman myth: god of the sea

History:
1882 February 25: Laid down at Brest
1887 May 7: Launched
1892 December 22: Completed
1902-03 Refit, reboilered
1908 Discarded
1913 Broken up

Normandie

Type: Broadside Ship
Class: 'Gloire' (1858)
Nomenclature: A province of France on the English Channel

History:
1858 September 14: Laid down at Cherbourg
1860 March 10: Launched
1862 May 13: Completed
1862 July: First armoured ship to cross Atlantic, on voyage to Mexico
1870 North Sea and Baltic; blockade of Prussia
1872 Discarded

Normandie

Type: Dreadnought
Class: 'Normandie' (1912)

History:
1913 April 18: Laid down by Loire
1914 October 19: Launched
1915 Construction suspended when 65% complete
1924-25 Broken up in Italy

Océan

Type: Central Battery Ship
Class: 'Océan' (1865)
Nomenclature: Ship of 1752

History:
1865 April 18: Laid down at Brest
1868 October 15: Launched
1870 July 21: Completed
1870 North Sea and Baltic, blockade of Prussia
1894 Discarded and broken up

Top left:
***Lorraine* — Battleship of 1912 demilitarised at Alexandria, 1943. Notice tricolour on turrets.** *IWM*

Centre left:
***Magnanime* — Armoured frigate of 'Flandre' class, improved 'Gloire' type.** *Marius Bar*

Bottom left:
***Marceau* — Barbette ship of 1880 after reconstruction of 1902 with lightened superstructure and masts.** *Photomatic*

Onondaga

Type: Monitor
Class: 'Onondaga' (1867)
Nomenclature: Former name retained

History:
1862 Laid down by Continental
1863 July 29: Launched
1864 March 24: Completed as US ***Onondaga***
1867 March 2: Sold to France
1867 September 2: Left New York for Halifax
1868 June 15: Left Halifax
1868 July 2: Arrived at Brest in tow
1869 June 15: Commissioned
1890 Guardship, St Malo
1903 Discarded and broken up

Painlevé

Type: Aircraft Carrier
Class: 'Joffre' (1937)
Nomenclature: Paul Painlevé (1863-1933), statesman, Premier of France

History:
1939 Laid down by Penhoet
1940 Construction suspended

Paris

Type: Dreadnought
Class: 'Courbet' (1910)
Nomenclature: Capital city of France

History:
1911 November 11: Laid down at La Seyne
1912 September 28: Launched
1914 August 22: Completed
World War 1: 1914-18 Adriatic, Malta, Corfu
1922-23 Refit
1925 September: Operated with Spanish fleet off Melilla against the Rifs
1927-29 Reconstructed
1931 Training ship
1934-35 Refit
World War 2: 1940 British, later Free French
1940 June: Fire support at Le Havre
1940 June 11: Damaged by aircraft bomb at Le Havre
1940 June 18: Evacuated 1,600 naval cadets from Brest to Plymouth
1940 July 3: Seized by British at Plymouth, used as accommodation ship for Polish personnel
—— Returned to Free French
1945 August 21: Towed to Brest, not used
1955 December 21: Discarded as *Q64* and broken up at La Seyne

Patrie

Type: Pre-dreadnought
Class: 'République' (1900)
Nomenclature: Fatherland

History:
1902 April 1: Laid down at La Seyne
1903 December 17: Launched
1906 Completed
World War 1: 1916-17 Aegean
1918 4×164mm guns removed for Army in Macedonia

1920 Training ship for electrical and torpedo apprentices, Toulon; 12×164mm AA, 3×450mm TT
1927 Discarded
1937 Broken up

Pothuau

Type: Armoured Cruiser
Class: 'Pothuau' (1892)
Nomenclature: Louis Pothuau (1815-1882), admiral and Minister of Marine

History:
1893 May 25: Laid down at Graville
1895 August 22: First attempt at launching unsuccessful
1895 September 19: Launched
1897 June 5: Completed
1897 At Kronstadt where treaty was signed between the Tsar and President Faure of France
1906 Gunnery school ship
1914 July: Recommissioned
World War 1: 1914 Mediterranean, Cameroons, 1916-17 Defence of Suez Canal
1915-16 Refit
1918 Kite balloon ship
1919 Gunnery school ship
1927 November 3: Discarded
1929 September 25: Sold and broken up

Provence

Type: Broadside Ship
Class: 'Flandre' (1860)
Nomenclature: A province of southeast France

History:
1861 January 1: Laid down at Toulon
1863 October 29: Launched
1865 February 1: Completed
1886 May 3: Discarded
1893 November 10: Sold and broken up

Provence

Type: Dreadnought
Class: 'Bretagne' (1912)

History:
1912 May 21: Laid down at Lorient
1913 April 20: Launched
1916 January 20: Completed
World War 1: 1916 Mediterranean Fleet (flagship), 1916 September-December: Greece, 1917-18 Corfu, 1919 Black Sea
1922-23 Reconstructed
1925-27 Refit
1931-34 Refit
1937 Naval patrol, Spain
1939 Refit
World War 2: 1939-40 South Atlantic, 1940 Mediterranean
1940 July 3: Damaged by British warships at Mers-el-Kebir and beached
1940 November 8: Returned to Toulon and placed in reserve
1942 November 27: Scuttled at Toulon
1943 July 11: Refloated by Germans, later used as a blockship
1949 April: Refloated and broken up

Redoutable

Type: Central Battery and Barbette Ship
Class: 'Redoutable' (1872)
Nomenclature: Redoubtable

History:
1873 July 10: Laid down at Lorient
1876 September 18: Launched
1882 January 28: Completed
1894 Reconstructed
1898 Refit, rearmed
1900 Far East
1902 Hulk at Saigon
1910 March: Discarded and broken up

Reine Blanche

Type: Armoured Corvette
Class: 'Belliqueuse' (1863)
Nomenclature: Blanche of Castile (1188-1252), Queen of France, mother of Saint Louis IX

History:
1865 October 1: Laid down at Lorient
1868 March 20: Launched
1869 Completed
1873 Blockade of Cartagena, Spain
1877 July 3: Rammed by corvette *Thétis* and run ashore off La Badine
1881 Operations off Sfax
1884 Pacific
1886 November 12: Discarded after fire; harbour service
1893 Broken up

République

Type: Pre-dreadnought
Class: 'République' (1900)
Nomenclature: Republic

History:
1901 December 2: Laid down at Brest
1902 September 4: Launched
1906 December: Completed
World War 1: 1917 Aegean
1918 Gunnery training ship, Toulon, main turrets removed
1921 Discarded

Requin

Type: Coast Defence Barbette Ship
Class: 'Terrible' (1876)
Nomenclature: Shark

Top right:
***Normandie* — Broadside ship, 'Gloire' class, with a ship-of-the-line behind.** *Marius Bar*

Centre right:
***Paris* — Battleship leaving Devonport 1940. Heavy tripod foremast installed during 1929 reconstruction.** *IWM*

Bottom right:
***Patrie* — Pre-dreadnought c1915. Notice false wave on bow.** *IWM*

History:
1879 Laid down by Gironde
1885 June 13: Launched
1886 December 23: Completed
1895-96 Reconstructed; rearmed, reboilered
World War 1: 1914-16 Defence of Suez Canal, Syria
1920 February 2: Discarded
1922 Broken up

Revanche

Type: Broadside Ship
Class: 'Flandre' (1860)
Nomenclature: Revenge

History:
1861 March 1: Laid down at Toulon
1865 December 28: Launched
1868 Completed
1870 North Sea
1877 March: Damaged by boiler explosion
1881 Operations at Sfax
1893 January 10: Discarded

Richelieu

Type: Central Battery Ship
Class: 'Richelieu' (1867)
Nomenclature: Armand Jean du Plessis, Cardinal and Duc de Richelieu (1585-1642), French statesman, minister of Louis XIII

History:
1868 December 1: Laid down at Toulon
1873 December 3: Launched
1875 April 12: Completed
1880 December 29: Caught fire and scuttled in Toulon harbour to prevent magazine explosion; refloated and repaired
1894 Reserve
1900 Discarded
1910 Lost in tow en route to breaking up

Richelieu

Type: Battleship
Class: 'Richelieu' (1935)

History:
1935 October 22: Laid down at Brest
1939 January 17: Launched
1940 June 15: Completed
1940 June 18: Left Brest for Dakar to escape advancing German armies prior to commissioning
World War 2: 1940-43 At Dakar, 1944-45 Indian Ocean
1940 July 8: Damaged by torpedo aircraft from British carrier *Hermes* in Dakar harbour
1940 September: Defended Dakar against British attack
1943 Refit at New York; completed, catapults removed, radar and AA guns fitted
1943 November 19: Commissioned
1945-46 Indochina
1956 In reserve
1960 Discarded
1968 August: Broken up at La Spezia

Top left:
***Redoutable* — Central battery and barbette ship of 1872, after reconstruction of 1894 with military masts. Notice prominent barbette on stern.** *Marius Bar*

Centre left:
***Richelieu* — Battleship of 1935, at New York 1943.**

Bottom left:
***Rochambeau* — Casemate ironclad in drydock, formerly the US *Dunderberg*, few photographs are known of this vessel.** *Marius Bar*

Rochambeau

Type: Casemate Ironclad
Class: 'Rochambeau' (1867)
Nomenclature: Jean Baptiste Donatien de Vimeur, Comte de Rochambeau (1725-1807), Marshal of France, a commander in the American Revolution and of the French Revolutionary Army

History:
1862 October 4: Laid down by Webb
1865 July 22: Launched as US ***Dunderberg***
1867 July: Sold to France, renamed ***Rochambeau***
1867 July 4: Sailed from New York with American crew
1867 Rearmed, bow rebuilt, engines improved
1870 North Sea, blockade of Prussia
1871 March 7: Decommissioned
1872 Discarded
1874 Broken up

Saint Louis

Type: Pre-dreadnought
Class: 'Charlemagne' (1893)
Nomenclature: Louis IX (1214-1270), King of France, a leader in the Crusades

History:
1895 March 25: Laid down at Lorient
1896 September 8: Launched
1900 September 1: Completed
1911 September 6: In collision with destroyer *Poignard* off Hyeres
1912 June 8: Sank submarine *Vendémiare* in collision during manoeuvres off Cap La Hogue
World War 1: 1914 Mediterranean convoys, 1915 Syria, 1916-17 Aegean
1915-16 Refit, bulges fitted
1917 Reserve
1919 Accommodation ship, mechanics' school, Toulon
1920 June 21: Discarded, hulk at Toulon
1933 April 25: Sold and broken up

Savoie

Type: Broadside Ship
Class: 'Flandre' (1860)
Nomenclature: Savoy, a region of southeastern France acquired from Piedmont in 1861

History:
1861 January 1: Laid down at Toulon
1864 September 29: Launched
1865 March 25: Completed
1888 Discarded and broken up

Solférino

Type: Broadside Ship
Class: 'Magenta' (1859)

Nomenclature: French and Sardinian victory over Austria, 24 June 1859

History:
1859 June 24: Laid down at Lorient
1861 June 24: Launched
1861 December 18: Completed
1868-69 Refit; rearmed and rerigged
1871 In reserve
1882 July 21: Discarded
1884 Broken up at Brest

Strasbourg

Type: Battleship
Class: 'Dunkerque' (1931)
Nomenclature: Capital city of Alsace

History:
1934 November 25: Laid down by Penhoet
1936 December 12: Launched
1938 December: Completed
World War 2: 1939-40 South Atlantic, 1940 Mediterranean
1940 July 3: Escaped to open sea during British attack on Mers-el-Kebir
1940-42 High Seas Naval Force (flag)
1942 November 27: Scuttled at Toulon
1943 July 17: Refloated by Italians
1944 August 18: Hulk sunk by US aircraft
1945 August: Refloated, hulk used for underwater tests until 1951
1955 May: Broken up

Suffren

Type: Central Battery Ship
Class: 'Océan' (1865)
Nomenclature: Pierre André de Suffren de St Tropez (1726-1788), admiral, noted naval commander

History:
1866 April 1: Laid down at Cherbourg
1870 October 26: Launched
1873 August 5: Completed
1897 July 15: Discarded

Suffren

Type: Pre-dreadnought
Class: 'Suffren' (1898)

History:
1899 January 16: Laid down at Brest
1899 July 25: Launched
1904 February 4: Completed
World War 1: 1915 Dardanelles
1915 March 18: Severely damaged by shore guns at Dardanelles
1916 November 26: Torpedoed and sunk by German submarine *U52* off Lisbon (648 dead, no survivors)

Sully

Type: Armoured Cruiser
Class: 'Amiral Aube' (1898)
Nomenclature: Maximilien de Bethune, Duc de Sully (1560-1641), statesman under King Henry IV

History:
1899 May 24: Laid down at La Seyne
1901 June 4: Launched
1904 June: Completed
1905 February 7: Went aground in Along Bay off Haiphong, Tonkin and foundered

Surveillante

Type: Broadside Ship
Class: 'Flandre' (1860)
Nomenclature: Guardian

History:
1861 January 28: Laid down at Lorient
1864 August 18: Launched
1867 August 21: Completed
1870 North Sea operations, blockade of Prussia (flag)
1870 November 12: Lost rudder in storm off coast of Germany
1881 Operations at Sfax
1887 Discarded, guardship at Cherbourg
1898 Broken up

Taureau

Type: Coast Defence Turret Ram
Class: 'Taureau' (1863)
Nomenclature: Bull

History:
1863 October 5: Laid down at Toulon
1865 June 10: Launched
1866 Completed
1879 In reserve
1890 October 25: Discarded

Tempête

Type: Coast Defence Turret Ship
Class: 'Tempête' (1872)
Nomenclature: Tempest

History:
1872 December 26: Laid down at Brest
1876 August 18: Launched
1878 Completed
1883 April 15: Commissioned
1881 Operations at Bizerte
1892 July 20: Sank torpedo boat *No 76* in collision at Brest
1907 Discarded
1912 Sold and broken up

Terrible

Type: Coast Defence Barbette Ship
Class: 'Terrible' (1876)
Nomenclature: Terrible

History:
1878 Laid down at Brest
1881 March 29: Launched
1886 July 13: Completed
1886 Refitted, rearmed
1901 Reconstruction suspended
1908 Discarded
1914 Broken up

***Solférino* — Broadside ship, 'Magenta' class. Note large eagle figurehead on bow.** *Marius Bar*

Thétis

Type: Armoured Corvette
Class: 'Belliqueuse' (1863)
Nomenclature: Greek myth: chief of the Nereids (sea-nymphs)

History:
1865 July 20: Laid down at Toulon
1867 August 22: Launched
1869 July 14: Completed
1870 North Sea, blockade of Prussia
1873 Blockade of Cartagena, Spain
1877 July 3: In collision with corvette *Reine Blanche* off La Badine
1885 Floating battery, Noumea

***Suffren* — Central battery ship, 'Océan' class, on 4 April 1892.** *Marius Bar*

1895 Discarded
1896 Sold and broken up

Tigre

Type: Coast Defence Turret Ram
Class: 'Bélier' (1865)
Nomenclature: Tiger

History:
1868 Laid down at Rochefort
1871 March 9: Launched
1874 July 20: Completed
1892 February 13: Discarded
1920 Broken up

Tonnant

Type: Coast Defence Turret Ship
Class: 'Tonnant' (1873)

Nomenclature: Thundering

History:
1875 December 12: Laid down at Rochefort
1880 October 16: Launched
1882 Completed
1902 Discarded and broken up

Tonnerre

Type: Coast Defence Turret Ship
Class: 'Tonnerre' (1872)
Nomenclature: Thunder

History:
1873 October: Laid down at Lorient
1875 September 16: Launched
1877 September 15: Completed
1905 Discarded
1922 Broken up

Tourville

Type: Dreadnought
Class: 'Lyon' (1913)
Nomenclature: Anne Hilarion de Cotentin, Comte de Tourville (1642-1701), Marshal of France, commanded the French fleet at Beachy Head

History:
1914 Ordered from Lorient, never laid down
1915 Contract cancelled

Tréhouart, see *Amiral Tréhouart*

Trident

Type: Central Battery Ship
Class: 'Colbert' (1869)
Nomenclature: Trident; emblem of mastery of the sea

History:
1870 April 1: Laid down at Toulon
1876 November 9: Launched
1878 November 1: Completed
1881 Operations at Sfax
1900 September 11: Discarded, hulk
1904 Renamed ***Var***
1909 Sold and broken up

Triomphante

Type: Armoured Corvette
Class: 'Victorieuse' (1868)
Nomenclature: Triumphant

History:
1870 September 1: Laid down at Rochefort
1877 March 28: Launched
1878 June 5: Completed
1884 Battle of Foochow
1885 Reclassified armoured cruiser
1896 July 8: Discarded, hulk at Saigon
1903 Broken up

Turenne

Type: Second Class Battleship
Class: 'Turenne' (1875)
Nomenclature: Henri de la Tour d'Auvergne, Vicomte de Turenne (1611-1675), Marshal-General of France, one of the greatest French commanders

History:
1877 March 1: Laid down at Lorient
1879 October 16: Launched
1882 February: Completed
1885 Reclassified armoured cruiser
1885-90 Far East
1892 In reserve
1900 Discarded

Valeureuse

Type: Broadside Ship
Class: 'Flandre' (1860)
Nomenclature: Valorous

History:
1861 May 13: Laid down at Brest
1864 August 18: Launched
1867 February 27: Completed
1870 North Sea
1870 240mm gun exploded (10 dead)
1886 Stricken and broken up

Valmy

Type: Coast Defence Ship
Class: 'Bouvines' (1889)
Nomenclature: First important engagement of the French Revolutionary Wars, 20 September 1792

History:
1889 December 18: Laid down by Loire
1892 October 6: Launched
1896 Completed
1910 Discarded
1911 July: Sold and broken up

Vauban

Type: Second Class Battleship
Class: 'Vauban' (1875)
Nomenclature: Sébastien Le Prestre, Marquis de Vauban (1633-1707), Marshal of France, famed military engineer

History:
1877 April 1: Laid down at Cherbourg
1882 July 2: Launched
1885 Reclassified armoured cruiser
1886 March 9: Completed
1898 Station hulk, Saigon
1905 Discarded
1914 Broken up

Vendée, see *Béarn*

Vengeur

Type: Coast Defence Turret Ship
Class: 'Vengeur' (1873)
Nomenclature: Avenger

History:
1874 December 1: Laid down at Brest

***Waldeck-Rousseau* — Armoured cruiser of 1905 shortly after completion.** *Marius Bar*

1878 May 16: Launched
1882 May 30: Completed
1905 Discarded

Vergniaud

Type: Pre-dreadnought
Class: 'Danton' (1906)
Nomenclature: Pierre Victurnien Vergniaud (1753-1793), a leader of the French Revolution

History:
1907 November: Laid down by Gironde
1910 April 12: Launched
1911 December 18: Completed
World War 1: 1914 Mediterranean convoys, 1915 Adriatic, 1918 Aegean
1919 Black Sea
1921 October 27: Discarded, used as aircraft target
1928 November 27: Sold and broken up

Verité

Type: Pre-dreadnought
Class: 'Justice' (1902)
Nomenclature: Truth

History:
1903 April: Laid down by Gironde
1907 March 28: Launched
1908 March: Completed
World War 1: Aegean
1921 Discarded and broken up

Victor Hugo

Type: Armoured Cruiser
Class: 'Gambetta' (1900)
Nomenclature: Victor Marie Hugo (1802-1885), man of letters, poet and novelist

History:
1903 April: Laid down at Lorient
1904 March 30: Launched
1907 April 16: Completed
World War 1: Adriatic
1922 Far East
1928 January 20: Discarded
1930 November 26: Sold and broken up

Victorieuse

Type: Armoured Corvette
Class: 'Victorieuse' (1868)
Nomenclature: Victorious

History:
1869 December 1: Laid down at Toulon
1875 November 18: Launched
1876 November 1: Completed
1885 Reclassified armoured cruiser
1900 March 9: Discarded, harbour service; renamed ***Semiramis***
1904 Broken up

Voltaire

Type: Pre-dreadnought
Class: 'Danton' (1906)
Nomenclature: Pseudonym of François Marie Arouet (1694-1778), writer and philosopher

History:
1907 July 20: Laid down at La Seyne
1909 January 16: Launched
1911 August 1: Completed
World War 1: 1914 Mediterranean convoys, 1915 Adriatic, 1916-18 Aegean
1918 October 10: Twice torpedoed by German submarine *UB48* near Milos in the Aegean
1923-24 Refit
1935 Discarded, used as target
1938 May: Sold and broken up

Waldeck-Rousseau

Type: Armoured Cruiser
Class: 'Edgar Quinet' (1904)
Nomenclature: Pierre Marie René Waldeck-Rousseau (1846-1904), statesman, Premier of France

History:
1906 June 15: Laid down at Lorient
1908 March 4: Launched
1911 August 8: Completed
1911 February 2: Struck rock during trials
1914 February 22: Damaged by hurricane off Southern France
World War 1: Adriatic, Ionian and Aegean Seas
1919-20 Black Sea
1929-32 Far East
1936 June 14: Discarded; hulk, Landevennec near Brest
1940 June 18: Hulk scuttled at Brest

Germany

Prior to the formation of the German Empire in 1871, Prussia maintained only a small navy for coast defence. The first ironclads were built in Britain and another had originally been built for the Confederacy. The blockade of the coast by the French navy during the Franco-Prussian War convinced the government of the need for a larger navy. During the 1870s nine capital ships were begun, built mostly in German yards.

Emperor Wilhelm II was an admirer of British naval power and the theories of Adm Mahan. Under the administration of Adm Tirpitz a large number of capital ships was built in order to challenge the British navy. The comparative rapid build up of German strength caused anxiety in Britain; Germany replaced France as Britain's perceived rival.

The appearance of the *Dreadnought* in 1906 made all other battleships obsolete, wiping out Britain's lead in capital ships, and the completion of the first battlecruisers occurred shortly after. These events inspired Germany to attempt parity with Britain but these efforts were hampered by British secrecy. In addition, German yards were unable to compete with British shipbuilding capacity. The naval race of this period produced successively larger and more powerful ships.

At the outbreak of war in 1914 all major German warships were in the North Sea except the battlecruiser *Goeben* in the Mediterranean and von Spee's squadron in the Far East. The *Goeben* made its celebrated escape from British and French ships to Constantinople and was then transferred in name to Turkey. Spee's ships were eliminated at the Battle of the Falklands.

The German ships composed the High Seas Fleet which, although inferior in numbers to the British Grand Fleet, was capable of inflicting serious damage. The strategy of its commander, Adm Scheer, was to force the British to divide their strength before coming to action. In May 1916 the two fleets met at the Battle of Jutland as Scheer's strategy to trap part of the British fleet led him into a confrontation with the entire Grand Fleet. The German losses were considerable; the battlecruiser *Lutzow* and pre-dreadnought *Pommern* were sunk and several other ships suffered serious damage. Their narrow escape from destruction led to a more cautious attitude and the two fleets did not meet again. Some of the battleships were used in the Baltic against the Russians but for the next two years the ships were mainly inactive. In 1918 mutiny broke out in almost every capital ship. The armistice terms called for the German fleet to be interned and for six months the ships lay at Scapa Flow until they were scuttled there on June 22 1919.

Under the Treaty of Versailles, Germany was permitted to retain six pre-dreadnoughts. In 1929 the first 'pocket battleship' *Deutschland* caused considerable attention. When Hitler came to power in 1933, treaty limitations were disregarded and the battlecruisers *Scharnhorst* and *Gneisenau* were begun. In May 1938, 'Plan Z' authorised a fleet of eight super-battleships, five battlecruisers, three pocket battleships and two aircraft carriers, all to be completed by 1944. The outbreak of war in 1939 diverted resources and only the battleships *Bismarck* and *Tirpitz* were actually completed.

Germany conducted a commerce-raiding war at sea with its heavy ships with some success at first, losing only the *Graf Spee*. After the sinking of the *Bismarck* in 1941 German capital ships remained in or close to their ports. Their presence tied up considerable Allied naval strength although only the *Scharnhorst* was sunk in action. By 1945 all had been destroyed by Allied air attacks as they lay inactive in port.

Class Details

'Arminius' (1862)

Coast Defence Monitor: *Arminius*
Displacement: 1,600tons, 1,829f/l
Dimensions: 207′4(oa) 202′2(wl) 197′2(pp)×35′9×15′2
[63.2(oa) 61.6(wl) 60.1(pp)×10.9×4.6]
Machinery: 1 screw, horizontal direct-acting trunk engines (Penn), 4 rectangular boilers
IHP 1,440 = 10.5knots
Endurance: 1,000/8
Armament: 4×210mm BL
1881: 4×37mm, 1×350mm TT added
Armour: Belt 76-114mm, turret 119mm, c/t 114mm
Complement: 132
Class notes: Designed by Coles. Built as a speculation, near sister of Danish *Rolf Krake*. Iron hull with two twin turrets. Rigging removed c1870. Reconstructed 1888, funnel shortened and superstructure modified

'Prinz Adalbert' (1865)

Ironclad Ram: *Prinz Adalbert*
Displacement: 1,440tons;
Dimensions: 186′9(oa) 165′8(wl) 157′6(pp)×32′6×16′6
[56.9(oa) 50.5(wl) 48(pp)×9.9×5.0]
Machinery: 2 screws, horizontal direct-acting engines (Mazeline), 2 boilers
IHP 1,200 = 10knots
Endurance: 1,200/8
Armament: *Designed:* 3×36 pdr
1865: 1×210mm BL, 2×177mm
Armour: Belt 127mm, turret 114mm
Complement: 130
Class notes: Built for the Confederate government under the cover name *Cheops*. Sister *Stonewall* (*Sphinx*) became Japanese *Azuma*. Purchased 1865 and rearmed. Single turret aft, single funnel, wood hull and brig rig. First twin screw ship in the German navy

'Friedrich Carl' (1865)

Central Battery Ship: *Friedrich Carl* (see later photo)
Displacement: 5,971tons, 6,932f/l
Dimensions: 308′9(oa) 298′10(wl) 290′6(pp)×54′6×26′5
[94.1(oa) 91.1(wl) 88.6(pp)×16.6×8.1]
Machinery: 1 screw, HSE engines (F C Med), 6 boilers
IHP 3,550 = 13knots
Endurance: 2,210/10
Armament: *Designed:* 26×72pdr
Completed: 16×210mm
Armour: Belt 114-127mm, battery and c/t 114mm
Complement: 531
Class notes: Iron hull armoured frigate with single funnel and bark rig

'Kronprinz' (1866)

Central Battery Ship: *Kronprinz*

Displacement: 5,767tons, 6,760f/l
Dimensions: 293'4(oa) 289'4(wl) 282'7(pp)×49'10×25'9 [89.4(oa) 88.2(wl) 86.1(pp)×15.2×7.9]
Machinery: 1 screw, HSE engines (Penn), 8 boilers
IHP 4,500 = 13.5knots
Endurance: 3,220/10
Armament: *Designed:* 32×72pdr
Completed: 16×210mm
Armour: Belt 124-176mm, battery 121mm, c/t 50mm
Complement: 541
Class notes: Designed by Reed. Armoured frigate with iron hull, two funnels and bark rig. Similar to *Friedrich Carl*

'König Wilhelm' (1867)

Broadside Ship: *König Wilhelm*
Displacement: 9,757tons, 10,761f/l
Dimensions: 368'2(oa) 356'4(wl)×60×28'3 [112.2(oa) 108.6(wl)×18.3×8.6]
Machinery: 1 screw, HSE engines (Maudslay), 8 boilers
IHP 8,000 = 14 knots
Endurance: 1,300/10
Armament: *Designed:* 33×72pdr
Completed: 18×240mm, 5×210mm
1886: 22×240mm, 18×88m, 5×350mm TT
Armour: Belt 127-305mm, battery 152-203mm
Complement: 730
Class notes: Armoured frigate designed by Reed. Laid down for Turkey and purchased prior to launching. Iron hull with ram bow and three masts, ship rig. Reconstructed 1896, rigging removed and replaced with military masts, ram removed and armoured conning tower added

'Hansa' (1871)

Armoured Corvette: *Hansa*
Displacement: 3,950tons, 4,404f/l
Dimensions: 241'1(oa) 235'3(wl) 224'5(pp)×46'3×22'3 [73.5(oa) 71.7(wl) 68.4(pp)×14.1×6.8]
Machinery: 1 screw, single expansion engines (Vulcan), 4 boilers
IHP 3,275 = 12knots
Endurance: 1,330/10
Armament: 8×210mm BLR
Armour: Belt 114-152mm, battery 114mm
Complement: 399
Class notes: Small central battery ship built for foreign service. Wood hull. First German designed armoured vessel

'Preussen' Class (1872)

Turret Ships: *Friedrich der Grosse, Grosser Kurfürst, Preussen* (see later photo)
Displacement: 6,821tons, 7,718f/l
Dimensions: 317(oa) 310(wl) 307(pp)×53'6×23'3 [96.6(oa) 94.5(wl) 93.6(pp)×16.3×7.1]
Machinery: 1 screw, HSE engines (Egells; *Preussen:* Vulcan), 6 box boilers
IHP 5,400 = 14knots
Endurance: 2,500/10
Armament: 4×260mm, 2×177mm
1889: 6×88mm and 5-350mm TT added
Armour: Belt 102-229mm, turrets 203-254mm, c/t 50mm
Complement: 543
Class notes: Armoured full rig ship similar to British *Monarch*. Iron hulls with two turrets on the centre line, single funnel and three masts. *Preussen* and *Friedrich der Grosse* reconstructed 1890, rigging and masts removed and single mast fitted abaft funnel, reboilered

'Kaiser' Class (1873)

Central Battery Ships: *Deutschland, Kaiser* (see also later photo)
Displacement: 7,645tons, 8,940f/l
Dimensions: 293(oa) 290'4(wl) 279'10(pp)×62'8×26 [89.3(oa) 88.5(wl) 85.3(pp)×9.1×7.9]
Machinery: 1 screw, horizontal direct-acting trunk engines (Penn), 8 box boilers
IHP 8,000 = 14knots
Endurance: 2,470/10
Armament: 8×260mm, 1×210mm, 7×150mm
1882: 5×350mm TT added
Armour: Belt 127-254mm, battery 178-203mm, deck 38-50mm, c/t 50mm
Complement: 638
Class notes: Designed by Reed. Central battery on main deck with four guns on each side. Ship rigged on iron hull. Similar to British *Hercules* and the last ships built for Germany in a foreign country. Reconstructed 1891-97, rigging removed and two military masts fitted, superstructure built up and additional guns added

'Sachsen' Class (1875)

Barbette Ships: *Baden, Bayern, Sachsen* (see later photo), *Württemberg*
Displacement: 7,635tons; *1896:* 7,400tons
Dimensions: 322'2(oa) 305'2(wl)×60'4×21'4 [98.2(oa) 93(wl)×18.4×6.5]
Machinery: 2 screws, single expansion engines (Markisch; *Sachsen* and *Württemberg:* Egells), 8 boilers; *1896:* compound engines, 8 Durr boilers (*Württemberg:* Thornycroft)
IHP 5,600 = 13knots; *1896:* IHP 6,000 = 14knots
Endurance: 1,940/10; *1896:* 3,000/10
Armament: 6×260mm/20, 6×87mm/24
1886: 3×350mm TT added
1896: 8×88mm added
Armour: Belt and citadel 203-254mm, inner belt 152mm, deck 50-75mm, barbettes 254mm, c/t 140mm
1896: Belt 355mm, citadel 254mm
Complement: 317
Class notes: Armoured corvettes with an armoured citadel containing four guns of the main battery in a barbette aft and two in a barbette forward. They had a single mast aft and four funnels in pairs side by side, and a ram bow. Reconstructed 1895-99, re-engined and reboilered, with only a single funnel

'Oldenburg' (1883)

Barbette Ship: *Oldenburg*
Displacement: 5,249tons, 5,743f/l
Dimensions: 261'10(oa) 257'3(wl) 246(pp)×59×20'8 [79.8(oa) 78.4(wl) 75(pp)×18×6.3]
Machinery: 2 screws, compound engines, 8 cylindrical boilers
IHP 3,900 = 14knots
Endurance: 1,370/10
Armament: 8×240mm, 4×150mm, 4×350mm TT
Armour: Belt 200-300mm, casemates 150-200mm, deck 30mm, c/t 50mm
Complement: 389
Class notes: Coast defence ship. Steel hull with armament in a central citadel. Intended as a unit of 'Sachsen' class, of little fighting value

'Siegfried' Class (1887-1891)

Coast Defence Ships: *Beowulf, Frithjof, Hagen* (see later

photo), *Heimdall, Hildebrand, Siegfried*
Displacement: 3,500tons, 3,741f/l; *1901:* 4,058tons, 4,225f/l
Dimensions: 259'2(oa) 250'8(wl)×48'10×18'9 [79(oa) 76.4(wl)×14.9×5.7]
1901: 282'6(oa) 278'3(wl) [86.1(oa) 84.8(wl)]
Machinery: 2 screws, VTE engines (builders), 4 locomotive boilers; *1901:* 8 Schulz-Thornycroft boilers
IHP 4,800 = 15knots
Endurance: 1,490/10; *1901:* 3,980/10
Armament: 3×240mm/35, 8×88mm, 4×350mm TT
1901: 3×450mm TT, 1×350mm TT, 2×88mm added
Armour: Belt 180-240mm, barbettes and turrets 200mm, deck 30mm, c/t 180mm
Complement: 276 (*Hildebrand:* 304); *1902:* 207 (*Hildebrand:* 350)
Class notes: Small steel hull vessels with three single turrets, two abreast forward and one aft. All reconstructed and lengthened 1898-1904, with new boilers and two funnels instead of one. Built for coastal defence against small French battleships

'Brandenburg' Class (1889)

Pre-dreadnoughts: *Brandenburg, Kurfürst Friedrich Wilhelm, Weissenburg, Wörth* (see later photo)
Displacement: 10,013tons, 10,670f/l
Dimensions: 379'8(oa) 373'9(wl)×64'8×26 [115.7(oa) 113.9(wl)×19.7×7.9]
Machinery: 2 screws, VTE engines (builders), 12 cylindrical boilers
IHP 10,000 = 16knots
Endurance: 4,500/10
Armament: 4×280mm/40, 2×280mm/35, 6×105mm/35, 8×88mm/30, 12×37mm, 6×450mm TT
1905: 2×105mm/35 added, 3×450mm TT removed
Armour: Belt 300-400mm, barbettes 300mm, deck 60mm, turrets 50-150mm, c/t 300mm
Complement: 585
Class notes: First modern battleships built by Germany for 20 years. Main armament in three twin turrets on the centreline but amidships turret with guns of shorter calibre had restricted arc of fire. Inferior armour protection. Modernised 1901-05; reboilered and rearmed. *Kurfürst Friedrich Wilhelm* and *Weissenburg* sold to Turkey 1910

'Odin' Class (1892)

Coast Defence Ships: *Ägir, Odin*
Displacement: 3,550tons, 3,754f/l
Dimensions: 259'2(oa) 250'8(wl)×48'10×18'4 [79(oa) 76.4(wl)×14.9×5.6]
1904: 282'10(oa) 273'3(wl) [86.2(oa) 84.8(wl)]
Machinery: 2 screws, VTE engines (builders), 8 Schulz-Thornycroft boilers
IHP 5,000 = 15knots
Endurance: 2,200/10; *1905:* 3,500/10
Armament: 3×240mm/35, 10×88mm, 4×350mm TT
Armour: Belt 180-240mm, barbettes and turrets 200mm, deck 50-70mm, bulkheads 200mm, c/t 180mm
Complement: 307
Class notes: Similar to 'Siegfried' class. *Ägir* built with one funnel. Both reconstructed 1901-04 as 'Siegfried' class

'Kaiser Friedrich III' Class (1894-1897)

Pre-dreadnoughts: *Kaiser Barbarossa, Kaiser Friedrich III, Kaiser Karl de Grosse, Kaiser Wilhelm II, Kaiser Wilhelm der Grosse*
Displacement: 11,097tons, 11,785f/l
Dimensions: 411(oa) 396'8(wl)×66'11×27 [125.3(oa) 120.9(wl)×20.4×8.2]
Machinery: 3 screws, VTE engines (builders: *Kaiser Wilhelm II* and *Kaiser Wilhelm der Grosse:* Germania); Boilers: *Kaiser Barbarossa:* 4 Schulz-Thornycroft and 6 cylindrical: *Kaiser Friedrich III:* 4 Schulz-Thornycroft and 8 cylindrical; *Kaiser Karl der Grosse:* 6 cylindrical, 2 Marine-Doppel and 2 Marine: *Kaiser Wilhelm II:* 4 Marine and 8 cylindrical; *Kaiser Wilhelm der Grosse;* 4 Marine and 6 cylindrical
IHP 13,500 = 17.5knots
Endurance: 2,250/12
Armament: 4×240mm/40, 18×150mm/40, 14×88mm/30, 6×450mm TT
1907: 4×150mm and 1 TT removed
Armour: Belt 150-300mm, turrets 250mm, casemates 150mm, deck 60mm, c/t 250mm
Complement: 622
Class notes: Larger vessels than previous class with less powerful armament and weaker protection. Two twin turrets fore and aft and secondary armament in casemates and turrets. All except *Kaiser Karl der Grosse* modernised 1908-10, new funnels and casemates, and pole masts replaced military masts

'Fürst Bismarck' (1895)

Armoured Cruiser: *Fürst Bismarck*
Displacement: 10,700tons, 11,461f/l
Dimensions: 416'8(oa) 412'4(pp)×67×27'6 [127(oa) 125.7(pp)×20.4×8.4]
Machinery: 3 screws, VTE engines (Germania), 4 Schulz-Thornycroft and 8 cylindrical boilers
IHP 13,500 = 18knots
Endurance: 4,560/10
Armament: 4×240/40, 12×150/40, 10×88mm, 6×450mm TT
Armour: Belt 100-200mm, turrets 200mm, casemates 100mm, c/t 200mm
Complement: 593
Class notes: First German armoured cruiser. Enlarged 'Victoria Louise' type with heavier armament and additional armour

'Prinz Heinrich' (1897)

Armoured Cruiser: *Prinz Heinrich*
Displacement: 8,900tons, 9,800f/l
Dimensions: 415(oa) 409'9(wl)×64'4×26'3 [126'5(oa) 124.9(pp)×19.6×8]
Machinery: 3 screws, VTE engines, 14 Durr boilers
IHP 15,000 = 20knots
Endurance: 4,580/10
Armament: 2×240mm/40, 10×150mm/40, 10×88mm/30, 4×450mm TT
Armour: Belt 80-100mm, turrets 150mm, c/t 150mm

Top left:
***Arminius* — Monitor, after removal of rigging in 1871.** *Foto Druppel*

Centre left:
***Kronprinz* — Armoured frigate, completed in 1867, at a review in the 1870s.** *IWM*

Bottom left:
***König Wilhelm* — Armoured frigate before reconstruction. Designed for Turkey but purchased by Prussia in 1867 prior to launching.** *IWM*

Top left:
***Friedrich der Grosse* — Turret ship, 'Preussen' class, as completed with full rig.** *Foto Druppel*

Top centre:
***Kaiser* — Central battery ship, as completed with square rig.** *Foto Druppel*

Top right:
***Baden* — Barbette ship of 'Sachsen' class as reconstructed, 1902.** *IWM*

Far left:
***Oldenburg* — Barbette ship of 1883. Notice three guns in gunports and the single one above in the central citadel.** *IWM*

Left:
***Beowulf* — 'Siegfried' class coast defence ship, after reconstruction, c1906.** *Foto Druppel*

Below left:
***Brandenburg* — Pre-dreadnought as completed 1893. Notice distinctive masts.** *IWM*

Below:
***Kaiser Friedrich III* — Pre-dreadnought shortly after completion 1900.** *US Naval Historical Centre*

Complement: 567
Class notes: Built for foreign service, more lightly armed and armoured than *Fürst Bismarck*

'Mecklenburg' Class (1899-1900)

Pre-dreadnoughts: *Mecklenburg, Schwaben, Wettin, Wittelsbach* (see later photo), *Zähringen*
Displacement: 11,774tons, 12,798f/l
Dimensions: 416(oa) 410'9(wl)×74'10×26'9 [126.8(oa) 125.2(wl)×22.8×8]
Machinery: 3 screws, VTE engines (builders), 6 Marine and 6 cylindrical boilers; (*Mecklenburg* and *Wettin:* 6 Schulz-Thornycroft and 6 cylindrical)
IHP 15,000 = 18knots
Endurance: 5,850/10
Armament: 4×240mm/40, 18×150mm/40, 12×88mm/30, 6×450mm TT
Armour: Belt 100-225mm, turrets 250mm, casemates 140mm, c/t 250mm
Complement: 683
Class notes: Improved 'Kaiser Friedrich' class. Slow and weakly armed. *Schwaben* and *Wittelsbach* converted to minesweeper depot ships and carriers 1919, turrets removed and platform for carrying 12 F-boats erected. *Zähringen* became target ship 1926

'Prinz Adalbert' Class (1899)

Armoured Cruisers: *Friedrich Carl, Prinz Adalbert*
Displacement: 9,050tons, 9,875f/l
Dimensions: 415(oa) 409'9(pp)×64'4×25'8 [126.5(oa) 124.9(pp)×19.6×7.8]
Machinery: 3 screws, VTE engines (builders), 14 Durr boilers; *1908: Friedrich Carl:* Schulz-Thornycroft
IHP 16,200 = 20knots; *Friedrich Carl:* IHP 17,000 = 20.5knots
Endurance: 6,750/10
Armament: 4×210mm/40, 10×150mm/40, 12×88mm/35, 4×450mm TT
Armour: Belt 80-100mm, turrets 150mm, casemates and citadel 100mm, deck 80mm, c/t 150mm
Complement: 591
Class notes: Similar to *Prinz Heinrich* with three funnels and twin main turrets. Poorly designed with weak protection

'Braunschweig' Class (1900-1902)

Pre-dreadnoughts: *Braunschweig, Elsass, Hessen* (see later photo), *Lothringen, Preussen*
Displacement: 13,200tons, 14,394f/l
Dimensions: 419(oa) 413'4(wl)×84×26'6 [127.7(oa) 126(wl)×25.6×8.1]

Top left:
***Fürst Bismarck* — Armoured cruiser of 1895.**
Foto Druppel

Centre left:
***Schwaben* — Battleship of 'Mecklenburg' class, underway.** *Foto Druppel*

Bottom left:
***Prinz Adalbert* — Armoured cruiser underway c1905.**
Foto Druppel

Machinery: 3 screws, VTE engines (builders), 8 Schulz-Thornycroft and 6 cylindrical boilers; *Hessen, 1923:* cylindrical replaced by two Oil Marine
IHP 16,000 = 18knots
Endurance: 6,500/10
Armament: 4×280mm/40, 14×170mm/40, 18×88mm/35, 6×450mm TT
Braunschweig, Elsass and *Hessen, 1924:* 4×280mm/40, 12×170mm/40 (*Elsass:* 10; *Hessen:* 14), 4×88mm/45, 4×500mm TT (*Braunschweig:* 2)
Armour: Belt 100-225mm, turrets 250mm, casemates 150mm, secondary turrets 150mm, citadel 140mm, deck 40mm, c/t 300mm
Complement: 743
Class notes: Improved 'Mecklenburg' class with new rapid loading and heavier guns. Three funnels and some secondary guns in turrets. *Lothringen* and *Preussen* converted to minesweeper depot ships in same manner as *Schwaben*. *Braunschweig, Elsass* and *Hessen* remained in service after World War 1 with revised armament. *Hessen* became target ship 1935

'Roon' Class (1901)

Armoured Cruisers: *Roon, Yorck*
Displacement: 9,500tons, 10,260fl
Dimensions: 419'3(oa) 417'8(wl)×66'3×25'3 [127.8(oa) 127.3(wl)×20.2×7.7]
Machinery: 3 screws, VTE engines (builders), 16 Durr boilers
IHP 19,000 = 21knots
Endurance: 4,300/12
Armament: 4×210mm/40, 10×150mm/40, 14×88mm/35, 4×450mm TT
Armour: Belt 80-100mm, turrets 150mm, casemates 100mm, deck 60mm, c/t 150mm
Complement: 633
Class notes: Improved 'Prinz Adalbert' class with four funnels but not very successful. Poor protection. Conversion of *Roon* to seaplane depot ship abandoned 1917

'Deutschland' Class (1902-1904)

Pre-dreadnoughts: *Deutschland, Hannover, Pommern, Schlesien, Schleswig-Holstein* (see later photo)
Displacement: 13,191tons, 14,218f/l
Dimensions: 418'8(oa) 413(wl)×72'10×27 [127.6(oa)125.9(wl)×22.2×8.2]
Machinery: 3 screws, VTE engines (builders), 12 Schulz-Thornycroft boilers
IHP 20,000 = 18knots
Endurance: 4,800/12
Armament: 4×280mm/40, 14×170mm/40, 20×88mm/35, 6×450mm TT
Hannover, Schlesien and *Schleswig-Holstein, 1922:* 4×280mm/40, 14×150mm/45 (*Hannover:* 14×170mm/45), 4×88mm/45
All three, 1935: 4×500mm TT added
All three, 1937: 6×105mm added
c1939: 150mm removed
Armour: Belt 100-240mm (*Deutschland:* 100-225mm), turrets 280mm, citadel 170mm (*Deutschland:* 160mm), deck 40mm, c/t 300mm
Complement: 743
Class notes: Last pre-dreadnoughts similar to 'Braunschweig' class with better protected turrets and all secondary guns in casemates. *Hannover, Schlesien* and *Schleswig-Holstein* retained in postwar fleet and rearmed. Latter two reconstructed 1931-35, two forward funnels trunked together

'Scharnhorst' Class (1903)

Armoured Cruisers: *Gneisenau* (see later photo), *Scharnhorst*
Displacement: 11,600tons, 12,900f/l
Dimensions: 474'4(oa) 471'10(wl)×70'10×26 [144.6(oa) 143.8(wl)×21.6×7.9]
Machinery: 3 screws, VTE engines (builders), 18 Schulz-Thornycroft boilers
IHP 26,000 = 22.5knots
Endurance: 5,120/12
Armament: 8×210mm/40, 6×150mm/40, 18×88mm/35, 4×450mm TT
Armour: Belt 80-150mm, turrets 170mm, casemates and citadel 150m, bulkhead 40-55mm, deck 60mm, c/t 200mm
Complement: 764
Class notes: Enlarged 'Roon' class with greater armament in two twin turrets and four guns in casemates

'Blücher' (1905)

Armoured Cruiser: *Blücher*
Displacement: 15,550tons, 17.500f/l
Dimensions: 530'10(oa) 528'6(wl)×80'5×28'10 [161.8(oa) 161.1(wl)×24.5×8.8]
Machinery: 3 screws, VTE engines (builder), 18 Schulz-Thornycroft boilers
IHP 34,000 = 24.8knots
Endurance: 6,600/12
Armament: 12×210mm/45, 8×150mm/45, 16×88mm/45, 4×450mm TT
Armour: Belt 80-180mm, turrets 180mm, citadel 160mm, deck 70mm, c/t 250mm
Complement: 888
Class notes: Built as reply to British secret 'Invincible' class. Design based on purposely misleading information and was outgunned as a battlecruiser. Tripod foremast fitted 1913

'Nassau' Class (1906)

Dreadnoughts: *Nassau, Posen, Rheinland, Westfalen*
Displacement: 18,873tons, 20,535f/l
Dimensions: 479'4(oa) 477'8(wl) 451'6(pp)×88'4×28'9 [146.1(oa) 145.6(wl) 137.6(pp)×26.9×8.7]
Machinery: 3 screws, VTE engines (builders), 12 Schulz-Thornycroft boilers
IHP 22,000 = 19.5knots
Endurance: 9,400/10
Armament: 12×280mm/45, 12×150mm/45, 16×88mm/45, 6×450mm TT
1915: 2×88mm AA replaced 2×88mm
Armour: Belt 100-290mm, turrets 220-280mm, deck 80mm, casemates 160mm, c/t 304mm
Complement: 1,008
Class notes: First German dreadnoughts. Shorter and wider than *Dreadnought* and less heavily armed but well protected. Poor disposition of main armament with two turrets on each side amidships and one each fore and aft limited broadside fire

'Von der Tann' (1907)

Battlecruiser: *Von der Tann*
Displacement: 19,370tons, 21,300f/l
Dimensions: 563'4(oa) 562'9(wl)×87'3×29'10 [171.7(oa) 171.5(wl)×26.6×9.1]
Machinery: 4 screws, Parsons turbines (builder), 18 Schulz-Thornycroft boilers
IHP 42,000 = 24.75knots
Endurance: 4,400/14
Armament: 8×280mm/45, 10×150mm/45, 16×88mm/45, 4×450mm TT
1915: 4×88mm AA replaced 4×88mm
Armour: Belt 100-250mm, turrets 230mm, barbettes 175-230mm, deck 50-75mm, secondary battery 150mm, c/t 250mm
Complement: 910
Class notes: First German battlecruiser and first major German warship built with turbines and four screws. Better protection than contemporary British battlecruisers. Four twin turrets all able to fire on broadside

'Helgoland' Class (1908)

Dreadnoughts: *Helgoland, Oldenburg, Ostfriesland* (see later photo), *Thüringen*
Displacement: 22,800tons, 24,700f/l
Dimensions: 548'6(oa) 546'3(wl)×93'6×29'3 [167.2(oa) 166.5(wl)×28.5×8.9]
Machinery: 3 screws, VTE engines (builders), 15 Schulz-Thornycroft boilers
IHP 28,000 = 20.3knots
Endurance: 3,600/18
Armament: 12×305mm/50, 14×150mm/45, 14×88mm/45, 6×500mm TT
1914: 2×88mm AA replaced 2×88mm
1916: 12×88mm removed
Armour: Belt 170-300mm, turrets 100-300mm, deck 60mm, c/t 300mm
Complement: 1,100
Class notes: Enlarged 'Nassau' class with 305mm guns. Only German dreadnoughts with three funnels, and very small superstructure. Funnels raised after completion

'Moltke' Class (1908-1909)

Battlecruisers: *Goeben* (see later photo), *Moltke*
Displacement: 22,979tons, 25,400f/l
Dimensions: 611'10(oa) 610'3(wl)×96'9×30'2 [186.5(oa) 186(wl)×29.5×9.2]
Machinery: 4 screws, Parsons turbines (builders), 24 Schulz-Thornycroft boilers
SHP 52,000 = 25.5knots
Endurance: 4,120/14
Armament: 10×280mm/50, 12×150mm/45, 12×88mm/45, 4×500mm TT
1915: 4×88mm AA replaced 4×88mm
Armour: Belt 95-265mm, turrets 230mm, battery 125mm, deck 50mm, c/t 350mm
Complement: 1,107
Class notes: Enlarged 'Von der Tann' type with stronger protection, an additional turret aft and turret arrangement as in 'Kaiser' class battleships. *Goeben* was the only German capital ship to serve outside the High Seas Fleet during the war and was transferred to Turkey

'Kaiser' Class (1909-1910)

Dreadnoughts: *Friedrich Der Grosse* (see later photo), *Kaiser* (see also later photo), *Kaiserin, König Albert, Prinzregent Luitpold*

Above right:
***Elsass* — Pre-dreadnought of 'Braunschweig' class.**
Foto Druppel

Below right:
***Roon* — Armoured cruiser in Kiel Canal 1910.**
US Naval Historical Centre

Displacement: 24,724tons, 27,000f/l
Dimensions: 565′8(oa) 563′8(wl)×95′2×29′9 [172.4(oa) 171.8(wl)×29×9.1]
Machinery: 3 screws, Parsons turbines (*Friedrich der Grosse:* Curtis; *König Albert:* Schichau), 16 Schulz-Thornycroft boilers; *Prinzregent Luitpold:* 2 screws, Parsons turbines and diesel (builder), 1 Germania and 14 naval boilers
SHP 31,000 = 21knots; *Prinzregent Luitpold:* SHP 26,000 = 20knots
Endurance: 7,900/12
Armament: 10×305mm/50, 14×150mm/45, 8×88mm/45, 4×88mm AA, 5×500mm TT
1916: 88mm removed
Armour: Belt 150-350mm, turrets 80-305mm, deck 100mm, casemates 170mm, c/t 355-400mm
Complement: 1,088
Class notes: First German battleships with turbines and with a superfiring turret (aft). *Prinzregent Luitpold* designed to have a combination of turbine and diesel machinery but diesel engines never installed. *Friedrich der Grosse* built as fleet flagship and, with *Kaiser,* had heavy foremast fitted in 1914

'Seydlitz' (1910)

Battlecruiser: *Seydlitz* (see also later photo)
Displacement: 24,988tons, 28,550f/l
Dimensions: 658′2(oa) 656′2(wl)×93′6×30′6 [200.6(oa) 200(wl)×28.5×9.3]
Machinery: 4 screws, Parsons turbines (builder), 27 Schulz-Thornycroft boilers
SHP 67,000 = 26.5knots
Endurance: 4,200/14
Armament: 10×280mm/50, 12×150mm/45, 12×88mm/45, 4×500mm TT
1916: All 88mm removed, 2×88mm AA added
Armour: Belt 100-300mm, turrets 250mm, casemates 150mm, deck 30-80mm, c/t 300mm
Complement: 1,108
Class notes: Enlarged 'Moltke' type. Excellent sea boat. Survived very heavy damage at Jutland reaching harbour with forecastle awash

'König' Class (1911)

Dreadnoughts: *Grosser Kurfürst, König, Kronprinz, Markgraf* (see later photo)
Displacement: 25,796tons, 28,600f/l
Dimensions: 575′6(oa) 573′3(wl)×96′9×30′2 [175.4(oa) 174.7(wl)×29.5×9.2]
Machinery: 3 screws, Parsons turbines (*Grosser Kurfürst:* AEG; *Markgraf:* Bergmann), 15 Schulz-Thornycroft boilers
SHP 31,000 = 21knots
Endurance: 8,000/12
Armament: 10×305mm/50, 14×150mm/45, 8×88mm/45, 8×88mm AA, 5×500mm TT
1916: 88mm removed

Top left:
***Schlesien* — Battleship of 'Deutschland' class as reconstructed, April 1937.** *R. Perkins*

Centre left:
***Scharnhorst* — Armoured cruiser as completed, 1907.** *IWM*

Bottom left:
***Blücher* — Armoured cruiser, after fitting of tripod foremast, 1913. Sunk at the Doggerbank 1914.** *Foto Druppel*

Armour: Belt 120-350mm, turrets 300mm, casemates 170mm, deck 100mm, c/t 355-400mm
Complement: 1,150
Class notes: First German battleships with all turrets on the centreline. Better protection than contemporary ships. All were planned to have diesel engines in place of one turbine. *König* and *Grosser Kurfürst* built with pole masts but heavy foremast fitted in all by 1916

'Derfflinger' Class (1912-1913)

Battlecruisers: *Derfflinger* (see later photo), *Hindenburg, Lützow*
Displacement: 26,600 tons, 31,200f/l; *Hindenburg:* 26,947tons, 31,500f/l
Dimensions: 690′4(oa) 689(wl)×95′2×31′2 [210.4(oa) 210(wl)×29×9.5]
Hindenburg: 698′2(oa) 697′2(wl) [212.8(oa) 212.5(wl)]
Machinery: 4 screws, Parsons geared turbines, 14 twin and 2 double-ended boilers
SHP 63,000 = 26.5knots; *Hindenburg:* SHP 72,000 = 27knots
Endurance: 5,300/14
Armament: *Derfflinger:* 8×305mm/50, 12×150mm/45, 12×88mm/45, 4×500mm TT
Hindenburg and *Lützow:* 8×305mm/50, 14×150mm/45, 4×88mm/45 AA, 4×600mm TT
Armour: Belt 100-300mm, turrets 270mm, casemates 150mm, citadel 270mm, deck 30-80mm, c/t 300mm
Complement: 1,215
Class notes: Called the best capital ships of their time. Carried 305mm guns in four twin turrets. *Hindenburg* completed with tripod foremast and *Derfflinger* modified similarly 1916. Funnels differed in all three

'Baden' Class (1913)

Dreadnoughts: *Baden, Bayern* (see later photo), *[Sachsen, Württemberg]*
Displacement: 28,600tons, 32,200f/l; *Sachsen:* 28,800tons, 32,500f/l
Dimensions: 590′6(oa) 588′6(wl)×98′6×30′6 [180(oa) 179.4(wl)×30×9.3]
Sachsen: 600(oa) 598′6(wl) [183(oa) 182.4(wl)]
Machinery: 3 screws, Parsons geared turbines (*Bayern:* Schichau; *Württemberg:* AEG), 11 boilers; *Sachsen:* Parsons turbines and diesel-electric engines
SHP 35,000 = 22knots
Endurance: 5,000/12
Armament: 8×381mm/45, 16×150mm/45, 8×88mm/45, 5×600mm TT
Armour: Belt 170-350mm, turrets 250-350mm, casemates 170mm, deck 100mm, c/t 400mm
Complement: 1,171
Class notes: Modified 'König' type without central barbette; 381mm guns and tripod foremast. Built as a reply to and generally similar to the British 'Queen Elizabeth' class but slower. *Baden* was fleet flagship. Pole mainmast added 1918. *Sachsen* designed with combination turbine and diesel-electric engines

'Mackensen' Class (1914)

Battlecruisers: *[Graf Spee, Mackensen* (see later photo), + *Fürst Bismarck, Prinz Eitel Friedrich]*
Displacement: 31,000tons, 35,300f/l
Dimensions: 734′10(oa) 731′8(wl)×99′7×30′6 [224(oa) 223(wl)×30.4×9.3]
Machinery: 4 screws, Parsons geared turbines, 16 double

ended boilers (*Mackensen:* 8 double-ended and 24 single-ended boilers)
SHP 90,000 = 27knots
Endurance: 5,500/14
Armament: 8×356mm/50, 14×150mm/45, 8×88mm/45 AA, 5×600mm TT
Armour: Belt 120-300mm, turrets 100-300mm, deck 30mm, c/t 350mm
Complement: 1,186
Class notes: Improved and enlarged 'Derfflinger' type with 356mm guns. Names of the last two are intended names as they were never launched, the time of official naming. None was ever completed

'Ersatz Yorck' Class (1915)

Battlecruisers: *[Ersatz Yorck, Ersatz Gneisenau, Ersatz Scharnhorst]*
Displacement: 33,500tons, 38,000f/l
Dimensions: 748(oa)×99'9×30'6 [228(oa)×30.4×9.3]
Machinery: 4 screws, Parsons geared turbines, 16 double-ended boilers
SHP 90,000 = 27.25knots
Endurance: 5,500/14
Armament: 8×381mm/45, 12×150mm/45, 8×88mm/45 AA, 3×600mm TT
Armour: Belt 100-300mm, turrets 150-250mm, deck 90mm, c/t 350mm
Complement: 1,227
Class notes: Originally planned to be of same class as 'Mackensen' type but redesigned in 1916 as response to British 'Renown' class. 381mm guns and single massive funnel. Never assigned names

'Deutschland' Class (1928-1931)

Armoured Ships: *Admiral Graf Spee, Admiral Scheer* (see later photo), *Deutschland*
Displacement: 11,700tons, 15,900f/l; *Graf Spee:* 12,100tons, 16,200f/l
Dimensions: 610'3(oa) 596'2(wl)×67'9×23'9 [186(oa) 181.7(wl)×20.7×7.2]
Graf Spee: 71'2 [21.7] beam ; *Scheer* and *Deutschland, 1940:* 616'6(oa) [187.9(oa)]
Machinery: 2 screws, diesel engines
BHP 55,400 = 26knots
Endurance: 10,000/20
Armament: 6×280mm/54, 8×150mm/55, 3×88mm/45 AA, 8×533mm TT
1935: 88mm replaced by 6×88mm/76 AA
1938: 88mm replaced by 6×105mm/65 AA
Armour: Belt 50-80mm, turrets 140mm, deck 18-40mm, c/t 150mm
Complement: 926
Class notes: Designed under restrictions of Versailles Treaty as raiders with large radius of action. Popularly known as 'pocket battleships' as they were too small for a battleship but more powerful and faster than most other warships. Electrically welded construction, less armour protection and diesel engines saved weight and permitted high speed. *Scheer* and *Graf Spee* had large armoured towers but this was replaced in *Scheer* in 1940 with lighter pole type mast as in *Deutschland.* Both were given prominent funnel caps and increased AA protection 1939-40. *Scheer* and *Deutschland* were reclassified heavy cruisers 1940

'Scharnhorst' Class (1933-1934)

Battlecruisers: *Gneisenau, Scharnhorst*
Displacement: 31,850tons, 34,900f/l
Dimensions: 754(oa) 741'6(wl)×98'6×32'6 [229.8(oa) 226(wl)×30×9.9] *1939:* 770'6(oa) [234'9]
Machinery: 3 screws, Brown-Boveri (*Scharnhorst*), Germania (*Gneisenau*), geared turbines, 12 Wagner boilers
SHP 160,000 = 31knots
Endurance: 8,800/19
Armament: 9×280mm/54, 12×150mm/55, 14×105mm/65 AA, 16×37mm AA, 6×533mm TT
Armour: Belt 70-350mm, turrets 150-360mm, barbettes 200-350mm, deck 50-105mm, c/t 350mm
Complement: 1,800
Class notes: Design based on 'Mackensen' class. Sacrificed weight of armament by retaining 280mm guns instead of protection to obtain high speed. Straight stem altered to clipper bow in 1939. Mainmast stepped abaft funnel but in *Scharnhorst* was moved further aft in 1939. Funnel caps added in both. Plan to replace 280mm turrets with twin 380mm turrets abandoned

'Bismarck' Class (1935-1937)

Battleships: *Bismarck* (see later photo), *Tirpitz*
Displacement: *Bismarck:* 41,700tons, 50,900f/l
Tirpitz: 42,900tons, 52,600f/l
Dimensions: 813'8(oa) 788(wl)×118'2×33'9 [248(oa) 240.2(wl)×36×10.2]; *1940:* 823'6(oa)/[251(oa)]
Machinery: 3 screws, Brown-Boveri geared turbines, 12 Wagner boilers
SHP 138,000 = 29knots
Endurance: *Bismarck:* 8,100/19; *Tirpitz:* 9,000/19
Armament: 8×380mm/47, 12×150mm/55, 16×105mm/65 AA, 16×37mm AA
Tirpitz, 1942: 8×533mm TT
Armour: Belt 220-320mm, turrets 360mm, secondary turrets 100mm, citadel 145mm, deck 100-120mm, c/t 350mm
Complement: 2,400
Class notes: Largest German battleships actually built with large percentage of weight given to armour protection. Straight stem of original design changed to clipper bow after launching

'Graf Zeppelin' (1935)

Aircraft Carriers: *[Graf Zeppelin]* + 1 unnamed
Displacement: 23,200tons, 33,550f/l
Dimensions: 861'3(oa) 820'3(wl)×118'9×27'10 [262.5(oa) 250(wl)×36.2×8.5]
Machinery: 4 screws, Brown-Boveri geared turbines, 16 LaMont boilers
SHP 200,000 = 33.75knots
Endurance: 8,000/19
Aircraft: 42
Armament: 16×150mm/55, 12×105mm/65, 22×37mm AA
Armour: Belt 80-100mm, deck 60mm, c/t 150mm
Complement: 1,760+aircrew
Class notes: Only German aircraft carrier planned. Lack of experience with this type of vessel resulted in design changes and delays in construction which was finally halted in 1943. Flightdeck and hangars were unprotected

'H' Class (1938)

Battleships: *[H, J, K, L, M, N]*
Displacement: 56,200tons, 68,000f/l
Dimensions: 911'5(oa) 872'9(pp)×123'4×36'9 [277.8(oa) 266(pp)×37.6×11.2]
Machinery: 3 screws, MAN geared diesel engines

BHP 165,000 = 30knots
Endurance: 19,000/16
Armament: 8×406mm/47, 14×150mm/55, 16×105mm/65, 6×533mm TT
Armour: Belt 220-320mm, turrets 385mm, secondary turrets 100mm, deck 100-120mm, c/t 350mm
Complement: 2,600
Class notes: *H* and *J* were laid down before plans were completed. Heavier armour protection and larger guns than in 'Bismarck' class. Were to have diesel propulsion. Last four were projected only and never named. Builders were to be Weser (*K*), Wilhelmshaven (*L*), Blohm & Voss (*M*) and Deutsche Werke (*N*). Final design included four twin turrets, two large funnels and tower superstructure.

'Q' Class (1939)

Battlecruisers: *[O, P, Q]*
Displacement: 32,300 tons, 38,200f/l
Dimensions: 841'6(oa) 807(wl)×98'6×36'9 [265.5(oa) 246(wl)×30×11.2]
Machinery: 3 screws, Brown Boveri geared turbines and MAN geared diesel engines
SHP 116,000+60,000 = 33.5knots
Endurance: 14,000/19
Armament: 6×381mm/47, 6×150mm/48, 8×105mm/65 AA, 8×37mm AA, 6×533mm TT
Armour: Belt 100-180mm, turrets 210mm, deck 80-110mm, citadel 80mm, c/t 200mm
Complement: 1,965
Class notes: Design sacrificed armament and protection for speed with only six guns of main armament in twin turrets but strong deck armour against air attack. Combined diesel and turbine propulsion. Projected only, builders were to be Deutsche Werke (*O*), Wilhelmshaven (*P*) and Germania (*Q*). Never named

Individual Ships

Admiral Graf Spee

Type: Armoured Ship
Class: 'Deutschland' (1929)
Nomenclature: Count Maximilian von Spee (1861-1914), vice-admiral, commander at Coronel and the Falklands

History:
1932 October 1: Laid down by Wilhelmshaven as *Ersatz Braunschweig*
1934 June 30: Launched
1936 January 6: Completed
1936-37 Spain
World War 2
1939 September-November: Sortie into South Atlantic, sinking or capturing merchant ships *Clement*, *Newton Beach*, *Ashlea*, *Huntsman*, *Trevanion*, *Africa Shell*, *Doric Star*, *Tairoa* and *Streonshah*
1939 December 13: Damaged in action with British cruisers off the River Plate estuary
1939 December 17: Scuttled off Montevideo

Admiral Scheer

Type: Armoured Ship
Class: 'Deutschland' (1929)
Nomenclature: Reinhard Scheer (1864-1928), admiral, commander of German High Seas Fleet at Jutland

History:
1931 June 25: Laid down by Wilhelmshaven as *Ersatz Lothringen*
1933 April 1: Launched
1934 November 12: Completed
1937 May 31: Shelled Almeria, Spain, in retaliation for bombing of sistership *Deutschland*
1939-40 Refit; raked bow, new c/t and foremast replaced armoured tower, increased AA armament
World War 2: Atlantic raids, 1942 Arctic, 1943-45 Baltic
1940 October: Commenced five-month raid into Atlantic and Indian Oceans
1940 November 5: Attacked convoy HX84 sinking auxiliary cruiser *Jervis Bay* and merchant ships *Maiden*, *Trewellard*, *Beaverford*, *Kenbane Head* and *Fresno City*; also sank *Port Hobart*, *Tribesman* and captured *Duquesa* in December
1941 January: Sank merchant ships *Sandefjord*, *Barnevelt* and *Stanpark* in South Atlantic
1941 February: Sank merchant ships *Canadian Cruiser*, *British Advocate*, *Rantaupandjang* and *Grigonos CII* in Indian Ocean
1942 August: Sortie into Kara Sea, bombarded shore stations and sank icebreakers *Aleksandr Sibiriakov*, *Taimyr* and *Valerian Kuibyshev*
1944 November-1945 February: Fire support for ground forces in Baltic Sea
1945 April 9: Capsized at dock at Kiel after being damaged by British aircraft bombs (32 dead)

Ägir

Type: Coast Defence Ship
Class: 'Odin' (1892)
Nomenclature: Norse myth: the god of the sea

History:
1892 Laid down by Kiel as *T*
1895 April 3: Launched
1896 October 15: Completed
1899 August 28: Damaged in collision with British merchant ship *Aberfoyle* in North Sea
1903-04 Reconstructed at Danzig
World War 1: 1915 Coast defence
1916 Accommodation ship, Wilhelmshaven
1919 June 17: Stricken
1922 Converted to motorship for use as merchant ship
1929 December 8: Wrecked off Karlso LH, Gotland

Arminius

Type: Coast Defence Monitor
Class: 'Arminius' (1862)
Nomenclature: Arminius (c17BC-21AD), German national hero who organised a rebellion against the Roman armies

History:
1863 Laid down by Samuda as a speculation
1864 August 20: Launched
1865 April 22: Completed
1870 Defence of the Elbe Estuary
1870 October 18: Damaged in collision with despatch vessel *Falke* off Wilhelmshaven
1872 Engineer's training ship
1892 Icebreaker, Kiel
1901 March: Sold and broken up 1902 at Hamburg

Baden

Type: Barbette Ship

Above left:
***Nassau* — The first German dreadnought, during inclining tests.** *Foto Druppel*

Above centre:
***Von der Tann* — Germany's first battlecruiser as completed.** *Foto Druppel*

Above right:
***Thüringen* — Dreadnought of 'Helgoland' class, as completed.** *Foto Druppel*

Right:
***Moltke* — Battlecruiser of 'Moltke' class.** *Foto Druppel*

Far right:
***Kaiser* — Dreadnought at wharf, 1914, with *Kaiserin* behind.** *Conway Photo Library*

Below:
***Seydlitz* — Battlecruiser as completed, 1913.** *Foto Druppel*

Below right:
***König* — Dreadnought of 'König' class.** *Foto Druppel*

Class: 'Sachsen' (1875)
Nomenclature: Baden, a sovereign grand duchy of the German Empire

History:
1876 Laid down by Kiel as *D*
1880 July 28: Launched
1883 October 13: Completed
1896-97 Reconstructed at Germania
1910 October 24: Stricken, gate hulk
1920 Target hulk
1938 April 23: Sold and broken up at Kiel

Baden

Type: Dreadnought
Class: 'Baden' (1913)

History:
1913 September 29: Laid down by Schichau as *Ersatz Wörth*
1915 October 30: Launched
1916 October 19: Completed
World War 1: High Seas Fleet 1917-18
1917-18 Fleet Flagship
1918 December 14: Interned at Scapa Flow
1919 June 21: Scuttled at Scapa Flow, towed ashore and beached
1919 July: Refloated; used as gunnery target
1921 August 16: Sunk as a target by British warships off Portsmouth

Above:
***Hindenburg* — Battlecruiser of 'Derfflinger' class as completed with tripod mast, at Scapa Flow.**
Foto Druppel

Left:
***Baden* — Dreadnought, 1918.**

Below:
***Admiral Graf Spee* — Armoured ship or 'pocket battleship', at the Coronation Review, May 1937. Note 11" turret and massive tower foremast.** *Wright & Logan*

Bayern

Type: Barbette Ship
Class: 'Sachsen' (1875)
Nomenclature: Bavaria, a sovereign kingdom of the German Empire

History:
1874 Laid down by Kiel as *A*
1878 May 13: Launched
1882 April 1: Completed
1895-98 Reconstructed by Schichau
1910 February 19: Stricken, target ship
1919 May 5: Sold and broken up at Kiel

Bayern

Type: Dreadnought
Class: 'Baden' (1913)

History:
1913 September 20: Laid down by Howaldt as *T*
1915 February 18: Launched
1916 March 18: Completed
World War 1: 1917 Gulf of Riga, High Seas Fleet 1917-18
1917 October 12: Damaged by a mine in Baltic Sea
1918 November 26: Interned at Scapa Flow
1919 June 21: Scuttled at Scapa Flow
1934 September: Refloated and broken up at Rosyth

Beowulf

Type: Coast Defence Ship
Class: 'Siegfried' (1887)
Nomenclature: Mythical hero of an old English epic story

Top:
Gneisenau — Battlecruiser after modifications of 1939. Notice mainmast on funnel and clipper bow.
Foto Druppel

Above:
Graf Zeppelin — Hull of incomplete aircraft carrier (at Gdynia or Stettin) June 1941. *Erich Groner Archiv*

Top right:
Keel of an 'H' class battleship, to be named *Grossdeutschland*, 1939.

Right:
***Admiral Scheer* — 'Pocket battleship' now classified as a heavy cruiser with new foremast replacing armoured tower, 1941.**

022 61

History:
1890 Laid down by Weser as *P*
1890 November 8: Launched
1892 April 1: Completed
1902-04 Reconstructed at Danzig
World War 1: 1915 Coast defence, 1916 U-boat target ship
1918 Icebreaker in Baltic Sea
1919 June 17: Stricken
1921 Broken up at Danzig

Bismarck

Type: Battleship
Class: 'Bismarck' (1935)
Nomenclature: Prince Otto Eduard Leopold von Bismarck-Schönhausen (1815-1898), Prussian statesman and first chancellor of the German Empire

History:
1936 July 1: Laid down by Blohm & Voss as *F* or *Ersatz Hannover*
1939 February 14: Launched
1940 August 24: Completed
1941 May 24: Sank British battlecruiser *Hood* in action off Iceland
1941 May 27: Sunk by gunfire and torpedoes of British fleet 300 miles northwest of Brest (1,977 dead); flagship of Vice-Adm Gunther Lutjens who was lost

Blücher

Type: Armoured Cruiser
Class: 'Blücher' (1905)
Nomenclature: Gebhard Leberecht von Blücher, Prince von Wahlstatt (1742-1819), Prussian field marshal during the Napoleonic Wars, joint victor of Waterloo

History:
1906 October: Laid down by Kiel as *E*
1908 April 11: Launched
1909 October 1: Completed
1911 Refit, regunned
1913 Refit, tripod foremast fitted
1911-14 Gunnery training ship
World War 1: Doggerbank
1915 January 24: Sunk by gunfire of British warships at Battle of the Doggerbank (792 dead)

Borussia, see **Preussen**

Brandenburg

Type: Pre-dreadnought
Class: 'Brandenburg' (1889)
Nomenclature: A province of Prussia

Top left:
***Bayern* — Dreadnought of 'Baden' class, 1917.**
Foto Druppel

Centre left:
***Bismarck* — Battleship leaving the shipyard, 1940.**

Bottom left:
***Derfflinger* — Battlecruiser of 'Derfflinger' class, 1917, with tripod foremast.** *Foto Druppel*

History:
1890 Laid down by Vulcan as *A*
1891 September 21: Launched
1893 November 19: Completed
1903-04 Refitted at Wilhelmshaven
World War 1: 1915 Coast defence
1916 Accommodation and distilling ship, Libau
1918 Conversion to target ship cancelled
1919 May 13: Stricken
1920 Broken up at Danzig

Braunschweig

Type: Pre-dreadnought
Class: 'Braunschweig' (1900)
Nomenclature: Brunswick, a sovereign duchy of the German Empire

History:
1901 October 24: Laid down by Germania as *H*
1902 December 20: Launched
1904 October 15: Completed
1916 Drill and accommodation ship, Kiel
1921-22 Refitted and rearmed by Wilhelmshaven
1931 March 31: Stricken and hulked

Derfflinger

Type: Battlecruiser
Class: 'Derfflinger' (1912)
Nomenclature: Baron Georg von Derfflinger (1606-1695), Brandenburg field marshal

History:
1912 January: Laid down by Blohm & Voss as *K*
1913 June 14: First attempt to launch unsuccessful
1913 July 12: Launched
1914 September 1: Completed
World War 1: High Seas Fleet 1914-18, Doggerbank, Jutland
1914 December 16: Bombarded Scarborough and Whitby
1915 January 24: Damaged at Battle of the Doggerbank
1915 August: Operations in Gulf of Riga
1916 April 25: Bombarded Lowestoft and Yarmouth
1916 May 31: Severely damaged at Battle of Jutland (21 hits, 157 dead)
1918 November 24: Interned at Scapa Flow
1919 June 21: Scuttled at Scapa Flow
1934 Refloated and broken up at Rosyth

Deutschland

Type: Central Battery Ship
Class: 'Kaiser' (1873)
Nomenclature: Germany

History:
1872 Laid down by Samuda
1874 September 12: Launched
1875 July 20: Completed
1882 Refit, renamed
1894-97 Reconstructed at Wilhelmshaven
1895 Redesignated armoured cruiser
1904 May 3: Harbour service
1904 November 22: Renamed ***Jupiter***
1906 May 21: Stricken, target ship
1908 Sold and broken up at Hamburg

Above:
***Friedrich Carl* — Armoured frigate, completed in 1867.**
IWM

Below:
***Friedrich der Grosse* — Dreadnought, 'Kaiser' class 1913, before heavy foremast was installed.**
Foto Druppel

Deutschland

Type: Pre-dreadnought
Class: 'Deutschland' (1902)

History:
1903 June 20: Laid down by Germania as *N*
1904 November 19: Launched
1906 August 3: Completed
1906-12 Fleet flagship
World War 1: High Seas Fleet 1914-16, Jutland
1917 Accommodation ship, Wilhelmshaven
1920 January 25: Stricken
1922 Broken up at Wilhelmshaven

Deutschland

Type: Armoured Ship
Class: 'Deutschland' (1928)

History:
1929 February 5: Laid down by Deutsche Werke as *A* or *Ersatz Preussen*
1931 May 19: Launched
1933 April 1: Completed
1937 May 29: Damaged by two bombs from Spanish Republican aircraft off Ibiza (22 dead)
World War 2: 1939 North Atlantic sortie, Norway, Arctic 1942, 1944-45 Baltic
1939 October: Sortie into North Atlantic, sank merchant ships *Stonegate* and *Lorentz W. Hanson* and captured American *City of Flint*
1939 November 15: Renamed ***Lützow***
1940 February: Reclassified heavy cruiser
1940 April 8-9: Damaged by three hits from shore batteries during landings at Oslo
1940 April 11: Severely damaged by torpedo in stern from British submarine *Spearfish* in Kattegat
1940-41 Repairs and refit
1941 June 13: Severely damaged by torpedo from British aircraft off Norway while en route to Atlantic sortie
1942 July 3: Went aground off Narvik
1943 September: Refit at Gdynia
1944 October-1945 February: Fire support for ground forces in Baltic Sea
1945 April 16: Sunk in shallow water at Swinemunde by bombs from British aircraft
1945 May 4: Wreck blown up to prevent capture
1947 September: Wreck refloated by Russians, towed to Leningrad and broken up 1948

Elsass

Type: Pre-dreadnought
Class: 'Braunschweig' (1900)
Nomenclature: Alsace, a French province annexed in 1871

History:
1901 September 5: Laid down by Schichau as *J*
1903 May 26: Launched
1904 November 29: Completed
1912 March 23: In collision with Swedish merchant vessel *Pollux*, which sank, in North Sea
1916 Drill and accommodation ship, Kiel
1923-24 Refitted and rearmed at Wilhelmshaven
1931 March 31: Stricken
1932 Broken up

Friedrich Carl

Type: Central Battery Ship
Class: 'Friedrich Carl' (1865)
Nomenclature: Prince Fredrick Charles Nicholas of Prussia (1862-1885), field marshal, army commander in wars against Denmark, Austria and France

History:
1866 Laid down by La Seyne
1867 January 16: Launched
1867 October 3: Completed
1873 Blockade of Cartagena, Spain
1873 July 24: Seized insurgent sloop *Vigilanta*
1873 August 2: Accepted surrender of insurgent battleship *Vitoria*
1892 Torpedo school ship
1902 January 21: Harbour service, renamed ***Neptun***
1905 June 22: Stricken and broken up in Holland

Friedrich Carl

Type: Armoured Cruiser
Class: 'Prinz Adalbert' (1899)

History:
1901 August: Laid down by Blohm & Voss as *Ersatz König Wilhelm*
1902 June 21: Launched
1903 December 12: Completed
1905 March 31: In collision with British battleship *Prince George* off Gibraltar
1908-14 Torpedo training ship
1914 November 17: Sunk by mine off Memel (seven dead)

Friedrich der Grosse

Type: Turret Ship
Class: 'Preussen' (1872)
Nomenclature: Fredrick the Great, Frederick II, King of Prussia (1712-1796), notable military commander and patron of the arts

History:
1869 Laid down by Kiel
1874 September 20: Launched
1877 November 22: Completed
1889-90 Refit at Wilhelmshaven, modernised
1903 November 12: Harbour service
1906 May 21: Stricken, coal hulk
1919 June 27: Sold and broken up 1920 at Ronnabeck

Friedrich der Grosse

Type: Dreadnought
Class: 'Kaiser' (1909)

History:
1910 January 26: Laid down by Vulcan as *Ersatz Heimdall*
1911 June 10: Launched
1912 October 15: Completed
1912-17 Fleet flagship
World War 1: High Seas Fleet 1914-18, Jutland, 1917 Baltic
1918 November 25: Interned at Scapa Flow
1919 June 21: Scuttled at Scapa Flow
1937 April 29: Refloated and broken up

Frithjof

Type: Coast Defence Ship
Class: 'Siegfried' (1887)
Nomenclature: Hero of an Icelandic legend

History:
1890 Laid down by Weser as *Q*
1891 July 21: Launched
1893 February 23: Completed
1902-03 Reconstructed at Danzig
World War 1: 1915 Coast defence
1916 Accommodation ship, Danzig
1919 June 17: Stricken and sold to Arnold Bernstein
1923 Converted to merchant ship
1930 Broken up at Danzig

Fürst Bismarck

Type: Armoured Cruiser
Class: 'Fürst Bismarck' (1895)
Nomenclature: Prince Otto Eduard Leopold von Bismarck-Schönhausen (1815-1898), Prussian statesman and first chancellor of the German Empire

History:
1896 April 1: Laid down by Kiel as *Ersatz Leipzig*
1897 September 25: Launched
1900 April 1: Completed
1910 Refit
1914 Seagoing torpedo school ship
World War 1: Coastal defence
1916 Engineers' training ship
1919 June 17: Stricken and broken up

Fürst Bismarck

Type: Battlecruiser
Class: 'Mackensen' (1914)

History:
1915 November 3: Laid down by Wilhelmshaven as *A*
1917 Summer: Construction suspended when 26 months to completion; broken up on the slip

Gneisenau

Type: Armoured Cruiser
Class: 'Scharnhorst' (1903)
Nomenclature: Count August Neithardt von Gneisenau (1760-1831), Prussian field marshal, active against Napoleon

History:
1904 June: Laid down by Weser as *D*
1906 June 14: Launched
1908 March 6: Completed
———-1914 Asiatic squadron
World War 1: Coronel, Falklands
1914 December 8: Sunk by British battlecruisers at the Battle of the Falklands (598 dead)

Gneisenau

Type: Battlecruiser
Class: 'Scharnhorst' (1933)

History:
1935 March: Laid down by Deutsche Werke as *E* or *Ersatz Hessen*
1936 December 8: Launched
1938 May 21: Completed
1939 Refit
World War 2: 1939 and 1940 Atlantic sorties, Norway, 'Channel dash'
1939 November: Sortie into North Atlantic with *Scharnhorst*, sank British auxiliary cruiser *Rawalpindi*
1940 April 9: Damaged by gunfire of British battlecruiser *Renown* off Norway
1940 June 8: Sank British aircraft carrier *Glorious* and destroyers *Acasta* and *Ardent* off Norway, with *Scharnhorst*
1940 June 20: Torpedoed by British submarine *Clyde* off Trondheim
1941 January-March: Sortie into North Atlantic with *Scharnhorst*, sank 22 ships
1941 April 6: Torpedoed by British aircraft at Brest
1941 April 10: Damaged by four aircraft bombs at Brest
1942 February 13: Damaged by mine off Terschelling during sortie from Brest to Germany
1942 February 27: Severely damaged in bow by aircraft bombs at Kiel
1942 July 1: Decommissioned, turrets removed
1943 January: Repairs suspended
—— Towed to Gdynia
1945 March 27: Hulk sunk as blockship at Gdynia
1947-51 Broken up

Goeben

Type: Battlecruiser
Class: 'Moltke' (1908)
Nomenclature: August von Goeben (1816-1880), Prussian general, distinguished during the Franco-Prussian War

History:
1909 December 7: Laid down by Blohm & Voss as *H*
1911 March 28: Launched
1912 July 2: Completed
1912 Mediterranean
1914 August 4: Bombarded Bone and Philippeville
1914 August: Arrived at Constantinople after evading British Mediterranean Fleet
1914 August 16: In Turkish service as ***Yavuz Sultan Selim***
1914 November 18: Damaged in action with Russian battleships off Samsoun
1914 December 26: Struck two mines in approaches to the Bosphorus
1915 May 10: Damaged in action with Russian battleships in Black Sea
1918 January 20: Sank British monitors *Raglan* and *M28* in attack on Mudros, hit two mines and ran aground; refloated
1918 May: Drydocked at Sevastopol
1918 November 2: Formally handed over to Turkey (see Turkey: *Yavuz Sultan Selim*)

Graf Spee

Type: Battlecruiser
Class: 'Mackensen' (1914)
Nomenclature: Count Maximilian von Spee (1861-1914), vice admiral, commander at Coronel and the Falklands

History:
1915 November 30: Laid down by Schichau as *Ersatz Blücher*
1917 September 15: Launched

Above right:
***Gneisenau* — Armoured cruiser of 'Scharnhorst' class of 1903.** *Foto Druppel*

Below right:
***Goeben* — Battlecruiser of 1908 'Moltke' class, which later became the Turkish *Yavuz*.** *Foto Druppel*

1917 Construction suspended when 18 months to completion
1919 November 17: Stricken
1921 October 28: Sold and broken up incomplete at Kiel

Graf Spee, see *Admiral Graf Spee*

Graf Zeppelin

Type: Aircraft Carrier
Class: 'Graf Zeppelin' (1935)
Nomenclature: Count Ferdinand von Zeppelin (1838-1917), inventor of the rigid airship

History:
1936 December 28: Laid down by Deutsche Werke as *A*
1938 December 8: Launched
1940 May: Construction suspended when 85% complete, towed to Gdynia
1941 Towed to Stettin
1942 December: Towed to Kiel
1943 January: Construction again suspended
1943 April: Towed to the Oder River
1945 April 25: Scuttled incomplete near Stettin
1946 March: Towed to Swinemunde by Russians
1947 September 29: Struck mine and sank north of Danzig, or possibly severely damaged and broken up at Leningrad

Grosser Kurfürst

Type: Turret Ship
Class: 'Preussen' (1872)
Nomenclature: The Great Elector, ie Frederick William, Elector of Brandenburg (1620-1688), distinguished military leader

History:
1868 Laid down by Wilhelmshaven
1875 September 17: Launched
1878 May 6: Completed
1878 May 31: Sank after being rammed by ironclad *König Wilhelm* in the Straits of Dover (269 dead)

Grosser Kurfürst

Type: Dreadnought
Class: 'Konig' (1911)

History:
1911 October: Laid down by Vulcan as *Ersatz Kurfürst Friedrich Wilhelm*
1913 May 5: Launched
1914 July 30: Completed
World War 1: High Seas Fleet 1914-18, Jutland, 1917 Baltic
1916 May 31: Damaged at Battle of Jutland (eight hits)
1916 November 5: Torpedoed by British submarine *J1* off Utsira
1917 March 5: Damaged in collision with battleship *Kronprinz* in Heligoland Bight
1918 November 26: Interned at Scapa Flow
1919 June 21: Scuttled at Scapa Flow
1936 Refloated and broken up at Rosyth

Above left:
***Hagen* — Coast defence ship of 'Siegfried' class, as reconstructed, 1901.** *IWM*

Below left:
***Hessen* — Battleship of 1900 at sea in the 1920s with a sister ship.** *Foto Druppel*

Hagen

Type: Coast Defence Ship
Class: 'Siegfried' (1887)
Nomenclature: German legend: the slayer of Siegfried

History:
1891 Laid down by Kiel as *S*
1893 October 21: Launched
1894 October 2: Completed
1898-1900 Reconstructed at Kiel
1916 Accommodation ship, Swinemunde
1919 June 17: Stricken
—— Broken up

Hannover

Type: Pre-dreadnought
Class: 'Deutschland' (1902)
Nomenclature: Hanover, a province of Prussia, formerly a kingdom of the German Empire

History:
1904 April: Laid down by Wilhelmshaven as *P*
1905 September 29: Launched
1907 October 1: Completed
World War 1: High Seas Fleet 1914-16, Jutland
1917 Guardship
1920-21 Refitted at Wilhelmshaven, rearmed
1929-30 Refit
1935 Stricken, conversion to radio controlled target ship for aircraft cancelled
1944-46 Broken up at Bremerhaven

Hansa

Type: Armoured Corvette
Class: 'Hansa' (1871)
Nomenclature: Mercantile league of German Baltic towns during the Middle Ages

History:
1868 Laid down by Danzig
1872 October 26: Launched
1875 May 19: Completed
1878-80 South America
1880 Guardship at Kiel
1888 September 6: Stricken; stokers' training ship
1906 Sold and broken up at Swinemunde

Heimdall

Type: Coast Defence Ship
Class: 'Siegfried' (1887)
Nomenclature: Norse myth: watchman of the gods

History:
1891 Laid down by Wilhelmshaven as *U*
1892 July 27: Launched
1894 April 7: Completed
1901-02 Reconstructed at Kiel

World War 1: 1915 Coast defence
1916 Accommodation ship, Emden
1919 June 17: Stricken, conversion to salvage ship cancelled
1921 Broken up at Ronnebeck

Helgoland

Type: Dreadnought
Class: 'Helgoland' (1908)
Nomenclature: Fortified German island in the North Sea

History:
1908 November 24: Laid down by Howaldt as *Ersatz Siegfried*
1909 September 25: Launched
1911 August 23: Completed
World War 1: High Seas Fleet 1914-18, Jutland
1916 May 31: Damaged at Battle of Jutland (one hit)
1918 October: Mutiny on board
1919 November 5: Stricken
1920 August 5: Allocated to Great Britain
1924 Broken up at Morecambe

Hessen

Type: Pre-dreadnought
Class: 'Braunschweig' (1900)
Nomenclature: Hesse, a sovereign grand duchy of the German Empire

History:
1902 April 15: Laid down at Germania as *L*
1903 September 18: Launched
1905 September 19: Completed
1917 Tender, Brunsbuttel
1923-25 Refitted and rearmed at Wilhelmshaven
1935 March 31: Stricken, converted to radio controlled target ship
1946 Seized by Soviet Union, renamed ***Tsel***

Hildebrand

Type: Coast Defence Ship
Class: 'Siegfried' (1887)
Nomenclature: Tragic hero of an old German epic

History:
1890 Laid down by Kiel as *R*
1892 August 6: Launched
1893 October 28: Completed
1901-02 Reconstructed at Danzig
World War 1: 1915 Coast defence
1916 Accommodation and distilling ship, Windau
1919 June 17: Stricken
1919 December 21: Stranded on Dutch coast en route to breaking up
1933 Wreck broken up

Hindenburg

Type: Battlecruiser
Class: 'Derfflinger' (1912)
Nomenclature: Paul Ludwig Hans Anton von Beneckendorff und von Hindenburg (1847-1934), field marshal, most celebrated German commander of World War 1 and later President of Germany

History:
1913 June 30: Laid down by Wilhelmshaven as *Ersatz Hertha*
1915 August 1: Launched
1917 May 10: Completed
World War 1: High Seas Fleet 1917-18
1918 November 24: Interned at Scapa Flow
1919 June 21: Scuttled at Scapa Flow
1930 July 22: Refloated and broken up at Rosyth

Kaiser

Type: Central Battery Ship
Class: 'Kaiser' (1873)
Nomenclature: Emperor

History:
1872 Laid down by Samuda
1874 March 19: Launched
1875 February 13: Completed
1882 Refit, rearmed
1891-95 Reconstructed at Wilhelmshaven, reboilered
1895 April 27: Redesignated armoured cruiser
1904 May 3: Harbour service
1905 October 12: Renamed ***Uranus***
1906 May 21: Stricken, accommodation ship
1920 Broken up at Hamburg

Kaiser

Type: Dreadnought
Class: 'Kaiser' (1909)

History:
1909 October: Laid down by Kiel as *Ersatz Hildebrand*
1911 March 22: Launched
1912 August 1: Completed
World War 1: High Seas Fleet 1914-18, Jutland, 1917 Baltic
1916 May 31: Damaged at Battle of Jutland (two hits)
1918 November 25 Interned at Scapa Flow
1919 June 21: Scuttled at Scapa Flow
1929 March 20: Refloated and broken up at Rosyth

Kaiser Barbarossa

Type: Pre-dreadnought
Class: 'Kaiser Friedrich III' (1894)
Nomenclature: Emperor Frederick I Barbarossa (1123-1190), Holy Roman Emperor 1152-90, one of the most esteemed German leaders

History:
1898 September: Laid down by Schichau as *A*
1900 April 21: Launched
1901 June 10: Completed
1907-10 Refit at Kiel
1916 Prison ship, Wilhelmshaven
1919 December 6: Stricken and broken up 1920 at Rustringen

Kaiser Friedrich III

Type: Pre-dreadnought
Class: 'Kaiser Friedrich III' (1894)
Nomenclature: Frederick III (1831-1888), German Emperor and King of Prussia, a leading army commander in wars against Austria and France

History:
1895 April 5: Laid down by Wilhelmshaven as *Ersatz Preussen*
1896 July 1: Launched
1898 October 7: Completed
1908-09 Refit by Wilhelmshaven
1916 Prison ship, Wilhelmshaven
1919 December 6: Stricken and broken up 1920 at Rustringen

Kaiser Karl der Grosse

Type: Pre-dreadnought
Class: 'Kaiser Friedrich III' (1894)
Nomenclature: Charlemagne, Emperor of the West (742-814)

History:
1898 August: Laid down by Blohm & Voss as *B*
1899 October 18: Launched
1902 February 4: Completed
1916 Prison ship, Wilhelmshaven
1919 December 6: Stricken and broken up 1920 at Rostock

Kaiser Wilhelm II

Type: Pre-dreadnought
Class: 'Kaiser Friedrich III' (1894)
Nomenclature: William II (1859-1941), Emperor of Germany 1888-1918

History:
1896 July: Laid down by Wilhelmshaven as *Ersatz Friedrich der Grosse*
1897 September 14: Launched
1900 February 13: Completed
1901-06 Fleet Flagship
1910 Refit at Wilhelmshaven
1915 Headquarters ship, Wilhelmshaven
1921 March 17: Stricken and broken up at Hamburg

Kaiser Wilhelm der Grosse

Type: Pre-dreadnought
Class: 'Kaiser Friedrich III' (1894)
Nomenclature: William I the Great (1797-1888), King of Prussia and German Emperor, ruler during the unification of Germany

History:
1897 December 17: Laid down by Germania as *Ersatz König Wilhelm*
1899 June 1: Launched
1901 May 5: Completed
1908-10 Refit at Kiel
1916 Depot ship and torpedo range ship, Kiel
1919 December 6: Stricken and broken up 1920 at Kiel

Kaiserin

Type: Dreadnought
Class: 'Kaiser' (1909)
Nomenclature: Empress

History:
1910 July: Laid down by Howaldt as *Ersatz Hagen*
1911 November 11: Launched
1913 May 14: Completed
World War 1: High Seas Fleet 1914-18, Jutland, 1917 Baltic
1918 November 25: Interned at Scapa Flow
1919 June 21: Scuttled at Scapa Flow
1936 May 14: Refloated and broken up at Rosyth

König

Type: Dreadnought
Class: 'König' (1911)
Nomenclature: King

History:
1911 October: Laid down by Wilhelmshaven as *S*
1913 March 1: Launched
1914 August 10: Completed
World War 1: High Seas Fleet 1914-18, Jutland
1916 May 31: Damaged at Battle of Jutland (10 hits)
1917 October: Gulf of Riga
1918 October 28: Crew mutinied
1918 November 5: Officers shot by crew
1918 December 6: Interned at Scapa Flow
1919 June 21: Scuttled at Scapa Flow, not refloated

König Albert

Type: Dreadnought
Class: 'Kaiser' (1909)
Nomenclature: Albert, King of Saxony (1828-1902), German field marshal, army commander in the Franco-Prussian War

History:
1910 July: Laid down by Schichau as *Ersatz Odin*
1912 April 27: Launched
1913 July 31: Completed
World War 1: High Seas Fleet 1914-18
1917 October: Gulf of Riga
1918 November 25: Interned at Scapa Flow
1919 June 21: Scuttled at Scapa Flow
1935 July 31: Refloated and broken up at Rosyth

König Wilhelm

Type: Broadside Ship
Class: 'König Wilhelm' (1867)
Nomenclature: William III, King of Prussia (1797-1888), later German Emperor as William I

History:
1865 Laid down by Thames for Turkey as ***Fatikh***
1867 February 6: Purchased by Prussia, renamed ***Wilhelm I***
1867 December 14: Renamed ***König Wilhelm***
1868 April 25: Launched
1869 February 20: Completed
1878 May 31: Damaged in collision with ironclad *Grosser Kürfurst* in English Channel
1896 Rebuilt by Blohm & Voss
1897 January 25: Redesignated armoured cruiser
1904 May 3: Harbour service, boys' school ship, Kiel, 16×88mm guns only
1921 January 4: Stricken and sold, broken up

Kronprinz

Type: Central Battery Ship
Class: 'Kronprinz' (1866)
Nomenclature: Crown Prince

History:
1866 Laid down by Samuda

1867 May 6: Launched
1867 September 17: Completed
—— Refit, reboilered
1901 August 22: Stricken, engineering hulk, Kiel
1921 October 3: Sold and broken up at Rendsdorf

Kronprinz

Type: Dreadnought
Class: 'Konig'(1911)
Nomenclature: Crown Prince, ie Friedrich Wilhelm, Crown Prince of Germany (1882-1951)

History:
1912 May: Laid down by Germania as *Ersatz Brandenburg*
1914 February 21: Launched
1914 November 8: Completed
World War 1: High Seas Fleet 1914-18, Jutland
1916 November 5: Torpedoed by British submarine *J1* off Utsira
1917 March 5: In collision with battleship *Grosser Kurfürst* in Heligoland Bight
1917 October: Gulf of Riga
1918 January 27: Renamed ***Kronprinz Wilhelm***
1918 November 26: Interned at Scapa Flow
1919 June 21: Scuttled at Scapa Flow
1938 Refloated and broken up at Rosyth

Kronprinz Wilhelm see *Kronprinz*

Kurfürst Friedrich Wilhelm

Type: Pre-dreadnought
Class: 'Brandenburg' (1889)
Nomenclature: Frederick William, Elector of Brandenburg (1620-1688), the Great Elector (see *Grosser Kurfürst*)

History:
1890 Laid down by Wilhelmshaven as *D*
1891 June 30: Launched
1894 April 29: Completed
1902 June 11: In collision with battleship *Weissenburg* off Kiel
1904-05 Refit by Wilhelmshaven
1910 September 12: Sold to Turkey, renamed ***Hairredin Barbarossa***

Lothringen

Type: Pre-dreadnought
Class: 'Braunschweig' (1900)
Nomenclature: Lorraine, a French province annexed in 1871

Top left:
***Kaiser* — Central battery ship in 1889 prior to reconstruction. Notice armoured battery amidships.** *IWM*

Centre left:
***Kaiser* — Dreadnought of 1909 with heavy pole foremast fitted.** *Foto Druppel*

Bottom left:
***Mackensen* — Battlecruiser launched 1917 but never completed.** *Foto Druppel*

History:
1903 March 31: Laid down by Schichau as *M*
1904 May 27: Launched
1906 May 18: Completed
1916 Guardship, 10×170mm guns only
1917 Drillship and engineers' training ship, Wilhelmshaven
1918 Disarmed
1919 Converted to minesweeper depot ship
1931 March 31: Stricken, broken up at Wilhelmshaven

Lutzow

Type: Battlecruiser
Class: 'Derfflinger' (1912)
Nomenclature: Baron Ludwig Adolf Wilhelm von Lützow (1782-1834), Prussian military commander during the Napoleonic Wars
History:
1912 July: Laid down by Schichau as *Ersatz Kaiserin Augusta*
1913 November 29: Launched
1915 August 8: Completed
1915 Suffered turbine damage during trials
World War 1: High Seas Fleet 1915-16, Jutland
1916 April 25: Bombarded Lowestoft and Yarmouth
1916 June 1: Sunk by German destroyer *G38* after being heavily damaged at Battle of Jutland (116 dead)

Lützow, see *Deutschland*

Mackensen

Type: Battlecruiser
Class: 'Mackensen' (1914)
Nomenclature: August von Mackensen (1849-1945), German field marshal during World War 1

History:
1915 January 30: Laid down by Blohm & Voss as *Ersatz Victoria Luise*
1917 April 21: Launched
1917 Construction suspended, 12 months before completion date
1919 November 17: Stricken
1923 Broken up incomplete at Kiel

Markgraf

Type: Dreadnought
Class: 'Konig' (1911)
Nomenclature: Margrave

History:
1911 November: Laid down by Weser as *Ersatz Weissenburg*
1913 June 4: Launched
1914 October 1: Completed
World War 1: High Seas Fleet 1914-18, Jutland
1916 May 31: Damaged by gunfire at Battle of Jutland (five hits)
1917 October 29: Damaged by mine during operations in Gulf of Riga
1918 November 26: Interned at Scapa Flow
1919 June 21: Scuttled at Scapa Flow
1937 Refloated and broken up at Rosyth

Mecklenburg

Type: Pre-dreadnought
Class: 'Mecklenburg' (1899)
Nomenclature: Two sovereign grand duchies of the German Empire

History:
1900 May 15: Laid down by Vulcan as *G*
1901 November 9: Launched
1903 June 25: Completed
1916 Prison ship, Kiel
1918 Accommodation ship, Kiel
1920 January 25: Stricken
1921 August 16: Sold and broken up at Kiel

Moltke

Type: Battlecruiser
Class: 'Moltke' (1908)
Nomenclature: Count Helmuth Karl Bernhard von Moltke (1800-1891), German field marshal, architect of German victories in 1866 and 1870
History:
1908 December 7: Laid down by Blohm & Voss as *G*
1910 April 7: Launched
1911 September 30: Completed
World War 1: High Seas Fleet 1914-18, Doggerbank, Jutland
1914 November 3: Bombarded Yarmouth
1914 December 16: Bombarded Hartlepool
1915 August 19: Torpedoed by British submarine *E1* during operations in Gulf of Riga
1916 April 25: Bombarded Lowestoft and Yarmouth
1916 May 31: Damaged (four hits) at Battle of Jutland
1917 October: Operations in Gulf of Riga
1918 April 25: Torpedoed by British submarine *E42* in North Sea
1918 November 24: Interned at Scapa Flow
1919 June 21: Scuttled at Scapa Flow
1927 Refloated, broken up at Rosyth

Nassau

Type: Dreadnought
Class: 'Nassau' (1906)
Nomenclature: A province of Germany

History:
1907 July 22: Laid down by Wilhelmshaven as *Ersatz Bayern*
1908 March 7: Launched
1909 October 1: Completed
World War 1: High Seas Fleet 1914-18, Jutland
1916 May 31: Damaged at Battle of Jutland (two hits). Sank British destroyer *Spitfire* by ramming
1919 November 5: Stricken
1920 April 7: Allocated to Japan
1920 June: Sold and broken up at Dordrecht

Odin

Type: Coast Defence Ship
Class: 'Odin' (1892)
Nomenclature: Norse myth: chief of the Gods

History:
1893 Laid down by Danzig as *V*
1894 November 3: Launched
1896 July 7: Completed
1901-03 Reconstructed at Danzig
World War 1: 1915 Coast defence
1917 Tender, Wilhelmshaven
1919 December 6: Stricken and sold to Arnold Bernstein
1922 Converted to motorship for use as merchant ship
1935 Broken up

Oldenburg

Type: Barbette Ship
Class: 'Oldenburg' (1883)
Nomenclature: A sovereign grand duchy of the German Empire

History:
1883 Laid down by Vulcan as *E*
1884 December 20: Launched
1886 April 8: Completed
1899 March: Went aground in a snowstorm in Strand Bay, Holstein
1900 Harbour defence guardship
1912 January 13: Stricken, target ship
1919 May 5: Sold and broken up at Wilhelmshaven

Oldenburg

Type: Dreadnought
Class: 'Helgoland' (1908)

History:
1909 March 1: Laid down by Schichau as *Ersatz Frithjof*
1910 June 30: Launched
1912 May 1: Completed
World War 1: High Seas Fleet 1914-18, Jutland
1916 May 31: Damaged by gun fire at Battle of Jutland (one hit)
1919 November 5: Stricken
1920 May 13: Allocated to Japan
1921 Broken up at Dordrecht

Ostfriesland

Type: Dreadnought
Class: 'Helgoland' (1908)
Nomenclature: East Friesland, a province of Germany

History:
1908 October 19: Laid down by Howaldt as *Ersatz Oldenburg*
1909 September 30: Launched
1911 August 1: Completed
World War 1: High Seas Fleet 1914-18, Jutland
1916 June 1: Damaged by mine after Battle of Jutland
1919 November 5: Stricken
1920 April 7: Allocated to United States
1921 July 21: Sunk as target by US aircraft off Cape Henry, Virginia

Top right:
***Markgraf* — Dreadnought of 'König' class, 1917. Note heavy pole foremast.** *Foto Druppel*

Centre right:
***Ostfriesland* — Battleship of 1908.** *Foto Druppel*

Bottom right:
***Preussen* — Turret ship, as completed, c1885. Notice turrets on either side of funnel.** *IWM*

Pommern

Type: Pre-dreadnought
Class: 'Deutschland' (1902)
Nomenclature: Pomerania, a province of Germany

History:
1904 April: Laid down by Vulcan as *O*
1905 December 2: Launched
1907 August 6: Completed
World War 1: High Seas Fleet 1914-16, Jutland
1916 June 1: Torpedoed and sunk by British destroyers during night action at Battle of Jutland (839 dead, no survivors)

Posen

Type: Dreadnought
Class: 'Nassau' (1906)
Nomenclature: A province of Germany

History:
1907 June 11: Laid down by Germania as *Ersatz Baden*
1908 December 12: Launched
1910 May 31: Completed
World War 1: High Seas Fleet 1914-18, Jutland, 1918 Finland
1916 May 31: Collided with cruiser *Elbing* at Jutland
1919 November 5: Stricken
1920 May 13: Allocated to Great Britain
1922 Broken up at Dordrecht

Preussen

Type: Turret Ship
Class: 'Preussen' (1872)
Nomenclature: Prussia, a sovereign kingdom of the German Empire

History:
1870 Laid down by Vulcan as ***Borussia***, renamed ***Preussen***
1873 November 22: Launched
1876 July 4: Completed
1889-90 Modernised at Wilhelmshaven
1891 Guardship at Wilhelmshaven
1903 November 12: Renamed ***Saturn***
1906 May 21: Stricken, coal hulk
1919 June 27: Sold, broken up at Wilhelmshaven

Preussen

Type: Pre-dreadnought
Class: 'Braunschweig' (1900)

History:
1902 June 14: Laid down by Vulcan as *K*
1903 October 30: Launched
1905 July 12: Completed
1916 Guardship
1917 Depot ship, Wilhelmshaven
1919 Converted to minesweeper depot ship
1922 Reserve
1929 April 5: Stricken
1931 February 25: Sold and broken up

Prinz Adalbert

Type: Ironclad Ram
Class: 'Prinz Adalbert' (1865)
Nomenclature: Prinz Adalbert of Prussia (1811-1873), admiral and navy commander, founder of the Prussian navy

History:
1863 Laid down for Confederate Navy by Arman
1864 Launched under cover name *Cheops*
1865 October 29: Purchased by Prussia, named ***Prinz Adalbert***
1866 June 9: Completed
1868-69 Refit at Geestemunde
1875 Disarmed
1878 May 28: Sold and broken up at Wilhelmshaven

Prinz Adalbert

Type: Armoured Cruiser
Class: 'Prinz Adalbert' (1899)

History:
1900 April: Laid by Germania as *B*
1901 June 22: Launched
1904 January 12: Completed
1904-14 Gunnery training ship
1915 July 2: Torpedoed by British submarine *E9* off Danzig
1915 October 23: Torpedoed and sunk by British submarine *E8* off Libau (672 dead)

Prinz Eitel Friedrich

Type: Battlecruiser
Class: 'Mackensen' (1914)
Nomenclature: Prince Eitel Frederick of Prussia (1883-1942), second son of Kaiser Wilhelm II

History:
1915 May 1: Laid down by Blohm & Voss as *Ersatz Freya*
1917 Construction suspended, 21 months before completion date
1920 March 13: Hull launched to clear slip
1922 Broken up at Hamburg

Prinz Heinrich

Type: Armoured Cruiser
Class: 'Prinz Heinrich' (1897)
Nomenclature: Prince Henry of Prussia (1862-1929), grand admiral, brother of Kaiser Wilhelm II

History:
1898 December 1: Laid down by Kiel as *A*
1900 March 22: Launched
1902 March 11: Completed
1914 Refit
1916 Headquarters ship, Kiel
1920 January 25: Stricken and broken up

Prinzregent Luitpold

Type: Dreadnought
Class: 'Kaiser' (1909)
Nomenclature: Prince Luitpold of Bavaria (1821-1912), Regent of Bavaria 1886-1912

History:
1910 November: Laid down by Germania as *Ersatz Ägir*
1912 February 17: Launched
1913 August 19: Completed
World War 1: High Seas Fleet 1914-18, Jutland
1917 October: Gulf of Riga

1918 November 25: Interned at Scapa Flow
1919 June 21: Scuttled at Scapa Flow
1931 July 9: Refloated and broken up 1933 at Rosyth

Rheinland

Type: Dreadnought
Class: 'Nassau' (1906)
Nomenclature: Rhineland, a province of Germany

History:
1907 June 1: Laid down by Vulcan, Stettin, as *Ersatz Württemberg*
1908 September 26: Launched
1910 April 30: Completed
World War 1: High Seas Fleet 1914-17, Jutland
1916 May 31: Damaged at Battle of Jutland (one hit)
1918 April 11: Went aground in Aland Sea during landings in Finland
1918 July 9: Refloated after forward turret guns and armour removed, towed to Kiel, not repaired
1918 Accommodation ship, Kiel
1919 November 5: Stricken
1920 June 28: Sold
1921 Broken up at Dordrecht

Roon

Type: Armoured Cruiser
Class: 'Roon' (1901)
Nomenclature: Count Albrecht Theodor Emil von Roon (1803-1879), Prussian field marshal, instrumental in the victories of the Franco-Prussian War

History:
1902 August 1: Laid down by Kiel as *Ersatz Kaiser*
1903 June 27: Launched
1906 April 5: Completed
1916 Accommodation ship, Kiel
1918 Projected conversion to seaplane carrier cancelled
1920 November 25: Stricken and broken up at Kiel

Sachsen

Type: Barbette Ship
Class: 'Sachsen' (1875)
Nomenclature: Saxony, a sovereign kingdom of the German Empire

History:
1875 Laid down by Vulcan as *B*
1877 July 21: Launched
1878 October 20: Completed
1897-99 Reconstructed at Kiel
1900 February 27: Ran aground off Kiel
1910 February 19: Stricken, target ship
1919 May 5: Sold and broken up at Wilhelmshaven

Sachsen

Type: Dreadnought
Class: 'Baden' (1913)

History:
1914 Laid down by Germania as *Ersatz Kaiser Friedrich III*
1916 November 21: Launched
1917 Construction suspended
1919 November 3: Stricken and broken up 1920 incomplete at Kiel

Scharnhorst

Type: Armoured Cruiser
Class: 'Scharnhorst' (1903)
Nomenclature: Gerhard Johann David von Scharnhorst (1755-1813), Prussian general

History:
1905 May: Laid down by Blohm & Voss as *C*
1906 March 22: Launched
1907 October 24: Completed
——-1914 Asiatic Squadron
World War 1: Coronel, Falklands
1914 December 8: Sunk by British battlecruisers at the Battle of the Falklands, flagship of Vice-Adm Count von Spee (860 dead, no survivors)

Scharnhorst

Type: Battlecruiser
Class: 'Scharnhorst' (1933)

History:
1934 April 2: Laid down by Wilhelmshaven as *D* or *Ersatz Elsass*
1936 October 3: Launched
1939 January 7: Completed
World War 2: 1939 and 1941 Atlantic sorties, Norway, 'Channel dash', 1943 Arctic
1939 November: Sortie into North Atlantic with *Gneisenau*, sank British auxiliary cruiser *Rawalpindi*
1940 April 9: In action with British battlecruiser *Renown* off Norway
1940 June 8: Sank British aircraft carrier *Glorious* and destroyers *Acasta* and *Ardent* off Norway, with *Gneisenau*; torpedoed by *Acasta*
1941 January-March: Sortie into North Atlantic with *Gneisenau*, sank 22 ships
1941 July 22: Damaged by five aircraft bombs at La Pallice
1942 February 13: Twice mined in English Channel en route from Brest to Kiel
1943 September 8: Bombarded Spitzbergen
1943 December 26: Sunk in action with British battleship *Duke of York* off North Cape (1,803 dead)

Schlesien

Type: Pre-dreadnought
Class: 'Deutschland' (1902)
Nomenclature: Silesia, a province of Germany

History:
1905 Laid down by Schichau as *R*
1906 May 28: Launched
1908 May 5: Completed
World War 1: High Seas Fleet 1914-18, Jutland
1917 Drillship and accommodation ship, Kiel
1918 Cadet training ship
1926-27 Refit
1935 Reconstructed; two fore funnels trunked
1936 Cadet training ship
1945 May 4: Damaged by aircraft mine at Swinemunde and scuttled

Schleswig-Holstein

Type: Pre-dreadnought
Class: 'Deutschland' (1902)
Nomenclature: Schleswig-Holstein, a province in northern Germany

History:
1905 August: Laid down by Germania as *Q*
1906 December 7: Launched
1908 July 6: Completed
World War 1: High Seas Fleet 1914-16, Jutland
1917 Depot ship, Bremerhaven
1918 Accommodation ship, Kiel
1925-26 Refit
1930-31 Refit, 2 fore funnels trunked
1935 Cadet training ship
World War 2
1939 September 1: Fired opening shots of the war at Westerplatte
1944 December 18: Severely damaged by aircraft bombs at Gdynia
1945 March 21: Scuttled at Gdynia

Schwaben

Type: Pre-dreadnought
Class: 'Mecklenburg' (1899)
Nomenclature: Swabia, a historic region of south Germany

History:
1900 October 18: Laid down by Wilhelmshaven as *F*
1901 August 19: Launched
1904 April 13: Completed
1911 Gunnery training ship
1916 Drill ship, Wilhelmshaven
1919 Converted at Wilhelmshaven to minesweeper depot ship
1921 March 8: Stricken and broken up at Kiel

Seydlitz

Type: Battlecruiser
Class: 'Seydlitz' (1910)
Nomenclature: Friedrich Wilhelm von Seydlitz (1721-1773), Prussian cavalry commander

History:
1911 February 4: Laid down by Blohm & Voss as *J*
1912 March 30: Launched
1913 May 22: Completed
World War 1: High Seas Fleet 1914-18, Doggerbank, Jutland
1914 November 3: Bombarded Yarmouth
1914 December 16: Bombarded Hartlepool
1915 January 24: Severely damaged by two hits at Battle of the Doggerbank, two after turrets burned out (165 dead)
1915 August: Operations in Gulf of Riga
1916 April 25: Damaged by mine en route to bombardment of Lowestoft
1916 May 31: Severely damaged by 23 hits and torpedoes at Battle of Jutland, two turrets burned out (98 dead)
1918 November 24: Interned at Scapa Flow
1919 June 21: Scuttled at Scapa Flow
1928 November 2: Refloated
1930 Broken up at Rosyth

Siegfried

Type: Coast Defence Ship
Class: 'Siegfried' (1887)
Nomenclature: Legendary German hero

History:
1888 Laid down at Germania as *O*
1889 August 10: Launched
1890 April 29: Completed
1903-04 Reconstructed at Danzig
1915 Coast defence
1916 Accommodation ship, Wilhelmshaven
1919 June 17: Stricken, conversion to salvage ship cancelled
1920 Broken up at Kiel

Thüringen

Type: Dreadnought
Class: 'Helgoland' (1908)
Nomenclature: Thuringia, a province of Germany

History:
1908 November 2: Laid down by Weser as *Ersatz Beowulf*
1909 November 27: Launched
1911 July 1: Completed
World War 1: High Seas Fleet 1914-18, Jutland
1918 October: Crew mutinied
1919 November 5: Stricken
1920 April 29: Allocated to France
1921 Target ship
1923 Broken up at Lorient

Tirpitz

Type: Battleship
Class: 'Bismarck' (1935)
Nomenclature: Alfred von Tirpitz (1849-1930), grand admiral, creator of the modern German navy

History:
1936 October 24: Laid down by Wilhelmshaven as *G* or *Ersatz Schleswig-Holstein*
1939 April 1: Launched
1941 February 25: Completed
World War 2: Based in Norway from early 1942
1943 September 8: Bombarded Spitzbergen
1943 September 22: Damaged by British midget submarine attack in Altafjord
1944 April 3: Damaged by carrier aircraft bombs (14 hits, 122 dead)
1944 September 15: Damaged by aircraft bombs, no longer seaworthy
1944 November 12: Hit by British aircraft bombs and capsized off Tromso (902 dead)

Von der Tann

Type: Battlecruiser
Class: 'Von der Tann' (1907)
Nomenclature: Ludwig Arthur Samson, Freiherr von und zu der Tann-Rothsamhausen (1815-1881), Bavarian general of infantry

History:
1908 March 25: Laid down by Blohm & Voss as *F*
1909 March 20: Launched
1910 September 1: Completed

Top right:
***Sachsen* — Barbette ship of 1875, prior to reconstruction.** *Foto Druppel*

Centre right:
***Schleswig-Holstein* — Battleship of 'Deutschland' class, 1920s.** *Foto Druppel*

Bottom right:
***Seydlitz* — Battlecruiser of 1910.** *Foto Druppel*

1911 Cruise to South Africa
World War 1: High Seas Fleet 1914-18, Jutland
1914 November 3: Bombarded Yarmouth
1914 December 16: Bombarded Scarborough and Whitby
1915 August: Operations in Gulf of Riga
1916 April 25: Bombarded Lowestoft and Yarmouth
1916 May 31: Damaged at Battle of Jutland (four hits)
1918 November 24: Interned at Scapa Flow
1919 June 21: Scuttled at Scapa Flow
1930 December 7: Refloated
1934 Broken up at Rosyth

Weissenburg

Type: Pre-dreadnought
Class: 'Brandenburg' (1889)
Nomenclature: German victory over the French, 6 August 1870

History:
1890 Laid down by Vulcan as *C*
1891 December 14: Launched
1894 June 5: Completed
1900 April 7: Damaged by striking submerged object in Baltic Sea
1902 June 11: In collision with battleship *Kurfürst Friedrich Wilhelm* off Kiel after steering failure
1903-04 Refit by Wilhelmshaven
1910 September 12: Sold to Turkey, renamed ***Torgud Reis***

Westfalen

Type: Dreadnought
Class: 'Nassau' (1906)
Nomenclature: Westphalia, a province of Germany

History:
1907 August 12: Laid down by Weser as *Ersatz Sachsen*
1908 July 1: Launched
1909 November 16: Completed
World War 1: High Seas Fleet 1914-18, Jutland, 1918 Finland
1916 May 31: Damaged at Battle of Jutland (one hit)

***Wittelsbach* — Pre-dreadnought of 1899.**

1916 August 19: Torpedoed by British submarine *E23* in North Sea
1918 September 1: Gunnery training ship
1919 November 5: Stricken
1920 August 5: Allocated to Great Britain
1924 Broken up at Birkenhead

Wettin

Type: Pre-dreadnought
Class: 'Mecklenburg' (1899)
Nomenclature: Ruling dynasty of the kingdom of Saxony

History:
1899 October 10: Laid down by Schichau as *D*
1901 June 6: Launched
1902 October 1: Completed
1911-14 Artillery school ship
1916 Drill and depot ship
1920 March 11: Stricken
1921 November 21: Sold and broken up at Ronnebeck

Wilhelm I, see *Konig Wilhelm*

Wittelsbach

Type: Pre-dreadnought
Class: 'Mecklenburg' (1899)
Nomenclature: Ruling dynasty of the Kingdom of Bavaria

History:
1899 September 30: Laid down by Wilhelmshaven as *C*
1900 July 3: Launched
1902 October 15: Completed
1916 Drillship, Kiel
—— Tender, Wilhelmshaven
1919 Converted at Wilhelmshaven to minesweeper depot ship
1921 March 8: Stricken
1921 July 7: Sold and broken up at Wilhelmshaven

Wörth

Type: Pre-dreadnought
Class: 'Brandenburg' (1889)
Nomenclature: German victory over the French, 4 August 1870

History:
1890 Laid down by Germania as *B*
1892 August 6: Launched
1893 October 31: Completed
1899 November 25: Damaged by striking a rock in Eckernforder Bay
1901-03 Refitted at Wilhelmshaven; reboilered, new guns
World War 1: 1915 Coast defence
1916 Accommodation ship, Danzig
1919 May 13: Stricken and broken up at Danzig

Württemberg

Type: Barbette Ship
Class: 'Sachsen' (1875)
Nomenclature: Wurttemberg, a sovereign kingdom of the German Empire

History:
1876 Laid down by Vulcan as *C*
1878 November 9: Launched
1881 May 9: Completed
1898-99 Reconstructed at Wilhelmshaven
1906 Torpedo school ship, armament only 4×88mm guns and 7×450mm TT
1920 October 20: Sold and broken up at Wilhelmshaven

Württemberg

Type: Dreadnought
Class: 'Baden' (1913)

History:
1915 January 4: Laid down by Vulcan as *Ersatz Kaiser Wilhelm II*
1917 June 20: Launched
1917 Construction suspended
1919 November 3: Stricken
1921 Broken up incomplete at Hamburg

Wörth **— Pre-dreadnought of 'Brandenburg' class, shortly after completion.** *Photomatic*

Yorck

Type: Armoured Cruiser
Class: 'Roon' (1901)
Nomenclature: Count Hans David Ludwig Yorck von Wartenburg (1759-1830), Prussian field marshal prominent in the Napoleonic Wars

History:
1903 April 25: Laid down by Blohm & Voss as *Ersatz Deutschland*
1904 May 14: Launched
1905 November 21: Completed
1913 March 4: Sank destroyer *S178* in collision during exercises off Helgoland
1914 November 4: Sunk by mine in Jade Estuary (336 dead)

Zähringen

Type: Pre-dreadnought
Class: 'Mecklenburg' (1899)
Nomenclature: Ruling dynasty of the Grand Duchy of Baden

History:
1899 November 21: Laid down by Germania as *E*
1901 June 12: Launched
1902 October 25: Completed
1916 Drillship, Kiel
1917 Stokers' training ship, Kiel
1920 March 11: Stricken
1926-27 Converted to radio controlled target ship
1944 December 18: Sunk by British aircraft at Gdynia

Great Britain

Britain's response to France's *Gloire*, the world's first seagoing armoured warship, was to order a series of broadside ironclads. The first of these was the *Warrior*, a vessel superior in most respects to *Gloire*. The new ships were built along the lines of the old wooden vessels with all guns firing through open ports along the hull, but superior industrial strength allowed Britain to outbuild France. In addition, effective strength was increased by converting wooden ships to ironclads.

The battle of Hampton Roads between the turret ship *Monitor* and the broadside ship *Virginia* had a profound effect; it was apparent that the *Monitor* outclassed even the new broadside ironclads. Experimental ships with turrets such as *Royal Sovereign* and *Prince Albert* were built, while Capt Cowper Coles prevailed against opposition in building his turret ship *Captain*.

The loss of the *Captain* in 1870 had a traumatic effect on the Royal Navy and set back several years the development of the turret ship. However in 1873 the *Devastation* was completed without masts or rigging with the guns able to fire in any direction. In time this was the design which prevailed over competing ideas such as the central battery, armoured redoubt and broadside vessel. The turret ship *Inflexible* was completed in 1881 with an underwater armoured deck. In 1877 came the Russo-Turkish War scare and a force of miscellaneous and obsolete types was hastily mobilised as the Particular Service Squadron.

Developments came rapidly, including breech loading guns, compound armour, guns mounted in armoured barbettes and triple-expansion engines. In 1888 the 'Royal Sovereign' class, a large group of barbette ships, set the basic style for capital ships for 20 years.

British policy was described as a 'two power standard' which kept the navy equal in numbers to any two foreign navies. Large numbers of battleships were built in the years up to 1906 to maintain this standard. Proceeding along parallel lines was the development of the armoured cruiser, which ships were actually longer if not as powerful as the heavier battleships.

The appearance of the *Dreadnought* in 1906 changed existing assumptions. Britain was forced to start at near equality with Germany and in order to maintain its superiority had to build greater numbers of battleships. The near simultaneous appearance of the first battlecruiser, whose speed was to replace armour as protection, led to an additional rivalry in the naval race. Both these revolutionary designs were the result of Lord Fisher's administration which brought forth many reforms in the navy including the wholesale scrapping of obsolete vessels.

By the outbreak of World War 1 Britain had 20 dreadnoughts and 12 under construction compared to Germany's 15 and six. Battlecruisers numbered nine to Germany's five. In addition three nearing completion for foreign navies were taken over. No base in the North Sea was large enough for this huge force, organised as the Grand Fleet, and Scapa Flow in the Orkneys was taken over for this purpose.

The early loss of the new dreadnought *Audacious* to a mine caused alarm and the new *Queen Elizabeth* was present at the Dardanelles but quickly withdrawn. When the two fleets met in 1916 at the battle of Jutland almost all the dreadnoughts in the Royal Navy were present. The loss of three battlecruisers was telling evidence of their vulnerability.

Construction of capital ships during the war was limited to the 'Renown' and 'Hood' classes of more heavily protected battlecruisers. The first aircraft carriers, *Furious* and *Argus* (both conversions), made their appearance late in the war, while a purpose-built vessel, *Hermes*, was begun.

Nevertheless, British naval thinking, obsessed by Jutland, concentrated on battleships rather than carriers, while a dispute with the RAF prevented creation of a naval air arm until the late 1930s.

Ever larger battleships and battlecruisers were designed but these efforts were aborted by the Washington Naval Treaty of 1922 limiting Britain to parity with the United States, and only the two 'Nelson' class ships were built. Other battleships were modernised and two large cruisers were converted to carriers. New construction was not initiated until the 1930s when the carrier *Ark Royal* was built and the 'King George V' class battleships were begun. Six carriers and four battleships were ordered in 1938-39 but after the war began construction of the 'Lion' class was stopped.

Thus Britain entered the war deficient in aircraft carriers and naval aircraft as well as in submarine and anti-submarine warfare. During World War 2 British battleships were active in both the North Atlantic and Mediterranean. Although enemy capital ships were engaged on a few occasions, the British ships remained useful as a foil to possible enemy activity. The loss of the *Hood* to the German battleship *Bismarck* and the new *Prince of Wales* and battlecruiser *Repulse* to Japanese aircraft in 1941 caused deep shock to Britain. The carrier attack on the Italian fleet base at Taranto in 1940, on the other hand, marked the first and successful use of this naval weapon against battleships. In 1945 British carriers escorted by fast battleships joined their American counterparts in the war against Japan in the Pacific.

The battleship *Vanguard*, the last of its type, was not completed until after the war and only six of the carriers incomplete at the end of the war were finished. A large attack carrier proposed in 1966 was cancelled and after that time the Royal Navy gradually changed its emphasis from large carriers to submarine and anti-submarine warfare.

Class Details

'Warrior' Class (1859)

Broadside Ships: *Black Prince* (see later photo), *Warrior*
Displacement: 9,210tons
Dimensions: 419'4(oa) 380(pp)×58'3×26 [127.8(oa) 115.8(pp)×17.7×7.9]
Machinery: 1 screw, horizontal trunk single expansion engines (Penn), 10 rectangular boilers
IHP 5,270 (*Warrior*), 5,770 (*Black Prince*) = 14knots
Endurance: 2,000/10
Armament: 26×68pdr, 10×110pdr BL, 4×70pdr BL
1867: 28×7" MLR (*Black Prince:* 24), 4×8" MLR, 4×20pdr BL
Armour: Belt and bulkheads 4.5"(114mm)
Complement: 707
Class notes: First seagoing iron hulled armoured warships, built to overtake and destroy any other warship. Designed by Watts. Extreme length precluded wood construction. Fully rigged armoured frigates with two funnels. Breech loading rifles replaced by muzzle loaders 1868

'Defence' Class (1859)

Broadside Ships; *Defence, Resistance*
Displacement: *Defence:* 6,070tons; *Resistance:* 6,150tons
Dimensions: 291'4(oa) 280(pp)×54×25 [88.8(oa) 85.3(pp)×16.5×7.7]
Machinery: 1 screw, trunk engines (Penn), 4 rectangular boilers
IHP 2,540 = 10.75knots
Endurance: 1,670/10
Armament: *Defence:* 8×7" (178mm) BL, 10×68pdr, 4×5" (127mm) BL
Resistance: 6×7" (178mm) BL, 10×68pdr, 2×32pdr
Both, 1867: 2×8" MLR, 14×7" (178mm) MLR
Armour: Belt and bulkheads 4.5" (114mm)
Complement: 460
Class notes: Designed by Watts. Smaller and slower than *Warrior* with ram bow and single funnel but with entire battery behind the belt. Bark rig, but *Defence* changed to full ship rig in 1866

'Hector' Class (1860)

Broadside Ships: *Hector, Valiant*
Displacement: 6,710tons
Dimensions: 280(pp)×56'3×25 [85.3(pp)×17.2×7.7]
Machinery: 1 screw, return connecting-rod engines (*Hector:* Napier; *Valiant:* Maudslay), 6 boilers
IHP 3,260 (*Hector*) 3,560 (*Valiant*) = 11.5knots
Endurance: 1,395/10
Armament: *Hector:* 4×7" BL, 20×68pdr
Both, 1867: 2×8" MLR, 16×7" MLR
Armour: Belt 4.5" (114mm), battery 2.5-4.5" (63-114mm), bulkheads 4.5" (114mm)
Complement: 530
Class notes: Modified 'Defence' class with end-to-end battery armour but a shorter belt. Straight stem and bark rig. Completion of *Valiant* delayed by financial failure of the builder and then by change from breech loading to muzzle loading guns

'Achilles' (1860)

Broadside Ship: *Achilles* (see later photo)
Displacement: 9,820tons
Dimensions: 386'6(oa) 380(pp)×58'3×27'3 [117.8(oa) 115.8(pp)×17.8×8.3]
Machinery: 1 screw, horizontal trunk engines (Penn), 10 rectangular boilers
IHP 5,270 = 14.3knots
Endurance: 2,260/10
Armament: 14×100pdr SB
1865: 6×68pdr SB and 4×7" SB added
1868: 22×7" MLR, 4×8" MLR
1874: 2×7" MLR, 14×9" MLR
1889: 7" replaced by 2×6" BLR, 8×3pdr added
Armour: Belt 2.5-4.5" (64-114mm), battery and bulkheads 4.5" (114mm)
Complement: 709
Class notes: Designed by Watts and regarded as a highly successful design. Iron hull with a complete waterline belt. The only British warship with four masts. The bowsprit and bow mast were removed in 1865 but bowsprit replaced 1866. Ship rigged until 1875 when it became a bark

'Minotaur' Class (1861)

Broadside Ships: *Agincourt* (see later photo), *Minotaur, Northumberland*
Displacement: 10,690tons; *Northumberland:* 10,780tons
Dimensions: 411(oa) 400(pp)×59'6×27'9 [125.3(oa) 121'9(pp)×18.1×8.5]
Machinery: 1 screw, horizontal trunk engines (Penn); *Agincourt:* return connecting-rod engines (Maudslay), 10 rectangular boilers
IHP 6,700 = 14knots
Endurance: *Agincourt:* 2,735/10; *Minotaur:* 1,765/10; *Northumberland:* 2,825/10
Armament: 4×9" MLR, 24×7" MLR, 8×24pdr
1875: 17×9" MLR, 2×20pdr, 4 TT
Northumberland: 4×9" MLR, 22×8" MLR, 2×7" MLR
Northumberland: 1875: 7×9" MLR, 20×8" MLR, 2×20pdr, 4 TT
Armour: Belt 4.5-5.5" (114mm-140mm); *Northumberland:* c/t 4.5" (114mm)
Complement: 800
Class notes: Designed as sisters by Watts but *Northumberland* was altered by Reed before launching. The longest single-screw warships built, they had five masts and two funnels. *Northumberland* armed with the new 8" guns and had side armour reduced. *Minotaur* served as flagship during active career

'Royal Oak' (1861)

Broadside Ship: *Royal Oak*
Displacement: 6,360tons
Dimensions: 273(pp)×58'3×25 [83.2(pp)×17.8×7.6]
Machinery: 1 screw, horizontal direct-acting engines (Maudslay), 6 rectangular boilers
IHP 3,000 = 12.5knots
Armament: 11×7" BLR, 24×68pdr
1867: 4×8" MLR, 20×7" MLR
Armour: Sides 3-4" (76-101mm), battery 3-4.5" (76-114mm)
Complement: 585
Class notes: Laid down as wood hull line-of-battle ship, converted and lengthened before launching. First British ironclad with complete end-to-end armour protection from waterline to battery. Rearmed and bark rig altered to ship rig 1867

'Prince Consort' Class (1861)

Broadside Ships: *Caledonia* (see later photo), *Ocean, Prince Consort*
Displacement: 6,830tons
Dimensions: 273(pp)×58'6×26'9 [83.2(pp)×17.8×8.2]
Machinery: 1 screw, horizontal direct-acting engines (Maudslay), 8 rectangular boilers
IHP 4,200 = 12.5knots
Endurance: 2,000/5
Armament: *Prince Consort:* 7×7" BLR, 8×100pdr SB, 16×68pdr SB
Caledonia: 10×7" BLR, 8×100pdr SB, 12×68pdr SB
Ocean: 24×7" MLR
All, 1867: 4×8" MLR, 20×7" MLR
Prince Consort, 1871: 7×9" MLR, 8×8" MLR
Armour: Sides 3-4" (76-101mm), battery 3-4.5" (76-114mm)
Complement: 605
Class notes: Wood hull. Laid down as line-of-battle ships, converted while under construction. Similar to *Royal Oak* with more powerful engines and two funnels

'Prince Albert' (1862)

Turret Ship: *Prince Albert*
Displacement: 3,880tons

Dimensions: 244(oa) 240(pp)×48′1×20′6 [74.4(oa) 73.2(pp)×14.7×6.2]
Machinery: 1 screw, horizontal direct acting engines (Humphrys), 4 rectangular boilers
IHP 2,130 = 11.3knots
Endurance: 810/10
Armament: 4×9″ (230mm) 250pdr MLR
Armour: Sides 3.4-4.5″ (85-114mm), turrets 5-10″ (127-254mm)
Complement: 201
Class notes: First British turret ship, designed by Watts after plans by Coles. Hinged bulwarks provided additional freeboard and four single turrets on the centreline. Iron hull. Although long on the Navy list, was in reserve most of its career

'Royal Sovereign' (1862)

Turret Ship: *Royal Sovereign*
Displacement: 5,080tons
Dimensions: 240′6(pp)×62×25 [73.3(pp)×18.9×7.6]
Machinery: 1 screw, return connecting-rod engines (Maudslay), 6 boilers
IHP 2,460 = 11knots
Armament: 5×10.5″ (267mm) 300pdr MLR
Armour: Turrets 5.5-10″ (140-254mm), sides and c/t 5.5″ (140mm)
Complement: 300
Class notes: 131-gun wood line-of-battle ship converted to a turret ship, with hull cut down to the lower deck following a plan of Coles. Had one twin and three single turrets on the centreline and single funnel forward. First British turret ship to be completed

'Pallas' (1862)

Armoured Corvette: *Pallas*
Displacement: 3,794tons
Dimensions: 225(pp)×50×24′3 [68.6(pp)×15.2×7.4]
Machinery: 1 screw, horizontal compound engines (Humphreys), 4 rectangular boilers
IHP 3,580 = 12knots
Armament: 2×7″ (177mm) BL, 4×7″ (177mm) MLR
1866: 2×7″ (177mm) BL, 4×8″ (203mm) MLR, 2×5″ (127mm) BL
1871: 4×6″ (152mm) MLR, 4×8″ (203mm) MLR
Armour: Belt and battery 4.5″ (114mm)
Complement: 253
Class notes: First British warship designed as a ram and first to have compound engines. Designed by Reed. Iron hull. Rig and guns sacrificed for speed. Never realised expectations

'Lord Clyde' Class (1863)

Broadside Ships: *Lord Clyde, Lord Warden*
Displacement: *Lord Clyde:* 7,750tons; *Lord Warden:* 7,940tons
Dimensions: 280(pp)×59×27 (*Lord Warden:* 28) [85.3(pp)×18×8.2 (*Lord Warden:* 8.5)]
Machinery: 1 screw, *Lord Clyde:* trunk engines (Ravenhill); *Lord Warden:* return connecting-rod engines (Maudslay); 9 rectangular boilers
IHP 6,700 = 13.5knots
Armament: *Lord Clyde:* 24×7″ (177mm) MLR
Lord Warden, as designed: 16×8″ (203mm) MLR, 4×7″ (177mm) BLR
Both, 1867-70: 2×9″ (228mm) MLR, 14×8″ (203mm) MLR, 2×7″ (177mm) MLR, 2×20pdr BL
Armour: Belt 4.5-5.5″ (114-140mm), c/t 4.5″ (114mm)
Complement: 605
Class notes: Designed by Reed. The largest and fastest wooden warships ever built. Wood hull with ram bow, two funnels and ship rig. *Lord Clyde* given new engines and screw in 1868 but the wood hull was rotten by 1872

'Bellerophon' (1863)

Central Battery Ship: *Bellerophon*
Displacement: 7,550tons
Dimensions: 319′10(oa) 300(pp)×56×26′6 [97.5(oa) 91.4(pp)×17.1×8.1]
Machinery: 1 screw, trunk engines (Penn), 8 rectangular boilers
IHP 6,500 = 14knots
Endurance: 1,650/10
Armament: 10×9″ (228mm) MLR, 5×7″ (177mm) MLR
1885: 10×8″/25 (203mm) BL, 4×6″/26 (152mm) BL, 6×4″ (102mm) BL, 2×14″ (356mm) TT
Armour: Belt 5″ (127mm), battery 6″ (152mm), c/t 6-8″ (152-203mm)
Complement: 650
Class notes: Designed by Reed. The first large ironclad incorporating his ideas, of iron and steel construction. Built on the bracket-frame system. Full ship rig

'Scorpion' Class (1863)

Turret Ships: *Scorpion, Wivern* (see later photo)
Displacement: 2,750tons
Dimensions: 224′6(pp)×42′6×17 [68.4(pp)×12.9×5.2]
Machinery: 1 screw, horizontal direct-acting engines (Laird), 4 boilers
IHP 1,450 = 10knots
Endurance: 1,300/10
Armament: 4×9″ (228mm) MLR
Armour: Sides 2-4.5″ (50-114mm), turrets 5-10″ (127-254mm)
Complement: 153
Class notes: Iron hull. Similar to Danish *Rolf Krake*. First British turret ships with a poop and forecastle. Ordered for the Confederate government but seized by Britain in 1863. Bark rig altered to fore and aft rig 1868

'Zealous' (1863)

Central Battery Ship: *Zealous*
Displacement: 6,100tons
Dimensions: 252(pp)×58′6×25′9 [76.8(pp)×17.8×7.9]
Machinery: 1 screw, return connecting-rod engines (Maudslay), 6 rectangular boilers
IHP 3,450 = 11.7knots
Armament: 20×7″ (177mm) MLR
Armour: Belt 2.25-4.5″ (57-114mm), battery 4.5″ (114mm), bulkheads 3″ (76mm)
Complement: 510
Class notes: Laid down as wood line-of-battle ship and converted while under construction. Single funnel and full ship rig with straight stem. Comparatively weak, lightly armed with less protection than other conversions

Top right:
***Resistance* — Broadside ironclad of 'Defence' class, shown c1878.** *IWM*

Centre right:
***Valiant* — Broadside ship of 'Hector' class, 1863.** *P. A. Vicary*

Bottom right:
***Minotaur* — Broadside ship of 1861 after 1875 when two masts were removed.** *IWM*

Above:
***Royal Oak* — Wood broadside ship, 1863, with windsails rigged. Notice guns protruding from gunports.**
P. A. Vicary

Below:
***Prince Consort* — Wood broadside ship as completed 1864.** *IWM*

Above:
***Prince Albert* — The first British turret ship.**
Martin Holbrook Collection, IWM

Below:
***Royal Sovereign* — Wood battleship converted to turret ship as completed in 1864. Three turrets on centreline aft of funnel.** *IWM*

'Royal Alfred' (1863)

Central Battery Ship: *Royal Alfred*
Displacement: 6,700tons
Dimensions: 273(pp)×58'6×27 [83.2(pp)×17.8×8.3]
Machinery: 1 screw, horizontal return connecting-rod engines (Maudslay), 6 rectangular boilers
IHP 3,230 = 12.4knots
Endurance: 2,200/5
Armament: 10×9" (228mm) MLR, 8×7" (177mm) MLR
Armour: Belt 4-6" (101-152mm), battery 4.5-6" (114-152mm), bulkheads 4.5" (114mm)
Complement: 605
Class notes: Laid down as wood line-of-battle ship and converted while under construction to design by Reed. Heavier armament than *Zealous* and more protection. Full ship rig replaced bark rig prior to commissioning

'Penelope' (1863)

Armoured Corvette: *Penelope*
Displacement: 4,470tons
Dimensions: 265(pp)×50×17'9 [80.8(pp)×15.2×5.4]
Machinery: 2 screws, horizontal direct-acting engines (Maudslay), 4 rectangular engines
IHP 4,700 = 12.7knots
Armament: 8×8" (203mm) MLR, 3×5" (127mm) 40pdr BLR, 2×20pdr BLR
Armour: Belt 5-6" (127-152mm), battery 6" (152mm)
Complement: 350
Class notes: Designed by Barnaby. Iron hull. Central battery ship with twin screws and very shallow draft

Top left:
***Pallas* — Armoured corvette of 1862.**
Martin Holbrook Collection, IWM

Centre left:
***Bellerophon* — Central battery ship 1865, shortly after completion.** *P. A. Vicary*

Bottom left:
***Zealous* — Wood central battery ship on completion, 1866.** *IWM*

Below:
***Royal Alfred* — Wood central battery ship, 1866.**
P. A. Vicary/Martin Holbrook Collection

'Hercules' (1865)

Central Battery Ship: *Hercules* (see later photo)
Displacement: 8,680tons
Dimensions: 340'6(oa) 325(pp)×59×26'6 [103.8(oa) 99.1(pp)×18×8.1]
Machinery: 1 screw, trunk engines (Penn), 9 rectangular boilers; *1892:* ITE engines (Greenock Foundry), 8 cylindrical boilers
IHP 6,750 = 14.7knots; *1892:* IHP 8,500 = 14.6knots
Endurance: 2,160/10
Armament: 8×10" (254mm) MLR, 2×9" (228mm), 4×7" (177mm)
1892: 7" replaced by 2×6" (152mm) and 6×4.7" (119mm)
Armour: Belt 6-9" (152-228mm), bulkheads 5-6" (127-152mm)
Complement: 630
Class notes: Designed by Reed. Improved 'Bellerophon' type. Iron hull with ram bow, ship rig. Reconstructed 1892-93, rigging and masts replaced by two military masts and new funnel, new engines and boilers

'Monarch' (1865)

Turret Ship: *Monarch*
Displacement: 8,300tons
Dimensions: 341'3(oa) 330(pp)×57'6×26'7 [104(oa) 100.6(pp)×17.5×8.1]
Machinery: 1 screw, return connecting-rod engines (Humphrys), 9 rectangular boilers; *1896:* VTE engines (Maudslay), 8 cylindrical boilers
IHP 7,840 = 14.9knots; *1896:* IHP 8,200 = 15.75knots
Armament: 4×12" (305mm) MLR, 3×7" (177mm) MLR
1871: 4×12" (305mm) MLR, 2×9" (228mm) MLR, 1×7" (177mm) MLR
1890: 4×12pdr and 2×14" (356mm) TT added
Armour: Sides 4.5-7" (114-177mm), turrets 8-10" (203-254mm), bulkheads 4-4.5" (102-114mm), c/t 8" (203mm)
Complement: 530
Class notes: Designed by Reed. Iron hull. First seagoing turret ship, forecastle and full ship rig. Two twin turrets amidships with limited arc of fire. Reduced to bark 1872. Reconstructed 1890-97, sails and rigging removed and fighting tops added to masts, tall funnel and bridge added

***Penelope* — Armoured corvette, 1886, at the end of its active career.** *IWM*

'Captain' (1865)

Turret Ship: *Captain*
Displacement: 7,767tons
Dimensions: 334(oa) 320(pp)×53'3×25'6 [101.8(oa) 97.5(pp)×16.2×7.8]
Machinery: 2 screws, trunk engines (Laird), 8 rectangular boilers
IHP 5,400 = 14.25knots
Armament: 4×12" (305mm) MLR, 2×7" (177mm) MLR
Armour: Belt 4-7" (102-178mm), turret 8-10" (203-254mm), c/t 7" (178mm)
Complement: 500
Class notes: Iron hull. Design based on plans by Coles. The ship floated too deeply because of overweight material being used in construction, giving a freeboard of only 6'6 instead of the already low 8'6 as designed. Designed displacement was 6,950 tons and designed draft was 23'6. Differed from *Monarch* in having two decks with turrets on the lower deck and rigging on the flying deck above.

'Repulse' (1866)

Central Battery Ship: *Repulse*
Displacement: 6,190tons
Dimensions: 252(pp)×59×26 [76.8(pp)×18×7.9]
Machinery: 1 screw, trunk engines (Penn), 6 rectangular boilers
IHP 3,350 = 12.5knots
Armament: 12×8" (203mm) MLR
1877: 4×16" TT added
Armour: Belt 4.5-6" (114-152mm), battery 6" (132mm)
Complement: 515
Class notes: The last wood hull capital ship in the Royal Navy. Single funnel and ship rig. Engines were built for wood battleship *Prince of Wales,* never completed

'Audacious' Class (1867)

Central Battery Ships: *Audacious, Invincible* (see later photo), *Iron Duke, Vanguard*
Displacement: 6,010tons
Dimensions: 341'3(oa) 280(pp)×54×23'2 [104(oa) 85.3(pp)×16.5×7.1]
Machinery: 2 screws, horizontal return connecting-rod engines (Ravenhill; *Invincible:* Napier; *Vanguard:* Laird), 6 rectangular boilers
IHP 4,830 = 13knots
Endurance: 1,260/10
Armament: 10×9" (229mm) MLR), 4×6" (152mm) MLR, 6×20pdr
1878: 4×14" (356mm) TT added
1885: 20pdr replaced by 6 or 8×4" BL
Armour: Belt 6-8" (152-203mm), battery 4-6" (102-152mm), bulkheads 4-5" (102-127mm)
Complement: 450
Class notes: Second class battleships designed for foreign service as a reply to French 'Alma' class. Designed by Reed to provide a steady gun platform under steam in a seaway with good sail performance and axial fire from main armament. *Audacious* had rigging removed in 1890 and fighting tops added to masts

'Sultan' (1867)

Central Battery Ship: *Sultan*
Displacement: 9,290tons
Dimensions: 337'(oa) 325(pp)×59×28 [103(oa) 99.1(pp)×18×8.5]
Machinery: 1screw, trunk engines (Penn); *1896:* ITE engines (Thomson), 8 boilers
IHP 7,720 = 14knots; *1896:* IHP 6,500 = 14.6knots
Endurance: 2,140/10
Armament: 8×10" (254mm) MLR, 4×9" (229mm) MLR, 7×20pdr BL
1896: 8×10" (254mm) MLR, 4×9" (229mm) MLR, 4×4.7" (119mm), 9×6pdr, 13×3pdr, 4×14" (356mm) TT

Armour: Belt 6-9″ (152-229mm), battery 8-9″ (203-229mm), bulkheads 4.5-6″ (114-152m)
Complement: 633
Class notes: Designed by Reed. Modified 'Hercules' type, with upper deck armoured battery. Iron hull with full ship rig, reduced to bark 1876. Reconstructed following salvage 1893-96. Masts and rigging replaced by two military masts, new tall funnels, new engines and boilers

'Cerberus' Class (1867)

Breastwork Monitors: *Cerberus, Magdala*
Displacement: 3,340tons
Dimensions: 235′3(oa) 225(pp)×45×15′3 [71.7(oa) 68.6(pp)×13.7×4.6]
Machinery: 2 screws, horizontal direct-acting engines (*Cerberus:* Maudslay; *Magdala:* Ravenhill)
Cerberus: IHP 1,370 = 9.75knots; *Magdala:* IHP 1,430 = 10.6knots
Endurance: 450/10
Armament: 4×10″ (254mm) MLR
Magdala, 1892: 4×8″ (203mm)/25 BLR
Armour: Sides 6-8″ (152-203mm), breastwork 8-9″ (203-229mm), turrets 9-10″ (229-254mm), deck 1.5″ (37mm)
Complement: 155
Class notes: Designed by Reed. *Cerberus* was the first British ship built with no sail power and first with a central superstructure and fore and aft turrets. Built for colonial harbour defence. Temporary sail rig fitted for passage to Indian Ocean

'Abyssinia' (1867)

Breastwork Monitor: *Abyssinia*
Displacement: 2,900tons
Dimensions: 236′6(oa) 225(pp)×42×14′6 [72.1(oa) 68.6(pp)×12.8×4.4]

***Monarch* — The first seagoing turret ship, c1889. Notice turrets amidships under flying deck.** *IWM*

Machinery: 2 screws, inclined direct-acting engines (Dudgeon)
IHP 1,200 = 9.6knots
Endurance: 600/10
Armament: 4×10″ (254mm) MLR
1892: 4×8″ (203mm)/25 BLR
Armour: Sides 6-7″ (152-178mm), breastwork 7-8″ (178-203mm), turrets 8-10″ (203-254mm)
Complement: 100
Class notes: Designed by Reed. Similar to *Cerberus*. Sailed to India without sails

'Glatton' (1867)

Breastwork Monitor: *Glatton* (see later photo)
Displacement: 4,910tons
Dimensions: 263′2(oa) 245(pp)×54×19′6 [80.2(oa) 74.7(pp)×16.5×5.9]
Machinery: 2 screws, horizontal direct-acting engines (Laird)
IHP 2,870 = 12.1knots
Endurance: 2,000/10
Armament: 2×12″ (305mm) MLR
Later: 3×6pdr added
Armour: Sides 10-12″ (254-305mm), breastwork 12″ (305mm), turret 12-14″ (305-355mm), c/t 6-9″ (152-229mm)
Complement: 185
Class notes: Designed by Reed. Described by Parkes as 'the acme of uselessness.' Single turret monitor with very low freeboard but deep draft for harbour defence

'Hotspur' (1867)

Breastwork Monitor and Ram: *Hotspur*
Displacement: 4,010tons

Dimensions: 251(oa) 235(pp)×50×20'9 [76.5(oa) 71.6(pp)×15.2×6.3]
Machinery: 2 screws, horizontal direct-acting engines (Napier)
IHP 3,500 = 12.6knots
Endurance: 950/10
Armament: 1×12" (305mm) MLR, 2×64pdr MLR
1883: 2×12" (305mm) MLR, 2×6" (152mm) BL, 8×3" (76mm), 2×14" TT
Armour: Belt 8-11" (203-279mm), breastwork 8" (203mm), deck 1-2.75" (26-70mm), turret 8.5-10" (216-254mm, c/t 10" (254mm)
Complement: 209
Class notes: Designed by Reed as a ram with a single fixed turret. Reconstructed 1881-83 with revolving twin turret, new boilers and the internal breastwork replaced by side armour

'Swiftsure' Class (1868)

Central Battery Ships: *Swiftsure, Triumph*
Displacement: *Swiftsure:* 6,910tons; *Triumph:* 6,640tons
Dimensions: 291'3(oa) 280(pp)×55×26'1 [88.8(oa) 85.3(pp)×16.8×7.8]
Machinery: 1 screw, horizontal return connecting-rod engines (Maudslay), rectangular boilers
IHP 4,900 = 12.6knots
Endurance: *Swiftsure:* 1,450/10; *Triumph:* 1,770/10
Armament: 10×9" (229mm) MLR, 4×6" (152mm) MLR, 6×20pdr

Above:
***Captain* — The ill-fated turret ship lost in 1870.** *IWM*

Top right:
***Abyssinia* — Double turret monitor after being rearmed, 1892.**

Centre right:
***Cyclops* — Breastwork monitor, underway at Spithead.** *IWM*

Bottom right:
***Shannon* — The first armoured cruiser.**
National Maritime Museum

1882: 6" replaced by 4×5" (*Triumph*) or 8×4" (*Swiftsure*), 4×14" TT added
Armour: Belt 6-8" (152-203mm), battery 4-6" (102-152mm), bulkheads 4-5" (102-127mm)
Complement: 450
Class notes: Designed by Barnaby for foreign service. Similar to 'Audacious' class with single hoisting screw but different hull form. Full ship rig gave good sailing qualities; reduced to bark 1881

'Devastation' Class (1868)

Turret Ships: *Devastation* (see later photo), *Thunderer* (see later photo)

Displacement: 9,330tons
Dimensions: 311(oa) 285(pp)×62′3×27′6 [94.8(oa) 86.9(pp)×19×8.4]
Machinery: 2 screws, *Devastation:* direct-acting trunk engines (Penn); *Thunderer:* horizontal direct-acting engines (Humphrys), 8 rectangular boilers; *Both, 1891:* ITE engines (Maudslay), cylindrical boilers
IHP 6,650 = 13.5knots; *1891:* IHP 7,200 = 14.2knots
Armament: *Devastation:* 4×12″ (305mm) MLR
Thunderer: 2×12.5″ (317mm) MLR, 2×12″ (305mm) MLR
Both, 1891: 4×10″ (254mm)/32 BL, 6×6pdr, 8×3pdr, 2×14″ (355mm) TT
Armour: Belt 8.5-12″ (216-305mm), turret 10-14″ (254-355mm), breastwork 10-12″ (254-305mm), deck 2-3″ (51-76mm), c/t 6-9″ (152-229mm)
Complement: 358
Class notes: Designed by Reed and modified by Barnaby. Of revolutionary design, generally condemned at the time, with no sail power, masts or rigging, yet built for sea duty. Nevertheless a successful innovation. Two twin turrets fore and aft, two funnels and a single mast. Reconstructed 1889-92 with new engines and boilers, new masts and breech loading guns

'Dreadnought' (1869)

Turret Ship: *Dreadnought*
Displacement: 10,886 tons
Dimensions: 320(pp)×63′9×26 [97.5(pp)×19.5×7.9]
Machinery: 2 screws, compound vertical engines (Humphrys), 12 boilers
IHP 8,210 = 14knots
Endurance: 5,200/10
Armament: 4×12.5″ (317mm) MLR, 6×6pdr, 12×3pdr, 2×14″ TT
Armour: Belt 8-14″ (203-355mm), turrets 14″ (355mm), bulkheads 13″ (330mm), c/t 6-14″ (152-355mm), deck 2.5-3″ (63-76mm)
Complement: 369
Class notes: Originally designed by Reed and laid down as *Fury* with low freeboard. Redesigned by Barnaby with breastwork extended to the sides of the hull which was built up fore and aft. Two turrets fore and aft and two funnels with superstructure amidships. The first ship with a longitudinal bulkhead amidships. Funnels raised 1899

'Rupert' (1869)

Breastwork Monitor: *Rupert* (see later photo)
Displacement: 5,440tons
Dimensions: 267′4(oa) 250(pp)×53×23′8 [81.5(oa) 76.2(pp)×16.2×7.2]
Machinery: 2 screws, horizontal direct-acting engines (Napier); *1893:* VTE engines
IHP 4,200 = 12knots; *1893:* IHP 6,000 = 14knots
Endurance: 2,000/10
Armament: 2×10″ (254mm) MLR, 2×64pdr
1887: 64pdr replaced by 2×6″ (152mm) BLR
1892: 2×9.2″ (234mm)/25 BL, 2×6″ (152mm) BL, 4×6pdr, 4×14″ TT
Armour: Belt 9-11″ (229-279mm), breastwork 12″ (305mm), turret 12-14″ (305-355mm), c/t 12″ (305mm), deck 2-3″ (51-76mm)
Complement: 217
Class notes: Designed by Barnaby as modified 'Hotspur' with twin turret and increased armour protection. Reconstructed 1893, re-engined and reboilered, breech loading guns and single military mast

Above left:
***Nelson* — Armoured frigate as modernised in 1892 with military masts.** *National Maritime Museum*

Below left:
***Inflexible* — Turret ship, c1882 at Malta. Notice 16″ turret; other turret hidden by superstructure.**

'Cyclops' Class (1869)

Breastwork Monitors: *Cyclops, Gorgon, Hecate, Hydra*
Displacement: 3,480tons
Dimensions: 238′2(oa) 225(pp)×45×16′3 [72.6(oa) 68.6(pp)×13.7×4.9]
Machinery: 2 screws, compound engines (John Elder); *Gorgon* and *Hecate:* horizontal direct-acting engines (Ravenhill)
IHP 1,500 = 11knots
Endurance: 3,000/10
Armament: 4×10″ (254mm) MLR
Armour: Belt 6-8″ (152-203mm), turret 9-10″ (229-254mm), c/t 6-9″ (152-229mm), breastwork 8-9″ (203-229mm)
Complement: 191
Class notes: Designed for harbour defence. Launched in quick time after being ordered but completion delayed thereafter. Unsatisfactory as ironclads

'Alexandra' (1872)

Central Battery Ship: *Alexandra* (see later photo)
Displacement: 9,490tons
Dimensions: 325(pp)×63′8×26′6 [99.1(pp)×19.4×8.1]
Machinery: 2 screws, vertical inverted compound engines (Humphrys), 12 cylindrical boilers
IHP 8,610 = 15.1knots
Endurance: 2,700/10
Armament: 2×11″ (279mm) MLR, 10×10″ (254mm) MLR, 6×13cwt BL
1891: 4×9.2″ (234mm)/25 BL, 8×10″ (254mm) MLR, 6×4″ (102mm) BL, 4×14″ (356mm) TT
1897: 4″ replaced by 4.7″
Armour: Belt 6-12″ (152-305mm), bulkheads 5-8″ (127-203mm), battery 8-12″ (203-305mm), deck 2″ (52mm)
Complement: 674
Class notes: Designed by Barnaby. Central battery ship with both broadside and bow fire. Fastest battleship afloat when completed. Bark rig. Reconstructed 1889-91, military masts replaced sails and rigging, rearmed with breech loading guns, reboilered, conning tower added between funnels

'Shannon' (1872)

Armoured Cruiser: *Shannon*
Displacement: 5,390tons
Dimensions: 260(pp)×54×23′4 [79.3(pp)×16.5×7.1]
Machinery: 1 screw, horizontal compound return connecting-rod engines (Laird), 8 cylindrical boilers
IHP 3,370 = 12.25knots
Endurance: 2,260/10
Armament: 2×10″ (254mm) MLR, 7×9″ (229mm) MLR, 6×20pdr
1881: 6×4″, 2×14″ TT added
Armour: Belt 6-9″ (152-229mm), bulkheads 8-9″ (203-229mm), c/t 4-9″ (102-229mm), deck 1-3″ (25-76mm)
Complement: 452
Class notes: Designed by Barnaby. The first British armoured cruiser, officially called second class battleship. First ship with a protective deck. Full ship rig, single funnel and ram bow. Reduced to bark 1876 after trials

'Northampton' Class (1873)

Armoured Frigates: *Nelson, Northampton*
Displacement: *Nelson:* 7,473tons; *Northampton:* 7,630tons
Dimensions: 280(pp)×60×25'9 [85.5(pp)×18.3×7.8]
Machinery: 2 screws, inverted compound engines (*Nelson:* Elder; *Northampton:* Penn), 10 oval boilers
Nelson: IHP 6,600 = 14knots; *Northampton:* IHP 6,000 = 13.1knots
Endurance: 5,000/10.5
Armament: 4×10" (254mm) MLR, 8×9" (229mm) MLR, 6×20pdr
Nelson, 1889: 4×4.7"
Both later: 4×14" TT added
Armour: Belt 6-9" (152-229mm), bulkheads 6-9" (152-229mm), c/t 9" (229mm), deck 2-3" (51-76mm)
Complement: 560
Class notes: Designed by Barnaby. Improved 'Shannon' type with main armament in central battery. Two funnels, bark rig and ram bow. *Nelson* modernised 1889, sail rig replaced by military masts

'Temeraire' (1873)

Central Battery and Barbette Ship: *Temeraire*
Displacement: 8,450tons
Dimensions: 285(pp)×62×27'3 [86.9(pp)×18.9×8.3]
Machinery: 2 screws, vertical inverted compound engines (Humphrys), 12 boilers
IHP 7,520 = 14.6knots
Endurance: 2,700/10
Armament: 4×11" (279mm) MLR, 4×10" (254mm) MLR, 6×20pdr
1897: 4×9.2" (234mm)/25 BL, 4×8" (203mm), 6×4" (102mm), 4×6pdr, 2×14" (356mm) TT
Armour: Belt 5.5-11" (140-279mm), forward barbette 10" (254mm), aft barbette 8" (203mm), battery 8-9" (203-229mm), bulkheads 5-8" (127-203mm), deck 1.5-2" (37-52mm)
Complement: 580
Class notes: First British barbette ship with single 11" guns mounted in barbettes fore and aft with other guns in battery. Two funnels and brig rig, removed 1899

'Inflexible' (1873)

Turret Ship: *Inflexible*
Displacement: 11,880tons
Dimensions: 344(oa) 320(pp)×75×26'6 [104.8(oa) 97.5(pp)×22.9×8.1]
Machinery: 2 screws, inverted compound engines (John Elder), 12 boilers
IHP 8,400 = 14.75knots
Endurance: 3,400/10
Armament: 4×16" (406mm) MLR, 6×20pdr
1885: 20pdr replaced by 8×4" BL, 4×6pdr and 4×14" (356mm) added
Armour: Citadel 16-24" (406-609mm), bulkheads 14-22" (355-559mm), turrets 16-17" (406-432mm), c/t 12" (305mm), deck 3" (76mm)
Complement: 440
Class notes: Designed by Barnaby. Built as a reply to the Italian *Duilio*. First capital ship with an underwater armoured deck in place of vertical armour on the waterline. Had the thickest armour ever and two twin turrets en echelon amidships. Brig rig replaced by fighting tops 1885

Top left:
***Ajax* — Turret ship of 1875.** *Marius Bar*

Centre left:
***Belleisle* — Small central battery ship taken over from Turkey in 1878; shown in 1886 as guardship at Kingstown, Ireland.** *IWM*

Bottom left:
***Superb* — Central battery ship, the last British broadside ironclad, at Algiers 1886.** *IWM*

'Ajax' Class (1875)

Turret Ships: *Agamemnon* (see later photo), *Ajax*
Displacement: 8,510tons
Dimensions: 301'9(oa) 280(pp)×66×24 [92(oa) 85.3(pp)×20.1×7.3]
Machinery: 2 screws, inverted compound engines (Penn), 10 return tubular boilers
IHP 6,000 = 13knots
Endurance: 4,500/12
Armament: 4×12.5" (317mm) MLR, 2×6" (152mm) BL
Later: 6×6pdr, 2×14" (356mm) TT added
Armour: Citadel 15-18" (381-457mm), turrets 14-16" (355-406mm), bulkheads 13.5-16.5" (343-419mm), c/t 12" (305mm), deck 3" (76mm)
Complement: 345
Class notes: Designed by Barnaby. Smaller and cheaper version of *Inflexible* with two turrets en echelon amidships and armoured deck. The last British battleships with muzzle loading guns. Unsatisfactory design, stability could not have been maintained in case of severe damage

'Belleisle' Class (1878)

Central Battery Ships: *Belleisle, Orion*
Displacement: 4,870tons
Dimensions: 245(pp)×52×21'1 [74.7(pp)×15.8×6.4]
Machinery: 2 screws, horizontal direct-action engines (Maudslay), 4 rectangular boilers
IHP 3,200 = 12.25knots
Endurance: 1,850/10
Armament: 4×12" (305mm) MLR, 4×20pdr
Later: 6×6" and 2×14" (356mm) TT (*Orion:* 4)
Armour: Belt 6-12" (152-305mm), battery 8-10" (203-254mm), c/t 9" (229mm), bulkheads 5-9" (127-229mm), deck 1-3" (25-76mm)
Complement: 249
Class notes: Coast defence rams designed in Constantinople for the Turkish navy and taken over in 1878 during the Russo-Turkish War. Unsuitable for fleet operations. Last British central battery ships. *Belleisle* briefly had square rig when completed and had short funnel raised 1879

'Superb' (1878)

Central Battery Ship: *Superb*
Displacement: 9,710tons
Dimensions: 332'3(pp)×59×26'6 [101.3(pp)×18×8.1]
Machinery: 1 screw, horizontal direct-acting engines (Maudslay), 9 rectangular boilers; *1887:* VTE engines (Humphrys), 5 cylindrical boilers
IHP 6,580 = 13.25knots; *1887:* IHP 8,500 = 14.5knots
Endurance: 2,000/10
Armament: 16×10" (254mm) MLR, 6×20pdr
1885: 20pdr replaced by 6×4", 4×14" (356mm) TT added
1891: 12×10" (254mm) MLR, 10×6' (152mm)/35 BL, 6×6pdr, 10×3pdr, 4×14" (356mm) TT
Armour: Belt 7-12" (178-305mm), battery 12" (305mm), c/t 8" (203mm), bulkheads 5-10" (127-254mm), deck 1.5" (38mm)
Complement: 640

Class notes: Designed by Reed. Built for Turkey but detained in Britain during Russo-Turkish War and purchased 1878. Last and best protected British broadside ironclad. Ram bow, two funnels and bark rig. Reconstructed 1887-91, new engines and boilers, rigging replaced by military masts, armament modified

'Neptune' (1878)

Turret Ship: *Neptune*
Displacement: 9,310tons
Dimensions: 300(pp)×63×25 [91.4(pp)×19.2×7.6]
Machinery: 1 screw, horizontal trunk engines (Penn), 8 rectangular boilers
IHP 8,500 = 14.25knots
Endurance: 1,480/10
Armament: 4×12.5″ (318mm) MLR, 2×9″ (229mm) MLR, 6×20pdr, 2×14″ (356mm) TT
Armour: Belt 9-12″ (229-305mm), redoubt 8-10″ (203-254mm), turrets 11-13″ (279-330mm), c/t 6-8″ (152-203mm), bulkheads 6-8″ (152-203mm), decks 2-3″ (51-76mm)
Complement: 541
Class notes: Designed by Reed as the Brazilian *Independencia*, a 'Devastation' with rigging which, with the poop and forecastle, deprived the turrets of axial fire. Purchased by Britain 1878, but considered a poor addition to the navy. Rigging replaced by military masts 1886

'Colossus' Class (1878)

Turret Ships: *Colossus* (see later photo), *Edinburgh*
Displacement: 9,150tons, 9,520f/l
Dimensions: 325(pp)×68×26′4 [99.1(pp)×20.7×8]
Machinery: 2 screws, inverted direct compound engines (*Colossus:* Maudslay; *Edinburgh:* Humphrys), 10 elliptical tubular boilers
IHP 6,000 = 14knots
Endurance: 6,200/10
Armament: 4×12″ (305mm)/25 BLR, 5×6″ (152mm) BLR, 4×6pdr, 10×3pdr, 2×14″ (356mm) TT
Armour: Citadel 14-18″ (355-457mm), bulkheads 13-16″ (330-406mm), turrets, 14-16″ (355-406mm), c/t 14″ (355mm), deck 3″ (76mm)
Complement: 396
Class notes: First British battleship with breech-loading guns and with compound armour instead of iron. Enlarged version of 'Ajax' class with two twin turrets en echelon amidships, single funnel and two military masts

'Conqueror' Class (1879-1882)

Turret Ships: *Conqueror* (see later photo), *Hero*
Displacement: *Conqueror:* 6,200tons; *Hero:* 6,440tons
Dimensions: 288(oa) 270(pp)×58×24′3 [87.8(oa) 82.3(pp)×17.7×7.4]
Machinery: 2 screws, inverted compound engines (*Conqueror:* Humphrys; *Hero:* Rennie), 8 cylindrical boilers
IHP 4,500 = 14knots
Endurance: 5,200/10
Armament: 2×12″ (305mm)/25, 4×6″ (152mm), 7×6pdr QF, 6×14″ (356mm) TT
Armour: Belt 8-12″ (203-305mm), citadel 10.5-12″ (267-305mm), turret 12-14″ (305-355mm), c/t 6-12″ (152-305mm), deck 2.5″ (63mm)
Complement: 330
Class notes: Designed by Barnaby. Too small for the seagoing fleet and good only for harbour service. A development of the 'Rupert' type

'Collingwood' (1879)

Barbette Ship: *Collingwood* (see later photo)
Displacement: 9,500tons
Dimensions: 325(pp)×68×26′11 [99.1(pp)×20.7×8.2]
Machinery: 2 screws, inverted compound engines (Humphrys), 12 cylindrical boilers
IHP 9,600 = 15.5knots
Endurance: 7,000/10
Armament: 4×12″ (305mm)/25, 6×6″ (152mm)/26, 12×6pdr, 4×14″ (356mm) TT
Armour: Belt 8-18″ (203-457mm), bulkheads 7-16″ (178-406mm), barbettes 10-11.5″ (254-292mm), c/t 2-12″ (51-305mm), deck 2.5″ (63mm)
Complement: 498
Class notes: Designed by Barnaby. Set the standard for future battleship designs for the next 25 years. Main guns mounted in twin barbettes fore and aft with smaller guns in batteries. Short narrow waterline belt

'Imperieuse' Class (1880)

Armoured Cruisers: *Imperieuse* (see later photo), *Warspite*
Displacement: 8,500tons
Dimensions: 315(pp)×62×27′3 [96(pp)×18.9×8.3]
Machinery: 2 screws, inverted compound engines (*Imperieuse:* Maudslay; *Warspite:* Penn) cylindrical and oval boilers
IHP 10,000 = 16.7knots
Endurance: 5,500/10
Armament: 4×9.2″ (234mm)/25, 10×6″ (152mm), 4×6pdr, 6×14″ (356mm) TT
Armour: Belt 10″ (254mm), barbettes 8″ (203mm), bulkheads 9″ (229mm), c/t 9″ (229m), deck 4″ (102mm)
Complement: 555
Class notes: Poorly designed with brig rig and breech loading guns. *Imperieuse* rerigged with single mast between the funnels and *Warspite* completed with new rig

'Admiral' Class (1881)

Barbette Ships: *Anson, Benbow* (see later photo), *Camperdown, Howe, Rodney*
Displacement: 10,600tons; *Howe* and *Rodney:* 10,300tons
Dimensions: 330(pp)×68′6×28′4 [100.5(pp)×20.9×8.6]
Howe and *Rodney:* 325(pp)×65×28′4 [99.1(pp)×19.8×8.6]
Machinery: 2 screws, inverted compound engines (Humphrys; *Benbow* and *Camperdown:* Maudslay), 12 cylindrical boilers
IHP 11,500 = 17.4knots
Armament: 4×13.5″ (343mm)/30, 6×6″ (152mm)/25, 12×6pdr, 10×3pdr, 5×14″ (356mm) TT (*Rodney:* 4)
Benbow: 2×16.25″ (413mm)/30, 10×6″/25
Armour: Belt 8-18″ (203-457mm), bulkheads 7-16″ (178-406mm), barbettes 12-14″ (305-355mm), c/t 12″ (305mm), deck 2.5-3″ (63-76mm)
Howe and *Rodney*, barbettes: 10-11.5″ (254-292mm)
Complement: 525
Class notes: Improved 'Collingwood' type with larger guns

Top right:
***Neptune* — Turret ship taken over from Brazil, as it appeared with military masts in 1895.** *IWM*

Centre right:
***Edinburgh* — 'Colossus' class turret ship of 1878.**
P. A. Vicary

Bottom right:
***Hero* — Turret ship, 'Conqueror' class, 1890s.**
P. A. Vicary/Martin Holbrook Collection

'Victoria' Class (1884)

Turret Ships: *Sans Pareil, Victoria*
Displacement: 10,470tons
Dimensions: 340(pp)×70×29 [103.6(pp)×21.3×8.8]
Machinery: 2 screws, VTE engines (Humphrys), 8 4-furnace boilers
IHP 14,000 = 17knots
Endurance: 7,000/10
Armament: 2×16.25" (413mm)/30, 1×10" (254mm)/32, 12×6" (152mm)/26, 12×6pdr, 6×14" (356mm) TT
Armour: Belt 16-18" (406-457mm), bulkheads 6-16" (152-406mm), turret 17" (432mm), redoubt 18" (457mm), c/t 10-14" (254-355mm), deck 3" (76mm)
Complement: 430
Class notes: Designed by Barnaby. First battleships with triple expansion engines. Reversion to one turret with two tall funnels side by side

'Orlando' Class (1884)

Armoured Cruisers: *Aurora, Australia, Galatea, Immortalité, Narcissus, Orlando, Undaunted*
Displacement: 5,600tons
Dimensions: 300(pp)×56×26 [91.4(pp)×17.1×7.9]
Machinery: 2 screws, HTE engines (*Aurora:* Thompson; *Australia* and *Galatea:* Napier; *Immortalité* and *Narcissus:* Earle; *Orlando* and *Undaunted:* Palmer), 4 double-ended boilers
IHP 8,500 = 18knots
Endurance: 8,000/10
Armament: 2×9.2" (234mm)/25, 10×6" (152mm)/25, 3×9pdr, 10×3pdr (47mm), 4×14" (356mm) TT
1897-1900: 2×9.2"/30, 10×6" QF, TT removed
Armour: Belt 10" (254mm), bulkheads 16" (406mm), deck 2-3" (51-76mm), c/t 12" (305mm)
Complement: 484
Class notes: Armoured or 'belted' cruisers lacking protection for the guns, with two single turrets fore and aft, secondary armament in gunhouses amidships, two funnels and two masts. Shorter funnels on *Undaunted*

'Trafalgar' Class (1885)

Turret Ships: *Nile, Trafalgar*
Displacement: 12,590tons
Dimensions: 345(pp)×73×30 [105.2(pp)×22.2×9.1]
Machinery: 2 screws, VTE engines (*Nile:* Maudslay; *Trafalgar:* Humphrys), 6 cylindrical boilers
IHP 12,000 = 16.75knots
Endurance: 6,500/10
Armament: 4×13.5" (343mm)/30, 6×4.7" (119mm), 8×6pdr, 9×3pdr (47mm), 6×14" (356mm) TT
1896: 4.7" replaced by 6" QF
Armour: Belt 14-20" (355-508mm), bulkheads 14-16" (355-406mm), turrets 18" (457mm), c/t 14" (355mm), deck 3" (76mm)
Complement: 577
Class notes: Two twin turrets fore and aft with two funnels side by side and military mast. First British battleships with quick-firing guns. *Trafalgar* completed with short funnels which were raised 1891. *Nile* completed with taller funnels which extended beyond the casings

Top left:
***Camperdown* — 'Admiral' class barbette ship.** *IWM*

Centre left:
***Sans Pareil* — 'Victoria' class turret ship, 1890s.** *IWM*

Bottom left:
***Australia* — 'Orlando' class armoured cruiser, with short funnels, 1891.** *Photomatic*

'Barfleur' Class (1888)

Barbette Ships: *Barfleur, Centurion*
Displacement: 10,500tons
Dimensions: 360(wl)×70×25'6 [109.7(wl)×21.3×7.8]
Machinery: 2 screws, VTE engines (Greenock Foundry), 8 cylindrical boilers
IHP 13,000 = 18.5knots
Endurance: 6,000/10
Armament: 4×10" (254mm)/32, 10×4.7" (119mm) QF, 8×6pdr, 12×3pdr, 7×18" (457mm) TT
1901: 4.7" replaced by 6", 4TT removed
Armour: Belt 12" (305mm), bulkheads 8" (203mm), barbettes 6-9" (152-229mm), c/t 12" (305mm), casemates 4" (102mm), deck 2" (51mm)
Complement: 620
Class notes: Second class battleships intended for foreign service. Similar to 'Royal Sovereign' class but with hooded barbettes. Reconstructed 1901-04 with new casemates and foremast removed

'Royal Sovereign' Class (1888-1889)

Barbette Ships: *Empress of India, Ramillies, Repulse, Resolution* (see later photo), *Revenge, Royal Oak, Royal Sovereign*
Turret Ship: *Hood* (see later photo)
Displacement: 14,150tons, 15,585f/l
Dimensions: 410'6(oa) 380(wl)×75×30 [125.1(oa) 115.8(wl)×22.9×9.1]
Machinery: 2 screws, VTE engines (Humphrys; *Resolution* and *Revenge:* Palmers; *Royal Oak:* Laird; *Ramillies:* Thomson), 8 cylindrical boilers
IHP 11,000 = 16.5knots
Endurance: 4,720/10
Armament: 4×13.5" (343mm) 30, 10×6" (152mm) 26/QF, 16×6pdr (*Hood:* 10), 12×3pdr, 7×18" (457mm) TT
1905: 4 TT removed
Armour: Belt 14-18" (355-457mm), bulkheads 14-16" (355-406mm), barbettes (*Hood:* turrets) 11-17" (279-432mm), forward c/t 14" (355mm), casemates 6" (152mm), decks 3" (76mm)
Complement: 712
Class notes: A highly successful design and faster than any contemporary battleships. Designed by White with big guns in separate redoubts separated by the secondary battery and with high freeboard. Presented a symmetrical profile with fore and aft barbettes, two military masts and two funnels side by side. *Hood* was similar except big guns were in turrets and had one less deck, a less desirable arrangement. Secondary battery in casemates, and upper guns put in casemates 1902-04

'Renown' (1892)

Pre-dreadnought: *Renown* (see later photo)
Displacement: 12,350tons
Dimensions: 380(wl)×72'4×26'9 [115.8(wl)×22.0×8.1]
Machinery: 2 screws, VTE engines (Maudslay), 8 cylindrical boilers
IHP 12,000 = 18knots
Endurance: 8,500/15
Armament: 4×10" (254mm)/40, 10×6" (152mm) QF,

Above left:
***Trafalgar* — Turret ship of 1885.** *Marius Bar*

Above right:
***Barfleur* — Barbette ship of 1888.** *Marius Bar*

Far left:
***Mars* — 'Majestic' class battleship, c1904.**

Left:
***Vengeance* — 'Canopus' class pre-dreadnought, 1903.**

Below left:
***Formidable* — Pre-dreadnought at Spithead Review, July 1914, sunk in 1915.**

Below:
***Good Hope* — 'Drake' class armoured cruiser, sunk with all hands at Coronel, 1914.**

12×12pdr (76mm), 12×3pdr (47mm), 5×18″ (457mm) TT
1902: 6×6″ removed
1905: All 6″ removed
Armour: Belt 6-8″ (152-203mm), bulkheads and barbettes 6-10″ (152-254mm), c/t 9″ (229mm), casemates 6″ (152mm), deck 2-3″ (51-76mm)
Complement: 674
Class notes: Designed by White as modified 'Barfleur' type with all steel armour

'Majestic' Class (1893-94)

Pre-dreadnoughts: *Caesar, Hannibal, Illustrious, Jupiter* (see later photo), *Magnificent, Majestic, Mars, Prince George, Victorious*
Displacement: 14,890tons, 16,060f/l
Dimensions: 421(oa) 399(wl) 390(pp)×75×30 [128.3(oa) 121.6(wl) 118.9(pp)×22.9×9.1]
Machinery: 2 screws, VTE engines (*Caesar:* Maudslay; *Hannibal:* Harland; *Illustrious* and *Magnificent:* Penn; *Jupiter:* Thomson; *Majestic*, Vickers; *Mars:* Laird; *Prince George:* Humphrys; *Victorious:* Hawthorn), 8 cylindrical boilers
IHP 12,000 = 17knots
Endurance: 7,600/10
Armament: 4×12″ (305mm)/35, 12×6″ (152mm)/40, 16×12pdr (76mm), 12×3pdr (47mm), 5×18″ (457mm) TT
Armour: Belt 9″ (229mm), bulkheads 12-14″ (305-355mm), c/t 14″ (355mm), casemates 6″ (152mm), decks 4″ (102mm)
Complement: 672
Class notes: Designed by White, Improved 'Renown' with new 12″ guns. Served as a pattern for battleship design until *Dreadnought*. Two oval barbettes and two military masts with secondary armament in casemates. *Magnificent, Mars, Hannibal* and *Victorious* had main guns removed 1915 for use in new monitors

'Canopus' Class (1896)

Pre-dreadnoughts: *Albion, Canopus, Glory* (see later photo), *Goliath, Ocean, Vengeance*
Displacement: 12,950tons, 14,320f/l
Dimensions: 418(oa) 400(wl) 390(pp)×74×26′6 [127.4(oa) 121.9(wl) 118.8(pp)×22.6×8.1]
Machinery: 2 screws, VTE engines (*Albion:* Maudslay; *Canopus:* Greenock Foundry; *Glory:* Laird; *Goliath:* Penn; *Ocean:* Hawthorn; *Vengeance:* Vickers), 20 Belleville boilers
IHP 13,500 = 18.25knots
Endurance: 8,000/10
Armament: 4×12″ (305mm)/35, 12×6″ (152mm)/40 (*Canopus* and *Glory:* 8), 12×12pdr (76mm), 6×3pdr (47mm), 4×18″ (457mm) TT
1916: 4×6″ and 6×12pdr removed
Armour: Belt 2-6″ (51-152mm), bulkheads and barbettes 6-12″ (152-306mm), c/t 12″ (305mm), casemates 6″ (152mm), deck 2.5″ (63mm)

Top left:
***Cornwallis* — 'Duncan' class pre-dreadnought, torpedoed and sunk by a U-boat in 1917.** *Marius Bar*

Centre left:
***Cornwall* — 'Monmouth' class armoured cruiser, 1909.**

Bottom left:
***King Edward VII* — Pre-dreadnought, 1911.** *P. A. Vicary*

Complement: 750
Class notes: Improved 'Majestic' class with thinner armour and circular barbettes. First British battleships with watertube boilers. Two uneven funnels fore and aft. Main deck casemate guns removed 1916

'Formidable' Class (1897-1900)

Pre-dreadnoughts: *Bulwark, Formidable, Implacable, Irresistible, London* (see later photo), *Prince of Wales, Queen, Venerable*
Displacement: 15,000tons, 15,640f/l
Dimensions: 431′9(oa) 411(wl) 400(pp)×75×26′10 [131.6(oa) 125.3(wl) 121.9(pp)×22.9×8.2]
Machinery: 2 screws, VTE engines (*Bulwark:* Hawthorn; *Formidable* and *London* : Earle; *Implacable:* Laird; *Irresistible* and *Venerable:* Maudslay; *Prince of Wales:* Greenock Foundry; *Queen:* Harland), 20 Belleville boilers (*Queen:* 15 B&W)
IHP 15,000 = 18knots
Endurance: 8,000/10
Armament: 4×12″ (305mm)/40, 12×6″ (152mm)/45, 16×12pdr (76mm), 6×3pdr (47mm), 4×18″ (457mm) TT
Implacable, London and *Venerable, 1916:* 4×6″ and 8×12pdr removed
Armour: Belt 9″ (229mm), bulkheads 9-12″ (229-305mm), barbettes 6-12″ (152-305mm), c/t 14″ (355mm), casemates 6″ (152mm), deck 3″ (76mm)
Complement: 780
Class notes: Improved 'Canopus' class with heavier armour and new 12″ guns. *Formidable, Irresistible* and *Implacable* were 1897 programme and remaining ships were officially a separate ('London') class with modifications to the armour arrangement. *London* fitted with flying off platform for seaplane experiments 1912. In 1917 *London* was converted to minelayer and main guns were removed

'Cressy' Class (1898)

Armoured Cruisers: *Aboukir, Bacchante* (see later photo), *Cressy, Euryalus* (see later photo), *Hogue, Sutlej*
Displacement: 12,000tons
Dimensions: 472(oa) 454(wl) 440(pp)×69′6×25′9 (143.9(oa) 138.4(wl) 134.1(pp)×21.2×7.8]
Machinery: 2 screws VTE engines (*Aboukir* and *Cressy:* Fairfield; *Bacchante* and *Sutlej*; John Brown; *Euryalus* and *Hogue:* Vickers), 30 Belleville boilers
IHP 21,000 = 21knots
Armament: 2×9.2″ (234mm)/40, 12×6″ (152mm)/45, 12×12pdr (76mm), 2×18″ (457mm) TT
Armour: Belt 2-6″ (51-152mm), bulkheads 5″ (127mm), turrets 6″ (152mm), casemates 5″ (127mm), deck 3″ (76mm), c/t 12″ (305mm)
Complement: 760
Class notes: Modified 'Diadem' class with armour belt on waterline and larger guns, the armour modelled on 'Canopus' class battleships. Four funnels, two single turrets fore and aft and secondary armament in casemates amidships. Conversion of *Euryalus* to minelayer cancelled 1918

'Drake' Class (1898)

Armoured Cruisers: *Drake* (see later photo), *Good Hope, King Alfred, Leviathan*
Displacement: 14,100tons
Dimensions: 529′6(oa) 515(wl) 500(pp)×71×26 [161.4(oa) 157(wl) 152.4(pp)×21.6×7.9]
Machinery: 2 screws, VTE engines, (*Drake:* Humphrys; *Good Hope:* Fairfield; *King Alfred:* Vickers; *Leviathan:* John Brown), 43 Belleville boilers

IHP 30,000 = 23knots
Armament: 2×9.2" (234mm)/40, 16×6" (152mm)/45, 14×12pdr (76mm), 2×18" (457mm) TT
Armour: Belt 3-6" (76-152mm), bulkheads 8" (203mm), turrets 5" (127mm), barbettes and casemates 6" (152mm), c/t 12" (305mm)
Complement: 900
Class notes: Designed by White. Enlarged 'Cressy' class with pole masts, more armour and improved engines. Main deck guns could not be used at high speed

'Duncan' Class (1898)

Pre-dreadnoughts: *Albemarle, Cornwallis, Duncan, Exmouth, Montagu, Russell*
Displacement: 14,000tons
Dimensions: 432(oa) 418(wl) 405(pp)×75'6×26'3 [131.6(oa) 127.4(wl) 123.4(pp)×23×8]
Machinery: 2 screws, VTE engines (Thames; *Exmouth* and *Montagu:* Laird; *Russell:* Palmer), 24 Belleville boilers
IHP 18,000 = 19knots
Armament: 4×12" (305mm)/40, 12×6" (152mm)/45, 10×12pdr (76mm), 6×3pdr (47mm), 4×18" (457mm) TT
Albemarle, 1917: 4×6" and 6×12pdr removed
Armour: Belt 3-7" (76-178mm), bulkheads 7-11" (178-279mm), barbettes 4-11" (102-279mm), c/t 12" (305mm), deck 2.5" (63mm)
Complement: 720
Class notes: Modified 'Formidable' class, faster, with slightly less protection. Main deck battery of *Albemarle* removed to upper deck 1917

'Monmouth' Class (1899-1900)

Armoured Cruisers: *Bedford, Berwick, Cornwall, Cumberland, Donegal, Essex, Kent, Lancaster* (see later photo), *Monmouth, Suffolk* (see later photo)
Displacement: 9,800tons
Dimensions: 463'6(oa) 440(wl)×66×24'6 [141.3(oa) 134.1(wl)×20.1×7.5]
Machinery: 2 screws, VTE engines (*Bedford* and *Donegal:* Fairfield; *Berwick* and *Suffolk:* Humphrys; *Cornwall, Lancaster* and *Kent:* Hawthorn; *Cumberland* and *Monmouth:* London & Glasgow; *Essex:* John Brown), 31 Belleville boilers (*Cornwall:* 24 B&W; *Berwick* and *Suffolk:* Niclausse)
IHP 22,000 = 23knots
Armament: 14×6" (152mm)/45, 10×12pdr (76mm), 3×3pdr (47mm), 2×18" (457mm) TT
Armour: Belt 2-4" (51-102mm), bulkheads 5" (127mm), turrets 5" (127mm), casemates 4" (102mm), c/t 10" (254mm)
Complement: 678
Class notes: Designed by White for commerce protection with two twin turrets fore and aft and balance of guns in broadside casemates. Three funnels and two masts, high freeboard

'King Edward VII' Class (1901-1903)

Pre-dreadnoughts: *Africa, Britannia, Commonwealth, Dominion, Hibernia, Hindustan, King Edward VII, New Zealand* (see later photo)
Displacement: 16,350tons, 17,500f/l
Dimensions: 453'9(oa) 439(wl) 425(pp)×78×26'9 [138.3(oa) 133.8(wl) 129.5(pp)×23.8×8.1]
Machinery: 2 screws, VTE engines (*Africa* and *Hindustan:* John Brown; *Britannia* and *New Zealand:* Humphrys; *Commonwealth:* Fairfield; *Dominion:* Vickers; *Hibernia* and *King Edward:* Harland), 16 B&W boilers (*Africa, Britannia, Hibernia* and *Hindustan:* 12 B&W and 3 cylindrical; *King Edward:* 10 B&W and 6 cylindrical; *New Zealand:* 12 Niclausse and 3 cylindrical)
IHP 18,000 = 18.5knots
Endurance: 7,000/10
Armament: 4×12" (305mm)/40, 4×9.2" (234mm)/45, 10×6" (152mm)/50, 14×12pdr (76mm), 14×3pdr (47mm), 5×18" (457mm) TT
Commonwealth and *Zealandia, 1918:* 6×6" and 4×12pdr removed
Armour: Belt 4-9" (102-229mm), bulkheads 8-12" (203-305mm), barbettes 6-12" (152-305mm), c/t 12" (305mm), battery 7" (178mm), deck 2" (51mm)
Complement: 777
Class notes: Design started by White and completed by Watts. Had 9.2" secondary battery and fire control positions instead of fighting tops on both masts. *Hibernia* fitted with flying off platform for seaplane experiments 1912. *Commonwealth* and *Zealandia* (ex-*New Zealand*) were altered for coastal bombardment and fitted with tripod foremast 1918

'Devonshire' Class (1901)

Armoured Cruisers: *Antrim, Argyll, Carnarvon, Devonshire, Hampshire, Roxburgh*
Displacement: 10,750tons
Dimensions: 475(oa) 450(pp)×68'6×25'3 [144.8(oa) 137.2(pp)×20.9×7.7]
Machinery: 2 screws, VTE engines (*Antrim:* John Brown; *Argyll:* Greenock Foundry; *Carnarvon:* Humphrys; *Devonshire:* Thames; *Hampshire:* Hawthorn; *Roxburgh:* London & Glasgow), 17 Yarrow boilers (*Argyll:* 16 B&W; *Carnarvon:* 17 Niclausse; *Devonshire:* 15 Niclausse and 2 B&W; *Roxburgh:* 17 Durr and 6 cylindrical)
IHP 21,000 = 22.5knots
Armament: 4×7.5" (190mm)/50, 6×6" (152mm)/50, 2×12pdr (76mm), 17×3pdr (47mm), 2×18" (457mm) TT
Armour: Belt 2-6" (51-152mm), bulkheads 6" (152mm), barbettes and casemates 6" (152mm), deck 1.5" (38mm), c/t 12" (305mm)
Complement: 655
Class notes: Designed by Watts. Improved 'Monmouth' class with 7.5" guns fore and aft and greater protection. Had four funnels and two masts, all raked for the first time

'Duke of Edinburgh' Class (1902)

Armoured Cruisers: *Black Prince, Duke of Edinburgh* (see also later photo)
Displacement: 13,550tons, 14,500f/l
Dimensions: 505'6(oa) 480(pp)×73'6×27'1 [154(oa) 146.3(pp)×22.4×8.2]
Machinery: 2 screws, VTE engines (*Black Prince:* Thames; *Duke of Edinburgh:* Hawthorn), 20 B&W and 6 cylindrical boilers
IHP 23,000 = 22.75knots
Endurance: 8,130/10
Armament: 6×9.2" (234mm)/45, 10×6" (152mm)/50, 20×3pdr (47mm), 3×18" TT (457mm)
Armour: Belt 3-6" (76-152mm), turrets 4.5-7.5" (114-190mm), barbettes 3-6" (76-152mm), battery 6" (152mm), c/t 10" (254mm), decks 1-1.5" (26-37mm)
Complement: 789
Class notes: Designed by Watts. Were to serve with the battle fleet rather than for commerce protection. Cruiser version of 'King Edward VII' class with 12" guns omitted; 6" batteries placed too low to be used except in calm sees. *Duke*

Above:
***Argyll* — 'Devonshire' class armoured cruiser, c1916.**
IWM

Below:
***Duke of Edinburgh* — Armoured cruiser, c1906.**

***Swiftsure* — Pre-dreadnought purchased from Chile in 1903.** *Marius Bar*

of *Edinburgh* modified 1916, with tripod replacing forward mast and 6" batteries placed in mounts on upper deck

'Swiftsure' Class (1903)

Pre-dreadnoughts: *Swiftsure, Triumph*
Displacement: 11,800tons, 13,840f/l
Dimensions: 479'9(oa) 458(wl) 436(pp)×71×25'4 [146.2(oa) 139'6(wl) 132.9(pp)×21.6×7.7]
Machinery: 2 screws, VTE engines (*Swiftsure:* Humphrys; *Triumph:* Vickers), 12 Yarrow boilers
IHP 12,500 = 19knots
Endurance: 6,250/10
Armament: 4×10" (254mm)/45, 14×7.5" (190mm)/50, 14×14pdr, 4×6pdr (57mm), 2×18" (457mm) TT
Armour: Belt 3-7" (76-178mm), barbettes 3-10" (76-254mm), c/t 11" (279mm), battery and casemates 7" (178mm), deck 3" (76mm)
Complement: 802
Class notes: Designed by Reed. Built for Chile and purchased prior to completion. Smaller than other British battleships but the first to record 20knots

'Warrior' Class (1903)

Armoured Cruisers: *Achilles, Cochrane, Natal* (see also later photo), *Warrior*
Displacement: 13,350tons, 14,500f/l
Dimensions: 505'6(oa) 480(pp)×73'5×27'6 [154.1(oa) 146.3(pp)×22.4×8.4]
Machinery: 2 screws, VTE engines (*Achilles:* Hawthorn; *Cochrane:* Fairfield; *Natal:* Vickers; *Warrior:* Wallsend), 19 Yarrow and 6 cylindrical boilers
IHP 23,000 = 23knots
Endurance: 7,960/10
Armament: 6×9.2" (234mm)/45, 4×7.5" (190mm)/50, 24×3pdr (47mm), 3×18" (457mm) TT
Armour: Belt 3-6" (76-152mm), turrets 4.5-7.5" (114-190mm), barbettes 6" (152mm), deck 1.5" (37mm), c/t 10" (254mm)
Complement: 712
Class notes: Laid down as 'Duke of Edinburgh' class but modified by having secondary armament raised one deck and mounted in turrets. Had the reputation of being the best cruisers ever built. Funnels raised 1912. *Achilles* and *Cochrane* refitted 1916 with tripod foremast and director tops

'Minotaur' Class (1904)

Armoured Cruisers: *Defence, Minotaur, [Orion], Shannon* (see later photo)
Displacement: 14,600tons, 16,100f/l
Dimensions: 519(oa) 490(pp)×74'6×26 [158.2(oa) 149.4(pp)×22.7×7.9]; *Shannon*: beam 75'6 [22.9]
Machinery: 2 screws, VTE engines (*Defence:* Scotts; *Minotaur:* Harland; *Shannon:* Humphrys), 24 Yarrow boilers (*Minotaur:* 25 B&W)
IHP 27,000 = 23knots
Endurance: 8,150/10
Armament: 4×9.2" (234mm)/50, 10×7.5" (190mm)/50, 16×12pdr (76mm), 5×18mm (457mm) TT
Armour: Belt 3-6" (76-152mm), turrets 4.5-8" (114-203mm), barbettes 7" (178mm), c/t 10" (254mm), decks 1-2" (25-51mm)
Complement: 755
Class notes: Designed by Watts. Funnels raised 1909 and tripod foremast fitted 1917. Enlarged 'Warrior' class with twin turrets fore and aft. Funnels raised 1909. *Minotaur* and *Shannon* refitted 1917 with tripod foremasts and director tops. *Orion* never built. Last armoured cruisers built, being actually completed after the first battlecruisers entered service

'Lord Nelson' Class (1904)

Pre-dreadnoughts: *Agamemnon, Lord Nelson*
Displacement: 16,500tons, 17,820f/l
Dimensions: 443'6(oa) 435(wl) 410(pp)×79'6×27 [135.2(oa) 132.6(wl) 125(pp)×24.2×8.2]
Machinery: 2 screws, VTE engines (*Agamemnon:* Hawthorn; *Lord Nelson:* Palmer), 15 Yarrow boilers (*Lord Nelson:* B&W)
IHP 16,750 = 18knots
Endurance: 9,180/10
Armament: 4×12" (305mm)/45, 10×9.2 (234mm)/50, 24×12pdr (76mm), 5×18" (457mm) TT

***Natal* — 'Warrior' class armoured cruiser, March 1907, on trials.**

Armour: Belt 4-12" (102-305mm), barbettes 3-12" (76-305mm), turrets 12" (305mm), bulkheads 8" (203mm), citadel 8" (203mm), c/t 12" (305mm)
Complement: 817
Class notes: Designed by Watts with battery of mixed large calibre guns in turrets. First British battleships with a tripod mast and the last with twin screws and reciprocating engines. Funnels raised 1917. *Agamemnon* converted to radio controlled target ship 1923

'Dreadnought' (1905)

Dreadnought: *Dreadnought* (see also later photo)
Displacement: 17,900tons, 21,845f/l
Dimensions: 527(oa) 520(wl) 490(pp)×82×26'6 [160.6(oa) 158.5(wl) 149.4(pp)×25×8.1]
Machinery: 4 screws, Parsons turbines (Vickers), 18 B&W boilers
SHP 23,000 = 21knots
Endurance: 6,620/10
Armament: 10×12" (305mm)/45, 27×12pdr (76mm), 5×18 (457mm) TT
Armour: Belt and barbettes 4-11" (102-279mm), bulkheads 8" (203mm), turrets 11" (279mm), c/t 11" (279mm), decks 1-4" (26-102mm)
Complement: 697
Class notes: First battleship with main armament of a single calibre; also first with steam turbines and quadruple screws. Design outclassed and made obsolete all other battleships afloat and ship's name was thereafter used to describe all battleships with single calibre armament. Two funnels with single tripod mast just abaft forward funnel and a small tripod aft. Built in record time, being completed one year after being laid down. Withdrawn from the Grand Fleet 1916 before Jutland as too slow

'Invincible' Class (1905)

Battlecruisers: *Indomitable, Inflexible, Invincible*
Displacement: 17,250tons, 20,125f/l
Dimensions: 567(oa) 560(wl) 530(pp)×78'5×26'8 [172.8(oa) 170.7(wl) 161.5(pp)×23.9×8.1]
Machinery: 4 screws, Parsons turbines (*Indomitable:* Fairfield; *Inflexible:* John Brown; *Invincible:* Humphrys), 31 Yarrow boilers (*Indomitable:* B&W)
IHP 41,000 = 25knots
Endurance: 3,000/25
Armament: 8×12" (305mm)/45, 16×4" (102mm)/45, 1×3" (76mm), 5×18" (457mm) TT
1917: 4×4" replaced by 1×4" AA and 1×3" AA
Armour: Belt 4-6" (102-152mm), barbettes 2-7" (51-178mm), turrets 7" (178mm), bulkheads 6-7" (152-178mm), c/t 10" (254mm), decks 1.5-2.5" (37-63mm)
Complement: 784
Class notes: The first battlecruisers, built under great secrecy, with protection sacrificed for speed. Similar to *Dreadnought* with 12" guns, turbines, tripod masts and great length. *Indomitable* and *Inflexible* had the fore funnel raised 1910-11 and *Invincible* 1914. Modifications to armour protection made after Jutland

'Bellerophon' Class (1906)

Dreadnoughts: *Bellerophon, Superb, Temeraire* (see later photo)
Displacement: 18,600tons, 22,100f/l
Dimensions: 526(oa) 520(wl) 490(pp)×82'5×27'2 [160.3(oa) 158.5(wl) 149.4(pp)×25.1×8.3]
Machinery: 4 screws, Parsons turbines (*Bellerophon:* Fairfield; *Superb:* Wallsend; *Temeraire:* Hawthorn), 18 B&W boilers (*Temeraire:* Yarrow)
IHP 23,000 = 20.75knots
Endurance: 5,720/10
Armament: 10×12" (305mm)/45, 16×4" (102mm)/50, 4×3pdr (47mm) 3×18" (457mm) TT
1918: 2×4" (102mm) AA added
Armour: Belt 5-10" (127-254mm), barbettes 5-9" (127-229mm), turrets 11" (279mm), bulkheads 8" (203mm), c/t 8-11" (203-279mm), decks 1.5-4" (37-102mm)
Complement: 733
Class notes: Repeat 'Dreadnought' type with two tripod masts each forward of one of the two funnels. Anti-torpedo bulkheads were added to the longitudinal bulkheads of previous types

Above left:
Minotaur **— 'Minotaur' class armoured cruiser, 1917. Notice new tripod mast and dazzle camouflage.** *IWM*

Above right:
Lord Nelson **— The last pre-dreadnought, 1918, after funnels were raised. Notice 9.2" turrets amidships.**
P. A. Vicary

Left:
Dreadnought **— The first all big-gun battleship, 1907. It was considered too slow by 1916 and missed the Battle of Jutland.**

KING GEORGE V
ADMIRAL JELLICOE

'St Vincent' Class (1907)

Dreadnoughts: *Collingwood, St Vincent* (see later photo), *Vanguard*
Displacement: 19,250tons, 23,030f/l
Dimensions: 536(oa) 530(wl) 500(pp)×84×28'7 [163.4(oa) 161.5(wl) 152.4(pp)×25.6×8.7]
Machinery: 4 screws, Parsons turbines (*Collingwood:* Hawthorn; *St Vincent:* Scotts, *Vanguard:* Vickers), 18 B&W boilers (*Collingwood:* Yarrow)
IHP 24,500 = 21knots
Endurance: 6,900/10
Armament: 10×12" (305mm)/50, 20×4" (102mm)/50, 4×3pdr (47mm), 3×18mm (457mm) TT
By 1917: Only 12×4"; also 1×4" AA, 1×3" AA, only 2 TT
Armour: Belt 7-10" (178-254mm), turrets 11" (279mm), barbettes 5-9" (127-229mm), bulkheads 4-8" (102-203mm), c/t 8-11" (203-279mm), decks 1.5-3" (37-76mm)
Complement: 758
Class notes: Improved 'Bellerophon' type with new 12" guns

'Neptune' Class (1908-09)

Dreadnoughts: *Colossus, Hercules, Neptune*
Displacement: 20,000tons, 23,050f/l; *Neptune:* 19,900tons, 22,720f/l
Dimensions: 546(oa) 540(wl) 510(pp)×85×28'6 [166.4(oa) 164.6(wl) 155.4(pp)×25.9×8.7]
Machinery: 4 screws, Parsons turbines (*Colossus:* Scotts; *Hercules:* Palmer; *Neptune;* Harland), 18 Yarrow boilers (*Colossus:* B&W)
IHP 25,000 = 21knots
Endurance: 6,680/10
Armament: 10×12" (305mm)/50, 16×4" (102mm)/50, 4×3pdr (47mm), 3×21" (457mm) (*Neptune:* 18")
1917: Only 13×4", 1×4" AA, 1×3" AA, 2×21" TT
Armour: Belt 7-11" (178-279mm), bulkeads 4-10" (102-254mm), decks 1.5-3" (38-76mm), barbettes 4-11" (102-279mm), turrets 11" (279mm), c/t 11" (279mm)
Neptune: belt 7-10" (178-254mm), bulkheads 4-8" (102-203mm), barbettes 5-9" (127-229mm)
Complement: 755
Class notes: New turret arrangement to provide greater broadside fire with amidships turrets en echelon and 'X' turret superfiring over 'Y' turret. Flying bridge admidships. *Colossus* and *Hercules* differed in having stronger armour and only one tripod mast again fitted abaft forward funnel. Fore funnel raised 1912. *Neptune* had forward flying bridge removed 1914 and after control top removed. Others had after flying bridge removed 1914

'Indefatigable' Class (1908-09)

Battlecruisers: *Australia, Indefatigable* (see later photo), *New Zealand*
Displacement: 18,800tons, 22,080f/l
Dimensions: 590(oa) 578(wl) 555(pp)×80×27 [179.8(oa) 176.2(wl) 169.2(pp)×24.4×8.2]

Top left:
***Indomitable* — Battlecruiser of 'Invincible' class, with the King on board.** *Marius Bar*

Centre left:
***Vanguard* — 'St Vincent' class dreadnought, 1910, as completed.**

Bottom left:
***Colossus* — Dreadnought, completed 1911.**

Machinery: 4 screws, Parsons turbines (John Brown; *New Zealand:* Fairfield), 31 B&W boilers
IHP 44,000 = 25knots
Endurance: 6,330/10
Armament: 8×12" (305mm)/45, 16×4" (102mm)/50, 4×3pdr (76mm), 2×18" (457mm) TT
Armour: Belt 4-6" (102-152mm), barbettes 3-7" (76-178mm), turrets 7" (178mm), c/t 10" (254mm), bulkheads 4" (102mm), decks 1-2.5" (26-63mm)
Complement: 800
Class notes: Enlarged 'Invincible' class with similar weak protection. Forward funnel raised later. Australia and New Zealand paid for two of this class and *Australia* was actually flagship of the Royal Australian Navy

'Orion' Class (1909)

Dreadnoughts: *Conqueror, Monarch, Orion, Thunderer*
Displacement: 22,500tons, 25,870f/l
Dimensions: 581(oa) 576'3(wl) 545(pp)×88'6×27'6 [177.1(oa) 175.6(wl) 166.1(pp)×27×8.4]
Machinery: 4 screws, Parsons turbines (*Conqueror:* Beardmore; *Monarch:* Hawthorn; *Orion:* Wallsend; *Thunderer:* Thames), 18 B&W boilers (*Monarch:* Yarrow)
IHP 27,000 = 21knots
Endurance: 6,730/10
Armament: 10×13.5" (343mm)/45, 16×4" (102mm)/50, 4×3pdr, 3×21" (533mm) TT
1917: 8×4" removed and 2×4" AA added; only 2 TT
Armour: Belt 8-12" (203-305mm), barbettes 3-10" (76-254mm), turrets 11" (279mm), bulkheads 3-10" (76-254mm), c/t 11" (279mm), decks 1-4" (26-102mm)
Complement: 752
Class notes: First British dreadnoughts with 13.5" guns all on the centreline in superfiring turrets. Tripod mast abaft forward funnel. First class to have director firing system

'Lion' Class (1909-10)

Battlecruisers: *Lion, Princess Royal* (see later photo), *Queen Mary*
Displacement: 26,350tons, 29,680f/l
Dimensions: 700(oa) 675(wl) 660(pp)×88'6×28'10 [213.4(oa) 205.7(wl) 201.2(pp)×27×8.8]
Machinery: 4 screws, Parsons turbines (Vickers; *Queen Mary:* John Brown), 42 Yarrow boilers
IHP 70,000 = 26knots
Endurance: 5,610/10
Armament: 8×13.5" (343mm)/45, 16×4" (102mm)/50, 4×3pdr (47mm), 2×21" (533mm) TT
Armour: Belt 4-9" (102-229mm), barbettes 3-9" (76-229mm), turrets 9" (229mm), c/t 10" (254mm), bulkheads 4" (102mm), decks 1" (26mm)
Complement: 997
Class notes: First battlecruisers which surpassed battleships in size. Retained amidships turret with limited arc of fire. *Lion* completed with tripod foremast aft of the fore funnel. *Lion* was altered and others completed with funnels raised and light pole foremast forward of funnels. In 1917-18 foremast changed to tripod

'King George V' Class (1910)

Dreadnoughts: *Ajax* (see later photo), *Audacious* (see later photo), *Centurion, King George V*
Displacement: 23,000tons, 25,700f/l
Dimensions: 597'6(oa) 589'6(wl) 555(pp)×89×28'8 [182.1(oa) 179.7(wl) 169.2(pp)×27.1×8.7]; *King George V*: 594'4(oa) [180.1(oa)]
Machinery: 4 screws, Parsons turbines (*Ajax:* Scotts;

Audacious: Laird; *Centurion:* Hawthorn; *King George V:* Parsons), 18 B&W boilers (*Audacious* and *Centurion:* Yarrow)
IHP 31,000 = 21.75knots
Endurance: 4,060/18
Armament: 10×13.5 (343mm)/45, 16×4″ (102mm)/50, 4×3pdr (47mm), 3×21″ (533mm) TT
1917: 4×4″ replaced by 2×4″ AA, 1 TT removed
Armour: Belt 8-12″ (203-305mm), barbettes 3-10″ (76-254mm), turrets 11″ (279mm), bulkheads 4-10″ (102-254mm), c/t 11″ (279mm), decks 1-4″ (26-102mm)
Complement: 782; *later:* 1,132
Class notes: Improved 'Orion' class with pole mast forward of funnels, later modified to a tripod. *Centurion* converted to radio controlled target ship 1926

'Iron Duke' Class (1911)

Dreadnoughts: *Benbow, Emperor of India* (see later photo), *Iron Duke, Marlborough*
Displacement: 26,100tons, 30,380f/l
Dimensions: 622′9(oa) 614′3(wl) 580(pp)×90×29′6 [189.8(oa) 187.2(wl) 176.8(pp)×27.4×9]
Machinery: 4 screws, Parsons turbines (*Benbow:* Beardmore; *Emperor of India:* Yarrow; *Iron Duke:* Laird; *Marlborough:* Hawthorn), 18 B&W boilers (*Emperor of India* and *Marlborough:* Yarrow)
IHP 29,000 = 21knots
Endurance: 7,780/10
Armament: 10×13.5″ (343mm)/45, 12×6″ (152mm)/45, 4×3pdr (47mm), 4×21″ (533mm) TT
1917: 2×4″ AA added
Armour: Belt 4-12″ (102-305mm), barbettes 3-10″ (76-254mm), bulkheads 2-8″ (51-203mm), battery 2-6″ (51-152mm), c/t 11″ (279mm), decks 1-2.5″ (26-64mm)
Complement: 925; *later;* 1,193
Class notes: Similar to 'King George V' class with 6″ secondary battery and greater underwater protection. Two thin funnels of equal size and heavy tripod mast. *Iron Duke* was last battleship completed with anti-torpedo nets, removed after trials. *Iron Duke* became training ship 1931 with 'B' and 'Y' turrets, belt armour and conning tower removed

'Tiger' (1911)

Battlecruiser: *Tiger*
Displacement: 28,500tons, 35,160f/l
Dimensions: 704(oa) 698(wl) 660(pp)×90′6×32′4 [214.6(oa) 212.8(wl) 201.2(pp)×27.6×10.4]
Machinery: 4 screws, Brown-Curtis turbines (John Brown), 39 B&W boilers
IHP 108,000 = 29knots
Endurance: 5,700/12
Armament: 8×13.5″ (343mm)/45, 12×6″ (152mm)/45, 4×3pdr (47mm), 4×21″ (533mm) TT
1917: 4×4″ AA added
Armour: Belt 3-9″ (76-229mm), barbettes 3-9″ (76-229mm), turrets 9″ (229mm), c/t 10″ (254mm), decks 1-3″ (26-76mm)
Complement: 1,121
Class notes: Planned as fourth unit of 'Lion' class, redesigned after advent of Japanese *Kongo*. Secondary armament, beam and horsepower increased. Three large funnels and single tripod mast forward. 'Q' turret shifted aft of funnels for unobstructed axial fire. In 1918 topmast shifted to mainmast position forward of third funnel

'Queen Elizabeth' Class (1912)

Dreadnoughts: *Barham* (see later photo), *Malaya* (see later photo), *Queen Elizabeth, Valiant, Warspite* (see later photo), *[Agincourt]*
Displacement: 27,500tons, 33,000f/l; *World War 2:* 31,000tons, 35,000f/l
Dimensions: 640(oa) 634′6(wl) 600(pp)×90′6×34′1 [195(oa) 193.4(wl) 182.9(pp)×27.6×10.4]; *1924-29:* beam 104 [31.7]
Machinery: 4 screws, Parsons (*Barham* and *Valiant:* Brown-Curtis) turbines (*Barham:* John Brown; *Malaya* and *Queen Elizabeth:* Wallsend; *Valiant:* Fairfield; *Warspite:* Hawthorn), 24 B&W boilers (*Barham* and *Warspite:* Yarrow)
IHP 75,000 = 24knots
Endurance: 6,450/10knots
Armament: 8×15″ (381mm)/42, 14×6″ (152mm)/45, 2×3″ (76mm) AA, 4×3pdr (76mm), 4×21″ (533mm) TT

Top right:
***New Zealand* — Battlecruiser of 'Indefatigable' class, c1920.** *Marine Photos*

Above right:
***Thunderer* — Dreadnought of 'Orion' class, after World War 1, c1922.** *Wright & Logan*

Right:
***Lion* — Battlecruiser, showing tripod foremast resited forward.**

Top left:
King George V **— Dreadnought, c1914.** *Tom Molland*

Top right:
Iron Duke **— Dreadnought, 1914, as flagship of the Home Fleet.**

Above left:
Tiger **— Battlecruiser, c1921.**

Above:
Queen Elizabeth **— Battleship, prior to reconstruction, in 1926.** *Wright & Logan*

Left:
Valiant **— Battleship of 'Queen Elizabeth' class after second reconstruction, 1940, having been completely rebuilt amidships.**

Agincourt* — The former Turkish dreadnought *Sultan Osman I.

1916: 2×6″ replaced by 2×4″ AA
1920s: 3″ replaced by 4×4″ AA
Malaya and *Barham, 1936:* 8×4″ AA
Armour: Belt 6-13″ (152-330mm), barbettes 4-10″ (102-254mm), turrets 11-13″ (279-330mm), c/t 11″ (279mm), bulkheads 4-6″ (102-152mm), decks 1-3″ (26-76mm)
Complement: 951; *later:* 1,297

***Queen Elizabeth, Valiant* and *Warspite* after second reconstruction**
Displacement: 31,000tons, 35,000f/l
Dimensions: As above
Machinery: 4 screws, Parsons geared turbines, 8 Admiralty 3-drum boilers (*Warspite:* 6)
SHP 80,000 = 24knots
Armament: 8×15″ (381mm)/42, 20×4.5″ (114mm)
Warspite: 8×15″, 8×6″, 8×4″ AA, 4×3pdr
Armour: As above
Complement: 1,124
Class notes: Designed as fast battleships to replace battlecruisers as the offensive wing of the battle fleet able to engage enemy battleships. First battleships with 15″ guns and oil firing. Distinctive appearance with two massive funnels, heavy tripod foremast and pole mainmast. *Agincourt* not built after *Malaya* was donated by Federated Malay States. All were reconstructed 1924-30, bulges fitted, fore funnel trunked into second, bridge remodelled, AA guns fitted. *Malaya* refitted 1934-36, hangars and catapult fitted, TT removed. *Warspite, Queen Elizabeth* and *Valiant* reconstructed 1934-40, new engines and boilers, tower superstructure and pole mast, single funnel, amidships hangar fitted, main battery elevation increased. Latter two had new secondary armament. Reconstruction of *Barham* cancelled because of the war

'Royal Sovereign' Class (1913)

Dreadnoughts: *Ramillies* (see later photo), *Resolution* (see later photo), *Revenge, Royal Oak, Royal Sovereign* (see later photo), + *[Renown, Repulse, Resistance]*
Displacement: 27,500tons, 31,200f/l; *1937:* 29,150tons, 33,000f/l
Dimensions: 624′3(oa) 614′6(wl) 580(pp)×88′6×28′7 [190.3(oa) 187.3(wl) 176.8(pp)×27×8.7]
1930: beam (oa) 102.6 [31.2]
Machinery: 4 screws, Parsons direct and geared turbines (*Ramillies:* Beardmore; *Resolution:* Palmer; *Revenge:* Vickers; *Royal Oak:* Hawthorn; *Royal Sovereign:* Parsons), 18 B&W boilers (*Resolution* and *Royal Oak:* Yarrow)
SHP 40,000 = 23knots
Endurance: 6,800/10
Armament: 8×15″ (381mm)/42, 14×6″ (152mm)/45, 2×3″ (76mm) AA, 4×3pdr, 4×21″ (533mm) TT
1924-25: 3″ AA replaced by 8×4″ AA
1928: 2×6″ removed, 2 TT removed (*Resolution* and *Royal Oak:* all)
1930: All TT removed
Armour: Belt 4-13″ (102-330mm), barbettes 4-10″ (102-254mm), turrets 5-13″ (127-330mm), bulkheads 4-6″ (102-152mm), c/t 11″ (279mm), decks 1-4″ (26-102mm)
Complement: 936
Class notes: Improved 'Iron Duke' class with 15″ guns arranged as in *Queen Elizabeth* with a large single funnel. Converted from coal to mixed fuel during construction. Three units not built. *Ramillies* fitted with bulges when built, added to others 1926-30. *Royal Oak, Resolution* and *Ramillies* had tripod mainmast later, but *Resolution* reverted to pole mast 1942

'Erin' (1914)

Dreadnought: *Erin* (see later photo)
Displacement: 23,000tons, 25,250f/l
Dimensions: 559′6(oa) 525(pp)×91′7×30′11 [170.5(oa) 160(pp)×27.9×9.4]
Machinery: 4 screws, Parsons turbines (Vickers), 15 B&W boilers
SHP 26,500 = 21knots
Endurance: 5,300/10
Armament: 10×13.5″ (343mm)/45, 16×6″ (152mm)/50, 6×6pdr, 2×3″ AA, 4×21″ (533mm) TT
1916: 6pdr removed
Armour: Belt 4-12″ (102-305mm), barbettes 3-10″ (76-254mm), turrets 3-11 (76-279mm), c/t 4-12″ (102-305mm), bulkheads 4-8″ (102-203mm), decks 1-3″ 26-76mm)
Complement: 1,070
Class notes: Designed by Sir Richard Thurston for Turkey and taken over by Britain 1914. Shorter and wider than contemporary British battleships yet had offensive power of an 'Iron Duke'. Two narrow funnels and tripod foremast with legs stepped forward

'Agincourt' (1914)

Dreadnought: *Agincourt*
Displacement: 27,500tons, 30,250f/l
Dimensions: 671′5(oa) 668(wl) 632(pp)×89×30′6 [204.7(oa) 203.6(wl) 192.6(pp)×27.1×9.3]

Canada* — Battleship in service during World War 1, returned to Chile 1920 as *Almirante Latorre.

Machinery: 4 screws, Parsons turbines (Vickers), 22 B&W boilers
SHP 34,000 = 22knots
Endurance: 4,000/10
Armament: 14×12" (305mm)/45, 20×6" (152mm)/50, 10×3" (76mm), 2×3" AA, 3×21" (533mm) TT
1916: 2×3" and stern TT removed
Armour: Belt 4-9" (102-229mm), barbettes 3-9" (76-229mm), turrets 8-12" (203-305mm), bulkheads 3-6" (76-152mm), c/t 12" (305mm), decks 1-2.5" (26-63mm)
Complement: 1,115; *later:* 1,267
Class notes: Laid down for Brazil, purchased by Turkey and taken over in August 1914. Was the longest battleship in the world carrying the largest number of main battery guns in seven turrets. Two tripod masts and two widely spaced funnels with flying deck between which was removed on acquisition by Britain. Tripod main mast reduced to pole 1917 and later removed

'Canada' (1914)

Dreadnought: *Canada*
Displacement: 28,000tons, 32,120f/l
Dimensions: 661(oa) 654'10(wl) 625(pp)×92'6×32 [201.5(oa) 199.6(wl) 190.5(pp)×28.2×9.8]
Machinery: 4 screws, Brown-Curtis and Parsons turbines (Clydebank), 21 Yarrow boilers
SHP 37,000 = 22.75knots
Endurance: 4,400/10
Armament: 10×14" (355mm)/45, 16×6" (152mm)/50, 2×3" AA, 4×3pdr, 4×21" (533mm) TT
1918: 4×6" removed
Armour: Belt 4-9" (102-229mm), barbettes 4-10" (102-254mm), turrets 10" (254mm), c/t 11" (279mm), bulkheads 3-4.5" (76-114mm), decks 1-4" (26-102mm)
Complement: 1,167
Class notes: Laid down for Chile and taken over in August 1914. Sistership became aircraft carrier *Eagle*. Lengthened 'Iron Duke' type with 14" guns. Two large unequal funnels and high tripod foremast with pole mainmast. Sold back to Chile 1920 and renamed *Almirante Latorre*

'Renown' Class (1914)

Battlecruisers: *Renown* (see also later photo), *Repulse* (see later photo)
Displacement: 26,500tons, 32,727f/l; *Repulse, 1936:* 32,000tons; *Renown, 1939:* 33,725tons, 37,400f/l
Dimensions: 794(oa) 787'9(wl) 750(pp)×90×30'3 [242(oa) 240.1(wl) 228.6(pp)×27.4×9.2]
1926: beam 102'8 [31.2]
Machinery: 4 screws, Brown-Curtis turbines (*Renown:* Fairchild; *Repulse:* John Brown), 42 B&W boilers; *Renown, 1939:* Parsons geared turbines (Cammell Laird), 8 Admiralty 3-drum boilers
Endurance: 4,200/10
SHP 112,000 = 30knots; *Renown, 1939:* SHP 130,000 = 29.9knots
Armament: 6×15" (381mm)/42, 17×4" (102mm)/40, 2×3" AA, 4×3pdr, 2×21" (533mm) TT
Repulse, 1936: 6×15", 12×4"/40, 8×4" AA, 4×3pdr, 8×18" TT
Renown, 1939: 6×15", 20×4.5", 24×2pdr pompom, 8×18" TT
Renown, 1943: 4×2pdr pompom added, 4×18" TT removed
Armour: Belt 3-6" (76-152mm), barbettes 4-7" (102-178mm), turrets 7-11" (178-279mm), bulkheads 3-4" (76-102mm), c/t 10" (254mm), decks 1-3.5" (26-89mm), *1921-26:* Belt 9" (229mm)
Complement: 967
Class notes: Reversion to original battlecruiser idea with protection sacrificed for speed. Three twin turrets on hull of great length only lightly armoured. First capital ships to have bulges as part of original design. Materials from two cancelled 'Royal Sovereign' class battleships used in their construction, which was completed in record time. Fore funnel raised after trials. *Repulse* altered 1919-20 with additional armour protection. In 1934-36 *Repulse* fitted with hangar and catapult, additional armour and increased AA armament. *Renown* reconstructed 1936-39 with new engines and boilers, tower superstructure and light tripod mast, new deck armour protection, elevation of main guns increased

'Abercrombie' Class (1914)

Monitors: *Abercrombie, Havelock, Raglan* (see later photo), *Roberts* (see later photo)
Displacement: 6,150tons
Dimensions: 334'6(oa) 320(pp)×90×10 [102(oa) 97.5(pp)×27.4×3]
Machinery: 2 screws, TE engines (*Raglan* and *Roberts:* QE engines) (builders), 2 B&W boilers
IHP 2,000 = 6knots
Endurance: 670/6
Armament: 2×14" (355mm)/45, 2×12pdr, 1×3pdr
1916: 2×6" added (*Havelock:* 1×7.5")
Armour: Deck 4" (102mm), guns 7-10" (178-254mm)

Complement: 198
Class notes: Designed as seagoing vessels for shore bombardment. One twin 14" turret on low hull with shallow draft, single funnel and tripod mast. Bulges added on outside of hull underwater. Guns made in US for Greek battlecruiser *Salamis* under construction in Germany. American names originally given were changed just after completion

'Lord Clive' Class (1914)

Monitors: *Earl of Peterborough, General Craufurd, General Wolfe, Lord Clive, Prince Eugene, Prince Rupert, Sir John Moore, Sir Thomas Picton*
Displacement: 5,900tons
Dimensions: 335'6(oa) 320(pp)×87'2×9'7 [102.3(oa) 97.5(pp)×26.5×2.9]
Machinery: 2 screws, VTE engines (builder; *Prince Rupert* and *General Wolfe:* McKie & Baxter)
IHP 2,300 = 6.5knots
Endurance: 550/6.5
Armament: 2×12" (305mm)/35, 2×12pdr, 1×3" AA
1918: 1×18" (457mm)/40 (*Wolfe, Clive*), 2×12"/35 4×4" (*Clive, Moore*), 2×3" (except *Moore*), 2×12pdr (except *Clive, Wolfe* and *Eugene*), 2×6" (*Craufurd:* 4; *Picton:* 1; *Clive, Moore* and *Peterborough:* none)
Armour: Deck 4" (102mm), guns 7-10" (178-254mm), c/t 6" (152mm)
Complement: 194
Class notes: Similar to 'Abercrombie' class with 12" turrets taken from old battleships. *General Wolfe* and *Lord Clive* fitted with 18" gun from *Furious* in fixed mount aft trained to starboard 1917-18. Addition of 18" gun to *Prince Eugene* cancelled October 1918

'Marshal Ney' Class (1914)

Monitors: *Marshal Ney, Marshal Soult* (see also later photo)
Displacement: 6,670tons
Dimensions: 355"8(oa) 340(pp)×90'3×10'6 [108.4(oa) 103.6(pp)×27.5×3.2]
Machinery: 2 screws, diesel engines (*Ney:* White; *Soult:* Vickers)
BHP 1,500 = 6.5knots
Endurance: 1,000/5 (*Soult*)
Armament: 2×15" (381mm), 2×12pdr, 1×3" AA
Ney, 1916: 6×6' (152mm), 2×3" AA
Soult, 1916: 8×4" added
Armour: Deck 4" (102mm), guns 13" (330mm)
Complement: 228
Class notes: Built to use spare 15" turrets remaining from cancelled battleship programme. Turret mounted on tall barbette, small funnel. Engines taken from oilers under construction. *Ney's* engines were a failure and the turret was removed 1916 and transferred to *Terror*. Both ships too slow, far below designed speed

Top left:
***Renown* — Battlecruiser, June 1932, prior to reconstruction of 1936-39.** *Wright & Logan*

Centre left:
***Raglan* — 'Abercrombie' class monitor at Mudros 1918. Notice camouflaged turret and upperworks.**

Bottom left:
***Sir John Moore* — Monitor of 'Lord Clive' class.** *IWM*

'Hood' Class (1915)

Battlecruisers: *Hood* (see also later photo) [*Anson, Howe, Rodney*]
Displacement: 41,200tons, 45,200f/l
Dimensions: 860'7(oa) 850(wl) 810(pp)×105×31'6 [262.3(oa) 259.1(wl) 246.9(pp)×32×9.6]
Machinery: 4 screws, Brown-Curtis geared turbines (builders), 24 Yarrow boilers
SHP 144,000 = 32knots
Endurance: 6,300/12
Armament: 8×15" (381mm)/42, 12×5.5" (140mm)/50, 4×4" (102mm) AA, 4×3pdr (45mm), 6×21" (533mm) TT
1940: 5.5" removed and 8×4" AA added, 2×21" TT removed
Armour: Belt 5-12" (127-305mm), barbettes 5-12" (127-305mm), turrets 11-15" (279-381mm), c/t 9-11" (229-381mm), bulkheads 4-5" (102-127mm), decks 1-3" (26-76mm)
Complement: 1,477
Class notes: Designed as an enlarged 'Queen Elizabeth' type as a response to German 'Mackensen' class battlecruisers. Original design modified after Jutland to include greater armour protection, but remained poorly protected. Last three suspended after work on 'Mackensen' class ceased. *Hood* completed as the largest warship in the world and remained such until World War 2. Reconstruction proposed in 1939 cancelled by the war

'Courageous' Class (1915)

Light Battlecruisers: *Courageous, Glorious*
Displacement: 18,600tons, 22,690f/l
Dimensions: 786(oa) 735(pp)×81×23'4 [239.6(oa) 224(pp)×24.7×7.1]
Machinery: 4 screws, Parsons geared turbines (*Courageous:* Parsons; *Glorious:* Harland & Wolff), 18 Yarrow boilers
SHP 90,000 = 32knots
Endurance: 3,200/19
Armament: 4×15" (381mm)/42, 18×4" (102mm)/50, 2×3" AA, 12×21" (533mm) TT
Armour: Belt 2-3" (51-76mm), barbettes 3-7" (76-178mm), turrets 4.5-13" (114-330mm), c/t 10" (254mm), decks 1-3" (26-76mm)
Complement: 842
Class notes: Actually very large cruisers with 15" guns, no proper armour but very fast. Intended for Lord Fisher's Baltic invasion plan. Two twin turrets, single large funnel and two tripod masts on long hull. Of little use, used as cruisers and converted for minelaying 1917. Both converted to aircraft carriers 1924

'Furious' (1915)

Light Battlecruiser: *Furious*
Displacement: 19,513tons, 22,890f/l
Dimensions: 786'6(oa) 750(pp)×88×24 [239.7(oa) 228.6(pp)×26.8×7.3]
Machinery: 4 screws, Brown-Curtis geared turbines (Wallsend), 18 Yarrow boilers
SHP 94,000 = 31.5knots
Armament: 1×18" (457mm)/40, 11×5.5" (140mm)/50, 4×3" AA, 4×3pdr, 18×21" (533mm) TT
1918: 18" and 1×5.5" removed
Armour: Belt 2-3" (51-76mm), barbettes 4-7" (102-178mm), turret 4.5-13" (114-330mm), c/t 10" (254mm)
Complement: 880
Class notes: Modified 'Courageous' type designed with two 18" guns in two single turrets. Completed with single turret aft and flightdeck and hangar forward and as such considered an aircraft carrier. Turret and mainmast removed at end of 1917 and second flightdeck built aft. Completely rebuilt as aircraft carrier 1921

'Erebus' Class (1915)

Monitors: *Erebus* (see also later photo), *Terror*
Displacement: 8,000tons, 8,450f/l
Dimensions: 405(oa) 380(pp)×88′2×11′8 [123.4(oa) 115.8(pp)×26.9×3.6]
Machinery: 2 screws, VTE engines (Harland & Wolff), 4 B&W boilers
IHP 6,000 = 12knots
Endurance: 1,240/12
Armament: 2×15″ (381mm)/42, 2×6″, 2×12pdr, 1×3″ AA
1919: 6″ replaced by 8×4″, 12pdr removed
Terror, 1939: 8×4″ replaced by 6×4″ AA, 3″ removed
Erebus, 1940: 6×4″ AA added
Armour: Sides 6″ (152mm), barbette 8″ (203mm), turret 13″ (330mm), c/t 6″ (152mm), deck 2″ (51mm)
Complement: 223
Class notes: Longer but different form of hull resulted in faster vessels than previous types. Turret of *Terror* taken from *Marshal Ney*. *Erebus* modified 1941 with AA guns, topmast removed. New topmast fitted 1944, reduced freeboard and bulge submerged

'Gorgon' Class (1915)

Coast Defence Ships: *Glatton* (see later photo), *Gorgon*
Displacement: 5,700tons
Dimensions: 310(oa) 295′3(pp)×73′7×16′6 [95.5(oa) 90(pp)×22.4×5]
Machinery: 2 screws, VTE engines (Hawthorn), 4 Yarrow boilers
IHP 4,000 = 13knots
Endurance: 2,700/11
Armament: 2×9.2″ (234mm)/51, 4×6″ (152mm), 2×3″ AA
Armour: Sides 7″ (178mm), turret 8″ (203mm), c/t 8″ (203mm), deck 2″ (51mm)
Complement: 323
Class notes: Built for Norway and acquired 1915 prior to completion. Modified after acquisition and construction suspended for 14 months. Bulges added, elevation of guns increased, tripod mast fitted abaft funnel

'Argus' (1916)

Aircraft Carrier: *Argus*
Displacement: 15,775tons, 17,000f/l
Dimensions: 565(oa) 560(wl) 535(pp)×68×21 [172.2(oa) 170.7(wl) 163.1(pp)×20.7×6.4]; *1926:* beam 75′9 [23]
Machinery: 4 screws, Parsons turbines (Beardmore), 12 cylindrical boilers; *1937:* 6 Yarrow boilers
SHP 20,000 = 20.25knots
Aircraft: 20
Armament: 2×4″ (102mm)/50, 4×4″ AA, 4×3pdr
1937: Guns removed
Complement: 495
Class notes: Laid down as passenger liner, acquired for conversion 1916. First aircraft carrier with large hangar and full-length flightdeck. Bulges fitted 1925-26. Flightdeck altered forward 1938. Employed as training carrier and aircraft ferry in World War 2

'Eagle' (1917)

Aircraft Carrier: *Eagle* (see later photo)
Displacement: 22,600tons, 26,400f/l
Dimensions: 667(oa) 627(pp)×92′9×27 [203.3(oa) 190.5(pp)×28.3×8.2]
Machinery: 4 screws, Brown-Curtis geared turbines (John Brown), 32 Yarrow boilers
SHP 50,000 = 24knots
Aircraft: 21
Armament: 9×6″ (152mm)/50, 5×4″ AA
Armour: Belt 4.5″ (114mm), deck 1.5″ (38mm)
Complement: 748
Class notes: Laid down as battleship for Chile (sister to battleship *Canada*) and acquired 1917 for conversion to aircraft carrier. Extensively modified after trials and rebuilt. Full-length flightdeck and heavy gun armament. First carrier with an island superstructure

'Hermes' (1917)

Aircraft Carrier: *Hermes*
Displacement: 10,850tons, 12,900f/l
Dimensions: 598(oa) 548(pp)×70×21′6 [182.3(oa) 167(pp)×21.3×6.6]
Machinery: 2 screws, Parsons geared turbines (Parsons), 6 Yarrow boilers
SHP 40,000 = 25knots
Aircraft: 15
Armament: 6×5.5″ (140mm)/50, 3×4″ AA, 4×3pdr AA
Armour: Belt 3″ (76mm), deck 1″ (25mm)
Complement: 664
Class notes: First vessel designed as an aircraft carrier, having a small cruiser type hull and engines, full flightdeck and large island

'Furious' (1920)

Aircraft Carrier: *Furious*
Displacement: 22,450tons
Dimensions: 786′3(oa) 735(pp)×90×27′9 [239.6(oa) 224(pp)×27.4×8.5]
Machinery: 4 screws, Brown-Curtis geared turbines (Wallsend), 18 Yarrow boilers
SHP 94,000 = 32.5knots
Aircraft: 33
Armament: 12×4″ (102mm) AA
1925: 10×5.5″ (140mm), 6×4″ AA, 4×3pdr
1938: 12×4″ AA
Armour: Belt 3″ (76mm), deck 3″ (76mm)
Complement: 890
Class notes: Fully converted from light battlecruiser (qv), bridge and funnel removed and fore and aft flightdecks joined to make full-length flightdeck with a flying-off deck forward. Rearmed 1938 and small island with pole mast fitted

'G3' Class (1921)

Battlecruisers: 4 unnamed
Displacement: 48,400tons
Dimensions: 862(oa) 850(wl) 820(pp)×106×32′6 [262.7(oa) 259(wl) 250(pp)×32.3×9.9]
Machinery: 4 screws, Parsons geared turbines, 24 boilers
SHP 160,000 = 31knots
Endurance: 6,500/12
Armament: 9×16″ (406mm)/45, 16×6″ (152mm)/50, 6×4.7″ (119mm)/43 AA, 2×24.5″ (622mm) TT

Top right:
***Marshal Soult* — Monitor, 1918, with mast camouflaged in a checkerboard pattern.** *Marius Bar*

Centre right:
***Hood* — Battlecruiser, 1924.** *Marine Photos*

Bottom right:
***Courageous* — Light battlecruiser, 1917.** *P. A. Vicary*

Top left:
***Furious* — Light battlecruiser with 18″ gun aft and flightdeck forward, 1917. The gun was removed shortly afterwards.** *IWM*

Top right:
***Erebus* — Monitor, as recommissioned, August 1939.**
Wright & Logan

Centre left:
***Gorgon* — Coast defence ship acquired from Norway, 1918. Notice guns trained to starboard.**
Conway Photo Library

Bottom left:
***Argus* — The first aircraft carrier with full length flightdeck, c1930.** *Wright & Logan*

Above:
***Hermes* — Aircraft carrier, after completion 1925.**
Abrahams

Armour: Belt 12-14" (305-355mm), turrets 8-17" (203-432mm), barbettes 14" (355mm), c/t 6-12" (152-305mm), deck 8" (203mm)
Complement: 1,716
Class notes: Designed by Goodall to have all main armament forward in three triple turrets and machinery aft so as to save weight of armour. Tower foremast was widely copied. Four units ordered from Beardmore, Swan Hunter, Fairfield and John Brown were never named. None laid down and construction cancelled 9 February 1922 to comply with Washington Treaty

'Nelson' Class (1922)

Battleships: *Nelson* (see later photo), *Rodney*
Displacement: 33,950tons, 38,000f/l
Dimensions: 710(oa) 702(wl) 660(pp)×106×30 [216.4(oa) 214(wl) 201.2(pp)×32.3×9.1]
Machinery: 2 screws, Brown-Curtis geared turbines (*Nelson:* Wallsend; *Rodney:* Cammell Laird) 8 Yarrow boilers
SHP 45,000 = 23knots
Endurance: 16,500/12
Armament: 9×16" (406mm)/45, 12×6" (152mm)/50, 6×4.7" (119mm) AA, 8×2pdr pompom, 2×24.5" (622mm) TT
1938: TT removed
1945: 16×40mm AA added
Armour: Belt 11-14" (279-355mm), barbettes 15" (381mm), turrets 9-16" (229-406mm), bulkheads 14" (355mm), deck 6.5" (165mm), c/t 13.5" (343mm)
Complement: 1,314
Class notes: Designed by d'Eyncourt. Reduced version of the 1921 battlecruisers with three triple turrets grouped forward of the tower foremast and tripod mainmast aft of the funnel. *Rodney* carried a catapult 1934-43

'Courageous' Class (1924)

Aircraft Carriers: *Courageous* (see later photo), *Glorious*
Displacement: 22,500tons, 26,500f/l

Above:
***Furious* — Aircraft carrier, following removal of aft 18" gun but prior to full conversion.** *IWM*

Below:
***Rodney* — Battleship of 'Nelson' class, c1938.**

Dimensions: 786′3(oa) 735(pp)×90′6×28′6 [239.6(oa) 224(pp)×27.6×8.7]
Machinery: 4 screws, Parsons geared turbines (*Courageous:* Parsons; *Glorious:* Harland), 18 Yarrow boilers
SHP 90,000 = 30knots
Aircraft: 48
Armament: 16×4.7″ (119mm) AA, 4×3pdr
Armour: Belt and deck 3″ (76mm)
Complement: 1,216
Class notes: Converted 1924-30 from light battlecruisers. Superstructure removed and flightdeck and hangar built over hull. A short flying-off deck forward was not long used. Island with pole mast and large funnel on starboard side. Light tripod replaced pole mast in *Courageous* 1936 and flightdeck extended aft in *Glorious*

'Ark Royal' (1934)

Aircraft Carrier: *Ark Royal* (see later photo)
Displacement: 22,000tons, 27,720f/l
Dimensions: 800(oa) 721′6(wl) 685(pp)×94′9×28 [243.8(oa) 219.9(wl) 208.8(pp)×28.9×8.5]
Machinery: 3 screws, Parsons geared turbines (builder), 6 Admiralty 3-drum boilers
SHP 102,000 = 30.75knots
Endurance: 7,620/20
Aircraft: 60
Armament: 16×4.5″ (114mm) DP, 48×2pdr AA
Armour: Belt 4.5″ (114mm), deck 2.5″ (63mm)
Complement: 1,575
Class notes: Combined best features of previous designs with full length flightdeck overhanging the stern. Island had large funnel and light tripod

'King George V' Class (1936-37)

Battleships: *Anson, Duke of York, Howe* (see later photo), *King George V, Prince of Wales*
Displacement: 36,750tons, 44,460f/l
Dimensions: 745(oa) 739′8(wl) 700(pp)×103×35′6 [227.1(oa) 225.4(wl) 213.4(pp)×31.4×10.8]
Machinery: 4 screws, Parsons geared turbines (*Anson:* Wallsend; *Duke of York:* John Brown; *Howe:* Fairfield; *King George V:* Vickers, Barrow; *Prince of Wales:* Cammell Laird), 8 Admiralty 3-drum boilers
SHP 125,000 = 27.5knots
Endurance: 14,000/10
Armament: 10×14″ (355mm)/50, 16×5.25″ (133mm), 24×2pdr pompom, 10×40mm AA
Later: 88×2pdr pompom
Armour: Belt 5.4-14.7″ (137-374mm), turrets 6.8-12.8″ (174-324mm), barbettes 12″ (304mm), bulkheads 14.7″ (374mm), decks 2-6″ (51-152mm), c/t 4.5″ (114mm)
Complement: 1,640
Class notes: Designed as replacement for 'Royal Sovereign' class. Reverted to 14″ guns mounted in two quadruple and one twin turrets. Aircraft hangar built in but removed 1943. Two funnels and two light tripod masts

'Illustrious' Class (1936-37)

Aircraft Carriers: *Formidable, Illustrious* (see also later photo), *Indomitable* (see also later photo), *Victorious* (see later photo)
Displacement: 23,200tons, 28,619f/l; *Indomitable:* 24,680tons, 29,730f/l
Dimensions: 753′6(oa) 710(wl) 673(pp)×95′9×28 [229.7(oa) 216.4(wl) 205.1(pp)×29.2×8.5]

Machinery: 3 screws, Parsons geared turbines, (Vickers, Barrow; *Victorious:* Wallsend; *Formidable:* Harland), 6 Admiralty 3-drum boilers
SHP 110,000 = 31knots
Endurance: 11,000/14
Aircraft: 36
Armament: 16×4.5" (114mm) AA, 48×2pdr AA
Armour: Belt 4.5" (114mm), deck 3" (76mm)
Complement: 1,392

***Victorious* as modified:**

Displacement: 30,000tons, 37,000f/l
Dimensions: 781(oa) 673(pp)×103'4×31 [238(oa) 216.4(pp)×31.5×9.4]
Machinery: 3 screws, Parsons geared turbines, 6 Foster-Wheeler boilers
SHP 110,000 = 31knots
Aircraft: 72
Armament: 12×3" AA, 6×40mm
Complement: 2,200
Class notes: Differed from previous carriers in having an armoured hangar which significantly reduced number of aircraft carried. *Indomitable* modified while building to provide additional hangar space aft. Reconstruction of *Victorious* so costly that plans to modernise others were cancelled

'Implacable' Class (1938-39)

Aircraft Carriers: *Implacable, Indefatigable*
Displacement: 26,000tons, 32,110f/l
Dimensions: 766'2(oa) 673(pp)×95'9×29 [233.5(oa) 205.1(pp)×29.2×8.8]
Machinery: 4 screws, Parsons geared turbines (*Implacable:* Vickers; *Indefatigable:* John Brown), 8 Admiralty 3-drum boilers
SHP 148,000 = 32knots
Aircraft: 72
Armament: 16×4.5" (114mm), 48×2pdr AA
1949: 2pdrs replaced by 12×40mm AA
Armour: Belt 4.5" (114mm), deck 3" (76mm)
Complement: 1,785
Class notes: Similar to 'Illustrious' class with additional hangar space and modified bow. Light tripod mast on island

'Lion' Class (1938-39)

Battleships: *[Conqueror, Lion, Thunderer, Temeraire]*
Displacement: 40,550tons, 46,400f/l
Dimensions: 793(oa) 780(wl) 740(pp)×108×30 [241.7(oa) 237.7(wl) 225.6(pp)×32.9×9.1]
Machinery: 4 screws, Parsons geared turbines (builders), 8 Admiralty 3 drum boilers
SHP 130,000 = 30knots
Armament: 9×16"(406mm)/45, 16×5.25" (132mm)/50, 6×8-barrel 2pdr pompom
Armour: Belt 5.2-14.7" (132-373mm), turrets 5.9-14.7" (150-373mm), barbettes 11.7-14.7" (297-373mm), deck 6" (152mm), c/t 4.5" (114mm)

Top left:
***Glorious* — Aircraft carrier, August 1935. The hull's cruiser lines can still be seen despite addition of bulges.** *Wright & Logan*

Centre left:
***Anson* — Battleship, 'King George V' class, after World War 2.**

Bottom left:
***Illustrious* — Aircraft carrier, 1944.** *IWM*

Complement: 1,680
Class notes: Enlarged 'King George V' type with 16" guns in three triple turrets. Construction suspended 1940. Above particulars are as originally designed; improvements were made and recommended during the war

'Roberts' Class (1940-41)

Monitors: *Abercrombie, Roberts*
Displacement: *Roberts:* 7,970tons, 9,150f/l; *Abercrombie:* 8,536tons, 9,717f/l
Dimensions: 373'3(oa)×89'9×14'4 [113.8(oa)×27.4×4.4]
Machinery: 2 screws, Parsons geared turbines (*Roberts:* John Brown; *Abercrombie:* Parsons), 2 Admiralty 3-drum boilers
SHP 4,800 = 12knots
Endurance: 1,340/12
Armament: 2×15" (381mm)/42, 8×4" (102mm) AA 16×2pdr AA
Armour: Belt 5" (127mm), turret 5-13" (127-330mm), deck 4-6" (102-152mm) c/t 3" (76mm)
Complement: 450
Class notes: Similar to 'Erebus' class with additional superstructure, AA armament and external sloping armour belt on top of the bulges. Turret for *Roberts* taken from *Marshal Soult*

'Vanguard' (1940)

Battleship: *Vanguard* (see also later photo)
Displacement: 44,500tons, 51,420f/l
Dimensions: 814'4(oa) 800(wl) 760(pp)×108'6×36 [248.2(oa) 243.8(wl) 231.6(pp)×33.1×11]
Machinery: 4 screws, Parsons geared turbines (John Brown), 8 Admiralty 3-drum boilers
SHP 130,000 = 30knots
Endurance: 9,000/20
Armament: 8×15" (381mm)/42, 16×5.25" (133mm), 71×40mm AA
Armour: Belt 3.8-12.8" (97-325mm), turrets 5.8-12.8" (147-325m), barbettes 11.8-12.8" (300-325mm), deck 6" (152mm), c/t 2.9" (74mm)
Complement: 1,600
Class notes: Enlarged 'King George V' type with longer hull to accommodate four twin turrets utilising guns originally mounted in *Courageous* and *Glorious*. Designed to be completed rapidly but construction was delayed and many modifications were made

'Audacious' Class (1940-43)

Aircraft Carriers: *[Africa], Ark Royal* (see also later photo), *[Eagle], Eagle* (ex-*Audacious*) (see later photo)
Displacement: 36,800tons; *Ark Royal:* 43,340tons, 53,340f/l; *Eagle:* 43,060tons, 53,000f/l
Dimensions: 803'9(oa) 720(pp)×112'4×33'4 [245(oa) 219.5(pp)×34.2×10.2]
Ark Royal, 1970: 845(oa)×166(oa beam) [257.6(oa)×50.06(oa beam)]
Machinery: 4 screws, Parsons geared turbines (builders), 8 Admiralty 3-drum boilers
SHP 152,000 = 31.5knots
Aircraft: 100; *Ark Royal, 1970:* 36
Armament: 16×4.5" (114mm) DP, 58×40mm AA
Ark Royal, 1956: 12×4.5", 34×40mm
Ark Royal, 1959: 8×4.5", 32×40mm
Ark Royal, 1970: 4 Seacat SAM
Eagle, 1964: 8×4.5", 24 Seacat
Armour: Belt 4.5" (114mm), flightdeck 4" (102mm)
Complement: 2,300

Class notes: Improved 'Implacable' type with greatly enlarged armoured hangar. Construction delayed during the war and *Africa* and original *Eagle* were cancelled 1945. *Eagle* (ex-*Audacious*) completed to near original design. *Ark Royal* modified with steam catapult and deck edge elevator. *Eagle* reconstructed 1959-64 with angled flightdeck, steam catapult and missile armament. *Ark Royal* reconstructed 1967-70 with fully angled flightdeck and missile armament

'Colossus' Class (1942)

Light Aircraft Carriers: *Colossus, [Edgar], Glory, [Mars], Ocean, Theseus, Triumph* (see later photo), *Venerable, Vengeance, Warrior*
Displacement: 13,190tons, 18,000f/l; *Edgar, Theseus, Triumph* and *Warrior:* 13,350tons
Dimensions: 695(oa) 630(pp)×80'3×21'4 [211.8(oa) 192(pp)×24.5×6.5]; *Vengeance*: 693'4(oa) [211.3(oa)]
Machinery: 2 screws, Parsons geared turbines (*Colossus:* Parsons; *Edgar* and *Mars:* Vickers-Barrow; *Glory* and *Warrior:* Harland; *Ocean:* Stephen; *Theseus:* Fairfield; *Triumph:* Hawthorn; *Venerable:* Cammell Laird; *Vengeance:* Wallsend), 4 Admiralty 3-drum boilers
SHP 42,000 = 25knots
Endurance: 12,000/14
Aircraft: 48
Armament: Varied, 24×2pdr pompom AA, 19×40mm AA
Complement: 1,076
Class notes: A wartime expedient, small unarmoured carriers which could be built quickly at additional yards. Destroyer machinery fitted and single hangar. *Edgar* and *Mars* completed as aircraft maintenance ships. Several were eventually transferred to foreign navies

'Majestic' Class (1942)

Light Aircraft Carriers: *[Hercules, Leviathan, Magnificent, Majestic, Powerful, Terrible]*
Displacement: 15,700tons, 19,500f/l
Dimensions: 694'4(oa) 630(pp)×80'3×26 [211.6(oa) 192(pp)×24.5×7.9]
Machinery: 2 screws, Parsons geared turbines (*Hercules* and *Terrible:* Parsons; *Leviathan:* Wallsend; *Magnificent* and *Powerful:* Harland; *Majestic:* Vickers-Barrow), 4 Admiralty 3-drum boilers
SHP 42,000 = 24.5knots
Endurance: 12,000/14
Aircraft: 34
Armament: 30×40mm AA
Complement: 1,100
Class notes: Repeat 'Colossus' class with internal modifications. None saw active service in the British Navy. All but *Leviathan* were completed for Commonwealth navies

'Hermes' Class (1943)

Light Aircraft Carriers: *Albion* (see also later photo), *[Arrogant], Bulwark* (see later photo), *Centaur* (see later photo), *[Hermes]* (see later photo), *Hermes* (ex-*Elephant*) (see later photo), *[Monmouth, Polyphemus]*
Displacement: 18,300tons, 25,760f/l; *Completed:* 22,000tons, 27,000f/l
Dimensions: 737'9(oa) 650(pp)×90×27 [224.9(oa) 198.1(pp)×27.4×8.2]; *Hermes, 1958*: 744'3(oa) [226.8(oa)]
Machinery: 2 screws, Parsons geared turbines (*Albion:* Wallsend; *Bulwark* and *Centaur:* Harland; *Hermes:* Vickers-Barrow), 4 Admiralty 3-drum boilers
SHP 83,000 = 28knots
Aircraft: 50
Armament: 32×40mm AA
Hermes: 14×3" AA
Hermes, 1969: 2 quadruple Seacat SAM
Complement: 1,330
Class notes: Enlarged 'Majestic' class with higher speed and better protection. Four cancelled in 1945 and construction of others suspended in 1947, work resumed 1950. *Centaur* completed to near original design; *Albion* and *Bulwark* completed with partly angled flightdeck and steam catapults, and *Centaur* was modified in 1957. *Hermes* (ex-*Elephant*) completed with further modifications; *Bulwark* and *Albion* converted to commando carriers 1959-62. *Hermes* reconstructed 1964-66 with fully angled flightdeck and missile armament

'Gibraltar' Class (1943)

Aircraft Carriers: *[Gibraltar, Malta, New Zealand]*
Displacement: 46,950tons, 56,800f/l
Dimensions: 916'6(oa) 850(wl) 820(pp)×115.7×34.6 [279.3(oa) 259(wl) 250(pp)×35.2×10.5]
Machinery: 4 screws, Parsons geared turbines (builders), 8 Admiralty 3-drum boilers
SHP 200,000 = 32knots
Aircraft: 81
Armament: 16×4.5" (114mm), 55×40mm AA
Armour: Sides 3-4" (76-102mm), flightdeck 1" (25mm)
Complement: 3,535
Class notes: Designed without previous armoured hangar in order to accommodate larger number of aircraft. Armoured around machinery, fuel and magazines. None was completed

'CVA 01' (1966)

Aircraft Carrier: Unnamed
Displacement: 53,000tons
Dimensions: 925(oa)×122(wl) 184(fd) [281.9(oa)×37.2(wl) 56.1(fd)]
Machinery: 3 screws, geared turbines
SHP 135,000 = 31knots
Aircraft: 70
Class notes: Contract cancelled, never laid down

'Invincible' Class (1972)

Aircraft Carriers: *Ark Royal, Illustrious, Invincible*
Displacement: 16,000tons, 19,500f/l
Dimensions: 677(oa) 632(wl)×90×24 [206.3(oa) 192.6(wl)×27.4×7.3]
Machinery: 2 screws, gas turbines
SHP 112,000 = 28knots
Endurance: 5,000/18
Aircraft: 14
Armament: Twin Sea Dart SAM
Complement: 1,318
Class notes: Originally designated 'through-deck cruisers', these eventually received classification of aircraft carriers. Only aircraft carried are VTOL planes and helicopters. Flight deck has 'ski jump' inclination forward and is slightly off centre

Top left:
***Indefatigable* — Aircraft carrier, 'Implacable' class, 1945.** *Marine Photos*

Centre left:
***Abercrombie* — 'Roberts' class monitor, October 1945.** *A. & J. Pavia*

Bottom left:
***Vanguard* — Battleship, as completed 1946.** *IWM*

Individual Ships

Abercrombie

Type: Monitor
Class: 'Abercrombie' (1914)
Nomenclature: Sir Ralph Abercromby (1731-1801), general, mortally wounded at the Battle of Aboukir

History:
1914 December 12: Laid down as ***Farragut*** at Harland & Wolff
1914 December: Renamed ***Admiral Farragut***
1915 April 15: Launched
1915 May 29: Completed
1915 May 31: Renamed ***M1***
1915 June 19: Renamed ***Abercrombie***
World War 1: 1915-16 Dardanelles
1927 June 25: Sold and broken up at Inverkeithing

Abercrombie

Type: Monitor
Class: 'Roberts' (1940)

History:
1941 May 26: Laid down at Vickers, Tyne
1942 March 31: Launched
1943 May 5: Completed
World War 2: Sicily, Salerno
1943 September 9: Damaged by mine off Salerno
1944 August 21: Damaged off Malta by two mines
1954 December: Broken up at Barrow

Aboukir

Type: Armoured Cruiser
Class: 'Cressy' (1898)
Nomenclature: The Battle of the Nile, 1 August 1798, at which Nelson annihilated the French fleet in Aboukir Bay

History:
1898 November 9: Laid down at Fairfield
1900 May 16: Launched
1901 March 9: Completed
1902-05 Mediterranean
1907-12 Mediterranean
World War 1: North Sea
1914 September 22: Torpedoed and sunk by *U9* in North Sea (527 dead)

Left, top to bottom:

***Ark Royal* — 'Audacious' class aircraft carrier, December 1964, after first modification.** *Wright & Logan*

***Theseus* — Light aircraft carrier of 'Colossus' class, 1951, at Auckland.** *Marine Photos*

***Magnificent* — Light aircraft carrier, 'Majestic' class, as completed for Canada.**

***Albion* — 'Hermes' class light aircraft carrier, 1959.** *Marine Photos*

Abyssinia

Type: Breastwork Monitor
Class: 'Abyssinia' (1867)
Nomenclature: British military expedition to Ethiopia, 1868

History:
1868 July 23: Laid down at Dudgeon
1870 February 19: Launched
1870 October: Completed
1871 Guardship, Bombay
1892 Rearmed
1903 January: Sold

Achilles

Type: Broadside Ship
Class: 'Achilles' (1860)
Nomenclature: Greek myth, the foremost hero of the Trojan War

History:
1861 August 1: Laid down at Chatham
1863 December 23: Launched
1864 November 26: Completed
1865 Bow mast removed
1868 Refit, rearmed with ML guns
1874 Rearmed again
1877 Rerigged, reduced to bark
1878-80 Mediterranean
1878 February 14: Naval demonstration in the Dardanelles
1879 October: In collision with battleship *Alexandra*
1885 Paid off
1890 Reboilered
1902 Depot ship, Malta; renamed ***Hibernia***
1904 March: Renamed ***Egmont***
1914 Depot ship, Chatham
1916 June 19: Renamed ***Egremont***
1919 June 6: Renamed ***Pembroke***
1923 January 16: Sold and broken up

Achilles

Type: Armoured Cruiser
Class: 'Warrior' (1903)

History:
1904 February 22: Laid down at Armstrong
1905 June 17: Launched
1907 April 22: Completed
World War 1: 1914-17 Grand Fleet, 1917-18 Convoy escort
1914 November 30: Damaged by gun explosion
1917 February: In collision with cruiser *Bacchante* in Irish Sea
1917 March 16: With armed boarding steamer *Dundee* sank the German raider *Leopard* north of the Shetland Islands
1918 Stokers' training ship, Chatham
1921 May 9: Sold and broken up at Briton Ferry 1923

Admiral Farragut, see *Abercrombie*

Nomenclature: See *Farragut*

Africa, see *Good Hope*

***Achilles* — Broadside ship of 1860, as it appeared after being rearmed and rerigged in 1874.** *IWM*

Africa

Type: Pre-dreadnought
Class: 'King Edward VII' (1901)
Nomenclature: 46-gun ship of 1694

History:
1904 January 27: Laid down at Chatham
1905 May 20: Launched
1906 November 6: Completed
1907 March 23: In collision with merchant ship *Ormuz* off Portland
1912 April: Fitted with temporary flightdeck for seaplane experiments
World War 1: 1914-15 Grand Fleet, 1915 Adriatic
1919 April: Accommodation ship
1920 June 30: Sold and broken up at Newcastle

Africa

Type: Aircraft Carrier
Class: 'Audacious' (1940)

History:
1943 July 12: Ordered from Fairfield; never laid down
1945 October: Cancelled

Agamemnon

Type: Turret Ship
Class: 'Ajax' (1875)
Nomenclature: Greek myth: King of Mycenae and commander of the Greek army in the Trojan War

History:
1876 May 9: Laid down at Chatham
1879 September 17: Launched
1883 March 29: Completed
1884-86 Far East
1884 Ran aground in the Suez Canal
1886 Refit at Malta, stern altered
1886-89 East Indies and Zanzibar, Mediterranean
1903 January 13: Sold and broken up in Germany

Agamemnon

Type: Pre-dreadnought
Class: 'Lord Nelson' (1904)

History:
1905 May 15: Laid down at Beardmore
1906 June 23: Launched
1908 June 25: Completed
1909 August 18: Went aground near Longsands Range
1911 February 11: Damaged when grazed an uncharted rock at Ferrol
World War 1: 1914 Channel. 1915-16 Dardanelles, 1916-18 Aegean
1915 February 19 and 25: Hit over 50 times in action with forts in the Dardanelles
1915 March 18: Again hit 12 times in the Dardanelles
1916 May 15: Shot down Zeppelin *L85* at Salonika
1920 September: Converted to radio controlled target ship
1927 January 24: Sold and broken up at Newport

Agincourt

Type: Broadside Ship
Class: 'Minotaur' (1861)
Nomenclature: Military victory of Henry V in France, 25 October 1415

History:
1861 October 30: Laid down at Laird as ***Captain***, renamed ***Agincourt***
1865 March 27: Launched
1868 June 1: Completed
1871 July 1: Damaged by grounding on Pearl Rock, Gibraltar; refloated July 4
1875 Rearmed
1877-78 Mediterranean and Dardanelles

***Agamemnon* — Turret ship of 'Ajax' class in 1884. Notice turrets under flying deck.**

1878 February 14: Naval demonstration in the Dardanelles
1888 July 17: In collision with merchant ship *Sestos* off Falmouth
1889 Paid off
1893 Training ship, Portland
1904 March: Renamed ***Boscawen III***
1906 June 21: Renamed ***Ganges II***
1908 September: Coal hulk, Sheerness, renamed ***C109***
1960 Broken up at Grays

Agincourt

Type: Dreadnought
Class: 'Queen Elizabeth' (1912)

History:
1914 Ordered from Portsmouth; never laid down
1914 August 26: Contract cancelled

Agincourt

Type: Dreadnought
Class: 'Agincourt' (1914)

History:
1911 September 14: Laid down at Armstrong for Brazil as ***Rio de Janeiro***
1913 January 22: Launched
1914 January 9: Sold to Turkey, renamed ***Sultan Osman I***
1914 August 2: Seized by British government, renamed ***Agincourt***
1914 August 20: Completed
World War 1: 1914-18 Grand Fleet, Jutland
1916 Refit, tripod mainmast replaced by short pole mast
1921 December 19: Sold and broken up at Rosyth

Ajax

Type: Turret Ship
Class: 'Ajax' (1875)
Nomenclature: Greek myth: a hero of the Trojan War

History:
1876 March 21: Laid down at Pembroke
1880 March 10: Launched
1883 March 30: Completed
1886 Refit at Chatham, stern altered
1887 In collision with battleship *Devastation* off Portland
1889 September 4: Explosion of 12.5" ML gun
1904 March 1: Sold and broken up at Northfleet

Ajax

Type: Dreadnought
Class: 'King George V' (1910)

History:
1911 February 27: Laid down at Scotts
1912 March 21: Launched
1913 October 31: Completed
World War 1: 1914-18 Grand Fleet, Jutland
1919-24 Mediterranean, Black Sea
1926 November 9: Sold and broken up at Rosyth

Albemarle

Type: Pre-dreadnought
Class: 'Duncan' (1898)
Nomenclature: George Monck, Duke of Albemarle (1608-1670), British naval commander

History:
1900 January 8: Laid down at Chatham
1901 March 5: Launched
1903 November 12: Completed
1903-05 Mediterranean
1907 February 11: In collision with battleship *Commonwealth* off Lagos
1912 Refit
World War 1: 1914 Grand Fleet, 1915 Channel patrol, 1916 White Sea, ice breaker at Archangel
1917 Main deck battery suppressed, reserve

1917 Accommodation ship, Devonport
1919 November 19: Sold
1922 Broken up at Swansea

Albion

Type: Pre-dreadnought
Class: 'Canopus' (1896)
Nomenclature: Ancient name for Britain

History:
1896 December 3: Laid down at Thames
1898 June 21: Launched, 34 spectators drowned
1901 June 25: Completed
1901-05 Far East
1905 September 26: In collision with battleship *Duncan* at Lerwick
World War 1: 1914 Channel, 1914-15 Cape of Good Hope and East Africa, Dardanelles, 1916-18 English East Coast
1915 April 28 and May 2: Damaged by shore batteries at the Dardanelles
1918 Accommodation ship, Devonport
1919 December 11: Sold and broken up at Morecambe

Albion

Type: Light Aircraft Carrier
Class: 'Hermes' (1943)

History:
1944 March 23: Laid down at Swan Hunter
1947 May 6: Launched and laid up
1949 October 18: Damaged in collision with merchant ship *Maystone* while in tow to Rosyth; later taken to Vickers, Tyne for completion
1954 May 26: Completed
1956 Suez
1958 Far East
1961-62 Converted to commando carrier at Portsmouth
1962 Far East
1973 November: Broken up at Faslane

Alexandra

Type: Central Battery Ship
Class: 'Alexandra' (1872)
Nomenclature: Alexandra, Princess of Wales (1844-1925), later Queen of England

History:
1873 March 5: Laid down at Chatham as ***Superb***
1874 March 4: Renamed ***Alexandra***
1875 April 7: Launched
1877 January 31: Completed
1877-89 Mediterranean
1878 February 13: Went aground in the Dardanelles
1879 October: In collision with ironclad *Achilles*
1882 July 11: Damaged by 34 hits during bombardment of Alexandria
1889-91 Reconstructed; military rig, rearmed
1901 Reserve
1903 April: Mechanics' training ship, Chatham
1908 October 6: Sold

Anson

Type: Barbette Ship
Class: 'Admiral' (1881)
Nomenclature: George, Lord Anson (1697-1762), British admiral and naval reformer, 'father of the navy'

History:
1883 April 24: Laid down at Pembroke
1886 February 17: Launched
1889 May 28: Completed, having been delayed by late delivery of armament
1891 March 17: Liner *Utopia* foundered with loss of 533 persons after colliding with *Anson's* underwater ram while anchored in Gibraltar Bay
1893-1900 Mediterranean
1896 Refit
1898 October 11: Damaged by collision with merchant vessel *Cuzco* while lying at anchor at Gibraltar
1904 Paid off
1909 July 13: Sold and broken up at Upnor

Anson

Type: Battlecruiser
Class: 'Hood' (1915)

History:
1916 November 9: Laid down at Armstrong
1917 March 9: Construction suspended
1919 March 17: Contract cancelled

Anson, see Duke of York

Anson

Type: Battleship
Class: 'King George V' (1936)

History:
1937 July 20: Laid down at Swan Hunter as ***Jellicoe***
1940 February 21: Renamed ***Anson***
1940 February 24: Launched
1942 June 22: Completed
World War 2: 1942-45 Home Fleet, Arctic 1942-43
1944-45 Refit
1945 August: Arrived in Pacific too late for hostilities
1945 August: Occupation of Hong Kong
1945-46 Far East
1949 November: Reserve
1957 December: Broken up at Faslane

Antrim

Type: Armoured Cruiser
Class: 'Devonshire' (1901)
Nomenclature: A county of Northern Ireland

History:
1902 August 27: Laid down at John Brown
1903 October 8: Launched
1905 June 23: Completed
World War 1: 1914-15 North Sea, 1916 North Russia, 1916-18 North America and West Indies
1920 March: Wireless telegraph training ship
1922 December 19: Sold and broken up at Blyth

Argus

Type: Aircraft Carrier
Class: 'Argus' (1916)

Nomenclature: Greek myth: 100-eyed giant killed by Hermes

History:
1914 June: Laid down at Beardmore as Italian passenger liner ***Conte Rosso***
1916 August: Purchased by British government for conversion to the first aircraft carrier with full-length flightdeck, renamed ***Argus***
1917 December 2: Launched
1918 September 14: Completed
World War 1: 1918-19 Grand Fleet
1925-26 Refit, bulges added
1927-28 China
1930 Reserve
1937 Refit; flightdeck made level forward
1938 Training ship
World War 2: 1939-40 Mediterranean, 1940-41 Home Fleet, 1941 Arctic, 1941-42 North Africa, Atlantic Convoys, 1942 Force 'H', Malta Convoys, 1943-44 Home Fleet
1942 November: Damaged by aircraft bombs off Algeria
1944-45 Accommodation ship, Chatham
1946 December 5: Sold and broken up at Inverkeithing

Argyll

Type: Armoured Cruiser
Class: 'Devonshire' (1901)
Nomenclature: A county of Scotland

History:
1902 September 1: Laid down at Scotts
1904 March 3: Launched
1905 December: Completed
1912 December 28: Went aground in Plymouth Sound
World War 1: 1914-15 North Sea
1915 October 28: Wrecked in heavy weather near Dundee (none lost)

Ark Royal

Type: Aircraft Carrier
Class: 'Ark Royal' (1934)
Nomenclature: Traditional name first used for a ship of 1587

History:
1935 September 16: Laid down at Cammell Laird
1937 April 13: Launched
1938 November 16: Completed
World War 2: 1939 Home Fleet, 1940 Mediterranean; Norwegian campaign, Cape Spartivento, 'Bismarck' operations, Malta convoys, Oran, Dakar
1941 November 13: Torpedoed by *U81* in western Mediterranean and sank in tow the following day (one dead)

Ark Royal

Type: Aircraft Carrier
Class: 'Audacious' (1940)

History:
1943 May 3: Laid down at Cammell Laird as ***Irresistible***
1945 Renamed ***Ark Royal***
1950 May 3: Launched
1955 February 22: Completed
1958 Refit
1961 Far East
1967-70 Reconstructed; fully angled flightdeck, missile armament
1970 February 24: Reconstructed
1979 February 13: Decommissioned
1980 Sold and broken up

Ark Royal

Type: Aircraft Carrier
Class: 'Invincible' (1972)

History:
1978 December 14: Laid down by Swan Hunter
1981 June 4: Launched

Arrogant

Type: Light Aircraft Carrier
Class: 'Hermes' (1943)
Nomenclature: 3rd rate of 1705

History:
1943 July 12: Ordered from Swan Hunter; never laid down
1945 October: Contract cancelled

Audacious

Type: Central Battery Ship
Class: 'Audacious' (1867)
Nomenclature: 3rd rate of 1785

History:
1867 June 26: Laid down at Napier
1869 February 27: Launched in a gale and damaged
1870 September 10: Completed at Plymouth
1874-78 Far East
1876 In collision during a typhoon at Yokohama
1880-83 Refit; reboilered
1889-90 Refit; sails removed, new guns added
1894 Laid up
1902 Boys' training ship
1904 April: Renamed ***Fisgard***
1914 Receiving ship, Scapa, renamed ***Imperieuse***
1919 Receiving ship, Rosyth, renamed ***Victorious***
1929 March 15: Sold and broken up at Inverkeithing

Audacious

Type: Dreadnought
Class: 'King George V' (1910)

History:
1911 March 23: Laid down at Laird
1912 September 14: Launched
1913 October 21: Completed
1914 October 27: Sunk by mine northeast of Tory Island near Lough Swilly (none lost)

Audacious, see Eagle

Aurora

Type: Armoured Cruiser
Class: 'Orlando' (1884)
Nomenclature: Roman myth; goddess of Dawn

History:
1886 February 1: Laid down at Pembroke
1887 October 28: Launched

Top left:

***Agincourt* — Broadside ship, 'Minotaur' class, with five masts, c1870.** *IWM*

Top right:

***Ajax* — 'King George V' class dreadnought, on completion 1913.** *S. Cribb*

Centre left:

***Albion* — 'Hermes' class aircraft carrier, after conversion to commando carrier, April 1964.** *P. A. Vicary*

Above:

***Alexandra* — Central battery ship, leaving Portsmouth 1889 just before reconstruction.** *IWM*

Bottom left:

***Ark Royal* — Aircraft carrier, June 1939.** *Wright & Logan*

Top left:
***Ark Royal* — Aircraft carrier, 1957.**
British Information Services

Top right:
***Audacious* — Sinking after hitting a mine in October 1914, just one year after being commissioned.**

Above:
***Bacchante* — 'Cressy' class armoured cruiser, c1904.**
Marius Bar

Left:
***Barham* — 'Queen Elizabeth' class battleship, as reconstructed, in the Mediterranean 1941, just before its loss.** *IWM*

1890 July 1: Completed
1900 China
1907 October 2: Sold and broken up at Milford Haven

Australia

Type: Armoured Cruiser
Class: 'Orlando' (1884)
Nomenclature: The continent southeast of Asia, a British territory

History:
1885 April 21: Laid down at Fairfield
1886 November 25: Launched
1889 November 19: Completed
1900 China
1905 April 4: Sold and broken up at Troon

Australia

Type: Battlecruiser
Class: 'Indefatigable' (1908)

History:
1910 June 23: Laid down at John Brown for Royal Australian Navy
1911 October 25: Launched
1913 June 21: Completed
World War 1: 1914 North America and West Indies, 1915-18 Grand Fleet
1916 April 22: Damaged in collision with battlecruiser *New Zealand* in fog (missed Battle of Jutland)
1917 December 12: Damaged in collision with battlecruiser *Repulse*
1921 December 12: Decommissioned
1924 April 12: Sunk as target off Sydney

Bacchante

Type: Armoured Cruiser
Class: 'Cressy' (1898)
Nomenclature: Greek myth: a female devotee of Bacchus

History:
1899 March 8: Laid down at John Brown
1901 February 21: Launched
1901 December 7: Completed
1902-05 Mediterranean
1906-12 Mediterranean
World War 1: North Sea, Heligoland, Suez Canal defence 1915, Dardanelles, 1917-18 Gibraltar
1917 February: Damaged in collision with cruiser *Achilles* in Irish Sea
1920 July 1: Sold and broken up at Plymouth

Barfleur

Type: Pre-dreadnought
Class: 'Barfleur' (1888)
Nomenclature: Naval victory over the French off Cape Barfleur, 19 May 1692

History:
1890 October 12: Laid down at Chatham
1892 August 10: Launched
1894 June: Completed
1895-98 Mediterranean
1898-1902 China, Boxer Rebellion
1902-04 Reconstruction, casemates fitted, rearmed, foremast removed
1904 August 5: In collision with battleship *Canopus* in Mounts Bay
1905 China
1910 July 12: Sold and broken up at Glasgow

Barham

Type: Dreadnought
Class: 'Queen Elizabeth' (1912)
Nomenclature: Charles Middleton, Lord Barham (1762-1813), admiral and naval administrator

History:
1913 February 24: Laid down at John Brown
1914 December 31: Launched
1915 October 19: Completed
World War 1: 1914-18 Grand Fleet, Jutland
1916 May 31: Received six hits at Jutland (26 dead)
1924-27 Mediterranean
1927-28 Reconstructed; bridge remodelled, two funnels trunked into one, bulges fitted
1928-29 Mediterranean
1931-34 Refit
1935-39 Mediterranean
1940 Planned reconstruction like *Valiant* cancelled because of the war
World War 2: 1939-40 Home Fleet, 1940 Force 'H', 1940-41 Mediterranean; Dakar, Matapan, Crete
1939 December 12: Sank destroyer *Duchess* in collision off West Coast of Scotland
1939 December 28: Damaged by torpedo from *U-30* off the Clyde Estuary
1940 September 25: Damaged by gunfire of French battleship *Richelieu* during attack on Dakar
1941 January 3: Bombarded Bardia, Libya
1941 May 27: Damaged by aircraft bomb off Crete
1941 November 25: Torpedoed three times by *U-331*, capsized and blew up off Sollum, Egypt (862 dead)

Beatty, see **Howe**

Nomenclature: David Beatty, Earl Beatty (1871-1936), Admiral of the Fleet, commander of the Grand Fleet in World War 1

Bedford

Type: Armoured Cruiser
Class: 'Monmouth' (1899)
Nomenclature: County in central England

History:
1900 February 19: Laid down at Fairfield
1901 August 31: Launched
1902 May 14: Completed
1907-10 Far East
1910 August 21: Wrecked in Straits of Korea on Quelpart Island (18 dead)

Belleisle

Type: Central Battery Ship
Class: 'Belleisle' (1878)
Nomenclature: Island off Brittany captured 7 June 1761

History:
1874 Laid down at Samuda for Turkey as ***Peyk-i-Shereef***

1876 February 12: Launched
1878 February 20: Taken over by British government during Russo-Turkish War, renamed ***Belleisle***
1878 July 19: Completed
1879-93 Coastguard ship, Kingstown (Ireland)
1900 May: Target ship
1903 September 3: Sunk as torpedo target off Portsmouth
1904 Refloated, hulk broken up in Germany

Bellerophon

Type: Central Battery Ship
Class: 'Bellerophon' (1863)
Nomenclature: Greek myth: a hero who slew the monster Chimaera

History:
1863 December 28: Laid down at Chatham
1865 April 26: Launched
1866 April 11: Completed
1868 Damaged in collision with ironclad *Minotaur* in Belfast Lough
1871-72 Mediterranean
1873-81 North America
1873 Sank merchant vessel *Flamsteed* in collision in North Atlantic
1881-85 Refit; reboilered, rearmed with BL guns, rerigged, reduced to bark
1885-92 North America and West Indies
1904 March: Stokers' training ship, Devonport, renamed ***Indus III***
1922 December 12: Sold, broken up at Bo'ness

Bellerophon

Type: Dreadnought
Class: 'Bellerophon' (1906)

History:
1906 December 3: Laid down at Portsmouth
1907 July 27: Launched
1909 February 2: Completed
1911 May 26: In collision with battlecruiser *Inflexible* at Portland
1914 August 28: In collision with merchant vessel *St Clair*
World War 1: 1914-18 Grand Fleet, Jutland
1921 November 8: Sold and broken up in Germany

Benbow

Type: Barbette Ship
Class: 'Admiral' (1881)
Nomenclature: John Benbow (1653-1702), admiral, killed in battle in West Indies

History:
1882 November 1: Laid down at Thames
1885 June 15: Launched
1888 June: Completed
1888-91 Mediterranean
1904 April: Paid off
1909 July 13: Sold and broken up at Morecambe

Benbow

Type: Dreadnought
Class: 'Iron Duke' (1911)

History:
1912 May 30: Laid down at Beardmore
1913 November 12: Launched
1914 October 7: Completed
World War 1: 1914-18 Grand Fleet, Jutland
1919-26 Mediterranean, Black Sea
1931 March: Sold and broken up at Rosyth

Berwick

Type: Armoured Cruiser
Class: 'Monmouth' (1899)
Nomenclature: County in northern England

History:
1901 April 19: Laid down at Beardmore
1902 September 20: Launched
1903 September: Completed
1908 April 2: Sank destroyer *Tiger* in collision off the Isle of Wight
1909-12 West Indies
World War 1: 1914-18 South Atlantic and West Indies, Convoy escort
1920 July 1: Sold and broken up 1922 in Germany

Black Prince

Type: Broadside Ship
Class: 'Warrior' (1859)
Nomenclature: Edward, Prince of Wales (1330-1376), eldest son of King Edward III, a great military leader called the Black Prince

History:
1859 October 12: Laid down at Napier as ***Invincible***
1859 Renamed ***Black Prince***
1861 February 27: Launched
1861 Capsized in dock at Greenock, damaging masts
1862 September 12: Completed
1867-68 Rearmed
1875 Refit
1878 Armoured Cruiser, in reserve
1896 Boys' training ship, Queenstown
1903 Depot ship, renamed ***Emerald***
1910 Renamed ***Impregnable III***
1923 February 21: Sold and broken up at Dover

Black Prince

Type: Armoured Cruiser
Class: 'Duke of Edinburgh' (1902)

History:
1903 June 3: Laid down at Thames
1904 November 8: Launched
1906 January: Completed
1913-14 Mediterranean
World War 1: 1914 Mediterranean and Red Sea, 'Goeben' operations, 1914-16 Grand Fleet, Jutland
1916 May 31: Sunk by gunfire and torpedoes during night action at Battle of Jutland (857 dead, no survivors)

Brave, see ***Warrior***

Britannia

Type: Pre-dreadnought
Class: 'King Edward VII' (1901)
Nomenclature: Roman name for Britain

History:
1904 February 4: Laid down at Portsmouth
1904 December 10: Launched
1906 September 8: Completed
1910 July 14: In collision with bark *Loch Trool* in English Channel
World War 1: 1914-15 Grand Fleet
1915 January: Badly damaged by grounding at Inchkeith
1918 November 9: Torpedoed and sunk by *UB50* off Cape Trafalgar (40 dead)

Bulwark

Type: Pre-dreadnought
Class: 'Formidable' (1897)
Nomenclature: Solid part of a ship's side extending above the deck

History:
1899 March 20: Laid down at Devonport
1899 October 18: Launched
1902 March 11: Completed
1902-07 Mediterranean
1907 October 26: Went aground near Lemonlight, in North Sea
1912 May: Went aground twice on Barrow Deep off the Nore
World War 1: 1914 Channel Patrol
1914 November 26: Blew up and sank while anchored off Sheerness (781 dead)

Bulwark

Type: Light Aircraft Carrier
Class: 'Hermes' (1943)

History:
1945 May 10: Laid down at Harland & Wolff
1948 June 22: Launched
1954 November 4: Completed
1956 Suez
1957 Far East
1959-60 Converted to commando carrier at Portsmouth
1960-62 Far East
1971 November 26: Damaged by boiler room fire at Trieste
1981 March 27: Decommissioned

CVA 01

Type: Aircraft Carrier
Class: 'CVA 01' (1966)

History:
1966 February: Contract cancelled; never laid down

Top left:
***Benbow* — 'Admiral' class barbette ship with 16" guns.** *IWM*

Centre left:
***Black Prince* — Broadside ship, 1862, 'Warrior' class, with funnels lowered.** *P. A. Vicary*

Bottom left:
***Bulwark* — 'Hermes' class commando carrier, January 1972.** *G. E. P. Brownell*

Caesar

Type: Pre-dreadnought
Class: 'Majestic' (1893)
Nomenclature: Gaius Julius Caesar (102-44BC), Roman general and statesman

History:
1895 March 25: Laid down at Portsmouth
1896 September 2: Launched
1898 January 13: Completed
1898-1903 Mediterranean
1905 June 3: Damaged in collision which sank bark *Afghanistan* in fog off Dungeness
World War 1: 1914 Channel Fleet, 1915-18 North America and West Indies, 1918-19 Mediterranean and Black Sea
1918 November: Depot ship, Malta
1921 November 8: Sold and broken up in Germany

Caledonia

Type: Broadside Ship
Class: 'Prince Consort' (1861)
Nomenclature: Roman name for Scotland

History:
1860 October 1: Laid down at Woolwich as wood line-of-battle ship
1861 May 27: Reordered as ironclad
1862 October 24: Launched
1865 July 6: Completed; completion delayed by late-delivery of guns
1866-69 Mediterranean
1867 Rearmed with ML guns
1875 Paid off
1886 September 30: Sold

Camperdown

Type: Barbette Ship
Class: 'Admiral' (1881)
Nomenclature: Adam Duncan, Viscount Duncan of Camperdown (1731-1804), British admiral, victor of Camperdown, 1797

History:
1882 December 18: Laid down at Portsmouth
1885 November 24: Launched
1889 July: Completed
1889-90 Mediterranean
1892-95 Mediterranean
1893 June 22: Damaged in collision which sank battleship *Victoria* off coast of Syria
1896-97 Refit
1903 Paid off
1908 October: Berthing ship for submarines, Harwich
1911 July 11: Sold and broken up at Swansea

Canada

Type: Dreadnought
Class: 'Canada' (1914)
Nomenclature: A British dominion in North America

History:
1911 November 27: Laid down at Armstrong for Chile as ***Almirante Latorre***
1913 November 27: Launched

1914 September 9: Purchased by British government, renamed ***Canada***
1915 September: Completed
World War 1: 1915 18 Grand Fleet, Jutland
1920 August 1: Returned to Chile, renamed ***Almirante Latorre***

Canopus

Type: Pre-dreadnought
Class: 'Canopus' (1896)
Nomenclature: Ancient Egyptian city near Aboukir, scene of the Battle of the Nile, 1798

History:
1897 January 4: Laid down at Portsmouth
1897 October 13: Launched
1899 December 5: Completed
1900-03 Mediterranean
1903-04 Refit
1904 August 5: Slight damage in collision with battleship *Barfleur* in Mounts Bay
1908-09 Mediterranean
World War 1: 1914 South Atlantic; 1915 Dardanelles
1916 Accommodation ship, Chatham
1917 Main deck battery suppressed
1920 February 18: Sold and broken up at Dover

Captain, see *Agincourt*

Captain

Type: Turret Ship
Class: 'Captain' (1865)
Nomenclature: 3rd rate of 1678

History:
1867 January 30: Laid down at Laird
1869 March 27: Launched
1870 January: Completed
1870 September 7: Capsized and sank in gale at sea off Cape Finisterre. Capt Coles, the designer, among those lost (473 lost)

Carnarvon

Type: Armoured Cruiser
Class: 'Devonshire' (1901)
Nomenclature: A county of Wales

History:
1902 October 1: Laid down at Beardmore
1903 October 7: Launched
1905 May 29: Completed
1905-07 Mediterranean
World War 1: 1914-15 South Atlantic, Falklands, 1915-18 North America and West Indies
1916 February 22: Damaged by grounding on Abrolhos Rocks
1919-21 Cadet training ship
1921 November 8: Sold and broken up in Germany

Centaur

Type: Light Aircraft Carrier
Class: 'Hermes' (1943)
Nomenclature: Greek myth: a monster with the head, trunk and arms of a man on the body of a horse

History:
1944 May 30: Laid down at Harland & Wolff
1947 April 22: Launched
1953 September 1: Completed
1957 Refit, steam catapults fitted
1958 Far East
1961 Refit
1972 September: Broken up at Cairnryan

Centurion

Type: Pre-dreadnought
Class: 'Barfleur' (1888)
Nomenclature: A commander in the Roman Army

History:
1890 March 30: Laid down at Portsmouth
1892 August 3: Launched
1894 February: Completed
1894-1901 China, Boxer Rebellion
1901-03 Reconstructed, casemates fitted, rearmed, foremast removed
1903-05 China
1904 April 17: In collision with battleship *Glory*
1910 July 12: Sold and broken up at Morecambe

Centurion

Type: Dreadnought
Class: 'King George V' (1910)

History:
1911 January 16: Laid down at Devonport
1911 November 18: Launched
1912 December 9: Sank Italian steamer *Derna* in collision while on trials
1913 May 22: Completed
World War 1: 1914-18 Grand Fleet, Jutland
1919-24 Mediterranean, Black Sea
1926 Converted to remote controlled target ship
1941 April: Converted to dummy battleship (*Anson*)
1944 January: Floating AA battery south of Suez
1944 June 9: Sunk as blockship at Normandy for artificial port

Cerberus

Type: Breastwork Monitor
Class: 'Cerberus' (1867)
Nomenclature: Greek myth: a three-headed dog guarding the entrance to Hades

History:
1867 September 18: Laid down at Palmers for the State of Victoria
1868 December 2: Launched

Top right:
Caledonia **— Wood hull armoured broadside ship, completed in 1865.**

Centre right:
Centaur **— 'Hermes' class light aircraft carrier, July 1960.** *Wright & Logan*

Bottom right:
Collingwood **— Barbette ship of 1879.** *P. A. Vicary*

R08

Above:
***Colossus* — Turret ship, completed 1886. First British battleship with breech loading guns.**

Below:
***Conqueror* — Turret ship of 1879, c1900.**
Martin Holbrook Collection

1870 September: Completed; based at Melbourne
1900 Depot ship
1918 Renamed ***Platypus II***
1924 April 23: Sold
1924 July 26: Sunk as breakwater at Melbourne

Cochrane

Type: Armoured Cruiser
Class: 'Warrior' (1903)
Nomenclature: Thomas, Lord Cochrane, Earl of Dundonald (1775-1860), British naval commander and Chilean admiral

History:
1904 March 24: Laid down at Fairfield
1905 May 20: Launched
1907 February 21: Completed
World War 1: 1914-17 Grand Fleet, Jutland, 1917-18 North America and West Indies, 1918 North Russia
1918 November 14: Ran aground and broke in two in fog in the Mersey Estuary (none lost)

Collingwood

Type: Barbette Ship
Class: 'Collingwood' (1879)
Nomenclature: Cuthbert, Lord Collingwood (1748-1810), British admiral, second in command at Trafalgar

History:
1880 July 12: Laid down at Pembroke
1882 November 22: Launched
1886 May 4: Faulty 12" gun burst on trials
1887 July 1: Completed
1889-97 Mediterranean
1897 Refit, reboilered
1899 January 23: In collision with cruiser *Curacoa* at Portsmouth
1903 Reserve
1909 May 11: Sold and broken up at Dunston

Collingwood

Type: Dreadnought
Class: 'St Vincent' (1907)

History:
1908 February 3: Laid down at Devonport
1908 November 7: Launched
1910 April 19: Completed
World War 1: 1914-18 Grand Fleet, Jutland
1919 Gunnery training ship
1922 December 12: Sold and broken up at Newport

Colossus

Type: Turret Ship
Class: 'Colossus' (1878)
Nomenclature: The Colossus of Rhodes, a statue of Apollo, one of the seven wonders of the ancient world

History:
1879 June 6: Laid down at Portsmouth
1882 May 21: Launched
1886 October 31: Completed; completion delayed by late delivery of armament
1887-93 Mediterranean
1901 Paid off
1904 January: Depot ship, tender to *Excellent*
1908 October 6: Sold and broken up at Briton Ferry

Colossus

Type: Dreadnought
Class: 'Neptune' (1908)

History:
1909 July 8: Laid down at Scotts
1910 April 9: Launched
1911 July: Completed
World War 1: 1914-18 Grand Fleet, Jutland
1916 May 31: Received two hits at Battle of Jutland
1919 Cadet training ship
1922 July: Sold and broken up at Alloa

Colossus

Type: Light Aircraft Carrier
Class: 'Colossus' (1942)

History:
1942 June 1: Laid down at Vickers, Tyne
1943 September 30: Launched
1944 December 16: Completed
World War 2: 1945 Pacific Fleet
1946 August 6: Loaned to France, renamed ***Arromanches***

Commonwealth

Type: Pre-dreadnought
Class: 'King Edward VII' (1901)
Nomenclature: The Commonwealth of Australia

History:
1902 June 17: Laid down at Fairfield
1903 May 13: Launched
1905 March 14: Completed at Devonport
1907 February 11: Severely damaged in collision with battleship *Albemarle* off Lagos
1907 August 23: Went aground at entrance to Lamlash
World War 1: 1914-15 Grand Fleet
1918 Refit; main deck battery suppressed, waterline bulges fitted, tripod mast fitted
1918 Gunnery training ship, Invergordon
1921 November 18: Sold and broken up in Germany

Conqueror

Type: Turret Ship
Class: 'Conqueror' (1879)
Nomenclature: Ship of 1745

History:
1879 April 28: Laid down at Chatham
1881 September 8: Launched
1886 March: Completed
1889 Tender to gunnery school
1900 July 11: Went aground on the Shambles
1902 Paid off
1907 April 9: Sold and broken up

Conqueror

Type: Dreadnought
Class: 'Orion' (1909)

History:
1910 April 5: Laid down at Beardmore

1911 May 1: Launched
1912 November: Completed
World War 1: 1914-18 Grand Fleet, Jutland
1914 December 27: Damaged in collision with battleship *Monarch*
1922 December 19: Sold and broken up at Upnor

Conqueror

Type: Battleship
Class: 'Lion' (1938)

History:
1939 August 16: Ordered from John Brown, never laid down
1939 October: Construction suspended
1941 September: Contract cancelled

Cornwall

Type: Armoured Cruiser
Class: 'Monmouth' (1899)
Nomenclature: A county in southwest England

History:
1901 March 11: Laid down at Pembroke
1902 October 29: Launched
1904 September: Completed
1908-12 North America and West Indies
1911 July 31: Went aground off Cape Sable while towing off stranded Canadian cruiser *Niobe*
World War 1: 1914 South Atlantic, Falklands, 1915 Southwest and East Africa, Dardanelles, 1916 China, 1917-18 Convoy escort
1919 Cadet training ship
1920 June 7: Sold and broken up at Briton Ferry

Cornwallis

Type: Pre-dreadnought
Class: 'Duncan' (1898)
Nomenclature: The Hon Sir William Cornwallis (1743-1819), British admiral

History:
1899 July 19: Laid down at Thames
1901 July 13: Launched
1904 February 9: Completed
1904-05 Mediterranean
1904 September 17: In collision with Greek bark *Angelica*
1910-12 Mediterranean
World War 1: 1914 Channel patrol, 1915 Mediterranean, Dardanelles
1917 January 9: Torpedoed and sunk by *U32* off Malta (15 dead)

Courageous

Type: 1) Light Battlecruiser, 2) Aircraft Carrier
Class: 1) 'Courageous' (1915), 2) 'Courageous' (1924)
Nomenclature: Prize of 1761

History:
1915 March 28: Laid down at Armstrong
1916 February 5: Launched
1917 January: Completed
World War 1: 1917-18 Grand Fleet
1917 November 27: Damaged in action in the North Sea
1924 June 27: Decommissioned for conversion to aircraft carrier
1928 February 21: Recommissioned
1933 September 25: Went aground off Yarmouth
1936 Refit, light tripod mast fitted
World War 2: Home Fleet
1939 September 17: Torpedoed and sunk by *U29* southwest of Iceland (515 dead)

Cressy

Type: Armoured Cruiser
Class: 'Cressy' (1898)
Nomenclature: Military victory of Edward III over the French at Crecy, 26 August 1346

History:
1898 October 12: Laid down at Fairfield
1899 December 4: Launched
1900 September 25: Completed
1901-04 China
1907-09 North America and West Indies
World War 1: Heligoland Bight
1914 September 22: Torpedoed and sunk by *U9* in North Sea (560 dead)

Cumberland

Type: Armoured Cruiser
Class: 'Monmouth' (1899)
Nomenclature: A county in northern England

History:
1901 February 19: Laid down at London & Glasgow
1902 December 16: Launched
1903 November: Completed
World War 1: Cameroons, 1915-18 Atlantic convoy escort
1914 September 27: Captured 10 German merchant ships at Duala, Cameroons
1921 May 9: Sold and broken up 1923 at Briton Ferry

Cyclops

Type: Breastwork Monitor
Class: 'Cyclops' (1869)
Nomenclature: Greek myth: a one-eyed giant

History:
1870 September 10: Laid down at Thames
1871 July 18: Launched
1877 May 4: Completed, having been delivered in 1872
1878 Particular Service Squadron
1887-89 Refit
1903 July 7: Sold

Defence

Type: Broadside Ship
Class: 'Defence' (1859)
Nomenclature: 10-gun ship of 1588

History:
1859 December 14: Laid down at Palmer
1861 April 24: Launched
1861 December 4: Completed
1867 Rearmed with ML guns
1869-70 North America
1870-72 Mediterranean
1871 Went aground off Pantellaria Island
1872-74 Refit
1878 Mediterranean and Dardanelles

1879 Paid off
1884 July 20: Damaged in collision with ironclad *Valiant* in Lough Swilly
1890 Floating workshop, Devonport
1898 June: Renamed ***Indus***
1935 Broken up at Plymouth

Defence

Type: Armoured Cruiser
Class: 'Minotaur' (1904)

History:
1905 February 22: Laid down at Pembroke
1907 April 24: Launched
1909 February 9: Completed
1912-14 Mediterranean
World War 1: 1914 Mediterranean, 'Goeben' operations, Cape of Good Hope, 1915-16 Grand Fleet, Jutland
1916 May 31: Sunk by gunfire of German battleship *Friedrich der Grosse* at Jutland. Flagship of Rear-Adm Sir Robert Arbuthnot who was lost (893 dead)

Delhi, see Emperor of India

Nomenclature: Capital of India

Devastation

Type: Turret Ship
Class: 'Devastation' (1868)
Nomenclature: Bomb ship of 1804

History:
1869 November 12: Laid down at Portsmouth
1871 July 12: Launched
1873 April 19: Completed
1874 July: Rammed in collision with ironclad *Resistance* at Portland
1874-78 Mediterranean
1879 Refit; searchlights, torpedoes and machine guns fitted
1887 In collision with battleship *Ajax*
1891-92 Refit, rearmed, re-engined and reboilered
1898-1902 Guardship, Gibraltar
1900 August 28: Gun explosion while at Gibraltar
1907 Non-effective
1908 May 12: Sold and broken up at Morecambe

Devonshire

Type: Armoured Cruiser
Class: 'Devonshire' (1901)
Nomenclature: A county of southwest England

History:
1902 March 25: Laid down at Chatham
1904 April 30: Launched
1905 August 24: Completed
World War 1: 1914-16 North Sea, 1916-18 North America and West Indies
1921 May 9: Sold
1923 Broken up at Barrow

Dominion

Type: Pre-dreadnought
Class: 'King Edward VII' (1901)
Nomenclature: The Dominion of Canada

History:
1902 May 23: Laid down at Vickers
1903 August 25: Launched
1905 June 6: Completed
1906 August 16: Damaged by hitting a rock in Chalon Bay, St Lawrence River
1911 Refit; reboilered
World War 1: 1914-15 Grand Fleet
1921 May 9: Sold
1924 Broken up at Preston

Donegal

Type: Armoured Cruiser
Class: 'Monmouth' (1899)
Nomenclature: A county of Northern Ireland

History:
1901 February 14: Laid down at Fairfield
1902 September 4: Launched
1903 October 1: Completed
1906 March 2: Ran aground near Suez en route to China station
1909 December 8: In collision with merchant vessel *Malaga* at Gibraltar
World War 1: 1914 South Atlantic, 1915 Grand Fleet, North Russia, 1917-18 North America and West Indies
1920 July 1: Sold and broken up

Drake

Type: Armoured Cruiser
Class: 'Drake' (1898)
Nomenclature: Sir Francis Drake (1540-1596), English admiral and navigator, the foremost British sailor of his time

History:
1899 April 24: Laid down at Pembroke
1901 March 5: Launched
1903 January 13: Completed
World War 1: Convoy escort, 1915-17 Grand Fleet
1917 October 2: Torpedoed and sunk by *U79* north of Ireland (19 dead)

Dreadnought

Type: Turret Ship
Class: 'Dreadnought' (1869)
Nomenclature: Elizabethan compound name, first used 1573

History:
1870 September 10: Laid down as ***Fury*** at Pembroke
1871 Construction suspended, redesigned
1875 February 1: Renamed ***Dreadnought***
1875 March 8: Launched
1879 February 15: Completed
1884 First commissioned
1884-94 Mediterranean
1897 Refit; funnels raised, reboilered
1902 Torpedo boat depot ship, Devonport
1908 July 14: Sold and broken up at Barrow

Dreadnought

Type: Dreadnought
Class: 'Dreadnought' (1905)

Top left:
Courageous **— Aircraft carrier, 1935, before addition of tripod mast.** *R. Perkins*

Top right:
Devastation **— Turret ship of 1868, after being rearmed with breech loading guns in 1892.** *IWM*

Centre left:
Drake **— 'Drake' class armoured cruiser, c1912, sunk by a U-boat in 1917.**

Above:
Dreadnought **— Shortly after completion.**

Far left:
Duke of Edinburgh **— Armoured cruiser, 1913, entering Malta.**

Left:
Eagle **— Aircraft carrier, August 1937.** *Wright & Logan*

***Eagle* — 'Audacious' class aircraft carrier, April 1955.**
Wright & Logan

History:
1905 October 2: Laid down at Portsmouth
1906 February 10: Launched
1906 October 3: Completed
World War 1: 1914-15 Grand Fleet, 1916-18 Thames Estuary
1915 March 18: Rammed and sank *U29* in North Sea
1921 May 9: Sold and broken up 1923 at Inverkeithing

Duke of Edinburgh

Type: Armoured Cruiser
Class: 'Duke of Edinburgh' (1902)
Nomenclature: Prince Alfred, Duke of Edinburgh (1844-1900), Admiral of the Fleet, second son of Queen Victoria

History:
1903 February 11: Laid down at Pembroke
1904 June 14: Launched
1905 December: Completed
1913-14 Mediterranean
World War 1: 1914 Mediterranean and Red Sea, 1914-17 Grand Fleet, Jutland, 1917 Convoy escort, 1918 North America and West Indies
1917 May: Refit; main deck 6" batteries suppressed, tripod foremast fitted
1920 April 12: Sold and broken up at Blyth

Duke of York

Type: Battleship
Class: 'King George V' (1936)
Nomenclature: Title of King George VI before he became king

History:
1937 May 5: Laid down at John Brown as ***Anson***
1938 December 21: Renamed ***Duke of York***
1940 February 28: Launched
1941 November 4: Completed
World War 2: 1941-45 Home Fleet, North Africa, Arctic, 1942-43, North Cape
1941 December: Carried Prime Minister Churchill to US
1943 December 26: Sank German battleship *Scharnhorst* off North Cape
1944-45 Refit
1945-46 Pacific Fleet
1945 August: Arrived in Pacific too late for hostilities
1951 November 6: Laid up in reserve
1958 February: Broken up at Faslane

Duncan

Type: Pre-dreadnought
Class: 'Duncan' (1898)
Nomenclature: Adam Duncan, Viscount Duncan of Camperdown (1731-1804), British admiral, victor of Camperdown, 1797

History:
1899 July 10: Laid down at Thames
1901 March 21: Launched
1903 October 8: Completed
1903-05 Mediterranean
1905 September 26: Rammed battleship *Albion* in collision at Lerwick
1906 July: Went aground on Lundy Island while assisting wrecked battleship *Montagu*
World War 1: 1914 Northern patrol, Dover patrol; 1915-17 Mediterranean
1917 Reserve
1920 February 18: Sold and broken up at Dover

Eagle

Type: Aircraft Carrier
Class: 'Eagle' (1917)
Nomenclature: Name first used 1592

History:
1913 January 22: Laid down by Armstrong as Chilean battleship ***Almirante Cochrane***
1917 Purchased by British government for conversion to aircraft carrier and renamed ***Eagle***
1918 June 8: Launched
1920 April 13: Completed
1920-23 Refit after trials
1923 September 19: Recommissioned
1931-32 Refit
1933 April 28: Damaged by explosion at Portsmouth
1933-35 and 1937-39 Far East
World War 2: 1939-40 West Indies, 1940-41 Mediterranean, 1941-42 South Atlantic, 1942 Force 'H', Malta Convoys
1940 March 14: Damaged by accidental bomb explosion off Ceylon
1940 Carrier raids on Libyan ports

1942 August 11: Torpedoed and sunk by *U73* south of Balearic Islands during operations supporting Malta convoy 'Pedestal' (163 dead)

Eagle

Type: Aircraft Carrier
Class: 'Audacious' (1940)

History:
1942 April 19: Laid down at Vickers, Tyne
1945 Contract cancelled

Eagle

Type: Aircraft Carrier
Class: 'Audacious' (1940)

History:
1942 October 24: Laid down at Harland & Wolff as ***Audacious***
1946 January 21: Renamed ***Eagle***
1946 March 19: Launched
1951 October 1: Completed
1955 Refit, partially angled flightdeck
1956 Suez
1959-64 Reconstructed at Devonport; angled flightdeck, steam catapults fitted, new radar, missile armament
1967 April 11: Damaged by fire in boiler room
1972 Decommissioned
1978 Broken up at Cairnryan

Earl Roberts, see *Roberts*

Earl of Peterborough

Type: Monitor
Class: 'Lord Clive' (1914)
Nomenclature: Charles Mordaunt, Earl of Peterborough (1658-1735), military commander during the War of the Spanish Succession

History:
1914 December: Laid down at Harland & Wolff as ***M8***
1915 June: Renamed ***Earl of Peterborough***
1915 August 28: Launched
1915 September 5: Completed
World War 1: Dardanelles, Adriatic
1921 November 8: Sold and broken up in Germany

Edgar

Type: Light Aircraft Carrier
Class: 'Colossus' (1942)
Nomenclature: Edgar, King of the English 959-975

History:
1942 June 1: Laid down at Vickers, Tyne, as ***Edgar***
1944 March 26: Launched as ***Perseus***
1945 October 19: Completed as aircraft maintenance ship
1958 May: Broken up at Port Glasgow

Edinburgh

Type: Turret Ship
Class: 'Colossus' (1878)
Nomenclature: Capital of Scotland

History:
1879 March 20: Laid down at Pembroke as ***Majestic***
1882 March 16: Renamed ***Edinburgh***
1882 March 18: Launched
1883 September: Ran trials; completion delayed by late delivery of armament
1887 July 8: Completed
1887-94 Mediterranean
1899 October: Gunnery ship, tender to *Wildfire*
1908 Used as target
1910 October 11: Sold and broken up at Briton Ferry

Elephant, see *Minotaur*

Elephant, see *Hermes*

Emperor of India

Type: Dreadnought
Class: 'Iron Duke' (1911)
Nomenclature: A title of the King of England

History:
1912 May 31: Laid down at Vickers, as ***Delhi***
1913 October: Renamed ***Emperor of India***
1913 November 27: Launched
1914 October 12: Completed
World War 1: 1914-18 Grand Fleet
1919-26 Mediterranean
1922 Refit
1931 July 1: Sunk as target off Owers Bank, refloated and broken up at Rosyth

Empress of India

Type: Pre-dreadnought
Class: 'Royal Sovereign' (1888)
Nomenclature: A title of Queen Victoria

History:
1889 July 9: Laid down at Pembroke as ***Renown***
1890 Renamed ***Empress of India***
1891 May 7: Launched
1893 September 11: Completed

1897-1901 Mediterranean, Crete operations
1902 Refit
1906 April 30: In collision with submarine *A10* in Plymouth Sound
1911 In collision with German bark *Winderhudder* while under tow to lay up
1911 Target ship
1913 November 4: Sunk as target off Portland Bill

Erebus

Type: Monitor
Class: 'Erebus' (1915)
Nomenclature: Greek myth: the entrance to Hades

History:
1915 October 12: Laid down at Harland & Wolff, Govan
1916 June 19: Launched
1916 September 2: Completed
World War 1: 1916-18 Dover patrol, Zeebrugge, 1919 North Russia, Baltic
1917 October 28: Damaged by radio-controlled boat
1937 Cadet training ship
World War 2: 1940 English Channel, 1941 North Sea, Sicily, Normandy, Walcheren
1943 July 18: Damaged by aircraft bombs off Sicily
1947 January: Broken up at Inverkeithing

Erin

Type: Dreadnought
Class: 'Erin' (1914)
Nomenclature: A poetic name for Ireland

History:
1911 August 1: Laid down at Vickers for Turkey as ***Sultan Mehmed Reshad V***
1913 September 3: Launched as ***Reshadieh***
1914 August: Seized by British government, renamed ***Erin***
1914 August 22: Completed
World War 1: 1914-18 Grand Fleet, Jutland
1922 December 19: Sold and broken up at Queenborough

Essex

Type: Armoured Cruiser
Class: 'Monmouth' (1899)
Nomenclature: A county of England

History:
1900 January 1: Laid down at Pembroke
1901 August 29: Launched
1903 December: Completed
1906 July 4: Damaged by 6" gun explosion at Devonport
World War 1: 1914-15 North America and West Indies, 1915-18 Escort and patrol
1914 Captured two German merchant ships in North Atlantic, also one in 1916
1921 November 8: Sold and broken up in Germany

Ethalion, see *Mars*

Euryalus

Type: Armoured Cruiser
Class: 'Cressy' (1898)
Nomenclature: Greek myth: a hero of the Trojan War

History:
1899 July 18: Laid down at Vickers
1901 May 20: Launched
1901 June 11: Damaged by fire while fitting out; towed to Cammell Laird for drydocking but severely damaged when she slipped off the blocks
1903 June 27: In collision with auxiliary vessel *Traveller* at Devonport
1904 January 5: Completed
1904-06 Australian station
1906-09 North America and West Indies
World War 1: Heligoland, Suez Canal defence 1915, Dardanelles, Red Sea 1917, Far East 1918
1917 November: Conversion to minelayer cancelled
1920 July 1: Sold
1922 September: Broken up in Germany

Exmouth

Type: Pre-dreadnought
Class: 'Duncan' (1898)
Nomenclature: Sir Edward Pellew, Viscount Exmouth (1757-1833), British admiral

History:
1899 August 10: Laid down at Laird
1901 August 31: Launched
1903 June 2: Completed
1903-04 Mediterranean
1908-12 Mediterranean
World War 1: 1914 Grand Fleet, Channel patrol, 1915 Dardanelles
1917 Reserve
1920 January 15: Sold and broken up in Holland

Farragut, see *Abercrombie*

Nomenclature: David Glasgow Farragut (1801-1870), American admiral

Formidable

Type: Pre-dreadnought
Class: 'Formidable' (1897)
Nomenclature: Something of alarming strength

History:
1898 March 21: Laid down at Portsmouth
1898 November 17: Launched
1901 October 10: Completed
1901-08 Mediterranean
World War 1: Channel patrol
1915 January 1: Torpedoed twice and sunk by *U24* off Portland Bill (547 dead)

Top right:
***Emperor of India* — 'Iron Duke' class battleship, after World War 1.**

Centre right:
***Erebus* — Monitor of 1915, during World War 2.** *IWM*

Bottom right:
***Erin* — Former Turkish battleship seized 1914, late in the war.**

***Euryalus* — 'Cressy' class armoured cruiser, during World War 1.** *National Maritime Museum*

Formidable

Type: Aircraft Carrier
Class: 'Illustrious' (1936)

History:
1937 June 17: Laid down at Harland & Wolff
1939 August 17: Launched
1940 November 24: Completed
World War 2: 1941 East Indies and Mediterranean, 1942 Indian Ocean, 1943 Force 'H', 1944 Home Fleet, 1945 Pacific Fleet; Matapan, Crete, North Africa, Sicily, Salerno, Okinawa, Japan raids 1945
1941 May 26: Damaged by aircraft bombs off Crete
1941-42 Repaired at Norfolk
1945 May 4: Damaged by kamikaze off Okinawa
1945 May 9: Again hit by kamikaze off Okinawa
1948 Reserve
1953 November: Broken up at Inverkeithing

Foudroyant, see *Neptune*

Furious

Type: 1) Light Battlecruiser, 2) Aircraft Carrier
Class: 1) 'Furious' (1915), 2) 'Furious' (1920)
Nomenclature: Name first used 1797

History:
1915 June 8: Laid down at Armstrong
1916 August 15: Launched
1917 June 26: Completed
World War 1: 1917-18 Grand Fleet
1917 September 1: Refit; 18" gun and mainmast removed and flightdeck and hangar installed aft
1918 March 15: Recommissioned
1918 July 19: First successful carrier-borne raid carried out on Zeppelin base at Tondern

***Furious* — Aircraft carrier, December 1931, after full conversion.** *Wright & Logan*

1921-25 Converted to aircraft carrier with complete flightdeck
1925 September 1: Recommissioned
1931-32 Refit
1937 January 16: Small fire in engine room at Devonport
1939 Refit; rearmed, small island added
World War 2: 1939-44 Home Fleet; Narvik, Norwegian campaign, North Africa, Malta convoys
1941-42 Refit at Philadelphia
1942 Ferried aircraft to Malta
1944 Reserve
1948 January 23: Sold and broken up at Troon

Fury, see *Dreadnought*

Galatea

Type: Armoured Cruiser
Class: 'Orlando' (1884)
Nomenclature: Greek myth: a sea-nymph

History:
1885 April 21: Laid down at Fairfield
1887 March 10: Launched
1889 March: Completed
1905 April 4: Sold and broken up at Troon

General Abercrombie, see *Abercrombie*

General Craufurd

Type: Monitor
Class: 'Lord Clive' (1914)
Nomenclature: Robin Craufurd (d1812), major-general, killed at the Battle of Ciudad Rodrigo

History:
1915 January: Laid down at Harland & Wolff as ***M7***
1915 June 1: Renamed ***General Craufurd***
1915 July 8: Launched
1915 August: Completed
World War 1: 1915-18 Dover patrol, Zeebrugge
1921 May 9: Sold and broken up at New Holland

General Grant, see Havelock

Nomenclature: Ulysses Simpson Grant (1822-1885), American general

General Wolfe

Type: Monitor
Class: 'Lord Clive' (1914)
Nomenclature: James Wolfe (1727-1759), major-general, killed at the Battle of Quebec

History:
1914 December: Laid down at Palmer as ***M9***
1915 June: Renamed ***Sir James Wolfe***
1915 June: Renamed ***General Wolfe***
1915 September 9: Launched
1915 November 6: Completed
World War 1: 1916-18 Dover patrol
1918 Rearmed with 18" gun
1921 May 9: Sold and broken up at Hayle

Gibraltar

Type: Aircraft Carrier
Class: 'Gibraltar' (1943)
Nomenclature: Strategic British fortress at the western entrance to the Mediterranean, captured 1704

History:
1943 July 15: Ordered from Vickers, Tyne; never laid down
1945 December 21: Contract cancelled

Glatton

Type: Breastwork Monitor
Class: 'Glatton' (1867)
Nomenclature: Village where the builder of the first ship of the name (1755) owned an estate

History:
1868 August 10: Laid down at Chatham
1871 March 8: Launched
1872 February 24: Completed
1872-1901 Based at Portsmouth
1878 Particular Service Squadron
1903 July 7: Sold

Glatton

Type: Coast Defence Ship
Class: 'Gorgon' (1915)

History:
1913 May 26: Laid down at Armstrong for Norway as ***Bjorgvin***
1914 August 8: Launched
1915 January 31: Purchased by British government, renamed ***Glatton***
1918 September 8: Completed
World War 1: 1918 Dover patrol
1918 September 16: Caught fire after internal explosion at Dover and sunk by a destroyer (77 dead)

Glorious

Type: 1) Light Battlecruiser, 2) Aircraft Carrier
Class: 1) 'Courageous' (1915), 2) 'Courageous' (1924)
Nomenclature: First ship of name

History:
1915 May 1: Laid down at Harland & Wolff
1916 April 20: Launched
1917 January: Completed
World War 1: 1917-18 Grand Fleet
1924 February 14: Decommissioned for conversion to aircraft carrier
1930 February 24: Recommissioned
1934-35 Refit, flightdeck extended aft
1931 April 1: Bow damaged in collision with French liner *Florida*
World War 2: 1939-40 Mediterranean, 1940 Home Fleet, Norwegian campaign
1940 June 8: Sunk by German battlecruisers *Scharnhorst* and *Gneisenau* off Norway (about 800 dead)

Glory

Type: Pre-dreadnought
Class: 'Canopus' (1896)
Nomenclature: First used 1763

History:
1896 December 1: Laid down at Laird
1899 March 11: Launched
1900 November 1: Completed
1900-01 Far East
1904 April 17: Damaged in collision with battleship *Centurion*

1907-09 Mediterranean
World War 1: 1914 Channel Fleet, Atlantic escort, North America, 1915 Mediterranean, Suez Canal, 1916-19 North Russia
1917 Refit, main deck battery suppressed
1919 Depot ship, Rosyth
1920 April: Renamed ***Crescent***
1922 December 19: Sold

Glory

Type: Light Aircraft Carrier
Class: 'Colossus' (1942)

History:
1942 August 28: Laid down at Harland & Wolff
1943 November 27: Launched
1945 April 22: Completed
World War 2: 1945 Pacific Fleet
1946-47 Pacific
1949 Mediterranean
1950-53 Korea
1955-56 Refit
1961 August: Sold and broken up at Inverkeithing

Goliath

Type: Pre-dreadnought
Class: 'Canopus' (1896)
Nomenclature: Biblical legend: Philistine giant slain by David

History:
1897 January 4: Laid down at Chatham
1898 March 23: Launched
1900 March 27: Completed
1900-03 Far East
World War 1: 1914 Channel and Scapa defence, Ostend, East Indies, 1915 Dardanelles
1915 April 25 and May 2: Damaged by shore batteries at the Dardanelles
1915 May 13: Twice torpedoed by Turkish destroyer *Muavenet* and sank off Cape Helles (570 dead)

Good Hope

Type: Armoured Cruiser
Class: 'Drake' (1898)
Nomenclature: Cape Colony (Cape of Good Hope)

History:
1899 September 11: Laid down at Fairfield as ***Africa***
1899 October 2: Renamed ***Good Hope***
1901 February 21: Launched
1902 November 18: Completed
World War 1: 1914 Western Atlantic, Coronel
1914 November 1: Sunk in action with German warships off Coronel, Chile. Flagship of Rear-Adm Sir Christopher Cradock who was lost (919 dead, all lost)

Top left:
***Glatton* — Single turret monitor, a vessel of little value.** *IWM*

Centre left:
***Glatton* — Coast defence ship, purchased from Norway 1915.** *IWM*

Bottom left:
***Glory* — 'Canopus' class battleship of 1896.**
National Maritime Museum

Gorgon

Type: Breastwork Monitor
Class: 'Cyclops' (1869)
Nomenclature: Greek myth: a female monster with serpents in place of hair

History:
1870 September 5: Laid down at Palmer
1871 October 14: Launched
1872 April: Delivered and held in reserve
1874 March 19: Completed
1878 Particular Service Squadron
1888-89 Refit
1903 May 12: Sold

Gorgon

Type: Coast Defence Ship
Class: 'Gorgon' (1915)

History:
1913 June 11: Laid down at Armstrong for Norway as ***Nidaros***
1914 June 9: Launched
1915 January 31: Purchased by British government, renamed ***Gorgon***
1918 July 4: Completed
World War 1: 1918 Dover patrol
1928 August 28: Sold and broken up at Pembroke

Hampshire

Type: Armoured Cruiser
Class: 'Devonshire' (1901)
Nomenclature: A county of southwest England

History:
1902 September 1: Laid down at Armstrong
1903 September 24: Launched
1905 July 15: Completed
1911-12 Mediterranean
1912-14 Far East
World War 1: 1914 Far East, 1914-15 Grand Fleet, 1915 North Russia, Jutland
1916 June 5: Sunk by mine north of Scapa Flow en route to Russia with Field Marshal Earl Kitchener of Khartoum and staff on board (655 dead including Lord Kitchener)

Hannibal

Type: Pre-dreadnought
Class: 'Majestic' (1893)
Nomenclature: Carthaginian general of the Second Punic War (247-183BC)

History:
1894 May 1: Laid down at Pembroke
1896 April 28: Launched
1898 May 10: Completed
1903 October 17: In collision with battleship *Prince George* off Cape Finisterre
1905 June 3: In collision in fog with schooner *Emma Louise* off Dungeness
1906 Refit, fire control added
1909 August 19: Severely damaged when struck a submerged reef in Babbacombe Bay
1909 October 29: In collision with torpedo boat *No 105* off Torbay
World War 1: 1914 Guardship (Humber and Scapa), 1915

Mediterranean as troopship, 1916 East Indies and Egypt
1915 September: Turrets removed
1920 January 28: Sold and broken up in Italy

Havelock

Type: Monitor
Class: 'Abercrombie' (1914)
Nomenclature: Sir Henry Havelock (1795-1857), major-general, killed at the relief of Lucknow

History:
1914 November: Laid down at Harland & Wolff as ***General Grant***
1915 April 29: Launched
1915 May 31: Renamed ***M2***
1915 June 11: Completed
1915 June 20: Renamed ***Havelock***
World War 1: Dardanelles
1927 June 25: Sold and broken up at Preston

Hecate

Type: Breastwork Monitor
Class: 'Cyclops' (1869)
Nomenclature: Thracian goddess of sorcery

Left:
***Hercules* — Central battery ship, as completed in 1868.**
IWM

Below:
***Hermes* — Light aircraft carrier, May 1966 after reconstruction, with angled flightdeck.**
Ministry of Defence

History:
1870 September 5: Laid down at Dudgeon
1871 September 30: Launched
1872 April: Delivered, held in reserve
1877 May 24: Completed
1878 Particular Service Squadron
1885-86 Refit
1903 May 12: Sold

Hector

Type: Broadside Ship
Class: 'Hector' (1860)
Nomenclature: Greek myth: noted defender of Troy, killed by Achilles

History:
1861 March 8: Laid down at Napier
1862 September 26: Launched
1864 February 22: Completed
1867-68 Refit, rearmed with ML guns
1878 Particular Service Squadron
1886 Paid off
1900 Torpedo training ship, Portsmouth, experimental wireless vessel
1905 July 11: Sold and broken up at Portsmouth

Hercules

Type: Central Battery Ship
Class: 'Hercules' (1865)
Nomenclature: Mythological hero renowned for his physical strength; son of Zeus

Right:
***Hood* — Battleship of 1889, similar to 'Royal Sovereign' class, with turrets instead of barbettes.** *Marius Bar*

History:

1866 February 1: Laid down at Chatham
1868 February 10: Launched
1868 November 21: Completed
1872 December 25: In collision with ironclad *Northumberland* at Funchal
1874-75 Refit
1875-77 Mediterranean
1878 Particular Service Squadron
1892-93 Reconstructed
1893 Reserve
1905 Depot ship, Gibraltar
1909 Renamed ***Calcutta***
1914 Training ship, Portsmouth
1915 April: Renamed ***Fisgard II***
1932 July: Broken up at Preston

Hercules

Type: Dreadnought
Class: 'Neptune' (1908)

History:

1909 July 30: Laid down at Palmer
1910 May 10: Launched
1911 August: Completed
1913 March 22: In collision with a steamer in Portland Roads
World War 1: 1914-18 Grand Fleet, Jutland
1921 November 8: Sold and broken up at Kiel

Hercules

Type: Light Aircraft Carrier
Class: 'Majestic' (1942)

History:

1943 October 14: Laid down at Vickers, Tyne
1945 September 22: Launched
1946 May: Construction suspended 75% complete
1957 January: Sold to India, renamed ***Vikrant*** Reconstructed and completed by Harland & Wolff, angled flightdeck
1961 March 4: Commissioned

Hermes

Type: Aircraft Carrier
Class: 'Hermes' (1917)
Nomenclature: Greek myth: messenger of the gods

History:

1918 January 15: Laid down at Armstrong
1919 September 11: Launched
1920 Towed to Devonport for completion
1924 February 19: Completed
1925-26 Far East
1927 Refit
1928-33 Far East
1933-34 Refit
1934-37 Far East
World War 2: 1939 Home Fleet, 1939-42 East Indies (Dakar, Iraq 1941), 1942 Indian Ocean
1940 July 11: Damaged in collision with armed merchant cruiser *Corfu* off Freetown
1942 April 9: Sunk by Japanese carrier aircraft off Ceylon (302 dead)

Hermes

Type: Light Aircraft Carrier
Class: 'Hermes' (1943)

History:

1944 Laid down at Cammell Laird
1945 October: Contract cancelled

Hermes

Type: Light Aircraft Carrier
Class: 'Hermes' (1943)

History:

1944 June 21: Laid down at Vickers, Barrow, as ***Elephant***
1945 November 5: Renamed ***Hermes***
1953 February 16: Launched
1959 November 18: Completed
1964-66 Reconstructed; angled flightdeck, missile armament
1971-73 Converted to Commando Carrier at Devonport
1976 Converted to ASW carrier
1980-81: Refit, 'ski jump' takeoff ramp fitted to bow
1982 April: Falkland Islands Task Force (flag)

Hero

Type: Turret Ship
Class: 'Conqueror' (1882)
Nomenclature: Greek myth: a priestess of Apollo whose lover Leander swam the Hellespont every night to see her

History:

1884 April 11: Laid down at Chatham
1885 October 27: Launched
1888 May: Completed
1888 Tender to gunnery school
1907 November: Target ship
1908 February 18: Sunk as a target off Kentish Knock

Hibernia

Type: Pre-dreadnought
Class: 'King Edward VII' (1901)
Nomenclature: Roman name for Ireland

History:

1904 January 6: Laid down at Devonport
1905 June 17: Launched
1907 January 2: Completed
1912 May: Fitted with temporary flightdeck for aircraft experiments
1912 May 4: First seaplane flight from a British warship by C. R. Samson took place
World War 1: 1914-15 Grand Fleet, 1915 Dardanelles
1919 Accommodation ship, The Nore
1921 November 8: Sold and broken up in Germany

Hindustan

Type: Pre-dreadnought
Class: 'King Edward VII' (1901)
Nomenclature: Persian name for India

History:

1902 October 25: Laid down at John Brown
1903 December 19: Launched
1905 February 28: Completed

World War 1: 1914-15 Grand Fleet, 1915 Thames Estuary
1921 May 9: Sold and broken up 1923 at Preston

Hogue

Type: Armoured Cruiser
Class: 'Cressy' (1898)
Nomenclature: Naval battle, second phase of the Battle of Barfleur, 1692

History:
1898 July 14: Laid down at Vickers
1900 August 13: Launched
1902 November 19: Completed
1904 March 11: In collision with merchant ship *Meurthe* off Europa Point
1904-06 China
1906-08 North America and West Indies
1909 October 26: Damaged by coal bunker explosion at Devonport (two dead)
World War 1: Heligoland
1914 September 22: Torpedoed and sunk by *U9* in North Sea (48 dead)

Hood

Type: Turret Ship
Class: 'Royal Sovereign' (1888)
Nomenclature: Several distinguished admirals, including Samuel, Viscount Hood (1724-1816), and Sir Samuel Hood (1762-1814)

History:
1889 August 12: Laid down at Chatham
1891 July 30: Launched
1893 May: Completed
1893-1900 and 1901-02 Mediterranean
1901 April 18: In collision with merchant ship *Eugene Periere* at Malta
1902-03 Refit
1910 Receiving ship, Queenstown
1911 Reserve, used as target
1914 November 4: Sunk as blockship in Portland Roads

Hood

Type: Battlecruiser
Class: 'Hood' (1915)

History:
1916 September 1: Laid down at John Brown
1918 August 22: Launched
1920 March 5: Completed
1923-24 World cruise
1929-31 Refit, catapult fitted
1935 January 23: In collision with battlecruiser *Renown* in Atlantic
1936-38 Mediterranean
1938 September 20: Went aground at Gibraltar
1939 Refit, submerged TT removed, AA battery increased
World War 2: 1939-41 Home Fleet, 1940 Mediterranean, Oran
1940 Refit: AA armament increased, catapult removed
1941 May 24: Sunk by gunfire of German battleship *Bismarck* in action in Denmark Strait. Flagship of Vice-Adm L. E. Holland who was lost (1,338 dead)

Hotspur

Type: Breastwork Monitor and Ram
Class: 'Hotspur' (1867)
Nomenclature: Nickname of Sir Henry Percy (1364-1403), eldest son of the 1st Earl of Northumberland

History:
1868 October 2: Laid down at Napier
1870 March 19: Launched
1871 November 17: Completed
1870 In collision with a merchant vessel
1876-78 Mediterranean
1881-83 Reconstructed by Laird; rearmoured, regunned, reboilered
1893 In reserve
1897-1903 Guardship, Bermuda
1904 August 2: Sold

Howe

Type: Barbette Ship
Class: 'Admiral' (1881)
Nomenclature: Richard, Earl Howe (1726-1799), Admiral of the Fleet, victor of the Glorious First of June, 1794

History:
1882 June 7: Laid down at Pembroke
1885 April 28: Launched
1889 July 18: Completed; completion delayed by late delivery of armament
1892 November 2: Went aground on rocks off Ferrol, Spain
1893 March 30: Refloated and repaired at Ferrol and Chatham
1904 September: Paid off
1911 October 11: Sold and broken up at Morecambe

Howe

Type: Battlecruiser
Class: 'Hood' (1915)

History:
1916 October 16: Laid down at Cammell Laird
1917 March 9: Construction suspended
1919 March 17: Contract cancelled

Howe

Type: Battleship
Class: 'King George V' (1936)

History:
1937 January 1: Laid down at Fairfield as ***Beatty***
1940 February 21: Renamed ***Howe***
1940 April 9: Launched
1942 August 29: Completed
World War 2: 1942-43 Home Fleet, 1943 Force H, 1943-44 Home Fleet, 1944 Indian Ocean, 1945 Pacific Fleet; Arctic convoys 1942-43, Sicily, Okinawa
1944 Refit
1951 Reserve
1958 May: Broken up at Inverkeithing

Hydra

Type: Breastwork Monitor
Class: 'Cyclops' (1869)

Nomenclature: Greek myth: a serpent with nine heads, slain by Hercules

History:
1870 September 5: Laid down at Napier
1871 December 28: Launched
1872 August: Delivered, held in reserve
1876 May 31: Completed
1878 Particular Service Squadron
1888-89 Refit
1903 July 7: Sold and broken up at Genoa

Illustrious

Type: Pre-dreadnought
Class: 'Majestic' (1893)
Nomenclature: Highly distinguished; first used 1789

History:
1895 March 11: Laid down at Chatham
1896 September 17: Launched
1898 May 10: Completed
1898-1904 Mediterranean
World War 1: Guardship and detached service
1916-17 Ammunition storeship, Tyne
1917-19 Storeship, Portsmouth
1920 June 18: Sold and broken up at Barrow

Illustrious

Type: Aircraft Carrier
Class: 'Illustrious' (1936)

History:
1937 April 27: Laid down at Vickers, Barrow
1939 April 5: Launched
1940 May 21: Completed
World War 2: 1940-41 Mediterranean, 1942-43 Indian Ocean, 1943 Force H, 1944 Indian Ocean, 1945 Pacific Fleet; Taranto, Malta convoys, Diego Suarez, Salerno, Sabang and Palembang raids, Okinawa
1941 January 10: Damaged by enemy aircraft off Malta
1941 January 19: Again damaged by aircraft while repairing at Malta dockyard
1941 Repaired at Norfolk
1946 Trials carrier
1948 Refit
1954 December: Decommissioned
1956 November: Broken up at Faslane

Illustrious

Type: Aircraft Carrier
Class: 'Invincible' (1972)

History:
1976 October 7: Laid down by Swan Hunter

Top:
***Hood* — Battlecruiser, 1930s. Was the largest warship in the world until World War 2.**

Centre:
***Howe* — 'King George V' class battleship, 1946.**
Marine Photos

Bottom:
***Illustrious* — Aircraft carrier, at Malta, September 1943.** *P. A. Vicary*

1978 December 14: Launched
1982 June 20: Completed

Immortalité

Type: Armoured Cruiser
Class: 'Orlando' (1884)
Nomenclature: Prize name, taken 1798

History:
1886 January 18: Laid down at Chatham
1887 June 7: Launched
1890 July 1: Completed
1907 January 1: Sold and broken up at Blackwall

Imperieuse

Type: Armoured Cruiser
Class: 'Imperieuse' (1880)
Nomenclature: Prize name, taken 1793

History:
1881 August 10: Laid down at Portsmouth
1883 December 18: Launched
1886 September: Completed
1887 Refit; single mast between funnels replaced two masts and brig rig
1889-94 Far East
1894 Refit, QF guns added
1896-99 Pacific
1905 February: Destroyer depot ship, Portland, renamed ***Sapphire II***
1909 June: Renamed ***Imperieuse***
1913 September 24: Sold and broken up at Morecambe

Implacable

Type: Pre-dreadnought
Class: 'Formidable' (1897)
Nomenclature: Not to be appeased; first used 1805

History:
1898 July 13: Laid down at Devonport
1899 March 11: Launched
1901 September 10: Completed
1901-08 Mediterranean
1905 July 12: Severely damaged by burst steam pipe (seven dead)
1906 August 16: Again damaged by boiler explosion
World War 1: 1914 Channel patrol, Dardanelles, 1915 Adriatic, East Indies and Egypt; 1918-19 Northern Patrol
1916 Armament altered
1921 November 8: Sold and broken up in Germany

Implacable

Type: Aircraft Carrier
Class: 'Implacable' (1938)

History:
1939 February 21: Laid down at Fairfield
1942 December 10: Launched
1944 August 28: Completed
World War 2: 1944 Home Fleet, 1945 Pacific Fleet, Norway raids 1944, Japan raids 1945
1948-49 Refit
1955 November: Broken up at Inverkeithing

Indefatigable

Type: Battlecruiser
Class: 'Indefatigable' (1908)
Nomenclature: Incapable of being tired out

History:
1909 February 23: Laid down at Devonport
1909 October 28: Launched
1911 February 24: Completed
1913-14 Mediterranean
World War 1: 'Goeben' operations, Dardanelles 1914, Grand Fleet 1915-16
1916 May 31: Destroyed by direct hits scored by German battlecruiser *Von der Tann* at Battle of Jutland (1,017 dead)

Indefatigable

Type: Aircraft Carrier
Class: 'Implacable' (1938)

History:
1939 November 3: Laid down at John Brown
1942 December 8: Launched
1944 May 3: Completed
World War 2: 1944 Home Fleet, 1945 Pacific Fleet; Palembang raid, Okinawa, Japan raids 1945
1956 Broken up at Dalmuir

India

Type: Dreadnought
Class: 'Canada' (1914)
Nomenclature: Name proposed for Chilean battleship *Almirante Cochrane* (later completed as aircraft carrier *Eagle*)

Indomitable

Type: Battlecruiser
Class: 'Invincible' (1905)
Nomenclature: That which cannot be overcome

History:
1906 March 1: Laid down at Fairfield
1907 March 16: Launched
1908 June 25: Completed
1910 Refit, forefunnel raised
1913-14 Mediterranean
World War 2: 'Goeben' operations, Dardanelles, 1915-18 Grand Fleet, Doggerbank, Jutland
1921 December 1: Sold and broken up at Dover

Top right:
***Imperieuse* — Armoured cruiser, c1905. It was originally rigged as a bark on completion in 1886.**

Centre right:
***Indefatigable* — Battlecruiser, after fore funnel was raised.**

Bottom right:
***Indomitable* — Aircraft carrier, modified 'Illustrious' class, June 1946.** *Wright & Logan*

***Invincible* — 'Audacious' class central battery ship, as completed in 1870.** *IWM*

1890-93 Mediterranean
1897 October: Reserve
1903 September 15: Sold and broken up at Preston

Indomitable

Type: Aircraft Carrier
Class: 'Illustrious' (1936)

History:
1937 November 10: Laid down at Vickers, Barrow
1940 March 26: Launched
1941 October 1: Completed
1940-41 Modified while building, additional hangar added
World War 2: 1941 Home Fleet, 1942 Indian Ocean, 1942-43 Home Fleet, 1943 Force 'H', 1944 Indian Ocean, 1945 Pacific Fleet; Malta convoys, Diego Suarez, Sicily, Palembang raid, Okinawa
1941 November 3: Went aground off Kingston, Jamaica, while working up
1941 Repaired at Norfolk
1943 July 16: Torpedoed by Italian aircraft off Sicily
1948 Refit, forward flightdeck rebuilt
1953 Reserve
1955 September: Broken up at Faslane

Inflexible

Type: Turret Ship
Class: 'Inflexible' (1873)
Nomenclature: Unyielding; first used 1780

History:
1874 February 24: Laid down at Portsmouth
1876 April 27: Launched
1881 October 18: Completed
1881-85 Mediterranean
1882 July 11: Damaged by shell hit during bombardment of Alexandria
1885 Refit; sails removed, fighting tops fitted to masts

Inflexible

Type: Battlecruiser
Class: 'Invincible' (1905)

History:
1906 February 5: Laid down at John Brown
1907 June 16: Launched
1908 October 20: Completed
1911 Refit; forefunnel raised
1911 May 26: Bow damaged in collision with battleship *Bellerophon* in English Channel
1912-14 Mediterranean
World War 1: 'Goeben' operations, Falklands, Dardanelles, 1915-18 Grand Fleet, Jutland
1915 March 18: Severely damaged by shore batteries and mine during bombardment in the Dardanelles
1918 January 31: Sank submarine *K4* in collision off May Island during night exercises
1921 December 1: Sold and broken up in Germany

Invincible, see *Black Prince*

Invincible

Type: Central Battery Ship
Class: 'Audacious' (1867)
Nomenclature: That which cannot be conquered

History:
1867 June 28: Laid down at Napier
1869 May 29: Launched
1870 October 1: Completed

1872-76 Mediterranean
1873 Blockade of Cartagena, Spain
1876 Refit; re-engined and reboilered
1878-86 Mediterranean
1882 Bombardment of Alexandria
1887 Far East
1901 Torpedo boat depot ship
1904 April: Renamed ***Erebus***
1906 January: Training ship, Portsmouth, renamed ***Fisgard II***
1914 September 17: Foundered in tow off Portland en route to Scapa (21 dead)

Invincible

Type: Battlecruiser
Class: 'Invincible' (1905)

History:
1906 April 2: Laid down at Armstrong
1907 April 13: Launched
1908 March 20: Completed
1913 Mediterranean
1913 March 17: In collision with submarine *C34* in Stokes Bay
World War 1: 1914-16 Grand Fleet, Heligoland Bight, Falklands, Jutland
1914 December 8: Slightly damaged in action at Battle of the Falklands
1915 Refit, fore funnel raised
1916 May 31: Blew up and sank after being hit at Battle of Jutland, Flagship of Rear-Adm the Hon H. L. A. Hood, who was lost (1,026 dead)

Invincible

Type: Aircraft Carrier
Class: 'Invincible' (1972)

History:
1973 July 20: Laid down by Vickers
1977 May 3: Launched
1980 June 11: Commissioned
1982 April: Falkland Islands Task Force

Iron Duke

Type: Central Battery Ship
Class: 'Audacious' (1867)
Nomenclature: Sobriquet of Arthur Wellesley, Duke of Wellington (1769-1852), foremost British military leader of the Napoleonic Wars

History:
1868 August 23: Laid down at Pembroke
1870 March 1: Launched
1871 January 21: Completed
1871-75 Far East
1875 September 1: Sank sistership *Vanguard* in collision off Dublin
1877-78 Refit
1878-83 Far East
1879 Aground on Woosung Reef for five days
1880 Went aground off Hokkaido
1883-85 Refit, reboilered
1890 Reserve
1900 Coal hulk, Kyles of Bute
1906 June 15: Sold and broken up at Glasgow

Iron Duke

Type: Dreadnought
Class: 'Iron Duke' (1911)

History:
1912 January 12: Laid down at Portsmouth
1912 October 12: Launched
1914 March 10: Completed
World War 1: Grand Fleet 1914-18, Fleet Flagship 1914-16 Jutland
1919-26 Mediterranean, Black Sea
1931 Gunnery and boys' training ship; 'B' and 'Y' turrets, conning tower and armour belt removed
1939 October 17: Beached after being damaged by near misses of German aircraft bombs at Scapa
1946 March 2: Sold and broken up at Faslane

Irresistible

Type: Pre-dreadnought
Class: 'Formidable' (1897)
Nomenclature: That which cannot be withstood

History:
1898 April 11: Laid down at Chatham
1898 December 15: Launched
1902 February 4: Completed
1902-08 Mediterranean
1902 March 3: Seriously damaged in collision with merchant vessel *Clive*
1905 October 9: Went aground at Malta
World War 1: Channel patrol, Belgian coast operations, Ostend, 1915 Dardanelles
1915 March 18: Sunk by mine in the Dardanelles after being damaged by shore batteries (none lost)

Irresistible, see *Ark Royal*

Jellicoe, see *Anson*

Nomenclature: John Rushworth Jellicoe, Earl Jellicoe (1859-1935), Admiral of the Fleet, Commander at Jutland

Jupiter

Type: Pre-dreadnought
Class: 'Majestic' (1893)
Nomenclature: The supreme god of the ancient Romans

History:
1894 April 26: Laid down at Thomson
1895 November 18: Launched
1897 June 8: Completed
1905 Refit
1909-10 Refit, fire control added
World War 1: 1914 Humber and Tyne defence; 1915 Icebreaker at Archangel; 1915-16 East Indies and Egypt
1919 Paid off
1920 January 15: Sold and broken up on the Tyne

Kent

Type: Armoured Cruiser
Class: 'Monmouth' (1899)
Nomenclature: A county of southeast England

History:
1900 February 12: Laid down at Portsmouth
1901 March 6: Launched
1903 August 1: Completed
1905 March 15: Went aground in the Firth of Forth
1906-13 Far East
World War 1: 1914 South Atlantic, Falklands, 1915 Pacific, 1916-18 Convoy escort, 1918-19 China, Vladivostok
1915 March 14: Caught German cruiser *Dresden,* which was scuttled, at Mas a Fuera Island
1920 June 20: Sold at Hong Kong

King Alfred

Type: Armoured Cruiser
Class: 'Drake' (1898)
Nomenclature: Alfred the Great, King of England (849-901), founder of the English navy

History:
1899 August 11: Laid down at Vickers
1901 August 28: Launched
1903 December 22: Completed
1905 May 5: Went aground off Sheerness
1906-13 Far East

Left:
***Jupiter* — 'Majestic' class battleship.** *Real Photographs*

Below:
***Lancaster* — 'Monmouth' class armoured cruiser, during World War 1.** *IWM*

World War 1: 1914 Convoy escort, 1915-17 Grand Fleet, 1918 North America and convoy escort
1920 January 30: Sold and broken up in Holland

King Edward VII

Type: Pre-dreadnought
Class: 'King Edward VII' (1901)
Nomenclature: Edward VII (1841-1910), King of Great Britain 1901-1910

History:
1902 March 8: Laid down at White
1903 July 23: Launched
1905 February 7: Completed
World War 1: Grand Fleet 1914-15
1916 January 6: Damaged by mine off Cape Wrath, capsized and sank after tow failed (none lost)

King George V, see Monarch

King George V

Type: Dreadnought
Class: 'King George V' (1910)
Nomenclature: George V (1865-1936), King of Great Britain 1910-1936

History:
1911 January 11: Laid down at Portsmouth as ***Royal George***
1911 Renamed ***King George V***
1911 October 9: Launched
1912 November 16: Completed
World War 1: 1914-18 Grand Fleet, Jutland
1919-23 Mediterranean
1923-26 Gunnery training ship
1926 December: Sold and broken up at Rosyth

King George V

Type: Battleship
Class: 'King George V' (1936)

History:
1937 January 2: Laid down at Vickers, Tyne
1939 February 21: Launched
1940 December 11: Completed
World War 2: 1941-43 Home Fleet, 1943 Force 'H' 1943-44 Home Fleet, 1945 Pacific Fleet; 'Bismarck' operations, Arctic 1942-43, Sicily, Salerno, Okinawa, Japan raids
1941 January: Voyaged to US with Prime Minister Churchill on board
1942 May 1: Bow damaged by depth charges when in collision with destroyer *Punjabi* which sank in the Arctic
1944 Refit
1949 December 4: Decommissioned
1958 January: Broken up at Troon and Dalmuir

Lancaster

Type: Armoured Cruiser
Class: 'Monmouth' (1899)
Nomenclature: A county of northern England

History:
1901 March 4: Laid down at Armstrong
1902 March 22: Launched
1904 March: Completed
1904-09 Mediterranean
1913-14 West Indies
World War 1: 1914-15 West Indies, 1915-16 Grand Fleet, 1916-18 Pacific
1920 March 3: Sold and broken up at Preston

Leviathan

Type: Armoured Cruiser
Class: 'Drake' (1898)
Nomenclature: Biblical sea monster

History:
1900 January 22: Laid down at John Brown
1901 July 3: Launched
1902 March 11: Completed
1903 Far East
1904-06 Mediterranean
World War 1: 1914-15 Convoy escort, 1915-18 North America and West Indies, convoy escort
1920 March 3: Sold and broken up at Blyth

Leviathan

Type: Light Aircraft Carrier
Class: 'Majestic' (1942)

History:
1943 October 18: Laid down at Swan Hunter
1945 June 7: Launched
1946 May: Construction suspended when 80% complete; laid up at Portsmouth
1961 December: Construction cancelled
1968 May: Broken up incomplete at Faslane

Lion

Type: Battlecruiser
Class: 'Lion' (1909)
Nomenclature: First used 1511

History:
1909 November 29: Laid down at Devonport
1910 August 6: Launched
1912 May: Completed
1913 Refit; tripod mast replaced by pole and resited, rangefinders fitted
World War 1: 1914-18 Grand Fleet, flagship of Battlecruiser Fleet, Heligoland, Doggerbank, Jutland
1915 January 24: Damaged by gunfire (18 hits) at the Battle of the Doggerbank
1916 May 31: Severely damaged by 12 hits, narrowly escaped blowing up, at Battle of Jutland (99 dead)
1924 January 31: Sold and broken up at Blyth

Lion

Type: Battleship
Class: 'Lion' (1938)

History:
1939 July 4: Laid down at Vickers, Tyne
1939 October: Construction suspended
1944 Contract cancelled

London

Type: Pre-dreadnought
Class: 'Formidable' (1897)
Nomenclature: Capital city of England

History:
1898 December 8: Laid down at Portsmouth
1899 September 21: Launched
1902 February 7: Completed
1902-07 Mediterranean
1908 Refit
1912 May: Fitted for seaplane launching experiments
1912 May 11: In collision with merchant vessel *Don Benito* off Hythe
World War 1: 1914 Channel patrol, 1915 Mediterranean, Dardanelles
1917-18 Converted to minelayer; after barbette removed, 3×6", 1×4", 240 mines
1920 June 4: Sold and broken up in Germany 1922

Lord Clive

Type: Monitor
Class: 'Lord Clive' (1914)
Nomenclature: Robert, Lord Clive (1725-1774), victor of the Battle of Plassey and a founder of the British empire in India

History:
1915 January 9: Laid down at Harland & Wolff as ***M6***
1915 June: Renamed ***Lord Clive***
1915 June 10: Launched
1915 July 10: Completed
World War 1: 1916-18 Dover patrol, Zeebrugge
1918 Rearmed with 18" gun
1927 October 10: Sold and broken up at Bo'ness

Lord Clyde

Type: Broadside Ship
Class: 'Lord Clyde' (1863)
Nomenclature: Sir Colin Campbell, Lord Clyde (1792-1863), field marshal, commander in India and victor of Balaclava

History:
1863 September 29: Laid down at Pembroke
1864 October 13: Launched
1866 June 2: Completed
1868-69 Mediterranean
1869 Refit; rearmed and re-engined
1871 Mediterranean
1871 Went aground off Pantellaria, taken to Plymouth, hull found to be rotten
1876 Hulked
1884 Broken up

Lord Nelson

Type: Pre-dreadnought
Class: 'Lord Nelson' (1904)
Nomenclature: Horatio, Viscount Nelson (1758-1805), British admiral, victor of the Nile, Copenhagen and Trafalgar

History:
1905 May 18: Laid down at Palmer
1906 September 4: Launched
1908 December 1: Completed
World War 1: 1914 Channel Fleet (flag), Dardanelles (flag), Aegean, Black Sea
1920 January 4: Sold and broken up in Germany

***London* — Pre-dreadnought, in 1912 with flying-off platform on bow.** *National Maritime Museum*

Lord Raglan, see ***Raglan***

Lord Warden

Type: Broadside Ship
Class: 'Lord Clyde' (1863)
Nomenclature: Lord Warden of the Cinque Ports, an honorary office

History:
1863 December 24: Laid down at Chatham
1865 May 27: Launched
1867 August 30: Completed
1867-75 Mediterranean
1873 Blockade of Cartagena, Spain
1878 Particular Service Squadron
1885 Decommissioned
1889 Sold

M1, see ***Abercrombie***

M2, see ***Havelock***

M3, see ***Raglan***

M4, see ***Roberts***

M5, see ***Sir John Moore***

M6, see ***Lord Clive***

M7, see ***General Craufurd***

M8, see ***Earl of Peterborough***

M9, see ***General Wolfe***

M10, see ***Prince Rupert***

M11, see ***Prince Eugene***

M12, see ***Sir Thomas Picton***

M13, see ***Marshal Ney***

M14, see ***Marshal Soult***

Magdala

Type: Breastwork Monitor
Class: 'Cerberus' (1867)
Nomenclature: British victory in Ethiopia, 1868

History:
1868 October 6: Laid down at Thames
1870 March 2: Launched
1870 November: Completed
1871 Guardship, Bombay
1892 Rearmed
1903 January: Sold

Magnificent

Type: Pre-dreadnought
Class: 'Majestic' (1893)
Nomenclature: First used 1766

History:
1893 December 18: Laid down at Chatham
1894 December 19: Launched
1895 December 12: Completed
1905 June 15: Gun explosion

1907-08 Refit, fire control added
1911 February: Turret drill ship, tender to *Vivid*
1912 May: Seagoing gunnery training ship
1913 June 16: Went aground in fog near Cawsand
World War 1: 1914 Guardship (Humber), 1915 Dardanelles
1915 September: Turrets removed, used as transport
1921 May 9: Sold and broken up at Inverkeithing

Magnificent

Type: Light Aircraft Carrier
Class: 'Majestic' (1942)

History:
1943 July 29: Laid down at Harland & Wolff
1944 November 16: Launched
1948 May 21: Completed for Royal Canadian Navy
1957 June 14: Returned to the Royal Navy
1965 July: Broken up at Faslane

Majestic, see Edinburgh

Majestic

Type: Pre-dreadnought
Class: 'Majestic' (1893)
Nomenclature: First used 1785

History:
1894 February 4: Laid down at Portsmouth
1895 January 31: Launched
1895 December 12: Completed
1904 December 14: Coal gas explosion while in the Channel
1907-08 Refit, fire control and wireless fitted
1912 July 14: In collision with battleship *Victorious*
World War 1: Atlantic escort duty, Channel and Dover patrol, 1915 Mediterranean
1915 May 27: Torpedoed and sunk by *U21* while at anchor off Gaba Tepe, Dardanelles (40 dead)

Majestic

Type: Light Aircraft Carrier
Class: 'Majestic' (1942)

History:
1943 April 13: Laid down at Vickers, Barrow
1945 February 28: Launched
1946 Construction suspended
—— Design modified; angled flightdeck and steam catapults added
1955 October 28: Completed for Australia, renamed ***Melbourne***
1964 February 10: Sank destroyer *Voyager* in collision during exercises south of Sydney (79 dead)
1968 Refit, converted to ASW
1969 June 3: Damaged in collision which sank US destroyer *Frank E. Evans* in South China Sea
1978 Refit; flightdeck extended
1982 June 30: Decommissioned

Malaya

Type: Dreadnought
Class: 'Queen Elizabeth' (1912)
Nomenclature: The ship was donated by the Federated Malay States

History:
1913 October 20: Laid down at Armstrong
1915 March 18: Launched
1916 February 19: Completed
World War 1: 1914-18 Grand Fleet, Jutland
1915 May 31: Received seven hits at Jutland (63 dead)
1921 Visited Malaya
1922-27 Mediterranean
1922 Carried the Sultan of Turkey to exile in Malta
1927-29 Reconstructed; bridge remodelled, two funnels trunked into one, bulges fitted
1929-30 Mediterranean
1934-36 Reconstructed; hangars added, AA protection increased, torpedo tubes removed
1937-39 Mediterranean
World War 2: 1939-40 Atlantic, 1941 Force 'H', 1941-42 Home Fleet; Calabria, Malta convoys, 1944 English Channel
1941 February 9: Bombardment of Genoa
1941 March 20: Torpedoed by *U106* 250 miles northwest of Cape Verde while escorting convoy SL68. Repaired at New York
1943 December-1944 June: Decommissioned
1945 May: Torpedo training depot
1948 February 20: Sold and broken up at Faslane

Malta

Type: Aircraft Carrier
Class: 'Gibraltar' (1943)
Nomenclature: Strategic British island base in the Mediterranean

History:
1944 December: Laid down at John Brown
1945 December 21: Contract cancelled

Marlborough

Type: Dreadnought
Class: 'Iron Duke' (1911)
Nomenclature: John Churchill, Duke of Marlborough (1650-1722), victor of Blenheim, Ramillies, Oudenarde and Malplaquet

History:
1912 January 25: Laid down at Devonport
1912 October 24: Launched
1914 June 2: Completed
World War 1: 1914-18 Grand Fleet, Jutland
1916 May 31: Severely damaged when torpedoed by German cruiser at Jutland
1919-26 Mediterranean, Black Sea
1920-22 Refit
1932 June 27: Sold and broken up at Rosyth

Mars

Type: Pre-dreadnought
Class: 'Majestic' (1893)
Nomenclature: The Roman god of war

History:
1894 June 2: Laid down at Laird
1896 March 30: Launched
1897 June 8: Completed
1902 April 14: Gun explosion
1905 Refit, first battleship to burn oil fuel
World War 1: 1914 Humber defence, 1915 Mediterranean, Dardanelles

***Malaya* — 'Queen Elizabeth' class battleship, after reconstruction, 1933 with funnels trunked.** *R. Perkins*

1915 September: Turrets removed, used as a transport
1916 Depot ship, Invergordon
1921 May 9: Sold and broken up at Briton Ferry

Mars

Type: Light Aircraft Carrier
Class: 'Colossus' (1942)

History:
1942 December 2: Laid down at Vickers, Barrow as ***Ethalion***
1943 Renamed ***Mars***
1944 May 20: Launched
1944 June: Renamed ***Pioneer***
1945 February 8: Completed as aircraft maintenance ship
1954 September: Broken up at Inverkeithing

Marshal Ney

Type: Monitor
Class: 'Marshal Ney' (1914)
Nomenclature: Michel Ney (1769-1815), Marshal of France under Napoleon

History:
1915 January: Laid down at Palmer as ***M13***
1915 June: Renamed ***Marshal Ney***
1915 June 17: Launched
1915 August 26: Completed
World War 1: 1915-18 Dover patrol
1916 Turret removed
1922 June: Base ship, renamed ***Vivid***, disarmed and hulked
1934 January 1: Renamed ***Drake***
1947 Renamed ***Alaunia II***
1957 October: Broken up at Milford Haven

Marshal Soult

Type: Monitor
Class: 'Marshal Ney' (1914)
Nomenclature: Nicolas Jean de Dieu Soult (1769-1851), Marshal of France under Napoleon

***Marshal Soult* — Monitor, at Chatham showing enormous bulges extending on beam. Destroyer *Velox* (D34) at left.**

History:
1915 February: Laid down at Palmer as ***M14***
1915 June: Renamed ***Marshal Soult***
1915 August 24: Launched
1915 November 2: Completed
World War 1: 1915-18 Dover patrol, Zeebrugge
1925-40 Gunnery training ship
1940 Base ship, disarmed and hulked
1946 August: Broken up at Troon

Minotaur

Type: Broadside Ship
Class: 'Minotaur' (1861)
Nomenclature: Greek myth: a monster, half bull and half man, slain by Theseus

History:
1861 September 12: Laid down at Thames, projected name *Elephant*
1863 December 12: Launched
1868 December 19: Completed, completion delayed by change in design
1868 In collision with ironclad *Bellerophon* in Belfast Lough
1873-75 Refit; rearmed, two masts removed
1887 Paid off to reserve
1890 Reboilered, training ship, Portland
1904 March: Renamed ***Boscawen II***
1906 June 11: Renamed ***Ganges***; depot ship, Harwich
1908 April 25: Renamed ***Ganges II***
1922 January 30: Sold, broken up at Swansea

Minotaur

Type: Armoured Cruiser
Class: 'Minotaur' (1904)

History:
1905 January 2: Laid down at Devonport
1906 June 6: Launched
1908 April 1: Completed
1910-14 Far East
World War 1: 1914 Australian convoys, Cape of Good Hope, 1915-18 Grand Fleet, Jutland
1920 April 20: Sold and broken up at Milford Haven

Monarch

Type: Turret Ship
Class: 'Monarch' (1865)
Nomenclature: Prize name, taken 1747

History:
1866 June 1: Laid down at Chatham
1868 May 25: Launched
1869 June 12: Completed
1869-70 Voyaged to US
1871 Refit, rearmed
1876 Mediterranean
1877 Refit
1878-85 Mediterranean
1882 Egyptian campaign, bombardment of Alexandria
1885 Broke down at sea, towed to Malta for repairs
1890-97 Reconstructed; sails removed, fighting tops added to masts, tall raked funnel added, re-engined and reboilered
1898-1902 Guardship, Capetown
1902 Depot ship, Simonstown
1904 March: Renamed ***Simoom***
1905 April 4: Sold and broken up

Monarch

Type: Dreadnought
Class: 'Orion' (1909)

History:
1910 April 1: Laid down at Armstrong as ***King George V***
1910 Renamed ***Monarch***
1911 March 30: Launched
1912 April 6: Completed
World War 1: 1914-18 Grand Fleet, Jutland
1914 December 27: Severely damaged in collision with battleship *Conqueror*
1922 Decommissioned; target ship
1925 January 20: Sunk as target by battleship *Revenge* off Scilly Islands

Monmouth

Type: Armoured Cruiser
Class: 'Monmouth' (1899)
Nomenclature: A county of Wales

History:
1899 August 29: Laid down at London & Glasgow
1901 November 13: Launched
1903 November: Completed
1906-13 Far East
World War 1: Sunk in action with German warships off Coronel, Chile (735 dead, all lost)

Monmouth

Type: Light Aircraft Carrier
Class: 'Hermes' (1943)

History:
1943 July 12: Ordered from Fairfield; never laid down
1945 October: Contract cancelled

Montagu

Type: Pre-dreadnought
Class: 'Duncan' (1898)
Nomenclature: Sir Edward Montagu, Earl of Sandwich (1625-1672), British admiral, killed at the Battle of Sole Bay

History:
1899 November 23: Laid down at Devonport
1901 March 5: Launched
1903 October: Completed
1903-05 Mediterranean
1906 May 30: Wrecked in dense fog on Lundy Island

Narcissus

Type: Armoured Cruiser
Class: 'Orlando' (1884)
Nomenclature: Greek myth: a beautiful youth who fell in love with his own image

History:
1885 April 27: Laid down at Earle
1886 December 15: Launched
1889 July: Completed
1906 September 11: Sold and broken up at Briton Ferry

***Natal* — 'Warrior' class armoured cruiser, 1911. Notice turrets amidships replacing casemates.** *P. A. Vicary*

Natal

Type: Armoured Cruiser
Class: 'Warrior' (1903)
Nomenclature: Colony in South Africa

History:
1904 January 6: Laid down at Vickers
1905 September 30: Launched
1907 April 5: Completed
World War 1: 1914-15 Grand Fleet
1915 December 30: Destroyed by an ammunition explosion in after magazine in Cromarty Firth (415 dead)

Nelson

Type: Armoured Frigate
Class: 'Northampton' (1873)
Nomenclature: Horatio, Viscount Nelson (1785-1805), British admiral, victor of the Nile, Copenhagen and Trafalgar

History:
1874 November 2: Laid down at Elder
1876 November 4: Launched
1881 July 26: Completed
1881-85 Australian station
1889-92 Refit; military rig and 4.7" guns added
1901 December: Stokers' training ship, Portsmouth
1910 July 12: Sold and broken up in Holland

Nelson

Type: Battleship
Class: 'Nelson' (1922)

History:
1922 December 28: Laid down at Armstrong
1925 September 3: Launched
1927 June: Completed
1927-41 Fleet flagship
World War 2: 1939-42 Home Fleet, 1943 Force 'H', 1943-44 Home Fleet, 1945 East Indies; Malta convoys, North Africa, Sicily, Salerno, Normandy
1939 December 4: Damaged by mine off Loch Ewe (under repair until August 1940)
1941 September 27: Torpedoed by Italian aircraft during Malta convoy Operation 'Halberd' (under repair until August 1942)
1943 September 29: Armistice with Italy signed on board
1944 July 12: Torpedoed by German MTB *S138* off Normandy
1944 Repaired at Philadelphia
1948 February: Sold and broken up at Inverkeithing

Neptune

Type: Turret Ship
Class: 'Neptune' (1878)
Nomenclature: Roman god of the sea

History:
1873 Laid down at Dudgeon for Brazil as ***Independencia***
1874 July 30: Launch incomplete and stuck in mud on the ways until 10 September 1874
—— Repaired at Samuda
1878 March: Purchased by British government, renamed ***Neptune,*** rearmed
1881 September 3: Completed
1885-86 Mediterranean
1886 Refit, rerigged
1903 September 15: Sold
1903 October 23: While being towed through Portsmouth harbour, rammed old *Victory*, collided with battleship *Hero* and narrowly missed other ships; broken up at Bremerhaven

Neptune

Type: Dreadnought
Class: 'Neptune' (1908)

History:
1909 January 19: Laid down at Portsmouth as ***Foudroyant***
1909 Renamed ***Neptune***
1909 September 30: Launched
1911 January 19: Completed
1912 Refit, fore funnel raised
World War 1: 1914-18 Grand Fleet, Jutland
1916 April 23: In collision with neutral merchant ship in fog in the North Sea
1922 September 1: Sold and broken up at Blyth

New Zealand

Type: Pre-dreadnought
Class: 'King Edward VII' (1901)
Nomenclature: Dominion of New Zealand

History:
1903 February 9: Laid down at Portsmouth
1904 February 4: Launched
1905 June 24: Completed
1911 December 1: Renamed ***Zealandia***
World War 1: 1914-15 Grand Fleet, 1915 Dardanelles
1918 Refit; main deck battery suppressed, tripod mast fitted
1919 Accommodation ship, Portsmouth
1921 November 8: Sold and broken up in Germany

New Zealand

Type: Battlecruiser
Class: 'Indefatigable' (1908)

History:
1910 June 20: Laid down at Fairfield
1911 July 1: Launched
1912 November 9: Completed
1913 World cruise
World War 1: 1914-18 Grand Fleet, Heligoland, Doggerbank, Jutland
1916 April 22: Damaged in collision with battlecruiser *Australia*
1916 May 31: Received one hit at Battle of Jutland
1920 Tour of Dominions with Admiral Jellicoe aboard
1922 December 19: Sold and broken up at Rosyth

New Zealand

Type: Aircraft Carrier
Class: 'Gibraltar' (1943)

History:
1943 July 15: Ordered from Cammell Laird; never laid down
1945 December 21: Contract cancelled

Nile

Type: Turret Ship
Class: 'Trafalgar' (1885)
Nomenclature: Battle in Aboukir Bay in which Nelson annihilated the French fleet, 1 August 1798

History:
1886 April 8: Laid down at Pembroke
1888 March 27: Launched

1891 July 10: Completed
1891-98 Mediterranean
1912 July 9: Sold and broken up at Briton Ferry

Northampton

Type: Armoured Frigate
Class: 'Northampton' (1873)
Nomenclature: City in the Midlands of England

History:
1874 October 26: Laid down at Napier
1876 November 18: Launched
1878 December 7: Completed
1879-86 North America and West Indies
1894 Seagoing training ship for boys
1905 April 5: Sold and broken up at Morecambe

Northumberland

Type: Broadside Ship
Class: 'Minotaur' (1861)
Nomenclature: A county in the north of England

History:
1861 October 10: Laid down at Mare
1866 March 17: Launch incomplete, stuck on the ways for one month
1866 April 17: Launched
1868 October 8: Completed
1872 December 25: Damaged in collision with ironclad *Hercules* at Funchal
1875-79 Refit; rearmed, second and fourth masts removed
1882 Egyptian campaign
1885-87 Refit

Above:
***Nelson* — 'Nelson' class battleship.**

Below:
***New Zealand* — 'King Edward VII' class pre-dreadnought, 1909, renamed *Zealandia* 1911.**

1898 Stokers' training ship, The Nore
1904 March: Renamed ***Acheron***
1909 Coal hulk
1914 Renamed ***C68***
1926 Renamed ***C8***
1927 June: Sold, became merchant hulk *Steamowna* at Dakar
1935 Broken up

Ocean

Type: Broadside Ship
Class: 'Prince Consort' (1861)
Nomenclature: Commemorates the Battle of Lagos, 1761, in which the French flagship *L'Océan* was sunk

History:
1860 August 23: Laid down at Devonport as wood line-of-battle ship
1861 May 27: Reordered as ironclad
1863 March 19: Launched
1866 July: Completed
1866 Mediterranean
1867-72 Far East; the only armoured ship to double the Cape of Good Hope under sail
1882 Sold

Ocean

Type: Pre-dreadnought
Class: 'Canopus' (1896)

History:
1897 February 15: Laid down at Devonport
1898 July 5: Launched
1900 February 20: Completed
1900 Mediterranean
1900-05 Far East, Boxer Rebellion
1908 Mediterranean
World War 1: 1914 Channel, East Indies, Persian Gulf, 1915 Suez, Dardanelles
1915 March 18: Struck a mine and sank in the Dardanelles after being damaged by shore batteries

Ocean

Type: Light Aircraft Carrier
Class: 'Colossus' (1942)

History:
1942 November 8: Laid down at Stephen
1944 July 8: Launched
1945 June 30: Completed
1945-47 Mediterranean
1949 Far East
1952-53 Korea
1956 Suez
1962 May: Broken up at Faslane

Orion

Type: Central Battery Ship
Class: 'Belleisle' (1878)
Nomenclature: Greek myth: a great hunter

History:
1874 Laid down at Samuda for Turkey as ***Boordji-Zafer***
1878 February 20: Taken over by British government during Russo-Turkish War, renamed ***Orion***
1879 January 23: Launched
1882 July 3: Completed
1882-88 Mediterranean
1882 Egyptian campaign, bombardment of Alexandria
1882 In collision with battleship *Temeraire*
1888-90 Singapore
1902 Destroyer depot ship, Malta
1910 September 12: Renamed ***Orontes***; storeship
1913 June 19: Sold at Malta and broken up in Italy

Orion

Type: Armoured Cruiser
Class: 'Minotaur' (1904)

History:
1905 Projected, never ordered

Orion

Type: Dreadnought
Class: 'Orion' (1909)

History:
1909 November 29: Laid down at Portsmouth
1910 August 20: Launched
1912 January 2: Completed
1912 January 7: In collision with old battleship *Revenge* in Portsmouth harbour
World War 1: 1914-18 Grand Fleet, Jutland
1922 December 19: Sold and broken up at Upnor

Orlando

Type: Armoured Cruiser
Class: 'Orlando' (1884)
Nomenclature: A character in Shakespeare's *As You Like It*

History:
1885 April 23: Laid down at Palmer
1886 August 3: Launched
1888 May 24: Completed
1900 China
1905 July 11: Sold and broken up at Morecambe

Pallas

Type: Armoured Corvette
Class: 'Pallas' (1862)
Nomenclature: Greek myth: the goddess Athene

History:
1863 October 19: Laid down at Woolwich
1865 March 14: Launched
1866 March 6: Completed
1870-72 Refit, rearmed
1872-79 Mediterranean
1873 Blockade of Cartagena, Spain
1879 Paid off
1886 April 20: Sold

Penelope

Type: Armoured Corvette
Class: 'Penelope' (1863)
Nomenclature: Greek myth: the wife of Odysseus

History:
1865 September 4: Laid down at Pembroke
1867 June 18: Launched
1868 June 27: Completed
1878 Particular Service Squadron
1882 Mediterranean
1882 July 11; Bombardment of Alexandria, damaged
1887 Paid off
1888 Receiving ship, Simonstown
1897 January: Prison hulk
1912 Sold and broken up at Capetown

Polyphemus

Type: Light Aircraft Carrier
Class: 'Hermes' (1943)
Nomenclature: Greek myth: chief of the Cyclops

History:
1943 August 11: Ordered from Devonport; never laid down
1945 October: Contract cancelled

Powerful

Type: Light Aircraft Carrier
Class: 'Majestic' (1942)
Nomenclature: First used 1783

History:
1943 November 27: Laid down by Harland & Wolff
1945 February 27: Launched
1946 Construction suspended
—— Design modified; angled flightdeck, steam catapault
1952 Construction resumed for Canada
1956 Renamed ***Bonaventure***
1957 January 17: Completed
1966-67 Refit
1970 July 1: Decommissioned; broken up in Taiwan

Prince Albert

Type: Turret Ship
Class: 'Prince Albert' (1862)
Nomenclature: Prince Albert, the Prince Consort (1819-1861), husband of Queen Victoria

History:
1862 April 29: Laid down by Samuda
1864 May 23: Launched
1866 February 23: Completed
1878 Particular Service Squadron
1878 Reboilered
1899 March 16: Sold and broken up at Preston

Prince Consort

Type: Broadside Ship
Class: 'Prince Consort' (1861)
Nomenclature: Prince Albert, the Prince Consort (1819-1861), husband of Queen Victoria

History:
1860 August 13: Laid down by Pembroke as wood line-of-battle ship ***Triumph***
1861 May 27: Reordered as ironclad
1862 February 14: Renamed ***Prince Albert***
1862 June 26: Launched
1864 February 6: Completed
1867 Rearmed with ML guns
1867-71 Mediterranean
1871 Again rearmed, laid up
1882 March: Sold

Prince Eugene

Type: Monitor
Class: 'Lord Clive' (1914)
Nomenclature: Prince Eugene of Savoy (1663-1736), brilliant Austrian general and ally of Marlborough during the War of the Spanish Succession

History:
1915 February 1: Laid down by Harland & Wolff, Govan as ***M11***
1915 June: Renamed ***Prince Eugene***
1915 July 14: Launched
1915 September 21: Completed
World War 1: 1915-18 Dover patrol, Zeebrugge, Ostend
1921 May 9: Sold and broken up at Preston

Prince George

Type: Pre-dreadnought
Class: 'Majestic' (1893)
Nomenclature: Prince George of Wales (1865-1936), later Duke of York and King George V

History:
1894 September 10: Laid down at Portsmouth
1895 August 22: Launched
1896 November 26: Completed
1903 October 17: In collision with battleship *Hannibal* off Cape Finisterre and beached at Ferrol
1904 Refit, fire control added
1905 March 31: Damaged in collision with German cruiser *Freidrich Carl* at Gibraltar
1909 December 5: Broke adrift and damaged in collision with cruiser *Shannon* at Portsmouth
World War 1: 1914 Channel Fleet, 1915 Mediterranean, Dardanelles
1915 May 2: Damaged by shore batteries at the Dardanelles
1916 January 9: Hit by submarine torpedo which failed to explode during evacuation of Cape Helles
1916 Destroyer depot ship, harbour service
1918 July: Renamed ***Victorious II***
1919 February: Renamed ***Prince George***
1921 September 21: Sold
1921 December 30: Foundered in tow off Kamperduin en route to breaking up in Germany

Prince of Wales

Type: Pre-dreadnought
Class: 'Formidable' (1897)
Nomenclature: The title conferred on the eldest son of the sovereign

History:
1901 March 20: Laid down by Chatham
1902 March 25: Launched
1904 April 7: Completed
1904-07 Mediterranean
1905 July 29: In collision with merchant vessel *Enidwen* off Oran
1906 April 16: Damaged by engine room explosion off Malta (three dead)
1909 July 2: Damaged by stokehold explosion

1913 June 2: Run into by submarine *C32* during exercises off Isle of Wight
World War 1: Channel patrol, 1915 Dardanelles, 1915-18 Adriatic
1920 April 12: Sold and broken up at Milford Haven

Prince of Wales

Type: Battleship
Class: 'King George V' (1936)

History:
1937 January 2: Laid down by Cammell Laird
1939 May 3: Launched
1941 March 31: Completed
World War 2: 1940-41 Home Fleet, 1941 East Indies
1941 May 21: Damaged by seven hits in action with German battleship *Bismarck* and cruiser *Prinz Eugen* off Iceland
1941 August: Carried Prime Minister Churchill to meeting with President Roosevelt in Newfoundland; Atlantic Charter signed on board
1941 December 10: Sunk by Japanese aircraft bombs and torpedoes off east coast of Malaya. Flag of Adm Sir Tom Phillips who was lost (327 dead)

Prince Rupert

Type: Monitor
Class: 'Lord Clive' (1914)
Nomenclature: Prince Rupert of the Rhine (1619-1682), royalist general during the English Civil War

History:
1915 January 12: Laid down by Hamilton as ***M10***
1915 May 20: Launched
1915 June: Renamed ***Prince Rupert***
1915 July 12: Completed
World War 1: 1915-18 Dover patrol
1918 Addition of 18" gun cancelled
1922 February 24: Base ship, renamed ***Pembroke***
1922 September 1: Renamed ***Prince Rupert***
1923 May: Sold and broken up at Glasgow

Princess Royal

Type: Battlecruiser
Class: 'Lion' (1909)
Nomenclature: Title conferred on the eldest daughter of the sovereign

History:
1910 May 2: Laid down by Vickers
1911 April 29: Launched
1912 November 14: Completed
1913 Refit, tripod mast replaced by pole and resited, rangefinders fitted
World War 1: 1914-18 Grand Fleet, Heligoland, Doggerbank, Jutland
1916 May 31: Damaged by gunfire, nine hits, at Battle of Jutland (22 dead)
1922 December 29: Sold and broken up at Rosyth

Queen

Type: Pre-dreadnought
Class: 'Formidable' (1897)
Nomenclature: First used 1225

History:
1901 March 12: Laid down by Devonport
1902 March 8: Launched
1904 May 18: Completed
1904-08 Mediterranean
1905 August 28: Went aground off Malta

Princess Royal **— Battlecruiser of 'Lion' class.**

1913 January 13; In collision with tender *Starling* at Sheerness
World War 1: 1914 Channel patrol, 1915 Dardanelles, 1915-18 Adriatic
1920 November 4: Sold and broken up at Birkenhead and Preston

Queen Elizabeth

Type: Dreadnought
Class: 'Queen Elizabeth' (1912)
Nomenclature: Elizabeth I (1533-1603), Queen of England 1558-1603

History:
1912 October 21: Laid down by Portsmouth
1913 October 16: Launched
1915 January 19: Completed
World War 1: 1915 Dardanelles, 1915-18 Grand Fleet, 1916-18 Fleet flagship
1924-26 Mediterranean
1926-27 Reconstructed at Portsmouth; bridge remodelled, two funnels trunked into one, bulges fitted
1929-37 Mediterranean
1937-40 Reconstructed at Portsmouth; re-engined and reboilered, tower superstructure and pole mast, rearmed; completed at Rosyth
1941 January 31: Recommissioned
World War 2: 1941 Mediterranean, Crete, 1943-44 Home Fleet, 1944-45 Indian Ocean; Burma, Sabang raid
1941 December 19: Severely damaged by Italian frogmen at Alexandria
1942 Repaired at Norfolk
1943 June: Recommissioned
1948 March 19: Sold and broken up at Dalmuir & Troon

Queen Mary

Type: Battlecruiser
Class: 'Lion' (1909)
Nomenclature: Queen Mary (1867-1953), wife of King George V

History:
1911 March 6: Laid down by Palmer
1912 March 20: Launched
1913 August 30: Completed
World War 1: 1914-16 Grand Fleet, Heligoland, Jutland
1916 May 31: Blew up after direct hit from German battlecruiser *Derfflinger* at Battle of Jutland (1,266 dead)

Raglan

Type: Monitor
Class: 'Abercrombie' (1914)
Nomenclature: Fitzroy James Henry Somerset, Lord Raglan (1788-1855), field marshal, commander-in-chief during the Crimean War

History:
1914 November: Laid down by Harland & Wolff, Govan, as ***Robert E. Lee***
1915 April 29: Launched
1915 May 31: Renamed ***M3***
1915 June 13: Completed
1915 June 20: Renamed ***Lord Raglan***
1915 June 23: Renamed ***Raglan***
World War 1: Dardanelles
1918 January 20: Sunk by gunfire of Turkish battlecruiser *Yavuz Sultan Selim* (*Goeben*) off Imbros (122 dead)

Ramillies

Type: Pre-dreadnought

***Raglan* — 'Abercrombie' class monitor, at Mudros, 1915.** *P. A. Vicary*

Ramillies — **Battleship, 'Royal Sovereign' class, c1930.**

Class: 'Royal Sovereign' (1889)
Nomenclature: Victory of Marlborough during the War of the Spanish Succession, 23 May 1706

History:
1890 August 11: Laid down by Thomson
1892 March 1: Launched
1893 October 17: Completed
1893-1903 Mediterranean
1903-04 Refit
1906 June 15: In collision with battleship *Resolution* near Sheerness
1906 Refit
1911 Paid off
1913 October 7: Sold and broken up at Swansea

Ramillies

Type: Dreadnought
Class: 'Royal Sovereign' (1913)

History:
1913 November 12: Laid down by Beardmore
1916 September 12: Launched, rudder damaged; towed to Cammell Laird for completion
1917 September: Completed
World War 1: 1917-18 Grand Fleet
1920-24 Mediterranean
1924-27 Refit
1927-32 Mediterranean
1932-33 Refit, tripod mainmast fitted
1933-35 Mediterranean
World War 2: 1939 Home Fleet, 1940 East Indies and Mediterranean, 1941 Atlantic convoys, 1942-43 Indian Ocean; Cape Spartivento, Diego Suarez, Normandy, Southern France
1942 May 30: Torpedoed by midget submarine from Japanese *I20* off Diego Suarez
1944 Torpedo training ship, Portsmouth
1948 February 20: Sold and broken up at Cairnryan

Redoubtable, see *Revenge*

Nomenclature: To be feared

Renown, see *Empress of India*

Renown, see *Victoria*

Renown

Type: Pre-dreadnought
Class: 'Renown' (1892)
Nomenclature: Ship of 1651

History:
1893 February: Laid down by Pembroke
1895 May 8: Launched
1897 January: Completed
1897-99 North America and West Indies
1899-1902 Mediterranean
1902 Refit, main deck 6" guns removed
1904-05 Refit, all 6" guns removed
1909 Stokers' training ship, Portsmouth
1911 September 26: Damaged when run into by water tanker *Aid* at Portsmouth
1914 February 2: Sold and broken up at Blyth

Renown

Type: Dreadnought
Class: 'Royal Sovereign' (1913)

History:
1913 Ordered from Fairfield; never laid down
1914 Contract cancelled

Renown

Type: Battlecruiser
Class: 'Renown' (1914)

***Renown* — Battleship , modified 'Barfleur' class, in 1905.**

History:
1915 January 25: Laid down by Fairfield
1916 March 4: Launched
1916 September 12: Completed
World War 1: 1916-18 Grand Fleet
1923-26 Refit, bulges added and catapult fitted
1935 January 23: Damaged bow in collision with battlecruiser *Hood*
1936-39 Reconstructed at Portsmouth, re-engined, tripod mainmast replaced by pole, forward tripod replaced by tower superstructure
World War 2: 1939 South Atlantic, 1940-41 Force 'H', 1942-43 Home Fleet, 1944 Indian Ocean, 1945 East Indies; Atlantic convoys 1940, Norwegian campaign, Cape Spartivento, 'Bismarck' operations, Malta convoys, Arctic 1942, North Africa, Sabang raid
1940 April 9: Damaged in action with German warships off Narvik
1941 February 9: Bombardment of Genoa
1945 Harbour service
1948 March 19: Sold and broken up at Faslane

Repulse

Type: Central Battery Ship
Class: 'Repulse' (1866)
Nomeclature: Galleon of 1595

History:
1859 August 29: Laid down by Woolwich as wood line-of-battle ship
1861 August: Reordered as ironclad
1866 October 25: Conversion to ironclad commenced
1868 April 25: Launched
1870 January 31: Completed at Sheerness
1872-77 Eastern Pacific
1877 Only British armoured ship to round Cape Horn under sail
1877-80 Refit
1885 Paid off
1889 February: Sold

Repulse

Type: Pre-dreadnought
Class: 'Royal Sovereign' (1889)

History:
1890 January 1: Laid down by Pembroke

***Renown* — Battlecruiser, 1940, after reconstruction.**

1892 February 27: Launched
1894 April 25: Completed
1896 July 18: In collision with battleship *Resolution*
1902-03 Mediterranean
1903 Refit
1911 July 11: Sold and broken up at Morecambe

Repulse

Type: Dreadnought
Class: 'Royal Sovereign' (1913)

History:
1913 Ordered from Palmer; never laid down
1914 Contract cancelled

Repulse

Type: Battlecruiser
Class: 'Renown' (1914)

History:
1915 January 25: Laid down by John Brown
1916 January 8: Launched
1916 August 14: Completed
World War 1: 1916-18 Grand Fleet
1917 December 12: In collision with battlecruiser *Australia*
1919-21 Refit, armour increased, TT added
1923-24 World cruise
1932-36 Refit, superstructure built up, hangar and catapult added, AA armament increased
1936-38 Mediterranean
World War 2: 1939-41 Home Fleet, 1941 Far East; Norwegian campaign, 'Bismarck' operations
1941 December 10: Sunk by Japanese aircraft bombs and torpedoes off east coast of Malaya (327 dead)

Resistance

Type: Broadside Ship
Class: 'Defence' (1859)
Nomenclature: First used 1782

History:
1859 December 21: Laid down by Westwood & Baillie
1861 April 11: Launched
1862 August 21: Completed
1864-67 Mediterranean (first British ironclad on that station)
1867-69 Refit, rearmed with ML guns
1874 July: In collision with battleship *Devastation* at Portland

Above:
***Repulse* — Battlecruiser, June 1929, prior to major refit.** *Wright & Logan*

Above right:
***Resolution* — 'Royal Sovereign' class battleship of 1888, c1909.** *National Maritime Museum*

Right:
***Resolution* — Battleship, January 1939, with tripod mainmast and funnel cap.** *Wright & Logan*

1878 Particular Service Squadron
1880 Paid off
1885 Target Ship
1898 Sold
1899 March 4: Foundered in tow off Holyhead

Resistance

Type: Dreadnought
Class: 'Royal Sovereign' (1913)

History:
1914 Ordered from Devonport; never laid down
1914 August 26: Contract cancelled

Resolution

Type: Pre-dreadnought
Class: 'Royal Sovereign' (1889)
Nomenclature: 64 gun ship of 1650

History:
1890 June 14: Laid down by Palmer
1892 May 28: Launched
1893 December 5: Completed
1896 July 18: In collision with battleship *Repulse*
1906 July 15: In collision with battleship *Ramillies* near Sheerness
1911 Paid off
1912 Damaged by collision with merchant vessel *Seapoint* while laid up at Motherbank
1914 April 2: Sold and broken up in Holland

Resolution

Type: Dreadnought
Class: 'Royal Sovereign' (1913)

History:
1913 November 29: Laid down by Palmer
1915 January 14: Launched
1916 December 30: Completed
World War 1: 1916-18 Grand Fleet
1920 Mediterranean
1921-24 Refit
1924 January 10: Sank submarine *L24* in collision off Portland
1924-30 Mediterranean
1930-31 Refit
1931-35 Mediterranean
World War 2: 1939-40 Home Fleet, Atlantic convoys, 1942-43 Indian Ocean; Norwegian campaign, Oran, Dakar
1940 May 18: Hit by aircraft bomb at Tjeldsundet near Narvik
1940 September 24: Damaged by French shore batteries at Dakar
1940 September 25: Torpedoed by French submarine *Beveziers* off Dakar
1941 Repaired and refit at Philadelphia
1944 May: Stokers' training depot ship, Gairloch
1948 May 5: Sold and broken up at Faslane

Revenge

Type: Pre-dreadnought
Class: 'Royal Sovereign' (1889)

Nomenclature: Drake's flagship against the Spanish Armada, 1588

History:
1891 February 12: Laid down by Palmer
1892 November 3: Launched
1894 March 22: Completed
1896-1900 Mediterranean, Crete operations
1902 Refit
1908 January 7: In collision with merchant vessel *Bengore Head*
1912 January 7: Broke away from moorings and drifted on to bows of battleship *Orion* in Portsmouth harbour, severely damaged
1914 Ordered to be sold
1914 August: Returned to service as bombarding ship, guns relined and reduced to 12", bulges added
1915 August 2: Renamed ***Redoubtable***
World War 1: Served off Belgian coast
1919 November 6: Sold and broken up at Briton Ferry

Revenge

Type: Dreadnought
Class: 'Royal Sovereign' (1913)

History:
1913 December 22: Laid down by Vickers
1915 May 29: Launched

1916 March: Completed
World War 1: 1916-18 Grand Fleet, Jutland
1918 November 5: In collision in Scapa Flow with aircraft carrier *Campania*, which sank
1920 Mediterranean
1928-29 Refit
1930-31 Refit
1936-37 Refit
World War 2: 1939-41 Home Fleet, Atlantic convoys, 1942-43 Indian Ocean
1940 September: Bombarded German positions at Cherbourg
1941 September 2: In collision with cruiser *Orion*
1944 May: Stokers' training depot ship, Gairloch
1948 September: Sold and broken up at Inverkeithing

Robert E. Lee, see ***Raglan***

Nomenclature: Robert Edward Lee (1807-1870), Confederate general

Roberts

Type: Monitor
Class: 'Abercrombie' (1914)
Nomenclature: Sir Frederick Sleigh Roberts, Earl Roberts (1832-1914), field marshal, commander during the Boer War

History:
1914 November: Laid down by Swan Hunter as ***Stonewall Jackson***
1915 April 15: Launched
1915 May 31: Renamed ***M4***
1915 June 8: Completed
1915 June 19: Renamed ***Earl Roberts***
1915 June 22: Renamed ***Roberts***
World War 1: Dardanelles
1936 September: Sold and broken up at Preston

Roberts

Type: Monitor

***Roberts* — 'Abercrombie' class monitor, 1915.**
P. A. Vicary

Class: 'Roberts' (1940)

History:
1940 April 30: Laid down by John Brown
1941 February 1: Launched
1941 October 27: Completed
World War 2: North Africa, Sicily, Salerno, Normandy, Walcheren
1942 November 11: Damaged by aircraft bombs at Bougie, Algeria
1965 August: Broken up at Inverkeithing

Rodney

Type: Barbette Ship
Class: 'Admiral' (1881)
Nomenclature: George Brydges Rodney, Lord Rodney (1719-1792), admiral, commander at the Battle of the Saintes

History:
1882 February 6: Laid down by Chatham
1884 October 8: Launched
1888 June 20: Completed
1894-97 Mediterranean
1901 February: Paid off
1909 May 11: Sold and broken up at Morecambe

Rodney, see ***Vanguard***

Rodney

Type: Battlecruiser
Class: 'Hood' (1915)

History:
1916 October 9: Laid down by Fairfield
1917 March 9: Construction suspended
1919 March 17: Contract cancelled

Rodney

Type: Battleship
Class: 'Nelson' (1922)

History:
1922 December 28: Laid down by Cammell Laird
1925 December 17: Launched
1927 August: Completed
World War 2: 1939-42 Home Fleet, 1943 Force 'H', 1943-45 Home Fleet; Norwegian campaign, Atlantic convoys, 'Bismarck' operations, Malta convoys, North Africa, Sicily, Salerno, Normandy, Arctic 1944
1940 April 9: Damaged by aircraft bomb in the North Sea
1941 Repaired and refit at Boston
1948 February: Sold and broken up at Inverkeithing

Roxburgh

Type: Armoured Cruiser
Class: 'Devonshire' (1901)
Nomenclature: A county of southern Scotland

History:
1902 June 13: Laid down by London & Glasgow
1904 January 19: Launched
1905 September 5: Completed
World War 1: 1914-16 North Sea, 1916-18 North America and West Indies
1915 June 20: Torpedoed by *U39* off Norwegian coast
1918 February 12: Rammed and sank *U89* while on convoy duty north of Ireland
1919-20 Wireless training ship
1921 November 8: Sold and broken up in Germany

Royal Alfred

Type: Central Battery Ship
Class: 'Royal Alfred' (1863)
Nomenclature: Prince Alfred, Duke of Edinburgh (1844-1900), a son of Queen Victoria

History:
1859 December 1: Laid down by Portsmouth as wood line-of-battle ship
1861 May 27: Reordered as ironclad
1864 October 15: Launched
1867 March 23: Completed
1867-69 and 1870-74 North America and West Indies
1872 Damaged by grounding on Bahama Bank
1874 January: Paid off
1885 Sold

Royal George, see *King George V*

Royal Oak

Type: Broadside Ship
Class: 'Royal Oak' (1861)
Nomenclature: Tree near Boscobel in which King Charles II hid after his defeat at Worcester 1651

History:
1860 May 1: Laid down by Chatham as wood line-of-battle ship
1861 May 8: Reordered as ironclad
1862 September 10: Launched
1863 May 23: Completed
1863-67 Mediterranean
1867 Refit, rearmed with ML guns
1868 In collision with ironclad *Warrior*
1869-71 Mediterranean
1869 November: Went aground off Port Said at the opening of the Suez Canal
1871 Paid off
1885 September 30: Sold and broken up

Royal Oak

Type: Pre-dreadnought
Class: 'Royal Sovereign' (1889)

History:
1890 May 29: Laid down by Laird
1892 November 5: Launched
1894 June 12: Completed
1897-1902 Mediterranean
1902 Refit
1905 May 11: Had small arms explosion at Chatham
1914 January 14: Sold and broken up at Briton Ferry

Royal Oak

Type: Dreadnought
Class: 'Royal Sovereign' (1913)

History:
1914 January 15: Laid down by Devonport
1914 November 17: Launched
1916 May: Completed
World War 1: 1916-18 Grand Fleet, Jutland
1922-24 Refit
1926-34 Mediterranean
1934-35 Refit, tripod mainmast fitted
World War 2: 1939 Home Fleet
1939 October 14: Torpedoed and sunk by *U47* in Scapa Flow (833 dead)

Royal Sovereign

Type: Turret Ship
Class: 'Royal Sovereign' (1862)
Nomenclature: First used 1660

History:
1849 December 17: Laid down by Portsmouth as 131-gun wood line-of-battle ship
1857 April 25: Launched
1862 Completed
1862 April 4: Conversion to turret ship commenced
1864 August 20: Conversion completed
1873 Reserve
1885 May: Sold

Royal Sovereign

Type: Pre-dreadnought
Class: 'Royal Sovereign' (1889)

History:
1889 September 30: Laid down by Portsmouth
1891 February 26: Launched
1892 May: Completed
1897-1902 Mediterranean
1901 November: Sustained explosion of 6" gun
1903 Refit

1913 October 7: Sold and broken up at Genoa

Royal Sovereign

Type: Dreadnought
Class: 'Royal Sovereign' (1913)

History:
1914 January 15: Laid down by Portsmouth
1915 April 29: Launched
1916 May: Completed
World War 1: 1916-18 Grand Fleet
1927-28 Refit
1937 Refit
World War 2: 1939 Home Fleet, 1940-41 Atlantic convoys, 1942-43 Indian Ocean
1941 Refit at Norfolk
1944 May 30: Loaned to Soviet Union, renamed ***Arkhangelsk***
1949 February 4: Returned to Royal Navy, renamed ***Royal Sovereign***
1949 April 5: Sold and broken up at Inverkeithing

Rupert

Type: Breastwork Monitor
Class: 'Rupert' (1869)
Nomenclature: Prince Rupert of the Rhine (1619-1682), royalist admiral and general during the English Civil War

History:
1870 June 9: Laid down by Chatham
1872 March 12: Launched
1874 July 1: Completed
1876-86 Mediterranean
1891-93 Reconstructed; rearmed and re-engined
1895-1902 Guardship, Gibraltar and Egypt
1904-07 Guardship, Bermuda
1907 July 10: Sold

Russell

Type: Pre-dreadnought
Class: 'Duncan' (1898)
Nomenclature: Edward Russell, Earl of Orford (1652-1727), British admiral, victor of Barfleur

History:
1899 March 11: Laid down by Palmer
1901 February 19: Launched
1903 February 20: Completed
1903-04 Mediterranean
1908 July 16: In collision with cruiser *Venus* off Quebec
1909-12 Mediterranean
World War 1: 1914 Grand Fleet, Channel patrol, Belgian coast operations, 1915 Mediterranean, Dardanelles, Aegean
1916 April 27: Sunk by mine off Malta (126 dead)

Top left:
***Royal Sovereign* — Battleship, in wartime camouflage, October 1940.**

Centre left:
***Rupert* — Breastwork monitor of 1869.** *Marius Bar*

Bottom left:
***St Vincent* — Dreadnought, c1910.**

St Vincent

Type: Dreadnought
Class: 'St Vincent' (1907)
Nomenclature: Sir John Jervis, Earl of St Vincent (1734-1833), Admiral of the Fleet, victor of the Battle of Cape St Vincent

History:
1907 December 30: Laid down by Portsmouth
1908 September 10: Launched
1910 January: Completed
World War 1: 1914-18 Grand Fleet, Jutland
1921 December 1: Sold and broken up at Dover

Sans Pareil

Type: Turret Ship
Class: 'Victoria' (1884)
Nomenclature: Prize name, taken 1794

History:
1885 April 21: Laid down by Thames
1887 May 9: Launched
1891 July 8: Completed
1892-95 Mediterranean
1898 August 9: Sank schooner *East Lothian* in collision off Lands End
1904 January: Paid off
1907 April 9: Sold and broken up at Preston

Scorpion

Type: Turret ship
Class: 'Scorpion' (1863)
Nomenclature: First used 1746

History:
1862 April: Laid down by Laird for Confederate government, to be named ***North Carolina***; built under cover name *El Tousson*
1863 July 4: Launched
1863 October 2: Seized by British government, renamed ***Scorpion***
1865 October 10: Completed
1869 Coast defence ship, Bermuda
1901 Sunk as target at Bermuda
1903 February: Hulk sold
1903 June 17: Foundered in tow en route to Boston for breaking up

Shannon

Type: Armoured Cruiser
Class: 'Shannon' (1872)
Nomenclature: A river in Ireland

History:
1873 September 29: Laid down by Pembroke
1875 November 11: Launched
1877 September 17: Completed
1878 China
1879-81 Pacific
1881 Refit, TT added
1893 Reserve
1899 December 15: Sold

Shannon

Type: Armoured Cruiser
Class: 'Minotaur' (1904)

History:
1905 January 2: Laid down by Chatham
1906 September 20: Launched
1908 March 10: Completed
1909 December 5: Damaged in collision with battleship *Prince George* which broke adrift at Portsmouth
World War 1: 1915-17 Grand Fleet, 1918 Convoy escort, Jutland
1920-22 Accommodation ship
1922 December 22: Sold and broken up at Bo'Ness

Sir James Wolfe, see *General Wolfe*

Sir John Moore

Type: Monitor
Class: 'Lord Clive' (1914)
Nomenclature: Sir John Moore (1761-1809), lieutenant-general, mortally wounded during the retreat to Corruna

History:
1915 January 13: Laid down by Scotts as ***M5***
1915 May 31: Launched
1915 June: Renamed ***Sir John Moore***
1915 July 20: Completed
World War 1: 1915-18 Dover patrol
1921 November 8: Sold and broken up in Germany

Sir Thomas Picton

Type: Monitor
Class: 'Lord Clive' (1914)
Nomenclature: Sir Thomas Picton (1758-1815), lieutenant-general, killed at Waterloo

History:
1914 December: Laid down by Harland & Wolff as ***M12***
1915 June: Renamed ***Sir Thomas Picton***
1915 September 30: Launched
1915 November: Completed
World War 1: Dardanelles, Adriatic
1921 November 8: Sold and broken up in Germany

Stonewall Jackson, see *Roberts*

Nomenclature: Thomas Jonathan Jackson (1824-1863), Confederate general

Suffolk

Type: Armoured Cruiser
Class: 'Monmouth' (1899)
Nomenclature: A county of England

History:
1901 March 25: Laid down by Portsmouth
1903 January 15: Launched
1904 April: Completed
1904-07 Mediterranean
1909-12 Mediterranean
1913-14 West Indies

Above:
***Minotaur* and *Shannon* — Armoured cruisers of the 'Minotaur' class, 1918, with new tripod masts and wearing dazzle camouflage.** *IWM*

Right:
***Suffolk* — 'Monmouth' class armoured cruiser, 1906.**
P. A. Vicary

World War 1: 1914-16 North America and West Indies, 1917-18 Far East, 1919 Vladivostok
1919 Cadet training ship
1920 July 1: Sold and broken up 1922 in Germany

Sultan

Type: Central Battery Ship
Class: 'Sultan' (1867)
Nomenclature: Named in honour of Abdul Aziz, Sultan of Turkey, who visited Britain in 1869

History:
1868 February 29: Laid down by Chatham
1870 May 31: Launched
1871 October 10: Completed
1876 Refit, reduced to bark
1876-79 Mediterranean
1879 Refit, reboilered
1882-84 Mediterranean
1882 Egyptian campaign, bombardment of Alexandria
1884 December: Sank a French transport in collision in the Tagus River
1886-89 Mediterranean
1889 March 6: Went aground in Comino Channel off Malta and sank, 14 March
1889 August 26: Raised and taken to Malta; repaired at Portsmouth
1893-96 Reconstructed; military rig, two tall funnels, new guns, re-engined
1896 Reserve
1906 Artificers' training ship, Portsmouth
1906 January 1: Renamed ***Fisgard IV***
1931 Mechanical training ship
1932 Renamed ***Sultan***
1940-45 Depot ship for minesweepers, Portsmouth
1946 August 13: Sold and broken up at Dalmuir

Superb, see *Alexandra*

Superb

Type: Central Battery Ship
Class: 'Superb' (1878)
Nomenclature: Ship of 1710

History:
1873 Laid down by Thames for Turkey as ***Hamidieh***
1875 November 16: Launched
1878 February 20: Taken over by British government during Russo-Turkish War and detained, purchased and renamed ***Superb***
1880 November 15: Completed
1880-87 Mediterranean
1882 Egyptian campaign, bombardment of Alexandria
1887-91 Reconstructed, sail rig removed, rearmed, re-engined, and reboilered
1904 Accommodation ship
1906 May 15: Sold

Superb

Type: Dreadnought
Class: 'Bellerophon' (1906)

History:
1907 February 16: Laid down by Armstrong
1907 November 7: Launched
1909 May 29: Completed
World War 1: 1914-18 Grand Fleet, Jutland, 1918 Mediterranean
1920 Gunnery target vessel
1922 December 12: Sold and broken up at Dover

Sutlej

Type: Armoured Cruiser
Class: 'Cressy' (1898)
Nomenclature: Two victories of the Sikh War, 1846, on the Sutlej River

History:
1898 August 15: Laid down by John Brown
1899 November 18: Launched
1901 February 5: Completed
1903 September 18: Sank bark *Charles Chalmers* in collision in North Sea
1904-06 Far East
1906-09 North America and West Indies
1910 July 15: Damaged by boiler explosion while on manoeuvres, 40 miles off Berehaven (four dead)
World War 1: Regular patrol and escort duties
1918 January: Depot ship, Rosyth; renamed ***Crescent***
1919 Renamed ***Sutlej***
1921 May 9: Sold and broken up 1924 at Preston

Swiftsure

Type: Central Battery Ship
Class: 'Swiftsure' (1868)
Nomenclature: Elizabethan compound name meaning Swift Pursuer; first used 1573

History:
1868 August 31: Laid down by Palmer
1870 June 15: Launched
1872 June 27: Completed
1872-78 Mediterranean
1873 Blockade of Cartagena, Spain; accepted surrender of insurgent battleship *Vitoria* 2 August
1881 Refit, reduced to bark
1882-85 Pacific
1885 Refit, reboilered
1888-90 Pacific
1893 Reserve
1901 Store hulk, Portsmouth
1904 March: Renamed ***Orontes***
1908 July 14: Sold and broken up

Swiftsure

Type: Pre-dreadnought
Class: 'Swiftsure' (1903)

History:
1902 March 13: Laid down by Armstrong for Chile as ***Constitucion***
1903 January 12: Launched
1903 December 3: Purchased by British government, renamed ***Swiftsure***
1904 June 21: Completed
1905 June 3: In collision with sister-ship *Triumph* in fog off Dungeness
1909-12 Mediterranean
1913 East Indies
World War 1: 1914 Red Sea, Defence of Suez Canal, 1915 Dardanelles
1916 Reserve
1919 Target ship
1920 June 18: Sold

Top left:
***Temeraire* — Dreadnought of 'Bellerophon' class of 1906.**

Centre left:
***Thunderer* — Turret ship of 'Devastation' class, as completed 1876 and awaiting trials.**

Bottom left:
***Triumph* — Light aircraft carrier of 'Colossus' class, May 1946.** *Wright & Logan*

Temeraire

Type: Central Battery and Barbette Ship
Class: 'Temeraire' (1873)
Nomenclature: Prize name, taken 1759

History:
1873 August 18: Laid down by Chatham
1876 May 9: Launched
1877 August 31: Completed
1877-87 Mediterranean
1882 Egyptian campaign, bombardment of Alexandria
1888 Damaged when rammed by battleship *Orion*
1888-91 Mediterranean
1891 Paid off
1892-94 Refit; pole masts, tall funnels fitted, rearmed
1902 Depot ship, Devonport
1904 April: Renamed ***Indus II;*** floating workshop
1915 January: Renamed ***Akbar;*** reformatory ship, Liverpool
1921 May 26: Sold

Temeraire

Type: Dreadnought
Class: 'Bellerophon' (1906)

History:
1907 January 1: Laid down by Devonport
1907 August 24: Launched
1909 May 15: Completed
1909 July 31: Damaged by gun explosion during naval review
World War 1: 1914-18 Grand Fleet, Jutland, 1918 Mediterranean
1919 Seagoing cadet training ship
1921 December 7: Sold and broken up at Dover

Temeraire

Type: Battleship
Class: 'Lion' (1938)

History:
1939 June 1: Laid down by Cammell Laird
1939 October: Construction suspended
1944 Contract cancelled

Terrible

Type: Light Aircraft Carrier
Class: 'Majestic' (1942)
Nomenclature: First used 1694

History:
1943 April 19: Laid down by Devonport
1944 September 30: Launched
1948 October 16: Renamed ***Sydney;*** completed for Australia
1951-53 Korea
1955 May: Training Ship refit cancelled
1962 March: Troop Transport

1973 November: Decommissioned
1975 October 7: Sold and broken up in Korea

Terror

Type: Monitor
Class: 'Erebus' (1915)
Nomenclature: First used 1696

History:
1915 October: Laid down by Harland & Wolff
1916 May 18: Launched
1916 August 2: Completed
World War 1: 1916-18 Dover patrol, Zeebrugge
1917 October 19: Damaged by torpedo attack
World War 2: 1940-41 Libya
1941 February 22: Damaged by German aircraft at Bengazi and sank in tow two days later, off Derna

Theseus

Type: Light Aircraft Carrier
Class: 'Colossus' (1942)
Nomenclature: Legendary Greek hero, son of Aegeus, King of Athens

History:
1943 January 6: Laid down by Fairfield
1944 July 6: Launched
1946 January 9: Completed
1947-48 Pacific
1950-51 Korea
1956 Suez
1962 May: Broken up at Inverkeithing

Thunderer

Type: Turret Ship
Class: 'Devastation' (1868)
Nomenclature: First used 1760

History:
1869 June 26: Laid down by Pembroke
1872 March 25: Launched
1876 July 14: Damaged by boiler explosion during trials at Spithead
1877 May 26: Completed
1878 Particular Service Squadron
1878-81 Mediterranean
1879 January 2: Damaged by explosion of 38-ton gun while off Ismid, Turkey
1881 Refit; searchlights, torpedoes and MGs fitted
1889-91 Refit; rearmed, re-engined and reboilered
1891-92 Mediterranean
1900 Reserve
1907 Non-effective
1909 July 13: Sold

Thunderer

Type: Dreadnought
Class: 'Orion' (1909)

History:
1910 April 13: Laid down by Thames
1911 February 1: Launched
1912 June 15: Completed
World War 1: 1914-18 Grand Fleet, Jutland
1922 Seagoing cadet training ship
1926 December 10: Sold
1924 December 24: Ran aground en route to breaking up at Blyth

Thunderer

Type: Battleship
Class: 'Lion' (1938)

History:
1939 September: Not ordered, intended builder Fairfield
1941 September: Construction cancelled

Tiger

Type: Battlecruiser
Class: 'Tiger' (1911)
Nomenclature: Ship of 1546

History:
1912 June 20: Laid down by John Brown
1913 December 15: Launched
1914 October 3: Completed
World War 1: 1914-18 Grand Fleet, Doggerbank, Jutland
1915 January 24: Received three hits at Battle of the Doggerbank (12 dead)
1916 May 31: Damaged by 17 hits at the battle of Jutland (24 dead)
1917 Flying off platform added to 'Q' turret
1924 Mainmast fitted, AA guns added, flying off platform removed
1932 February: Sold and broken up at Inverkeithing

Trafalgar

Type: Turret Ship
Class: 'Trafalgar' (1885)
Nomenclature: British naval victory over French and Spanish fleets off Cape Trafalgar, 21 October 1805

History:
1886 January 18: Laid down by Portsmouth
1887 September 21: Launched
1890 March: Completed; completion delayed by late delivery of armament
1891 Refit, funnels raised
1890-97 Mediterranean
1900 July 30: In collision with merchant ship *King Orry*
1905 Refit
1911 May 9: Sold

Triumph, see *Prince Consort*

Triumph

Type: Central Battery Ship
Class: 'Swiftsure' (1868)
Nomenclature: First used 1561

History:
1868 August 31: Laid down by Palmer
1870 September 27: Launched
1873 April 8: Completed
1873-77 Mediterranean
1873 Blockade of Cartagena, Spain
1877-82 Pacific
1882 Refit, reboilered

1882-88 Pacific
1892 Reserve
1900 Depot ship, Plymouth
1903 Boys' training ship, Chatham
1904 April: Renamed ***Tenedos***
1912 Renamed ***Indus IV***
1914 Floating store ship, Invergordon
1916 January 15: Renamed ***Algiers***
1921 January: Sold and broken up at Sunderland

Triumph

Type: Pre-dreadnought
Class: 'Swiftsure' (1903)

History:
1902 March 13: Laid down by Vickers for Chile as ***Libertad***
1903 January 15: Launched
1903 December 3: Purchased by British government, renamed ***Triumph***
1904 June 21: Completed
1904 September 17: Run into by Trinity House steamer *Siren* at Pembroke
1905 June 3: Damaged in collision with sister-ship *Swiftsure* off Dungeness
1909-12 Mediterranean
1913-14 Far East
World War 1: 1914 Tsingtao, 1915 Dardanelles
1915 May 25: Torpedoed and sunk by *U21* off Gaba Tepe in the Dardanelles (73 dead)

Triumph

Type: Light Aircraft Carrier
Class: 'Colossus' (1942)

History:
1943 January 27: Laid down by Hawthorn Leslie
1944 October 2: Launched
1946 April 9: Completed
1947-49 Mediterranean
1949 Far East
1950 Korea
1958-64 Converted to repair ship

Undaunted

Type: Armoured Cruiser
Class: 'Orlando' (1884)
Nomenclature: Fearless

History:
1885 April 23: Laid down by Palmer
1886 November 25: Launched
1890 September 18: Completed
1900 China
1907 April 9: Sold and broken up at Falmouth

Valiant

Type: Broadside Ship
Class: 'Hector' (1860)
Nomenclature: First used 1759

History:
1861 February 1: Laid down by Westwood & Baillie
1863 October 14: Launched; completion delayed by financial failure of builder and late delivery of armament
1868 September 15: Completed by Thames
1878 Particular Service Squadron
1884 July 20: Damaged in collision with ironclad *Defence* in Lough Swilly
1885 Paid off
1898 Depot ship, Portsmouth
1904 Renamed ***Indus IV***
1915 Kite balloon ship
1918 Renamed ***Valiant III***
1926 Floating oil tank
1956 Broken up at Zeebrugge

Valiant

Type: Dreadnought
Class: 'Queen Elizabeth' (1912)

History:
1913 January 31: Laid down by Fairfield
1914 November 4: Launched
1916 February 19: Completed
World War 1: 1914-18 Grand Fleet, Jutland
1924-29 Mediterranean
1929-30 Reconstructed at Portsmouth; bridge remodelled, two funnels trunked into one, bulges fitted
1933-37 Mediterranean
1937-39 Reconstructed at Devonport; re-engined and reboilered, tower superstructure and pole mast, rearmed
1939 December: Recommissioned
World War 2: 1940 Home Fleet, 1940-43 Mediterranean, 1944-45 Indian Ocean, Norwegian campaign, Oran, Malta convoys, Matapan, Crete, Sicily, Salerno, Sabang raid
1940 December 18: Bombarded Valona, Albania
1941 January 3: Bombarded Bardia, Libya
1941 May 22: Damaged by two aircraft bombs off Crete
1941 December 19: Severely damaged by Italian frogmen at Alexandria
1942 July: Repairs completed at Durban but with only two screws operating
1944 August 8: Severely damaged during drydocking operation at Trincomalee when drydock collapsed
1944 October 21: Ran aground at south end of Suez Canal while en route for Britain to repairs
1945 August: Repairs suspended
1948 March 19: Sold and broken up at Cairnryan & Troon

Vanguard

Type: Central Battery Ship
Class: 'Audacious' (1867)
Nomenclature: First used 1586

History:
1867 October 21: Laid down by Laird
1870 January 3: Launched
1870 September 28: Completed
1875 September 1: Rammed and sunk in collision by sister-ship *Iron Duke* in fog off Dublin (none dead)

Vanguard

Type: Dreadnought
Class: 'St Vincent' (1907)

History:
1908 April 2: Laid down by Vickers as ***Rodney;*** renamed ***Vanguard***
1909 February 22: Launched

***Vanguard* — Battleship, c1950.** *Foto Druppel*

1910 March 1: Completed
World War 1: 1914-17 Grand Fleet, Jutland
1917 July 9: Destroyed by internal explosion at Scapa Flow, probably caused by unstable cordite (804 dead)

Vanguard

Type: Battleship
Class: 'Vanguard' (1940)

History:
1941 October 2: Laid down by John Brown
1944 November 30: Launched
1946 April 25: Completed
1947 Royal Tour to South Africa
1947-48 Refit
1949 Mediterranean
1951 Refit
1954 Refit
1956 Reserve
1960 June 7: Decommissioned
1960 August 4: Sold and broken up at Faslane

Venerable

Type: Pre-dreadnought
Class: 'Formidable' (1897)
Nomenclature: First used 1784 (3rd Rate)

History:
1899 January 2: Laid down by Chatham
1899 November 2: Launched
1902 November 12: Completed
1902-08 Mediterranean
World War 1: 1914 Belgian coast operations; 1915 Dardanelles, 1915-18 Adriatic
1920 June 4: Sold and broken up in Germany

Venerable

Type: Light Aircraft Carrier
Class: 'Colossus' (1942)

History:
1942 December 3: Laid down by Cammell Laird
1943 December 30: Launched
1945 January 17: Completed
World War 2: 1945 Pacific Fleet
1945-47 Pacific
1948 April 1: Transferred to Netherlands, renamed ***Karel Doorman***

Vengeance

Type: Pre-dreadnought
Class: 'Canopus' (1896)
Nomenclature: First used 1758 (6th Rate)

History:
1898 August 23: Laid down by Vickers
1899 July 25: Launched
1902 April 8: Completed
1902-03 Mediterranean
1903-05 Far East
1908 June 13: In collision with merchant vessel *Benyon Head*
1909 February 28: Went aground in London River
1910 November 29: In collision with tender *Biter* in fog at Sheerness
World War 1: 1914 Channel, Cameroons; 1915 Mediterranean, Dardanelles; 1915-17 Egypt and East Indies
1918-19 Ordnance Depot, Devonport
1921 December 1: Sold and broken up at Dover

Vengeance

Type: Light Aircraft Carrier
Class: 'Colossus' (1942)

History:
1942 November 16: Laid down by Swan Hunter
1944 February 23: Launched
1945 January 15: Completed
World War 2: 1945 Pacific Fleet
1952 November 13: Loaned to Australia
1955 August 12: Returned to Royal Navy
1956 December 13: Sold to Brazil, renamed ***Minas Gerais***

Victoria

Type: Turret Ship
Class: 'Victoria' (1884)
Nomenclature: Queen Victoria (1819-1901)

History:
1885 April 23: Laid down by Armstrong as ***Renown***
1887 March 18: Renamed ***Victoria***
1887 April 9: Launched
1890 March 19: Completed
1890-92 Mediterranean
1892 January 29: Went aground at Snipe Point, Platea, Greece; refloated 4 February
1893 June 22: Sunk in collision when rammed by battleship *Camperdown* off coast of Syria. Flagship of Vice-Adm Sir George Tryon who was lost (358 dead)

Victorious

Type: Pre-dreadnought
Class: 'Majestic' (1893)
Nomenclature: First used 1785

History:
1894 May 28: Laid down by Chatham
1895 October 19: Launched
1897 June 8: Completed
1898 February 14: Went aground in the Suez Canal near Port Said
1898-1900 Far East
1900-05 Mediterranean

***Victorious* — Aircraft carrier, as reconstructed with angled flightdeck, underway in the Indian Ocean May 1961.** *P. A. Vicary*

1904 July 14: Damaged in collision with torpedo boat *No 113* in the Hamoaze
1909 Refit, fire control added
1910 June 6: Damaged by explosion in coal bunker at Barrow Deep
1912 July 12: In collision with battleship *Majestic*
World War 1: 1914 Guardship (Humber and Scapa)
1916-19 Base ship and repair ship, Scapa
1920 Renamed ***Indus II***
1922 December 19: Sold and broken up at Dover

Victorious

Type: Aircraft Carrier
Class: 'Illustrious' (1936)

History:
1937 May 4: Laid down by Vickers, Tyne
1939 September 14: Launched
1941 May 15: Completed
World War 2: 1941-43 Home Fleet, 1943 South Pacific, 1944 Home Fleet, 1944 Indian Ocean, 1945 Pacific Fleet; Norwegian raids 1941-44; 'Bismarck' operations, Arctic 1941-42, North Africa, Malta convoys, Sabang and Palembang raids, Okinawa, Japan raids 1945
1947 Training ship
1950-57 Reconstructed at Portsmouth; angled flightdeck, steam catapults, new radars, reboilered, rearmed
1960 Far East
1963 Refit
1967 November 11: Damaged by fire at Portsmouth while refitting
1969 July: Broken up at Faslane

***Warspite* — 'Queen Elizabeth' class battleship, after reconstruction in 1937.**

Warrior

Type: Broadside Ship
Class: 'Warrior' (1859)
Nomenclature: First used 1781

History:
1859 May 25: Laid down by Mare & Co
1860 December 29: Launched
1861 October 24: Completed
1864-67 Rearmed with MLR
1868 In collision with ironclad *Royal Oak*
1875-78 Refit, poop fitted
1878 Particular Service Squadron
1881-84 RNR training ship, Clyde
1884 Armoured cruiser, in reserve
1893 Refit, reboilered
1902 July: Torpedo depot ship, Portsmouth
1904 March: Renamed ***Vernon III***
1923 Renamed ***Warrior***
1929 March: Oil hulk
1945 Renamed ***C77***
1979 Acquired by the maritime trust for restoration and display at Portsmouth

Warrior

Type: Armoured Cruiser
Class: 'Warrior' (1903)

History:
1903 November 5: Laid down by Pembroke
1905 November 25: Launched
1907 January: Completed
1913-14 Mediterranean
World War 1: 1914 Adriatic, Egypt, 1914-16 Grand Fleet, Jutland
1916 May 31: Severely damaged by German warships at Jutland and foundered in tow the following day (71 dead)

Warrior

Type: Light Aircraft Carrier
Class: 'Colossus' (1942)

History:
1942 December 12: Laid down by Harland & Wolff
1944 May 20: Launched
1946 January 24: Completed and loaned to Canada
1948 May 21: Returned to Royal Navy
1952-53 Refit, lattice foremast fitted
1953-54 Far East
1955-56 Reconstructed: angled flightdeck
1957 Headquarters ship, Christmas Island nuclear experiments
1958 October 4: Sold to Argentina, renamed ***Independencia***

Warspite

Type: Armoured Cruiser
Class: 'Imperieuse' (1880)
Nomenclature: Elizabethan compound name, a term of defiance, first used 1596

History:
1881 October 25: Laid down by Chatham
1884 January 29: Launched; modified as *Imperieuse* prior to completion
1888 June: Completed
1890-93 Pacific
1899-1902 Pacific
1905 April 4: Sold and broken up at Preston

Warspite

Type: Dreadnought
Class: 'Queen Elizabeth' (1912)

History:
1912 October 31: Laid down by Devonport
1913 November 26: Launched
1915 March 19: Completed
World War 1: 1915-18 Grand Fleet, Jutland

1915 Damaged in collision with sister-ship *Barham*
1916 May 31: Severely damaged by 13 hits at Jutland (14 dead)
1916 August: Damaged in collision with sister-ship *Valiant*
1924-26 Reconstructed at Portsmouth; bridge remodelled, two funnels trunked into one, bulges fitted
1926-30 Mediterranean
1934-37 Reconstructed at Portsmouth; re-engined and reboilered, tower superstructure and pole mast
1937 June 29: Recommissioned
1937-39 Mediterranean
World War 2: 1939-42 Mediterranean, Home Fleet, 1942-43 Indian Ocean, 1943 Mediterranean, 1944 Home Fleet; Narvik, Norwegian campaign, Calabria, Malta convoys, Matapan, Crete, Sicily, Salerno, Normandy, Walcheren
1940 December 18: Bombarded Valona, Albania
1941 January 3: Bombarded Bardia, Libya
1941 May 22: Severely damaged by aircraft bomb at Crete, repaired at Bremerton
1943 September 16: Severely damaged by radio-controlled bombs off Salerno; only partially repaired
1944 June 13: Damaged by mine off Harwich
1945 Reserve
1946 July 12: Sold
1947 April 23: Went aground in Mounts Bay, Cornwall, while in tow en route to breaking up

Wivern

Type: Turret Ship
Class: 'Scorpion' (1863)
Nomenclature: Heraldic monster, a dragon with two legs

History:
1862 April: Laid down by Laird for Confederate government, was to be named ***Mississippi***; built under cover name *El Monassir*
1863 August 29: Launched
1863 October: Seized by British government, renamed ***Wivern***
1865 October 10: Completed
1867 Gun explosion
1880 Coast defence ship, Hong Kong
1904 Workshop and distilling ship, Hong Kong
1922 May: Sold at Hong Kong

Zealandia, see *New Zealand*

Zealous

Type: Central Battery Ship
Class: 'Zealous' (1863)
Nomenclature: First used 1785

History:
1859 October 26: Laid down by Pembroke as wood line-of-battle ship
1861 June: Reordered as ironclad
1864 March 7: Launched
1866 October 4: Completed
1866-72 Eastern Pacific
1872 Struck uncharted rock in Straits of Magellan
1873 Refit
1875 Paid off
1886 September: Sold

***Wivern* — Turret ship built for the Confederate navy, on completion 1865, with bulwarks down.** *IWM*

Greece

Although a small nation with a long seafaring tradition, Greece had only a small navy whose main purpose was defence against the Turks. Two small ironclads were built in 1868 and these remained the principal vessels until the 'Hydra' class of 1887.

After 1900 steps were taken to increase the size of the navy and in 1911 the armoured cruiser *Averof* was acquired. With these forces Greece defeated Turkey with its larger navy in 1912. Under the command of Adm Condouriotis the fleet seized the Aegean islands and fought several actions with Turkish ships. In 1912 the large battlecruiser *Salamis* was ordered in Germany and in 1914 two pre-dreadnoughts were purchased from the United States. A larger dreadnought was ordered in France in 1914 but neither it nor the *Salamis* was ever completed.

The former American battleships were no longer effective by the 1930s and only the *Averof* remained to serve in World War 2, although in a subsidiary capacity.

Class Details

'Vasilevs Georgios' (1865)

Central Battery Ship: *Vasilevs Georgios*
Displacement: 1,774tons
Dimensions: 213'3(oa) 200'3(pp)×33'2×20 [65(oa) 61(pp)×10.1×6.1]
Machinery: 2 screws, HSE (builder)
IHP 2,100 = 13.8knots
Endurance: 1,300/12
Armament: 2×229mm MLR, 2×145mm
1880: 2×210mm BL, 1×136mm
Armour: Belt 114-178mm, battery 152mm
Complement: 120
Class notes: Armoured corvette with hexagonal redoubt within which the guns could be moved, designed by Mackrow. Iron hull with schooner rig and one funnel

'Vasilissa Olga' (1866)

Central Battery Ship: *Vasilissa Olga*
Displacement: 2,030tons
Dimensions: 250(oa) 229'8(pp)×39×22'8 [76.2(oa) 70(pp)×11.9×6.9]
Machinery: 1 screw
IHP 1,950 = 10knots
Armament: 2×229mm MLR, 10×178mm 70pdr
1890: 4×170mm/25 BLR, 2×170mm/20 BLR, 4×75mm
Armour: Belt 100-150mm, battery 119mm
Class notes: Armoured corvette, one of two vessels ordered by Chile and purchased in 1868. Wood hull with armoured redoubt, bark rig and single funnel. Rearmed 1880 and reconstructed 1897 when sail rig was replaced by two military masts

'Hydra' Class (1887)

Barbette Ships: *Hydra, Psara, Spetsai* (see later photo)
Displacement: 4,885tons
Dimensions: 344'6(oa) 331(wl) 320(pp)×51'10×24 [105(oa) 100.9(wl) 97.5(pp)×15.8×7.3]
Machinery: 2 screws, HTE engines (F C Med), 4 cylindrical boilers; *1897:* 4 Belleville boilers
IHP 6,700 = 17.5knots
Armament: 2×270mm/36, 1×270mm/30, 5×150mm/45 (*Spetsai:* 4), 1×380mm TT, 2×355mm TT
Armour: Belt 120-300mm, forward battery 350mm, aft barbette 300mm, c/t 300mm
Complement: 440
Class notes: Small battleships with two guns in a forward barbette firing to port and starboard and one in turret aft. Two funnels and three military masts. Reconstructed 1897-1900 when fore and aft masts were modernised. Only *Psara* retained middle mast

'Averof' (1911)

Armoured Cruiser: *Georgios Averof* (see later photo)
Displacement: 9,960tons
Dimensions: 462'6(oa) 430(pp)×69×24'8 [141(oa) 131.1(pp)×21×7.5]
Machinery: 2 screws, VTE engines (Odero), 22 Belleville boilers
IHP 21,200 = 23knots
Endurance: 7,125/10
Armament: 4×235mm/45, 8×190mm/45, 16×76mm, 3×450mm TT
1927: 2×76mm AA added
1943: 4×40mm AA added
Armour: Belt 76-203mm, turrets 165mm, barbettes 203mm, c/t 178mm
Complement: 550
Class notes: Sister of Italian *Pisa*, built as a speculation and purchased by Greece. Main and secondary armament in turrets. Three funnels and two tripod masts. Modernised 1927, reboilered and heavy tripod foremast fitted

'Kilkis' Class (1914)

Pre-dreadnoughts: *Kilkis, Lemnos*
Displacement: 13,000tons
Dimensions: 382(oa) 375(wl)×77×24'8 [116.4(oa) 114.3(wl)×23.5×7.5]
Machinery: 2 screws, VTE engines, 8 B&W boilers
IHP 10,000 = 17knots
Endurance: 5,775/10
Armament: 4×305mm/45, 8×230mm/45, 8×178mm/45, 12×76mm/50, 2×533mm TT
Armour: Belt 102-229mm, turrets 203-305mm, barbettes 190-254mm, battery 178mm, deck 76mm, c/t 229mm
Complement: 801
Class notes: Small by contemporary standards. Purchased from US in 1914 and little changed in Greek service. Two funnels and two cagemasts

'Salamis' (1912)

Battlecruiser: *[Salamis]*
Displacement: 19,193tons
Dimensions: 570'9(wl)×82×25'3 [174(wl)×25×7.7]

Machinery: 3 screws, AEG-Curtis turbines (Vulcan), 18 Yarrow boilers
SHP 40,000 = 22knots
Endurance: 5,000/10
Armament: 8×356mm/45, 12×152mm/50, 12×75mm, 5×500mm TT
Armour: Belt 80-250mm, turrets 250m, c/t 300mm, deck 40-75mm
Class notes: Originally projected as a small battleship, redesigned as a battlecruiser with four twin turrets fore and aft similar to German designs. The 356mm (14") guns ordered from US could not be delivered after 1914 and were purchased by Britain being mounted in 'Abercrombie' class monitors. Incomplete hull refused by Greece in 1919 and it was never completed

'Vasilevs Konstantinos' (1913)

Dreadnought: *[Vasilevs Konstantinos]*
Displacement: 23,000tons
Dimensions: 551(oa) 541(pp)×91'6×29'6 [168(oa) 165(pp)×27.9×9]
Machinery: 4 screws, Parsons turbines
SHP 28,000 = 20knots
Endurance: 4,200/10
Armament: 10×340mm/45, 22×140mm, 12×76mm
Armour: Belt 180-300mm, turrets 320mm, deck 70mm
Complement: 1,100
Class notes: Would have been similar to French 'Provence' class but little work was done. Acquisition by France in 1914 as *Savoie* considered but contract was cancelled

Individual Ships

Georgios Averof

Type: Armoured Cruiser
Class: 'Averof' (1911)
Nomenclature: Georgios Averof, benefactor of the Greek navy, leaving it £300,000

***Hydra* — Barbette ship of 1887, with middle mast removed.** *Marius Bar*

History:
1907 Laid down by Orlando as a speculation
1910 March 12: Launched
1911 February: Acquired by Greece, named ***Georgios Averof***
1912 Completed
1912-13 Balkan Wars
1912 December 16 and 22: Slightly damaged in actions with the Turkish fleet off the Dardanelles
1925-27 Refit at La Seyne, new tripod mast fitted, reboilered
1935 Name shortened to ***Averof***
World War 2: Indian Ocean
1946 In reserve
1952 Naval museum and memorial at Poros

Hydra

Type: Barbette Ship
Class: 'Hydra' (1887)
Nomenclature: An island in the Aegean Sea, whose inhabitants were among the first to revolt against Turkey in 1821

History:
1887 Laid down by Loire
1889 May 15: Launched
1891 Completed
1900 Reconstructed by La Seyne
1912-13 Balkan Wars
1912 December 16: In action with Turkish warships off the Dardanelles
1920 Navigational training ship, Poros
1929 Broken up

Kilkis

Type: Pre-dreadnought
Class: 'Kilkis' (1914)
Nomenclature: Greek victory in Macedonia during Second Balkan War, 4 July 1913

History:
1904 May 12: Laid down by Cramp as US ***Mississippi***
1905 September 30: Launched
1908 February 1: Completed
1914 June 23: Purchased from US, renamed ***Kilkis***
1932 Cadet training ship
1937 Hulked, disarmed
1941 April 10: Hulk sunk by German aircraft at Salamis

Lemnos

Type: Pre-dreadnought
Class: 'Kilkis' (1914)
Nomenclature: Island in the Aegean, captured from Turkey 1912

History:
1904 May 12: Laid down by Cramp as US ***Idaho***
1905 December 9: Launched
1908 April 1: Completed
1914 June 23: Purchased from US, renamed ***Lemnos***
1937 Accommodation and AA ship
World War 2:
1941 April 23: Sunk by German and Italian aircraft at Salamis

Psara

Type: Barbette Ship
Class: 'Hydra' (1887)
Nomenclature: Island in the Aegean near Chios, captured by the Turks 1824 after a heroic resistance

Above:
***Lemnos* — Battleship, formerly US *Idaho*.** *IWM*

Above right:
***Averof* — Armoured cruiser, at Piraeus 1944.** *IWM*

Below right:
***Spetsai* — Barbette ship of 1887, as it appeared in 1901.** *Marius Bar*

History:
1888 Laid down at Graville
1890 February 20: Launched
1892 Completed
1897 Reconstructed at La Seyne
1912-13 Balkan Wars
1912 December 16: In action with Turkish warships off the Dardanelles
1920 Gunnery training ship, Poros
1932 Broken up

Salamis

Type: Battlecruiser
Class: 'Salamis' (1912)
Nomenclature: Greek naval victory over the Persians, 480BC

History:
1913 July 23: Laid down by Vulcan as US ***Vasilevs Georgios***
1913 Renamed ***Salamis***
1914 November 11: Launched

1914 December: Construction suspended
1919 Incomplete hull refused by Greek government
1932 Broken up incomplete

Spetsai

Type: Barbette Ship
Class: 'Hydra' (1887)
Nomenclature: Island near Corinth, which contributed a large squadron during the War of Independence 1821

History:
1887 Laid down at Graville
1889 October 26: Launched
1891 Completed
1900 Reconstructed at La Seyne
1912-13 Balkan Wars
1912 December 16: In action with Turkish warships off the Dardanelles
1919 Signals training ship, Poros
1929 Broken up

Vasilevs Georgios

Type: Central Battery Ship
Class: 'Vasilevs Georgios' (1865)
Nomenclature: George I, King of Greece (1845-1913)

History:
—— Laid down by Thames
1867 December 28: Launched
1869 November: Completed
1897 Refit, re-engined
1915 Broken up

Vasilevs Georgios, see Salamis

Vasilevs Konstantinos

Type: Dreadnought
Class: 'Vasilevs Konstantinos' (1913)
Nomenclature: Constantine I, King of Greece (1868-1923)

History:
1914 July 9: Laid down by Penhoët
1914 August: Renamed ***Vasilevs Georgios***
1914 August: Work suspended and broken up on slip

Vasilissa Olga

Type: Central Battery Ship
Class: 'Vasilissa Olga' (1866)
Nomenclature: Queen Olga (1851-1926), wife of King George I

History:
1868 Laid down by Stab Tecnico
1869 Launched
1871 Completed
1897 Refit; re-engined, rerigged with military masts; gunnery training ship
1925 Broken up

Italy

The Italian navy, founded in 1860 upon the unification of Italy, built a number of ironclads in foreign yards including two armoured frigates in the United States. The innovative turret ram *Affondatore* was ready just in time for the war with Austria in 1866 which ended with the disastrous Battle of Lissa. Two Italian ironclads were sunk and others damaged and the Italian commander was later court martialled

Italy was fortunate to have the capable naval engineer Benedetto Brin whose designs created much interest. The powerful *Duilio* and *Dandalo* with their huge guns inspired competitive vessels in other countries. Units of the highly successful 'Garibaldi' class of armoured cruisers were sold to Spain, Argentina and Japan. In 1903 the eminent Italian naval engineer Vittorio Cuniberti published an article advocating the all-big gun battleship, an idea which led to the construction of the *Dreadnought*. Nevertheless, the first Italian dreadnought was not laid down until 1909. The Italian fleet controlled the sea against the inferior Turkish fleet during the Balkan wars of 1911-12.

When Italy entered the war in 1915 the fleet included six dreadnoughts with four more under construction. The main fleet base was moved to Taranto away from Austrian aerial attacks, but the battle fleet did little during the war. The dreadnoughts under construction were not completed, and the postwar fleet by 1930 was reduced to the four remaining battleships. These underwent major reconstruction in the 1930s and new ships of the 'Vittorio Veneto' class were begun.

With these vessels the Italian navy was the major power when war began in the Mediterranean in 1940. The battle fleet was used in a defensive manner, especially after the British carrier strike on Taranto when three battleships were put out of action. When Italy surrended in 1943, all battleships in commission joined the Allies but the newest vessel, *Roma,* was sunk by German air attack. At the end of the war only two of the old reconstructed ships were retained and these were scrapped in 1956.

Italian development of aircraft carriers, at first deemed unnecessary because of the numerous shore bases available, was aborted by the surrender in 1943. The incomplete *Aquila* was captured by the Germans and the projected conversion of *Sparviero* was abandoned.

Class Details

'Terribile' Class (1860)

Broadside Ships: *Formidabile* (see also later photo), *Terribile*
Displacement: 2,725tons
Dimensions: 215'10(oa) 210(pp)×44'7×17'8 [65.8(oa) 64(pp)×13.6×5.4]
Machinery: 1 screw, single expansion engines (F C Med), 6 rectangular boilers
IHP 1,100 = 10knots
Armament: 16×164mm, 4×203mm 72pdr
1878: 8×203mm MLR
Formidabile, 1885: 4×152mm BLR, 8×119mm, 4 TT
Terribile, 1885: 8×203mm, 6×75mm, 4 TT
Armour: Belt 109mm, redoubt 100mm
Complement: 371
Class notes: Iron hull armoured corvettes with ram bow and schooner rig. Built for the Sardinian navy and originally designed as floating batteries. Reboilered 1873 and rearmed 1878

'Carignano' Class (1860)

Broadside Ships: *Conte Verde, Messina, Principe de Carignano*
Displacement: 3,930tons, 4,313f/l; *Carignano:* 3,501tons, 4,086f/l
Dimensions: 248'8(oa) 238'2(pp)×49'10×21'4 [75.8(oa) 72.6(pp)×15.2×6.5]
Machinery: 1 screw, single expansion engines (Penn; *Conte Verde:* Ansaldo), 6 cylindrical boilers (*Carignano:* 4)
IHP 1,900 = 12knots
Armament: 4×203mm 72pdr MLR, 18×164mm
Carignano: 10×203mm, 12×164mm
Conte Verde, 1870: 6×254mm, 1×203mm
Messina, 1870: 2×254mm, 4×203mm, 8×164mm
Carignano, 1870: 4×203mm, 16×164mm
Armour: Belt 120mm
Complement: 572
Class notes: *Carignano* and *Messina* converted to armoured vessels after construction began. Armoured frigates with full belt and ram bow, bark rig. *Conte Verde* laid down as ironclad but with incomplete protection

'Re d'Italia' Class (1861)

Broadside Ships: *Re d'Italia, Re di Portogallo*
Displacement: 5,700tons
Dimensions: 294(oa) 276'6(pp)×54'5×23'8 [89.6(oa) 84.3(pp)×16.6×7.2]
Machinery: 1 screw, single expansion engines, 6 boilers
IHP 1,800 = 12knots
Endurance: 3,120/12
Armament: *Re d'Italia:* 6×203mm, 30×164mm, 4×72pdr SB
Re di Portogallo: 2×254mm MLR, 26×164mm
Re di Portogallo, 1870: 14×164mm replaced by 6×203mm
Armour: Belt 114mm
Complement: 550
Class notes: Large armoured frigates built of green wood in the US, designed after French *Gloire*. Bark rig with single funnel

'Regina Maria Pia' Class (1861)

Broadside Ships: *Regina Maria Pia* (see later photo), *San Martino*
Displacement: 4,268tons, 4,600f/l
Dimensions: 266'4(oa) 247'9(pp)×49'9×20'8 [81.2(oa) 75.5(pp)×15.2×6.3]
Machinery: 1 screw, HSE engines (F C Med), 6 rectangular boilers
IHP 2,500 = 13knots
Endurance: 2,600/10
Armament: 4×203mm, 22×164mm
1892: 8×152mm, 5×119mm, 4×57mm, 3 TT
Armour: Belt 76-120mm, battery 108mm
Complement: 484
Class notes: Iron hulled armoured vessels with ram bow and

***Formidabile* — Armoured corvette of 1861, as reconstructed, c1880.**

schooner, later bark, rig. Rearmed in 1870s. Reconstructed 1889-92, rigging removed and replaced by two military masts, new funnel fitted, new engines and rearmed

'Castelfidardo' Class (1861)

Broadside Ships: *Ancona, Castelfidardo* (see later photo)
Displacement: 4,224tons, 4,600f/l
Dimensions: 268'9(oa) 249'6(pp)×47'10×20'6 [81.8(oa) 76(pp)×14.6×6.3]
Machinery: 1 screw, horizontal compound engines (*Castelfidardo:* Mazeline), 8 rectangular boilers
IHP 2,500 = 13knots
Endurance: 2,600/10
Armament: 4×203mm, 23×16mm
Later: 2×220mm MLR, 9×203mm MLR
1890: 8×152mm, 6×119mm, 4×57mm, 2 TT
Armour: Belt 76-108mm, battery 108mm, bulkhead 108mm
Complement: 484
Class notes: Similar to 'Maria Pia' class and similarly reconstructed

'Affondatore' (1862)

Turret Ship: *Affondatore*
Displacement: 4,376tons, 4,540f/l
Dimensions: 307'9(oa) 294(pp)×40×21'4 [93.8(oa) 89.6(pp)×12.2×6.5]
Machinery: 1 screw, horizontal compound engines (Maudslay), 8 boilers
IHP 2,700 = 12knots
Endurance: 1,650/10
Armament: 2×254mm MLR
1885: 6×119mm, 4×57mm and 4 TT added
Armour: Belt 102-127mm, turrets 127mm, deck 50mm
Complement: 309
Class notes: Armoured turret ram of iron hull with two single turrets fore and aft and two tall funnels. 26' ram bow. Rigging replaced by single mast following salvage, in 1867-73. Reconstructed 1885, new engines, superstructure and two military masts and additional guns fitted

'Roma' Class (1862)

Broadside Ship: *Roma*
Central Battery Ship: *Venezia*
Displacement: 5,814tons, 6,250f/l
Dimensions: 261'4(pp)×57'5×25 [79.6(pp)×17.5×7.6]
Machinery: 1 screw, single expansion engines (Maudslay), 6 cylindrical boilers
IHP 3,670 = 13knots
Endurance: 1,940/10
Armament: *Roma:* 5×254mm MLR, 12×203mm MLR
Roma, 1875: 11×254mm
Venezia: 18×254mm MLR
Venezia, 1875: 8×254mm, 1×220mm
Armour: Belt 150mm, battery (*Venezia*) 120mm
Complement: 550
Class notes: *Roma* completed as broadside ironclad but *Venezia*, delayed in construction, completed with central battery. Wood hulls with bark rig

'Palestro' Class (1863)

Coast Defence Ships: *Palestro, Varese*
Displacement: *Palestro:* 2,200tons, 2,600f/l; *Varese:* 2,000tons, 2,400f/l
Dimensions: 212'8(oa) 200(pp)×42'8×14'2 [64.8(oa) 61(pp)×13×4.3]
Machinery: 2 screws, compound engines (F C Med), 2 double boilers
IHP 930 = 8knots
Armament: 4×203mm MLR, 1×165mm
Armour: Belt 120mm, citadel 120mm
Complement: 250
Class notes: Iron hull armoured gunboats with ram bow, bark rig and single funnel forward

'Principe Amedeo' Class (1865)

Central Battery Ship: *Palestro* (see later photo), *Principe Amedeo*
Displacement: 5,854tons, 6,274f/l
Dimensions: 261'6(pp)×57'4×24'8 [79.7(pp)×17.5×7.5]

Machinery: 1 screw, compound engines (Maudslay), 6 cylindrical boilers
IHP 3,310 = 13knots
Endurance: 1,780/10
Armament: *Designed:* 12×160mm MLR
Completed: 1×280mm MLR, 6×250mm MLR
Later: 6×75mm and 2 TT added
Armour: Belt 127-225mm, battery 140mm, bulkhead 100mm, c/t 60mm
Complement: 548
Class notes: Wood hull armoured frigates with two redoubts differing in details. Bark rig

'Duilio' Class (1872)

Turret Ships: *Dandalo, Duilio*
Displacement: 11,138tons, 12,265f/l
Dimensions: 358'3(oa) 339'7(pp)×64'8×28'10 [109.2(oa) 103.5(pp)×19.7×8.8]
Machinery: 2 screws, vertical compound engines (*Dandalo:* Maudslay; *Duilio:* Penn), 10 rectangular boilers
IHP 7,710 = 15knots
Endurance: 3,760/10
Armament: 4×450mm/20 MLR, 3×120mm, 2×75mm, 8×57mm, 22×37mm
Dandalo, 1898: 4×254mm/40, 7×152mm, 5×119mm, 16×57mm, 4×457mm TT
Armour: Belt 550mm, turrets 430mm, barbettes 250mm, bulkheads 400mm, deck 50mm, c/t 350mm
Complement: 410
Class notes: Designed by Brin. Largest, fastest and most powerful battleships of their day with huge guns. Two twin turrets in an armoured citadel placed amidships en echelon between two funnels with single mast in between. Design changed for progressively larger guns during construction. The muzzle loading guns were so long they had to be loaded outside the turret. *Dandalo* modified with compound engines. Short thick belt amidships and protective underwater deck. Refit in 1895-1900. *Dandalo* received new engines, boiler and guns, single mast replaced by two military masts

'Italia' Class (1875)

Barbette Ships: *Italia, Lepanto*
Displacement: 13,898tons, 15,900f/l
Dimensions: 409'2(oa) 400'3(pp)×73'10×30'6 [124.7(oa) 122(pp)×22.5×9.3]
Machinery: 2 screws, vertical compound engines (Penn), 26 cylindrical boilers (*Lepanto:* 24)
Italia: IHP 12,000 = 17knots; *Lepanto:* IHP 16,000 = 18knots
Endurance: 8,700/10
Armament: 4×431mm/27, 8×152mm, 4×120mm, 2×75mm, 12×57mm, 4×355mm TT
Armour: Belt none, redoubt 480mm, funnel base 406mm, deck 76mm, deck 102mm, c/t 102mm
Complement: 756
Class notes: Designed by Brin, sacrificing armour for big guns and speed. High freeboard with no armour belt or citadel, protection being restricted to redoubt, ammunition hoists and submerged protective deck. Became obsolescent at time of completion and were more like big protected cruisers. *Italia* had six funnels, *Lepanto* four in two groups, with two barbettes en echelon amidships. *Italia* reconstructed 1905-06, four funnels and two masts fitted

Top left:
***Affondatore* — Turret ship, 1866, as built.** *P. A. Vicary*

Centre left:
***Roma* — Broadside ironclad completed in 1869.**
US Naval Historical Centre

Bottom left:
***Principe Amedeo* — Central battery ship of 1872.**

'Ruggiero di Lauria' Class (1880)

Barbette Ships: *Andrea Doria* (see later photo), *Francesco Morosini, Ruggiero di Lauria*
Displacement: 11,204tons, 11,726f/l
Dimensions: 347'5(oa) 328'2(pp)×65×27'6 [105.9(oa) 100(pp)×19.8×8.4]
Machinery: 2 screws, vertical compound engines (Hawthorne; *Lauria:* Maudslay), 8 cylindrical boilers
IHP 10,300 = 16knots
Endurance: 4,500/10
Armament: 4×431mm, 2×152mm, 4×120mm, 2×75mm, 10×57mm, 5×355mm TT
Armour: Belt 450mm, redoubt and barbettes 360mm, deck 76mm, bulkheads 355mm, c/t 250mm
Complement: 506
Class notes: Designed by Micheli as modified but smaller 'Duilio' type. Improve armour belt with guns in hooded barbettes amidships

'Re Umberto' Class (1883)

Barbette Ships: *Re Umberto* (see later photo), *Sardegna, Sicilia*
Displacement: *Re Umberto:* 13,300tons, 15,000f/l; *Sardegna:* 13,860tons, 15,800f/l; *Sicilia:* 13,400tons 15,100f/l
Dimensions: 429'6(oa) 410'4(pp)×77'5×29'6 [130.9(oa) 125.1(pp)×23.6×9]
Re Umberto: 418'8(oa) 400'3(pp)×76'9×29'6 [127.6(oa) 122(pp)×23.4×9]
Machinery: 2 screws, vertical compound engines (*Re Umberto:* Maudslay; *Sicilia*: Ansaldo); *Sardegna:* VTE engines (Hawthorn), 18 cylindrical boilers
IHP 19,500 = 18.6knots; *Sardegna:* IHP 21,000 = 20knots
Endurance: 6,000/10
Armament: 4×343mm/30, 8×152mm, 16×120mm, 20×57mm (*Re Umberto:* 16), 10×37mm, 5×450mm TT
Armour: Belt 100mm, turrets 100mm, barbettes 350mm, battery 102mm, deck 51-108mm, c/t 300mm
Complement: 752
Class notes: Designed by Brin with two twin barbettes placed fore and aft and three funnels, two side by side forward and one aft with single pole mast between. Side armour strengthened during construction. *Re Umberto* converted to assault ship 1918, guns and barbettes removed

'Marco Polo' (1888)

Armoured Cruiser: *Marco Polo*
Displacement: 4,580tons, 4,390f/l
Dimensions: 347'9(oa) 327'1(pp)×48'3×20'4 [106(oa) 99.7(pp)×14.7×6.2]
Machinery: 2 screws, VTE engines (Ansaldo), 4 cylindrical boilers
IHP 10,000 = 17knots
Endurance: 5,800/10
Armament: 6×152mm/40, 10×120mm/40, 9×57mm, 5×450mm TT
1910: 6×120mm, 3×57mm and 4 TT removed
Armour: Belt 100mm, gunshields 50mm, c/t 50mm
Complement: 394
Class notes: Originally designed as unarmoured cruiser of 'Piemonte' type but modified prior to launching. Lightly armed and armoured. Converted to troop transport 1917

'Pisani' Class (1891)

Armoured Cruisers: *Carlo Alberto, Vettor Pisani*
Displacement: *Carlo Alberto:* 6,832tons, 7,170f/l; *Vettor Pisani:* 6,720tons, 7,242f/l
Dimensions: 346'9(oa) 324'10(pp)×59'2×24'7 [105.7(oa) 99(pp)×18×7.5]
Machinery: 2 screws, VTE engines (*Vettor Pisani:* Hawthorn; *Carlo Alberto:* Ansaldo), 8 cylindrical boilers
IHP 13,000 = 19knots
Endurance: 5,400/10
Armament: 12×152mm/40, 6×120mm/40, 10×57mm, 5×450mm TT
Armour: Belt 110-150mm, deck 40mm, gun shields 114mm, c/t 150mm
Complement: 500
Class notes: More heavily armoured and more guns than *Marco Polo* but lacking in heavy guns. Two funnels and two military masts but only foremast in *Pisani. Carlo Alberto* converted to troop transport 1917

'Emanuele Filiberto' Class (1892)

Barbette Ships: *Ammiraglio di Saint Bon, Emanuele Filiberto*
Displacement: 9,800tons, 10,250f/l
Dimensions: 366'10(oa) 344'6(pp)×69'2×24'7 [111.8(oa) 105(pp)×21.1×7.5]
Machinery: 2 screws, VTE engines (*Saint Bon:* Ansaldo; *Emanuele Filiberto:* Hawthorn), 12 cylindrical boilers
IHP 14,000 = 18knots
Endurance: 7,000/10
Armament: 4×254mm/40, 8×152mm/40, 8×120mm, 6×76mm (*Saint Bon:* 8), 8×47mm (*Saint Bon:* 2), 4×450mm TT
Armour: Belt 100-250mm, barbettes 250mm, battery 150mm, deck 70mm, c/t 250mm
Complement: 531
Class notes: Designed by G. Pullino as reaction against previous large battleships with 10" guns and armour belt similar to foreign contemporaries. Two twin turrets fore and aft, low freeboard, two widely separated funnels and single mast. *St Bon* had shorter funnels

'Garibaldi' Class (1894-1899)

Armoured Cruisers: [*Giuseppe Garibaldi* (1), *Giuseppe Garibaldi* (2), *Giuseppe Garibaldi* (3), *Giuseppe Garibaldi* (4), *Francesco Ferruccio, Varese* (1), *Varese* (2), *Varese* (3)] (see later photo)
Displacement: 7,350tons, 8,100f/l
Dimensions: 366'6(oa) 343'10(pp)×59'8×24 [111.7(oa) 104.8(pp)×18.2×7.3]
Machinery: 2 screws, VTE engines (*Francesco Ferruccio:* Hawthorn; *Giuseppe Garibaldi:* Ansaldo; *Varese:* Orlando), 24 Niclausse boilers (*Varese:* Belleville)
IHP 13,500 = 20knots
Endurance: 5,400/10
Armament: 1×254mm/40, 2×203mm/45, 14×152mm/40, 10×76mm, 6×47mm, 4×450mm TT
1916: 12×152mm removed, 5×14pdr AA added
Armour: Belt 90-120mm, turrets 120mm, deck 38mm, c/t 120mm
Complement: 549
Class notes: Very successful class, four sold to Argentina and one to Spain prior to completion. Two similar vessels ordered by Argentina were sold to Japan. Final three vessels completed for Italy. Well armed, well protected and fast with turrets fore and aft, two funnels with mast between

'Regina Margherita' Class (1898)

Pre-dreadnoughts: *Benedetto Brin, Regina Margherita*
Displacement: 13,427tons, 14,574f/l
Dimensions: 454'9(oa) 426'6(pp)×78×28'2 [138.6(oa) 130(pp)×23.8×8.6]
Machinery: 2 screws, VTE engines (*Benedetto Brin:* Hawthorn; *Regina Margherita:* Ansaldo), 28 Niclausse boilers (*Benedetto Brin:* Belleville)
IHP 20,000 = 20knots
Endurance: 10,000/10
Armament: 4×305mm/40, 4×203mm/45, 12×152mm/40, 20×76mm, 2×47mm, 4×450mm TT
Armour: Belt 50-120mm, turrets 120mm, deck 38mm, c/t 120mm casemates 150mm
Complement: 797
Class notes: Design by Brin, modified by Micheli with higher freeboard, protection sacrificed for speed. Three funnels, two forward side by side and one on centreline

'Vittorio Emanuele' Class (1901-1902)

Pre-dreadnoughts: *Napoli, Roma* (see later photo), *Regina Elena, Vittorio Emanuele*
Displacement: *Vittorio Emanuele:* 13,035tons 14,192f/l; *Regina Elena:* 12,691tons, 13,804f/l; *Napoli:* 12,833tons 14,112f/l; *Roma:* 12,791tons, 13,950f/l
Dimensions: 474'4(oa) 435(pp)×73'6×26'9 [144.6(oa) 132.6(pp)×22.4×8]
Machinery: 2 screws, VTE engines (*Vittorio Emanuele:* Orlando; *Regina Elena:* Odero; *Napoli:* Hawthorn, *Roma:* Ansaldo), 28 Belleville boilers (*Napoli:* 22 B&W; *Roma:* 18 B&W)
IHP 19,000 = 21knots; *Napoli* and *Roma:* IHP 20,000 = 22knots
Endurance: 10,000/10
Armament: 2×305mm/40, 12×203mm/45, 16×76mm (*Napoli* and *Roma:* 24), 10×47mm (*Napoli* and *Roma:* 2), 2×450mm TT
Armour: Belt 100-250mm, turrets 200mm, secondary turrets 150mm, battery 75mm, deck 38mm, c/t 250mm
Complement: 700
Class notes: An innovative design but completed long after *Dreadnought.* Designed by Cuniberti with main battery and protection sacrificed for speed. Considered forerunner of the battlecruiser. Two single turrets and three funnels with two pole masts. *Napoli* and *Roma* had shorter funnels and only pole mainmast

'Pisa' Class (1904)

Armoured Cruisers: *Amalfi, Pisa*
Displacement: 10,600tons
Dimensions: 461(oa) 426'6(pp)×68'10×23 [140.5(oa) 130(pp)×21×7]

Top right:
***Duilio* — Turret ship of 1876, with turrets in armoured citadel amidships.** *Aldo Fraccaroli*

Centre right:
***Ruggiero di Lauria* — Barbette ship of 1884, with main battery amidships.** *Marius Bar*

Bottom right:
***Sicilia* — Barbette ship of 1891, c1901.** *Aldo Fraccaroli*

Top left:
***Marco Polo* — Armoured cruiser.**

Top centre:
***Vettor Pisani* — Armoured cruiser of 1895, c1908.**
Aldo Fraccaroli

Top right:
***Emanuele Filiberto* — Battleship of 1897, as it appeared in 1910.** *Aldo Fraccaroli*

Far left:
***Giuseppe Garibaldi* — Armoured cruiser, 1910.**
Aldo Fraccaroli

Left:
***Vittorio Emanuele* — Battleship of 1904, shown in 1917 with wartime additions.** *IWM*

Bottom left:
***Pisa* — Armoured cruiser of 1907.**

Bottom centre:
***San Marco* — Armoured cruiser of 1909.**

Bottom right:
***Leonardo da Vinci* — Dreadnought of 1911, destroyed by an explosion 1916.** *Aldo Fraccaroli*

Machinery: 2 screws, VTE engines (builders), 22 Belleville boilers
IHP 20,000 = 22.5knots
Endurance: 2,500/12
Armament: 4×254mm/45, 8×190mm/45, 16×14pdr, 8×47mm, 3×450mm TT
Armour: Belt 90-200mm, turrets 200mm, citadel 178mm, deck 50mm, c/t 178mm
Complement: 684
Class notes: Designed by G. Orlando and classified as second class battleships. Three large funnels and pole mainmasts. A similar vessel was built for Greece. Pole foremast fitted in Pisa 1917

'San Giorgio' Class (1904)

Armoured Cruisers: *San Giorgio, San Marco* (see later photo)
Displacement: *San Giorgio:* 10,170tons 11,300f/l; *San Marco:* 10,320tons, 11,900f/l
Dimensions: 462'4(oa) 429'9(pp)×68'10×24 [140.9(oa) 131(pp)×21×7.3]
Machinery: *San Marco:* 4 screws, Parsons turbines (Ansaldo), 14 B&W boilers
SHP 23,000 = 23knots
San Giorgio: 2 screws, VTE engines (Ansaldo), 14 Blechynden boilers
IHP 19,500 = 22.5knots
Endurance: *San Marco:* 4,800/10; *San Giorgio:* 6,270/10
Armament: 4×254/45, 8×190mm/45, 20×75mm (*San Giorgio:* 18) 3×450mm TT
1919: 10×76mm replaced by 6×76mm AA, 1 TT removed
Armour: Belt 60-200mm, turrets 200mm, bulkheads 100mm, c/t 250mm, citadel 178mm
Complement: 700
Class notes: Designed by Masdea. Two pairs of widely separated funnels and single pole mast forward of second pair, with guns arranged similar to 'Pisa' class. Machinery differed. Foremast mounted 1917

'Dante Alighieri' (1907)

Dreadnought: *Dante Alighieri*
Displacement: 19,500tons, 21,800f/l
Dimensions: 551'6(oa) 541'2(wl) 519'8(pp)×87'3×30'2 [168.1(oa) 165(wl) 158.4(pp)×26.6×9.2]
Machinery: 4 screws, Parsons turbines (Ansaldo), 23 Blechynden boilers
SHP 32,200 = 23knots
Endurance: 5,000/10
Armament: 12×305mm/46, 20×120mm/50, 16×76mm/40, 3×450mm TT
1917: 2×76mm removed, 6×76mm AA added
Armour: Belt 120-250mm, turrets 280mm, barbettes 230mm, c/t 203mm
Complement: 987
Class notes: First Italian dreadnought, designed by Masdea. First battleship with main armament in triple turrets with all on centreline to gain maximum broadside fire. Secondary armament partially in turrets. Two groups of funnels and mast widely separated by the second and third turrets amidships. Foremast replaced by tripod and moved forward 1923

'Cavour' Class (1909)

Dreadnoughts: *Conte di Cavour, Giulio Cesare* (see later photo), *Leonardo da Vinci*
Displacement: 23,088tons, 25,086f/l
Dimensions: 577'9(oa) 554'6(pp)×91'10×30'9 [176.1(oa) 169(pp)×28×9.4]
Machinery: 4 screws, Parsons turbines (*Cavour:* Orlando; *Cesare:* Odero; *Leonardo da Vinci,* Ansaldo), 20 Blechynden boilers (*Cesare:* 24 B&W)
IHP 31,000=21.5knots
Endurance: 4,800/10
Armament: 13×305mm/46, 18×120mm/50, 13×76mm/50 (*Leonardo da Vinci:* 14), 6×76mm/40, 3×450mm TT
1917: 3×76mm replaced by 6×76mm AA
Armour: Belt 127-250mm, turrets 280mm, barbettes 240mm, deck 170mm, c/t 280mm
Complement: 1,000

As reconstructed 1933:

Displacement: 28,800tons, 29,100f/l
Dimensions: 611'6(oa) 554'6(pp)×91'9×34'2 [186.4(oa) 169(pp)×28×10.4]
Machinery: 2 screws, Belluzzo geared turbines, 8 3-drum boilers
SHP 75,000 = 27knots
Endurance: 3,100/20
Armament: 10×320mm/44, 12×120mm/50, 8×100mm/47, 8×37mm
Armour: Belt 250mm, turrets 280mm, deck 135mm, c/t 260mm
Complement: 1,236
Class notes: Designed by Masdea with main armament in

three triple turrets and two twin superfiring turrets. Two large funnels and two tripod masts with fore funnel forward of foremast were separated by the amidships turret. *Cavour* had new tripod foremast fitted 1925.
Cavour and *Cesare* totally reconstructed 1933-37, new engines and boilers fitted, new main battery and AA armament, centre turret removed, new superstructure and funnel arrangement, hull lengthened, number of propellers reduced to two

'Duilio' Class (1911)

Dreadnoughts: *Andrea Doria* (see also later photo), *Caio Duilio*
Displacement: 22,964tons, 25,200f/l
Dimensions: 577'9(oa) 554'6(pp)×91'10×31'2 [176.1(oa) 169(pp)×28×9.5]
Machinery: 4 screws, Parsons turbines (Ansaldo), 20 Yarrow boilers
SHP 32,000 = 21.5knots
Endurance: 4,800/10
Armament: 13×305mm/46, 16×152mm/45, 13×76mm/45, 6×76mm/40 AA, 2×450mm TT
Armour: Belt 127-235mm, turrets 280mm, barbettes 240mm, deck 170mm, battery 170mm, c/t 280mm
Complement: 1,000

As reconstructed 1937:

Displacement: 28,700tons, 29,000f/l
Dimensions: 613'2(oa) 554'6(wl)×91'10×29'9 [186.9(oa) 169(pp)×28×9.1]
Machinery: 2 screws, Belluzzo geared turbines, 8 3-drum boilers
SHP 85,000 = 27knots
Endurance: 4,250/12
Armament: 10×320mm/44, 12×135mm/45, 10×90mm/50, 19×37mm
Class notes: Modified 'Cavour' class with 6" secondary armament. Both tripod masts placed forward of each funnel. Both reconstructed 1937-40 similar to 'Cavour' class, hull lengthened, new engines and boilers, new main battery and AA armament, centre turret removed, new superstructure and funnel arrangement, number of propellers reduced to two

'Caracciolo' Class (1914)

Dreadnoughts: *[Cristoforo Colombo, Francesco Caracciolo, Francesco Morosini, Marcantonio Colonna]*

***Conte de Cavour* — Battleship, after reconstruction, May 1938. Sister *Giulio Cesare* at right.** *Aldo Fraccaroli*

Displacement: 32,800tons, 34,000f/l
Dimensions: 695′10(oa) 661′5(pp)×97′2×31′2 [212.1(oa) 201.6(pp)×29.6×9.5]
Machinery: 4 screws, Parsons geared turbines, 20 Yarrow boilers
SHP 105,000 = 28knots
Endurance: 8,000/10
Armament: 8×381mm/40, 12×152mm/45, 12×40mm AA
Armour: Belt 150-300mm, turrets 150-400mm, barbettes 300mm, deck 35mm, casemates 150mm, c/t 340mm
Class notes: Super dreadnoughts designed by Ferrati with flush-decked hull and 15″ guns. Construction suspended 1915 and only *Caracciolo* was launched. None was completed

Above:
***Andrea Doria* — Battleship built in 1913, as reconstructed 1940.**

Right:
***Caracciolo* — Dreadnought, never completed, being launched 12 May 1920.** *Aldo Fraccaroli*

Below right:
***Roma* — Battleship of 1940, sunk by German bombs in 1943, shortly after completion.** *Aldo Fraccaroli*

'Vittorio Veneto' Class (1934-1938)

Battleships: *[Impero]* (see later photo), *Littorio, Roma, Vittorio Veneto* (see later photo)
Displacement: *Vittorio Veneto:* 41,167tons, 45,752f/l; *Littorio:* 41,377tons, 45,963f/l; *Roma:* 41,650tons, 46,215f/l
Dimensions: 780′2(oa) 762′6(wl) 736′7(pp)×107′10×34′5 [237.8(oa) 232.4(wl) 224.5(pp)×32.9×10.5] *Roma* and *Impero:* 789′9 [240.7(oa)]
Machinery: 4 screws, Belluzzo geared turbines, 8 Yarrow boilers
SHP 140,000 = 30knots
Endurance: 4,580/16
Armament: 9×381mm/50, 12×152mm/55, 12×90mm/50, 20×37mm AA
Armour: Belt 60-350mm, turrets 345-380mm, barbettes 345mm, deck 200mm, c/t 254mm
Complement: 1,920
Class notes: Designed by Pugliese as reply to French 'Dunkerque' class. Three triple turrets and secondary armament in four triple turrets. Good protection and fast. *Impero* was not completed. The bows of *Roma* and *Impero* differed from first two ships

'Aquila' (1941)

Aircraft Carrier: *[Aquila]* (see later photo)
Displacement: 23,350tons, 27,600f/l
Dimensions: 759′3(oa) 680′2(wl) 664(pp)×95′2×24′3 [231.4(oa) 207.3(wl) 202.4(pp)×29×7.4]
Machinery: 4 screws, geared turbines, 8 boilers
SHP 140,000 = 31knots
Endurance: 4,150/18
Aircraft: 51
Armament: 8×135mm/45 AA, 12×65mm AA
Complement: 1,410
Class notes: Converted from passenger liner *Roma*. Turbines taken from incomplete cruisers *Silla* and *Emilio*. Almost complete when Italy surrendered and fell into German hands. Conversion never completed

'Sparviero' (1942)

Aircraft Carrier: *[Sparviero]*
Class notes: Planned conversion from passenger liner *Augustus*, never completed because of seizure by Germans 1943

Individual Ships

Affondatore

Type: Turret Ship
Class: 'Affondatore' (1862)
Nomenclature: Sinker

History:
1863 April 11: Laid down by Harrison, Millwall
1865 November 3: Launched
1866 June 6: Commissioned
1866 June 20: Sailed incomplete from England
1866 July 20: Second flagship of Adm Persano at the Battle of Lissa, severely damaged by gunfire
1866 August 6: Foundered, as a result of previous damage, in storm in Ancona harbour
1866 October 25: Refloated, reconstructed at Genoa, single mast replaced rigging
1883-85 Reconstructed at La Spezia; superstructure and military masts added, armament increased
1891 Torpedo training ship
1904 Guardship, Venice
1907 Floating magazine, Taranto
1907 October 11: Stricken

Amalfi

Type: Armoured Cruiser
Class: 'Pisa' (1904)
Nomenclature: Town in Campania, former independent city-state

History:
1905 July 24: Laid down by Odero
1908 May 5: Launched
1909 September 1: Completed
1911 Operations off Libya
1912 Aegean Sea
1915 July 7: Torpedoed and sunk by Austrian submarine *U26* (German *UB14*) in northern Adriatic (67 dead)

Ammiraglio di Saint Bon

Type: Pre-dreadnought
Class: 'Emanuele Filiberto' (1892)
Nomenclature: Count Simone Arturo Pacoret di Saint Bon (1823-1892), admiral

History:
1894 July 18: Laid down at Venice
1897 April 29: Launched
1901 February 1: Commissioned
1912 Occupation of Tripoli
1912 Aegean Sea, occupation of Rhodes
World War 1: Adriatic
1920 June 18: Stricken and broken up

Ancona

Type: Broadside Ship
Class: 'Castelfidardo' (1861)
Nomenclature: Seaport on the Adriatic, scene of 1860 victory over Papal troops

History:
1862 August 11: Laid down by Arman
1864 October 17: Launched
1866 April: Completed
1866 July 20: Slightly damaged at Battle of Lissa
1870 Liberation of Rome
1876 Refit
1884 Red Sea, occupation of Massawa, Eritrea
1886 Operations at Crete
1892 Reconstructed
1900 Torpedo school ship
1903 August 30: Stricken, munitions hulk
1906 Broken up

Andrea Doria

Type: Barbette Ship
Class: 'Ruggiero di Lauria' (1880)
Nomenclature: Andrea Doria, Prince of Melfi (1468-1560), Genoese admiral and statesman

History:
1882 January 7: Laid down at La Spezia
1885 November 21: Launched
1891 July 1: Completed
1898 Refit
1900 June 27: Went aground at Taranto
1901 June 28: Went aground at Gallipoli
1903 Refit
1907 Artificers' training ship, Venice
1911 May 25: Stricken, floating oil storage hulk
1915 Converted to floating battery *GR104*, at Brindisi
1929 Broken up

Andrea Doria

Type: Dreadnought
Class: 'Duilio' (1911)

History:
1912 March 24: Laid down at La Spezia
1913 March 30: Launched
1916 March 13: Completed
World War 1: Southern Adriatic
1919 July: Levant
1919 October: Black Sea
1923 August: Corfu operation
1937 April: Reconstruction by Adriatico
1940 October 26: Recommissioned
World War 2: 1941-42 Mediterranean actions and convoy battles
1941 December 17: First Battle of Sirte
1942 March: Reserve
1943 September 9: Left Taranto on Italian surrender for internment at Malta
1944 June: Training ship
1949 Reactivated
1956 November 1: Stricken
1961 Broken up at La Spezia

Aquila

Type: Aircraft Carrier
Class: 'Aquila' (1941)
Nomenclature: Eagle

History:
1925 Laid down by Ansaldo as passenger liner ***Roma***
1926 February 26: Launched
1941 July: Conversion to aircraft carrier by Ansaldo commenced. Renamed ***Aquila***
1943 September: Seized by Germans when almost completed at Genoa on Italian surrender

1945 April 19: Severely damaged by Italian human torpedoes at Genoa to prevent ship being used by Germans as a blockship
1945 April 24: Found sunk at Genoa
1946 Refloated
1951 Broken up at La Spezia

Top:
***Andrea Doria* — Barbette ship of 1885, shown c1895.** *IWM*

Above:
***Andrea Doria* — Dreadnought of 1913, as it appeared in 1919.** *IWM*

Benedetto Brin

Type: Pre-dreadnought
Class: 'Regina Margherita' (1898)
Nomenclature: Benedetto Brin (1833-1898), navy minister and noted naval designer

History:
1899 January 30: Laid down at Castellammare
1901 November 7: Launched
1905 September 1: Completed
1911 Operations off Tripoli
1912 Aegean Sea
1915 September 27: Destroyed by magazine explosion at Brindisi caused either by sabotage or unstable cordite (421 dead)

Caio Duilio

Type: Dreadnought
Class: 'Duilio' (1911)
Nomenclature: See *Duilio*

History:
1912 February 24: Laid down at Castellammare
1913 April 24: Launched
1915 May 10: Completed
World War 1: Southern Adriatic
1919 April: Levant
1919 July: Black Sea
1923 Corfu operation
1925 April 8: Damaged by explosion in 'Q' turret at La Spezia

***Aquila* — Incomplete aircraft carrier, as it appeared in June 1946. Note bulges added to hull.** *Aldo Fraccaroli*

1937 April 1: Reconstructed at Tirreno
1940 July 15: Recommissioned
World War 2: 1940 Mediterranean actions, Taranto, 1942 Mediterranean convoy actions
1940 November 12: Damaged by aircraft torpedo at Taranto and beached
1942 March: Reserve
1943 September 9: Left Taranto on Italian surrender for internment at Malta
1944 June: Training ship
1956 September 15: Stricken
1957 Broken up at La Spezia

Carlo Alberto

Type: Armoured Cruiser
Class: 'Pisani' (1891)
Nomenclature: Charles Albert, King of Sardinia (1798-1849), leader in the war against Austria 1848

History:
1892 February 1: Laid down at La Spezia
1896 September 23: Launched
1898 May 1: Completed
1900-01 Far East
1901 Experimental vessel for wireless telegraphy
1902-03 Venezuelan blockade
1911 Operations off Tripoli
1917 Converted to troop transport
1918 April 4: Renamed ***Zenson***
1920 June 12: Stricken

Castelfidardo

Type: Broadside Ship
Class: 'Castelfidardo' (1861)
Nomenclature: Victory of Piedmont over the Papal army, 18 September 1860, which led to the unification of Italy

History:
1862 July 27: Laid down by Gouin
1863 August 1: Launched
1864 May: Completed
1866 July 20: Battle of Lissa
1869 November 10: Damaged by boiler explosion at Brindisi
1870 Liberation of Rome
1871 Refit
1881 Refit
1881 Operations at Tunis
1884-85 Red Sea
1889-90 Reconstructed
1900 Torpedo school ship, La Spezia
1910 December 4: Stricken and broken up

Conte de Cavour

Type: Dreadnought
Class: 'Cavour' (1909)
Nomenclature: Count Camillo Benso di Cavour (1810-1861), statesman and architect of the unification of Italy

History:
1910 August 10: Laid down at La Spezia
1911 August 10: Launched
1915 April 1: Completed
World War 1: Southern Adriatic
1919 July: Cruise to US
1923 August: Corfu operation
1925 Refit, new forward tripod mast
1933 Reconstructed by Adriatico
1937 June 1: Recommissioned
World War 2: 1940 Mediterranean actions
1940 November 12: Sunk by aerial torpedoes during British carrier attack on Taranto
1941 July: Refloated
1941 December 22: Towed to Trieste for repairs
1943 September 10: Seized by Germans at Trieste while still under repair
1945 February 17: Sunk by aircraft bombs at Trieste
1947 February 27: Stricken

Conte Verde

Type: Broadside Ship
Class: 'Carignano' (1860)

***Castelfidardo* — Broadside ship of 1863, after reconstruction.**

Nomenclature: Green Count, sobriquet of Amedeo VI, Count of Savoy (1334-1383), who favoured wearing green costumes

History:
1863 March 2: Laid down at San Rocco
1867 July 29: Launched
1871 December: Completed
1878 Ammunition storeship
1880 May 27: Stricken
1898 Broken up

Cristoforo Colombo

Type: Dreadnought
Class: 'Caracciolo' (1914)
Nomenclature: Christopher Columbus (1451-1506), discoverer of America

History:
1915 March 14: Laid down by Ansaldo
1915 Construction cancelled when 5.5% complete

Dandalo

Type: Turret Ship
Class: 'Duilio' (1872)
Nomenclature: Enrico Dandalo (1108-1205), Doge of Venice, who captured Constantinople in the Fourth Crusade

History:
1873 January 8: Laid down at La Spezia
1878 July 10: Launched
1882 April 11: Completed
1895-98 Reconstructed; re-engined, reboilered, new armament
1913 Guardship, Tobruk
World War 1: Local defence ship, Brindisi and Venice
1920 January 23: Stricken

Dante Alighieri

Type: Dreadnought
Class: 'Dante Alighieri' (1907)
Nomenclature: Dante Alighieri (1265-1321), poet

History:
1909 June 6: Laid down at Castellammare
1910 August 20: Launched
1913 January 15: Completed
World War 1: Southern Adriatic (flag); inactive
1923 Refit; tripod foremast fitted and moved forward
1928 November 1: Stricken

Duilio

Type: Turret Ship
Class: 'Duilio' (1872)
Nomenclature: Gaius Duilius (200 BC), Roman general who helped establish Roman sea power

History:
1873 April 24: Laid down at Castellammare
1876 May 8: Launched
1880 January 6: Completed
1880 March 6: 450mm gun in after turret burst during firing trial
1887 Refit
1909 June 27: Stricken; floating tank (*GM40*)

Emanuele Filiberto

Type: Pre-dreadnought
Class: 'Emanuele Filiberto' (1892)
Nomenclature: Emanuel Philibert, Duke of Savoy (1528-1580), allied with Spain against France, winning the battle of Saint Quentin, 1557

History:
1893 October 5: Laid down at Castellammare
1897 September 29: Launched
1901 September 6: Commissioned
1902 April 16: Completed
1911 Operations at Tripoli

***Formidabile* — Broadside ship, the first Italian ironclad.**

1912 Aegean Sea, occupation of Rhodes
World War 1: Adriatic
1920 March 29: Stricken

Formidabile

Type: Broadside Ship
Class: 'Terribile' (1860)
Nomenclature: Formidable

History:
1860 December: Laid down at La Seyne
1861 October 1: Launched
1862 May: Completed
1866 July 17: Damaged by shore batteries at Porto San Giorgio, Lissa (three dead)
1870 September: Liberation of Rome
1871-75 Decommissioned, refit
1878 Refit
1887 Gunnery and torpedo school ship, La Spezia
1904 July 25: Stricken

Francesco Caracciolo

Type: Dreadnought
Class: 'Caracciolo' (1914)
Nomenclature: Prince Francesco di Caracciolo (1752-1799), admiral in the service of King Ferdinand IV of Naples, hanged on Nelson's orders after surrendering

History:
1914 October 12: Laid down at Castellammare
1916 March: Construction suspended
1920 May 12: Launched
1920 October 25: Sold for conversion to passenger liner; not converted and broken up

Francesco Ferruccio

Type: Armoured Cruiser
Class: 'Garibaldi' (1894)
Nomenclature: Francesco Ferruccio (1489-1530), famous Florentine soldier

History:
1899 September 18: Laid down at Venice
1902 April 23: Launched
1905 September 1: Completed
1911 Operations off Tripoli
1912 February 24: Bombardment of Beirut, sank Turkish destroyer *Angora*
World War 1: 1915 Levant, 1916 southern Adriatic
1923 January 4: Training ship
1930 April 1: Stricken

Francesco Morosini

Type: Barbette Ship
Class: 'Ruggiero di Lauria' (1880)
Nomenclature: Francesco Morosini (1618-1694), Doge of Venice, military and naval commander

History:
1881 December 4: Laid down at Venice
1885 July 30: Launched
1889 April 21: Completed
1909 August 3: Stricken
1909 September 15: Sunk as torpedo target in La Spezia harbour

Francesco Morosini

Type: Dreadnought
Class: 'Caracciolo' (1914)

History:
1915 June 27: Laid down by Orlando
1915 Construction cancelled

Giulio Cesare

Type: Dreadnought
Class: 'Cavour' (1909)
Nomenclature: Gaius Julius Caesar (100 BC- 44 BC), Roman general and statesman

History:
1910 June 24: Laid down by Ansaldo
1911 October 15: Launched
1914 May 14: Completed
World War 1: Southern Adriatic
1923 Corfu operation
1925 Refit, new forward tripod mast
1933 October: Reconstructed by Tirreno
1937 October 1: Recommissioned

***Giulio Cesare* — Battleship, following complete reconstruction, at Malta 1938.** *A. & J. Pavia*

World War 2: 1940-41 Mediterranean actions with British fleet
1940 July 9: Hit in action with British battleship *Warspite* in Ionian Sea
1941 January 8: Damaged by near miss in air raid at Naples
1941 December 17: First Battle of Sirte
1943 January: Training and accommodation ship, Pola
1943 September 9: Left Pola for Taranto on Italian surrender, arrived at Malta for internment September 12 1943
1948 December 15: Stricken
1949 February 3: Transferred to Soviet Union under peace treaty, renamed ***Novorossisk***

Giuseppe Garibaldi (1)

Type: Armoured Cruiser
Class: 'Garibaldi' (1894)
Nomenclature: Giuseppe Garibaldi (1807-1882), Italian patriot

History:
1894 Laid down by Ansaldo
1895 May 27: Launched
1895 July: Sold to Argentina, name retained

Giuseppe Garibaldi (2)

Type: Armoured Cruiser
Class: 'Garibaldi' (1894)

History:
1895 Laid down by Ansaldo
1896 August: Sold prior to launching to Spain, renamed ***Cristobal Colon***

Giuseppe Garibaldi (3)

Type: Armoured Cruiser
Class: 'Garibaldi' (1894)

History:
1896 Laid down by Ansaldo
1897 September 25: Launched
1897 Sold to Argentina, renamed ***Pueyrredon***

Giuseppe Garibaldi (4)

Type: Armoured Cruiser
Class: 'Garibaldi' (1894)

History:
1898 September 21: Laid down by Ansaldo
1899 June 26: Launched
1900 July 12: Damaged by boiler explosion
1901 January 1: Completed
1911 Operations off Tripoli
1912 February 24: Bombardment of Beirut
1912 Aegean Sea
1915 July 18: Torpedoed and sunk by Austrian submarine *U4* in Adriatic off Gravosa (53 dead)

Impero

Type: Battleship
Class: 'Vittorio Veneto' (1934)
Nomenclature: Empire

History:
1938 May 14: Laid down by Ansaldo
1939 November 15: Launched
1940 June 1: Towed incomplete from Genoa to Brindisi to avoid French air attack
1942 January: Again towed to Venice, then Trieste
1943 September 8: Seized by Germans on Italian surrender
1845 February 17: Incomplete hull sunk by British air attack at Trieste
1946 Refloated and towed to Venice
1947 March 27: Stricken and broken up

Italia

Type: Barbette Ship
Class: 'Italia' (1875)
Nomenclature: Italy

History:
1876 January 3: Laid down at Castellammare
1880 September 29: Launched
1885 October 16: Completed at La Spezia
1905 Reconstructed; six funnels reduced to four, single central mast replaced two military masts
1909 Torpedo school ship
1914 June 1: Stricken, towed to Brindisi
1915 May 23: Reinstated as auxiliary first class, floating battery, Brindisi

1917 December: Converted to commercial vessel as bulk grain carrier
1921 November 16: Stricken and broken up

Italia, see *Littorio*

Leonardo da Vinci

Type: Dreadnought
Class: 'Cavour' (1909)
Nomenclature: Leonardo da Vinci (1452-1519), Florentine painter, architect, engineer and scientist

History:
1910 July 18: Laid down by Odero
1911 October 14: Launched
1914 May 17: Completed
World War 1: Southern Adriatic
1916 August 2: Caught fire, blew up and capsized at Taranto, caused by unstable cordite or Austrian sabotage (249 dead)
1919 September 17: Refloated upside down, righted January 24 1921, not repaired
1923 March 22: Stricken and broken up

Lepanto

Type: Barbette Ship
Class: 'Italia' (1875)
Nomenclature: Naval battle of 1571 in which Christian powers under John of Austria defeated the Turks

History:
1876 November 4: Laid down by Orlando
1883 March 17: Launched
1887 August 16: Completed
1902 Gunnery training ship
1910 Depot ship, Spezia
1913 Guardship, Derna
1914 January 15: Stricken
1915 March 27: Sold and broken up

Littorio

Type: Battleship
Class: 'Vittorio Veneto' (1934)
Nomenclature: Lictor, an official of ancient Rome who bore the fasces, adopted by the Fascists as their symbol

Far left:
***Impero* — Battleship of 'Vittorio Veneto' class, prior to launching, 15 November 1939, never completed.**

Above left:
***Palestro* — Central battery ship of 1871.**

Below left:
***Re Umberto* — Barbette ship of 1888, photo taken c1893.** *Photomatic*

History:
1934 October 28: Laid down by Ansaldo
1937 August 22: Launched
1940 May 6: Completed
World War 2: Mediterranean actions, Taranto, Battles of Sirte
1940 November 12: Severely damaged by three aerial torpedoes during carrier raid on Taranto, beached
1942 June 15: Torpedoed by British aircraft during attack on Malta convoy
1943 June 19: Hit by US aircraft bombs at La Spezia
1943 July 30: Renamed ***Italia***
1943 September 9: Left La Spezia on Italian surrender for Malta, damaged by German radio controlled bomb
1943 September: Interned at Lake Amaro in Suez Canal until February 1946
1948 June 1: Stricken
1960 Broken up

Marcantonio Colonna

Type: Dreadnought
Class: 'Caracciolo' (1914)
Nomenclature: Marc Antonio Colonna, Duke of Paliano (d1584), general-admiral of the Christian fleet against the Turks at Lepanto, 1571

History:
1915 March 3: Laid down by Odero
1915 Construction cancelled

Marco Polo

Type: Armoured Cruiser
Class: 'Marco Polo' (1888)
Nomenclature: Marco Polo (1254?-1324?), famous traveller

History:
1890 January 7: Laid down at Castellammare
1892 October 27: Launched
1894 July 21: Completed
1898-99 Far East
1901-03 Far East
1905-07 Far East
1911-12 Operations in Libya
1913-15 Far East
World War 1: Northern Adriatic
1918 April 4: Renamed ***Cortellazzo***, converted to troop transport
1920 October 1: Renamed ***Europa***
1921 January 16: Stricken
1921 Reinstated and renamed ***Volta***
1922 January 5: Stricken and broken up

Messina

Type: Broadside Ship
Class: 'Carignano' (1860)
Nomenclature: Seaport in Sicily

History:
1861 September 28: Laid down at Castellammare
1864 December 20: Launched
1867 February: Completed
1870 September: Liberation of Rome, went aground in the mouth of the Tiber River
1880 May 27: Stricken

Napoli

Type: Pre-dreadnought
Class: 'Vittorio Emanuele' (1901)
Nomenclature: Naples

History:
1903 October 21: Laid down at Castellammare
1905 September 10: Launched
1908 September 1: Completed
1911 Operations at Tobruk, bombardment of Bengazi
1912 Dardanelles, Aegean Sea, occupation of Rhodes
World War 1: Southern Adriatic
1926 September 3: Stricken
1927 May: Broken up at Savona

Palestro

Type: Coast Defence Ship
Class: 'Palestro' (1863)
Nomenclature: Victory of Piedmont and France over Austria, 31 May 1859

History:
1864 August: Laid down at La Seyne
1865 September 5: Launched
1866 January 28: Completed
1866 July 20: Damaged by gunfire and blew up during Battle of Lissa (227 dead)

Palestro

Type: Central Battery Ship
Class: 'Principe Amedeo' (1865)

History:
1865 August: Laid down at La Spezia
1871 October 2: Launched
1875 July 11: Completed
1881-82 Refit
1886 Refit
1889 Local defence, La Maddalena
—— Boys' training ship, Spezia
1900 April 15: Stricken
1902-04 Broken up

Pisa

Type: Armoured Cruiser
Class: 'Pisa' (1904)
Nomenclature: Town in Tuscany, former independent city-state

History:
1905 May 20: Laid down by Orlando
1907 September 15: Launched
1909 September 1: Completed
1911 Operations in Libya
1912 Dardanelles, Aegean Sea
World War 1: Southern Adriatic
1917 October 27: Hit by Austrian aircraft bomb at Brindisi
1919 Black Sea
1937 April 28: Stricken

Principe Amedeo

Type: Central Battery Ship
Class: 'Principe Amedeo' (1865)
Nomenclature: Prince Amedeo of Savoy, Duke of Aosta (1845-1890), King of Spain 1870-73, son of King Victor Emmanuel II

History:
1865 August: Laid down at Castellammare
1872 January 15: Launched
1874 December 15: Completed
1886 Operations off Crete
1888 Local defence, Taranto
1895 March 28: Stricken, ammunition hulk, Taranto
1910 Broken up

Principe di Carignano

Type: Broadside Ship
Class: 'Carignano' (1860)
Nomenclature: Prince Eugenio of Savoy-Carignan (1816-1888), Italian admiral

History:
1861 January: Laid down by Foce
1863 September 15: Launched
1865 June 11: Completed
1865-66 Aegean Sea
1866 July 20: Damaged at Battle of Lissa
1869 Refit
1870 Liberation of Rome
1875 March 31: Stricken
1877-79 Broken up

Re d'Italia

Type: Broadside Ship
Class: 'Re d'Italia' (1861)
Nomenclature: King of Italy: Victor Emmanuel II, first king of united Italy

History:
1861 November 21: Laid down by Webb
1863 April 18: Launched
1864 April: Arrived in Italy
1864 September 18: Commissioned
1866 July 20: Flag of Admiral Persano at the Battle of Lissa; rammed and sunk by Austrian ironclad *Ferdinand Max* (383 dead)

Re di Portogallo

Type: Broadside Ship
Class: 'Re d'Italia' (1861)
Nomenclature: Luis I, King of Portugal (1838-1889), son-in-law of King Victor Emmanuel II

History:
1861 December: Laid down by Webb
1863 August 29: Launched
1864 March 12: Completed
1864 October 4: Arrived in Italy
1866 July 20: Rammed by Austrian ship *Kaiser* at Battle of Lissa

1872 Artillery school ship, La Spezia
1875 March 31: Stricken and broken up 1877-79

Re Umberto

Type: Barbette Ship
Class: 'Re Umberto' (1883)
Nomenclature: Humbert I, King of Italy (1844-1900)

History:
1884 July 10: Laid down at Castellammare
1888 October 17: Launched
1893 July 21: Completed
1911 Refit
1911 Operations at Tripoli
1912 October: Depot ship, Genoa
1914 May 10: Stricken, depot ship, La Spezia
1915 December 9: Reinstated and converted to floating battery, at Brindisi and Valona
1918 Converted to troop transport; modified for use in forcing enemy harbour at Pola, turrets and barbettes removed and 8×76mm guns mounted, but war ended before the operation could take place
1920 July 4: Stricken

Regina Elena

Type: Pre-dreadnought
Class: 'Vittorio Emanuele' (1901)
Nomenclature: Queen Helene (1873-1952), wife of King Victor Emmanuel III

History:
1901 March 27: Laid down at La Spezia
1904 June 19: Launched
1907 September 11: Completed
1911 Occupation of Bengazi
1912 Aegean Sea, occupation of Rhodes
World War 1: Southern Adriatic
1923 March 15: Stricken

Regina Margherita

Type: Pre-dreadnought
Class: 'Regina Margherita' (1898)
Nomenclature: Queen Margaret (1851-1926), wife of King Humbert I

History:
1898 November 20: Laid down at La Spezia
1901 May 30: Launched
1904 April 14: Completed
1911-12 Refit
1912 Aegean Sea, occupation of Rhodes
World War 1: Adriatic
1916 December 11: Sunk by two mines off Valona laid by German submarine *UC14* (675 dead)

Regina Maria Pia

Type: Broadside Ship
Class: 'Regina Maria Pia' (1861)
Nomenclature: Maria Pia of Savoy (1847-1911), wife of King Luis I of Portugal, and daughter of King Victor Emmanuel II

History:
1862 July 22: Laid down at La Seyne
1863 Apr 28: Launched
1864 April 17: Completed
1866 July 20: Damaged at Battle of Lissa by shells and collision with *San Martino*
1874-75 Refit
1878 Protected Italian interests at Salonika
1881-83 Refit
1886 Operations at Crete
1892 Reconstructed, rigging replaced by two military masts
1900 Gunnery training ship
1904 May 22: Stricken, used as a target

Roma

Type: Broadside Ship
Class: 'Roma' (1862)
Nomenclature: Rome

History:
1863 February: Laid down by Foce
1865 December 18: Launched
1869 June 15: Completed
1870 Liberation of Rome
1873 Blockade of Cartagena, Spain
1895 May 5: Stricken, ammunition hulk
1896 July 28: Sunk to prevent explosion after catching fire at La Spezia
1896-97 Hulk broken up

Roma

Type: Pre-dreadnought
Class: 'Vittorio Emanuele' (1901)

History:
1903 September 20: Laid down at La Spezia
1907 April 21: Launched
1908 December 17: Completed
1911 Bombardment of Bengazi
1912 Dardanelles, Aegean Sea, Occupation of Rhodes
World War 1: Southern Adriatic, 1919 Black Sea
1927 October 13: Stricken, training ship
1932 Broken up at Pola

Roma

Type: Battleship
Class: 'Vittorio Veneto' (1934)

History:
1938 September 18: Laid down at Adriatico
1940 June 9: Launched
1942 June 14: Completed
World War 2: No active service
1943 June 5: Damaged by aircraft bombs at La Spezia
1943 September 9: Left La Spezia on Italian surrender for Malta, flagship of Admiral Bergamini; sunk by two German glider bombs off Sardinia (1,254 dead)

Ruggiero di Lauria

Type: Barbette Ship
Class: 'Ruggiero di Lauria' (1880)
Nomenclature: Roger of Loria (1250-1305), Sicilian naval commander

History:
1881 August 3: Laid down at Castellammare
1884 August 9: Launched
1888 December 1: Completed

Above:
***Regina Maria Pia* — Broadside ship, shown at Genoa, 17 July 1886. *Affondatore* at right and *Ancona* at left.**
US Naval Historical Centre

Below:
***Roma* — Pre-dreadnought of 'Vittorio Emanuele' class.**

1894 Refit
1897 Operations off Crete
1902 Refit, reboilered
1909 November 11: Stricken, floating oil depot, Spezia
1943 Hulk sunk by bombs
1946 Broken up

San Giorgio

Type: Armoured Cruiser
Class: 'San Giorgio' (1904)
Nomenclature: St George, patron saint of Genoa

History:
1905 July 4: Laid down at Castellemmare
1908 July 27: Launched
1910 July 1: Completed
1912 Operations off Libya
1913 November 21: Went aground in Straits of Messina, damaged
World War 1: Adriatic
1921 Refit
1925 Operations against rebels in Somalia
1937 Reconstructed at La Spezia; reboilered, new screws, new funnels, new AA guns, torpedo tubes removed
1938 June: Recommissioned
1940-41 Floating AA battery, Tobruk
1941 January 22: Scuttled in Tobruk harbour after being damaged by British aircraft
1952 Wreck raised and scuttled at sea

San Marco

Type: Armoured Cruiser
Class: 'San Giorgio' (1904)
Nomenclature: St Mark, patron saint of Venice

History:
1907 January 2: Laid down at Castellammare
1909 December 20: Launched
1911 February 7: Completed
1912 Operations in Libya
1912 Aegean Sea
World War 1: Adriatic
1931 Converted at La Spezia to target ship, two screws, SHP 13,000 = 18knots, eight boilers removed
1943 September 9: Captured by Germans at La Spezia
1945 Found sunk at La Spezia

San Martino

Type: Broadside Ship
Class: 'Regina Maria Pia' (1861)
Nomenclature: Victory of Piedmont and France over Austria, 24 June 1859

History:
1862 July 22: Laid down at La Seyne
1863 September 12: Launched
1864 November 9: Completed
1866 July 20: Damaged at Battle of Lissa by shells and collision with *Regina Maria Pia*
1873 Blockade of Cartagena, Spain
1875-76 Refit
1886 Refit
1890 Reconstructed
1894 Training ship, La Spezia
1903 August 30: Stricken
1906 June: Broken up

Sardegna

Type: Barbette Ship
Class: 'Re Umberto' (1883)
Nomenclature: Sardinia, an island in the Mediterranean

***San Marco* — Armoured cruiser, 1911.**

***Varese* — Armoured cruiser of 1899.**

History:
1885 October 24: Laid down at La Spezia
1890 September 20: Launched
1895 February 16: Completed
1911 Operations at Tripoli
World War 1: Guardship at Venice and Brindisi
1919-21 Constantinople
1923 January 4: Stricken

Sicilia

Type: Barbette Ship
Class: 'Re Umberto' (1883)
Nomenclature: Sicily

History:
1884 November 3: Laid down at Venice
1891 July 6: Launched
1895 May 4: Completed
1911 Operations at Tripoli
1914 July 9: Stricken, depot ship
1914 August 16: Reinstated as auxiliary, converted to repair ship
1923 March 4: Stricken and broken up

Sparviero

Type: Aircraft Carrier
Class: 'Sparviero' (1942)
Nomenclature: Sparrowhawk

History:
—— Laid down by Ansaldo as passenger liner ***Augustus***
1926 December 13: Launched
1927 Completed
1942 Conversion to aircraft carrier planned, renamed ***Falco***
1942 Renamed ***Sparviero***
1943 Captured by Germans at Genoa on Italian surrender
1944 October 5: Sunk in Genoa harbour as a blockship by Germans
1947 Refloated and broken up

Terribile

Type: Broadside Ship
Class: 'Terribile' (1860)
Nomenclature: Terrible

History:
1860 June: Laid down at La Seyne
1861 February 16: Launched
1861 September: Completed
1866 July 20: Battle of Lissa
1870 Liberation of Rome
1879 Refit
1885 Artillery school ship, La Spezia
1896 School ship at Taranto, later Venice
1903 August 30: Stricken
1906 Broken up

Varese

Type: Coast Defence Ship
Class: 'Palestro' (1863)
Nomenclature: Victory of Garibaldi's forces over Austria, 26 May 1859

History:
1864 August: Laid down at La Seyne
1865 December 23: Launched
1866 June 1: Completed
1866 July 20: Battle of Lissa
1870 Liberation of Rome
1880-83 Refit
1885 Red Sea
1886 Hospital ship
1891 May 29: stricken; depot and training ship
1901 Broken up

Varese (1)

Type: Armoured Cruiser
Class: 'Garibaldi' (1894)

History:
1895 Laid down by Orlando
1896 May 25: Launched
1896 October: Sold to Argentina, renamed ***San Martin***

Varese (2)

Type: Armoured Cruiser
Class: 'Garibaldi' (1894)

History:
1896 June: Laid down by Orlando
1897 July 25: Launched
1897 Sold to Argentina, renamed ***General Belgrano***

Varese (3)

Type: Armoured Cruiser
Class: 'Garibaldi' (1894)

History:
1898 September 15: Laid down by Orlando
1899 August 6: Launched
1901 April 5: Completed
1911 Operations off Tripoli
1912 February 24: Bombardment of Beirut
1912 Aegean Sea
World War 1: Southern Adriatic
1920 Training ship
1923 January 4: Stricken

Venezia

Type: Central Battery Ship
Class: 'Roma' (1862)
Nomenclature: Venice, ceded to Italy by Austria, 1866

History:
1863 February: Laid down by Foce
1869 January 21: Launched
1873 April 1: Completed
1873 Blockade of Cartagena
1881 October: Torpedo school ship
1895 February 24: Stricken and broken up at la Spezia

Vettor Pisani

Type: Armoured Cruiser
Class: 'Pisani' (1891)
Nomenclature: Vettor Pisani (d1380), Venetian admiral who defeated the Genoese fleet near Civitavecchia 1378

History:
1892 December 7: Laid down at Castellammare
1895 August 14: Launched
1898 April 1: Completed
1900-01 Far East, Boxer Rebellion, Taku forts
1903-04 Far East
1911 Operations off Albania
1912 Aegean Sea
World War 1: Northern Adriatic
1920 January 2: Stricken and broken up

Vittorio Emanuele

Type: Pre-dreadnought
Class: 'Vittorio Emanuele' (1901)
Nomenclature: Victor Emmanuel III (1869-1947), King of Italy 1900-1946

History:
1901 September 18: Laid down at Castellammare
1904 October 12: Launched
1908 August 1: Completed
1911 Operations off Tobruk, bombardment of Bengazi
1912 Aegean Sea, occupation of Rhodes
World War 1: Southern Adriatic 1915-17, Aegean 1918
1919 Constantinople
1923 April 1: Stricken

Vittorio Veneto

Type: Battleship
Class: 'Vittorio Veneto' (1934)
Nomenclature: Italian victory against the Austrian army in World War 1, 3 November 1918

History:
1934 October 28: Laid down by Adriatico
1937 July 22: Launched
1940 April 28: Completed
World War 2: Mediterranean actions, Taranto, Matapan
1941 March 28: Damaged by aircraft torpedo during Battle of Matapan
1941 December 14: Torpedoed by British submarine *Urge* while covering convoy to Libya
1943 June 5: Damaged by US aircraft bombs at La Spezia
1943 September 9: Left La Spezia on Italian surrender for Malta
1943 September: Interned at Lake Amaro in Suez Canal until February 1946
1948 February 1: Stricken
1960 Broken up at La Spezia

***Vittorio Veneto* — Battleship of 1937, as completed.**
Aldo Fraccaroli

Japan

The modern Japanese navy started with the construction of the ironclad *Fuso* and two armoured corvettes in 1875. Prior to that time the Confederate ironclad ram *Stonewall* had been acquired. It was with these ships and modern cruisers that Japan in 1894 defeated the obsolescent vessels of China at the Battle of the Yalu.

Two battleships were ordered in England in 1892 and additional units were built later. Armoured cruisers were ordered from yards in various countries. Japan participated with the European powers in the campaign in China in 1900 and signed an alliance with Britain in 1902.

In 1904 the navy included six battleships and eight armoured cruisers when Japan attacked the Russian base at Port Arthur, initiating the Russo-Japanese War. The Russian fleet was successfully shut up at Port Arthur and destroyed. A second Russian fleet from Europe was also destroyed at the Battle of Tsushima the next year. Eight Russian battleships were added to the Japanese navy at the end of the war in which Japan emerged as the major power in the Far East.

The large armoured cruiser *Tsukuba* was an innovative design but it was overshadowed by the contemporaneous appearance of the battlecruiser. The first dreadnoughts in 1908 were followed by the battlecruiser *Kongo*, an impressive vessel which outclassed all of its type. This was the last capital ship built outside of Japan as Japanese industry gained the technology to build large warships.

When war started in Europe in 1914, Japan declared war on Germany. Japanese naval forces captured the German base of Kiauchau in China and searched for German raiders in the Pacific, but a British request for the 'Kongo' class battlecruisers to serve with the Grand Fleet was turned down. In 1915 there was controversy with the US over Japanese policies in China and it was decided to build more battleships to attain parity with the US in the Pacific. The '8-8' fleet law was adopted calling for eight battleships and eight battlecruisers to be built by 1922. The ships laid down were of great size and power.

In the event, as a result of the Washington Treaty of 1922, only the first two battleships were completed and an additional two ships were completed as aircraft carriers. Japan accepted a ratio of three battleships for every five of the US and Great Britain. The ships retained under the treaty were successively reconstructed during the 1920s and 1930s. In 1937, disregarding treaty limitations, Japan laid down the huge 'Yamato'class battleships, the most powerful ever built. In addition the Japanese recognised the value of aviation and a force of aircraft carriers was constructed.

As relations between Japan and the US deteriorated in 1940-41, Japan determined that war was necessary to accomplish its aims in the Far East. On 7 December 1941 a carrier attack on the American base at Pearl Harbor achieved complete surprise and destroyed the American battle fleet.

At first Japanese forces were successful in overrunning Southeast Asia. Carrier forces made devastating attacks on Java, Ceylon and northern Australia before the first confrontation with US carriers in the Coral Sea. The next battle, Midway, was the turning point of the war as four Japanese carriers were lost together with many of their trained pilots and crews and the Japanese were unable to replace these losses. Of 21 new carriers projected only *Taiho* and three 'Unryu' class were completed because Japanese shipyards were unable to cope with wartime demands. A large programme of conversions was also authorised. The most spectacular was that of the battleship *Shinano* then in the early stages of construction, which was lost prior to being placed in service. The battleships *Ise* and *Hyuga* were converted to carry aircraft but as no aircraft were available they continued to serve as battleships.

Four more carriers were lost at the Battle of the Philippine Sea, again with a great number of trained pilots. At the Battle of Leyte Gulf the major Japanese attack was made up of battleships with the carriers, lacking aircraft, used as a diversion. Three battleships, including the huge *Musashi*, were lost together with four more carriers. The *Yamato* was sunk in April 1945 while on a mission against US forces off Okinawa carrying insufficient fuel to return to base.

The last capital ships of the Japanese navy were, towards the end of the war, confined to their bases by lack of fuel and escorts and most were sunk in shallow water in Japanese ports by US carrier aircraft. Of the battleships, only *Nagato* remained afloat, to be sunk a year later in the atomic tests at Bikini.

Class Details

'Azuma' (1867)

Ironclad Ram: *Azuma*
Displacement: 1,358tons
Dimensions: 186'9(oa) 165'9(wl) 157'6(pp)×32'6×16'6 [56.9(oa) 50.5(wl) 48(pp)×9.9×5]
Machinery: 2 screws, horizontal direct-acting engines (Mazeline), 2 boilers
IHP 1,200 = 9knots
Endurance: 1,200/8
Armament: 1×230mm SB, 4×160mm SB
Armour: Belt 90-115mm, casemate 115mm, c/t 140mm
Complement: 135
Class notes: Built for Confederate government as *Stonewall* and purchased from US in 1867 by the Shogunate government. Taken over by the Imperial government 1869. Ironclad ram with wood hull, twin coupled rudders and twin keels. Rated as coast defence ship

'Fuso' (1875)

Central Battery Ship: *Fuso*
Displacement: 3,718tons
Dimensions: 220(pp)×48×18 [67(pp)×14.6×5.5]
Machinery: 2 screws, horizontal trunk engines (Penn), 8 cylindrical boilers
IHP 3,500 = 13knots
Endurance: 4,500-10
Armament: 4×240mm/20 BLR, 3×170mm/25 BLR, 4×76mm BLR, 2×380mm TT
1894: 2×152mm QF replaced 2×170mm
1898: 240mm removed, 8×152mm added
1903: 2×152mm/50, 4×120mm/50, 11×47mm, 3×457mm TT
Armour: Belt 100-230mm, casemates 178-203mm, bulkheads 178mm
Complement: 250
Class notes: Designed by Reed. Armoured iron hull frigate with bark rig. First armoured vessel built for Japan. Rebuilt 1894, rigging removed and replaced by two military masts and rearmed. Salved after being wrecked in 1897 and recommissioned as coast defence ship

'Kongo' Class (1875)

Armoured Corvettes: *Hiei, Kongo*
Displacement: 2,248tons, 3,718f/l
Dimensions: 231(wl) 219'10(pp)×41×18 [70.4(wl) 67(pp)×12.5×5.5]
Machinery: 1 screw, horizontal compound engines (Earle), cylindrical boilers
IHP 2,450 = 13.75knots
Endurance: 3,100/10
Armament: 3×170mm/20 BLR, 6×150mm BLR, 2×355mm TT (*Hiei*)
1903: 2×76mm and 2×47mm added
Armour: Belt 90-115mm
Complement: 314
Class notes: Designed by Reed. *Hiei*, iron hull; *Kongo*, composite hull. Bark rig was removed in 1895

'Yashima' Class (1892)

Pre-dreadnoughts: *Fuji, Yashima*
Displacement: 12,533tons
Dimensions: 412(oa) 389'9(wl) 374(pp)×73'3×29 [125.5(oa) 118.8(wl) 114(pp)×22.3×8.8]
Machinery: 2 screws, VTE engines (Humphrys), 14 cylindrical boilers; *Fuji, 1910:* 10 Miyabara boilers
IHP 13,500 = 18.25knots
Endurance: 4,000/10
Armament: 4×305mm/40, 10×152mm/40, 20×47mm, 5×457mm TT
1900: 16×76mm replaced 16×47mm
Armour: Belt 355-457mm, turrets 152mm, barbettes 355mm, bulkheads 305-355mm, deck 63mm, c/t 355mm
Complement: 637
Class notes: The first battleships built for Japan. Ordered to bolster the fleet against China which had two modern battleships but the war ended long before their completion. Improved 'Royal Sovereign' type designed by G. C. Mackrow, with two twin turrets fore and aft, two tall funnels and military masts. *Fuji* refitted 1910, rearmed with Japanese guns

'Chin Yen' (1895)

Turret Ship: *Chin Yen*
Displacement: 7,220tons, 7,670f/l
Dimensions: 308'5(oa) 298'6(wl)×59×20 [93.9(oa) 91(wl)×18×6.1]
Machinery: 2 screws, horizontal compound engines (Vulcan), 8 cylindrical boilers
IHP 6,200 = 14.5knots
Endurance: 4,500/10
Armament: 4×305mm/20, 4×152mm/40, 2×57mm, 2×47mm
Armour: Belt 255-355mm, barbettes 305-355mm, casemates 203mm, deck 75mm, c/t 203mm
Complement: 250
Class notes: Built for China as *Chen Yuen*, captured 1895. Refitted and rearmed and commissioned in Japanese navy as second class battleship

Azuma — Ironclad ram, originally built for the Confederate navy as *Stonewall*. *IWM*

'Shikishima' Class (1894-95)

Pre-dreadnoughts: *Hatsuse* (see later photo), *Shikishima*
Displacement: *Shikishima:* 14,850tons, 15,453f/l; *Hatsuse:* 15,000, 15,255f/l
Dimensions: 438(oa) 415(wl) 400(pp)×75'6×28'2 [133.5(oa) 126.5(wl) 122(pp)×23×8.6]; *Hatsuse:* 439(oa)×76'9 [134(oa)×23.4]
Machinery: 2 screws, VTE engines (Humphrys), 25 Belleville boilers
IHP 14,500 = 18knots
Endurance: 5,000/10
Armament: 4×305mm/40, 14×152mm/45, 20×76mm, 12×47mm, 4×457mm TT (*Shikishima:* 5)
Armour: Belt 102-230mm, barbettes 203-355mm, casemates 50-152mm, deck 75-102mm, c/t 75-355mm
Complement: 741
Class notes: Near sisters designed by Mackrow as improved 'Majestic' type. *Shikishima* had different hull form; *Hatsuse* more like *Yashima*. Fighting tops removed 1904

'Asahi' Class (1896-97)

Pre-dreadnoughts: *Asahi* (see later photo), *Mikasa*
Displacement: *Asahi:* 15,200tons 15,374f/l; *Mikasa:* 15,140tons
Dimensions: 425'6(oa) 415(wl) 400'6(pp)×75'3×27'3 [129.6(oa) 126.5(wl) 122(pp)×22.9×8.3]; *Mikasa:* 432(oa) 414(wl) [131.7(oa) 125.5(wl)]
Machinery: 2 screws, VTE engines (*Asahi:* John Brown; *Mikasa:* Vickers), 25 Belleville boilers
IHP 15,000 = 18knots
Endurance: 9,000/10
Armament: 4×305mm/40, 14×152mm/45, 20×76mm, 12×47mm, 4×457mm TT
Armour: Belt 102-230mm, barbettes 203-355mm, casemates 50-152mm, deck 26-100mm, c/t 355mm
Complement: 773
Class notes: *Asahi* similar to British 'Canopus' class with different shape turrets. *Mikasa* was similar but more powerful. As the most modern vessel in the fleet during the Russo-Japanese War it was Togo's flagship and was later preserved as a memorial. *Asahi* converted to depot and repair ship 1923

'Asama' Class (1897)

Armoured Cruisers: *Asama, Tokiwa*
Displacement: 9,750tons, 10,500f/l
Dimensions: 442(oa) 408(pp)×67'3×24'4 [134.7(oa) 124.4(pp)×20.5×7.4]

Above:
***Fuso* — Central battery ship of 1877, first modern warship built for Japan.** *US Navy Official*

Top right:
***Fuji* — Battleship of 1896, the first built for Japan.** *IWM*

Centre right:
***Asama* — Armoured cruiser of 1898, in Victorian livery.** *Conway Photo Library*

Bottom right:
***Azuma* — French-built armoured cruiser of 1899.** *Conway Photo Library*

Machinery: 2 screws, VTE engines (Humphrys), 12 cylindrical boilers
IHP 18,000 = 21.3knots
Endurance: 10,000/10
Armament: 4×203mm/40, 14×152mm/40, 12×76mm, 8×47mm, 5×457mm TT
1922: 8×76mm/40 added
1937: 6×152mm removed
Armour: Belt 75-178mm, turrets and casemates 152mm, deck 75mm, c/t 355mm
Complement: 726
Class notes: British built units of 1897 cruiser programme designed by Watts. Two tall funnels and two military masts and main guns in two twin turrets. Given Japanese boilers and guns in 1910-17. *Tokiwa* converted to minelayer 1922

'Azuma' (1897)

Armoured Cruiser: *Azuma*
Displacement: 9,278tons, 9,953f/l
Dimensions: 452'5(oa) 431'6(pp)×68'9×23'6 [137.9(oa) 131.5(pp)×20.9×7.2]
Machinery: 2 screws, VTE engines (St Denis), 24 Belleville boilers
IHP 18,000 = 21knots
Endurance: 7,000/10
Armament: 4×203mm/40, 12×152mm/40, 12×76mm, 12×47mm, 5×457mm TT
1922: 4×152mm and 7×76mm removed
Armour: Belt 90-178mm, barbettes and casemates 152mm, deck 76mm, c/t 355mm
Complement: 726
Class notes: French built unit of 1897 cruiser programme with three unevenly spaced funnels. Slower than British built 'Asama' class

'Yakumo' (1897)

Armoured Cruiser: *Yakumo*
Displacement: 9,735tons, 10,288f/l
Dimensions: 434(oa) 408'11(pp)×64×23'8 [132.3(oa) 124.6(pp)×19.5×7.2]
Machinery: 2 screws, VTE engines (Vulcan), 24 Belleville boilers; *1927:* 6 Yarrow boilers
IHP 15,500 = 20knots; *1927:* IHP 7,000 = 16knots
Endurance: 7,000/10
Armament: 4×203mm/40, 12×152mm/40, 12×76mm, 12×47mm 5×457mm TT
1922: 4×152mm and 7×76mm removed
Armour: Belt 90-178mm, barbettes 152mm, turrets 160mm, c/t 355mm, deck 63mm
Complement: 670
Class notes: German built unit of 1897 cruiser programme. Three evenly spaced medium size funnels and two masts. Redesignated coast defence ship 1921

'Izumo' Class (1897)

Armoured Cruisers: *Iwate, Izumo* (see also later photo)
Displacement: 9,750tons, 10,235f/l
Dimensions: 435'8(oa) 400(pp)×68'6×24'3 [132.8(oa) 121.9(pp)×20.9×7.4]
Machinery: 2 screws, VTE engines (Humphrys), 24 Belleville boilers; *Iwate, 1931:* 6 Yarrow boilers; *Izumo, 1935:* 6 Kanpon boilers
IHP 14,700 = 20.75knots; *1931/35:* IHP 7,000 = 16knots
Endurance: 7,000/10
Armament: 4×203mm/40, 14×152mm/40, 12×76mm, 8×47mm, 5×457mm TT
1922: 6×152mm and 12×76mm removed, 2×78mm and 2×78mm AA added
Armour: Belt 90-178mm, barbettes 102-152mm, turrets 152mm, deck 63mm, c/t 355mm
Complement: 672
Class notes: Designed by Watts. British-built with improved

Above left:
***Yakumo* — German-built armoured cruiser of 1899, c1910.** *Marius Bar*

Below left:
***Izumo* — Armoured cruiser, entering Malta harbour 1919.**

Above:
***Katori* — Pre-dreadnought of 'Kashima' class, 1906.**

power and protection over previous cruisers. Three tall funnels. Redesignated coast defence ships 1921. Reboilered 1931-35

'Kashima' Class (1903)

Pre-dreadnoughts: *Kashima* (see later photo), *Katori*
Displacement: *Kashima:* 16,400tons, 17,200f/l; *Katori:* 15,590, 16,663f/l
Dimensions: 470'2(oa) 455(wl) 424'10(pp)×78'2×26'4 [143.3(oa) 138.7(wl) 129.5(pp)×23.8×8]
Katori: 456(oa) 425(wl) 420(pp)×78×27 [139(oa) 129.5(wl) 128(pp)×23.8×8.2]
Machinery: 2 screws, VTE engines (*Kashima:* Humphrys, *Katori:* Vickers), 20 Niclausse boilers
IHP 16,000 = 18.5knots
Endurance: 12,000/11
Armament: 4×305mm/45, 4×254mm/45, 12×152mm/45, 16×76mm, 3×47mm, 5×457mm TT
Armour: Belt 90-230mm, barbettes 127-305mm, casemates 50-152mm, deck 50-75mm, c/t 230mm
Complement: 864
Class notes: The last battleships built outside of Japan. Extremely powerful ships similar to British 'King Edward VII' class with heavier armament but slightly less armour protection

'Kasuga' Class (1903)

Armoured Cruisers: *Kasuga, Nisshin*
Displacement: *Kasuga:* 7,628tons, 8,591f/l; *Nisshin:* 7,698tons 8,384f/l
Dimensions: 366'6(oa) 357(wl) 344(pp)×61'4×25'3 [111.7(oa) 108.8(wl) 104.9(pp)×18.7×7.7]
Machinery: 2 screws, VTE engines (Ansaldo), 8 cylindrical boilers; *1914:* 12 Kanpon boilers
IHP 14,800 = 20.6knots
Endurance: 5,500/10
Armament: 4×203mm/45 (*Kasuga:* 1×254mm/45 and

2×203mm/45), 14×152mm/45, 10×76mm, 6×47mm (*Kasuga:* 4), 4×457mm TT
1914: TT removed
1924: 6×152mm and 6×76mm removed
Armour: Belt 73-152mm, barbettes 152mm, battery 152mm, c/t 152mm
Complement: 560
Class notes: Improved version of Italian 'Garibaldi' class designed by Masdea ordered by Argentina and sold to Japan prior to completion. Two large funnels with single mast between. Arrived in Japan just in time to join fleet for the war with Russia 1904. Redesignated coast defence ships 1921

'Tsukuba' Class (1904)

Armoured Cruisers: *Ikoma, Tsukuba*
Displacement: 13,750tons, 15,400f/l
Dimensions: 475(oa) 450(wl) 440(pp)×75×26 [144.8(oa) 137.2(wl) 134.1(pp)×22.9×7.9]
Machinery: 2 screws, VTE engines (builder), 20 Miyabara boilers
IHP 20,500 = 20.5knots
Armament: 4×305mm/45, 12×152mm/45, 12×120mm/50, 4×76mm/40, 3×457mm TT
1919: 2×152mm and 4×120mm removed
Armour: Belt 102-178mm, turrets 178mm, casemates 127mm, deck 50mm, c/t 203mm
Complement: 820
Class notes: A new type of warship outclassing all other armoured cruisers, but were made obsolete by the time of their completion by the appearance of the British battlecruisers. Redesignated battlecruisers 1912

'Kurama' Class (1904)

Armoured Cruisers: *Ibuki, Kurama*
Displacement: 14,636tons, 17,200f/l
Dimensions: 485(oa) 473'6(wl) 450(pp)×75'4×26'1 [147.8(oa) 144.3(wl) 137.2(pp)×23×8]
Machinery: 2 screws, *Kurama:* VTE engines (Yokosuka); *Ibuki:* Curtis turbines (Fore River); 28 Miyabara boilers (*Ibuki:* 18)
Kurama: IHP 22,500 = 21.25knots
Ibuki: SHP 24,000 = 21.5knots
Armament: 4×305mm/45, 8×203mm/45, 14×120mm/50, 4×76mm/40, 3×357mm TT
Armour: Belt 102-178mm, turrets 152-178mm, casemates 127mm, deck 50mm, c/t 203mm
Complement: 845
Class notes: Improved 'Tsukuba' type. Completion of *Kurama* was much delayed by financial difficulties which enabled it to be fitted with tripod masts, while *Ibuki* retained pole masts. *Ibuki* was first major ship of Japanese navy to be completed with turbines

'Satsuma' (1904)

Pre-dreadnought: *Satsuma*
Displacement: 19,372tons
Dimensions: 482(oa) 479(wl) 449(pp)×83'6×27'6 [146.9(oa) 146(wl) 136.9(pp)×25.5×8.4]
Machinery: 2 screws, VTE engines (Yokosuka), 20 Miyabara boilers
IHP 17,300 = 18.25knots
Armament: 4×305mm/45, 12×254mm/45, 12×120mm/50, 4×76mm/40, 5×357mm TT
Armour: Belt 102-230mm, turrets 178-240mm, casemates 152mm, deck 50-75mm, c/t 250mm
Complement: 800
Class notes: First large warship built in Japan, called 'semi-dreadnought' because secondary battery was 10" guns in six twin turrets. Construction delayed by financial difficulties which lessened impact of the design on naval thinking

'Aki' (1904)

Pre-dreadnought: *Aki*
Displacement: 20,100tons, 21,800f/l
Dimensions: 492(oa) 483(wl) 460(pp)×83'7×27'6 [150(oa) 147.2(wl) 140.2(pp)×25.5×8.4]
Machinery: 2 screws, Curtis turbines (Fore River), 15 Miyabara boilers
SHP 24,000 = 20knots
Armament: 4×305mm/45, 12×254mm/45, 8×152mm/45, 8×76mm/40, 5×357mm TT
Armour: Belt 102-230mm, turrets 178-240mm, casemates 152mm, deck 50-75mm, c/t 255mm
Complement: 931
Class notes: Near sister to *Satsuma* but with three funnels and turbine engines, increased secondary armament

'Iki' (1905)

Pre-dreadnought: *Iki*
Displacement: 8,440tons, 9,960f/l
Dimensions: 346'6(oa) 331'4(wl) 327'11(pp)×66.9×24'11 [105.6(oa) 101(wl) 100(pp)×20.4×7.6]
Machinery: 2 screws, VTE engines (Baltic Works), 16 Belleville boilers
IHP 8,000 = 16knots
Endurance: 4,900/10
Armament: 2×305mm/30, 6×152mm/40, 6×76mm
1910: 6×120mm replaced 152mm
Armour: Belt 102-356mm, turrets 254mm, deck 60mm, casemates 76-152mm, c/t 203mm
Complement: 611
Class notes: Former Russian *Imperator Nikolai I* captured after Tsushima, virtually undamaged. Served as training ship and coast defence ship

'Tango' (1905)

Pre-dreadnought: *Tango* (see later photo)
Displacement: 10,960tons, 11,400f/l
Dimensions: 375(oa) 368'6(wl) 340(pp)×69'9×25'6 [114.3(oa) 112.3(wl) 103.6(pp)×21.3×7.8]
Machinery: 2 screws, VTE engines (Humphrys), 16 Miyabara boilers
IHP 10,600 = 17knots
Endurance: 1,750/16
Armament: 4×305mm/40, 12×152mm/45, 6×47mm, 4×457mm TT
Armour: Belt 100-380mm, turrets 152-255mm, battery 127mm, deck 74mm, c/t 230mm
Complement: 700
Class notes: Former Russian *Poltava* sunk at Port Arthur, refloated and repaired. Refitted with Japanese boilers and guns. Returned to Russia 1916

'Mishima' Class (1905)

Coast Defence Ships: *Mishima, Okinoshima*
Displacement: 4,165tons, 5,050f/l
Dimensions: 286'6(oa) 277'6(wl) 265(pp)×52'2×19 [87.3(oa) 84.6(wl) 80.8(pp)×15.9×5.8]
Machinery: 2 screws, VTE engines (Humphrys), 18 Miyabara boilers (*Okinoshima:* 18 Belleville)
IHP 5,250 = 16knots
Endurance: 3,000/10

Above:
***Nisshin* — Armoured cruiser built in Italy 1903, seen in 1917.** *IWM*

Below:
***Tsukuba* — Armoured cruiser of 1905, later redesignated battlecruiser.** *IWM*

Armament: 4×229mm/45 (*Okinoshima:* 3×254mm/45), 6×152mm, 4×120mm
Armour: Belt 102-254mm, turrets 203mm, deck 38-63mm, c/t 203mm
Complement: 406
Class notes: Former Russian *Admiral Senyavin* and *General Admiral Apraksin* captured after Tsushima, slightly damaged. *Mishima* served as second class coast defence ship. *Okinoshima* used as a training ship

'Sagami' Class (1905)

Pre-dreadnoughts: *Sagami, Suwo*
Displacement: 12,674tons, 13,500f/l
Dimensions: 434'6(oa) 424(wl) 401'3(pp)×71'8×26 [132.4(oa) 129.2(wl) 122.3(oa)×21.8×7.9]
Machinery: 3 screws, VTE engines, Miyabara boilers
IHP 14,500 = 18knots
Endurance: 6,000/10
Armament: 4×254mm/45, 10×152mm/45, 16×78mm, 2×457mm TT
Armour: Belt 178-229mm, turrets 229mm (*Suwo:* 254mm), casemates 51-127mm, c/t 152mm (*Suwo:* 210mm)
Complement: 775
Class notes: Former Russian *Peresviet* and *Pobieda* salved at Port Arthur, and rebuilt with Japanese boilers and guns. Served as first class coast defence ships. *Sagami* returned to Russia 1916

'Hizen' (1905)

Pre-dreadnought: *Hizen*
Displacement: 12,700tons, 12,900f/l
Dimensions: 386'8(oa) 374(wl) 372(pp)×72'3×28'3 [117.8(oa) 114(wl) 113.4(pp)×22×8.6]
Machinery: 2 screws, VTE engines, Miyabara boilers
IHP 16,000 = 18knots
Endurance: 4,000/10
Armament: 4×305mm/45, 12×152mm/45, 14×78mm, 2×457mm TT
Armour: Belt 51-229mm, turrets 229mm, casemates 152mm, deck 51-76mm, c/t 254mm
Complement: 741
Class notes: Former Russian *Retvizan* salved at Port Arthur and rebuilt with Japanese boilers and Armstrong guns

'Iwami' (1905)

Pre-dreadnought: *Iwami*
Displacement: 13,516tons, 15,300f/l
Dimensions: 397'8(oa) 389'9(wl) 376'5(pp)×76×26 [121.2 (oa) 118.8(wl) 114.8(pp)×23.2×7.9]
Machinery: 2 screws, VTE engines, Miyabara boilers
IHP 15,800 = 18knots
Endurance: 5,000/10
Armament: 4×305mm/40, 6×203mm/45, 16×78mm, 20×47mm, 2×457mm TT

Top left:
***Kurama* — Armoured cruiser completed 1911, c1919. Its sister *Ibuki* had pole masts.** *Marius Bar*

Centre left:
***Mishima* — The former Russian coast defence ship *Admiral Senyavin*, captured 1905.**

Bottom left:
***Kongo* — Battlecruiser, on trials, 1913.**
US Naval Historical Centre

Armour: Belt 100-178mm, turrets 152-254mm, deck 29-64mm, c/t 208mm
Complement: 750
Class notes: Former Russian *Orel* captured after Tsushima, badly damaged. Repaired and reboilered, flying deck and other topweight removed and funnels shortened

'Aso' (1905)

Armoured Cruiser: *Aso*
Displacement: 7,726tons
Dimensions: 452(oa) 444'11(wl) 410'10(pp)×57×22 [137.8(oa) 135.6(wl) 125.2(pp)×17.4×6.7]
Machinery: 2 screws, VTE engines, Miyabara boilers
IHP 16,500 = 21knots
Endurance: 7,000/10
Armament: 2×203mm/45, 8×152mm/45, 16×78mm
1913: 203mm replaced by 2×152mm
Armour: Belt 60-203mm, turrets 152mm, deck 51mm, c/t 160mm
Complement: 570
Class notes: Former Russian *Bayan* salved at Port Arthur. Reconstructed with Japanese boilers and Armstrong guns. Converted to minelayer 1920

'Kawachi' Class (1908)

Dreadnoughts: *Kawachi, Settsu*
Displacement: *Kawachi:* 20,823tons, 22,900f/l; *Settsu:* 21,443tons
Dimensions: 526(oa) 500(pp)×84'3×27 [160.3(oa) 152.4(pp)×25.7×8.2] *Settsu:* 533(oa) [162.5(oa)]
Machinery: 2 screws, Curtis turbines (Kawasaki), 16 Miyabara boilers
SHP 25,000 = 21knots
Endurance: 2,700/18
Armament: 4×305mm/50, 8×305mm/45, 10×152mm/50, 8×120mm/50, 12×78mm, 5×457mm TT
1918: 12×78mm replaced by 4×78mm AA, 3 TT removed
Armour: Belt 102-305mm, turrets 280mm, casemates 152mm, deck 305mm, c/t 152-255mm
Complement: 999
Class notes: First true Japanese dreadnoughts. Strong armour protection, carried main battery in two calibres in six twin turrets one each fore and aft and two on each beam. Introduced tripod masts. *Settsu* had clipper type bow while *Kawachi* had a straight stem

'Kongo' Class (1910-1911)

Battlecruisers: *Haruna* (see later photo), *Hiei, Kirishima, Kongo*
Displacement: 27,500tons, 32,200f/l
Dimensions: 704(oa) 659'4(wl) 653'6(pp)×92×27'6 [214.6(oa) 201(wl) 199.2(pp)×28×8.4] *1924:* 102'4 [31.2] beam
Machinery: 4 screws (*Haruna:* 3), Parsons turbines (*Haruna:* Brown-Curtis *Kongo:* Vickers; *Hiei* and *Haruna:* Kawasaki; *Kirishima:* Mitsubishi), 36 Yarrow boilers (*Hiei:* Kanpon); *Haruna, 1924-31:* 16 Kanpon; *Kirishima* and *Kongo 1927-31:* 6 Kanpon
SHP 64,000 = 27.5knots
Endurance: 8,000/14
Armament: 8×355mm/45, 16×152mm/50, 8×78mm/40 (*Kongo:* 16×76mm), 8×78mm/28 (*Kongo:* 4) 8×533 TT
1924: 4×76mm added, 4×533mm TT removed
Armour: Belt 76-203mm, turrets 230mm, barbettes 255mm, bulkheads 140-230mm, c/t 255mm, casemates 152mm
Complement: 1,221

As reconstructed 1933-34:

Displacement: 32,156tons, 36,600f/l
Dimensions: 728'3(oa) 720'5(wl) 654'6(pp)×101'7×31'8 [222(oa) 219.6(wl) 199.5(pp)×31×9.6]
Machinery: 4 screws, Kanpon geared turbines, 8 Kanpon boilers (*Haruna:* 11)
SHP 136,000 = 30knots
Endurance: 10,000/18
Armament: 8×355mm/45, 14×152mm/50, 8×127mm AA (*Hiei:* 4), 4×40mm AA
Armour: As before except: turrets 280mm, deck 120mm
Complement: 1,437
Class notes: Designed by Sir G. R. Thurston as an improved 'Lion', *Kongo* was built in England, the last capital ship built outside Japan. With new arrangement of main armament turrets, heavy secondary armament and good protection and internal subdivision, they outclassed all contemporary ships. *Hiei* was first warship to be fitted with new Japanese Kanpon boilers, but much material was imported. Funnel arrangement and propulsion systems differed among these ships.
Between 1924 and 1931 all but *Hiei* were reconstructed, reboilered with new Kanpon boilers, some oil firing, bulges fitted and extra armour, funnels reduced to two, superstructure built up around tripod foremast, elevation of guns increased and catapults fitted. *Hiei* was demilitarised with armour removed and used as training ship.
Between 1933 and 1940 all four were again reconstructed and redesignated battleships. More extensive armour, stern redesigned and hull lengthened, again reboilered and re-engined and new AA armament added

'Fuso' Class (1911-1913)

Dreadnoughts: *Fuso, Yamashiro* (see later photo)
Displacement: 30,600tons, 35,900f/l
Dimensions: 673(oa) 665(wl) 630(pp)×94×28'3 [205.1(oa) 202.7(wl) 192(pp)×28.7×8.6]
Machinery: 4 screws, Brown-Curtis turbines (Kawasaki), 24 Miyabara boilers
SHP 40,000 = 22.5knots
Endurance: 8,000/14
Armament: 12×355mm/45, 16×152mm/50, 12×78mm/40, 4×78mm/28, 5×533mm TT
1928: 6×78mm added
Armour: Belt 102-305mm, turrets 114-305mm, barbettes 203mm, casemates 152mm, bulkheads 102-305mm, deck 50mm, c/t 350mm
Complement: 1,193

As reconstructed 1930-35:

Displacement: 34,700tons, 39,154f/l
Dimensions: 698(oa) 689(wl) 630(pp)×108'6×31'9 [212.8(oa) 210(wl) 192(pp)×33.1×9.7]
Machinery: 4 screws, Kanpon geared turbines, 6 Kanpon boilers
SHP 75,000 = 24.7knots
Endurance: 11,800/16
Armament: 12×355mm/45, 14×152mm/50, 8×127mm AA, 16×25mm AA
Armour: As before except: deck 50-100mm
Complement: 1,396
Class notes: When completed *Fuso* was the most powerfully armed and fastest battleship in the world. Main turrets all on

Above:
***Fuso* — Battleship of 1914, after reconstruction of 1933.** *IWM*

Below:
***Ise* — Dreadnought, at sea during the 1920s.**
US Naval Historical Centre

centreline with two funnels and two tripod masts of uneven height. 1927-28 modernisation included new AA armament and addition of searchlights and fire control platforms to tripod masts. Both were reconstructed 1930-35, new engines and boilers fitted, forward funnel removed, bulges added, elevation of main battery increased, tripod masts replaced by towers fore and aft. Catapults added on stern of *Yamashiro* and on 'P' turret in *Fuso*. A plan to convert them to carrier-battleships like *Ise* was cancelled in 1944

'Ise' Class (1914)

Dreadnoughts: *Hyuga, Ise* (see later photo)
Displacement: 31,260tons, 36,500f/l
Dimensions: 683(oa) 675(wl) 642(pp)×94×29'1 [208.2(oa) 205.7(wl) 195.7(pp)×28.7×8.9]
Machinery: 4 screws, Brown-Curtis (*Ise*) Parsons (*Hyuga*) turbines, 24 Kanpon boilers
SHP 45,000 = 23.5knots
Endurance: 9,680/14
Armament: 12×355mm/45, 20×140mm/50, 12×78mm/40, 4×78mm/28, 6×533mm TT
Armour: Belt 102-305mm, turrets 305mm, barbettes 305mm, casemates 152mm, deck 25-55mm, c/t 305mm
Complement: 1,360

As reconstructed 1934-37:

Displacement: 35,800tons, 40,169f/l; *1943:* 35,350tons, 38,676f/l
Dimensions: 708(oa) 700(wl) 642(pp)×104×30'2 [215.8(oa) 213.4(wl) 195.7(pp)×31.7×9.2]
1943: 720'6(oa) [219.6(oa)]
Machinery: 4 screws, Kanpon geared turbines, 8 Kanpon boilers
SHP 80,825 = 25.3knots
Armament: 12×355mm/45, 16×140mm/50, 8×127mm/40 AA, 20×25mm AA
1943: 8×355mm/45, 16×127mm, 57×25mm AA, 22 aircraft
Armour: As before except: deck 170mm
Complement: 1,376
Class notes: Improved 'Fuso' type with 'P' and 'Q' turrets repositioned aft of both funnels. During 1931 refit the tripod foremast was built up with superstructure.
From 1934 to 1937 both reconstructed with new engines and boilers, forward funnel removed, bulges added, thicker deck armour and catapults added as well as new pagoda foremast. In 1943 they were converted to carrier-battleships by removal of the two aft turrets and construction of a flightdeck aft. They carried no aircraft into combat as no planes or pilots were available

'Nagato' Class (1916-1917)

Dreadnoughts: *Mutsu, Nagato* (see later photo)
Displacement: 33,800tons, 38,500f/l
Dimensions: 708(oa) 699(wl) 660'9(pp)×95×30 [215.8(oa) 213.1(wl) 201.3(pp)×29×9.1]
Machinery: 4 screws, Gihon geared turbines (builders), 21 Kanpon boilers
SHP 80,000 = 26.7knots
Endurance: 5,500/16
Armament: 8×406mm/45, 20×140mm/50, 4×78mm AA, 8×533mm TT
Armour: Belt 100-300mm, turrets 355mm, barbettes 300mm, deck 75-178mm, c/t 367mm
Complement: 1,333

As reconstructed 1934-36:

Displacement: 39,130tons, 42,850f/l
Dimensions: 738(oa) 725'4(wl) 660'9(pp)×113'6×31'2 [224.9(oa) 221.1(wl) 201.4(pp)×34.6×9.5]
Machinery: 4 screws, Kanpon geared turbines, 10 Kanpon boilers
SHP 82,300 = 25knots
Endurance: 8,650/16
Armament: 8×406mm/45, 18×140mm/50, 8×127mm AA, 20×25mm AA
Nagato, 1944: 98×25mm AA
Complement: 1,368
Class notes: Designed by Hiraga. First battleships in the world with 16" guns, they were the first of the '8-8' Project of eight battleships and eight battlecruisers. In 1924 the forward funnel was trunked aft. *Mutsu* had clipper bow fitted in 1930 and *Nagato* in 1936.
Both reconstructed 1934-36 including new engines and boilers and removal of forward funnel. Bulges added, elevation of main battery increased and catapults added

'Kaga' Class (1918)

Dreadnoughts: *[Kaga, Tosa]*
Displacement: 39,930tons, 44,500f/l
Dimensions: 768'1(oa) 760'2(wl) 715(pp)×100×30'9 [234.1(oa) 231.7(wl) 217.9(pp)×30.5×9.4]
Machinery: 4 screws, Brown-Curtis geared turbines, 12 Kanpon boilers
SHP 91,000 = 26.5knots
Endurance: 5,500/16
Armament: 10×406mm/45, 20×140mm/50, 4×78mm AA, 8×610mm TT
Armour: Belt 254-280mm, turrets and barbettes 230-280mm, deck 100-163mm, bulkheads 254 and 229-280mm, c/t 254mm
Complement: 1,333
Class notes: Improved 'Nagato' type, designed by Hiraga. Increased armour protection and enlarged main battery. Cancelled 1922 to comply with Washington Treaty, but incomplete hull of *Kaga* completed as aircraft carrier

'Amagi' Class (1918-1919)

Battlecruisers: *[Akagi, Amagi, Atago, Takao]*
Displacement: 41,217tons, 47,000f/l
Dimensions: 826'1(oa) 820'3(wl) 770'1(pp)×101×31 [251.8(oa) 250(wl) 234.7(pp)×30.8×9.4]
Machinery: 4 screws, Gihon geared turbines, 19 Kanpon boilers
SHP 131,200 = 30knots
Endurance: 8,000/14
Armament: 10×406mm/45, 16×140mm/50, 4×120mm/45 AA, 6×610mm TT
Armour: Belt 229-254mm, turrets 229-279mm, bulkheads 230-280mm, c/t 355mm
Class notes: First four battlecruisers of '8-8' Project, designed by Hiraga to outclass British *Hood* and US *Lexington*. Main armament in five twin turrets, three aft of superstructure. Single funnel and pagoda tripod foremast. All suspended 1922 prior to launching to comply with Washington Treaty, but *Amagi* and *Akagi* were retained for conversion to aircraft carriers

'Kii' Class (1921)

Dreadnoughts: *[Kii, Owari]*, 2 unnamed
Displacement: 42,600tons, 48,500f/l
Dimensions: 826'9(oa) 820'6(wl) 770'1(pp)×100×31'9 [252(oa) 250(wl) 234.7(pp)×30.5×9.7]
Machinery: 4 screws, Gihon geared turbines, 19 Kanpon boilers

Top:
***Mutsu* — Battleship of 1920, as completed.** *IWM*

Above:
***Akagi* — Aircraft carrier, April 1939, after reconstruction.** *IWM*

SHP 131,200 = 29.75knots
Endurance: 8,000/14
Armament: 10×406mm/45, 20×140mm/50, 4×78mm AA, 8×610mm TT
Armour: Belt 292mm, barbettes 229-280mm, deck 115mm, c/t 355mm
Class notes: Final four battleships of '8-8' Project, designed by Hiraga. Battleship version of 'Amagi' class with similar hull and machinery. None were ever laid down

'No 13' Class (1921)

Battlecruisers: 4 unnamed
Displacement: 47,500tons
Dimensions: 915'4(oa) 900(wl) 850(pp)×101×32 [279(oa) 274.3(wl) 259.1(pp)×30.8×9.8]
Machinery: 4 screws, Gihon geared turbines, 22 Kanpon boilers
SHP 150,000 = 30knots
Armament: 8×457mm/45, 16×140mm/50, 4×120mm/45 AA, 8×610mm TT
Armour: Belt 330mm, barbettes 229-280mm, deck 127mm, c/t 355mm
Class notes: Never ordered, builders were to be Yokosuka, Kure, Mitsubishi and Kawasaki. The final four battlecruisers of '8-8' Project designed by Hiraga. Enlarged version of 'Kaga' class

'Hosho' Class (1921)

Aircraft Carriers: *Hosho, [Shokaku]*
Displacement: 7,470tons, 9,630f/l
Dimensions: 552'6(oa) 541(wl) 510(pp)×59'1×20'3 [168.4(oa) 164.9(wl) 155.4(pp)×18×6.2]
Machinery: 2 screws, Parsons geared turbines, 8 Kanpon boilers
SHP 30,000 = 25knots
Endurance: 8,680/12
Aircraft: 26
Armament: 4×140mm/40
1944: 140mm removed, 30×25mm AA added
Complement: 550
Class notes: Laid down as a naval tanker and converted during construction. Originally built with small island and tripod mast which were removed in 1923. Three hinged funnels on starboard side were fixed upright in 1934. The flightdeck sloped down at the bow and this was made horizontal in 1936

'Akagi' Class (1922)

Aircraft Carriers: *Akagi, [Amagi]*
Displacement: 26,900tons, 34,364f/l
Dimensions: 855'4(oa) 816'7(wl) 764'5(pp)×95×26'6 [260.7(oa) 248.9(wl) 233(pp)×29×8.1]

Machinery: 4 screws, Gihon geared turbines, 19 Kanpon boilers
SHP 131,200 = 31knots
Endurance: 8,000/14
Aircraft: 60
Armament: 10×203mm, 12×114mm

As reconstructed in 1936:

Displacement: 36,500tons, 41,300f/l
Dimensions: 855'3(wl) 770(pp)×102'9×28'7 [260.7(wl) 234.7(pp)×31.3×8.7]
Machinery: 4 screws, Kanpon geared turbines, 19 Kanpon boilers (new)
SHP 133,000 = 31.25knots
Aircraft: 91
Armament: 6×203mm/50, 12×120mm/45 AA, 28×25mm AA
Complement: 2,000
Class notes: Laid down as battlecruisers but hull of *Amagi* was irreparably damaged by the earthquake of 1923 and battleship *Kaga* was substituted. As converted had three flightdecks forward, no island and two funnels on starboard side, one pointing up, the other out and down. Reconstructed in 1935-38 when the two lower flightdecks forward were removed and the top flightdeck extended forward to the bow. An island was added on the port side and funnels modified

'Kaga' (1923)

Aircraft Carrier: *Kaga*
Displacement: 26,000tons, 33,693f/l
Dimensions: 771(wl) 715'1(pp)×97'6×26 [235(wl) 218(pp)×29.7×7.9]
Machinery: 4 screws, Brown-Curtis geared turbines, 12 Kanpon boilers
SHP 91,000 = 28.5knots
Endurance: 8,000/14
Aircraft: 60
Armament: 10×203mm/50, 12×120mm/45
Complement: 1,340

As reconstructed in 1934:

Displacement: 38,200tons, 42,541f/l
Dimensions: 812'6(wl) 738'2(pp)×106'8×31'1 [247.7(wl) 225(pp)×32.5×9.5]
Machinery: 4 screws, Kanpon geared turbines, 8 Kanpon boilers
SHP 127,400 = 28.5knots

Top left:
***Ryujo* — Light aircraft carrier of 1932, before reconstruction.** *IWM*

Above left:
***Hiryu* — Aircraft carrier, 1939.** *IWM*

Above right:
***Yamato* — Battleship of 1940, as completed.** *IWM*

Endurance: 10,000/16
Aircraft: 90
Armament: 10×203mm, 16×127mm, 22×25mm
Complement: 2,016
Class notes: Converted from incomplete hull of battleship similar to *Akagi* with three flightdecks forward. Smoke was vented by two long funnels almost the length of the flightdeck on each side. Was not a very satisfactory conversion. Reconstructed 1934-35 when flightdeck was extended the full length of the ship, an island was constructed on starboard side just forward of the new funnel projecting out and down which replaced the two long funnels

'Ryujo' (1927)

Light Aircraft Carrier: *Ryujo*
Displacement: 8,000tons, 10,150f/l; *1936:* 10,600tons, 12,732f/l
Dimensions: 575(wl) 548(pp)×66'8×18'3 [175.3(wl) 167(pp)×20.3×5.6]
Machinery: 2 screws, Kanpon geared turbines, 6 Kanpon boilers
SHP 65,000 = 29knots
Endurance: 10,000/14
Aircraft: 48
Armament: 12×127mm
1936: 4×127mm removed, 4×25mm added
1944: 24×25mm AA
Complement: 600
Class notes: Designed to conform to treaty limitations. Design was modified during construction to add a second hangar deck. This caused the ship to be top heavy and in 1934 it was reconstructed to improve stability. In 1936 further changes were made to the bow and bridge. Too small for first line action during the war

Soryu Class (1931-1932)

Aircraft Carriers: *Hiryu, Soryu*
Displacement: *Soryu:* 15,900tons, 18,800f/l; *Hiryu:* 17,300tons, 20,250f/l
Dimensions: *Soryu:* 746′5(oa) 729′9(wl) 677′7(pp)×69′11×25 [227.5(oa) 224.4(wl) 206.5(pp)×21.3×7.6]; *Hiryu:* 745′11(oa) 721′9(wl) 687′5(pp)×73′3×25′9 [227.4(oa) 220(wl) 209.6(pp)×22.3×7.8]
Machinery: 4 screws, Kanpon geared turbines, 8 Kanpon boilers
SHP 152,000 = 34.5knots
Endurance: *Soryu:* 7,750/18; *Hiryu:* 10,330/18
Aircraft: 73
Armament: 12×127mm, 28×25mm
Complement: 1,100
Class notes: A successful design which became standard for the Japanese Navy. Construction of *Hiryu* was delayed to include improvement in the design to better seakeeping ability. *Hiryu* also differed in having a larger island on the port side, as in *Akagi*, an apparent failure. Funnels on both were on the starboard side

'Yamato' Class (1937)

Battleships: *Musashi, Yamato, [Shinano],* 1 unnamed
Displacement: 67,123tons, 71,695f/l
Dimensions: 862′10(oa) 839′10(wl) 800′6(pp)×121′1×32′11 [263(oa) 256(wl) 244(pp)×36.9×10]
Machinery: 4 screws, Kanpon geared turbines, 12 Kanpon boilers
SHP 150,000 = 27knots
Endurance: 7,200/16
Armament: 9×460mm/45, 12×156mm/55 (*Shinano:* 6), 12×127mm/40 AA (*Shinano:* 20×100mm), 24×25mm AA
1943: 6×155mm removed, 12×25mm AA added
1944: 152×25mm AA
Armour: Belt 270-410mm, turrets 250-650mm, barbettes 558mm, bulkheads 300mm, decks 200-230mm, c/t 300-500mm
Complement: 2,500
Class notes: The largest and most powerful battleships ever built whose construction was carried out in great secrecy. Designed to be able to compete on equal terms with any group of enemy battleships. Three triple turrets and huge tower foremast and funnel. *Shinano* was completed as an aircraft carrier and the fourth vessel was never launched

'Shokaku' Class (1937)

Aircraft Carriers: *Shokaku* (see later photo), *Zuikaku*
Displacement: 25,675tons, 29,800f/l
Dimensions: 844′10(oa) 620′2(wl) 774′6(pp)×85′4×29′1 [257.5(oa) 250(wl) 236.1(pp)×26×8.9]
Machinery: 4 screws, Kanpon geared turbines, 8 Kanpon boilers
SHP 160,000 = 34.5knots
Endurance: 9,700/18
Aircraft: 84
Armament: 16×127mm/40, 42×25mm AA
1944: 70×25mm AA
Zuikaku, August 1944: 96×25mm
Armour: Belt 216mm, deck 170mm
Complement: 1,660
Class notes: Modified 'Hiryu' type designed to operate with the 'Yamato' class. Increase in size occurred as a result of strengthened flightdeck, high speed and increased offensive and defensive weapons. A highly successful design

'Taiho' (1939)

Aircraft Carrier: *Taiho*
Displacement: 29,300tons, 34,600f/l
Dimensions: 855(oa) 830′1(wl) 780′10(pp)×90′10×31′6 [260.6(oa) 253(wl) 238(pp)×27.7×9.6]
Machinery: 4 screws, geared turbines, 8 Kanpon boilers
SHP 160,000 = 33.5knots
Endurance: 8,000/18
Aircraft: 60
Armament: 12×100mm/65 AA, 71×25mm
Armour: Belt 150mm, flightdeck 100mm, hangar deck 125mm
Complement: 1,750
Class notes: Design similar to *Shokaku* with armoured flightdeck and large island with upright funnel. Two more of this class were planned (Nos 801-802). Five additional vessels of a modified 'Taiho' type (Nos 5021-25) were also planned but none of these was ever laid down

'Zuiho' Class (1940)

Light Aircraft Carriers: *Shoho, Zuiho*
Displacement: 11,262tons, 13,950f/l
Dimensions: 674′2(oa) 660′11(wl) 606′11(pp)×59′8×21′7 [205.5(oa) 201.4(wl) 185(pp)×18.2×6.6]
Machinery: 2 screws, Kanpon geared turbines, 4 Kanpon boilers

***Zuiho* — Light aircraft carrier converted in 1940 from incomplete submarine tender *Takasaki*, 1940.** *IWM*

SHP 52,000 = 28knots
Endurance: 7,800/18
Aircraft: 30
Armament: 8×127mm/40, 8×25mm AA
Zuiho, 1943: 48×25mm
Zuiho, 1944: 68×25mm
Complement: 785
Class notes: Built as submarine tenders with diesel engines and converted in 1940-41. *Zuiho* was converted from an incomplete hull, while *Tsurugizaki* had been in service prior to conversion to *Shoho*. Their diesel engines were replaced with turbines and the flightdeck built over the existing superstructure

'Junyo' Class (1940)

Aircraft Carriers: *Hiyo, Junyo*
Displacement: 24,140tons, 26,949f/l
Dimensions: 719'7(oa) 706'4(wl) 675'10(pp)×87'7×26'9 [219.3(oa) 215.3(wl) 206(pp)×26.7×8.2]
Machinery: 2 screws, geared turbines, 4 Kanpon and 2 Mitsubishi boilers (*Junyo*), 6 Kawasaki (*Hiyo*)
SHP 56,250 = 25.5knots
Endurance: 11,700/18
Aircraft: 53
Armament: 12×127mm/40, 24×25mm
1943: 40×25mm
1944: 76×25mm
Complement: 1,224
Class notes: Laid down as large passenger liners and taken over by the navy for conversion to carriers. First Japanese carriers with a funnel on the island. Retained merchant hulls which had little protection against damage

'Ryuho' (1941)

Ligth Aircraft Carrier: *Ryuho*
Displacement: 13,360tons, 15,300f/l
Dimensions: 707'6(oa) 689(wl) 647'4(pp)×64'3×21'9 [215.6(oa) 210(wl) 197.3(pp)×19.6×6.6]
Machinery: 2 screws, Kanpon geared turbines, 4 Kanpon boilers
SHP 52,000 = 26.5knots
Endurance: 8,000/18
Aircraft: 31
Armament: 8×127mm/40, 26×25mm AA
1944: 61×25mm
Complement: 989
Class notes: Converted from submarine tender *Taigei*. The unsuccessful diesel engines were replaced by destroyer turbines. In 1944 the flightdeck was extended to the bow

'Unryu' Class (1941-1942)

Aircraft Carriers: *Amagi, [Aso, Ikoma, Kasagi], Katsuragi, Unryu*
Displacement: 17,150tons, 20,100f/l
Dimensions: 745'11(oa) 731'8(wl) 679'2(pp)×72'2×25'9 [227.4(oa) 223(wl) 207(pp)×22×7.8]
Machinery: 4 screws, geared turbines, 8 Kanpon boilers
SHP 152,000 = 34knots; *Aso* and *Katsuragi:* SHP 104,000 = 32knots
Endurance: 8,000/18
Aircraft: 65
Armament: 12×127mm/40, 51×25mm (*Amagi* and *Katsuragi:* 89×25mm)
Armour: Side 140mm, flightdeck 53mm
Complement: 1,595
Class notes: Modified 'Hiryu' design with island on starboard side. Turbines from cancelled cruisers were used except in *Aso* and *Katsuragi* which had destroyer-type turbines. Eleven others projected. *Aso, Ikoma* and *Kasagi* were not completed

Shinano (1942)

Aircraft Carrier: *Shinano*
Displacement: 64,800tons, 71,890f/l
Dimensions: 872'2(oa) 839'11(wl) 800'6(pp)×119'1×33'10 [265.8(oa) 256(wl) 244(pp)×36.3×10.3]
Machinery: 4 screws, Kanpon geared turbines, 12 Kanpon boilers
SHP 150,000 = 27knots
Endurance: 10,000/18
Aircraft: 47
Armament: 16×127mm/40, 145×25mm AA, 12×120mm
Armour: Belt 205mm, flightdeck 81mm, hangar deck 198mm
Complement: 2,400
Class notes: Converted from 'Yamato' class battleship prior to launching. Designed as a replenishment ship for other carriers rather than as an attack carrier. Barbettes retained to

house high speed elevators. The single hangar deck built over the main deck housed only fighter aircraft for defence. Although commissioned, ship was never operational and was still incomplete when sunk

'Ibuki' (1942)

Light Aircraft Carrier: *[Ibuki]*
Displacement: 12,500tons, 14,800f/l
Dimensions: 658'2(oa) 650'9(wl) 616'2(pp)×69'7×20'8 [200.6(oa) 198.3(wl) 187.8(pp)×21.2×6.3]
Machinery: 2 screws, Kanpon geared turbines, 4 Kanpon boilers
SHP 72,000 = 29knots
Endurance: 7,500/18
Aircraft: 27
Armament: 4×80mm /40, 48×25mm
Complement: 1,015
Class notes: Laid down as cruiser of modified 'Suzuya' type, conversion to aircraft carrier never completed

'Chitose' Class (1943)

Light Aircraft Carriers: *Chitose, Chiyoda*
Displacement: 11,190tons, 13,647f/l
Dimensions: 631'7(oa) 605'10(wl) 570'10(pp)×68'3×24'8 [192.5(oa) 184.6(wl) 174(pp)×20.8×7.5]
Machinery: 2 screws, geared turbines and diesels, 4 Kanpon boilers
SHP 44,000 + IHP 12,800 = 28.9knots
Endurance: 11,000/18
Aircraft: 30
Armament: 8×127mm/45, 30×25mm
Class notes: Converted from seaplane carriers having previously (1941) been modified to carry midget submarines. Had no island. *Mizuho* of this class was lost prior to conversion

Individual Ships

Akagi

Type: 1) Battlecruiser, 2) Aircraft Carrier
Class: 1) 'Amagi' (1918), 2) 'Akagi' (1922)
Nomenclature: Mountain northwest of Tokyo

History:
1920 December 6: Laid down at Kure as battlecruiser
1922 February 5: Construction suspended when 40% complete to comply with Washington Treaty
1923 Reordered as aircraft carrier
1925 April 22: Launched
1927 March 25: Completed
1935-38 Reconstructed at Sasebo, full-length flightdeck and port island added
World War 2: China, Pearl Harbor, Rabaul, Darwin, Java, Ceylon, Midway
1942 June 4: Severely damaged by US aircraft at Battle of Midway and sunk by destroyers *Nowake* and *Arashi* (221 dead)

Aki

Type: Pre-dreadnought
Class: 'Aki' (1904)
Nomenclature: Province of western Honshu

History:
1906 March 15: Laid down at Kure
1907 April 15: Launched
1911 March 11: Completed
World War 1:
1919 Refit
1919 September 20: Stricken
1924 September 2: Sunk as a target by battleships *Hyuga* and *Kongo* in Tokyo Bay

Amagi

Type: 1) Battlecruiser, 2) Aircraft Carrier
Class: 1) 'Amagi' (1918)
Nomenclature: Mountain southwest of Tokyo

History:
1920 December 16: Laid down at Yokosuka
1922 February 5: Construction suspended when 40% complete to comply with Washington Treaty
1923 Reordered as aircraft carrier
1923 September 1: Hull badly damaged by earthquake, conversion cancelled
1924 April 14: Stricken and broken up on stocks

***Unryu* — Aircraft carrier, 1944.** *IWM*

Amagi

Type: Aircraft Carrier
Class: 'Unryu' (1941)

History:
1942 October 1: Laid down by Mitsubishi
1943 October 15: Launched
1944 August 11: Completed
1945 March 19: Damaged by US aircraft at Kure
1945 July 24: Capsized in shallow water at Kure after being damaged by US aircraft
1947 December: Refloated and broken up

Asahi

Type: Pre-dreadnought
Class: 'Asahi' (1896)
Nomenclature: Rising sun, poetic name for birth of the new Japan

History:
1897 August 1: Laid down by John Brown
1899 March 13: Launched
1900 July 31: Completed
1900 April 30: Damaged by grounding off Southsea en route to Japan
1904 Blockade of Port Arthur
1904 August 10: Battle of the Yellow Sea (one hit)
1904 October 26: Moderately damaged by mine off Port Arthur
1905 May 27: Damaged by gunfire at Battle of Tsushima (nine hits)
1914 Gunnery training ship
1917 Refit, rearmed with Japanese guns
1921 First class coast defence ship
1923 April 1: Submarine depot ship; disarmed, reboilered, one funnel removed, 11,441tons, four Kanpon boilers, 12knots
1938 Repair ship
1942 May 25: Torpedoed and sunk by US submarine *Salmon* 100 miles southwest of Cape Paderan in South China Sea

Asama

Type: Armoured Cruiser
Class: 'Asama' (1897)
Nomenclature: Mountain in central Honshu

History:
1896 September 20: Laid down by Armstrong
1898 March 22: Launched
1899 March 18: Completed
1904 Blockade of Port Arthur
1904 August 10: Battle of the Yellow Sea
1905 May 27: Severely damaged by gunfire at Battle of Tsushima (11 hits)
World War 1: 1914, 1st South Seas Squadron, search for Spee's squadron
1914 December 3: Damaged in Turtle Bay
1915 January 31: Wrecked in San Bartolome Bay, Baja California
1915 May 8: Refloated, repaired and refitted at Yokosuka, reboilered
1917 March: Recommissioned
1921 First class coast defence ship
1935 Severely damaged by running on rocks in Inland Sea, not repaired
1937 Stationary training ship, Kure
1947 March: Broken up at Hitachi

Aso

Type: Armoured Cruiser
Class: 'Aso' (1905)
Nomenclature: Mountain in Kyushu

History:
1899 March: Laid down at La Seyne for Russia as ***Bayan***
1900 June 12: Launched
1902 Completed
1904 December 8: Sunk at Port Arthur
1905 June 24: Refloated, rebuilt at Maizuru, renamed ***Aso***
1913 Refit
1920 Converted to minelayer, 420 mines
1930 April 1: Stricken, renamed ***Hai Kan No 4***
1932 August 8: Sunk as target by cruiser *Myoko* in Tokyo Bay

Aso

Type: Aircraft Carrier
Class: 'Unryu' (1941)

History:
1943 June 8: Laid down at Kure
1944 November 1: Launched
1945 January: Construction suspended when 60% complete
1945 July 24: Hull heavily damaged by US aircraft at Kure
1945 Trials hulk
1947 April: Broken up at Sasebo

Atago

Type: Battlecruiser
Class: 'Amagi' (1918)
Nomenclature: Mountain in central Honshu

History:
1921 November 22: Laid down by Kawasaki
1922 February 5: Construction suspended to comply with Washington Treaty
1924 April 14: Stricken and broken up

Azuma

Type: Ironclad Ram
Class: 'Azuma' (1867)
Nomenclature: The area east of Mount Fuji

History:
1863 Laid down by Arman for Confederate government
1864 June 21: Launched
1864 October: Commissioned as ***Stonewall***
1867 Sold by United States to Japan for the Shogunate government
1868 April 24: Arrived at Yokohama
1869 January: Officially transfered to the Emperor, renamed ***Kotetsu***
1869 June: Led government forces against rebels at Hakodate
1871 December: Renamed ***Azuma***
1888 January 28: Stricken, accommodation ship
c1908 Broken up

Azuma

Type: Armoured Cruiser
Class: 'Azuma' (1897)

***Asahi* — Battleship of 1899.** *Conway Photo Library*

History:
1898 March: Laid down by Loire
1899 June 24: Launched
1900 July 28: Completed
1904 February 9: Bombardment of Port Arthur
1904 August 14: Damaged by gunfire at Battle of the Yellow Sea (10 hits)
1905 May 27: Damaged by gunfire at Battle of Tsushima (16 hits)
1914 Training ship
1915 Refit
1924 Refit, rearmed
1941 Hulk
1945 July 18: Damaged by US aircraft at Yokosuka
1946 Broken up

Chin Yen

Type: Turret Ship
Class: 'Chin Yen' (1895)
Nomenclature: Former name retained

History:
1880 Laid down by Vulcan for China as ***Chen Yuen***
1882 November 28: Launched
1884 Completed
1895 February 9: Sunk at Wei Hai Wei, later captured by Japan
1895 Salved by Japan, named ***Chin Yen;*** refit, rearmed
1910 Training ship for pilots
1911 Stricken and broken up 1914

Chitose

Type: Light Aircraft Carrier
Class: 'Chitose' (1943)
Nomenclature: River in Hokkaido; a thousand years

History:
1934 November 26: Laid down at Sasebo as seaplane carrier
1936 November 29: Launched
1938 July 25: Completed
1941 Modified to carry midget submarines
1943 Converted to aircraft carrier, at Sasebo
1944 January 1: Completed
World War 2: Philippine Sea, Leyte Gulf
1944 February 1: Hit by two dud torpedoes from US submarine *Bonefish* off Tawi Taw
1944 October 25: Sunk by US aircraft off Cape Engano during Battle of Leyte Gulf

Chiyoda

Type: Light Aircraft Carrier
Class: 'Chitose' (1943)
Nomenclature: Ancient name for a castle in Tokyo; field of a thousand generations

History:
1936 December 14: Laid down at Yokosuka as seaplane carrier
1937 November 19: Launched
1938 December 15: Completed
1941 Modified to carry midget submarines
1943 Converted to aircraft carrier at Yokosuka
1943 October 27: Slightly damaged by fire on lower deck during conversion at Yokosuka
1943 October 31: Completed
World War 2: Philippine Sea, Leyte Gulf
1944 June 19: Damaged by aircraft bomb at Battle of the Philippine Sea
1944 October 25: Damaged by US aircraft and sunk by US cruisers off Cape Engano during Battle of Leyte Gulf

Fuji

Type: Pre-dreadnought
Class: 'Yashima' (1892)
Nomenclature: Highest mountain on Honshu

History:
1894 August 1: Laid down by Thames
1896 March 31: Launched
1897 August 17: Completed
1901 Refit
1904 February 9: Hit twice during bombardment of Port Arthur
1904 March 22: Bombarded Port Arthur

***Haruna* — Battleship, 1934, built as a battlecruiser, after second reconstruction.** *IWM*

1904 August 10: Battle of the Yellow Sea
1905 May 27: Damaged by gunfire at Battle of Tsushima (11 hits)
1905 Refit; reboilered, fighting tops removed
1910 Refit; rearmed with Japanese guns
—— First class coast defence ship; gunnery training ship
1922 September 1: Stricken; accommodation and training hulk, Yokosuka
1945 Tender to navigation school
1948 Broken up at Yokosuka

Fuso

Type: Central Battery Ship
Class: 'Fuso' (1875)
Nomenclature: Ancient name for Japan

History:
1875 September: Laid down by Samuda
1877 April 14: Launched
1878 January: Completed
1894 Reconstructed, mainmast removed
1894 September 17: Lightly damaged at Battle of Yalu
1897 October 29: Beached off Nagahama, Shikoku, after collision in gale with cruiser *Matsushima*
1898 September: Raised and repaired at Kure
1903 Coast defence ship, rearmed
1908 Stricken, broken up 1910

Fuso

Type: Dreadnought
Class: 'Fuso' (1911)

History:
1912 March 11: Laid down at Kure
1914 March 28: Launched
1915 November 8: Completed
1927-28 Refit; searchlights, fire control platforms and 6×78mm AA guns added
1930-33 Reconstructed at Kure; reboilered and re-engined, forefunnel removed, mast rebuilt, elevation of guns increased, anti-torpedo bulges added
1934-35 Refit
World War 2: Aleutians, Operation 'Kon', Leyte
1944 October 25: Sunk by gunfire and torpedoes in Surigao Strait during Battle of Leyte Gulf

Haruna

Type: Battlecruiser
Class: 'Kongo' (1910)
Nomenclature: Mountain in north central Honshu

History:
1912 March 16: Laid down by Kawasaki
1913 December 14: Launched
1915 April 19: Completed
1917 Summer: Damaged by German mine in South Pacific
1924-28 Reconstructed at Yokosuka
1933-34 Reconstructed at Kure, reclassified battleship
World War 2: Malaya landings, E Indies, Darwin, Ceylon, Midway, Guadalcanal, Santa Cruz, Philippine Sea, Leyte Gulf
1944 June 19: Damaged by aircraft bomb at Philippine Sea
1944 November 22: Stranded at Lingga
1945 March 19: Damaged by aircraft bombs at Kure
1945 July 28: Sunk in shallow water near Kure by US carrier aircraft
1946 Refloated and broken up at Harima

Hatsuse

Type: Pre-dreadnought
Class: 'Shikishima' (1894)
Nomenclature: New tide

History:
1898 January 10: Laid down by Armstrong
1899 June 27: Launched
1901 January 18: Completed
1904 May 15: Sank after hitting two mines southeast of Port Arthur (493 dead)

Hiei

Type: Armoured Corvette
Class: 'Kongo' (1875)
Nomenclature: Mountain near Kyoto, a place of pilgrimage

History:
1875 September: Laid down by Milford Haven
1877 June 12: Launched
1878 March 23: Completed
1894 September 17: Damaged by gunfire at Battle of the Yalu (19 dead)
1897 Surveying vessel
1911 April 1: Stricken

Hiei

Type: Battlecruiser
Class: 'Kongo' (1910)

History:
1911 November 4: Laid down at Yokosuka
1912 November 21: Launched
1914 August 4: Completed
World War 1: 1914 Search for Spee's squadron
1932 Cadet training ship; 19,500tons, 11 Kanpon boilers, 6×355mm, 16×152mm, 4×127mm AA, 4×76mm
1936-40 Reconstructed at Kure, reclassified battleship
World War 2: Pearl Harbor, East Indies, Ceylon, Midway, Eastern Solomons, Santa Cruz, Guadalcanal
1942 March 1: Sank US destroyer *Edsall* south of Java, with *Kirishima*
1942 November 13: Sunk by gunfire, torpedoes and air attack off Savo Island in First Battle of Guadalcanal

Hiryu

Type: Aircraft Carrier
Class: 'Soryu' (1931)
Nomenclature: Flying dragon

History:
1936 July 8: Laid down at Yokosuka
1937 November 16: Launched
1939 July 5: Completed
World War 2: China, Pearl Harbor, Wake Island, Rabaul, Ambon, Timor, Darwin, Java, Ceylon, Midway
1942 June 4: Severely damaged by US aircraft at Battle of Midway and sunk by escorting destroyers the following day (416 dead). Flag of Rear-Adm T. Yamaguchi who was lost

Hiyo

Type: Aircraft Carrier
Class: 'Junyo' (1940)
Nomenclature: Flying hawk

History:
1939 November 30: Laid down by Kawasaki as passenger liner ***Izumo Maru***
1940 August: Acquired for conversion to aircraft carrier, renamed ***Hiyo***
1941 June 24: Launched
1942 July 31: Completed
World War 2: Guadalcanal, Philippine Sea
1942 October 22: Damaged by fire in generator while at sea in Eastern Solomons
1943 June 10: Torpedoed by US submarine *Trigger* off Tokyo Bay, severely damaged
1944 June 20: Torpedoed and sunk by US aircraft 450 miles northwest of Yap Island, Battle of Philippine Sea

Hizen

Type: Pre-dreadnought
Class: 'Hizen' (1905)
Nomenclature: Province of northern Kyushu

History:
1898 December: Laid down by Cramp for Russia as ***Retvizan***
1900 October 23: Launched
1902 Completed
1904 December 6: Sunk by Japanese artillery in Port Arthur harbour
1905 September 22: Refloated by Japanese, repaired at Sasebo, renamed ***Hizen***
1908 November: Recommissioned
1913 Refit
1921 September: First class coast defence ship

***Hatsuse* — Pre-dreadnought of 1899, lost off Port Arthur.** *IWM*

***Ise* — Battleship of 1916, as converted to hybrid battleship/aircraft carrier with flightdeck replacing aft turrets.** *US Navy Official*

1922 Disarmed
1923 September 20: Stricken
1924 July: Sunk as target in Bungo Straits

Hosho

Type: Aircraft Carrier
Class: 'Hosho' (1921)
Nomenclature: Soaring phoenix

History:
1919 Projected as an auxiliary tanker designed to carry aircraft, named ***Hiryu***
1919 October 21: Renamed ***Hosho***
1919 December 16: Laid down by Asano
1921 October 13: Redesignated aircraft depot ship
1921 November 13: Launched
1922 December 27: Completed
1923 Refit: island and tripod mast removed
1936 Refit
1936-39 China
World War 2: Midway
1941-45 Training carrier
1944 September 27: Damaged at Seto
1945 March 19: Damaged by air attack at Kure
1945 April 20: Disarmed
1945 Repatriation transport
1947 April: Broken up at Osaka

Hyuga

Type: Dreadnought
Class: 'Ise' (1914)
Nomenclature: Province of southeast Kyushu

History:
1915 May 6: Laid down by Mitsubishi
1917 Janaury 27: Launched
1918 April 30: Completed
1934-36 Reconstructed at Kure; forefunnel removed, new pagoda foremast, re-engined and reboilered, elevation of guns increased, anti-torpedo bulges added; thicker deck armour
World War 2: Midway, Leyte Gulf
1943 July: Converted to battleship-carrier at Sasebo
1945 March 1: Deactivated
1945 July 24: Sunk in shallow water near Kure by US carrier aircraft
1952 Refloated and broken up

Ibuki

Type: Armoured Cruiser
Class: 'Kurama' (1904)
Nomenclature: Mountain in central Honshu

History:
1906 May 22: Laid down as Kure
1907 November 21: Launched
1909 November 1: Completed
1912 Redesignated battlecruiser
1918 Refit
World War 1: 1914 Search for *Emden* and convoy escort, Indian Ocean
1921 Redesignated first class cruiser
1923 September 20: Stricken and broken up 1924 at Kobe

Ibuki

Type: Light Aircraft Carrier
Class: 'Ibuki' (1942)

History:
1942 April 24: Laid down at Kure as heavy cruiser
1943 May 21: Launched, towed to Sasebo for completion as aircraft carrier
1945 March: Construction suspended when 80% complete
1947 August: Broken up at Sasebo

Iki

Type: Pre-dreadnought
Class: 'Iki' (1905)
Nomenclature: Island off Kyushu in the Straits of Korea

History:
1886 July 23: Laid down by Franco-Russian for Russia as ***Imperator Nikolai I***
1889 May 20: Launched
1892 Completed
1905 May 28: Captured after the Battle of Tsushima
1905 July: Recommissioned by Japan, renamed ***Iki***
1905-10 Gunnery training ship
1910-15 Coast Defence and training ship
1915 May 1: Stricken
1915 October: Sunk as a target off Ise by battlecruisers *Kongo* and *Hiei*

Ikoma

Type: Armoured Cruiser
Class: 'Tsukuba' (1904)

Izumo — **Armoured cruiser of 1899, as it appeared in 1931.** *Marius Bar*

Nomenclature: Mountain near Kyoto

History:
1905 March 15: Laid down at Kure
1906 April 9: Launched
1908 March 24: Completed
1912 Redesignated battlecruiser
World War 1: 1914 1st South Seas Squadron, Search for Spee's squadron
1919 Gunnery training ship
1921 Redesignated first class cruiser
1923 September 20: Stricken and broken up 1924 at Nagasaki

Ikoma

Type: Aircraft Carrier
Class: 'Unryu' (1942)

History:
1943 July 5: Laid down by Kawasaki
1944 November 17: Launched
1945 January: Construction suspended when 60% complete
1945 July 24: Hull heavily damaged by US aircraft in Ikei Bay
1947 March: Broken up at Tanamo

Ise

Type: Dreadnought
Class: 'Ise' (1914)
Nomenclature: Province of south central Honshu

History:
1915 May 10: Laid down by Kawasaki
1916 November 12: Launched
1917 December 15: Completed
1930-31 Refit
1935-37 Reconstructed at Kure
World War 2: Midway, Leyte Gulf
1943 July: Converted to battleship-carrier at Kure; two aft turrets removed and flightdeck added
1945 March 1: Deactivated
1945 July 28: Sunk in shallow water northwest of Kure by US carrier aircraft
1946 Refloated and broken up at Harima

Iwami

Type: Pre-dreadnought
Class: 'Iwami' (1905)
Nomenclature: Province of western Honshu

History:
1900 June 11: Laid down by Franco-Russian for Russia as ***Orel***
1902 July 19: Launched
1904 September: Completed
1905 May 28: Captured after the Battle of Tsushima, repaired at Kure, renamed ***Iwami***
1907 June: Recommissioned
World War 1: 1914 Attack on Tsingtao
1922 September 1: Stricken
1924 July: Sunk as aircraft target off Miura

Iwate

Type: Armoured Cruiser
Class: 'Izumo' (1897)
Nomenclature: Ancient province in northern Honshu

History:
1898 November 11: Laid down by Armstrong
1900 March 29: Launched
1901 February 16: Completed
1904 February 9: Bombardment of Port Arthur
1904 August 14: Severely damaged by gunfire at Battle of the Yellow Sea (23 hits)
1905 May 27: Damaged by gunfire at Battle of Tsushima (16 hits)
World War 1: 1914 1st South Seas Squadron, Search for Spee's squadron
1921 First class coast defence ship
1924 Rearmed
1931 Refit, reboilered
1942 First class cruiser
1943 Training ship; 4×152mm, 4×127mm, 3×79mm, 9×25mm AA guns
1945 July 24: Sunk in shallow water by US aircraft at Kure
1947 January: Broken up at Harima

Izumo

Type: Armoured Cruiser
Class: 'Izumo' (1897)
Nomenclature: Ancient province in western Honshu

History:
1898 May 16: Laid down by Armstrong
1899 September 19: Launched
1900 September 1: Completed
1904 February 9: Bombardment of Port Arthur

1904 August 14: Damaged by gunfire at Battle of the Yellow Sea (20 hits)
1905 May 27: Damaged by gunfire at Battle of Tsushima (nine hits)
1915 Refit
1921 First class defence ship
1924 Rearmed
1932-42 China Squadron (flag)
1935 Refit, reboilered
1941 December: Attack on Hong Kong
1943 Training ship, Etajima naval college
1945 July 28: Sunk by US aircraft at Kure
1947 September: Refloated and broken up at Harima

Junyo

Type: Aircraft Carrier
Class: 'Junyo' (1940)
Nomenclature: Falcon hawk

History:
1939 March 20: Laid down by Mitsubishi as passenger liner ***Kashiwara Maru***
1940 August: Acquired for conversion to aircraft carrier, renamed ***Junyo***
1941 June 26: Launched
1942 May 5: Completed
World War 2: Dutch Harbor, Aleutians, Santa Cruz, Guadalcanal, Philippine Sea
1943 November 5: Torpedoed by US submarine *Halibut* north of Rabaul
1944 December 9: Torpedoed by US submarine *Redfish* off Nagasaki, not repaired
1947 August: Broken up at Sasebo

Kaga

Type: 1) Battleship, 2) Aircraft Carrier
Class: 1) 'Kaga' (1918), 2) 'Kaga' (1923)
Nomenclature: Province of north central Honshu

History:
1920 July 20: Laid down by Kawasaki as battleship
1921 November 17: Launched
1922 February 5: Stricken to comply with Washington Treaty
1922 July: Towed to Yokosuka
1923 November 19: Incomplete hull substituted for damaged *Amagi* for conversion to aircraft carrier
1928 March 31: Completed
1934-35 Reconstructed at Sasebo; full-length flightdeck and starboard island added
1935 June 25: Recommissioned
World War 2: China, Pearl Harbor, Rabaul, Darwin, Java, Midway
1942 June 4: Sunk by US aircraft at Battle of Midway (800 dead)

Kasagi

Type: Aircraft Carrier
Class: 'Unryu' (1941)
Nomenclature: Mountain near Kyoto

History:
1943 April 14: Laid down by Mitsubishi
1944 October 19: Launched
1945 April 1: Construction suspended when 85% complete; hull towed to Sasebo
1947 November: Broken up

Kashima

Type: Pre-dreadnought
Class: 'Kashima' (1903)
Nomenclature: Shinto shrine north of Tokyo; 'deer island'

History:
1904 February 29: Laid down by Armstrong
1905 March 22: Launched
1906 May 23: Completed
1915 Refit
1923 September 20: Stricken
1924 Broken up at Nagasaki

Kasuga

Type: Armoured Cruiser
Class: 'Kasuga' (1903)
Nomenclature: An ancient shrine; 'a day in spring'

History:
1902 March 10: Laid down by Ansaldo for Argentina as ***Mitra***
1902 October 22: Launched as ***Rivadavia***
1903 December 20: Completed
1903 December 29: Purchased by Japan, renamed ***Kasuga***
1904 May 15: Sank cruiser *Yoshino* in collision off Elliot Island
1904 August 14: Damaged by gunfire at Battle of Yellow Sea (three hits)
1905 May 27: Damaged by gunfire at Battle of Tsushima (three hits)
1914 Refit, reboilered
1918 January 13: Went aground in Banka Straits, refloated in June
1927 Engineers' training ship
1942 Hulk
1945 July 18: Capsized at Yokosuka after being damaged by US aircraft
1948 August: Refloated and broken up at Uraga

Katori

Type: Pre-dreadnought
Class: 'Kashima' (1903)
Nomenclature: Shinto shrine north of Tokyo

History:
1904 April 27: Laid down by Vickers
1905 July 4: Launched
1906 May 20: Completed
1916 Refit
1923 September 20: Stricken
1925 January: Broken up at Maizuru

Katsuragi

Type: Aircraft Carrier
Class: 'Unryu' (1941)
Nomenclature: Mountain south of Osaka

History:
1942 December 8: Laid down at Kure
1944 January 19: Launched
1944 October 15: Completed
1945 March 19: Damaged by US aircraft at Kure
1945 July 28: Damaged by US aircraft at Kure
1945-46 Repatriation transport
1947 November: Broken up at Osaka

Kashima — Battleship of 1905, as completed with anti-torpedo defence net along hull. *IWM*

Kawachi

Type: Dreadnought
Class: 'Kawachi' (1908)
Nomenclature: Province of west central Honshu

History:
1909 April 11: Laid down at Kure
1910 October 15: Launched
1912 March 31: Completed
World War 1: Home defence
1918 July 12: Destroyed by magazine explosion in Tokuyama Bay (700 dead)

Kii

Type: Dreadnought
Class: 'Kii' (1921)
Nomenclature: Province of west central Honshu

History:
1921 Ordered from Yokosuka; never laid down
1922 February 5: Construction suspended to comply with Washington Treaty
1924 April 14: Cancelled

Kirishima

Type: Battlecruiser
Class: 'Kongo' (1910)
Nomenclature: Mountain in Kyushu

History:
1912 March 17: Laid down by Mitsubishi
1913 December 1: Launched
1915 April 19: Completed
1927-30 Reconstructed at Kure
1934-36 Reconstructed at Sasebo, reclassified battleship
World War 2: Pearl Harbor, East Indies, Darwin, Ceylon, Midway, Eastern Solomons, Santa Cruz, Gaudalcanal
1942 March 1: Sank US destroyer *Edsall* south of Java, with *Hiei*
1942 November 15: Sunk by gunfire of US battleship *Washington* during Second Battle of Guadalcanal

Kongo

Type: Armoured Corvette
Class: 'Kongo' (1875)
Nomenclature: Mountain in central Honshu

History:
1875 September: Laid down by Earle
1877 April: Launched
1878 January: Completed
1887 June: Went aground off coast of Japan
1896 Training ship
1901 April 1: Stricken and broken up

Kongo

Type: Battlecruiser
Class: 'Kongo' (1910)

History:
1911 January 17: Laid down by Vickers
1912 May 18: Launched
1913 August 16: Completed
World War 1: Search for Spee's squadron
1929-31 Reconstructed at Yokosuka, reboilered, increased armour protection, bulges added
1935-37 Reconstructed at Yokosuka, reclassified battleship, re-engined and reboilered
World War 2: Malaya landings, Ambon, Darwin, Ceylon, Midway, Guadalcanal, Santa Cruz, Philippine Sea, Leyte Gulf
1944 November 21: Torpedoed and sunk by US submarine *Sealion* 65 miles northwest of Keelung

Kurama

Type: Armoured Cruiser
Class: 'Kurama' (1904)
Nomenclature: Historical site in Kyoto

History:
1905 August 23: Laid down at Yokosuka
1907 October 21: Launched
1911 February 28: Completed
1912 Redesignated battlecruiser
World War 1: 1914 Search for *Emden* and convoy escort Indian Ocean, 1st South Seas Squadron, search for Spee's squadron

***Nagato* — Dreadnought of 1919, in 1932 with forward funnel trunked aft.** *Conway Photo Library*

1918 Refit
1921 Redesignated first class cruiser
1923 September 20: Stricken and broken up 1924 at Kobe

Mikasa

Type: Pre-dreadnought
Class: 'Asahi' (1896)
Nomenclature: Mountain near ancient Kyoto

History:
1899 January 24: Laid down by Vickers
1900 November 8: Launched
1902 March 1: Completed
1904-05 Flagship of Admiral Togo during Russo-Japanese War
1904 February 9: Hit three times during bombardment of Port Arthur
1904 August 14: Damaged by gunfire at Battle of the Yellow Sea (22 hits)
1905 May 27: Damaged by gunfire at Battle of Tsushima (32 hits)
1905 September 12: Sank at moorings at Sasebo after ammunition explosion in after magazine (114 dead)
1906 August 7: Refloated and recommissioned, reconstruction cancelled
1916 Refit
1921 September 17: Ran aground off Vladivostok on Askold Island
1923 September 20: Stricken, preserved as a memorial until 1945
1960 Restored as a memorial at Yokosuka

Mishima

Type: Coast Defence Ship
Class: 'Mishima' (1905)
Nomenclature: Island in the Straits of Korea

History:
1892 July 20: Laid down by New Admiralty for Russia as ***Admiral Senyavin***
1894 August 22: Launched
1896 Completed
1905 May 28: Captured after Battle of Tsushima
1905 July: Recommissioned by Japan, renamed ***Mishima***
1907 Spring: Damaged by ammunition explosion
1928 Submarine depot ship
1936 April 10: Hulk ***Hai Kan No 7***
1936 January 10: Sunk as a target by gunfire

Musashi

Type: Battleship
Class: 'Yamato' (1937)
Nomenclature: Province of east central Honshu

History:
1938 March 29: Laid down by Mitsubishi
1940 November 1: Launched
1942 August 5: Completed
World War 2: Philippine Sea, Leyte Gulf
1943 Flagship of Admiral Koga
1944 March 29: Torpedoed by US submarine *Tunny* off Palau
1944 October 24: Sunk in Battle of Leyte Gulf in Visayan Sea after being hit by numerous bombs and torpedoes from US carrier aircraft (1,039 dead)

Mutsu

Type: Dreadnought
Class: 'Nagato' (1916)
Nomenclature: Ancient name for the provinces of northern Honshu

History:
1918 June 1: Laid down at Yokosuka
1920 May 31: Launched
1921 October 24: Completed
1924 Refit, forward funnel trunked aft
1930 Refit, clipper bow fitted
1934-36 Reconnaissance at Yokosuka
World War 2: Midway, Eastern Solomons
1943 June 8: Sunk by magazine explosion in Hiroshima Bay (1,222 dead)

1935 April 1: Stricken, renamed ***Hai Kan No 6***
1935 Autumn: Sunk as target off Kure
1936 Refloated and broken up

Nagato

Type: Dreadnought
Class: 'Nagato' (1916)
Nomenclature: Province of western Honshu

History:
1917 August 28: Laid down at Kure
1919 November 9: Launched
1920 November 25: Completed
1924 Refit, forward funnel trunked aft
1934-36 Reconstructed at Kure; fore funnel removed, re-engined and reboilered, anti-torpedo bulges added, elevation of guns increased, clipper bow fitted
1941 Flagship of Combined Fleet
World War 2: Midway, Philippine Sea, Leyte Gulf
1944 October 25: Damaged by aircraft bombs off Samar
1945 January: Inoperative at Yokosuka, funnel and mainmast removed for camouflage
1945 September: Surrendered
1946 July: Target ship in nuclear tests at Bikini, 24 July 1946, severely damaged in second test, wreck sank 29 July 1946

Nisshin

Type: Armoured Cruiser
Class: 'Kasuga' (1903)
Nomenclature: 'Daily progression', ie a steady, methodical advance

History:
1902 March 29: Laid down by Ansaldo for Argentina as ***Roca***
1903 February 9: Launched as ***Moreno***
1903 December 29: Purchased by Japan, renamed ***Nisshin***
1904 January 17: Completed
1904 April 15: Damaged by gunfire of Russian battleship *Peresviet* off Port Arthur
1904 August 14: Damaged by gunfire at Battle of the Yellow Sea (three hits)
1905 May 27: Damaged by gunfire at Battle of Tsushima (11 hits)
1914 Refit, reboilered
World War 1: 1914 Indian Ocean, Search for Spee's squadron, 1918 Mediterranean
1927 Training and depot ship, Yokosuka

Okinoshima

Type: Coast Defence Ship
Class: 'Mishima' (1905)
Nomenclature: Island in the Straits of Korea

History:
1894 October 12: Laid down by New Admiralty for Russia as ***General Admiral Apraksin***
1896 May 12: Launched
1899 Completed
1905 May 28: Captured after the Battle of Tsushima
1905 July: Recommissioned by Japan, renamed ***Okinoshima***
1905 Training ship
1915 Disarmed, accommodation ship for cadets
1922 Stricken and hulked
1939 Broken up

Owari

Type: Dreadnought
Class: 'Kii' (1921)
Nomenclature: Province of south central Honshu

History:
1921 Ordered from Kure
1922 February 5: Construction suspended to comply with Washington Treaty
1924 April 14: Cancelled

Ryuho

Type: Light Aircraft Carrier
Class: 'Ryuho' (1941)
Nomenclature: Dragon phoenix

History:
1933 April 12: Laid down at Yokosuka as submarine depot ship ***Taigei***
1933 November 16: Launched
1935 March 31: Completed
1941 December: Converted to aircraft carrier, renamed ***Ryuho***
1942 November 28: Recommissioned
World War 2: Philippine Sea
1942 December 12: Torpedoed by US submarine *Drum* off Hachijo Island
1943 December 4: Torpedoed by US submarine *Sailfish* 200 miles south of Yokosuka
1944 June 20: Damaged by aircraft at Battle of Philippine Sea
1945 March 19: Damaged by aircraft bombs at Kure
1947 October: Broken up at Kure

Ryujo

Type: Light Aircraft Carrier
Class: 'Ryujo' (1927)
Nomenclature: Fighting dragon

History:
1929 November 26: Laid down at Yokohama
1932 April 2: Launched
1933 May 9: Completed at Yokosuka

1934-36 Reconstructed at Yukosuka, rearmed
1935 September 26: Damaged in typhoon east of Honshu
World War 2: China, Philippines, East Indies, Aleutians, Eastern Solomons
1942 August 24: Sunk by aircraft of US carrier *Saratoga* near Bradley Reef during Battle of the Eastern Solomons

Sagami

Type: Pre-dreadnought
Class: 'Sagami' (1905)
Nomenclature: Province of southeast Honshu

History:
1895 November 21: Laid down by Baltic for Russia as ***Peresviet***
1898 May 19: Launched
1901 Completed
1904 December 6: Scuttled at Port Arthur
1905 June 29: Refloated by Japan and reconstructed at Yokosuka, renamed ***Sagami***
1908 April: Recommissioned, designated first class coast defence ship
1916 April 5: Returned to Russia, renamed ***Peresviet***

Satsuma

Type: Pre-dreadnought
Class: 'Satsuma' (1904)
Nomenclature: Province of southwest Kyushu

History:
1905 May 15: Laid down at Yokosuka
1906 November 15: Launched
1910 March 25: Completed
World War 1: 1914 2nd South Seas Squadron at Truk, Search for Spee's squadron
1922 Disarmed
1923 September 20: Stricken, target ship
1924 September 7: Sunk as target in Tokyo Bay by battleships *Nagato* and *Mutsu*

Settsu

Type: Dreadnought
Class: 'Kawachi' (1908)
Nomenclature: Province of west central Honshu

History:
1909 January 18: Laid down at Yokosuka
1911 March 30: Launched
1912 July 1: Completed
World War 1: Home defence
1923 October 1: Stricken; converted to target ship
1935 Converted to radio controlled target ship; 16,310tons, 16knots
1940 Reboilered
1945 July 24: Sunk in shallow water at Kure by carrier aircraft
1947 July: Broken up at Harima

Shikishima

Type: Pre-dreadnought
Class: 'Shikishima' (1894)
Nomenclature: 'The outspread isles', a poetical name for Japan

***Shokaku* — Aircraft carrier, 1941.** *IWM*

History:
1897 March 29: Laid down by Thames
1898 November 1: Launched
1900 January 26: Completed
1904 February 9: Damaged during bombardment of Port Arthur
1904 August 10: Battle of the Yellow Sea
1905 May 27: Damaged by gunfire at Battle of Tsushima (10 hits)
1919 Refit
1921 September 1: First class coast defence ship; training ship
1923 April 1: Transport; seamen's training ship
1948 January: Broken up at Sasebo

Shinano

Type: 1) Battleship, 2) Aircraft Carrier
Class: 1) 'Yamato' (1937), 2) 'Shinano' (1942)
Nomenclature: Province of central Honshu

History:
1940 May 4: Laid down at Yokosuka
1942 July: Reordered as aircraft carrier when 50% complete
1943 November 11: Launched
1944 November 18: Completed
1944 November 29: Torpedoed and sunk by US submarine *Archerfish* 160 miles southeast of Cape Muroto while en route to fitting out (500 dead)

Shoho

Type: Light Aircraft Carrier
Class: 'Zuiho' (1940)
Nomenclature: Happy phoenix

History:
1934 December 3: Laid down at Yokosuka as submarine depot ship ***Tsurugizaki***
1935 June 1: Launched
1939 January 15: Completed
1941 Converted to aircraft carrier at Yokosuka; renamed ***Shoho***
1942 January 26: Completed
World War 2: Coral Sea
1942 May 7: Sunk by US aircraft off Woodlark Island during Battle of the Coral Sea (about 600 dead)

Shokaku

Type: Aircraft Carrier
Class: 'Hosho' (1921)
Nomenclature: Happy crane

History:
1923 November 19: Contract cancelled following order for conversion of *Akagi* and *Kaga*

1922 April 1: Stricken and hulked
1922 July 13: Capsized at Kure during removal of armour
1946 Broken up at Kure

Shokaku

Type: Aircraft Carrier
Class: 'Shokaku' (1937)

History:
1937 December 12: Laid down at Yokosuka
1939 June 1: Launched
1941 August 8: Completed
World War 2: Pearl Harbor, Rabaul, Darwin, Java, Ceylon, Coral Sea, Eastern Solomons, Santa Cruz, Philippine Sea
1942 May 8: Damaged by three bomb hits during Battle of Coral Sea
1942 October 26: Damaged by six bomb hits during Battle of Santa Cruz
1944 June 19: Torpedoed and sunk by US submarine *Cavalla* 140 miles north of Yap Island prior to Battle of the Philippine Sea (1,263 dead)

Soryu

Type: Aircraft Carrier
Class: 'Soryu'(1931)
Nomenclature: Blue dragon

History:
1934 November 20: Laid down at Kure
1935 December 23: Launched
1937 December 29: Completed
World War 2: China, Pearl Harbor, Wake Island, Rabaul, Ambon, Timor, Darwin, Java, Ceylon, Midway
1942 June 4: Sunk by US aircraft at Battle of Midway (718 dead)

Suwo

Type: Pre-dreadnought
Class: 'Sagami' (1905)
Nomenclature: Province of western Honshu

History:
1898 August 1: Laid down by Baltic for Russia as ***Pobieda***
1900 May 24: Launched
1903 Completed
1904 December 7: Sunk by Japanese artillery at Port Arthur
1905 October 17: Refloated by Japan and reconstructed at Yokosuka, renamed ***Suwo***
1908 October: Recommissioned, first class coast defence ship
1913 Refit
—— Training ship for engineers and cadets

Taiho

Type: Aircraft Carrier
Class: 'Taiho' (1939)
Nomenclature: Giant phoenix

History:
1941 July 18: Laid down by Kawasaki
1943 April 7: Launched
1944 March 7: Completed
World War 2: Philippine Sea
1944 June 19: Torpedoed by US submarine *Albacore* and sank five hours later northwest of Yap Island prior to Battle of the Philippine Sea

Takao

Type: Battlecruiser
Class: 'Amagi' (1918)
Nomenclature: Mountain in central Honshu

History:
1921 December 19: Laid down by Mitsubishi, original name ***Aiyo***
1922 February 5: Construction suspended to comply with Washington Treaty
1924 April 14: Stricken and broken up

Tango

Type: Pre-dreadnought
Class: 'Tango' (1905)
Nomenclature: Province on north coast of Honshu

History:
1892 February: Laid down by Baltic for Russia as ***Poltava***
1894 November 6: Launched
1898 Completed
1904 December 5: Sunk by Japanese artillery at Port Arthur
1905 July 21: Refloated by Japan and reconstructed at Maizuru, renamed ***Tango***
1908 November: Recommissioned, first class coast defence ship
1908 Refit; reboilered, rearmed
1916 April 5: Returned to Russia, renamed ***Poltava***, later ***Tchesma***

Tokiwa

Type: Armoured Cruiser
Class: 'Asama' (1897)

***Tango* — Pre-dreadnought, the former Russian *Poltava*, after being salvaged, without main battery.**

Nomenclature: Ancient name for a province in northern Japan

History:
1897 January 6: Laid down by Armstrong
1898 July 6: Launched
1899 April 18: Completed
1900 Boxer Rebellion
1904 Blockade of Port Arthur
1904 February 9: Bombardment of Port Arthur
1904 August 14: Damaged by gunfire at Battle of the Yellow Sea
1905 May 27: Damaged by gunfire at Battle of Tsushima (nine hits)
1911 Refit; reboilered and rearmed
World War 2: Search for Spee's squadron
1922 April 1: Reclassified minelayer, rearmed; 2×203mm, 8×152mm, 2×79mm guns, 200-300 mines
1927 August: Damaged by mine explosion
1937 Refit; reboilered, rearmed; 4×152mm, 1×76mm, 2×47mm, 35×25mm guns
1942 February 1: Damaged by US aircraft at Kwajalein
1945 April 14: Damaged by mine in Kanmon Strait
1945 August 8: Sunk in shallow water near Ominato by US aircraft
1947 September: Broken up

Tosa

Type: Dreadnought
Class: 'Kaga' (1918)
Nomenclature: Province of Shikoku

History:
1920 February 16: Laid down by Mitsubishi
1921 December 18: Launched
1922 February 5: Construction suspended to comply with Washington Treaty
1925 February 9: Hull sunk as a target in Bungo Straits

Tsukuba

Type: Armoured Cruiser
Class: 'Tsukuba' (1904)
Nomenclature: A mountain near Tokyo

History:
1905 January 14: Laid down at Kure
1905 December 26: Launched
1907 January 14: Completed
1912 Redesignated battlecruiser
World War 1: 1914 1st South Seas Squadron, Search for Spee's squadron
1917 January 14: Sunk by magazine explosion in Yokosuka Bay (305 dead)

***Yamashiro* — Battleship of 1915, on trials after reconstruction of 1934.** *IWM*

Unryu

Type: Aircraft Carrier
Class: 'Unryu' (1941)
Nomenclature: Cloudy dragon

History:
1942 August 1: Laid down at Yokosuka
1943 September 25: Launched
1944 August 6: Completed
1944 December 19: Torpedoed and sunk by US submarine *Redfish* 200 miles southeast of Shanghai

Yakumo

Type: Armoured Cruiser
Class: 'Yakumo' (1897)
Nomenclature: Province of northwest Japan

History:
1897 September 1: Laid down at Vulcan, Stettin
1899 July 8: Launched
1900 June 20: Completed
1904 August 14: Battle of the Yellow Sea
1905 May 27: Damaged by gunfire at Battle of Tsushima (seven hits)
1921 First class coast defence ship
1924 Rearmed
1927 Refit; reboilered
1942 July: First class cruiser
1945 January: Refit, rearmed
1945-46 Repatriation transport
1947 March: Broken up at Maizuru

Yamashiro

Type: Dreadnought
Class: 'Fuso' (1911)
Nomenclature: Ancient name for Kyoto

History:
1913 November 20: Laid down at Yokosuka
1915 November 3: Launched
1917 March 31: Completed
1927-28 Refit
1934-35 Reconstructed at Yokosuka
World War 2: Midway, Leyte Gulf
1943 December 9: Damaged in collision with submarine *Ro113* off Hiranezaki
1944 October 25: Sunk by gunfire and three torpedoes in Surigao Strait during Battle of Leyte Gulf. Flag of Vice-Adm Teiji Nishimura, who was among those lost

Yamato

Type: Battleship
Class: 'Yamato' (1937)
Nomenclature: Province of south central Honshu, also a poetical name for Japan

History:
1937 November 4: Laid down at Kure
1940 August 8: Launched
1941 December 16: Completed
1942 Flagship of Combined Fleet
World War 2: Midway, Philippine Sea, Leyte Gulf
1943 December 25: Torpedoed by US submarine *Skate* south of Truk
1944 October: Damaged by two bomb hits during Battle of Leyte Gulf
1945 April 7: Sunk by US carrier aircraft 130 miles southwest of Kagoshima (2,498 dead)

Yashima

Type: Pre-dreadnought
Class: 'Yashima' (1892)
Nomenclature: Island off coast of Japan

History:
1894 December 28: Laid down by Armstrong
1896 February 28: Launched
1897 September 9: Completed
1901 Refit
1904 February 9 and March 22: Bombardment of Port Arthur
1904 May 15: Damaged by mine 10 miles southeast of Port Aurthur and sank in tow

Zuiho

Type: Light Aircraft Carrier
Class: 'Zuiho' (1940)
Nomenclature: Lucky phoenix

History:
1935 June 20: Laid down at Yokosuka as submarine depot ship ***Takasaki***
1936 June 19: Launched
1940 Reordered as aircraft carrier, renamed ***Zuiho***
1940 December 27: Completed
World War 2: Philippines, Midway, Aleutians, Santa Cruz, Philippine Sea, Leyte Gulf
1942 October 26: Damaged by aircraft bombs at Battle of Santa Cruz
1944 October 25: Sunk by US aircraft northeast of Cape Engano during Battle of Leyte Gulf

Zuikaku

Type: Aircraft Carrier
Class: 'Shokaku' (1937)
Nomenclature: Lucky crane

History:
1938 May 25: Laid down at Kawasaki
1939 November 27: Launched
1941 September 25: Completed
World War 2: Pearl Harbor, Darwin, Java, Ceylon, Coral Sea, Aleutians, Eastern Solomons, Santa Cruz, Philippine Sea, Leyte Gulf
1944 June 19: Damaged by bomb hits at Philippine Sea
1944 October 25: Sunk by US aircraft 220 miles northeast of Cape Engano during Battle of Leyte Gulf

Netherlands

Although the Netherlands had been a maritime power of some importance the change from wooden sailing ships to iron steam ships caused the nation to decline as a power. The Dutch navy traditionally built all its ships in the Netherlands but the industrial plant did not have the capability of building the larger and increasingly more complex vessels required. A number of ironclads were built in the 1860s and 1870s but these were generally monitor types for coast defence.

Much of the navy was stationed in the East Indies and ships were shifted between the home and eastern fleets. In the 1890s small battleships or coast defence ships were built and these served as the capital ships of the Dutch navy for several decades. Battleships were contemplated just before World War 1, but nothing came of this, and during the 1920s most of the coast defence ships were relegated to harbour service.

In 1939 a class of battlecruisers was contemplated but the German invasion of the Netherlands ended this project. After World War 2 the Dutch navy briefly operated an aircraft carrier.

Class Details

'De Ruyter' (1863)

Broadside Ironclad: *De Ruyter*
Displacement: 2,828tons
Dimensions: 211'8×47'5×22'4 [64.5×14.5×6.8]
Machinery: IHP 1,750
Armament: 14×60pdr long SB
Later: 4×229mm MLR
Armour: Sides 152mm
Class notes: Converted wood screw frigate of 54 guns originally laid down as a 74-gun sailing vessel. Completed as a floating battery but apparently never commissioned

'Prins Hendrik' (1864)

Central Battery Turret Ship: *Prins Hendrik der Nederlanden*
Displacement: 3,375tons
Dimensions: 240'8(oa) 230(pp)×44×18'9 [73.4(oa) 70.1(pp)×13.4×5.7]
Machinery: 2 screws, horizontal return connecting-rod engines (Laird), 4 square boilers
IHP 2,000 = 11knots
Armament: 4×230mm MLR, 4×120mm
1890: 2×74mm added
Armour: Belt and redoubt 114mm, turrets 139-279mm, bulkhead 100mm
Complement: 243
Class notes: Central battery with guns in two revolving Coles type turrets. Iron hull, bark rig and ram bow. Enlarged 'Wivern' class built for service in East Indies

'Schorpioen' (1866)

Turret Ram: *Schorpioen*
Displacement: 2,175tons
Dimensions: 205(oa) 193'6(pp)×38×16'2 [62.5(oa) 59(pp)×11.6×4.9]
Machinery: 2 screws, compound engines (F C Med), 4 boilers
IHP 2,225 = 12knots
Endurance: 1,030/10
Armament: 2×230mm MLR
1884: 1×280mm BLR 7×37mm
Armour: Belt 76-152mm, turret 203-279mm, c/t 144mm
Complement: 110
Class notes: Iron hulled monitor with one twin turret. Full waterline belt and two masts

'Stier' (1866)

Turret Ram: *Stier*
Displacement: 2,069tons
Dimensions: 194'10(pp)×38×19'3 [59.4(pp)×11.6×5.9]
Machinery: 2 screws, horizontal trunk engines (Laird), square boilers
IHP 2,250 = 12knots
Armament: 2×230mm MLR
1882: 1×280mm BLR, 2×75mm
Armour: Belt 76-152mm, turret 280mm, c/t 114mm
Complement: 136
Class notes: Iron hull monitor similar to *Schorpioen*

'Buffel' Class (1867)

Turret Rams: *Buffel, Guinea*
Displacement: 2,198tons
Dimensions: 205'8(oa) 195'10(pp)×40'4×15'9 [62.7(oa) 59.7(pp)×12.3×4.8]
Machinery: 2 screws, compound engines (*Buffel:* Napier; *Guinea:* Amsterdam), 4 boilers
IHP 2,000 = 12.4knots
Armament: 2×230mm MLR, 4×30pdr ML
1888: 1×280mm, 2×75mm, 4×37mm
Armour: Belt 76-152mm, turret 203mm, c/t 144mm
Complement: 159
Class notes: Monitors with one twin turret. No sails or rigging, single funnel and two masts

'Heiligerlee' Class (1867)

Monitors: *Heiligerlee, Krokodil, Tijger*
Displacement: 1,530tons
Dimensions: 187(oa)×44'2×10 [57(oa)×13.5×3]
Machinery: 2 screws, trunk engines (Laird; *Tijger:* Napier)
IHP 680 = 8.5knots
Armament: 2×230mm
c1890: 1×280mm, 1×75mm
Armour: Sides 114-140mm, turrets 203-279mm, c/t 100mm
Complement: 117
Class notes: Iron hull coast defence ships with single twin turret

'Cerberus' Class (1867)

Monitors: *Bloedhond, Cerberus*
Displacement: *Cerberus:* 1,530tons, *Bloedhond:* 1,683tons
Dimensions: *Cerberus:* 185'6(oa)×44×9'10

[56.5(oa)×13.4×3]; *Bloedhond:* 182'9(oa)×46'7×10'6 [55.7(oa)×14.2×3.2]
Machinery: 2 screws, —— (Fijenoord)
IHP 680 = 7.5knots
Armament: 1×280mm, 1×75mm
Armour: Sides 114-140mm, turrets 203-279mm
Complement: 117
Class notes: Iron hulls. Improved 'Heiligerlee' type

'Panter' Class 1868)

Monitors: *Adder, Haai, Hyena, Luipaard, Panter, Wesp*
Displacement: 1,566tons
Dimensions: 192'3(oa) 186'4(pp)×44×10'2 [58.6(oa) 56.8(pp)×13.4×3.1]
Machinery: 2 screws, (*Adder, Haai* and *Luipaard:* Fijenoord; *others:* Amsterdam)
Armament: 2×230mm MLR
Luipaard and *Wesp, c1890;* 1×280mm
Armour: Sides 140mm, turrets 203-280mm, c/t 140mm
Complement: 134
Class notes: Small coast defence ships with single twin turret, no masts or rigging. Similar to 'Cerberus' type

'Koning der Nederlanden' (1871)

Turret Ship: *Koning der Nederlanden*
Displacement: 5,400tons
Dimensions: 279'6(oa) 268'4(pp)×49'10×19'3 [85.2(oa) 81.8(pp)×15.2×5.8]
Machinery: 2 screws, compound engines (Penn), 7 boilers
IHP 4,500 = 12knots
Armament: 4×280mm MLR, 4×120mm MLR
1890: 2×76mm added
Armour: Belt 150-200mm, turrets 230-305mm, deck 75mm
Complement: 256
Class notes: Iron hull second class battleship with two twin turrets, spar torpedoes and ram bow. Three funnels and bark rig. An innovative design using turret system with full rig

'Draak' Class (1874)

Monitors: *Draak, Matador*
Displacement: 2,156tons
Dimensions: *Draak:* 213'7(oa) 201'5(pp) 49'3×10'10 [65.1(oa) 61.4(pp)×15×3.3]; *Matador:* 209'8(oa)×47'5×10'6 [63.9(oa)×14.5×3.2]
Machinery: 2 screws, —— (*Draak:* Amsterdam; *Matador:* Fijenoord)
IHP 807 = 8knots
Armament: 2×280mm, 1×75mm
Armour: Belt 140-200mm, turret 230-305mm
Complement: 134
Class notes: Modified 'Buffel' type with one twin turret

'Koningin Wilhelmina' (1890)

Turret Ship: *Koningin Wilhelmina der Nederlanden*
Displacement: 4,600tons
Dimensions: 327'5(oa)×48'10×19'8 [99.8(oa)×14.9×6]
Machinery: 2 screws, VTE engines, cylindrical boilers
IHP 5,900 = 17knots
Armament: 1×280mm/35, 1×213mm/35, 2×170mm/22, 6×12 pdr, 3 TT
Armour: Belt none, turret and c/t 280mm, deck 60mm
Class notes: Single armoured turret forward. Single funnel and two military masts on steel hull, no armour belt. Re-engined 1899

'Evertsen' Class (1892)

Coast Defence Ships: *Evertsen* (see later photo), *Kortenaer, Piet Hein* (see later photo)
Displacement: 3,520tons
Dimensions: 282'9(oa) 267'8(pp)×47×16'10 [86.2(oa) 81.6(pp)×14.3×5.1]
Machinery: 2 screws, VTE engines, 4 cylindrical boilers
IHP 4,800 = 16knots
Endurance: 2,800/9
Armament: 3×210mm/35, 2×150mm/35, 6×75mm, 3×457mm TT
Armour: Belt 102-152mm, barbettes 240mm, c/t 240mm
Complement: 260
Class notes: Small battleships with one twin barbette forward and single barbette aft, guns being taken from old gunboats. One tall funnel and two military masts

'Koningin Regentes' Class (1898)

Coast Defence Ships: *De Ruyter, Hertog Hendrik, Koningin Regentes* (see later photo)
Displacement: 5,084tons
Dimensions: 316'8(oa) 312(pp)×49'8×19 [96.5(oa) 95.1(pp)×15.1×5.8]
Machinery: 2 screws, VTE engines, 6 Yarrow boilers
IHP 6,300 = 16knots
Endurance: 1,600/14.5
Armament: 2×240mm/40, 4×150mm/40, 8×75mm, 3×457mm TT
Hertog Hendrik, 1920: 1×240mm and 4×75mm and TT removed, 4×75mm AA added
Armour: Belt 102-152mm, turrets 127-254mm, deck 50mm, c/t 250mm
Complement: 347
Class notes: Enlarged 'Evertsen' type with two single turrets fore and aft. Single funnel and two pole masts

'Tromp' (1902)

Coast Defence Ship: *Marten Harpertszoon Tromp*
Displacement: 5,295tons
Dimensions: 331(pp)×50×18'8 [100.9(pp)×15.2×5.7]
Machinery: 2 screws, VTE engines, 6 Yarrow boilers
IHP 6,400 = 16knots
Endurance: 1,600/14
Armament: 2×240mm/40, 4×150mm/40, 8×75mm, 3×457mm TT
Armour: Belt 102-152mm, turrets 127-200mm, deck 50mm, c/t 200mm
Complement: 344
Class notes: Improved 'Koningin Regentes' type with secondary armament in single turrets. Single funnel and two masts

'Heemskerck' (1904)

Coast Defence Ship: *Jacob van Heemskerck* (see later photo)
Dimensions: 321'6(oa) 316'9(pp)×49'6×18'9 [98(oa) 96.5(pp)×15.1×5.7]
Machinery: 2 screws, VTE engines, 6 Yarrow boilers
IHP 6,000 = 16knots
Endurance: 3,300/10
Armament: 2×240mm/45, 6×150mm/40, 6×75mm, 2×457mm TT
Armour: Belt 102-152mm, turrets 102-120mm, bulkheads 152mm, deck 50mm, c/t 200mm

Top left:
***Prins Hendrik der Nederlanden* — Central battery ship; bulwarks are down to expose turrets.** *MoD, Den Haag*

Top centre:
***Schorpioen* — Turret ram with bulwarks down to reveal turret.** *Marius Bar*

Top right:
***Krokodil* — Monitor.** *MoD, Den Haag*

Above left:
***Cerberus* — Monitor of 1867.**
Vereeniging Nederlandsch Historisch Scheepvaart Museum

Above right:
***Marten Harpertszoon Tromp* — Coast defence ship.**
VNHSM

Far left:
***Koningin Wilhelmina der Nederlanden* — Turret ship of 1890.** *VNHSM*

Left:
***Hertog Hendrik* — Coast defence ship of 'Koningin Regentes' class, at Amboina 1905.** *MoD, Den Haag*

Complement: 351
Class notes: Modified 'Tromp' type with increased protection and armament. Two seaplanes added 1929

'De Zeven Provincien' (1907)

Coast Defence Ship: *De Zeven Provincien*
Displacement: 6,530tons
Dimensions: 339'6(oa) 331'4(pp)×56'3×20'3 [103.5(oa) 101(pp)×17.1×6.2]
Machinery: 2 screws, VTE engines, 8 Yarrow boilers (later only 3)
IHP 8,500 = 16knots
Endurance: 2,100/15
Armament: 2×280mm/42, 4×150mm/40, 10×75mm, 2×457mm TT
By 1919: No TT
Armour: Belt 102-152mm, turrets 250mm, barbettes 100-250mm, bulkheads 152mm, c/t 200mm
Complement: 411
Class notes: Last battleship built for the Dutch navy, with two single turrets, armament arranged as in *Tromp*. Two funnels

Battlecruisers (1940)

Battlecruisers: 3 unnamed
Displacement: 28,318tons
Dimensions: 791'4(oa) 777'9(wl)×101'3×25'6 [241.2(oa) 237.1(wl)×30.9×7.8]
Machinery: 3 screws, geared turbines, 8 boilers
SHP 180,000 = 34knots
Endurance: 4,500/20
Armament: 9×283mm/55, 12×120mm, 14×40mm AA
Armour: Belt 102-254mm, turrets 305mm, barbettes 254mm, deck 127mm, c/t 300mm
Class notes: Three vessels projected for service in East Indies as response to Japanese heavy cruisers. Protection and radius sacrificed for speed. Main armament in three triple turrets. Two funnels with hangar and catapult between. Authorised 10 February 1940 but not ordered before German invasion in May

'Karel Doorman' (1948)

Light Aircraft Carrier: *Karel Doorman* (see also later photo)
Displacement: 13,190tons; *1958:* 15,892tons, 19,896f/l
Dimensions: 695(oa) 630(pp)×80'3×21'4 [211.8(oa) 192(pp)×24.5×6.5]
Machinery: 2 screws, Parsons geared turbines (Cammell Laird), 4 Admiralty 3-drum boilers
SHP 42,000 = 25knots
Endurance: 12,000/14
Aircraft: 44; *1958:* 21
Armament: 10×40mm AA guns
Complement: 1,300
Class notes: Former British *Venerable* transferred in 1948. Reconstructed 1955-58 with angled flightdeck and steam catapults, and modified island. Sold to Argentina 1968

Individual Ships

Adder

Type: Monitor
Class: 'Panter' (1868)
Nomenclature: Adder

History:
1870 December 21: Laid down at Amsterdam
1871 September 28: Launched
1873 October 24: Completed
1882 July 5: Foundered in a gale off Scheveningen

Bloedhond

Type: Monitor
Class: 'Cerberus' (1867)
Nomenclature: Bloodhound

History:
1867 Laid down at Amsterdam
1869 Launched
1870 September 29: Completed (trials)
1907 Sold and broken up

Buffel

Type: Turret Ram
Class: 'Buffel' (1867)
Nomenclature: Water buffalo

***De Zeven Provincien* — Coast defence ship.**
MoD Den Haag

***Karel Doorman* — Aircraft carrier, 1960, after reconstruction.** *P. A. Vicary*

History:
1867 June 10: Laid down by Napier
1868 March 10: Launched
1868 July 22: Completed
1894-98 Converted to accommodation ship, Hellevoetsluis, later Den Helder
1940-45 Moored at Amsterdam
1945-46 Accommodation ship, Nieuwediep
1979 Museum at Rotterdam

Cerberus

Type: Monitor
Class: 'Cerberus' (1867)
Nomenclature: Greek myth: a three-headed dog guarding the entrance to Hades

History:
1867 November 30: Laid down at Amsterdam
1869 January 14: Launched
1870 July 7: Completed (trials)
1906 Sold and broken up

De Ruyter

Type: Broadside Ironclad
Class: 'De Ruyter' (1863)
Nomenclature: Michael Adrienszoon de Ruyter (1607-1676), Dutch admiral, regarded as the greatest of Dutch naval heroes

History:
1831 Laid down at Flushing as wood ship-of-the-line
1850 Converted to sail first class frigate, 54 guns
1853 Launched
1860 Converted to screw frigate, 45 guns
1863 Converted to broadside ironclad, floating battery
1874 Stricken, never commissioned

De Ruyter

Type: Coast Defence Ship
Class: 'Koningin Regentes' (1898)

History:
1900 May 12: Laid down by Fijenoord
1901 September 28: Launched
1902 October 29: Completed
1903-04 West Indies
1905 East Indies
1924 Broken up

De Zeven Provincien

Type: Coast Defence Ship
Class: 'De Zeven Provincien' (1907)
Nomenclature: The seven provinces of the Netherlands, ie those which declared their independence of Spain in 1581

History:
1908 February 7: Laid down at Amsterdam
1909 March 15: Launched
1910 October 6: Completed
1912 January: Went aground in East Indies
—— Cadets training ship
1933 February 4: Seized by mutineers at Obeleh, Sumatra, who surrendered 11 February
1936 October 21: Renamed ***Soerabaja***
1942 February 18: Sunk by Japanese aircraft at Surabaya (13 dead)
1944 Refloated but hulk wrecked off Djamoengan Reef

Draak

Type: Monitor
Class: 'Draak' (1874)
Nomenclature: Dragon

History:
1875 Laid down at Amsterdam
1877 August 22: Launched
—— Completed
1914 Sold and broken up

Evertsen

Type: Coast Defence Ship

Above left:
An 'Evertsen' class coast defence ship.

Above:
***Jacob van Heemskerck* — Coast defence ship.**
MoD, Den Haag

Above right:
***Karel Doorman* — Aircraft carrier, March 1955.**
A. & J. Pavia

Class: 'Evertsen' (1892)
Nomenclature: A distinguished Dutch naval family, including Jan Evertsen (1600-1666), and Cornelis Evertsen ('the Old') (1610-1666), both killed in actions against the British, also Cornelis Evertsen ('the Younger') (1628-1679) and Cornelis Evertsen ('the Youngest') (1642-1706). All were admirals taking a significant part in the naval wars of the 17th century

History:
1893 June 14: Laid down by de Schelde
1894 September 29: Launched
1896 February 1: Completed
1905 August 16: Went aground off Ijmuiden
1914 Broken up

Guinea

Type: Turret Ram
Class: 'Buffel' (1867)
Nomenclature: A former Dutch colony in West Africa

History:
1867 Laid down at Amsterdam
1870 May 5: Launched
1873 October 16: Completed (trials)
1897 Sold and broken up at Bolnes

Haai

Type: Monitor
Class: 'Panter' (1868)
Nomenclature: Shark

History:
1870 May 1: Laid down by NSM
1871 May 20: Launched
1872 September 12: Completed (trials)
1906 July: Sold and broken up

Heiligerlee

Type: Monitor
Class: 'Heiligerlee' (1867)
Nomenclature: Notable Dutch victory against Spain in 1568

History:
1867 Laid down by Laird as ***Panter***
1868 Renamed ***Heiligerlee***
1868 January 14: Launched
—— Completed
1910 Sold and broken up

Hertog Hendrik

Type: Coast Defence Ship
Class: 'Koningin Regentes' (1898)
Nomenclature: Duke Henry, ie Duke Henry of Mecklenburg-Schwerin (1876-1934), consort of Queen Wilhelmina

History:
1900 October 13: Laid down at Amsterdam
1902 June 7: Launched
1904 January 5: Completed
1905 July 3: Went aground near Makassar
1926 Cadet training ship, after turret removed
1939 August 30: Floating battery at Den Helder; renamed ***Vliereede***
1940 May 14: Scuttled in shallow water at Den Helder and seized by Germans
—— Refloated and towed to Antwerp; rebuilt as floating AA battery
1944 April: Renamed ***Ariadne***
1945 Returned to Netherlands, repaired as ***Hertog Hendrik***
1947 October 21: Accommodation ship, Amsterdam

Hyena

Type: Monitor
Class: 'Panter' (1868)
Nomenclature: Hyena

History:
1869 Laid down at Amsterdam
1870 Launched

1872 September 16: Completed (trials)
1906 July: Sold and broken up

Jacob van Heemskerck

Type: Coast Defence Ship
Class: 'Heemskerck' (1904)
Nomenclature: Jacob van Heemskerck (1567-1607), Dutch explorer and sea captain

History:
1905 August 15: Laid down at Amsterdam
1906 September 22: Launched
1908 April 22: Completed
1908 December: Arrested Venezuelan patrol boat *23 de Mayo* during blockade of Venezuela
1939 April: Guardship at Ijmuiden, renamed ***Ijmuiden***
1940 May 14: Scuttled at Ijmuiden
1940 July 16: Raised by Germans, converted at Kiel to AA ship and renamed ***Undine***, armament 8×105mm and 5×40mm guns
1945 Recovered by Netherlands
1948 February 25: Renamed ***Neptunus***

Karel Doorman

Type: Light Aircraft Carrier
Class: 'Karel Doorman' (1948)
Nomenclature: Karel W. F. M. Doorman (1889-1942), Dutch admiral, commander of Allied naval forces in the Dutch Indies, 1942, killed at the Battle of the Java Sea

History:
1942 December 3: Laid down at Cammell Laird as British ***Venerable***
1943 December 30: Launched
1945 January 17: Completed
1948 April 1: Transferred to Netherlands, renamed ***Karel Doorman***
1948 May 28: Commissioned
1968 October 15: Sold to Argentina, renamed ***Veinticinco de Mayo***

Koning der Nederlanden

Type: Turret Ship
Class: 'Koning Der Nederlanden' (1871)
Nomenclature: King of the Netherlands

History:
1871 December 31: Laid down at Amsterdam
1874 October 28: Launched
1877 July 26: Completed for trials
1895 April 1: Decommissioned, training ship
1899 December 1: Accommodation and guard ship, Surabaya
1942 March 2: Scuttled to prevent capture at Surabaya

Koningin Regentes

Type: Coast Defence Ship
Class: 'Koningin Regentes' (1898)
Nomenclature: Queen Regent, ie Queen Emma (1858-1934), Regent 1890-1898

History:
1898 December 3: Laid down at Amsterdam
1900 April 24: Launched
1901 August 9: Completed
1921 Broken up

Koningin Wilhelmina der Nederlanden

Type: Turret Ship
Class: 'Koningin Wilhelmina' (1890)
Nomenclature: Wilhelmina, Queen of the Netherlands (1880-1962)

History:
1891 April 22: Laid down at Amsterdam
1892 October 22: Launched
1894 April 17: Completed
1899 Refit; re-engined and reboilered
1910 Stricken

Kortenaer

Type: Coast Defence Ship
Class: 'Evertsen' (1892)
Nomenclature: Egbert Meussen Kortenaer (d1665), Dutch

admiral killed at the Battle of Lowestoft during the Second Anglo-Dutch War

History:
1893 June 13: Laid down at Amsterdam
1894 October 27: Launched
1895 December 17: Completed
1914 At Veracruz
1920 Broken up

Krokodil

Type: Monitor
Class: 'Heiligerlee' (1867)
Nomenclature: Crocodile

History:
1867 Laid down by Laird
1868 February 13: Launched
—— Completed
1906 Sold and broken up

Luipaard

Type: Monitor
Class: 'Panter' (1868)
Nomenclature: Leopard

History:
1875 Laid down by NSM
1876 Launched
—— Completed
1907 Sold and broken up

Marten Harpertszoon Tromp

Type: Coast Defence Ship
Class: 'Tromp' (1902)
Nomenclature: Marten Harpertszoon Tromp (1597-1653), Dutch admiral, prominent in the Anglo-Dutch wars, killed at Texel

History:
1903 May 2: Laid down at Amsterdam
1904 June 15: Launched
1905 November 17: Completed
1933 Broken up

Above:
***Koningin Regentes* — Coast defence ship, painted white for foreign service.** *VNHSM*

Right:
***Piet Hein* — Coast defence ship, c1905.** *Marius Bar*

Matador

Type: Monitor
Class: 'Draak' (1874)
Nomenclature: Matador

History:
1876 Laid down by NSM
1878 Launched
—— Completed
1914 Sold and broken up

Panter, see *Heiligerlee*

Panter

Type: Monitor
Class: 'Panter' (1868)
Nomenclature: Panther

History:
1869 Laid down at Amsterdam
1870 Launched
1872 October 28: Completed (trials)
1906 Sold and broken up

Piet Hein

Type: Coast Defence Ship
Class: 'Evertsen' (1892)
Nomenclature: Pieter Pieterszoon Hein (1578-1629), Dutch admiral, captured the Spanish treasure fleet in 1628

History:
1893 June 20: Laid down by Fijenoord
1894 August 16: Launched
1896 January 3: Completed
1914 Broken up

Prins Hendrik der Nederlanden

Type: Central Battery Turret Ship
Class: 'Prins Hendrik' (1864)
Nomenclature: Prince Henry of the Netherlands (1820-1879), Dutch admiral

History:
1865 August: Laid down by Laird
1866 October 9: Launched
1867 March: Completed
1876 Arrived in East Indies
1894 Expedition to Lombok
1899 May 5: Ammunition hulk, Surabaya
1925 Broken up

Schorpioen

Type: Turret Ram
Class: 'Schorpioen' (1866)
Nomenclature: Scorpion

History:
1867 August: Laid down at La Seyne
1868 January 18: Launched
1868 September 16: Completed
1886 August 9: Sank at dock at Willemsoord after collision; refloated
1906 November 28: Decommissioned
1909 Accommodation ship, Hellevoetsluis
1940 May 14: Seized by Germans at Den Helder
1941 Accommodation ship, Wesermunde
1945 Returned to Netherlands
1947 May 18: Accommodation ship, Den Helder as ***Internaat Prinses Margriet***

Stier

Type: Turret Ram
Class: 'Stier' (1866)
Nomenclature: Bull

History:
1867 June 7: Laid down by Laird
1868 April 9: Launched
—— Completed
1908 Decommissioned
1925 Sunk as target ship for aircraft off Den Helder

Tijger

Type: Monitor
Class: 'Heiligerlee' (1867)
Nomenclature: Tiger

History:
1867 Laid down by Napier
1868 Launched
1868 July 2: Completed (trials)
1896 Sold and broken up

Wesp

Type: Monitor
Class: 'Panter' (1868)
Nomenclature: Wasp

History:
1870 Laid down at Amsterdam
1871 Launched
1874 September 30: Completed (trials)
1906 October: Sold and broken up

Norway

Although Norway and Sweden were united in the person of the King of Sweden, Norway was an independent kingdom and maintained its own navy for the protection of its long coastline on the northern shore of Europe. Devoted solely to coast defence, Norway's armoured fleet consisted only of monitors and later small battleships. In 1905 the Norwegian parliament declared the union with Sweden dissolved. Norway remained neutral during World War 1, selling to Britain the two incomplete vessels then under construction. No further armoured vessels were built for Norway.

Class Details

'Skorpionen' (1864)

Monitor: *Skorpionen*
Displacement: 1,447tons
Dimensions: 199'5(pp)×45'4×11'6 [60.8(pp)×13.8×3.5]
Machinery: 1 screw
IHP 350 = 6knots
Armament: 2×267mm MLR
1897: 2×120mm, 2×65mm QF
Armour: Belt 124mm, turret 307mm
Complement: 80
Class notes: Iron hull vessel with one turret similar to Ericsson's Swedish types. Reconstructed and rearmed 1895-97

'Mjolner' Class (1866)

Monitors: *Mjolner, Thrudvang*
Displacement: 1,515tons
Dimensions: 204'7(oa) 187'8(pp)×45'6×10'9 (62.2(oa) 57.2(pp)×13.9×3.3]
Machinery: 1 screw
IHP 460 = 8.1knots; *Thrudvang:* IHP 500 = 8.5knots
Armament: 2×267mm MLR
Thrudvang, 1897: 2×120mm, 2×65mm QF
Armour: Belt 124mm, turret 307mm
Complement: 80
Class notes: Similar to *Skorpionen* and also reconstructed (1895-97)

'Thor' (1870)

Monitor: *Thor*
Displacement: 2,003tons
Dimensions: 204(oa)×47'6×13'2 [62.2(oa)×14.5×4]
Machinery: 1 screw
IHP 600 = 8.3knots
Armament: 2×267mm MLR
1897: 2×120mm, 2×65mm QF
Armour: Belt 127-176mm, turret 368mm
Complement: 90
Class notes: Single turret vessel also reconstructed 1895-97

'Harald Haarfagre' Class (1895)

Coast Defence Ships: *Harald Haarfagre* (see later photo), *Tordenskjold* (see also later photo)
Displacement: 3,400tons
Dimensions: 309(oa) 299(pp) 274'6(wl)×48'6×16'6 [94.2(oa) 91.1(pp) 83.7(wl)×14.8×5]
Machinery: 2 screws, VTE engines (Hawthorn Leslie), 3 cylindrical boilers
IHP 4,500 = 17.2knots
Armament: 2×210mm/44, 6×120mm/46, 6×76mm, 2×450mm TT
1918: 2×76mm AA added, TT removed
Armour: Belt 100-178mm, turrets 127-203mm, secondary shields 114mm, deck 50mm, c/t 152mm
Complement: 249
Class notes: Coastal battleships with two single turrets fore and aft. Single funnel and two military masts; fighting tops later removed.

'Norge' Class (1898)

Coast Defence Ships: *Eidsvold, Norge*
Displacement: 3,850tons 4,166f/l
Dimensions: 301'3(oa) 290(pp)×50'6×16'6 [91.8(oa) 88.4(pp)×15.4×5]
Machinery: 2 screws, VTE engines (Hawthorn Leslie), 8 Yarrow boilers
IHP 4,800 = 16.5knots
Armament: 2×210mm/44, 6×152mm/46, 8×76mm, 6×47mm, 2×450mm TT
1919: 2×47mm AA added, TT and old 47mm removed
Armour: Belt 102-152mm, turrets 203mm, c/t 203mm, casemates 127mm, deck 50mm
Complement: 270
Class notes: Improved 'Haarfagre' type with heavier secondary armament in casemates. Two funnels and two military masts. Belt amidships only

***Tordenskjold* — Coast defence ship of 1895, May 2 1905.** *Marius Bar*

Norge — **Coast defence ship as completed, 1902.** *IWM*

'Bjorgvin' Class (1912)

Coast Defence Ships: *[Bjorgvin, Nidaros]*
Displacement: 4,800tons
Dimensions: 310(oa) 295'3(pp)×54.9×16'6 [94.5(oa) 90(pp)×16.7×5]
Machinery: 2 screws, VTE engines (Hawthorn Leslie), 4 Yarrow boilers
IHP 4,000 = 13knots
Armament: 2×240mm/50, 4×150mm/50, 6×100mm, 1×76mm AA, 2×450mm TT
Armour: Belt 178mm, turrets 203mm, secondary turrets 152mm, deck 50mm, c/t 203mm
Class notes: Designed with two single turrets and secondary armament also in turrets. Both had been launched prior to sale to Great Britain late in 1914, being renamed *Glatton* and *Gorgon*

Individual Ships

Bjorgvin

Type: Coast Defence Ship
Class: 'Bjorgvin' (1912)
Nomenclature: Viking name for the city of Bergen

History:
1913 May 26: Laid down by Armstrong
1914 August 8: Launched
1915 January: Purchased by British government, renamed ***Glatton***

Eidsvold

Type: Coast Defence Ship
Class: 'Norge' (1898)
Nomenclature: Town north of Oslo where independence of Norway was proclaimed in 1814

History:
1899 Laid down by Armstrong
1900 June 14: Launched
1901 March 29: Completed
1940 April 9: Torpedoed and sunk by German destroyer *Wilhelm Heidkamp* at Narvik (178 dead)

Harald Haarfagre

Type: Coast Defence Ship
Class: 'Harald Haarfagre' (1895)
Nomenclature: Harald Haarfagre (Fairhaired) (860-940), first king of united Norway

History:
1896 Laid down by Armstrong
1897 January 4: Launched
1897 December 18: Completed
—— Accommodation ship, Horten
1940 April: Captured by Germans at Horten; rebuilt as AA ship, renamed ***Thetis***
1945 May: Recovered by Norway at Tromso, renamed ***Harald Haarfagre***
1945 Training ship
1947 Broken up at Stavanger

Mjolner

Type: Monitor
Class: 'Mjolner' (1866)
Nomenclature: Norse myth: the hammer of Thor

History:
—— Laid down by Motala
1868 Launched
1868 August 24: Completed
1895-97 Rebuilt, rearmed
1908 Stricken and broken up

***Harald Haarfagre* — Coast defence ship, in Victorian livery.** *IWM*

Nidaros

Type: Coast Defence Ship
Class: 'Bjorgvin' (1912)
Nomenclature: Viking name for the city of Trondheim

History:
1913 June 11: Laid down by Armstrong
1914 June 9: Launched
1915 January: Purchased by British government, renamed ***Gorgon***

Norge

Type: Coast Defence Ship
Class: 'Norge' (1898)
Nomenclature: Norway

History:
1899 Laid down by Armstrong
1900 March 31: Launched
1901 February 7: Completed
1940 April 9: Torpedoed and sunk by German destroyer *Bernd von Arnim* at Narvik (105 dead)

Skorpionen

Type: Monitor
Class: 'Skorpionen' (1864)
Nomenclature: Scorpion

History:
—— Laid down at Horten
1866 October 30: Launched
1867 June 15: Completed
1895-97 Rebuilt, rearmed
1908 Stricken and broken up

Thor

Type: Monitor
Class: 'Thor' (1870)
Nomenclature: Norse myth: Viking god of thunder

History:
—— Laid down at Horten
1872 June 5: Launched
1876 June 3: First commissioned
1897-98 Rebuilt, rearmed
1910 Stricken and broken up at Stavanger

Thrudvang

Type: Monitor
Class: 'Mjolner' (1866)
Nomenclature: Norse myth: the house of Thor

History:
—— Laid down at Horten
1869 May 3: Launched
1870 June 13: Completed
1895-97 Rebuilt, rearmed
1908 Stricken and broken up

Tordenskjold

Type: Coast Defence Ship
Class: 'Harald Haarfagre' (1895)
Nomenclature: Peder Wessel Tordenskjold (Thundershield) (1691-1720), Norwegian born Danish admiral, hero of the Great Northern War

History:
1896 Laid down by Armstrong
1897 March 18: Launched
1898 March 17: Completed
—— Accommodation ship, Horten
1940 April: Captured by Germans at Horten; rebuilt as AA ship, renamed ***Nymphe***
1945 May: Recovered by Norway at Tromso
—— Ran aground and lost in Raftsund near Svolvaer
1946 Broken up at Stavanger

***Tordenskjold* — As the German anti-aircraft ship *Nymphe* at Kiel, 1941.**

Peru

Two armoured vessels were built for Peru in the 1860s and two monitors were purchased from the United States. No further enlargement of the Peruvian navy was made. The *Huascar* made naval history when it was seized by mutineers and engaged the British cruiser *Shah* in 1877. During the War of the Pacific, from which Chile emerged victorious, Peru lost its ironclad ships.

Class Details

'Independencia' (1864)

Broadside Ship: *Independencia*
Displacement: 3,500tons
Dimensions: 215(pp)×44'9×22'6 [65.5(pp)×13.6×6.6]
Machinery: 1 screw (Penn)
IHP 2,200 = 12knots
Armament: 2×180mm MLR, 12×150mm MLR, 4×30pdr MLR
1879: 1×240mm and 1×180mm added
Armour: Belt and battery 114mm
Complement: 250
Class notes: Iron hull armoured corvette with ram bow, single funnel and bark rig. Reboilered 1878

'Huascar' (1864)

Turret Ship: *Huascar*
Displacement: 1,870tons
Dimensions: 190(oa)×35'6×16 [57.9(oa)×10.8×4.9]
Machinery: 1 screw, horizontal return connecting-rod engines (Laird), 4 rectangular boilers
IHP 1,100 = 9knots
Armament: 2×254mm MLR, 2×40pdr, 1×12pdr
Armour: Belt 63-115mm, bulkheads 150mm, turret 140-190mm, deck 50mm, c/t 75mm
Complement: 220
Class notes: Single turret ship with low freeboard, single funnel and brig rig. Captured by Chile 1879

'Atahualpa' Class (1867)

Monitors: *Atahualpa, Manco Capac*
Displacement: 2,100tons
Dimensions: 224(oa)×43'6×13'6 [68.6(oa)×13.3×4.1]
Machinery: 1 screw, horizontal vibrating-lever engines (builder), 2 boilers
IHP 320 = 8knots
Armament: 2×381mm SB
Armour: Sides 127mm, turret 254mm, pilot house 254mm
Complement: 85
Class notes: Former US *Catawba* and *Oneota* purchased 1867. Sailed down the Mississippi and around Cape Horn to Peru

Individual Ships

Atahualpa

Type: Monitor
Class: 'Atahualpa' (1867)
Nomenclature: Atahualpa (1502-1533), last Inca king of Peru

History:

——	Laid down by Swift Evans for US as ***Catawba***
1864	April 13: Launched
1865	June 10: Completed, not commissioned
1868	April 2: Sold to Peru, renamed ***Atahualpa***
1870	May 11: Arrived at Callao after voyage around Cape Horn
1880	January 16: Scuttled to prevent capture at Callao

***Huascar* — Turret ship, captured by Chilean navy in 1879.**

Huascar

Type: Turret Ship
Class: 'Huascar' (1864)
Nomenclature: Huascar (1495-1533), Inca prince

History:

——	Laid down by Laird
1865	October 6: Launched
——	Completed
1877	May 29: Fought celebrated action with HMS *Shah* off Peruvian coast while under control of mutineers; hit numerous times but only lightly damaged
1879	May 21: Rammed and sank Chilean sloop *Esmeralda* in action off Iquique, damaged
1879	October 8: Severely damaged and captured in action with Chilean vessels off Angamos. Adm Grau killed (about 60 dead)
1879	November 15: Recommissioned in Chilean Navy

Independencia

Type: Broadside Ship

Class: 'Independencia' (1864)
Nomenclature: Independence

History:
1864 Laid down by Samuda
1865 August 8: Launched
1866 December: Completed
1878 Refit, reboilered
1879 May 21: Blown up to prevent capture after running aground in action with Chilean gunboat *Covadonga* off Iquique

Manco Capac

Type: Monitor
Class: 'Atahualpa' (1867)
Nomenclature: Traditional founder of the Inca dynasty

History:
—— Laid down by Swift Evans for US as ***Oneota***
1864 May 21: Launched
1865 June 10: Completed, not commissioned
1868 April 2: Sold to Peru, renamed ***Manco Capac***
1869 January: Departed New Orleans in tow for Peru; sank steamer *Reyes* in collision off Cuba
1869 September 15: Went aground at Rio de Janeiro
1870 May 11: Arrived at Callao after voyage around Cape Horn
1870 Floating battery, Arica
1880 Engaged Chilean vessels at Arica
1880 June 7: Scuttled to prevent capture at Arica

Portugal

The single small Portuguese ironclad was of importance mainly to the Portuguese. This ship lasted long after its contemporaries only because a plan to increase the size of the navy in 1895, including construction of two coastal battleships, came to nought.

Above:
***Vasco da Gama* — Coast defence ship, 1895.** *IWM*

Below:
***Vasco da Gama* — Coast defence ship, as rebuilt.**
Foto Druppel

'Vasco da Gama' (1872)

Central Battery Ship: *Vasco da Gama*
Displacement: 2,479tons
Dimensions: 216(oa) 195(pp)×43'4×21 [65.8(oa) 59.4(pp)×13.2×6.4]
Machinery: 2 screws, vertical compound engines (Humphrys) IHP 3,600 = 13knots
Armament: 2×263mm, 1×150mm, 4×87mm
Armour: Belt 178-230mm, battery 230-250mm, deck 75mm
Complement: 218

As reconstructed 1903:

Displacement: 3,020tons
Dimensions: 232'9(pp)×40×18'4 [70.9(pp)×12.2×5.6]
Machinery: 2 screws, VTE engines, Yarrow boilers IHP 6,000 = 15.5knots
Armament: 2×203mm/40, 1×150mm/45, 1×76mm, 6×47mm
Armour: 178-228mm belt, 203mm barbettes
Complement: 270
Class notes: Armoured corvette intended for defence of Lisbon. Improved version of Greek *Vasilevs Georgios* with guns in an octagonal armoured redoubt. Iron hull with ram bow, single funnel and barkentine rig. Completely reconstructed 1903, lengthened, casemate removed, new engines and boilers, rearmed with main guns in sponsons. Two funnels and two military masts

Vasco da Gama

Type: Central Battery Ship
Class: 'Vasco da Gama' (1872)
Nomenclature: Vasco da Gama (1469-1524), Portuguese navigator

History:
—— Laid down by Thames
1875 December 1: Launched
1876 Completed
1902-03 Reconstructed by Orlando, relaunched 29 September 1902
1917 October 9: Severely damaged and beached during revolutionary fighting near Lisbon
1936 October 14: Stricken, broken up on the Clyde

Russia

As Russia was principally a military power, the naval arm was always secondary to the army. Nevertheless, two wooden vessels were converted to ironclads as early as 1861 and Russia's first armoured warship *Pervenietz* was ordered in Britain. A class of monitors designed by Ericsson and other ironclads were built at St Petersburg including the armoured frigates *Pozharski, Minin* and *General Amiral*. A number of interesting ships were designed by Russian naval constructors such as A. A. Popov. Among the most novel were his circular ironclads familiarly known as 'Popoffkas'.

These last were built for service in the Black Sea where Russia had been barred from maintaining a fleet under the Treaty of Paris ending the Crimean War; this ban had been denounced by Russia in 1871. Russia still had no substantial fleet when war broke out with Turkey in 1877 but the few successes were achieved by Russian spar torpedo boats.

Russia's geography meant that its navy was divided into separate fleets in the Baltic, Black Sea and Far East. Until the 1880s cruisers for commerce raiding were the basic offensive arm of the Russian fleet. As Russia moved to expand its power in the Far East, naval strength was increased. The fleet in the Black Sea was revived and a squadron stationed in the Far East at Port Arthur in 1895. A year earlier a base had been established in the Mediterranean near Nice, France.

The rise of Japan as a power inevitably led to contention and in 1904 the Japanese attacked Port Arthur without warning. The war was a series of disasters for Russia (including the death of the country's finest naval leader, Admiral Makarov) and led to the loss of its Asiatic Fleet. Late in 1904 the Baltic Fleet was sent on a voyage around the world to combat the Japanese and was annihilated at Tsushima. Those ships not sunk were captured and added to the Japanese fleet.

The losses incurred in this war led to political strife including the noted mutiny aboard the battleship *Potemkin*. It was several years before the fleet could be restored to any power. In 1909 the four dreadnoughts of the 'Gangut' class were begun in the Baltic followed by four more in the Black Sea in 1911. At the outbreak of World War 1 the reconstruction programme was only in its initial stages.

Little use was made of the dreadnoughts in the confined seas of the Baltic, but a more energetic policy was adopted in the Black Sea where the fleet was involved in several actions. The revolutions of 1917 destroyed the effectiveness of the fleet particularly that of the larger ships which were inactive. The ships, without their officers who had either been killed or were with the White forces, were controlled by the enlisted men and became ineffective through lack of maintenance. In the Black Sea the fleet lost its bases as the Germans advanced. Many of the battleships were abandoned at Sevastopol with their engines destroyed by the retreating Allies. The remaining vessels under White control went to Tunisia at the end of the Civil War in 1920 where they remained until scrapped.

The Soviets took steps to revive the navy and in the late 1920s the three remaining dreadnoughts, now renamed, were refitted and one was transferred to the Black Sea. The navy was still relatively unimportant, but in 1938 a class of large battleships was laid down. Two battlecruisers were begun in 1939 but none of these vessels ever reached launching stage as the war overwhelmed Russia. The three old dreadnoughts served throughout the war.

In 1944 the British battleship *Royal Sovereign* was given to Russia on loan in lieu of an Italian battleship and was returned in 1949 when Russia received its share of the Italian fleet. Salvage attempts on sunken or incomplete German major warships were unsuccessful.

Although large Soviet warships were reported under construction after the war, it was not until 1975 that the first aircraft carrier, *Kiev*, was completed. At least four vessels of this class have been built or are under construction. In 1981 Russia completed the first of a new class of warship, the battlecruiser *Kirov*, the largest nuclear-powered surface warship other than carriers to be built.

Class Details

'Petropavlovsk' (1861)

Broadside Ship: *Petropavlovsk*
Displacement: 6,175tons
Dimensions: 313'4(oa) 294'8(pp)×56'2×25'3 [95.5(oa) 89.8(pp)×17.1×7.7]
Machinery: 1 screw, horizontal return connecting-rod engines (Baird), rectangular boilers
IHP 2,460 = 11knots
Armament: 21×203mm BLR, 1×152mm, 10×90mm
Later: 24×203mm/22, 1×152mm/23, 10×87mm, spar torpedoes
Armour: Side and battery 114mm
Complement: 680
Class notes: Ironclad frigate, wood hull with 8' ram bow and ship rig. Converted to ironclad while under construction. Completion greatly delayed as ship had to be widened as part of the conversion. 152mm gun placed on pivot on forecastle

'Pervenietz' Class (1861)

Broadside Ships: *Nye Tron Menya, Pervenietz*
Displacement: *Nye Tron Menya:* 3,340tons; *Pervenietz:* 3,277tons
Dimensions: *Pervenietz:* 225'1(wl) 221'9(pp)×53'2×14'9 [68.6(wl) 67.6(pp)×16.2×4.5]; *Nye Tron Menya:* 227'8(oa) 215'9(pp) [69.4(oa) 65.8(pp)]
Machinery: 1 screw, horizontal direct-acting engines (*Pervenietz:* Maudslay; *Nye Tron Menya:* Humphrys), 2 rectangular boilers (*Nye Tron Menya:* 4)
IHP 1,000 = 9knots
Armament: *Pervenietz:* 6×203mm/22, 9×152mm/23, 4×9pdr, 4×85mm
Nye Tron Menya: 14×203mm/22, 4×85mm
Armour: Sides and battery 114mm, c/t 114mm
Complement: 394
Class notes: *Pervenietz* was first armoured warship in Russian navy, built in England. *Nye Tron Menya* built in Russia from British plans with engines taken from old battleship *Konstantin*. Iron hull with sloping sides and ram bow, single funnel and three masts with schooner rig. Poor sea boats

'Sevastopol' (1862)

Broadside Ship: *Sevastopol*
Displacement: 6,275tons, 7,075f/l
Dimensions: 314'10(oa) 303'6(pp)×51'1×26'4 [95.9(oa) 92.5(pp)×15.9×8]

Top left:
***Nye Tron Menya* — Broadside ship of 1864, as refitted c1890.** *US Naval Historical Centre*

Top centre:
***Kniaz Pozharski* — Armoured frigate, prior to reconstruction, with single lowering funnel.** *Marius Bar*

Top right:
***Minin* — Armoured frigate, following reconstruction in 1887, with two funnels.** *IWM*

Above left:
***Vieschun* — Monitor of 'Uragan' class, built 1864, as completed.** *US Naval Historical Centre*

Above right:
***Admiral Spiridov* — Turret ship of 1868.** *Marius Bar*

Left:
***Kreml* — Broadside ship of 1865, as completed.**
US Naval Historical Centre

Far left:
***Gerzog Edinburgski* — Central battery ship built in 1875, seen in 1901 following reconstruction. Notice central battery amidships.** *Marius Bar*

Machinery: 1 screw, horizontal return connecting-rod engines (Admiralty), rectangular boilers
IHP 3,090 = 12knots
Armament: 18×203mm BLR, 1×152mm, 10×80mm, 4×60pdr
Later: 16×203mm/22, 1×152mm/23, 8×87mm
Armour: Side and battery 114mm
Complement: 607
Class notes: Steam frigate converted to ironclad while under construction. Wood hull with cutaway forecastle and iron ram bow. Schooner rig

'Uragan' Class (1862)

Monitors: *Bronenosets, Koldun, Latnik, Lava, Perun, Strelets, Tifon, Uragan, Vieshchun, Yedinorog*
Displacement: 1,400tons, 1,566f/l
Dimensions: 201'1(wl)×46×12'7 [61.3(wl)×14×3.8]
Machinery: 1 screw, horizontal direct-acting engines, 2 rectangular boilers
IHP 450 = 7knots
Armament: 2×230mm SB
Later: 2×229mm/20
Armour: Sides 76-229mm, turret 280mm, pilot house 203mm
Complement: 138
Class notes: Similar to US *Monitor*, designed by Ericsson. Iron hulls without sails and one turret. Originally classed as second class battleships. *Vieshchun* and *Koldun* built in Belgium and reassembled in St Petersburg

'Smerch' (1862)

Monitor: *Smerch*
Displacement: 1,461tons, 2,013f/l
Dimensions: 189'8(oa) 183'4(wl) 172'3(pp)×38×11'4 [57.8(oa) 55.9(wl) 52.5(pp)×11.6×3.4]
Machinery: 2 screws, horizontal direct-acting engines (Maudslay), 3 rectangular boilers
IHP 700 = 8knots
Armament: *Designed:* 4×60pdr SB
As completed: 2×230mm SB
Later: 2×230mm/20, 4×37mm
Armour: Belt 102-114mm, turrets 114-152mm, c/t 114mm
Complement: 153
Class notes: Designed by Mitchell. Iron hull with two turrets of Coles type. Similar to Danish *Rolf Krake*

'Kniaz Pozharski' (1863)

Central Battery Ship: *Kniaz Pozharski*
Displacement: 4,506tons
Dimensions: 281'10(oa) 272'8(wl) 263'6(pp)×48'10×22'1 [85.9(oa) 83.1(wl) 80.3(pp)×14.9×6.7]
Machinery: 1 screw, horizontal direct-acting engine (Baird), 8 cylindrical boilers
IHP 2,835 = 11.7knots
Armament: 8×228mm/20 BLR, 8×250pdr
1885: 8×203mm/35, 2×152mm/23, 8×4pdr
1892: 2×380mm TT added
Armour: Belt 100mm, battery 112mm
Complement: 495
Class notes: Armoured frigate designed by A. F. Sobolev. Iron hull with ram bow and ship rig. Hull recessed to permit axial fire. Reconstructed 1885, two funnels replaced single lowering funnel, new boilers and armament

'Minin' (1864)

Armoured Cruiser: *Minin*
Displacement: 5,763tons
Dimensions: 309'4(oa) 298'6(pp)×49'3×23'7 [94.3(oa) 91(pp)×15×7.2]
Machinery: 1 screw, simple horizontal direct-acting engine (builder), 8 boilers; *1886:* 18 Belleville boilers
IHP 5,290 = 12.5knots
Endurance: 4,200/9
Armament: 4×203mm/30, 12×152mm/28, 4×87mm
1887: 3×355 TT added, 2×152mm removed
Armour: Belt 152-178mm
Complement: 540
Class notes: Designed as sister to *Pozharski* but postponed because of difficulties with *Pozharski's* design as well as introduction of new foreign types. Redesigned as turret ship, but construction suspended 1870 following loss of HMS *Captain*. Again redesigned, by Popov, as an armoured frigate with single funnel and three masts with ship rig. Reconstructed 1887, two funnels, new guns and watertube boilers fitted

'Kreml' (1864)

Broadside Ship: *Kreml*
Displacement: 3,412tons, 4,323f/l
Dimensions: 220'9(oa) 214'10(pp)×53'2×15 [67.4(oa) 65.5(pp)×16.2×4.6]
Machinery: 1 screw, horizontal direct-acting engines, 4 rectangular boilers
IHP 1,000 = 9.5knots
Armament: 8×203mm/22, 1×152mm/45, 2×152mm/35, 3×152mm SB, 7×47mm
Armour: Belt 114mm, battery 127mm, c/t 114mm
Complement: 430
Class notes: Improved 'Pervenietz' type with straight stem and iron hull with more vertical sides. Machinery taken from frigate *Ilya Murometz* and boilers from frigate *Osliabia*

'Rusalka' Class (1865)

Monitors: *Charodeika, Rusalka*
Displacement: 1,881tons, 2,100f/l
Dimensions: 210(oa) 206'4(wl) 200'2(pp)×42×12'5 [64(oa) 62.9(wl) 61(pp)×12.8×3.8]
Machinery: 2 screws, horizontal direct-acting engines (Baird), 2 rectangular boilers
IHP 786 = 8.7knots
Armament: 4×230mm SB
Later: 2×230mm/20, 2×230mm/22, 4×87mm
Armour: Belt 114mm, turrets 152mm, c/t 114mm
Complement: 172
Class notes: Improved 'Smerch' type with low freeboard, two Coles turrets and two pole masts. Bad sea boats and rolled heavily

'Admiral Greig' Class (1866)

Turret ships: *Admiral Greig* (see later photo), *Admiral Lazarev*
Displacement: 3,462tons
Dimensions: 263'5(oa) 254'10(wl) 247(pp)×43×20'4 [80.3(oa) 77.7(wl) 75.3(pp)×13.1×6.2]
Machinery: 1 screw, horizontal direct-acting engines (Carr & McPherson), 4 rectangular boilers; *1903:* cylindrical boilers
IHP 2,000 = 10.2knots
Armament: 6×230mm SB, 1×40pdr
1871: 3×280mm/20
1880s: 5×47mm added
Armour: Belt 89-114mm, turrets 152mm, c/t 127mm
Complement: 280

Class notes: Seagoing rigged turret ships. Iron hull with raised forecastle and ram bow with three Coles turrets. Sail rig removed 1870 after loss of HMS *Captain* and rearmed

'Admiral Spiridov' Class (1866)

Turret Ships: *Admiral Chichagov, Admiral Spiridov*
Displacement: 3,750tons
Dimensions: 254'5(wl) 251'8(pp)×43×18 [77.6(wl) 76.7(pp)×13.1×5.5]
Machinery: 1 screw, horizontal direct-acting engines (Poletika), 4 rectangular boilers; *1887:* cylindrical boilers
IHP 2,000 = 9.5knots
Armament: 4×230mm/20
1871: 2×280mm/20
1880s: 4×87mm added
Armour: Belt 152mm, turrets 152mm
Complement: 280
Class notes: Similar to 'Greig' type with only two turrets and heavier armour

'General Admiral' Class (1868)

Central Battery Ships: *General Admiral, Gerzog Edinburgski*
Displacement: 4,650tons
Dimensions: 285'8(oa) 280'10(pp)×47'11×22'1 [87(oa) 85.6(pp)×14.6×7.1]
Machinery: 1 screw, vertical compound engines (*General Admiral:* Baird; *Gerzog Edinburgski:* Carr & McPherson), 12 rectangular boilers
1897: Vertical compound engines (Elder); *General Admiral:* 3 double-ended and 2 single-ended cylindrical boilers; *Gerzog Edinburgski:* 4 double-ended cylindrical boilers
General Admiral: IHP 4,472 = 12knots; *Gerzog Edinburgski:* IHP 5,222 = 12.5knots
Endurance: 5,900/10
Armament: *General Admiral:* 6×230mm/22, 2×152mm/28, 4×87mm
General Admiral, 1886: 2×47mm and 2×381mm TT added
Gerzog Edinburgski: 4×203mm/30, 5×152mm/28, 6×107mm
Gerzog Edinburgski, later: 10×37mm and 2×381mm TT added
Armour: Belt 127-152mm, redoubt 152mm
Complement: 482
Class notes: Designed by Popov for foreign service with speed and endurance given top priority. Full ship rig and guns amidships in redoubt. Refitted 1890-95, re-engined and reboilered with two funnels replacing single lowering funnel and fixed propeller replacing lifting screw. Converted to minelayers 1909

'Petr Veliki' (1869)

Turret Ship: *Petr Veliki*
Displacement: 9,665tons, 10,406f/l
Dimensions: 333'3(oa) 330(wl) 320'10(pp)×63×27'2 [101.6(oa) 100.6(wl) 97.8(pp)×19.2×8.3]
Machinery: 2 screws, horizontal return connecting-rod engines (Baird), 12 rectangular boilers; *1882:* vertical compound engines (Elder), 6 cylindrical boilers
IHP 7,500 = 14.5knots
Armament: 4×305mm/20, 6×87mm, 2×380mm TT added later
1907: 4×230mm/50, 12×152mm/45, 12×76mm, 4×57mm, 8×47mm, 2×37mm
Armour: Belt 203-356mm, citadel 203-356mm, turrets 356mm, deck 76mm
Complement: 436
Class notes: Designed by A. A. Popov; of novel design with two turrets, no rigging and low freeboard. Contemporaneous with British *Devastation* but completed later. Unsatisfactory engines replaced 1882. Completely reconstructed 1907, turrets removed, hull built up and new armament resited, reboilered, two funnels and two military masts fitted

'Novgorod' (1871)

Circular Turret Ship: *Novgorod*
Displacement: 2,530tons
Dimensions: 101 (diameter)×12'6 [30.8 (diameter)×3.8]
Machinery: 6 (later 4) screws, horizontal compound engines (Baird), 8 cylindrical boilers
IHP 3,000 = 7knots; *later:* IHP 2,000 = 5.5knots
Armament: 2×280mm/20, 2×87mm
Armour: Sides 178-229mm, barbette 229mm, deck 60mm
Complement: 110; *later:* 149
Class notes: Designed by Vice-Adm Popov as a floating fort to be used in shallow areas in the Black Sea. Guns in single barbette and no rigging. Built in St Petersburg and reassembled at Nikolaiev. Lacked speed and manoeuvrability, tended to rotate after firing of guns

'Vice Admiral Popov' (1871)

Circular Turret Ship: *Vice Admiral Popov* (see later photo)
Displacement: 3,550tons
Dimensions: 120 (diameter)×13'6 [36.6 (diameter)×4.1]
Machinery: 6 (later 4) screws, horizontal compound engines, 8 cylindrical boilers
IHP 3,000 = 8.5knots; *later:* IHP 3,000 = 6knots
Armament: 2×305mm/20, 8×87mm
Armour: Sides 355-406mm, barbette 406mm
Complement: 120; *later:* 203
Class notes: Enlarged 'Novgorod' built at Nikolaiev, with same defects

'Vladimir Monomakh' (1880)

Armoured Cruiser: *Vladimir Monomakh*
Displacement: 5,754tons
Dimensions: 307'9(oa) 296(wl)×51'10×25 [93.8(oa) 90.2(wl)×15.8×7.6]
Machinery: 2 screws, vertical compound engines (Baltic), 6 cylindrical boilers; *1897:* VTE engines, 12 cylindrical boilers
IHP 7,000 = 16knots
Endurance: 6,200/10
Armament: 4×203mm/28, 12×152mm/28, 4×9pdr, 3×381mm TT
1897: 5×152mm/45, 6×120mm/45, 16×47mm, 4×37mm, 3×381mm TT
Armour: Belt 114-152mm, battery 76-102mm
Complement: 550
Class notes: Improved 'Minin' built for foreign service. Two funnels and full ship rig, guns in sponsons and casemates. Modernised 1897, rearmed with new guns and funnels, reboilered and re-engined, rigging removed. Mainmast removed prior to Battle of Tsushima

'Dmitri Donskoi' (1880)

Armoured Cruiser: *Dmitri Donskoi*
Displacement: 5,893tons, 6,200f/l
Dimensions: 306'6(oa) 296'8(wl) 295(pp)×52×25 [93.4(oa) 90.4(wl) 89.9(pp)×15.8×7.6]
Machinery: 2 screws, vertical compound engines (Baltic), 8 cylindrical boilers; *1895:* VTE engines
IHP 7,000 = 17knots

ебное судно
Двина"
Dvena

Top left:
***Petr Veliki* — Turret ship, after reconstruction in 1907 with turrets removed.**

Top centre:
***Novgorod* — Circular turret ship, Black Sea Fleet, popularly known as a *Popoffka*..** *Marius Bar*

Top right:
***Vladimir Monomakh* — Armoured cruiser, c1895.**

Far left:
***Dmitri Donskoi* — Armoured cruiser, in 1902 after reconstruction.** *Aldo Fraccaroli*

Left:
***Admiral Nakhimov* — Armoured cruiser of 1885 in the Far East, prior to reconstruction.** *US Navy Official*

Bottom left:
***Imperator Aleksandr II* — Barbette ship of 1887, after reconstruction of 1905. Note single barbette forward.**

Bottom centre:
***Dvina* — The former armoured cruiser *Pamiat Azova* after conversion to minelaying training ship, 1909.**

Bottom right:
***Navarin* — Turret ship of 1891 with unusual paired arrangement of funnels.** *Conway Picture Library*

Endurance: 4,800/10
Armament: 2×203mm/30, 14×152mm/28, 4×381mm TT
1895: 6×152mm/45, 10×119mm/45, 6×47mm, 4×381mm TT
1902: 6×119mm removed, 6×75mm and 2×47mm added
Armour: Belt 100-190mm, barbettes 254mm, bulkheads 254mm, deck 50mm, c/t 152mm
Complement: 570
Class notes: Near sister to *Vladimir Monomakh*. Iron hull and ship rig. Rigging removed 1895, rearmed, reboilered and re-engined

'Chesma' Class (1882)

Barbette Ships: *Chesma, Imperatritsa Ekaterina II*
Displacement: 10,250tons
Dimensions: 339'6(oa) 331(wl)×69×28'9 [103.5(oa) 100.9(wl)×21×8.8]
Machinery: 2 screws, vertical compound engines (*Ekaterina:* Baltic, *Chesma:* Cockerill), 14 cylindrical boilers; *Ekaterina, 1900:* 18 Belleville
IHP 10,000 = 15knots
Endurance: 1,350/14
Armament: 6×305mm/30, 7×152mm/35, 8×47mm, 4×37mm, 7×381mm TT
Armour: Belt 203-406mm, redoubt 305mm, deck 57mm, c/t 229mm
Complement: 657
Class notes: Main battery in twin barbettes, two side by side forward and one aft, and single military foremast

'Sinop' Class (1883)

Barbette Ships: *Georgi Pobiedonosets, Sinop*
Displacement: 10,280tons, 11,940f/l; *Sinop:* 10,100tons
Dimensions: 339'6(oa) 331(wl)×68'10×28'6 [103.5(oa) 100.9(wl)×21×8.7]
Machinery: 2 screws, VTE engines (*Pobiedonosets:* Maudslay; *Sinop:* Napier), 16 (*Pobiedonosets*), 14 (*Sinop*) cylindrical boilers; *Sinop, 1901:* 20 Belleville boilers
IHP 10,600 = 16.5knots
Armament: 6×305mm/30, 7×152mm/35, 8×47mm, 4×37mm (*Pobiedonosets:* 10), 7×381mm TT
Sinop, 1914: 6×305mm/30, 4×203mm, 8×152mm, 4×47mm, no TT
Pobiedonosets, 1914: No TT
Armour: Belt 203-406mm, redoubt 305mm, deck 57mm, c/t 229mm (*Pobiedonosets:* 305mm)
Complement: 657
Class notes: Modified 'Chesma' type. *Sinop* was first warship in the world with triple-expansion engines, and *Georgi Pobiedonosets* was first to have electrically-operated mechanism and hoists for main guns

'Admiral Nakhimov' (1883)

Armoured Cruiser: *Admiral Nakhimov* (see also later photo)
Displacement: 7,782tons, 8,524f/l
Dimensions: 338'10(oa)×332'8(pp)×61×27'6 [103.3(oa) 101.4(pp)×18.6×8.4]
Machinery: 2 screws, inverted compound engines, 12 cylindrical boilers; *1899:* VTE engines
IHP 9,000 = 17.5knots
Endurance: 8,000/10
Armament: 8×203mm/35, 10×152mm/35, 12×47mm, 3×381mm TT
1899: 8×152mm/45, 10×120mm/45, 14×47mm, 2×37mm, 4 TT
Armour: Belt 152-254mm, barbettes 76-203mm, deck 76mm, redoubt 152mm, c/t 152mm
Complement: 567
Class notes: Main battery in hooded barbettes instead of in battery replaced by turrets in 1900. Similar to British *Imperieuse* with brig rig. Reboilered and rearmed in 1900. Rigging removed and replaced by two military masts

'Imperator Aleksandr II' Class (1884)

Barbette Ship: *Imperator Aleksandr II*
Turret Ship: *Imperator Nikolai I*
Displacement: *Aleksandr:* 9,900tons; *Nikolai:* 9,700tons
Dimensions: 346'6(oa) 333'6(wl) 326'5(pp)×66'10×25'9 [105.6(oa) 101.7(wl) 99.5(pp)×20.4×7.8]
Machinery: 2 screws, vertical compound engines (Baltic); 12 cylindrical boilers; *1902-4:* VTE engines, 16 Belleville boilers
Endurance: 3,985/10
Armament: 2×305mm/30, 4×229mm/35, 8×152mm/35, 10×47mm (*Nikolai:* 16), 8×37mm (*Nikolai:* 2), 6×381mm TT
1902: 229mm and 152mm replaced by 13×152mm/45, no TT
Armour: Belt 102-356mm, barbette or turret 76-254mm, deck 60mm, casemates 76-152mm, c/t 254mm (*Nikolai:* 203mm)
Complement: 648
Class notes: Near sisters, differed in mountings for main battery, barbettes in *Aleksandr II*, turrets in *Nikolai I*, mounted forward. *Nikolai I* was reconstructed in 1901, re-engined, old masts replaced by military masts and rearmed. *Aleksandr II* reconstructed 1904

'Pamiat Azova' (1885)

Armoured Cruiser: *Pamiat Azova*
Displacement: 6,000tons, 6,734f/l
Dimensions: 385(oa) 377'9(wl)×51'2×26'10 [117.3(oa) 115.2(wl)×15.6×8.2]
Machinery: 2 screws, VTE engines, 6 cylindrical boilers; *1902:* 18 Belleville boilers
IHP 11,000 = 18.8knots
Endurance: 10,000/10
Armament: 2×203mm/35, 13×152mm/35, 7×47mm, 8×37mm, 3×457mm TT
1904: 12×152mm/45, 2×75mm, 10×47mm, 2×457mm TT
Armour: Belt 102-152mm, barbettes 203mm, deck 63mm, c/t 38mm
Complement: 525
Class notes: Steel hull with three funnels and bark rig. Armament modified prior to completion. Refitted 1905, rearmed, new watertube boilers, rig reduced

'Navarin' (1886)

Turret Ship: *Navarin*
Displacement: 9,475tons, 10,206f/l
Dimensions: 368'4(—) 338(wl)×67×27'6 [112.3(—) 103(wl)×20.4×8.4]
Machinery: 2 screws, VTE engines, 12 cylindrical boilers
IHP 9,000 = 16knots
Endurance: 3,050/10
Armament: 4×305mm/35, 8×152mm/35, 18×47mm, 12×37mm, 6×381mm TT
Armour: Belt 305-406mm, turrets 305mm, battery 127mm, deck 51-76mm, c/t 254mm
Complement: 690
Class notes: Designed with low freeboard for coastal operations. Main battery in two twin turrets fore and aft, four funnels side by side in pairs and large military mast aft

'Gangut' (1888)

Barbette Ship: *Gangut*
Displacement: 6,500tons
Dimensions: 289'9(wl) 278(pp)×62×21 [88.3(wl) 84.7(pp)×18.9×6.4]
Machinery: 2 screws, vertical compound engines, 8 cylindrical boilers
IHP 6,000 = 15knots
Armament: 1×305mm/30, 4×229mm/35, 4×152mm/35, 4×57mm, 6×381mm TT
Armour: Belt 254-406mm, barbette 178-229mm, battery 127mm, c/t 254mm
Complement: 420
Class notes: Small battleship with single 12" gun in forward barbette and secondary battery in casemates amidships. Single military mast and single funnel

'Dvenadtsat Apostolov' (1888)

Barbette Ship: *Dvenadtsat Apostolov*
Displacement: 8,113tons, 8,433f/l
Dimensions: 342(oa) 331'3(wl)×60×27'6 [104.2(oa) 101(wl)×18.3×8.4]
Machinery: 2 screws, VTE engines (Baltic), 8 cylindrical boilers
IHP 8,000 = 16knots
Armament: 4×305mm/30, 4×152mm/35, 12×47mm, 14×37mm, 6×381mm TT
Armour: Belt 229-356mm, barbettes 254-305mm, battery 305mm, bulkheads 254-350mm, deck 51-66mm, c/t 203mm
Complement: 611
Class notes: Second class battleship for coast defence in Black Sea. Two short funnels heightened in 1897. Two twin barbettes fore and aft

'Rurik' (1889)

Armoured Cruiser: *Rurik*
Displacement: 11,690tons, 11,930f/l
Dimensions: 435(oa) 425'10(pp)×67×29'9 [132.6(oa) 129.8(pp)×20.4×9.1]
Machinery: 2 screws, VTE engines (Baltic), 8 cylindrical boilers
IHP 13,500 = 18.8knots
Endurance: 19,000/10
Armament: 4×203mm/35, 16×152mm/35, 6×120mm/45, 10×47mm, 12×37mm, 4×381mm TT
Armour: Belt 203-254mm, battery 229-254mm, bulkheads 305 and 254mm, deck 51-76mm, c/t 152mm
Complement: 727
Class notes: Designed as a commerce raider with strong armament and light protective armour. Two funnels and bark rig. Unsuccessful with weak broadside and inadequate armour. Rigging reduced 1901

'Sisoi Veliki' (1890)

Turret Ship: *Sisoi Veliki*
Displacement: 9,000tons, 10,400f/l
Dimensions: 347'9(oa) 340'7(wl)×66'6×24 [106(oa) 103.8(wl)×20.3×7.3]
Machinery: 2 screws, VTE engines, 16 cylindrical boilers
IHP 8,500 = 16knots
Endurance: 2,000/10
Armament: 4×305mm/40, 6×152mm/45, 12×47mm, 12×37mm, 6×457mm TT
Armour: Belt 203-406mm, turrets 305mm, casemates 127mm, deck 51-76mm, c/t 152mm
Complement: 620
Class notes: Second class battleship with high freeboard, two funnels, one military mast and one pole mast. Two twin turrets fore and aft

'Tri Sviatitelia' (1890)

Pre-dreadnought: *Tri Sviatitelia*
Displacement: 12,540tons, 13,318f/l
Dimensions: 377'9(oa) 370'8(pp)×73×28'5 [115.1(oa) 113(pp)×22.2×8.7]
Machinery: 2 screws, VTE engines (Humphrys), 14 cylindrical boilers
IHP 10,600 = 16knots
Endurance: 3,980/10
Armament: 4×305mm/40, 8×152mm/45, 4×120mm/45, 10×47mm, 6×457mm TT
1912: 4×305mm/40, 14×152mm/45, 2×457mm TT
Armour: Belt 229-457mm, turrets 406mm, secondary guns 127mm, deck 76mm, c/t 305mm
Complement: 744
Class notes: Very well protected vessel with low freeboard. Similar to British *Trafalgar*. Two military masts replaced by pole masts, reboilered and armament modified 1912. First ship to have wireless installed 1899

'Petropavlovsk' Class (1891)

Pre-dreadnoughts: *Petropavlovsk, Poltava, Sevastopol*
Displacement: 10,960tons, 11,400f/l
Dimensions: 375(oa) 369(wl)×70'×27'3 [114.3(oa) 112.5(wl)×21.3×8.3]
Machinery: 2 screws, VTE engines (*Petropavlovsk:* Hawthorn; *Poltava:* Humphrys; *Sevastopol:* Baltic), 14 cylindrical boilers (*Sevastopol:* 16)
IHP 10,609 = 16knots
Endurance: 3,750/10
Armament: 4×305mm/40, 12×152mm/45, 12×47mm, 28×37mm, 6×457mm TT
Armour: Belt 208-406mm (*Petropavlovsk:* 229-369mm), turrets 254mm, secondary turrets 127mm, c/t 229mm (*Poltava:* 229-389mm)
Complement: 716
Class notes: Military foremast and pole mainmast, two funnels with searchlight mast between. *Poltava*, salved by Japanese at Port Arthur, was returned to Russia in 1916

'Admiral Ushakov' Class (1891)

Coast Defence Ships: *Admiral Senyavin, Admiral Ushakov, General Admiral Apraksin*
Displacement: 4,100tons
Dimensions: 286'6(oa) 277'6(wl) 265(pp)×51'9×19'6 [87.3(oa) 84.6(wl) 80.8(pp)×5.8×5.9]
Machinery: 2 screws, VTE engines (*Senyavin:* Humphrys; *Ushakov:* Maudslay; *Apraksin:* Franco-Russian), 8 cylindrical boilers (*Ushakov:* 4)
IHP 5,700 = 16knots
Endurance: 2,600/10
Armament: 4×229mm/45 (*Apraksin:* 3×254mm/45), 4×120mm/45, 6×47mm, 18×37mm, 4×457mm TT
Armour: Belt 102-254mm, turrets 203mm, deck 38-63mm, c/t 203mm
Complement: 422
Class notes: Built for coast defence in Baltic Sea with low freeboard, two tall funnels. *Senyavin* and *Apraksin* captured by Japanese 1905

'Rostislav' (1892)

Pre-dreadnought: *Rostislav*

Top left:
***Rurik* — Armoured cruiser of 1892.**
US Naval Historical Centre

Top centre:
***Sisoi Veliki* — Second class battleship of 1894, Black Sea Fleet.** *Conway Picture Library*

Top right:
***Poltava* — Battleship of 1894, later sunk at Port Arthur but returned to Russia in 1916.** *Conway Picture Library*

Above:
***General Admiral Apraksin* — Coast defence ship of the Baltic Fleet, lost at Tsushima. The stern turret had only a single gun.**

Above centre:
***Gromoboi* — Armoured cruiser of 1899, improved 'Rossia' type, as refitted after 1906.**

Above right:
***Tsesarevich* — Battleship, after removal of fighting tops from masts, c1910. The foremast was later removed.**

Right:
***Kniaz Potemkin Tavricheski* — Pre-dreadnought of 1900.** *Marius Bar*

Far right:
***Retvizan* — Battleship as completed in 1902. Later became the Japanese *Hizen*.** *IWM*

инейный корабль
Цесаревичъ"
Czarevitch

Displacement: 8,800tons
Dimensions: 351'10(oa) 345'2(pp)×68×22 [107.2(oa) 105.2(pp)×20.7×6.7]
Machinery: 2 screws, VTE engines (Baltic), 12 cylindrical boilers
IHP 8,500 = 16knots
Endurance: 3,000/10
Armament: 4×254mm/45, 8×152mm/45, 12×47mm, 14×37mm, 8×457mm TT
Armour: Belt 203-368mm, turrets 127-254mm, secondary turrets 127mm, deck 51-76mm, c/t 152mm
Complement: 641
Class notes: Improved 'Sisoi Veliki' with both main and secondary armament in turrets. First major warship in the world with oil fuel

'Peresviet' Class (1894)

Pre-dreadnoughts: *Peresviet* (see later photo), *Pobieda, Osliabia* (see later photo)
Displacement: 12,674tons
Dimensions: 434'6(oa) 426'6(wl) 401'3(pp)×71'6×26 [132.4(oa) 130(wl) 122.3(pp)×21.8×7.9]
Machinery: 3 screws, VTE engines (Baltic), 30 Belleville boilers
IHP 14,500 = 18knots
Endurance: 6,000/10
Armament: 4×254mm/45, 11×152mm/45, 20×75mm, 20×47mm, 8×37mm, 5×457mm TT
Armour: Belt 178-229mm, turrets 229mm (*Pobieda:* 254mm), casemates 51-127mm, c/t 152mm (*Pobieda:* 210mm)
Complement: 732
Class notes: First Russian battleships with quick-firing guns. High forecastle with secondary armament mounted on two decks. Designed with heavy armament and high speed but unsatisfactory in operation. Armour of *Pobieda* extended full length of hull. *Peresviet* and *Pobieda* were recommissioned by Japanese after Russo-Japanese War and former was returned to Russia 1916

'Rossia' (1894)

Armoured Cruiser: *Rossia*
Displacement: 12,200tons
Dimensions: 480(oa) 464(pp)×68×26 [146.3(oa) 141.4(pp)×20.7×7.9]
Machinery: 3 screws, VTE engines (Baltic), 32 Belleville boilers
IHP 18,000 = 20knots
Endurance: 19,000/10
Armament: 4×203mm/45, 16×152mm/45, 13×75mm, 18×47mm, 5×381mm TT
1907: 6×152mm added
Armour: Belt 127-203mm, battery 127mm, deck 51-76mm, c/t 305mm
Complement: 842
Class notes: Better protected than *Rurik* but unable to use all engines at full speed. Four funnels and three masts. Reboilered 1907

'Potemkin' (1896)

Pre-dreadnought: *Kniaz Potemkin-Tavricheski* (see also later photo)
Displacement: 12,582tons
Dimensions: 378'5(oa) 370'9(wl)×73×27 [115.3(oa) 113(wl)×22.3×8.2]
Machinery: 2 screws, VTE engines (Russo-Belgian), 22 Belleville boilers
IHP 10,600 = 16knots
Endurance: 3,400/10
Armament: 4×305mm/40, 16×152mm/45, 14×75mm, 6×47mm, 5×457mm TT
Armour: Belt 178-229mm, turrets 254mm, casemates 127mm, deck 38-76mm, c/t 229mm
Complement: 741
Class notes: Three tall funnels and two military masts with two twin turrets fore and aft. Seized by mutineers in 1905 becoming the focus of an enduring legend

'Gromoboi' (1897)

Armoured Cruiser: *Gromoboi*
Displacement: 13,220tons
Dimensions: 481(oa) 472'6(wl)×68'6×27'8 [146.6(oa) 144(wl)×20.9×8.4]
Machinery: 3 screws, VTE engines (Baltic), 32 Belleville boilers
IHP 14,500 = 19knots
Armament: 4×203mm/45, 16×152mm/45, 24×75mm, 18×37mm, 4 TT
1906: 6×152mm added
1916: 2×152mm removed, 2×203mm and 4×75mm AA added
Armour: Belt 152mm, casemates 171mm, deck 51-76mm, c/t 305mm
Complement: 868
Class notes: Similar to *Rossia* with better machinery. Four funnels and three masts; rearmed 1906

'Retvizan' (1897)

Pre-dreadnought: *Retvizan*
Displacement: 12,700tons
Dimensions: 386'8(oa) 382'3(wl) 376(pp)×72'2×26 [117.8(oa) 116.5(wl) 114.6(pp)×22×7.9]
Machinery: 2 screws, VTE engines (Cramp), 24 Niclausse boilers
IHP 16,000 = 18knots
Endurance: 4,000/10
Armament: 4×305mm/40, 12×152mm/45, 20×75mm, 24×47mm, 8×37mm, 6×457mm TT
Armour: Belt 51-229mm, turrets 229mm, casemates 152mm, deck 51-76mm, c/t 254mm
Complement: 778
Class notes: Built in United States, similar to 'Maine' class of 1898 with three tall funnels and two masts. Salved by Japanese in 1905

'Tsesarevich' (1898)

Pre-dreadnought: *Tsesarevich*
Displacement: 12,912tons, 13,380f/l
Dimensions: 401(oa) 388'9(wl) 384'6(pp)×76.2×26 [122.2(oa) 118.5(wl) 117.2(pp)×23.2×7.9]
Machinery: 2 screws, VTE engines (F C Med), 20 Belleville boilers
IHP 15,300 = 18knots
Endurance: 5,500/10
Armament: 4×305mm/40, 12×152mm/45, 20×75mm, 20×47mm, 2×37mm, 6×457mm TT
Armour: Belt 120-249mm, turrets 152-254mm, secondary turrets 152mm, deck 38-69mm, c/t 254mm
Complement: 774
Class notes: Built in France, somewhat top heavy and unstable with pronounced tumblehome. Two heavy military masts and two large funnels. Main and secondary armament in twin turrets. Fighting tops removed from masts and other topweight removed 1906

'Bayan' Class (1898-1905)

Armoured Cruisers: *Admiral Makarov, Bayan* (1), *Bayan* (2), *Pallada*
Displacement: 7,775tons
Dimensions: 449'7(oa) 443(wl)×57'4×21'3 [137(oa) 135(wl)×17.5×6.5]
Machinery: 2 screws, VTE engines (Franco-Russian; *Makarov* and *Bayan* (1): F C Med), 26 Belleville boilers
IHP 16,500 = 21knots
Armament: 2×203mm/45, 8×152mm/45, 22×75mm, 2×457mm TT
Bayan (1): 2×203mm/45, 8×152mm/45, 20×75mm, 8×47mm
Armour: Belt 89-222mm, turrets 146mm, casemates 57mm, deck 31mm, c/t 133mm
Bayan (1): Belt 60-203mm, turrets 152mm, deck 51mm, c/t 160mm
Makarov: Belt 90-175mm, turrets 132mm, deck 70mm, c/t 137mm
Complement: 568
Class notes: Smaller than previous armoured cruisers but of better design. Four funnels, two masts and two single turrets fore and aft. First *Bayan* salved by Japanese navy

'Borodino' Class (1898-1901)

Pre-dreadnoughts: *Borodino, Imperator Aleksandr III, Kniaz Suvorov, Orel, Slava* (see later photo)
Displacement: 13,516tons, 15,275f/l; *Slava:* 14,000tons
Dimensions: 397'8(oa) 389'9(wl) 376'5(pp)×76'1×26'2 [121.2(oa) 118.8(wl) 114.8(pp)×23.2×8]
Machinery: 2 screws, VTE engines (Baltic), 20 Belleville boilers (*Aleksandr:* 24 Niclausse)
IHP 15,800 = 18knots
Endurance: 6,624/10
Armament: 4×305mm/40, 12×152mm/45, 20×75mm, 20×47mm (*Slava:* 4), 8×37mm (*Slava:* none), 6×457mm TT (*Slava:* 2)
Armour: Belt 100-203mm (*Suvorov, Orel* and *Slava:* 102-178mm), turrets 152-254mm, secondary turrets 76mm, deck 29-64, c/t 208mm
Complement: 825
Class notes: Design based on *Tsesarevich*, an adaptation of French ideas with sloped sides, built up superstructure and gunports too low in the hull. Top heavy and unstable, they suffered heavily at Tsushima. *Slava* was modified before completion to reduce top heaviness. *Orel* recommissioned in Japanese navy 1905

'Admiral Butakov' (1899)

Coast Defence Ship: *[Admiral Butakov]*
Displacement: 5,985tons
Dimensions: 343'6×59'4×17'4 [104.7×18.1×5.3]
Machinery: 2 screws, VTE engines, Belleville boilers
IHP 7,000 = 16knots
Armament: 6×203mm/45, 16×47mm, 6 TT
Armour: Belt 102-178mm, turrets 152mm, deck 55mm
Complement: 470
Class notes: Modified 'Admiral Ushakov' type, not completed

'Andrei Pervozannyi' Class (1903)

Pre-dreadnoughts: *Andrei Pervozvannyi* (see also later photo), *Imperator Pavl I* (see later photo)
Displacement: 17,400tons, 18,580f/l
Dimensions: 460(oa) 454(wl)×80×28 [140.2(oa) 138.4(wl)×24.4×8.5]
Machinery: 2 screws, VTE engines (*Pavl I:* Baltic; *Pervozvannyi:* Franco-Russian), 25 Belleville boilers
IHP 17,600 = 18.6knots
Endurance: 6,000/12
Armament: 4×305mm/40, 14×203mm/50, 12×120mm/50, 4×75mm, 3×457mm TT
Armour: Belt 79-216mm, turrets 127-203mm, secondary turrets 102-152mm, battery 79-152mm, deck 35-60mm, c/t 203mm
Complement: 933
Class notes: Redesigned following experiences of Russo-Japanese War. Designed as improved 'Borodino' class but revised with lighter armour, more but lighter guns and cage masts replacing military masts, which greatly delayed completion. In 1916 cage masts were cut down to stumps and pole masts fitted

'Evstafi' Class (1903)

Pre-dreadnoughts: *Ioann Zlatoust, Sviatoi Evstafi*
Displacement: 12,840tons
Dimensions: 385'9(oa) 377(wl) 372(pp)×73'10×27 [117.6(oa) 114.9(wl) 113.4(pp)×22.5×8.2]
Machinery: 2 screws, VTE engines (Nikolaiev), 22 Belleville boilers
IHP 10,600 = 16knots
Endurance: 4,500/10
Armament: 4×305mm/40, 4×203mm/50, 12×152mm/45, 14×75mm, 10×47mm, 3×457mm TT
1916: 2×75mm AA added
Armour: Belt 152-244mm, turrets 254mm, battery 127-152mm, deck 38-76mm, c/t 229mm
Complement: 879
Class notes: Design altered during construction to incorporate lessons of Russo-Japanese War. Three funnels and two pole masts. Similar to *Potemkin*

'Rurik' (1905)

Armoured Cruiser: *Rurik* (see also later photo)
Displacement: 15,190tons, 16,930f/l
Dimensions: 529(oa) 490(pp)×75'2×26 [161.2(oa) 149.4(pp)×22.9×7.9]
Machinery: 2 screws, VQE engines (Vickers), 28 Belleville boilers
IHP 19,700 = 21knots
Endurance: 8,000/10
Armament: 4×254mm/50, 8×203mm/50, 20×120mm/50, 4×47mm, 2×457mm TT
Armour: Belt 76-155mm, turrets 178-203mm, deck 38mm, c/t 203mm
Complement: 899
Class notes: Long low profile with three funnels and pole mainmast. Guns in two twin turrets fore and aft and four twin turrets at corners of superstructure. A very successful design

'Gangut' Class (1908)

Dreadnoughts: *Gangut, Petropavlovsk, Poltava, Sevastopol* (see later photo)
Displacement: 23,400tons, 25,850f/l
Dimensions: 600(oa) 589'10(wl)×87×27'3 [182.9(oa) 179.8(wl)×26.5×8.3]
Machinery: 4 screws, Parsons turbines (Baltic; *Gangut* and *Poltava:* Franco-Russian), 24 Yarrow boilers
SHP 50,000 = 24.6knots
Endurance: 4,000/16
Armament: 12×305mm/52, 16×120mm/50, 4×47mm, 4×450mm TT

Top, left to right:
***Bayan* — Armoured cruiser, first of name, 1905.** *Druppel*

***Kniaz Suvorov* — Pre-dreadnought of 'Borodino' class, sunk at Tsushima.** *Marius Bar*

***Andrei Pervozvannyi* — Pre-dreadnought, 1910, with cagemasts.** *Druppel*

Far left:
***Rurik* — Armoured cruiser of 1906, Baltic Fleet** *(top);*
***Poltava* — Dreadnought of 1911, 'Gangut' class.** *IWM (below)*

Left:
***Marat* — Battleship, ex-*Petropavlovsk*, as seen from the air at the Coronation Review of May 1937.**

Bottom, left to right:
***General Alekseev* — Battleship of the White Russian Fleet, in the Black Sea, 1919, built as *Imperator Aleksander III*.** *IWM*

***Kiev* — The first Russian aircraft carrier, of 1976, in the Mediterranean. Notice the massive island and the missile launchers forward of flightdeck.** *Official US Navy*

***Admiral Grieg* — Turret ship of 1868, with three turrets. The funnels of another battleship appear between foremast and funnel.**

Armour: Belt 100-279mm, turrets 125-305mm, deck 76mm, c/t 250mm
Complement: 1,125

***Marat* (ex-*Petropavlovsk*) (1931), *Parizhskaya Kommuna* (ex-*Sevastopol*) (1936) as reconstructed:**

Displacement: 24,605tons, 25,727f/l
Dimensions: 603'8(oa) 590'7(wl)×88'3×30'6 [184(oa) 180(wl)×26.9×9.3]
Machinery: 4 screws, Parsons geared turbines, 22 Yarrow boilers
SHP 61,000
Endurance: 1,120/23
Armament: 12×305mm/50, 16×120mm, 6×76mm AA, 4×450mm TT
1941: TT and some 120mm replaced by AA guns

***Oktyabrskaya Revolutsia* (ex-*Gangut*) (1934) as reconstructed:**

Displacement: 23,256tons, 26,692f/l
Dimensions: 606'6(oa) 593'10(wl)×88'3×31 [184.9(oa) 181(wl)×26.9×9.4]
Machinery: 4 screws, Parsons geared turbines, 12 Yarrow-Normand boilers
SHP 57,500
Armament: As *Marat*
1941: 8×100mm AA and 12×37mm AA replaced some 120mm
Class notes: Original designs by Cuniberti modified by Krilov to include icebreaking bows and other differences. First Russian dreadnoughts, had main battery in four triple turrets. Three surviving vessels reconstructed 1931-39, re-engined and reboilered, and fore funnel raised and angled back. *Sevastopol* (*Parizhskaya-Kommuna*) transferred to Black Sea 1930. They differed in appearance

'Imperatritsa Maria' Class (1911)

Dreadnoughts: *Imperator Aleksandr III,* (see also later photo) *[Imperator Nikolai I], Imperatritsa Ekaterina Velikaya, Imperatritsa Maria*
Displacement: 22,800tons, 24,000f/l; *Nikolai I:* 27,300tons
Dimensions: 550'6(pp)×89'6×27'3 [167.8(pp)×27.3×8.3]
Nikolai I: 616'9(oa) 597'2(wl)×94'10×29'6 [188(oa)×182(wl)×28.9×9]
Machinery: 4 screws, *Maria* and *Ekaterina:* Parsons, *Aleksandr III* and *Nikolai I:* Brown-Curtis turbines, 20 Yarrow boilers (*Nikolai I:* 25 Yarrow)
SHP 26,500 = 21knots; *Nikolai I:* SHP 29,700
Endurance: 1,000/21
Armament: 12×305mm/52, 18×130mm/60 (*Nikolai:* 20), 4×75mm, 4×75mm AA, 4×47mm, 4×457mm TT
Armour: Belt 102-305mm, turrets 203-305mm, battery 127mm, deck 35mm, c/t 400mm
Complement: 1,252
Class notes: Similar to 'Gangut' class but slower with heavier armour and secondary armament. *Nikolai I* was to be slightly larger and more powerful but was never completed

'Borodino' Class (1912)

Battlecruisers: *[Borodino, Izmail, Kinburn, Navarin]*
Displacement: 32,500tons, 38,000f/l
Dimensions: 750(oa) 728(wl)×100×33'5 [228.6(oa) 221.9(wl)×30.5×10.2]
Machinery: 4 screws, Parsons turbines (Baltic Works; *Navarin:* Vulcan; *Izmail* and *Kinburn:* Franco-Russian), 25 Yarrow boilers
SHP 68,000 = 29.5knots
Endurance: 3,830/16
Armament: 12×356mm/45, 24×130mm/55, 8×75mm, 4×63mm, 6×533mm TT
Armour: Belt 100-240mm, turrets 152-240mm, deck 63mm
Complement: 1,250
Class notes: Similar in layout to 'Gangut' class with heavier guns and longer hull, more like battleships.
Construction suspended early 1917. Turbines for *Navarin* not delivered from Germany and were used in cruisers *Bremse* and *Brummer*. None was completed

'Sovietski Soyuz' Class (1937)

Battleships: *[Sovietskaya Bielorossia, Sovietskaya Rossia, Sovietskaya Ukraina, Sovietski Soyuz]*
Displacement: 59,150tons, 65,150f/l
Dimensions: 889(oa)×127'8×33'6 [271(oa)×38.9×10.2]
Machinery: 3 screws, turbo-electric engines
SHP 231,000 = 29knots
Endurance: 7,200/14.5
Armament: 9×406mm/50, 12×152mm/50; 8×100mm DP, 32×37mm
Armour: Belt 375-425mm, turrets 495mm, decks 25-150mm, secondary turrets 100mm, c/t 425mm
Class notes: Plans were sought in Italy and US but designs were Soviet made. Difficulty in obtaining equipment led to lengthy delays and eventual impossibility of completing these vessels. Construction suspended 1940

'Kronshtadt' Class (1938)

Battlecruisers: *[Kronshtadt, Sevastopol]*
Displacement: 35,240tons, 38,360f/l
Dimensions: 813'6(oa)×103×29'9 [248(oa)×31.4×9.1]
Machinery: 4 screws, geared turbines
SHP 150,000 = 32knots
Armament: 9×305mm, 8×152mm, 8×100mm DP, 24×37mm AA
Armour: Belt 230mm, turrets 305mm, deck 90mm
Class notes: Classed as heavy cruisers, these vessels would have been equivalent to US 'Alaska' class. Construction dependent on receiving armour and equipment from abroad

'Arkhangelsk' (1944)

Battleship: *Arkhangelsk*
Displacement: 29,150tons, 33,500f/l
Dimensions: 624'3(oa) 614'6(wl) 580(pp)×102'6×32 [190.3(oa) 187.3(wl) 176.8(pp)×31.2×9.8]
Machinery: 4 screws, Parsons geared turbines (Parsons), 18 B&W boilers
SHP 40,000 = 23knots
Armament: 8×381mm/42, 12×152mm/45, 8×102mm AA, 32×40mm
Armour: Belt 102-330mm, barbettes 102-254mm, turrets 127-330mm, bulkheads 102-152mm, c/t 279mm
Complement: 936
Class notes: Former British *Royal Sovereign* loaned in 1944

'Stalingrad' Class (1947)

Battlecruisers: *[Moskva, Stalingrad]*
Displacement: 38,420tons, 43,720f/l
Dimensions: 821'9(oa) 787'6(wl)×96'6×29 [250.5(oa) 240(wl)×29.4×8.9]

Armament: 9×305mm, 8×100mm
Class notes: Planned during World War 2, but not begun until 1950. Construction proceeded slowly and was abandoned during the 1950s following a change of naval policy. Details other than hull size are unknown or conjectural

'Novorossisk' (1948)

Battleship: *Novorossisk*
Displacement: 28,800tons, 29,100f/l
Dimensions: 611'6(oa) 554'4(pp)×91'9×34.2 [186.4(oa) 169(pp)×28×10.4]
Machinery: 2 screws, Belluzzo geared turbines, 8 3-drum boilers
SHP 75,000 = 28knots
Endurance: 3,100/20
Armament: 10×320mm/44, 12×120mm/50, 8×100mm/47, 8×37mm
Armour: Belt — 250mm, turrets 280mm, deck 135mm, c/t 260mm
Complement: 1,236
Class notes: Former Italian *Giulio Cesare* transferred after World War 2

'Kiev' Class (1968)

Aircraft Carriers: *Kharkov, Kiev, Minsk, Novorossisk*
Displacement: 32,000tons, 37,000f/l
Dimensions: 895'7(oa) 816'9(wl)×105×30 [273(oa) 249(wl)×32×9]
Machinery: 4 screws, steam turbines
SHP 180,000 = 32knots
Endurance: 13,000/18
Aircraft: 35-40 approx
Armament: 2 SA-N-3 SAM launchers, 4 SA-N-4 SAM launchers, 8 SSN-12 SSM launchers, 4×76mm DP guns, 10×533mm TT
Complement: 2,500
Class notes: The largest combatant vessels built in the Soviet Union. First Soviet aircraft carriers, officially designated large anti-submarine cruisers. Angled flightdeck extending forward only as far as the massive island. Heavily armed with AA, ASW and surface-to-surface cruise missiles. Aircraft limited to VTOL and helicopters

'Kirov' Class (1976)

Battlecruisers: *Kirov*
Displacement: 22,000tons, 25,000f/l
Dimensions: 820(oa)×90'2×32'9 [250(oa)×27.5×10]
Machinery: 2 screws, 2 nuclear reactors
SHP 150,000 = 35knots
Armament: 20 SS-N-19 SSM launchers, 12 SA-N-6 and 2 SA-N-4 SAM launchers, 1 twin SS-N-14 ASW launcher 2×100mm guns
Complement: 900
Class notes: The first Soviet nuclear powered surface warship and the largest warship other than carriers built since World War 2. Details given are approximate only. Others may be built

Individual Ships

Admiral Butakov

Type: Coast Defence Ship
Class: 'Admiral Butakov' (1899)
Nomenclature: Grigori Ivanovich Butakov (1820-1882), Russian admiral

History:
1900 May: Laid down at Galernii
1903 Construction cancelled

Admiral Chichagov

Type: Turret Ship
Class: 'Admiral Spiridov' (1866)
Nomenclature: Pavl Vasilievich Chichagov (1767-1849), navy minister

History:
1866 November 20: Laid down by Poletika as ***Chichagov***
1866 July 4: Renamed ***Admiral Chichagov***
1868 October 13: Launched
1869 Completed
1907 August 14: Stricken

Admiral Greig

Type: Turret Ship
Class: 'Admiral Greig' (1866)
Nomenclature: Samuel Greig (1736-1788), Russian admiral, commander at Chesma and Hogland

History:
1866 April 24: Laid down by Carr & McPherson as ***Greig***
1866 July 4: Renamed ***Admiral Greig***
1868 October 30: Launched
1869 Completed
1898 Reboilered
1909 December 22: Stricken

Admiral Lazarev

Type: Turret Ship
Class: 'Admiral Greig' (1866)
Nomenclature: Mikhail Petrovich Lazarev (1788-1851), commander of the Black Sea Fleet, promoted its development as well as that of ironclad and steam warships

History:
1867 Laid down by Carr & McPherson
1867 September 21: Launched
1868 Completed
1871 Rammed in collision with ironclad *Admiral Spiridov* at Kronstadt
1907 August 14: Stricken

Admiral Makarov

Type: Armoured Cruiser
Class: 'Bayan' (1898)
Nomenclature: Stepan Osipovich Makarov (1848-1904), commander of the Russian Far Eastern Squadron at Port Arthur killed when his flagship was sunk

History:
1905 April 3: Laid down at La Seyne
1906 May 9: Launched
1908 April: Completed
1922 Broken up at Stettin

Admiral Nakhimov

Type: Armoured Cruiser

Class: 'Admiral Nakhimov' (1883)
Nomenclature: Pavl Stepanovich Nakhimov (1802-1855), commander at the Battle of Sinop and a hero of the defence of Sevastopol

History:
1884 July: Laid down by Baltic
1885 November 2: Launched
1887 December 15: Completed
1888 Baltic Fleet
1889-91 Far East
1893 September: Lost bowsprit in collision with armoured cruiser *Pamiat Azova* at Cadiz
1894-98 Far East
1899 Reconstructed; re-engined and reboilered, new armament, rerigged
1900-02 Far East
1900 Boxer Rebellion
1904 October 15: Sailed for Far East, 2nd Pacific Squadron
1905 May 27: Battle of Tsushima; torpedoed by Japanese warships the following day and sank off Tsushima Island

Admiral Senyavin

Type: Coast Defence Ship
Class: 'Admiral Ushakov' (1891)
Nomenclature: Dmitri Nikolaievich Senyavin (1763-1831), Russian commander in the Mediterranean during the Napoleonic Wars

History:
1892 August 1: Laid down by New Admiralty
1894 August 22: Launched
1896 Completed
1895 Baltic Fleet
1905 February 16: Sailed for the Far East, 3rd Pacific Squadron
1905 May 27: At Tsushima; surrendered the following day. Taken into Japanese navy as ***Mishima***

Admiral Spiridov

Type: Turret Ship
Class: 'Admiral Spiridov' (1866)
Nomenclature: Grigori Andreyevich Spiridov, admiral, prominent in operations against the Turks in 18th century

History:
1866 November 20: Laid down by Poletika

Above left:
***Admiral Nakhimov* — Armoured cruiser seen after 1893. Note missing bowsprit lost in collision at Cadiz.**
Marius Bar

Above right:
***Andrei Pervozvannyi* — Pre-dreadnought of 1906, as it appeared after 1916 with pole masts replacing the cutdown cagemasts.** *IWM*

1868 August 28: Launched
1869 Completed
1871 In collision with ironclad *Admiral Lazarev* at Kronstadt
1907 August 14: Stricken

Admiral Ushakov

Type: Coast Defence Ship
Class: 'Admiral Ushakov' (1891)
Nomenclature: Fyodor Fyodorovich Ushakov (1743-1817), commander of the Black Sea Fleet in 1789 and victor of the Battles of Gadzhibey and Kaliakria

History:
1892 June 28: Laid down by Baltic
1893 November 4: Launched
1896 Completed
1896 Baltic Fleet
1905 February 16: Sailed for the Far East, 3rd Pacific Squadron
1905 May 27: Damaged by gunfire at Tsushima, again damaged the following day and scuttled by crew (60 dead)

Aleksandr Nevsky, see *Gerzog Edinburgski*

Nomenclature: Alexander Nevski (1220-1263), Russian ruler, defeated Swedes at the Neva River, 1240

Andrei Pervozvannyi

Type: Pre-dreadnought
Class: 'Andrei Pervozvannyi' (1903)
Nomenclature: Saint Andrew the Pre-eminent

History:
1903 April 28: Laid down at Galernii
1906 October 20: Launched
1910 September: Completed
1910 Baltic Fleet
1913 Went aground
World War 1: Baltic Fleet actions, inactive
1916-17 Refit, cagemasts replace with pole masts
1917 March 4: Mutiny on board, Adm Nebolsin killed
1917 October: Red Fleet
1919 August 18: Torpedoed by British torpedo boats at Kronstadt, refloated but not repaired
1923 Broken up

Arkhangelsk

Type: Battleship
Class: 'Arkhangelsk' (1944)
Nomenclature: Archangel, a port in northern Russia

History:
1914 January 15: Laid down at Portsmouth as British ***Royal Sovereign***
1915 April 29: Launched
1916 May: Completed
1944 May 30: Loaned to Soviet Union, renamed ***Arkhangelsk***; Arctic Fleet
1947 Autumn: Went aground and damaged in Barents Sea
1949 February 4: Returned to Great Britain

Bayan (1)

Type: Armoured Cruiser
Class: 'Bayan' (1898)
Nomenclature: A troubador

History:
1899 March: Laid down at La Seyne
1900 June 12: Launched
1903 April: Completed
—— Far East
1904 February 9: Damaged by gunfire in action off Port Arthur
1904 December 9: Sunk by siege batteries in Port Arthur harbour
1905 June 24: Refloated by Japanese and taken into service, renamed ***Aso***

Bayan (2)

Type: Armoured Cruiser
Class: 'Bayan' (1898)

History:
1905 August: Laid down by New Admiralty
1907 August 15: Launched
1911 February 13: Completed
1917 October 17: Damaged in action with German warships in Moon Sound
1922 Broken up at Stettin

Boretz za Svobodu, see ***Kniaz Potemkin Tavricheski***

Nomenclature: Fighter for liberty

Borodino

Type: Pre-dreadnought
Class: 'Borodino' (1898)
Nomenclature: Russian battle against Napoleon, 7 September 1812

History:
1900 May 25: Laid down by New Admiralty
1901 September 8: Launched
1904 September: Completed
1904 October 15: Sailed for Far East, 2nd Pacific Squadron
1905 May 27: Hit by gunfire of Japanese warships at Tsushima, blew up and sank (829 dead, one survivor)

Borodino

Type: Battlecruiser
Class: 'Borodino' (1912)

History:
1914 January 1: Laid down by New Admiralty
1915 July 1: Launched
1917 Early: Construction suspended
1923 Broken up at Bremen

Bronenosets

Type: Monitor
Class: 'Uragan' (1862)
Nomenclature: Ironclad

History:
1863 June 17: Laid down by Carr & McPherson
1864 March 24: Launched
1865 February 6: Completed
1905 August 5: Stricken

Charodeika

Type: Monitor
Class: 'Rusalka' (1865)
Nomenclature: Sorceress, enchantress

History:
1866 March: Laid down at Mitchell as ***Pyotr Veliki***
1867 September 12: Launched
1869 Completed

***Dmitri Donskoi* — Armoured cruiser of 1883.**

1872 Renamed ***Charodeika***
1907 April 7: Stricken and broken up

Chesma

Type: Barbette Ship
Class: 'Chesma' (1882)
Nomenclature: Russian naval victory over the Turks, 7 July 1770

History:
1883 November: Laid down at Ropit; Sevastopol
1886 May 18: Launched
1889 Completed; Black Sea Fleet
1903 Reconstructed, reboilered
1907 August 14: Stricken for harbour service, renamed *Blokshiv No 3*
1910 Stricken
1913 Sunk as a target

Chesma, see *Poltava*

Demokratiya, see *Imperator Nikolai I*

Nomenclature: Democracy

Dmitri Donskoi

Type: Armoured Cruiser
Class: Dmitri Donskoi' (1880)
Nomenclature: Dmitri Ivanovich, 'of the Don', Grand Duke of Moscow (1350-1389), victor against the Turks at Kulikovo

History:
1881 May 21: Laid down by New Admiralty
1883 August 30: Launched
1885 July: Completed
1885 Baltic Fleet
1885-87 Mediterranean
1887-89 Far East
1887 October 12: Went aground in Gulf of Amur
1892-93 Far East
1893-95 Reconstructed; re-engined and rearmed
1896-1902 Far East
1902 Reft, rearmed
1904 October 15: Sailed for Far East, 2nd Pacific Squadron
1905 May 27: Battle of Tsushima; sank damaged destroyer *Buini*, separated from other ships. Damaged in action with Japanese warships the following day and scuttled by crew off Tsushima Island

Dvenadtsat Apostolov

Type: Pre-dreadnought
Class: 'Dvenadtsat Apostolov' (1888)
Nomenclature: Twelve Apostles

History:
1889 July: Laid down at Nikolaiev Admy
1890 September 13: Launched
1892 December: Completed: Black Sea Fleet
1897 Refit; funnel raised
1911 March 19: Harbour service
1911 April 17: Stricken, hulk
1914 September 4: Renamed *Blokshiv No 8*
1922 Broken up

Gangut

Type: Barbette Ship
Class: 'Gangut' (1888)
Nomenclature: Hango, Russian naval victory over Sweden, 27 July 1714

History:
1889 June 1: Laid down by New Admiralty
1890 October 18: Launched
1893 Completed; Baltic Fleet
1897 June 12: Struck submerged rock off Transund near Viborg and sank (none lost)

Gangut

Type: Dreadnought
Class: 'Gangut' (1908)

History:
1909 July 13: Laid down by Admiralty
1911 October 7: Launched

1915 January 5: Completed
World War 1: Baltic Fleet
1917 Red Fleet
1925 July 7: Renamed ***Oktyabrskaya Revolutsia***
1926 Refit
1931 Autumn: Severely damaged when hull hit bottom in shallow water in Gulf of Finland
1931-34 Refit at Baltic; reboilered and re-engined, fore funnel raised and angled back
World War 2: Baltic Fleet, Defence of Leningrad
1939 December: Bombarded Finnish Coast
1941 September 23: Severely damaged when hit by six bombs at Leningrad
1942 April 4: Again hit by four bombs
1956-59 Broken up at Kronstadt

General Admiral

Type: Central Battery Ship
Class: 'General Admiral' (1868)
Nomenclature: Highest rank in the Imperial navy, named after Grand Duke Constantine Nikolaievitch (1827-1892)

History:
1870 November 27: Laid down by Nevski
1873 October 2: Launched
1875 Completed; Baltic Fleet
1875 Baltic Fleet
1875 Went aground in gale at Kronstadt
1884-85 Mediterranean
1886 Refit, reboilered
1892 Refit; re-engined by Elder, single funnel, fixed instead of lifting screw
1906 March 24: Training Ship
1909 October 25: Converted to minelayer, renamed ***Narova***
1913 Refit, reboilered
1918 Red Fleet
1922 Renamed ***Dvadsatpyatavo Oktyabrya*** (= *25 October*)
1938 Stricken; hulk at Leningrad
1959c Hulk expended as breakwater in Neva River

General Admiral Apraksin

Type: Coast Defence Ship
Class: 'Admiral Ushakov' (1891)
Nomenclature: Count Fedor Matveyevich Apraksin (1661-1728), victor of Gangut and founder of the navy

History:
1894 October 24: Laid down by New Admiralty
1896 May 12: Launched
1899 Completed; Baltic Fleet
1899 November 12: Went aground off Hogland
1900 May 2: Refloated and repaired
1905 February 16: Sailed for Far East, 3rd Pacific Squadron
1905 May 27: At Tsushima, surrendered the following day. Taken into Japanese navy as ***Okinoshima***

General Alekseev, see Imperator Aleksandr III

Nomenclature: Mikhail Vasilievich Alekseev (1857-1918), leading anti-Bolshevik general

Georgi Pobiedonosets

Type: Barbette Ship
Class: 'Sinop' (1883)
Nomenclature: St George the Victorious, patron saint of the Russian armed forces

History:
1889 July: Laid down by Ropit, Sevastopol
1892 March 9: Launched
1894 Completed
1894 Black Sea Fleet
—— Refit, reboilered
World War 1: Flagship of C-in-C Black Sea Fleet
1917 October: Red Fleet
1918 December: Seized by White Army at Sevastopol
1919 April 25: Machinery wrecked by Allied forces
1920 November: Towed to Bizerte with Wrangel fleet and interned, funnel collapsed on bridge during voyage
1924 October 24: Decommissioned
1936 Broken up

Gerzog Edinburgski

Type: Central Battery Ship
Class: 'General Admiral' (1868)
Nomenclature: Prince Alfred, Duke of Edinburgh (1844-1900), son-in-law of Emperor Alexander II

History:
1870 September 27: Laid down by Baltic as ***Aleksandr Nevsky***
1874 February 7: Renamed ***Gerzog Edinburgski***
1875 September 10: Launched
1877 Completed; Baltic Fleet
1881-84 Far East
1892 Refit; re-engined by Elder, rearmed, two funnels replaced single funnel
1906 March 24: Training ship
1909 October 25: Converted to minelayer, renamed ***Onega***
1915 October 14: Hulk, *Blokshiv No 9*
1920s Broken up

Grazhdanin, see Tsesarevich

Nomenclature: Citizen

Gromoboi

Type: Armoured Cruiser
Class: 'Gromoboi' (1897)
Nomenclature: Thunder

History:
1898 May 19: Laid down by Baltic
1899 May 20: Launched
1901 Completed; Baltic Fleet
—— Far East
1904 August 14: Damaged by 25 hits at Battle of the Yellow Sea
1904 November 12: Severely damaged when struck a reef in Possiet Bay near Vladivostok
1905 May 23: Damaged by mine off Vladivostok
1922 Went aground off Libau en route to breaking up
1922 Broken up

Imperator Aleksandr II

Type: Barbette Ship
Class: 'Imperator Aleksandr II' (1884)
Nomenclature: Alexander II, Emperor of Russia (1818-1881)

History:
1885 June 30: Laid down by New Admiralty
1887 July 26: Launched
1890 Completed; Baltic Fleet
1905 Reconstructed; reboilered and rearmed
1911 Gunnery training ship
1917 May 22: Renamed ***Zarya Svoboda***
1919 August 18: Damaged by British torpedo boats at Kronstadt
1922 Broken up

Imperator Aleksandr III

Type: Pre-dreadnought
Class: 'Borodino' (1898)
Nomenclature: Alexander III, Emperor of Russia (1845-1894)

History:
1899 September 5: Laid down by Baltic
1901 August 3: Launched
1903 November: Completed; Baltic Fleet
1904 October 15: Sailed for Far East, 2nd Pacific Squadron
1905 May 27: Capsized and sunk by gunfire of Japanese warships at Tsushima (823 dead, no survivors)

Imperator Aleksandr III

Type: Dreadnought
Class: 'Imperatritsa Maria' (1911)

History:
1911 November 30: Laid down by Russian
1914 April 15: Launched
1917 June 28: Completed
World War 1: Black Sea Fleet
1917 April 29: Renamed ***Volya***
1918 April: Captured by Germans at Sevastopol
1918 December: Seized by White (Russian) army at Sevastopol
1919 September: Renamed ***General Alekseev***
1920 October 31: Left Sevastopol with refugees and naval school cadets as flagship of Wrangel Fleet
1920 December: Interned at Bizerte
1924 October 29: Decommissioned at Bizerte
1936 Broken up

Imperator Nikolai I

Type: Turret Ship
Class: 'Imperator Aleksandr II' (1884)
Nomenclature: Nicholas I, Emperor of Russia (1796-1855)

History:
1886 August 4: Laid down by Franco-Russian
1889 June 1: Launched
1892 Completed; Baltic Fleet
1893-97 Mediterranean
1898 Refit, reboilered
1900 Refit, re-engined
1901 May 1: In collision with steamer *Saragossa* at Constantinople
1905 February 16: Sailed for Far East, 3rd Pacific Squadron, Flagship of Rear-Adm Nebogatoff
1905 May 27: Damaged by gunfire at Battle of Tsushima, and surrendered the following day. Taken into Japanese navy as ***Iki***

Above:
***Volya* — Dreadnought of the Black Sea Fleet, 1918.**
Druppel

Above right:
***Imperator Pavl I* — Pre-dreadnought of the Black Sea Fleet, as completed. The cagemasts were removed during World War 1.**

Imperator Nikolai I

Type: Dreadnought
Class: 'Imperatritsa Maria' (1911)

History:
1915 January 28: Laid down by Russian
1916 October 18: Launched
1917 October: Construction suspended when 40% complete
1917 April 29: Renamed ***Demokratiya***
1918 Incomplete hull damaged by German and White forces
1923 Broken up incomplete

Imperator Pavl I

Type: Pre-dreadnought
Class: 'Andrei Pervozvannyi' (1903)
Nomenclature: Paul I, Emperor of Russia (1754-1801)

History:
1904 April 15: Laid down by Baltic
1907 September 7: Launched
1910 October: Completed; Baltic Fleet
World War 1: Baltic Fleet actions
1917 March 4: Mutiny on board
1917 April 29: Renamed ***Respublika***
1917 October: Red Fleet
1923 Broken up

Imperatritsa Ekaterina II

Type: Barbette Ship
Class: 'Chesma' (1882)
Nomenclature: Catherine II the Great, Empress of Russia (1729-1796)

History:
1883 November: Laid down at Nikolaiev Admy
1886 May 22: Launched
1889 Completed; Black Sea Fleet
1900 Refit, reboilered
1907 August 14: Converted to target ship, *Blokshiv No 2*
1907 Damaged by gunfire and sunk near Tendra

Imperatritsa Ekaterina Velikaya

Type: Dreadnought
Class: 'Imperatritsa Maria' (1911)

Nomenclature: Empress Catherine the Great

History:
1912 September 1: Laid down at Nikolaiev as ***Ekaterina II***
1914 June 6: Launched
1915 June 27: Renamed ***Imperatritsa Ekaterina Velikaya***
1915 October 28: Completed
World War 1: Black Sea Fleet
1917 January : Raid on Turkish coastal shipping
1917 April 29: Renamed ***Svobodnaya Rossiya***
1917 November: Seized by crew, returned to Sevastopol
1918 April 6: Evacuated from Sevastopol to Novorossisk
1918 June 18: Scuttled on orders of Trotsky in Novorossisk harbour, being torpedoed by destroyer *Kerch*

Imperatritsa Maria

Type: Dreadnought
Class: 'Imperatritsa Maria' (1911)
Nomenclature: Marie Fedorovna (1847-1928), wife of Emperor Alexander III

History:
1911 October 30: Laid down by Russian
1913 November 1: Launched
1915 July 6: Completed
World War 1: Black Sea Fleet
1916 October 20: Scuttled in Sevastopol harbour following explosion in forward magazine probably caused by sabotage or unstable ammunition (225 dead)
1917-18 Refloated upside down
1926 Broken up

Ioann Zlatoust

Type: Pre-dreadnought
Class: 'Evstafi' (1903)
Nomenclature: John Chrysostom (the Golden-tongued) (345-407), one of the fathers of the Greek Church

History:
1903 November 14: Laid down at Sevastopol
1906 May 13: Launched
1910 August 11: Completed Sea Fleet actions
World War 1: Black Sea Fleet actions
1917 Red Fleet
1918 April: Captured by Germans at Sevastopol
1918 December: Seized by White Army at Sevastopol
1919 April 25: Machinery wrecked by Allied forces
1920 November: Seized by Red Army
1923 Broken up

Ivan Groznyi, see *Imperator Nikolai I*

Izmail

Type: Battlecruiser
Class: 'Borodino' (1912)
Nomenclature: Russian victory on the Danube over the Turks, 11 December 1790

History:
1914 January 1: Laid down by Baltic
1915 June 22: Launched
1917 Construction suspended
1931 Broken up at Leningrad

Kharkov

Type: Aircraft Carrier
Class: 'Kiev' (1968)
Nomenclature: City in the Ukraine

History:
1978 December: Laid down at Nikolaiev South
1981 Launched
1984 Completed

Kiev, see *Vice Admiral Popov*

Kiev

Type: Aircraft Carrier
Class: 'Kiev' (1968)
Nomenclature: Capital city of the Ukraine

History:
1970 September: Laid down at Nikolaiev South
1972 December: Launched
1975 May: Completed
1981 Northern (Arctic) Fleet

Kinburn

Type: Battlecruiser
Class: 'Borodino' (1912)
Nomenclature: Defensive action near Odessa against combined British and French fleets, 17 October 1854

History:
1914 January 1: Laid down by Baltic
1915 October 30: Launched
1917 Construction suspended
1923 Broken up at Kiel

Kirov

Type: Battlecruiser

Class: 'Kirov' (1976)
Nomenclature: Sergei Mironovich Kirov (1888-1934), Soviet revolutionary leader

History:
1973 Laid down at Baltic
1977 December: Launched
1981 Completed
1981 Northern (Arctic) Fleet

Kniaz Potemkin-Tavricheski

Type: Pre-dreadnought
Class: 'Potemkin' (1896)
Nomenclature: Prince Grigori Aleksandrovich Potemkin (1739-1791), statesman during the reign of Catherine the Great, builder of the Black Sea Fleet

History:
1898 October 8: Laid down at Nikolaiev Admy
1900 October 9: Launched
1903 Completed; Black Sea Fleet
1905 June 27: Seized by mutineers and sailed to Constantza, Romania, where ship was interned, July 8
1905 October 12: Renamed ***Panteleimon***
World War 1: Black Sea Fleet actions
1917 April 13: Renamed ***Potemkin***
1917 May 11: Renamed ***Boretz za Svobodu***
1918 April; Captured by the Germans at Sevastopol
1918 December: Seized by White Army at Sevastopol
1919 April 25: Machinery wrecked by Allied forces
1923 Broken up

Kniaz Pozharski

Type: Central Battery Ship
Class: 'Kniaz Pozharski' (1863)
Nomenclature: Prince Dmitri Mikhailovich Pozharski (1578-1642), leader with Minin against Polish invaders

History:
1864 November 30: Laid down by Mitchell as ***Pozharski***
1866 July 16: Renamed ***Kniaz Pozharski***
1867 September 12: Launched
1873 Completed
1873-75 and 1879-80 Pacific Squadron
1880 Baltic Fleet
1885 Refit; new main battery, reboilered, two funnels replaced single funnel
1885 Training ship
1892 February 13: Reclassified first class cruiser
1906 March 24: Reclassified training ship
1909 October 27: Hulk, *Blokshiv No 1*
1911 April 14: Stricken and broken up

Kniaz Suvorov

Type: Pre-dreadnought
Class: 'Borodino' (1898)
Nomenclature: Prince Aleksandr Vasilievich Suvorov (1730-1800), field marshal

History:
1901 September 8: Laid down by Baltic
1902 September 25: Launched
1904 August 27: Completed
1904 October 15: Sailed for Far East, 2nd Pacific Squadron. Flagship of Vice-Adm Rozhdestvensky
1905 May 27: Damaged by gunfire and sunk by torpedoes at Battle of Tsushima (830 dead)

Koldun

Type: Monitor
Class: 'Uragan' (1862)
Nomenclature: Sorcerer

History:
1863 Built by Cockerill
1863 November 9: Laid down at St Petersburg for reassembly
1864 May 8: Launched
1865 Completed
1900 August 5: Stricken

Kreiser, see *Petr Veliki*

Nomenclature: Cruiser

Kreml

Type: Broadside Ship
Class: 'Kreml' (1864)
Nomenclature: Kremlin

History:
1863 September 20: Laid down by Poletika
1865 August 14: Launched
1866 Completed
1869 August 3: Sank the wooden frigate *Oleg* in collision off Hogland Island (16 dead)
1905 October 12: Stricken
1906 Broken up

Kronshtadt

Type: Battlecruiser
Class: 'Kronshtadt' (1938)
Nomenclature: Naval base in the Baltic near Leningrad

History:
1939 July 15: Laid down by Marti
1940 Late: Construction suspended
1948-49 Hull broken up on slip

Latnik

Type: Monitor
Class: 'Uragan' (1862)
Nomenclature: Cuirassier

History:
1863 June 17: Laid down by Carr & McPherson
1864 March 22: Launched
1865 July 21: Completed
1900 August 5: Stricken

Lava

Type: Monitor
Class: 'Uragan' (1862)
Nomenclature: Avalanche

History:
1863 June 27: Laid down by Poletika
1864 June 8: Launched
1865 Completed
1911 April 14: Hulk, renamed *Blokshiv No 1*
1941 Still in existence

Marat, see ***Petropavlovsk***

Nomenclature: Jean Paul Marat (1743-1793), a leader of the French Revolution

Mikhail Frunze, see ***Poltava***

Nomenclature: Mikhail Vasilievich Frunze (1885-1925), Soviet army commander

Minin

Type: Armoured Cruiser
Class: 'Minin' (1864)
Nomenclature: Kuzma Minin (c1570-1616), leader with Pozharski against Polish invaders

History:
1866 November 24: Laid down by Baltic as turret ship
1869 November 3: Launched
1870 October: Construction suspended and redesigned as barbette ship
1878 Completed at Kronstadt
1878-81 Mediterranean and Far East
1883-85 Far East
1886-87 Reconstructed; two funnels replaced single lowering funnel, rig reduced, reboilered
1890 November 7: Damaged in hurricane off French coast
1891 Gunnery training ship
1901 Refit, rearmed
1909 Converted to minelayer
1909 October 25: Renamed ***Ladoga***
1915 August 15: Sunk by mine off Oero Island in Baltic

Minsk

Type: Aircraft Carrier
Class: 'Kiev' (1968)
Nomenclature: Capital city of White Russia

History:
1972 December: Laid down at Nikolaiev South
1975 August: Launched
1978 February: Completed
1979 Pacific Fleet

Moskva

Type: Battlecruiser
Class: 'Stalingrad' (1947)
Nomenclature: Capital city of the Soviet Union

History:
1950 Laid down by Baltic Yard
1954 Broken up on stocks

Navarin

Type: Barbette Ship
Class: 'Navarin' (1886)
Nomenclature: Navarino, Allied naval victory over Turkey, 27 October 1827

History:
1887 May 19: Laid down by Franco Russian
1891 October 20: Launched
1895 Completed
1895 Mediterranean
—— Baltic Fleet
1904 October 14: Sailed for Far East, 2nd Pacific Squadron
1905 May 27: Damaged by gunfire at Tsushima, torpedoed by torpedo boats, capsized and sank (619 dead)

Navarin

Type: Battlecruiser
Class: 'Borodino' (1912)

History:
1914 January 1: Laid down by Baltic
1916 November 22: Launched
1917 Early: Construction suspended
1923 Broken up at Hamburg

Novgorod

Type: Circular Turret Ship
Class: 'Novgorod' (1871)
Nomenclature: One of the oldest cities in Russia, on Lake Ilmen

History:
1871 December 29: Laid down at St Petersburg
1873 June 2: Launched
1874 Completed at Nikolaiev, having been disassembled and rebuilt
1874 Black Sea Fleet
1903 July 17: Stricken; storeship
1911 Broken up

Novorossisk

Type: Battleship
Class: 'Novorossisk' (1948)
Nomenclature: City on the Black Sea

History:
1910 June 24: Laid down by Ansaldo as Italian ***Giulio Cesare***
1911 October 15: Launched
1914 May 14: Completed
1949 February 3: Transferred from Italy under peace treaty, renamed ***Novorossisk***
1949 Black Sea Fleet
1955 November 4: Blew up and sank in Sevastopol harbour

Novorossisk

Type: Aircraft Carrier
Class: 'Kiev' (1968)

History:
1975 September: Laid down at Nikolaiev South
1978 December: Launched
1983 Completed

Nye Tron Menya

Type: Broadside Ship
Class: 'Pervenietz' (1861)
Nomenclature: Touch-me-not

History:
1863 November 19: Laid down at Mitchell
1864 June 11: Launched
1865 Completed
1897 Reboilered
1905 October 12: Stricken and broken up

Oktyabrskaya Revolutsia, see *Gangut*

Nomenclature: October Revolution

Orel

Type: Pre-dreadnought
Class: 'Borodino' (1898)
Nomenclature: Eagle, first large ship of Peter the Great's navy

History:
1900 June 11: Laid down by Galernii
1902 July 19: Launched
1904 September: Completed
1904 September 30: Went aground off Kronstadt
1904 October 15: Sailed for Far East, 2nd Pacific Squadron
1905 May 27: Severely damaged by gunfire at Battle of Tsushima, surrendered the following day. Taken into service by Japan, renamed ***Iwami***

Osliabia

Type: Pre-dreadnought
Class: 'Peresviet' (1894)
Nomenclature: A monk, a hero of the battle of Kulikovo, 1380

History:
1895 November 21: Laid down by New Admiralty
1898 November 8: Launched
1901 Completed
1901-04 Mediterranean
1904 October 15: Sailed for Far East, 2nd Pacific Squadron, flagship of Rear-Adm Folkersham
1905 May 27: Hit 15 minutes after start of the Battle of Tsushima, capsized and sank (515 dead)

Pallada

Type: Armoured Cruiser
Class: 'Bayan' (1898)
Nomenclature: Greek myth: Pallas, a name for the goddess Athene

History:
1905 August: Laid down by New Admiralty
1906 November 10: Launched
1911 December: Completed; Baltic Fleet
1914 October 11: Torpedoed and sunk by German submarine *U26* off Hango (594 dead)

Pamiat Azova

Type: Armoured Cruiser
Class: 'Pamiat Azova' (1885)
Nomenclature: Souvenir of the Azov, in honour of the wood line-of-battle ship *Azov,* distinguished at Navarino

History:
1886 July 24: Laid down by Baltic
1888 June 1: Launched
1889 Completed; Baltic Fleet
1890-91 Carried Tsarevitch Nicholas on visit to Far East
1891-92 Far East
1893-94 Mediterranean
1893 September: In collision with armoured cruiser *Admiral Nakhimov* at Cadiz
1894-99 Far East
1901-2 Refit; rearmed and reboilered
1906 July 19: Crew mutinied
1907 Training ship
1909 February 25: Renamed ***Dvina,*** minelaying training ship
1917 April 13: Renamed ***Pamiat Azova***
1917 Red Fleet
1919 August 18: Torpedoed and sunk by British torpedo boats at Kronstadt
1925 Refloated and broken up

Panteleimon, see *Kniaz Potemkin Tavricheski*

Nomenclature: A saint of the Orthodox Church

Below centre:
Panteleimon* — Pre-dreadnought, at Sevastopol 1918 flying the German naval ensign. The story of its seizure by mutineers in 1905 was told in the film *Battleship Potemkin.

Below left:
***Osliabia* — Battleship of 1898, seen in 1903. Notice high forecastle and casemates on two levels.** *Aldo Fraccaroli*

Below right:
***Peresviet* — Pre-dreadnought, the only battleship built in the US for a foreign power.**

Parizhskaya Kommuna, see ***Sevastopol***

Nomenclature: Paris Commune

Peresviet

Type: Pre-dreadnought
Class: 'Peresviet' (1894)
Nomenclature: A monk, a hero of the battle of Kulikovo, 1380

History:
1895 November 21: Laid down by Baltic
1898 May 19: Launched
1901 July: Completed; Pacific Fleet
1901 November 1: Went aground off Langeland
1904 February 9: Damaged by three hits in action off Port Arthur
1904 August 10: Severely damaged by 19 hits during Battle of the Yellow Sea
1904 September 30: Damaged by shore batteries at Port Arthur, and again on October 10 and 11 and November 24
1904 December 6: Scuttled in Port Arthur harbour
1905 July 3: Refloated by Japanese and taken into service, renamed ***Sagami***
1916 March: Returned to Russia, renamed ***Peresviet***
1916 May 23: Went aground off Vladivostok
1916 July: Refloated and repaired
1917 January 4: Sunk by two mines off Port Said (167 dead)

Perun

Type: Monitor
Class: 'Uragan' (1862)
Nomenclature: Thunderbolt

History:
1863 June 27: Laid down by Poletika
1864 June 30: Launched
1865 Completed
1900 August 5: Stricken

Pervenietz

Type: Broadside Ship
Class: 'Pervenietz' (1861)
Nomenclature: First Born

History:
1862 Laid down by Thames
1863 May 6: Launched
1863 August 3: Arrived at Kronstadt
1864 Completed
1905 October 12: Stricken and broken up

Petr Veliki

Type: Turret Ship
Class: 'Petr Veliki' (1869)
Nomenclature: Peter I the Great, Emperor of Russia (1672-1725)

History:
1869 May 29: Laid down at Galernii as ***Kreiser***
1872 June 12: Renamed ***Petr Veliki***
1872 August 27: Launched
1875 Completed; Baltic Fleet
1881 Refit, re-engined
1898 Training Ship
1907 Reconstructed by Franco-Russian, new superstructure and funnels, completely rearmed
1908 Gunnery training ship
1917 February: Renamed ***Barrikada*** (=*Barricade*)
1918 Captured by Bolsheviks at Helsingfors
1920 Hulk, mine depot ship
1959 Broken up at Leningrad

Petropavlovsk

Type: Broadside Ship
Class: 'Petropavlovsk' (1861)
Nomenclature: Town in Siberia where an Anglo-French landing was repulsed in 1854

History:
1861 September 9: Laid down at St Petersburg as unarmoured wood frigate
1861 October 19: Reordered as ironclad
1865 Launched
1867 August 16: Completed
1876 Mediterranean
1892 January 7: Stricken and broken up

Petropavlovsk

Type: Pre-dreadnought
Class: 'Petropavlovsk' (1891)

***Marat* — Battleship, ex-*Petropavlovsk*, May 1937.**
Wright & Logan

History:
1892 March 19: Laid down by Galernii
1894 November 9: Launched
1898 Completed; Pacific Squadron
1904 April 13: Sunk by mine off Port Arthur while leaving harbour to attack Japanese fleet. Among those lost were Vice-Adm Makarov and the painter Vereshchagin (652 dead)

Petropavlovsk

Type: Dreadnought
Class: 'Gangut' (1908)

History:
1909 July 13: Laid down by Baltic
1911 September 9: Launched
1915 November 3: Completed
World War 1: Baltic Fleet
1917 Red Fleet
1919 August 18: Claimed sunk in shallow water by British torpedo boats at Kronstadt, but some sources deny this. Was the only battleship in commission at the end of the Civil War
1921 March 7: Seized by crew and fought batteries at Kronstadt, surrendered 18 March
1921 March 31: Renamed ***Marat***
1926-28 Refit
1928-31 Refit at Baltic, reboilered, fore funnel raised and angled back
1935 July 25: Sank submarine *Tovarisch* in collision during manoeuvres in Gulf of Finland
World War 2: Baltic Fleet
1941 September 23: Severely damaged by bomb at Kronstadt, bow and 'A' turret destroyed and resting on bottom
1943 Renamed ***Petropavlovsk***
1946 Refloated, became artillery training ship ***Volkhov***
1953 Broken up

Pobieda

Type: Pre-dreadnought
Class: 'Peresviet' (1894)
Nomenclature: Victory

History:
1899 February 21: Laid down by Baltic
1900 May 24: Launched
1903 Completed; Pacific Squadron
1904 February 9: Slightly damaged by gunfire in action off Port Arthur
1904 April 13: Damaged by mine off Port Arthur
1904 August 10: Damaged by 11 hits at Battle of the Yellow Sea
1904 October-November: Repeatedly hit by Japanese shore batteries in Port Arthur harbour
1904 December 7: Sunk by siege batteries in Port Arthur harbour
1905 October 17: Refloated by Japanese and taken into service, renamed ***Suwo***

Poltava

Type: Pre-dreadnought
Class: 'Petropavlovsk' (1891)
Nomenclature: Decisive Russian military victory over Sweden, 9 July 1709

History:
1892 February: Laid down at New Admiralty
1894 November 6: Launched
1898 Completed
1900-04 Pacific Fleet
1900 January 16: Went aground near Libau
1904 August 10: Damaged by 14 hits during Battle of Yellow Sea
1904 December 5: Sunk by shore batteries in Port Arthur harbour
1905 July 21: Refloated by Japanese and taken into service renamed ***Tango***
1916 April 6: Returned to Russia at Vladivostok, renamed ***Poltava***
1917 Renamed ***Chesma***; White Sea Squadron
1918 Red Fleet at Murmansk during Allied intervention
1922 Broken up

Poltava

Type: Dreadnought
Class: 'Gangut' (1908)

History:
1909 July 13: Laid down at Admiralty
1911 July 10: Launched
1914 December 17: Completed
World War 1: Baltic Fleet, generally inactive
1917 Red Fleet
1921 Possibly renamed ***Mikhail Frunze***
1922 Severely damaged by fire and went aground in Neva River
1923 Disarmed and hulked
1941 Hulk used as blockship at Kronstadt

Potemkin, see *Kniaz Potemkin Tavricheski*

Pozharski, see *Kniaz Pozharski*

Pyotr Veliki, see *Charodeika*

Respublika, see *Imperator Pavl I*

Nomenclature: Republic

Retvizan

Type: Pre-dreadnought
Class: 'Retvizan' (1897)
Nomenclature: Pathfinder; name commemorates a famous ship of the Russian navy captured from Sweden in 1790

History:
1898 December: Laid down by Cramp
1900 October 23: Launched
1901 December: Commissioned at Kronstadt
1902 Pacific Fleet
1904 February 9: Torpedoed by Japanese torpedo boats at Port Arthur and went aground; refloated 8 March
1904 August 10: Damaged by gunfire at Battle of the Yellow Sea, suffered 18 hits
1904 December 6: Sunk by shore gunfire in Port Arthur harbour
1905 September 22: Refloated by Japanese and taken into service, renamed ***Hizen***

Rossia

Type: Armoured Cruiser
Class: 'Rossia' (1894)
Nomenclature: Russia

History:
1895 May 20: Laid down by Baltic
1896 May 12: Launched
1897 September: Completed; Baltic Fleet
1904 Far East
1904 August 14: Damaged by 22 hits in action with Japanese warships in Battle of the Yellow Sea
1907 Refit, funnels raised, rerigged, reboilered
1922 Broken up at Bremen

Rostislav

Type: Pre-dreadnought
Class: 'Rostislav' (1892)
Nomenclature: A Russian prince of the 12th century

History:
1894 Laid down at Nikolaiev Admy
1896 September 2: Launched
1898 Completed
1898 Black Sea Fleet
1909 January 11: Sank submarine *Kambala* in collision off Sevastopol
World War 1: Black Sea, support of land operations in Armenia
1917 October: Red Fleet
1918 December: Seized by White Army at Sevastopol
1919 April 25: Machinery wrecked by Allied forces
1919 Floating battery in Sea of Azov (White Army)
1920 November 16: Scuttled near Kertch
1922 Hulk broken up

Rurik

Type: Armoured Cruiser
Class: 'Rurik' (1889)
Nomenclature: Semi-legendary founder of Russia, d879

History:
1890 May 31: Laid down by Baltic
1892 November 3: Launched
1895 Completed; Baltic Fleet
1896-97 Far East
1902-04 Far East
1904 Made several sorties against Japanese shipping
1904 August 14: Damaged by gunfire of Japanese warships in Battle of the Yellow Sea and scuttled (192 dead)

Rurik

Type: Armoured Cruiser

Right:
***Rurik* — Armoured cruiser, as completed in 1908.**

Below:
***Rossia* — Armoured cruiser of 1896, as refitted.**

Class: 'Rurik' (1905)

History:
1905 September: Laid down by Vickers
1906 November 17: Launched
1908 September: Completed, Baltic Fleet
World War 1: Baltic Fleet
1915 February 13: Went aground near Faro lighthouse
1916 November 7: Severely damaged by mine off Hogland
1916-17 Refit, repaired and modernised; tripod mast fitted
1918 Red Fleet
1930s Broken up

Rusalka

Type: Monitor
Class: 'Rusalka' (1865)
Nomenclature: A siren or mermaid

History:
1866 Laid down by Mitchell
1867 September 12: Launched
1868 Completed
1869 Hit submerged rock in Gulf of Finland
1893 September 19: Disappeared at sea in Gulf of Finland en route Tallinn-Helsinki (178 dead)

Sevastopol

Type: Broadside Ship
Class: 'Sevastopol' (1862)
Nomenclature: Naval base in the Crimea, scene of a valiant defence during the Crimean War, 1854-55

History:
1862 March 16: Laid down at Kronstadt as unarmoured wood frigate
1862 July 26: Reordered as ironclad
1864 August 12: Launched
1865 July 9: Completed
1886 October 11: Stricken and broken up

Sevastopol

Type: Pre-dreadnought
Class: 'Petropavlovsk' (1891)

History:
1892 March: Laid down by Galernii
1895 June 1: Launched
1899 Completed; Pacific Squadron
1904 March 26: Damaged in collision with battleship *Peresviet* off Port Arthur
1904 June 27: Damaged by mine during action off Port Arthur
1904 August 10: Damaged by 14 hits during Battle of the Yellow Sea
1904 August 23: Again damaged by mine returning to Port Arthur
1904 December 16: Torpedoed in stern at Port Arthur
1905 January 2: Scuttled outside Port Arthur harbour following surrender of the city

Sevastopol

Type: Dreadnought
Class: 'Gangut' (1908)

Above:
***Sevastopol* — Dreadnought of 1911, 'Gangut' class, as completed.**

Above right:
***Slava* — Pre-dreadnought of 'Borodino' class, as modified after completion to reflect lessons of Tsushima, with top hamper reduced.**

History:
1909 July 13: Laid down by Baltic
1911 June 29: Launched
1914 November 17: Completed
World War 1: Baltic Fleet, inactive
1918 January: Red Fleet
1921 March 7: Seized by crew and damaged by batteries at Kronstadt, surrendered 18 March
1921 March 31: Renamed ***Parizhskaya Kommuna***
1926-28 Refit
1929 December: Transferred to Black Sea
1929 December 8: Damaged by heavy weather in Bay of Biscay, repaired at Brest
1930 January: Black Sea Fleet
1936-39 Refit at Sevastopol; reboilered, bulges added, fore funnel raised and angled back
World War 2: Black Sea Fleet, 1941-42 Defence of Sevastopol
1942 September: Damaged by German air attack at Sevastopol, not repaired and idle at Poti after April 1942
1943 Renamed ***Sevastopol***
1946 Repaired
1957 Broken up at Sevastopol

Sevastopol

Type: Battlecruiser
Class: 'Kronshtadt' (1938)

History:
1939 Laid down at Marti North
1940 Autumn: Construction suspended
1941 August: Seized by Germans on stocks when Nikolaiev was captured
1941-42 Hull broken up on stocks

Sinop

Type: Barbette Ship
Class: 'Sinop' (1883)
Nomenclature: Russian victory over the Turks, 30 November 1853

Слава“
Slava

History:
1884 April: Laid down at Ropit; Sevastopol
1887 June: Launched
1890 Completed; Black Sea Fleet
1901 Refit, reboilered
1910 Refit, rearmed
World War 1: 1914-17 Supported land operations in Romania; Guardship at Odessa and Sevastopol
1917 October: Decommissioned at Sevastopol, Red Fleet
1918 December: Seized by White Army
1919 April 25: Machinery wrecked by Allied forces
1922 Broken up

Sisoi Veliki

Type: Turret Ship
Class: 'Sisoi Veliki' (1890)
Nomenclature: St Sisoi the Great, Russian saint

History:
1891 July 25: Laid down by New Admiralty
1894 June 1: Launched
1896 August 18: Completed; Baltic Fleet
1897-98 Mediterranean
1897 March 15: Damaged by explosion in after turret while off Crete (23 dead)
1898-1902 Far East
1904 October 15: Sailed for Far East, 2nd Pacific Squadron
1905 May 27: Damaged by gunfire at Tsushima and by torpedoes the following day; scuttled by crew (50 dead)

Slava

Type: Pre-dreadnought
Class: 'Borodino' (1898)
Nomenclature: Glory

History:
1902 November 1: Laid down by Baltic
1903 August 29: Launched
1905 March: Completed; Baltic Fleet
1906 Refit; military tops removed from masts
1910 July: Engines failed while in Bay of Biscay, towed to Gibraltar. Refitted at La Seyne and reboilered
World War 1: Baltic Fleet actions
1915-16 Supported ground forces near Riga; actions with German battleships
1917 October: Damaged in action with German warships off Riga; trapped in Gulf of Riga
1917 October 17: Scuttled in Moonsund Strait, torpedoed by a Russian destroyer and sank (10 dead)

Smerch

Type: Monitor
Class: 'Smerch' (1862)
Nomenclature: Waterspout

History:
1863 November 19: Laid down by Mitchell
1864 June 23: Launched
1865 Completed; Baltic Fleet
1875 Rearmed
1904 Stricken; hulk, *Blokshiv No 2*
1941 Still in existence

Sovietskaya Bielorossia

Type: Battleship
Class: 'Sovietski Soyuz' (1937)
Nomenclature: Soviet White Russia

History:
1939 November 28: Laid down at Molotovsk
1940 October 19: Construction stopped

Sovietskaya Rossia

Type: Battleship
Class: 'Sovietski Soyuz' (1937)
Nomenclature: Soviet Russia

History:
1940 November 28: Laid down at Molotovsk; original name ***Strana Sovietov***
1940 Construction stopped

Sovietskaya Ukraina

Type: Battleship
Class: 'Sovietski Soyuz' (1937
Nomenclature: Soviet Ukraine

History:
1938 November 28: Laid down by Marti South
1941 August 16: Germans capture Nikolaiev, 75% complete. Was to be launched November 1942 but slip destroyed by Germans to prevent launch
1944-47 Hull broken up on slip

Sovietski Soyuz

Type: Battleship
Class: 'Sovietski Soyuz' (1937)

Nomenclature: Soviet Union

History:
1938 August 28: Laid down by Ordzhonikidze
1941 Summer: Construction halted when ready for launching; armour removed
1948-50 Hull broken up on slip

Stalingrad

Type: Battlecruiser
Class: 'Stalingrad' (1947)
Nomenclature: City on the Volga, scene of heroic defence and Russian victory in 1942

History:
1949 Laid down by Marti South
1953 Launched (about 60% complete)
1954 Hull used for naval weapons tests; grounded off Crimean coast and used as target ship

Strana Sovietov, see *Sovietskaya Rossia*

Nomenclature: Land of the Soviets

Strelets

Type: Monitor
Class: 'Uragan' (1862)
Nomenclature: A soldier of the medieval Russian army

History:
1863 June 13: Laid down by Galernii
1864 June 2: Launched
1865 July 15: Completed
1900 August 5: Stricken

Sviatoi Evstafi

Type: Pre-dreadnought
Class: 'Evstafi' (1903)
Nomenclature: Saint Eustace, Roman martyr of the 2nd century; patron of the chase

History:
1903 November 11: Laid down at Nikolaiev Admy
1906 November 3: Launched
1910 August 5: Completed; Black Sea Fleet
World War 1: Black Sea Fleet actions
1914 November 18: Sustained damage in action with German battlecruiser *Goeben* which was damaged
1917 Red Fleet
1918 April: Captured by Germans at Sevastopol
1918 December: Seized by White Army at Sevastopol
1919 April 25: Machinery wrecked by Allied forces
1920 November: Seized by Red Army
1922 Broken up

Svobodnaya Rossiya, see *Imperatritsa Ekaterina Velikaya*

Nomenclature: Free Russia

Tifon

Type: Monitor
Class: 'Uragan' (1862)
Nomenclature: Typhoon

History:
1863 July 8: Laid down by New Admiralty
1864 June 16: Launched
1865 Completed
1900 August 5: Stricken
1909 Hulk, *Blokshiv No 3*

Tri Sviatitelia

Type: Pre-dreadnought
Class: 'Tri Sviatitelia' (1890)
Nomenclature: Three Saints, ie of the Orthodox church; St Basil, St Gregory and St John Chrystostom

History:
1891 August 14: Laid down at Nikolaiev Admiralty
1893 November 12: Launched
1897 Completed; Black Sea Fleet

***Vice Admiral Popov* — Circular turret ship (*Popoffka*), in drydock, 1875. The ship's six propellers appear prominently in this view.** *P. A. Vicary*

1912 Refit; reboilered, military masts replaced by pole masts
World War 1: Black Sea Fleet actions
1918 April: Captured by Germans at Sevastopol
1918 December: Seized by White Army at Sevastopol
1919 April 25: Machinery wrecked by Allied forces
1920 November: Seized by Red Army
1922 Broken up

Tsesarevich

Type: Pre-dreadnought
Class: 'Tsesarevich' (1898)
Nomenclature: Title of the Czar's son, named for Grand Duke George Aleksandrovich (1871-1899)

History:
1899 May 18: Laid down by La Seyne
1901 February 23: Launched
1903 August: Completed
1903 Pacific Fleet
1904 February 9: Damaged by surprise Japanese torpedo attack at Port Arthur
1904 August 7: Hit by siege batteries at Port Arthur
1904 August 10: Damaged by 15 hits at Battle of the Yellow Sea; Flag of Rear-Adm Vitgeft who was killed. Interned at Kiauchau
1905 Baltic Fleet
1906 Refit, pole masts replaced military masts
World War 1
1917 April 13: Renamed ***Grazhdanin***
1917 October 5: Damaged by gunfire of German warships in Gulf of Riga
1918 Red Fleet
1923 Broken up

Uragan

Type: Monitor
Class: 'Uragan' (1862)
Nomenclature: Hurricane

History:
1863 July 2: Laid down by New Admiralty
1864 May 27: Launched
1865 Completed
1900 August 5: Stricken

Vice Admiral Popov

Type: Circular Turret Ship
Class: 'Vice Admiral Popov' (1871)
Nomenclature: Andrei Aleksandrovich Popov (1821-1898), admiral and designer of naval vessels

History:
1871 December 29: Laid down at Nikolaiev Admiralty as ***Kiev***
1873 October 21: Renamed ***Vice Admiral Popov***
1875 October 7: Launched
1876 Completed; Black Sea Fleet
1903 July 4: Stricken and broken up

Vieshchun

Type: Monitor
Class: 'Uragan' (1862)
Nomenclature: Prophet

***Vladimir Monomakh* — Armoured cruiser, as reconstructed, 1902. *Dmitri Donskoi* is behind.**
Aldo Fraccaroli

History:
1863 Built by Cockerill
1863 November 9: Laid down at St Petersburg for reassembly
1864 May 8: Launched
1865 Completed
1900 August 5: Stricken

Vladimir Monomakh

Type: Armoured Cruiser
Class: 'Vladimir Monomakh' (1880)
Nomenclature: Vladimir II, Prince of Kiev (1053-1125)

History:
1881 May 21: Laid down by Baltic
1882 October 22: Launched
1883 July 13: Completed; Baltic Fleet
1892 Refit
1896 Refit; re-engined, reboilered, rearmed
1900 Boxer Rebellion
1900 September: Sank merchant ship *Crown of Aragon* in Port Arthur harbour
1903-04 Refit
1905 February 16: Sailed for Far East, 3rd Pacific Squadron
1905 May 28: Torpedoed and sunk following Battle of Tsushima

Volya, see *Imperator Aleksandr III*

Nomenclature: Liberty

Yedinorog

Type: Monitor
Class: 'Uragan' (1862)
Nomenclature: Unicorn

History:
1863 June 13: Laid down by Galernii
1864 June 2: Launched
1865 July 15: Completed
1900 August 5: Stricken
1912 June 27: Stricken, renamed *Blockshiv No 4*
—— Renamed *Blokshiv No 2*
1941 Still in existence

Zarya Svoboda, see *Imperator Aleksandr II*

Nomenclature: Dawn of Freedom

Spain

As part of a programme to give Spain an advantage over the United States, six ironclad frigates were built or converted in the early 1860s. Two of these were completed in time to participate in Spanish fleet operations against Chile and Peru in 1865-66. During the 1873 Civil War the *Tetuán* was destroyed. No further capital ships were built until the *Pelayo* was laid down in 1885. A number of armoured cruisers was built in later years but the Spanish fleet was outclassed when war began with the United States in 1898.

The Pacific Squadron of old protected cruisers and gunboats was destroyed at the Battle of Manila Bay. A squadron of new armoured cruisers, including the *Cristóbal Colón* (sent without its main armament), was dispatched to the Caribbean. The ships remained blockaded in Santiago harbour until they emerged on 3 July 1898 to be sunk by the waiting American warships. A second Spanish squadron led by the *Pelayo* was halted en route to the Far East when the war ended. The loss of the war, its fleet and its colonies ended Spanish interest in naval construction for several years.

Three small dreadnoughts were started in 1909 although World War 1 delayed construction of the vessel. The *España* was wrecked off Morocco in 1923. The two remaining vessels were on opposite sides during the Civil War in 1937 and both were lost. Studies were made in 1913 for further battleships of 21,000tons, the 'Reina Victoria Eugenia' class, but the project was abandoned.

Class Details

'Numancia' (1861)

Broadside Ship: *Numancia*
Displacement: 7,305tons
Dimensions: 333(oa) 313'7(pp)×55'9×26'8 [101.5(oa) 95.6(pp)×17×8.1]
Machinery: 1 screw, compound return connecting-rod engines (F C Med) 8 boilers
IHP 3,700 = 12.9knots
Endurance: 3,000/10
Armament: 34×152mm 68pdr SB
1880: 6×239mm, 3×200mm, 8×164mm MLR
1890: 8×254mm, 7×203mm BLR
1898: 4×203mm/35, 3×164mm/35, 10×140mm, 12×47mm, 2 TT
Armour: Belt 100-130mm, battery 120mm
Complement: 600
Class notes: Iron hull armoured frigate built in France. Full ship rig and single funnel. Rearmed after completion. Reconstructed 1898, reboilered and rearmed, sail rig replaced by two military masts

'Zaragoza' (1861)

Broadside Ship: *Zaragoza*
Displacement: 5,600tons
Dimensions: 280(wl) 270'8(pp)×54'6×26'6 [85.3(wl) 82.5(pp)×16.6×8.1]
Machinery: 1 screw, compound trunk engines (Penn), 6 boilers
IHP 3,000 = 8knots
Armament: 21×152mm 68pdr SB
Later: 4×229mm MLR, 3×180mm, 8×164mm, 1×120mm, 6×12pdr
Armour: Belt 102-127mm, battery 102-127mm
Complement: 500
Class notes: Wood hull screw frigate converted to ironclad while under construction. Full ship rig and single funnel

'Tetuán' (1861)

Broadside Ship: *Tetuán*
Displacement: 6,200tons
Dimensions: 285'4 (oa) 279'1(wl)×55'9×21'8 [87(oa) 85(wl)×17×6.6]
Machinery: 1 screw, horizontal trunk engines (Penn), 8 boilers
IHP 4,520 = 10.25knots
Armament: 30×152mm 68pdr SB
1867: 2×120mm SB added
Armour: Belt and battery 130mm
Complement: 500
Class notes: Wood hull armoured frigate with full ship rig

'Arapiles' (1862)

Broadside Ship: *Arapiles*
Displacement: 3,441tons
Dimensions: 280(wl)×52'2×17 [85.3(wl)×15.9×5.2]
Machinery: 1 screw, compound trunk engines (Maudslay), 6 boilers
IHP 2,400 = 8knots
Armament: 2×254mm MLR, 5×203mm, 10×201mm BL
1878: 203mm and 201mm replaced by 12×160mm BL
Armour: Belt 114mm
Class notes: Wood hull screw frigate reordered as an ironclad while under construction in Britain. Full ship rig with single funnel. Reconstruction in 1882 halted because of poor condition of hull

'Vitoria' (1862)

Broadside Ship: *Vitoria*
Displacement: 7,250tons
Dimensions: 318'3(oa) 295(pp)×55'10×27'2 [97(oa) 89.9(pp)×17×8.3]
Machinery: 1 screw, compound engines (Penn)
IHP 2,500 = 11knots
Endurance: 2,400/10
Armament: 30×152mm 68pdr SB
c1875: 4×229mm, 3×203mm, 14×164mm
1898: 4×203mm/35, 4×164mm/35, 10×140mm
Armour: Belt 140mm, battery 120mm
Complement: 561
Class notes: Built in Britain to same specifications as *Numancia* with similar iron hull and rig but having two funnels. Reconstructed 1898, sail rig replaced by two auxiliary masts and rearmed

'Sagunto' (1862)

Broadside Ship: *Sagunto*

Displacement: 7,352tons
Dimensions: 294(oa) 279'3(pp)×55'10×31 [89.6(oa) 85.1(pp)×17×9.4]
Machinery: 1 screw, compound engines (F C Med), 8 boilers
IHP 3,700 = 8knots
Armament: 10×229mm BLR, 3×180mm BLR
Armour: Belt 152mm, battery 140mm, bulkheads 102mm, barbettes 127mm
Class notes: Laid down as wood screw ship-of-the-line and converted to ironclad prior to launching. Guns placed in armoured redoubt. Single funnel and full ship rig

'Mendez Nuñez' (1870)

Central Battery Ship: *Mendez Nuñez*
Displacement: 3,382tons
Dimensions: 236'2(wl)×49'3×21'11 [72(wl)×15×6.7]
Machinery: 1 screw, compound engines (Penn or Ferrol), 4 boilers
IHP 2,250 = 8knots
Armament: 4×230mm (250pdr) MLR, 2×203mm (180pdr) MLR
Armour: Belt and battery 127mm
Class notes: Completed as wood screw frigate *Resolucion* and converted 1867-70 to ironclad

'Pelayo' (1884)

Barbette Ship: *Pelayo*
Displacement: 9,900tons
Dimensions: 344'6(oa) 330(wl)×66'3×28'6 [105(oa) 100,5(wl)×20.2×8.7]
Machinery: 2 screw, vertical compound engines (F C Med), 12 cylindrical boilers; *1898:* 16 Niclausse boilers
IHP 9,000 = 15knots
Endurance: 5,000/12
Armament: 2×320mm/35, 2×280mm/35, 1×160mm, 12×120mm, 1×89mm
1898: 160mm and 120mm removed, 9×140/35, 12×57mm and 7 TT added
1914: 7 TT removed
Armour: Belt 300-450mm, barbettes 300-400mm, c/t 155mm, deck 63mm
Complement: 630
Class notes: Designed by Lagane and similar to French *Marceau* with pronounced tumblehome sides; 320mm main guns in single barbettes fore and aft and one 280mm on each beam. Two funnels and two masts. Reconstructed 1898 with rigging replaced by two military masts, reboilered

'Maria Teresa' Class (1888)

Armoured Cruisers: *Almirante Oquendo, Infanta Maria Teresa, Vizcaya* (see later photo)
Displacement: 6,890tons
Dimensions: 364(oa) 340(pp)×65'2×21'6 [110.9(oa) 103.6(pp)×19.9×6.6]
Machinery: 2 screws, VTE engines (Nervion), 6 cylindrical boilers
IHP 13,700 = 20.2knots
Endurance: 9,700/10
Armament: 2×280mm, 10×140mm, 8×57mm, 8 TT
Armour: Belt 255-305mm, barbettes 230mm, c/t 305mm, deck 50-75mm
Complement: 484
Class notes: Similar in design to British 'Orlando' class with heavy guns but narrow armour belt

'Emperador Carlos V' (1888)

Armoured Cruiser: *Emperador Carlos V*
Displacement: 9,090tons
Dimensions: 404'9(oa) 380'7(pp)×67×28'9 [123.4(oa) 116(pp)×20.4×8.7]
Machinery: 2 screws, VTE engines (Terrestre), 12 cylindrical boilers; *1925:* 8 Yarrow boilers
IHP 15,000 = 20knots
Endurance: 13,000/10
Armament: 2×280mm/35, 8×140mm/35, 4×100mm/35, 2×70mm, 4×57mm, 6×355mm TT
1912: 6×57mm added, 4 TT removed
Armour: Barbettes 250mm, belt 50mm, deck 165mm, c/t 308mm
Complement: 590
Class notes: Actually a large protected cruiser as there was no waterline belt. Three tall funnels and two military masts, two single turrets fore and aft

'Asturias' Class (1889)

Armoured Cruisers: *Cardenal Cisneros, Cataluña, Princesa de Asturias*
Displacement: 7,500tons
Dimensions: 363'10(oa) 347'10(pp)×60'8×22 [110.9(oa) 106(pp)×18.5×6.7]
Machinery: 2 screws, HTE engines (Terrestre), 6 cylindrical boilers
IHP 15,000 = 20knots
Endurance: 9,700/10
Armament: 2×240mm/40, 10×140mm/40, 8×57mm, 8×355mm TT
1910: 2 TT removed; all removed by 1925
Armour: Belt 150-305mm, barbettes 203mm, turrets 70mm, bulkheads 330mm, c/t 203mm
Complement: 497
Class notes: Improved 'Maria Teresa' class with better armament. Took over 12 years to complete

'Cristóbal Colón' (1896)

Armoured Cruiser: *Cristóbal Colón, [Pedro de Aragon]*

***Numancia* — Armoured frigate of 1863, after 1898 reconstruction, with military masts.** *Marius Bar*

Top left:

***Zaragoza* — Armoured frigate of 1867, shown c1885 in the Suez Canal.** *US Naval Historical Centre*

Top centre:

***Tetuan* — Broadside ship of 1863, sunk by insurgents in 1873.** *US Naval Historical Centre*

Top right:

***Vitoria* — Armoured frigate of 1865, after 1898 reconstruction, with military masts.** *Marius Bar*

Right:

***Pelayo* — Barbette ship, in the 1890s after completion.** *US Naval Historical Centre*

Far right:

***Infanta Maria Teresa* — Armoured cruiser of 1890, sunk at Santiago.** *IWM*

Bottom left:

***Emperador Carlos V* — Armoured or 'belted' cruiser, 1902.** *IWM*

Bottom centre:

***Cardenal Cisneros* — Armoured cruiser of 1897, wrecked in 1905 two years after completion.** *IWM*

Bottom right:

***Cristobal Colon* — Armoured cruiser, 1898, sunk at Santiago.** *Marius Bar*

Displacement: 6,840tons
Dimensions: 328(oa)×59′8×25′8 [100(oa)×18.2×7.8]
Machinery: 2 screws, VTE engines (Ansaldo), 24 Niclausse boilers
IHP 15,000 = 20knots
Endurance: 8,300/10
Armament: 2×254mm (not mounted), 10×152mm, 6×120mm, 18×57mm, 4×457mm TT
Armour: Belt 75-150mm, barbettes 150mm, c/t 152mm, deck 25-50mm
Complement: 500
Class notes: Purchased while under construction for Italian navy. *Colon* had main guns removed after completion to be replaced by Spanish guns but sailed for Caribbean in 1898 before the new guns were mounted. *Pedro de Aragon* never purchased

'España' Class (1908)

Dreadnoughts: *Alfonso XIII, España, Jaime I*
Displacement: 15,700tons
Dimensions: 459′6(oa) 438(wl)×78.9×26 [139.9(oa) 133.5(wl)×24×7.9]
Machinery: 4 screws, Parsons turbines (Vickers), 12 Yarrow boilers
IHP 15,500 = 19.5knots
Endurance: 6,000/10
Armament: 8×305mm/50, 20×102mm/50, 2×47mm, 3×457mm TT (not installed)
Armour: Belt 75-230mm, turrets 203-254mm, deck 38mm, c/t 254mm
Complement: 850
Class notes: Small battleships built in Spain with British technical assistance. Four twin turrets, single funnel and two tripod masts. Completion of *Jaime I* delayed when delivery of materiel from Britain held up by the war. Projected modernisation of 1932 never carried out

Individual Ships

Alfonso XIII

Type: Dreadnought
Class: 'España' (1908)
Nomenclature: Alfonso XIII (1886-1941), King of Spain 1886-1931

History:
1910 February 23: Laid down at Ferrol
1913 May 7: Launched
1915 August 16: Completed
1921 Operations off Morocco, Riff rebellion
1931 Planned refit cancelled, laid up
1931 April: Renamed ***España***
1936 July 20: Seized by crew when out of service at Ferrol. Bombarded Nationalists then surrendered when Ferrol was captured
1936 August-September and 1937 March-April: Blockade of Basque coast
1937 April 30: Sunk by mine off Bilbao (5 dead)

Almirante Oquendo

Type: Armoured Cruiser
Class: 'Maria Teresa' (1888)
Nomenclature: Antonio de Oquendo (1577-1639), admiral, defeated the Dutch off Pernambuco but killed in action with Tromp

History:
1889 Laid down at Bilbao
1891 August 3: Launched
1895 August 26: Completed
1898 July 3: Severely damaged by gunfire and beached during Battle of Santiago

Arapiles

Type: Broadside Ship
Class: 'Arapiles' (1862)
Nomenclature: Site of the Battle of Salamanca (1812) in which Wellington defeated the French

History:
1861 June: Laid down at Blackwall as unarmoured frigate
1862 August: Conversion to ironclad commenced
1864 October 17: Launched
1865 Completed as armoured broadside ship
1873 Went aground off Venezuela, repaired at Brooklyn, where it remained May 1873-January 1874. A lighter sank blocking drydock gates during US-Spanish crisis over the *Virginius* affair
1879 Hulked
1882 Reconstruction cancelled because of poor condition of wood hull. Broken up

Cardenal Cisneros

Type: Armoured Cruiser
Class: 'Asturias' (1889)
Nomenclature: Francisco Jimenez de Cisneros (1436-1517), prelate and statesman

History:
1890 September 1: Laid down at Ferrol
1897 March 19: Launched
1903 March 30: Completed
1905 October 28: Wrecked off coast of Galicia (none lost)

Cataluña

Type: Armoured Cruiser
Class: 'Asturias' (1889)
Nomenclature: Catalonia, a province of northeast Spain

History:
1890 January 23: Laid down at Cartagena
1900 September 24: Launched
1908 April 7: Completed
1911 Occupation of Larache, Morocco
1921-24 Operations off Morocco, Riff rebellion
1925 Cadet training ship
1929 Stricken and broken up

Cristóbal Colón

Type: Armoured Cruiser
Class: 'Cristobal Colon' (1896)
Nomenclature: Christopher Columbus (1451-1506)

History:
1895 Laid down by Ansaldo as Italian ***Giuseppe Garibaldi***
1896 August 14: Purchased by Spain and renamed ***Cristobal Colon***
1896 September 16: Launched
1897 May 16: Completed
1897 Main armament removed for replacement with Spanish guns

***España* — Dreadnought of 1912, wrecked off Morocco 1923.** *IWM*

1898 July 3: Damaged by gunfire of US warships at Battle of Santiago and capsized at Rio Tarquino

Emperador Carlos V

Type: Armoured Cruiser
Class: 'Emperador Carlos V' (1888)
Nomenclature: Charles V (1500-1558), King of Spain and Holy Roman Emperor

History:
1892 March 4: Laid down at Cadiz
1895 March 12: Launched
1900 March 13: Completed
1902-06 Operations in Morocco
1924 Decommissioned
1931 December: Stricken
1933 Broken up

España

Type: Dreadnought
Class: 'Espana' (1908)
Nomenclature: Spain

History:
1909 February 5: Laid down at Ferrol
1912 February 5: Launched
1913 October 23: Completed
1921 Operations off Morocco, Riff rebellion
1923 August 23: Wrecked in fog off Cape Tres Forces near Melilla, Morocco

España, see *Alfonso XIII*

Infanta Maria Teresa

Type: Armoured Cruiser
Class: 'Maria Teresa' (1888)
Nomenclature: Infanta Maria Teresa (1882-1912), second daughter of King Alfonso XII

History:
1889 July 24: Laid down at Bilbao
1890 August 30: Launched
1893 August: Completed
1898 July 3: Damaged by US warships at Battle of Santiago and beached
1898 September 24: Refloated and towed to Guantanamo
1899 Went aground in storm near Nassau, Bahamas while under tow to Norfolk. Broken up in place

Jaime I

Type: Dreadnought
Class: 'España' (1908)
Nomenclature: James I the Conqueror, King of Aragon (1208-1276)

History:
1912 February 5: Laid down at Ferrol
1914 September 21: Launched
1921 December 21: Completed
1922 At Constantinople to protect Spanish citizens
1922 December 15: Rammed by freighter *Grass* in collision at Constantinople
1923-25 Operations off Morocco during Riff rebellion
1936 July 20: Seized by crew at sea for Republican side at outset of Civil War
1936 August 9: Expeditionary force to Balearic Islands
1936 August 11: Bombarded Algeciras
1936 August 13: Damaged by aircraft bomb off Malaga
1936 September: Bombarded Ferrol
1937 May 22: Damaged by aircraft bombs at Almeria
1937 June 17: Sunk by an explosion at Cartagena (300+ dead)
1939 Refloated and broken up

Mendez Nuñez

Type: Central Battery Ship
Class: 'Mendez Nuñez' (1870)
Nomenclature: Don Casto Mendez Nuñez (1824-1869), commander of the Spanish fleet engaged with Chile and Peru, 1866

History:
1859 September 22: Laid down at Ferrol as frigate ***Resolución***

1861 September 19: Launched
1862 April 28: Completed
1866 Damaged during operations off Pacific coast
1867-70 Converted to armoured corvette at Cartagena
1870 August 21: Renamed ***Mendez Nuñez*** following conversion
1873 July: Seized by insurgents at Cartagena and placed in service
1873 October 11: Damaged in action with government vessels off Cartagena
1874 January 12: Sailed to Algeria with *Numancia* following fall of Cartagena
1886 Stricken
1896 Broken up

Numancia

Type: Broadside Ship
Class: 'Numancia' (1861)
Nomenclature: Ancient town near Soria which resisted repeated attempts to take it by the Romans, 143-133BC

History:
1862 April 22: Laid down at La Seyne
1863 November 19: Launched
1864 December 17: Completed
1865 Operations off Peru (flagship)
1866 March 27: Bombardment of Valparaiso
1866 April 30: Bombardment of Callao; sustained 51 hits from shore batteries but not damaged
1867-68 First armoured vessel to circumnavigate the world
1873 July: Seized by insurgents at Cartagena during Civil War
1873 October 11: Rammed and sank corvette *Fernando el Católico* in collision during naval engagement off Cartagena with government forces; damaged by gunfire
1874 January 13: Fled to Mers-el-Kebir following surrender of Cartagena; returned to Spanish government by French, 19 January
1897-98 Reconstructed at La Seyne, rearmed
1909-10 Operations in Morocco against the Riffs
1913 Boys' training ship
1916 December 17: Went aground off coast of Portugal while in tow

Pedro de Aragon

Type: Armoured Cruiser

Above:
***Jaime I* — Dreadnought as it appeared at the start of the Spanish Civil War, 1936.**

Above right:
***Vizcaya* — Armoured cruiser, sunk at Santiago.**
Marius Bar

Class: 'Cristobal Colon' (1896)
Nomenclature: Pedro III, King of Aragon and Valencia (1236-1285), founder of the powerful Aragonian navy

History:
1897 Ordered in Italy
1902 Cancelled

Pelayo

Type: Barbette Ship
Class: 'Pelayo' (1884)
Nomenclature: Pelayo (d737), first King of the Asturias

History:
1885 Laid down at La Seyne
1887 February 5: Launched
1888 September 9: Completed
1896-98 Refit at La Seyne, rearmed and reboilered
1898 Sailed for Philippines but recalled when held up at Port Said
1909 Operations in Morocco against Riffs
1910 Refit, TT removed, gunnery training ship
1922 October: Stricken
1925 Broken up

Princesa de Asturias

Type: Armoured Cruiser
Class: 'Asturias' (1889)
Nomenclature: Infanta Maria de las Mercedes, Princess of the Asturias (1880-1904), oldest daughter of King Alfonso XII

History:
1890 Laid down at Carraca
1896 October 17: Launched
1904 October: Completed
1929 Stricken
1932 Broken up

Sagunto

Type: Broadside Ship
Class: 'Sagunto' (1862)
Nomenclature: Town near Valencia besieged by Hannibal, 218BC

History:
1863 March 21: Laid down at Ferrol as ship of the line ***Principe Alfonso***
1868 Renamed ***Sagunto***
1869 April 26: Launched
1877 February 1: Completed as central battery ship
1885 Stricken

Tetuán

Type: Broadside Ship
Class: 'Tetuan' (1861)
Nomenclature: Town in Spanish Morocco

History:
1861 May: Laid down at Ferrol
1863 March: Launched
1866 January: Completed
1873 July: Seized by insurgents at Cartagena
1873 October 11: Damaged in action with government ironclad *Vitoria*
1873 December 30: Burned and blown up by insurgents to prevent capture (or by accident) at Cartagena
1874 Broken up

Vitoria

Type: Broadside Ship
Class: 'Vitoria' (1862)
Nomenclature: Town near Pamplona where Wellington defeated the French, 21 June 1813

History:
1863 Laid down by Thames
1865 November 4: Launched
1867 May: Completed
—— Refit, rearmed
1873 July: Seized by insurgents at Cartagena
1873 August 2: Surrendered to British battleship *Swiftsure* and German *Friedrich Carl* after crew went ashore at Escombera; returned to Spanish government 26 September
1873 October 11: Engaged insurgent warships off Cartagena during Civil War
1874 January 7: Sank British steamer *Ellen Constant* in collision off Cartagena
1897-98 Reconstructed at La Seyne, training ship
1912 Broken up

Vizcaya

Type: Armoured Cruiser
Class: 'Maria Teresa' (1888)
Nomenclature: One of the Basque provinces of Spain

History:
1889 October 7: Laid down at Bilbao
1891 July 8: Launched
1894 August: Completed
1898 July 3: Sunk in shallow water at Aseviados after being damaged by gunfire at Battle of Santiago

Zaragoza

Type: Broadside Ship
Class: 'Zaragoza' (1861)
Nomenclature: Capital of Aragon, site of heroic defence against siege by the French, 1808

History:
1861 October 4: Laid down at Cartagena as screw frigate; converted to armoured frigate
1867 February 6: Launched
1868 Completed
1873 July: Recalled from Cuban waters but arrived too late for action off Cartagena
1892 Torpedo school ship
c1903 Discarded

Sweden

Sweden had long been a power in European history but by the 1860s such matters were put aside and Sweden has maintained a neutral posture ever since. It has always had a strong defensive navy, which included monitors and small battleships as the mainstay of the fleet until after World War 2. Although united with Norway under the Swedish King until 1905, the Swedish and Norwegian navies were separate entities. Sweden's naval ships have always been Swedish-built, unique among smaller navies.

Class Details

'John Ericsson' Class (1863)

Monitors: *John Ericsson, Thordon, Tirfing*
Displacement: 1,500tons
Dimensions: 199'8(wl)×45'4×11'9 [60.9(wl)×13.8×3.6]
Machinery: 1 screw
IHP 380 = 6.5knots
Armament: *John Ericsson:* 2×381mm SB ML
John Ericsson, 1881: 2×240mm BLR
John Ericsson, 1895: 2×152mm, 2×57mm
Others: 2×240mm BLR
Others, 1903: 2×152mm, 8×57mm
Armour: Hull 118mm, turret 261mm, deck 25mm, c/t 237mm
John Ericsson: Hull 125mm, turret 270mm, deck 43mm, c/t 250mm
Complement: 80
Class notes: Designed by Ericsson similar to US monitors with one twin turret on hull with low freeboard. *John Ericsson* rearmed as others 1881 and reconstructed 1892-95 with new superstructure and new turret. Others reconstructed 1902-05 with new guns in original turrets

'Loke' (1866)

Monitor: *Loke*
Displacement: 1,600tons
Dimensions: 204'9(wl)×45'4×11'9 [62.4(wl)×13.8×3.6]
Machinery: 1 screw
IHP 430 = 7.8knots
Armament: 2×240mm BLR
Armour: Belt 125mm, deck 25mm, turret 370-450mm, c/t 240mm
Complement: 80
Class notes: Similar to 'John Ericsson' class but never reconstructed

'Svea' (1883)

Coast Defence Ship: *Svea*
Displacement: 2,900tons; *1904:* 3,100tons
Dimensions: 249'4(pp)×48'7×17 [75.7(pp)×14.8×5.2]
Machinery: 2 screws, horizontal compound engines, 6 cylindrical boilers
IHP 3,100 = 15.4knots
Endurance: 2,000/10
Armament: 2×254mm, 4×152mm, 2×38mm, 1×380mm TT
1897: 152mm and 38mm replaced by 4×120mm/45 and 6×57mm
1904: 1×210mm/45, 7×152mm/45, 11×57mm, 1×380mm TT
Armour: Belt 200-293mm, deck 50mm, turret 243-293mm, c/t 270mm
Complement: 232
Class notes: One twin turret forward with two funnels and single military mast. New secondary guns fitted 1897 and reconstructed 1903-04 with one single turret forward and seven small turrets and two masts

'Gota' (1886)

Coast Defence Ship: *Gota*
Displacement: 3,100tons; *1902:* 3,290tons
Dimensions: 258'6(pp)×47'10×16'9 [78.8(pp)×14.6×5.1]
Machinery: 2 screws, horizontal compound engines (builder), 6 cylindrical boilers
IHP 4,650 = 15knots
Endurance: 2,000/10
Armament: 2×254mm/34, 4×152mm, 5×57mm, 1×380mm TT
1902: 1×210mm/45, 7×152mm/45, 11×57mm, 1×380mm TT
Armour: Belt 250-300mm, turret 300mm, c/t 270mm, deck 50mm
Complement: 232
Class notes: Near sister to *Svea.* Similarly reconstructed 1901-02

'Thule' (1890)

Coast Defence Ship: *Thule*
Displacement: 3,150tons; *1903:* 3,300tons
Dimensions: 260'6(wl)×47'11×16'9 [79.5(wl)×14'6×5.1]
Machinery: 2 screws, horizontal compound engines, 6 cylindrical boilers
IHP 4,750 = 16knots
Endurance: 2,000/10
Armament: 2×254mm/45, 4×152mm/34, 5×57mm, 2×450mm TT
1903: 1×210mm/45, 7×152mm/34, 11×57mm, no TT
Armour: Belt 200-293mm deck 50mm, turret 243-293mm, c/t 270mm
Complement: 230
Class notes: Near sister to *Svea* and similarly reconstructed 1902-03

Top right:
***Gota* — Coast defence ship of 1886, prior to reconstruction.** *US Navy*

Centre right:
***Oden* — Coast defence ship of 1893, taken c1902.** *IWM*

Bottom right:
***Manligheten* — Coast defence ship of 1898, following reconstruction in 1941.**

'Oden' Class (1893)

Coast Defence Ships: *Niord, Oden, Thor*
Displacement: 3,300tons; *Oden:* 3,500tons
Dimensions: 278'3(wl)×48'7×17'4 [84.8(wl)×14.8×5.3]
Machinery: 2 screws, VTE engines (builders; *Niord:* Motala), 6 cylindrical boilers
IHP 5,350 = 16.5knots
Endurance: 2,530/10
Armament: 2×254mm/42, 6×120mm/45 (*Oden:* 4×120mm/45), 10×57mm, 1×450mm TT
1915: 2×120mm/45 added (*Oden*), 8×47mm added
Armour: *Oden:* Belt 243mm, turrets 250mm, deck 48mm, casemates 100mm, c/t 250mm
Others: Belt 240mm, turrets 200mm, deck 48mm, casemates 100mm, c/t 200mm
Complement: 250
Class notes: Improved 'Svea' class with two single turrets fore and aft and secondary armament in casemates. Two funnels and two military masts. Reconstructed 1915-17, with additional guns, single funnel and single tripod mast

'Dristigheten' (1897)

Coast Defence Ship: *Dristigheten* (see later photo)
Displacement: 3,450tons
Dimensions: 285(wl)×48'7×16 [86.9(wl)×14.8×4.9]
Machinery: 2 screws, VTE engines, 8 Yarrow boilers
IHP 5,550 = 16.8knots
Endurance: 2,040/10
Armament: 2×210mm/45, 6×152mm/45, 10×57mm, 2×450mm TT
Armour: Belt 240mm, turrets 200mm, deck 48mm, casemates 100mm, c/t 200mm
Complement: 270
Class notes: Modified 'Oden' type with different armament and watertube boilers. Funnels more widely spaced. Converted to aircraft tender 1930

'Aran' Class (1898)

Coast Defence Ships: *Aran, Manligheten, Tapperheten, Wasa*
Displacement: *Aran:* 3,650tons; *Manligheten* and *Tapperheten:* 3,840tons; *Wasa:* 3,745tons
Dimensions: 287(wl)×49'3×16'6 [87.5(wl)×15×5]
Machinery: 2 screws, VTE engines, 8 Yarrow boilers
IHP 6,500 = 17.2knots
Endurance: 2,000/10
Armament: 2×210mm/45, 6×152mm/45, 10×57mm, 2×450mm TT
1939: 4×57mm added, TT removed
Armour: Belt 175mm, turrets 190mm, deck 48mm, c/t 175mm
Complement: 300
Class notes: Similar to *Dristigheten* with secondary guns in turrets rather than casemates. Reconstructed 1932-42

'Oscar II' (1902)

Coast Defence Ships: *Oscar II*
Displacement: 4,270 tons
Dimensions: 313'8(wl)×50'6×17 [95.6(wl)×15.4×5.2]
Machinery: 2 screws, VTE engines, 12 Yarrow boilers
IHP 9,400 = 18.3knots
Endurance: 2,950/10
Armament: 2×210mm/45, 8×152mm/50, 10×57mm, 2×450mm TT
1939: 4×57mm added, TT removed
Armour: Belt 102-150mm, turrets 127-190mm, citadel 100mm, deck 50mm, c/t 175mm
Complement: 325
Class notes: Larger 'Aran' type with similar armament but secondary armament in twin turrets. Tripod foremasts and three funnels

'Sverige' Class (1911)

Coast Defence Ships: *Drottning Victoria* (see also later photo), *Gustaf V, Sverige* (see later photo)
Displacement: 6,842tons; *Sverige:* 6,582tons
Dimensions: 396'6(wl)×61×21'4 [120.9(wl)×18.6×6.5] *Sverige:* 392'8 [119.7(wl)]
Machinery: 4 screws, Westinghouse geared turbines (Motala), 12 Yarrow boilers; *Drottning Victoria* and *Gustaf V, 1935:* Penhoet boilers; *Sverige, 1935:* Curtis direct turbines (Bergsund), 12 Yarrow boilers
SHP 22,000 = 23knots; *Sverige:* SHP 20,000 = 27.5knots
Armament: 4×283mm, 8×152mm, 6×75mm, 2×450mm TT
1933: 4×75mm AA replaced old 75mm, TT removed
1938: 2×152mm replaced by 4×40mm and 4×25mm AA
1942: 2×40mm AA added
Drottning Victoria, 1942: 2×152mm replaced by 6×40mm AA and 4×25mm AA
Armour: Belt 200mm, turrets 200mm, deck 40mm, citadel 100mm, c/t 175mm
Complement: 450
Class notes: First ship cancelled after a change of government and funds were raised by public subscription. Considerably larger than previous vessels with two twin turrets fore and aft. Two funnels with tripod foremast and pole mainmast. *Gustaf V* reconstructed 1929-30 when funnels were trunked into one and superstructure changed. *Sverige* had fore funnel inclined aft 1932. *Drottning Victoria* received some new boilers 1934 and others in 1936-38. *Gustaf V* rearmed 1940

Above left:
***Oscar II* — Coast defence ship, March 1936.**
Wright & Logan

Above:
***Drottning Victoria* — Coast defence ship, as completed, 1922.**

Coast Defence Ships (1939)

Coast Defence Ships: 2 unnamed
Displacement: 8,000tons
Dimensions: 436'4(wl) 426'6(pp)×64×18'9 [133(wl) 130(pp)×19.5×5.7]
Machinery: SHP —— = 23knots
Armament: 4×254mm, 6×120mm AA, 8×40mm AA
Armour: Belt 250mm
Class notes: Ordered from Kockums & Gotaverken in 1939, but cancelled before construction began. Planned with two twin turrets fore and aft, single funnel and tower foremast

Individual Ships

Aran

Type: Coast Defence Ship
Class: 'Aran' (1898)
Nomenclature: Honour

History:
1899 Laid down by Lindholmens
1901 August 14: Launched
1902 August 25: Completed
1939 Reconstructed
1947 June 13: Stricken
1951 Broken up

Dristigheten

Type: Coast Defence Ship
Class: 'Dristigheten' (1897)
Nomenclature: Boldness

History:
1898 Laid down by Lindholmens
1900 April 28: Launched
1901 Completed
1929-30 Converted to seaplane tender, mainmast replaced by seaplane handling deck, armament only 4×76mm AA
1947 June 13: Converted to target ship
1961 Broken up

Drottning Victoria

Type: Coast Defence Ship
Class: 'Sverige' (1911)
Nomenclature: Queen Victoria (1862-1930), wife of King Gustaf V

History:
1915 July: Laid down by Gotaverken
1917 September 15: Launched
1921 March 12: Completed
1926-27 Refit, TT removed
1934-35 Reconstructed; reboilered, AA added
1940-42 Reconstructed
1947 March 22: Stricken
1959 Sold and broken up

Gota

Type: Coast Defence Ship
Class: 'Gota' (1886)
Nomenclature: Gotaland, the southern portion of Sweden

History:
1887 Laid down by Lindholmens
1889 September 30: Launched
1891 Completed
1901-02 Reconstructed at Karlskrona
1920 Accommodation ship
1943 Stricken and broken up

Gustaf V

Type: Coast Defence Ship
Class: 'Sverige' (1911)
Nomenclature: Gustaf V, King of Sweden (1858-1950)

History:
1914 December: Laid down by Kockums
1918 January 31: Launched
1922 December 12: Completed
1927-30 Reconstructed
1936-37 Refit; reboilered
1957 March 22: Stricken, machinists' training ship
1970 Sold and broken up at Goteborg

John Ericsson

Type: Monitor
Class: 'John Ericsson' (1863)
Nomenclature: John Ericsson (1803-1889), inventor, designer of the first monitor

History:
1864 July: Laid down by Motala
1865 March 17: Launched
1865 November 13: Completed
1881 Rearmed
1892-95 Reconstructed at Karlskrona
1918 November 12: Stricken
1919 Sold, converted to a barge

Loke

Type: Monitor

Class: 'Loke' (1866)
Nomenclature: Norse myth: Viking god of destruction

History:
1867 Laid down by Motala
1869 September 4: Launched
1871 October: Completed
1908 Stricken and broken up

Manligheten

Type: Coast Defence Ship
Class: 'Aran' (1898)
Nomenclature: Manliness

History:
1901 Laid down by Kockums
1903 December 1: Launched
1904 Completed
1941 Reconstructed
1950 February 24: Stricken and broken up 1952

Niord

Type: Coast Defence Ship
Class: 'Oden' (1893)
Nomenclature: Norse myth: a Viking god, the dispenser of riches

History:
1896 Laid down by Lindholmens
1898 March 30: Launched
1899 January 27: Completed
1916-17 Reconstructed
1928 Decommissioned
1935 Boys' accommodation ship
1945 Broken up

Oden

Type: Coast Defence Ship
Class: 'Oden' (1893)
Nomenclature: Norse myth: King of the Gods

History:
1894 Laid down by Finnboda
1896 March 9: Launched
1897 Completed
1915 Reconstructed
1919 Reserve
1937 Stricken

Oscar II

Type: Coast Defence Ship
Class: 'Oscar II' (1902)
Nomenclature: Oscar II, King of Sweden (1829-1907)

History:
1903 Laid down by Lindholmens
1905 June 6: Launched
1907 April 3: Completed
1939 Reconstructed
1950 February 24: Stricken; damage control training hulk
1974 Broken up at Goteborg

Svea

Type: Coast Defence Ship
Class: 'Svea' (1883)
Nomenclature: Svealand, the central portion of Sweden

Above left:
***Dristigheten* — Coast defence ship of 1897, following conversion in 1930 to aircraft tender.**

Above:
***Drottning Victoria* — Coast defence ship, May 1937, after modernisation with mainmast removed.**
Wright & Logan

Left:
***Sverige* — Coast defence ship, after modernisation, with forward funnel trunked aft.**

History:
1884 Laid down by Lindholmens
1885 December 12: Launched
1886 September: Completed
1897 Reconstructed
1903-04 Reconstructed
1921 Submarine depot ship, armament removed
1941 Receiving ship
1942 Stricken
1944 Broken up

Sverige

Type: Coast Defence Ship
Class: Sverige' (1911)
Nomenclature: Sweden

History:
1912 December 12: Laid down by Gotaverken
1915 May 3: Launched
1917 May 14: Completed
1926 Refit
1931-33 Refit
1938-40 Reconstructed
1953 January 30: Stricken
1958 Sold and broken up at Ronneby

Tapperheten

Type: Coast Defence Ship
Class: 'Aran' (1898)
Nomenclature: Bravery

History:
1899 Laid down by Kockums
1901 November 7: Launched
1903 Completed
1941 Reconstructed
1947 June 13: Stricken
1952 Broken up

Thor

Type: Coast Defence Ship
Class: 'Oden' (1893)
Nomenclature: Norse myth: god of Thunder

History:
1896 October 26: Laid down by Bergsund
1898 March 7: Launched
1899 August 7: Completed
1914-15 Reconstructed
1937 Stricken

Thordon

Type: Monitor
Class: 'John Ericsson' (1863)
Nomenclature: Thunder

History:
1865 April: Laid down by Motala
1865 December 1: Launched
1866 August: Completed
1903-05 Reconstructed at Karlskrona
1922 August 25: Stricken and broken up

Thule

Type: Coast Defence Ship
Class: 'Thule' (1890)
Nomenclature: Greek name for a northern European country

History:
1891 Laid down by Finnboda
1893 March 4: Launched
1893 Completed
1902-03 Reconstructed at Karlskrona
1923 Accommodation ship
1928 Stricken and broken up

Tirfing

Type: Monitor
Class: 'John Ericsson' (1863)
Nomenclature: Norse myth: a sword with supernatural qualities

History:
1865 Laid down by Motala
1866 August 1: Launched
1867 July 8: Completed
1902-03 Reconstructed by Bergsunds
1922 August 25: Stricken
1923 Broken up

Wasa

Type: Coast Defence Ship
Class: 'Aran' (1898)
Nomenclature: Name of the former Swedish royal dynasty

History:
1899 Laid down by Finnboda
1901 May 29: Launched
1902 October: Completed
1941 Stricken
1952 Damage control hulk
1961 Broken up

Turkey

In an effort to support the backward Turkish Empire against Russian expansionist policies aimed particularly at the Dardanelles, Britain gave considerable aid to Turkish efforts to build a powerful navy. In the 1860s and 1870s modern ironclad warships were built in Britain and France, so many that the Turkish navy became third in importance in size. Much of this development occurred under the administration of the British officer Hobart Pasha.

The Turkish navy did little during the war with Russia in 1877-78, losing two ironclads to inferior Russian forces on the Danube. Three capital ships under construction in Britain were seized under British neutrality laws and completed for the Royal Navy. Britain lost interest in a powerful Turkey following the peace settlement and the large navy became ever more antiquated. A single small battleship was built at Constantinople during this period while a second vessel had to be abandoned because of the builder's inefficiency.

As relations with Greece became more strained, two old battleships were acquired from Germany in 1910 and dreadnoughts were ordered from British yards. During the Balkan wars of 1911-12 the Turkish navy's weakness was apparent as Italian and then Greek warships controlled the seas.

Upon the outbreak of World War 1 the almost-completed dreadnoughts *Reshadieh* and *Sultan Osman I* were taken over by the Royal Navy. The spectacular arrival of the German battlecruiser *Goeben* at Constantinople in 1914 was a boon for Turkey as the ship was officially transferred, with its crew, to Turkey. During the war it operated as a Turkish ship but under German control and was active against the Russian fleet in the Black Sea.

After the war Turkey was permitted to keep the former *Goeben*, by then *Yavuz*, and it remained the flagship of the fleet until being scrapped in 1954.

Class Details

'Osmanieh' Class (1862)

Broadside Ships: *Azizieh, Mahmudieh, Orkanieh, Osmanieh* (see later photo)
Displacement: 6,400tons
Dimensions: 309(oa) 293(pp)×55'9×25'7 [94.2(oa) 89.3(pp)×17×7.8]
Mahmudieh: 253'9 [77.3] length
Machinery: 1 screw, horizontal direct-acting engines (Napier; *Mahmudieh:* Ravenhill; *Osmanieh:* Maudslay), 6 boilers; *1892:* 6 cylindrical boilers
IHP 3,740 = 12knots
Endurance: 1,600/10
Armament: 2×230mm MLR, 14×203mm MLR, 10×38pdr
Mahmudieh: 1×300pdr, 18×150pdr
1890s: 2×240mm/55, 8×210mm, 6×105mm, 2×355mm TT
Armour: Belt 76-140mm, battery 127mm, *1892:* barbettes 115mm
Complement: 340
Class notes: Armoured frigates with iron hull and bark rig similar to British *Minotaur*. Good sea boats. Reconstructed 1890-99 with sail rig replaced by two military masts, reboilered and rearmed with main armament in two barbettes and secondary armaments in casemates. A second reconstruction in 1904 was found not to be justified

'Fatikh' (1866)

Broadside Ship: *[Fatikh]*
Displacement: 9,700tons
Dimensions: 368'2(oa) 356'4(wl)×60×26'6 [112.2(oa) 108.6(wl)×18.3×8.1]
Machinery: 1 screw, HSE engines (Maudslay), 8 boilers
IHP 8,000 = 14knots
Endurance: 1,300/10
Armament: 33×72pdr
Armour: Belt 127-305mm, battery 150-200mm
Complement: 700
Class notes: Armoured frigate designed by Reed and sold to Prussia prior to launching, renamed *König Wilhelm*

'Assar-i-Shefket' Class (1867)

Central Battery Ships: *Assar-i-Shefket, Nedjim-i-Shefket*
Displacement: 2,050tons
Dimensions: 218(oa) 210(pp)×42'7×16'5 [66.4(oa) 64(pp)×13×5]
Machinery: 2 screws, (F C Med)
IHP 1,750 = 11knots
Endurance: 1,000/10
Armament: 5×230mm MLR,
c1886: 4×230 replaced by 4×178mm, 2×87mm added
Armour: Belt 75-150mm, battery 115mm, bulkheads 108mm, barbette 127mm
Complement: 220
Class notes: Armoured corvettes with iron hull, originally ordered by Egypt and taken over by Turkey prior to completion. Single funnel and two masts with brig rig and ram bow. Four guns in battery and one in barbette above

'Hafiz-i-Rahman' Class (1867)

Turret Ships (Monitors): *Hafiz-i-Rahman, Latif-i-Djelil*
Displacement: 2,540tons
Dimensions: 211'6(oa) 204(pp)×44'6×19'6 [64.5(oa) 62.2(pp)×13.6×5.9]
Machinery: 1 screw (Mazeline)
IHP 3,950 = 12knots
Armament: 2×203mm MLR, 2×178mm MLR, 1×120mm MLR
Hafiz-i-Rahman c1890: 2×150mm BLR, replaced 178mm, 2×37mm added
Armour: Belt 117-140mm, redoubt 75mm, turrets 127mm
Complement: 214
Class notes: Coastal defence vessels with two twin turrets. Iron hull with ram bow, single funnel and bark rig

'Assar-i-Tewfik' (1867)

Central Battery Ship; *Assar-i-Tewfik*
Displacement: 4,687tons
Dimensions: 285(oa) 275'5(pp)×52'6×24'11 [86.9(oa) 83.9(pp)×16×7.6]
Machinery: 1 screw, horizontal compound engine (F C Med), 6 cylindrical boilers; *1906:* Niclausse boilers
IHP 3,560 = 13.25knots
Endurance: 1,840/10
Armament: 8×230mm MLR, 2×203mm MLR

c1880s: 8×240mm BLR, 2×210mm BLR, 2×63mm
1907: 3×150mm/40, 7×120mm/40, 6×76mm
Armour: Belt 76-200mm, battery 152mm, barbettes 127mm
Complement: 600; *1906:* 320
Class notes: Ordered for Egypt and taken over by Turkey prior to launching. Smaller edition of French *Trident* with central redoubt and two guns in barbettes above the central redoubt. Iron hull with ram bow, single funnel and bark rig. Reconstructed 1903-06, completely rebuilt and rearmed, with single military mast and guns fore and aft.

'Avni Illah' Class (1867)

Central Battery Ships: *Avni Illah* (see later photo), *Muin-i-Zafer*
Displacement: 2,330tons
Dimensions: 244(oa) 230(pp)×36×16 [74.4(oa) 70.1(pp)×11×4.9]
Machinery: 2 screws (*Muin*), 1 screw (*Avni*), horizontal compound engines (Ravenhill), cylindrical boilers
IHP 2,200 = 12.5knots
Endurance: 1,270/10
Armament: 4×230mm MLR
Later: 1×120mm added
1907: 4×150mm/40, 6×120mm/40, 10×76mm
Armour: Belt 75-152mm, battery 152mm, bulkheads 127mm, deck 38mm
Complement: 220
Class notes: Armoured corvettes designed by Mackrow with guns in two central redoubts with single funnel between them amidships and brigantine rig. Reconstructed 1903-07, reboilered, conning tower added, rigging replaced by military mast amidships

'Idjlalieh' (1867)

Central Battery and Barbette Ship: *Idjlalieh* (see later photo)
Displacement: 2,240tons
Dimensions: 227(oa) 213'3(pp)×42'7×20'6 [69.2(oa) 65(pp)×13×6.2]
Machinery: 1 screw, — (Ravenhill)
IHP 1,800 = 11knots
Endurance: 1,170/10
Armament: 4×230mm MLR, 1×180mm MLR
1891: 1×150mm and 2×87mm added
Armour: Belt 100-150mm, barbette 127mm, battery 114mm
Complement: 220
Class notes: Armoured corvette with central redoubt and 180mm gun in barbette on upper deck. Iron hull with brig rig and prominent ram bow

'Feth-i-Bulend' Class (1868)

Central Battery Ships: *Feth-i-Bulend, Mukademeh-i-Hair*
Displacement: 2,720tons
Dimensions: 241(oa) 235(pp) ×39'4×18 [73.5(oa) 71.6(pp)×12×5.5]
Machinery: 1 screw, — (*Feth;* Humphrys; *Mukademeh:* Constantinople), 4 boilers
Feth: IHP 4,200 = 14knots; *Mukademeh:* IHP 3,000 = 12.5knots
Endurance: 1,040/10
Armament: 4×230mm MLR, 1×180mm MLR
Feth-i-Bulend, 1907: 4×150mm/40, 6×75mm, 10×6pdr
1890s: 180mm removed, 2×120mm added
Armour: Belt 102-230mm, battery 150-230mm, bulkhead 140mm
Complement: 219
Class notes: Designed by Reed. Armoured corvettes with octagonal central redoubt. Iron hull and brig rig with single funnel. *Feth-i-Bulend* reconstructed 1903-07

'Messudieh' Class (1872)

Central Battery Ships: *[Hamidieh], Messudieh*
Displacement: 8,990tons
Dimensions: 348(oa) 331'8(pp)×59×25'11 [106(oa) 101(pp)×18×7.9]
Machinery: 1 screw, horizontal direct-acting engines (Maudslay), 8 rectangular boilers
IHP 7,800 = 13.5knots
Endurance: 1,800/10
Armament: 16×254mm MLR, 4×180mm MLR
1890s: 4×254mm and 4×180mm removed, 3×150mm BLR added
Armour: Belt 178-305mm, battery 254-305mm, c/t 200mm, bulkheads 254mm
Complement: 600

***Messudieh* as rebuilt 1903:**

Displacement: 9,250tons
Dimensions: 338(oa) 315(pp)×59×27'3 [103(oa) 96(pp)×18×8.3]
Machinery: 2 screws, VTE engines (Ansaldo), 16 Niclausse boilers
IHP 11,000 = 16knots
Endurance: 2,200/10
Armament: 2×234mm/40, 12×152mm/45, 14×76mm, 10×57mm
Armour: As before except barbettes and turrets 152mm
Complement: 640
Class notes: Central battery ships designed by Reed based on British *Hercules* and built in Britain. Iron hull with two funnels and bark rig. *Hamidieh* purchased by Britain prior to completion 1876. *Messudieh* reconstructed 1898-1901 being completely rebuilt, new engines and boilers and fitted with two shafts, sail rig replaced by single military mast aft and armament arranged in turrets and casemates. The 234mm guns were never fitted and wood dummies put in their place

'Hamidieh' (1874)

Central Battery Ship: *Hamidieh*
Displacement: 6,700tons
Dimensions: 302(oa) 292(pp)×56×27'3 [92(oa) 89(pp)×17.1×8.3]
Machinery: 1 screw, single expansion engines (Maudslay),
IHP 6,800 = 13knots
Armament: 10×260mm, 2×165mm, 2×355mm TT
Armour: Belt 178-230mm, battery 127mm, deck 75mm
Complement: 600
Class notes: Reduced version of 'Messudieh' type built at Constantinople. Engines originally intended for frigate *Selimieh*. Single funnel and bark rig; 4×260mm guns mounted on upper deck fore and aft

'Peyk-i-Shereef' Class (1875)

Central Battery Ships: *[Boordji-Zafer, Peyk-i-Shereef]*
Displacement: 4,870tons
Dimensions: 245(pp)×52×21'1 [74.6(pp)×15.8×6.4]
Machinery: 2 screws, horizontal direct-action engines (Maudslay), 4 boilers
IHP 3,200 = 12.25knots
Endurance: 1,850/10
Armament: 4×254mm MLR
Armour: Belt 152-305mm, battery 203-254mm, bulkheads

Top, left to right:
***Mahmudieh* — Armoured frigate built in 1864, prior to reconstruction.** *Marius Bar*

***Nedjim-i-Shefket* — Armoured corvette of 1868, as completed.** *Marius Bar*

***Assar-i-Tewfik* — Central battery ship built 1868, prior to reconstruction.** *Marius Bar*

Above, left to right:
***Muin-i-Zafer* — Central battery ship built 1869, after reconstruction of 1907. Note single mast aft of funnel and guns in casemates in hull.** *P. A. Vicary*

***Feth-i-Bulend* — Armoured corvette.** *Marius Bar*

***Yavuz* — The former German battlecruiser *Goeben,* September 1945, in dazzle camouflage, with the crew lining the decks.** *IWM*

127-230mm, deck 25-76mm, c/t 230mm
Class notes: Coast defence vessels of Turkish design intended primarily as rams. Taken over by Britain during Russo-Turkish War 1878, renamed *Scorpion* and *Wivern*

'Abdul Kadir' (1892)

Barbette Ship: *[Abdul Kadir]*
Displacement: 10,650tons
Dimensions: 340×65×23'6 [103.6×19.8×7.2]
Machinery: 2 screws
IHP 11,500 = 17knots
Armament: 4×279mm, 6×150mm, 8×87mm, 6×355mm TT
Armour: Belt 178-355mm, barbettes 150mm, deck 76mm
Class notes: Laid down in 1892 but never completed as the blocks under the hull had moved before launching

'Hairredin Barbarossa' Class (1910)

Pre-dreadnoughts: *Hairredin Barbarossa, Torgud Reis*
Displacement: 10,013tons
Dimensions: 379'6(oa) 373'9(wl)×64'8×26 [115.7(oa) 113.9(wl)×19.7×7.9]
Machinery: 2 screws, VTE engines (builders), 12 cylindrical boilers
IHP 10,000 = 16knots
Endurance: 4,500/10
Armament: 4×279mm/40, 2×279mm/35, 8×105mm/35, 3×450mm TT
Armour: Belt 300-400mm, barbettes 300mm, deck 60mm, turrets 50-150mm, c/t 300mm
Complement: 585
Class notes: Built in 1891 as German *Kurfürst Friedrich Wilhelm* and *Weissenburg*. Purchased in 1910 as a reply to Greek coast defence ships

'Reshadieh' Class (1911)

Dreadnoughts: *[Reshadieh, Reshad-i-Hamiss]*
Displacement: 23,000tons, 25,250f/l
Dimensions: 559'6(oa) 525(pp)×91'7×28'2 [170.5(oa) 160(pp)×27.9×8.6]
Machinery: 4 screws, Parsons turbines (Vickers), 15 B&W boilers
SHP 26,500 = 21knots

Endurance: 5,300/10
Armament: 10×343mm/45, 16×152mm/50, 6×6pdr, 4×533mm TT
Armour: Belt 102-305mm, barbettes 76-254mm, turrets 76-280mm, c/t 305mm
Complement: 1,070
Class notes: Designed by Sir Richard Thurston on modified hull of 'King George V' type with improved armament and protection. *Reshad-i-Hamiss* cancelled in 1912 and *Reshadieh* seized by Britain 1914 and renamed *Erin*

'Sultan Osman I' (1914)

Dreadnought: *[Sultan Osman I]*
Displacement: 27,500tons, 30,250f/l
Dimensions: 671′6(oa) 632(pp)×89×27 [204.7(oa) 192.6(pp)×27.1×8.2]
Machinery: 4 screws, Parsons turbines (Vickers), 22 B&W boilers
SHP 34,000 = 22knots
Armament: 14×305mm/45, 20×152mm/50, 10×76mm, 3×533mm TT
Armour: Belt 102-230mm, barbettes 76-230mm, turrets 203-305mm, bulkhead 76-152mm, c/t 305mm
Complement: 1,115
Class notes: Laid down as Brazilian *Rio de Janeiro* and purchased while incomplete. Seized by Britain 1914 and renamed *Agincourt*. The longest battleship in the world mounting the largest number of big guns afloat in seven twin turrets

'Fatikh' (1914)

Dreadnoughts: *[Fatikh]*
Displacement: 24,700tons
Dimensions: 565(oa)×89′10×30′2 [172.2(oa)×29.5×9.2]
Machinery: SHP 27,500 = 21knots

'Yavuz Sultan Selim' (1914)

Battlecruiser: *Yavuz Sultan Selim*
Displacement: 22,979tons
Dimensions: 611′10(oa) 590′6(wl)×96′9×30′2 [186.5(oa) 180(wl)×29.5×9.2]
Machinery: 4 screws, Parsons turbines (Blohm & Voss), 24 Schulz-Thornycroft boilers
SHP 52,000 = 25.5knots
Endurance: 4,120/14
Armament: 10×280mm/50, 10×150mm/45, 12×88mm/45, 4×500mm TT
1928: Only 2×88mm and 4×88mm AA, 2 TT
1942: 4×88mm AA added
1948: 10×40mm AA added
Armour: Belt 95-265mm, turrets 200mm, battery 125mm, deck 75mm, c/t 250mm
Complement: 1,100
Class notes: Former German *Goeben* which eluded British interception in the Mediterranean in 1914 and was formally transferred to Turkey. Nevertheless the ship retained its German crew and control until the end of the war when the ship was interned heavily damaged. Completely refitted 1926-30, mainmast removed 1941

Individual Ships

Abdul Kadir

Type: Barbette Ship
Class: 'Abdul Kadir' (1892)
Nomenclature: Abdul Kadir Effendi (b1878), second son of Sultan Abdul Hamid II

History:
1892 October: Laid down at Constantinople
1905 Construction abandoned

Assar-i-Shefket

Type: Central Battery Ship
Class: 'Assar-i-Shefket' (1867)
Nomenclature: Sign of power

History:
1867 Laid down by La Seyne as Egyptian ***Kahera***
1868 Renamed ***Assar-i-Shefket***
1868 Launched
—— Completed
1877 August 23: Attacked by Russian torpedo boats at Sukhumkale, not damaged
1903-04 Broken up

Assar-i-Tewfik

Type: Central Battery Ship
Class: 'Assar-i-Tewfik' (1867)
Nomenclature: Sign of God's help

History:
1867 Laid down by La Seyne as Egyptian ***Ibrahimieh***
1868 Renamed ***Assar-i-Tewfk***
1868 November 30: Launched
1870 Completed
1899 Reconstruction by Ansaldo cancelled
1903-07 Rebuilt by Germania
1912 December 16: In action off the Dardanelles, and again on December 22, damaged
1913 February 11: Wrecked near Podima in the Bosphorus while supporting troops in action

Avni Illah

Type: Central Battery Ship
Class: 'Avni Illah' (1867)
Nomenclature: The help of God

History:
—— Laid down by Thames
1869 June: Launched
—— Completed
1903-07 Reconstructed by Ansaldo at Constantinople
1912 February 24: Sunk by gunfire of Italian cruiser *Giuseppe Garibaldi* at Beirut

Azizieh

Type: Broadside Ship
Class: 'Osmanieh' (1862)
Nomenclature: Abdul Aziz (1830-1877), Sultan of Turkey 1861-76

Above left:
***Assar-i-Tewfik* — Central battery ship, after reconstruction in 1906.**

Above right:
***Avni Illah* — Central battery ship of 1869, after being reconstructed in 1907.** *P. A. Vicary*

History:
1863 May: Laid down by Napier as ***Abdul Aziz***
1865 January: Launched
1865 December: Completed
1871 Renamed ***Azizieh***
1890-94 Rebuilt by Ansaldo as barbette ship
1911 Discarded
1919 Broken up

Boordji-Zafer

Type: Central Battery Ship
Class: 'Peyk-i-Shereef' (1875)
Nomenclature: Sign of victory

History:
—— Laid down by Samuda
1878 February 20: Purchased by Great Britain, renamed ***Orion***

Fatikh

Type: Broadside Ship
Class: 'Fatikh' (1866)
Nomenclature: Conqueror

History:
—— Laid down by Thames
1867 February 6: Purchased by Prussia, renamed ***Wilhelm I***, later ***König Wilhelm***

Fatikh

Type: Dreadnought
Class: 'Fatikh' (1914)

History:
1914 June 11: Laid down by Vickers
1914 August: Cleared from slip, never completed

Feth-i-Bulend

Type: Central Battery Ship

Class: 'Feth-i-Bulend' (1868)
Nomenclature: Great conqueror

History:
—— Laid down by Thames
1870 January 24: Launched
1870 July: Completed
1903-07 Rebuilt by Ansaldo at Constantinople
1912 October 31: Sunk by Greek torpedo boat *No 11* at Salonika

Hafiz-i-Rahman

Type: Turret Ship
Class: 'Hafiz-i-Rahman'(1867)
Nomenclature: Protector of the compassionate, an attribute of God

History:
—— Laid down by L'Ocean, Bordeaux
1868 Launched
1869 Completed
1877 November 9: Damaged by gunfire off Sulina
c1900 Broken up

Hairredin Barbarossa

Type: Pre-dreadnought
Class: 'Hairredin Barbarossa' (1910)
Nomenclature: Khair-ed-din Barbarossa II (1466-1546), Turkish seafarer, Dey of Algiers

History:
1890 Laid down by Wilhelmshaven for Germany as ***Kurfurst Friedrich Wilhelm***
1891 June 30: Launched
1894 April 29: Completed
1910 September 12: Purchased from Germany, renamed ***Hairredin Barbarossa***
1911 Defence of Chataldja
1912 November 12: Bombardment of Varna
1912 December 16: Damaged in action with Greek squadron off Dardanelles
1912 December 22: Again damaged off Dardanelles
1915 August 8: Torpedoed and sunk by British submarine *E11* in Dardanelles (253 dead)

Hamidieh

Type: Central Battery Ship
Class: 'Messudieh' (1872)
Nomenclature: Abdul Hamid II (1842-1918), Sultan of Turkey 1876-1909

History:
1873 Laid down by Thames as ***Memduhieh***
1875 November 16: Launched
1876 Renamed ***Hamidieh***
1877 Completed but detained in Britain because of the Russo-Turkish War
1878 February 20: Purchased by Great Britain, renamed ***Superb***

Hamidieh

Type: Central Battery Ship
Class: 'Hamidieh' (1880)

History:
1874 Laid down at Constantinople as ***Nusretieh***
1878 Renamed ***Hamidieh***
1885 Launched
1892 Completed
1913 Broken up

Idjlalieh

Type: Central Battery and Barbette Ship
Class: 'Idjlalieh' (1867)
Nomenclature: Glorious; majestic

History:
1868 May: Laid down by Stab Tecnico
1870 Launched
1872 January: Completed
1877 June 11: Attacked by Russian spar torpedo boat at Sulina, not damaged
1897 Training ship
1922 Broken up

Latif-i-Djelil

Type: Turret Ship
Class: 'Hafiz-i-Rahman'(1867)
Nomenclature: Favour of the great one; heavenly grace

History:
—— Laid down by L'Ocean, Bordeaux
1868 Launched
1869 Completed
1877 May 11: Sunk by Russian artillery in the Danube River near Galatz

Mahmudieh

Type: Broadside Ship
Class: 'Osmanieh' (1862)
Nomenclature: Mahmud II (1783-1839), Sultan of Turkey 1806-1839

History:
—— Laid down by Thames as ***Sultan Mahmud***
1864 December 13: Launched
1865 November: Completed
—— Renamed ***Mahmudieh***
1895-99 Rebuilt by Ansaldo as barbette ship
1911 Discarded
—— Broken up after World War 1

Memduhieh, see Hamidieh

Nomenclature: The praiseworthy one

Above left:
***Idjlalieh* — Armoured corvette of 1870. Note two gun ports amidships in central redoubt and barbette just forward of mainmast.** *Marius Bar*

Above right:
***Osmanieh* — Broadside ship of 1864, after reconstruction of 1894, with barbettes and military masts.** *Marius Bar*

Messudieh

Type: Central Battery Ship
Class: 'Messudieh' (1872)
Nomenclature: Bringer of good fortune

History:
1872 Laid down by Thames
1874 October 28: Launched
1876 Completed
1898-1903 Reconstructed by Ansaldo
1911 Defence of Chataldja
1912 November 12: Bombardment of Varna
1912 December 16: Action off Dardanelles with Greek squadron
1913 Main armament removed for relining, never remounted
1914 December 13: Torpedoed and sunk by British submarine *B11* off Chanak

Muin-i-Zafer

Type: Central Battery Ship
Class: 'Avni Illah' (1867)
Nomenclature: Contributor to victory

History:
—— Laid down by Samuda
1869 April: Launched
—— Completed
1904-07 Rebuilt by Ansaldo at Constantinople; reboilered
1925 Boys' training ship
1927 Broken up

Mukademeh-i-Hair

Type: Central Battery Ship
Class: 'Feth-i-Bulend' (1868)
Nomenclature: Promoter of charity

History:
—— Laid down at Constantinople
1872 November: Launched
—— Completed
c1910 Broken up

Nedjim-i-Shefket

Type: Central Battery Ship
Class: 'Assar-i-Shefket' (1867)
Nomenclature: Star of power

History:
1866 Laid down by La Seyne as Egyptian ***Moussafer***
1868 Renamed ***Nedjim-i-Shefket***
1868 Launched
—— Completed
1927 Depot ship
1929 Broken up in Italy

Nusretieh, see *Hamidieh*

Nomenclature: The victorious one

Orkanieh

Type: Broadside Ship
Class: 'Osmanieh' (1862)
Nomenclature: Orhan (1288-1362), Sultan of Turkey 1326-1362

History:
—— Laid down by Napier as ***Orhan***
1865 June 26: Launched
—— Completed as ***Orkanieh***
1895-99 Rebuilt by Ansaldo as barbette ship
1911 Discarded
—— Broken up after World War 1

Osmanieh

Type: Broadside Ship
Class: 'Osmanieh' (1862)
Nomenclature: Osman I (1259-1326), Sultan of Turkey 1299, founder of the Ottoman dynasty

History:
1863 March: Laid down by Napier as ***Osman Ghazi***
1864 September 2: Launched
—— Completed as ***Osmanieh***
1890-94 Rebuilt by Ansaldo as barbette ship

1911 Discarded
—— Broken up after World War 1

Peyk-i-Shereef

Type: Central Battery Ship
Class: 'Peyk-i-Shereef' (1875)
Nomenclature: Messenger of honour

History:
1875 Laid down by Samuda
1876 February 12: Launched
1878 February 20: Purchased by Great Britain, renamed ***Belleisle***

Reshad-i-Hamiss

Type: Dreadnought
Class: 'Reshadieh' (1911)
Nomenclature: Reshad V, ie Mohammed V (1884-1918), Sultan of Turkey 1909-1918

History:
1911 June: Ordered from Armstrong
1912 Contract cancelled

Reshadieh

Type: Dreadnought
Class: 'Reshadieh' (1911)
Nomenclature: Referring to Sultan Mohammed V (Reshad) (1844-1918)

History:
1911 August 1: Laid down by Vickers
1913 September 3: Launched
1914 August: Seized by Great Britain when complete, renamed ***Erin***

Sultan Mehmed Reshad V, see *Reshad-i-Hamiss*

Sultan Osman I

Type: Dreadnought
Class: 'Sultan Osman I' (1914)
Nomenclature: Sultan Osman I (1259-1326), founder of the Ottoman Empire

History:
1911 September 14: Laid down by Armstrong for Brazil as ***Rio de Janeiro***
1913 January 22: Launched
1914 January 9: Purchased by Turkey, renamed ***Sultan Osman I***
1914 August 2: Seized by British government, renamed ***Agincourt***

Torgud Reis

Type: Pre-dreadnought
Class: 'Hairredin Barbarossa' (1910)
Nomenclature: Torgud Reis (d1565) Turkish admiral, killed at the siege of Malta

History:
1890 Laid down by Vulcan for Germany as ***Weissenburg***
1891 December 14: Launched
1894 June 5: Completed
1910 September 12: Purchased by Turkey, renamed ***Torgud Reis***
1911 Defence of Chataldja
1912 November 12: Bombardment of Varna
1912 December 16: In action with Greek squadron off Dardanelles
1912 December 22: Damaged in action off Dardanelles
1924 Training ship, hulk in Bosphorus
1938 Broken up

Yavuz Sultan Selim

Type: Battlecruiser
Class: 'Yavuz Sultan Selim' (1914)
Nomenclature: Selim I the Grim (1467-1520), Sultan 1512-1520, conqueror of Egypt, Syria and the Hejaz

History:
1908 December 7: Laid down by Blohm & Voss for Germany as ***Goeben***
1911 March 8: Launched
1912 July 2: Completed
1914 August 10: Arrived at Constantinople after evading British warships in the Mediterranean
1914 August 16: In Turkish service as ***Yavuz Sultan Selim***
1914 October 29: Bombarded Sevastopol and sank Russian minelayer *Prut* in action, receiving three hits
1914 November 18: Damaged in action with Russian battleships off the Crimea (115 dead)
1914 December 10: Bombarded Batum
1914 December 26: Damaged by two mines in the Bosphorus
1915 May 10: Received two hits in action with Russian battleships
1916 January 8: In action with Russian battleship *Imperatritsa Ekaterina II*
1916 July 4: Bombarded Tuapse
1918 January 20: Sank British monitors *Raglan* and *M28* in raid on Mudros harbour, later struck a mine and ran aground. Refloated and drydocked at Sevastopol May 1918
1918 November 2: Formally handed over to Turkey
1918 November 5: Interned at Ismid
1927-30 Refit by Penhoet at Ismid
1930 August: Recommissioned
1936 Name shortened to ***Yavuz***
1938 Refit
1954 Decommissioned and broken up

USA

At the beginning of the Civil War in 1861 the government ordered construction of three ironclad designs. Of these the one by John Ericsson inaugurated a new era of naval warfare. This was the *Monitor*, the first warship without sails, 'the cheesebox on a raft'. The action at Hampton Roads with the Confederate ironclad *Virginia* marked a revolution which made obsolete all non-armoured vessels. The second vessel, *New Ironsides*, was of a more conventional design and was the most powerful vessel of the navy during the war. The third vessel, *Galena*, was a small gunboat with inadequate armour and not within the scope of this book.

The success of the *Monitor* led to construction of a number of similar vessels. Those incomplete at the end of the war were never finished and some were sold abroad. The monitors and *New Ironsides* fought actions with Confederate ironclads along the coasts of the Atlantic and Gulf of Mexico. After the war interest in the navy faded and monitors were thought to be the only vessels necessary for the purely coastal defence role envisioned for the navy. No money was appropriated for new vessels and new ships including five monitors were built under the guise of repairing old ones.

Nevertheless monitors soon became obsolete and support for new ships slowly gained support. In 1883 legislation was passed to start the 'New Navy'; the first new ships were based on foreign designs. The monitor faction was still strong and the first true battleships, the 'Indiana' class, were authorised as coast defence battleships with low freeboard.

The inexplicable destruction of the *Maine* at Havana led to the outbreak of war with Spain in 1898. The navy now included seven modern armoured vessels and the victories at Manila Bay and Santiago established the United States as a sea power. With these triumphs and the acquisition of territory in the Caribbean and the Far East, the navy's prestige soared and a succession of new vessels was built. Under the presidency of Theodore Roosevelt the Panama Canal was begun and the 'Great White Fleet' of 16 battleships was sent around the world as a gesture of American power.

Although these ships were already obsolescent as a result of the appearance of the *Dreadnought* two years earlier, the cruise was a success. The *South Carolina* with its main armament of a single calibre was ordered before the *Dreadnought*. Other significant innovations, many taken up by other navies, included the all-or-nothing protection of the *Nevada*, superfiring turrets, all turrets on the centreline and the cagemast which for a time identified vessels as American.

The navy in 1914 was unbalanced, strong in battleships but short of light cruisers and destroyers. The occupation of Veracruz in Mexico 1914-15 involved practically all battleships in service at the time. In 1916 a navy 'second to none' was authorised including 10 battleships and six battlecruisers. When the United States entered the war in 1917 a battleship squadron was sent to reinforce the British Grand Fleet in the North Sea and newer ships were stationed in Ireland to guard against possible German raiders.

At the end of the war naval construction continued in response to the Japanese '8-8' programme. The Washington Naval Treaty of 1922 gave the United States and Britain parity with five battleships each to each three Japanese ships (5-5-3). To accomplish parity the United States gave up 11 incomplete modern ships as against older completed British vessels, considered to be a greater sacrifice. Two incomplete vessels were completed as aircraft carriers and older battleships were modernised during the 1920s.

Carrier development continued with the smaller *Ranger* and the 'Yorktown' class in the 1930s, followed by the battleships of the 'North Carolina' class. These were overshadowed by the huge naval expansion acts of 1940 which authorised battleships of the 'Iowa' and 'Montana' classes, the large cruisers of the 'Alaska' class and the first 'Essex' class carriers. Although the neutrality of 1939 gradually slipped into a war footing by 1941, it was a terrible shock when the surprise Japanese attack on Pearl Harbor plunged the United States into war.

Five battleships were sunk and three damaged, but it was fortunate no carriers were present. With the battle fleet destroyed the navy was forced to rely on carriers as the first line of offence, avoiding the mistake of depending on obsolescent battleships. At the Battle of Midway, the American carrier planes sank all four Japanese carriers engaged while the surface fleets were never within sight of each other. It was the turning point of the war; in just 15 months, as new ships reached the Pacific, American fast carrier task forces commenced their attacks ranging further and deeper into enemy waters. With battleships relegated to escorts, carriers dominated the naval war. No fewer than 25 aircraft carriers were completed during the war.

Shore bombardment in support of amphibious landings became an important duty of the battleship in both the European and Pacific theatres of war. In 1942 at Guadalcanal, American and Japanese battleships were engaged, but it was in 1944 at Leyte Gulf that a major confrontation occurred, the last time two lines of opposing battleships met in combat. Ironically these all were ships built during World War 1.

The large 'Midway' class carriers were completed after the war. Larger ships able to handle larger aircraft were developed, the 'Forrestal' class of attack or super carriers appearing in the 1950s. New developments included angled flightdecks and steam catapults, but the major innovation was nuclear propulsion. The nuclear-powered aircraft carrier *Enterprise* was, on completion in 1961, the largest warship ever built. Since then, six additional nuclear-powered carriers have been built or begun, as well as eight conventionally powered supercarriers.

Although aircraft carriers replaced battleships as the capital ships of the fleet, only the United States has retained any battleships.

The *New Jersey* was briefly in service off Vietnam in 1968-69 as a gunnery support vessel. All four 'Iowa' class battleships were authorised to be recommissioned, with *New Jersey* the first in 1982.

Class Details

'New Ironsides' (1861)

Broadside Ship: *New Ironsides*
Displacement: 4,120tons
Dimensions: 232(oa)×57'6×15'8 [70.7(oa)×17.6×4.8]
Machinery: 1 screw, horizontal direct-acting engines (Merrick), 4 boilers
IHP 700 = 8knots
Armament: 14 or 16×11" (279mm) SB, 2×8" (203mm) 100pdr MLR, 4×24pdr howitzers
Armour: Sides 4" (102mm), c/t 10" (254mm)
Complement: 460
Class notes: Wood hull, bark rig, with ram bow. Draft too

great for inshore operations but ship was too slow for sea duty. Rigging was removed for combat. Proved almost invulnerable to enemy fire

'Monitor' (1861)

Monitor: *Monitor* (see later photo)
Displacement: 987tons
Dimensions: 172(oa)×41′6×10′6 [52.4(oa)×12.6×3.2]
Machinery: 1 screw, vibrating-lever engines (Delamater), 2 boilers
IHP 320 = 9knots
Armament: 2×11″ (279mm) SB
Armour: Turret 8″ (203mm), sides 4.5″ (114mm), pilot house 9″ (229mm)
Complement: 49
Class notes: Designed by Ericsson, a truly revolutionary design with a single turret on a flat deck. The first warship without rigging or sails having a flat-bottomed hull protected from gunfire and ramming. Extremely small freeboard to minimise area as a target limited its use outside of protected waters. Its emergence from combat with the Confederate ironclad *Virginia*, virtually undamaged and in control of the area, made obsolete all unarmoured vessels

'Dunderberg' (1862)

Ironclad Ram: *[Dunderberg]*
Displacement: 7,060tons
Dimensions: 377′4(oa) 358′8(pp)×72′10×21 [115(oa) 109.3(pp)×22.2×6.4]
Machinery: 1 screw, horizontal back-acting engines (Etna), 6 boilers
IHP 4,500 = 11.5 knots
Armament: 4×15″ (381mm) SB, 8×11″ (279mm) SB
Armour: Sides 3.5″ (89mm), casemates 4.5″ (114mm)
Complement: 590
Class notes: Designed by Lenthall. Originally designed with two turrets, but US armament never fitted. Similar to Confederate *Virginia* with battery in armoured casemate with sloping sides. Had double bottom and transverse bulkheads. Was the largest wood ship built. Not accepted by US Navy and returned to builder who sold the ship to France

'Roanoke' (1862)

Monitor: *Roanoke*
Displacement: 6,300tons
Dimensions: 265(oa)×52′6×23′6 [80.8(oa)×16×7.2]
Machinery: 1 screw, horizontal direct-acting trunk engines (Tredegar), 4 boilers
IHP 1,000 = 6knots
Armament: 2×150pdr, 2×15″ (381mm) SB, 2×11″ (279mm)
Armour: Sides 4.5″ (114mm), turrets 11″ (279mm), pilot house 9″ (229mm), deck 1.5″ (38mm)
Complement: 350
Class notes: Wood screw frigate cut down to gun deck and armour plated. Designed for four turrets on the centreline but only three could be mounted, which the hull was too weak to support. Each turret contained a combination of calibre of guns. An unsuccessful conversion with too deep a draft

'Puritan' (1862)

Monitor: *[Puritan]*
Displacement: 4,912tons
Dimensions: 340(oa)×50×21 [103.6(oa)×15.2×6.4]
Machinery: 2 screws, vibrating-lever engines (Allaire), 6 boilers
IHP —— = 15knots
Armament: 2×20″ (508mm) SB
Armour: Sides 6″ (152mm), turret 15″ (381mm), pilot house 12″ (305mm)
Class notes: Originally designed as a double-turret monitor but redesigned by Ericsson. Never completed because of delay in casting guns. Enlarged 'Dictator' type with iron hull. Incomplete hull officially repaired becoming a new vessel, BM-1

'Dictator' (1862)

Monitor: *Dictator*
Displacement: 4,438tons
Dimensions: 312(pp)×50×20′6 [95.1(pp)×15.2×6.2]
Machinery: 1 screw, vibrating-lever engines (Delamater), 6 boilers
IHP 1,000 = 15knots
Armament: 2×15″ (381mm) SB
Armour: Sides 11″ (279mm), turret 15″ (381mm), pilot house 12″ (305mm), deck 1.5″ (38mm)
Complement: 174
Class notes: Designed by Ericsson as a seagoing monitor with no overhang at bows, but did not reach contract speed. Single turret and single funnel on iron hull. The largest monitor completed during the Civil War. Spar torpedo fitted 1873

'Onondaga' (1862)

Monitor: *Onondaga* (see later photo)
Displacement: 2,592tons
Dimensions: 226′6(oa)×49′3×13 [69(oa)×15×4]
Machinery: 2 screws, horizontal back-acting engines (Morgan), 4 boilers
IHP 650 = 7knots
Armament: 2×150pdr rifles, 2×15″ (381mm) SB
Armour: Sides 5.5″ (140mm), turrets 11.75″ (298mm), deck 1″ (25mm)
Complement: 130
Class notes: Designed by George Quintard with iron hull. First double turret monitor completed for service. After active service during the Civil War was returned to builder and sold to France

'Passaic' Class (1862)

Monitors: *Camanche* (see later photo), *Catskill, Lehigh, Montauk, Nahant, Nantucket, Passaic, Patapsco, Sangamon, Weehawken*
Displacement: 1,875tons
Dimensions: 200(pp)×46×11′6 [61(pp)×14×3.5]
Machinery: 1 screw, trunk engines (*Camanche* and *Weehawken:* Fulton; *Catskill, Montauk* and *Passaic:* Delamater; *Lehigh* and *Sangamon:* Morris; *Nahant:* Loring; *Nantucket:* Atlantic; *Patapsco:* Harlan), 2 boilers
IHP 340 = 7knots
Armament: 1×15″ (381mm), 1×11″ (279mm)
Camanche: 2×15″ (381mm) SB
Patapsco: 1×150pdr, 1×15″ (381mm) SB
All, post 1875: 2×15″
Armour: Sides 5″ (127mm), turret 11″ (279mm), pilot house 8″ (203mm), deck 1″ (25mm)
Complement: 88
Class notes: Designed by Ericsson. Enlarged version of original *Monitor* with taller funnel. Following completion *Camanche* was shipped in pieces to the west coast

Above left:

***New Ironsides* — A rare photograph of the most powerful ship of the Federal navy during the Civil War.** *Smithsonian Institution*

Above right:

***Roanoke* — Former screw frigate cut down and armour plated. Each turret carried a combination of different calibre guns — notice varying size of gunports. At left is ship-of-the-line *Vermont*, the receiving ship at Brooklyn Navy Yard.** *Official Naval History*

Left:

***Jason* — Monitor of 'Passaic' class, c1898. Note low freeboard.** *US Navy*

Below left:

***Canonicus* — 'Canonicus' class monitor, 1904, at the Jamestown Exposition.** *US Navy*

Below:

***Tonawanda* — Double turret monitor, off Annapolis, c1870, with canvas awnings on the turrets. Its turrets were closer together than others of the class.** *Official Naval History*

Bottom:

A 'Kalamazoo' class monitor. Official sketch, the only known illustration of this class, none of which was built.

'Canonicus' Class (1862)

Monitors: *Canonicus, [Catawba], Mahopac* (see later photo), *Manayunk, Manhattan, [Oneota], Saugus, Tecumseh, Tippecanoe*
Displacement: 2,100tons
Dimensions: 235(oa)×43′6×13′6 [71.6(oa)×13.3×4.1] *Catawba* and *Oneota:* 225(oa), *Tippecanoe:* 224(oa), *Mahopac, Manhattan* and *Tecumseh:* 223(oa)
Machinery: 1 screw, vibrating-lever engines (*Canonicus:* Loring; *Catawba* and *Oneota:* Swift Evans; *Mahopac, Manhattan* and *Tecumseh:* Fulton; *Manayunk:* Snowden; *Saugus:* Harlan; *Tippecanoe:* Greenwood), 2 boilers
IHP 320 = 8knots
Armament: 2×15″ (381mm) SB
Armour: Sides 5″ (127mm), turret 10″ (254mm), pilot house 10″ (254mm)
Complement: 85
Class notes: Improved 'Passaic' class with armour protection around turret base and increased armament. *Oneota* and *Catawba* were never commissioned and sold to Peru. *Tippecanoe* saw no active service. *Canonicus* and *Wyandotte* (ex-*Tippecanoe*) had main deck raised 15″ 1874. *Ajax* (ex-*Manayunk*), *Mahopac* and *Manhattan* fitted with spar torpedo 1873

'Miantonomoh' Class (1862)

Monitors: *Agamenticus* (see later photo), *Miantonomoh, Monadnock, Tonawanda*
Displacement: 3,400tons; *Agamenticus* and *Monadnock:* 3,295tons
Dimensions: 250(oa)×53′8×12′3 [76.2(oa)×16.4×3.7]; *Tonawanda:* 259′6(oa)×52′10×13′5 [79.1(oa)×16.1×4.1]; *Miantonomoh:* Beam 50×14′9 [15.2×4.5]
Machinery: 2 screws, horizontal back-acting engines (*Miantonomoh:* Novelty; *Tonawanda:* Merrick); *Agamenticus* and *Monadnock:* vibrating-lever engines (Morris Towne); 4 boilers
IHP 1,400 = 9knots; *Miantonomoh:* IHP 800
Armament: 4×15″ (381mm) SB
Armour: Sides 5″ (127mm), turrets 11″ (279mm), pilot house 8″ (203mm)
Complement: 150

Class notes: Designed by Lenthall as double turreted monitors with wood hulls. *Miantonomoh* and *Tonawanda* engined by Isherwood, others by Ericsson. Only *Monadnock* completed in time to see active service during the Civil War, but it and *Miantonomoh* both made long ocean voyages. All officially repaired becoming new vessels as BM-2 to BM-5

'Kalamazoo' Class (1863)

Monitors: *[Kalamazoo, Passaconaway, Quinsigamond, Shackamaxon]*
Displacement: 5,660tons
Dimensions: 345'5(oa) 332'6(pp)×56'8×17'6 [105.3(oa) 101.3(pp)×17.3×5.3]
Machinery: 2 screws, horizontal direct-acting engines (Delamater; *Quinsigamond:* Atlantic; *Shackamaxon:* Pusey), 8 boilers
IHP —— = 10knots
Armament: 4×15" (381mm) SB
Armour: Sides 6" (152mm), turrets 10" (254mm)
Class notes: Designed by Delano and engined by Baird. Wood hulls, built of poorly seasoned timber, deteriorated rapidly on slips. The largest vessels ordered during the Civil War other than *Dunderberg* but none was ever launched

'Puritan' (1874)

Monitor: *Puritan* (BM-1)
Displacement: 6,060tons
Dimensions: 296'3(oa) 290'3(wl)×60'2×20 [90.3(oa) 88.5(wl)×18.3×6.1]
Machinery: 2 screws, horizontal compound engines (Morgan), 8 Scotch boilers
IHP 3,700 = 12.5knots
Endurance: 1,140/10
Armament: 4×12" (305mm)/35, 6×4" (102mm)/40, 6×6 pdr
Armour: Belt 6-14" (150-356mm), turrets 8" (203mm), c/t 10" (254mm), deck 2.5" (63mm)
Complement: 229
Class notes: A new vessel carried on the list as the original *Puritan* of 1862 'repaired' as funds for new construction had not been appropriated. Iron hull with low freeboard, two twin turrets, single funnel and military mainmast

Above:
***Puritan* (BM-1) — Monitor, on completion 1897; it had taken 20 years to build.**

Above right:
***Miantonomah* (BM-5) — Monitor; *Terror* had lower funnel.**

Right:
***Texas* — Battleship of 1886, as completed 1895. Starboard turret was aft of funnel.**

'Amphitrite' Class (1874)

Monitors: *Amphitrite* (BM-2), *Miantonomah* (BM-5) (see later photo), *Monadnock* (BM-3), *Terror* (BM-4)
Displacement: 3,990tons
Dimensions: 262'9(oa)×55'10×14'6 [80(oa)×17×4.4]
Machinery: 2 screws, inclined compound engines (builders; *BM-5:* Morgan), 6 Scotch boilers (*BM-2:* 4 B&W); *BM-3:* HTE engines (Mare Island), 4 Scotch boilers
IHP 1,600 = 12knots; *BM-3:* IHP 3,000 = 14knots
Endurance: 1,300/10
Armament: 4×10" (254mm)/30, 2×4" (102mm)/40, 2×6pdr
BM-5: 4×10"/35, 2×6pdr
Armour: Belt 4-7" (102-178mm) (*BM-2:* 5-9"/127-229mm), turrets 11.5" (292mm) (*BM-2* and *BM-3:* 7.5"/190mm), c/t 10" (254mm), deck 2" (51mm)
Complement: 155
Class notes: As *Puritan* they were officially 'repaired' old vessels from 1862. Two twin turrets, single funnel and military mainmast with variation among individual ships. Because of their low freeboard monitors were found unsuitable for extended operations but this quality proved them ideal for use as submarine depot ships

'Texas' (1886)

Battleship: *Texas*
Displacement: 6,315tons
Dimensions: 308'10(oa) 301'4(wl)×61'1×24'6 [94.1(oa) 91.9(wl)×19.5×7.5]
Machinery: 2 screws, VTE engines (Richmond), 4 double-ended cylindrical boilers

IHP 8,600 = 17.8knots
Endurance: 2,900/10
Armament: 2×12″ (305mm)/35, 6×6″ (152mm)/35, 12×6pdr, 4×18″ (457mm) TT (removed 1904)
Armour: Belt 8-12″ (203-305mm), bulkhead 12″ (305mm), turrets 12″ (305mm) deck 3″ (76mm), c/t 9″ (229mm)
Complement: 392
Class notes: Based on foreign designs with speed sacrificed for firepower. Two single turrets amidships arranged en echelon. Single funnel raised 1902

'Maine' (1886)

Battleship: *Maine* (see later photo)
Displacement: 6,682tons
Dimensions: 324′4(oa) 318(wl)×57×21′6 [98.8(oa) 96.9(wl)×17.4×6.6]
Machinery: 2 screws, VTE engines (Quintard), 8 cylindrical boilers
IHP 9,000 = 17knots
Endurance: 3,600/10
Armament: 4×10″ (254mm)/30, 6×6″ (152mm)/30, 7×6pdr, 4×18″ (457mm) TT
Armour: Belt 6-11″ (152-279mm), turrets 8″ (203mm), barbettes 12″ (305mm), c/t 10″ (254mm), deck 2-4″ (51-102mm)
Complement: 374
Class notes: Authorised as armoured cruiser, an enlarged copy of Brazilian *Riachuelo*. Originally bark rigged but mizzen mast removed in 1892 prior to completion, which was delayed by late delivery of armour. Two twin turrets arranged en echelon amidships

'New York' (1888)

Armoured Cruiser: *New York* (CA-2) (see also later photo)
Displacement: 8,150tons
Dimensions: 384(oa) 380′6(wl)×64′10×26′8 [117(oa) 116(wl)×19.8×8.1]
Machinery: 2 screws, VTE engines (Cramp), 8 cylindrical boilers; *1907:* 12 B&W boilers
IHP 16,000 = 21knots
Armament: 6×8″ (203mm)/35, 12×4″ (102mm)/40, 8×6pdr, 3×14″ (356mm) TT
1904: 4×8″/45, 10×5″/50, 8×3″, no TT
1917: 4×8″/45, 8×5″/50, 2×3″ AA
Armour: Belt 4″ (102mm), barbettes 4-6″ (102-152mm), turrets 6.5″ (165mm), deck 6″ (152mm), c/t 7″ (178mm)
Complement: 566
Class notes: An excellent ship, designed with two funnels but completed with three. Main guns in two twin turrets fore and aft and one on each beam in shields. Reconstructed 1903-04,

rearmed, new armour and boilers and funnels raised. Again rebuilt 1932 when boilers were reduced and one funnel removed

'Monterey' (1889)

Monitor: *Monterey* (BM-6)
Displacement: 4,084tons
Dimensions: 260'11(oa) 256'1(wl)×59×14'10 [79.5(oa) 78(wl)×18×4.5]
Machinery: 2 screws, VTE engines (Union), 4 Ward & Scotch boilers; *1904:* 4 B&W boilers
IHP 5,400 = 13.5knots
Endurance: 1,430/10
Armament: 2×12" (305mm)/35, 2×10" (254mm)/35, 6×6pdr
Armour: Belt 6-13" (152-330mm), 12" turret 14" (355mm), 10" turret 11.5" (292mm), deck 2" (51mm), c/t 10" (254mm)
Complement: 250
Class notes: Original designed armament of 1×16" (110tons) and 1×12" guns in barbettes and 1×5" dynamite gun in bow was too heavy and lighter armament was substituted. Two turrets with 12" guns forward and 10" aft

'Indiana' Class (1890)

Pre-dreadnougths: *Indiana* (BB-1), *Massachusetts* (BB-2) (see also later photo), *Oregon* (BB-3)
Displacement: 10,288tons, 11,688f/l
Dimensions: 350'11(oa) 348(wl)×69'3×27 [107(oa) 106.1(wl)×21.1×8.2]; *BB-3:* 351'2 [107(oa)]
Machinery: 2 screws, VTE engines, 4 Scotch boilers; *BB-1* and *BB-2, 1908:* 8 B&W
IHP 9,000 = 15.5knots
Endurance: 4,500/10
Armament: 4×13" (330mm)/35, 8×8" (203mm)/35, 4×6" (152mm)/40, 20×6pdr, 3×18" (457mm) TT (*BB-1:* 4)
1908-10: 12×3"/50 replaced 4×6"
c1908: TT removed
1918: 8×3" removed
Armour: Belt 15-18" (381-457mm), bulkheads 17" (432mm), turrets 15" (381mm), barbettes 17" (432mm), deck 3" (76mm), c/t 10" (254mm)
Complement: 650
Class notes: Authorised as coast defence battleships, they had low freeboard which prevented fighting the main battery in a seaway. Rolled heavily before fitting of bilge keels. Had heavier gun power and thicker armour than contemporary foreign ships. Two twin turrets fore and aft, two funnels and military foremast. Funnels raised 1900; cage mainmast fitted 1909-11

'Iowa' (1892)

Pre-dreadnought: *Iowa* (BB-4) (see also later photo)
Displacement: 11,410tons, 12,647f/l
Dimensions: 362'5(oa) 360(wl)×72'3×26'9 [110.5(oa) 109.7(wl)×22×8.2]
Machinery: 2 screws, VTE engines (Cramp), 5 cylindrical boilers (3 d/e, 2 s/e)
IHP 11,000 = 16knots
Endurance: 4,500/10
Armament: 4×12" (305mm)/35, 8×8" (203mm)/35, 6×4" (102mm)/40, 20×6pdr, 4×14" (356mm) TT
1906: TT removed
1910: 4×4" added
1918: 4×4" AA replaced old 4"
Armour: Belt 11-14" (279-356mm), bulkhead 12" (305mm), turrets 14" (356mm), deck 3" (76mm), c/t 10" (254mm)
Complement: 486
Class notes: Improved 'Indiana' type with decreased main battery and greater freeboard. Two tall funnels and single military mast forward. Reconstructed 1908, cage mainmast added

'Brooklyn' (1892)

Armoured Cruiser: *Brooklyn* (CA-3)
Displacement: 9,215tons, 10,068f/l
Dimensions: 402'7(oa) 400'6(wl)×64'8×28 [122.7(oa) 122.1(wl)×19.7×8.5]
Machinery: 2 screws, VTE engines (Cramp), 7 cylindrical boilers
IHP 16,000 = 20knots
Endurance: 7,500/10
Armament: 8×8" (203mm)/35, 12×5" (127mm)/40, 12×6pdr, 5×18" (457mm) TT
1909: TT removed
1918: Only 8×5" and 4×6pdr, 2×3" AA added
Armour: Belt 3" (76mm), barbettes 8" (203mm), deck 3-6" (76-152mm), c/t 7.5" (190mm)
Complement: 561
Class notes: Noticeable French influence in design which included ram bow, cruiser stern, pronounced tumblehome and great freeboard. Three tall funnels and two military masts; turrets arranged on French style one each fore and aft and one on each beam. Modernised 1909

'Kearsarge' Class (1895)

Pre-dreadnoughts: *Kearsarge* (BB-5), *Kentucky* (BB-6)
Displacement: 11,540tons, 12,905f/l
Dimensions: 375'4(oa) 368(wl)×72'3×26'2 [114.4(oa) 112.2(wl)×22×8]
Machinery: 2 screws, VTE engines (Newport News), 5 cylindrical boilers (3 d/e, 2 s/e), 8 Mosher boilers
IHP 10,000 = 16knots
Endurance: 5,300/10
Armament: 4×13" (330mm)/35, 4×8" (203mm)/35, 14×5" (127mm)/40, 20×6pdr, 4×18" (457mm) TT
1907: 8×6pdr and TT removed
1910: 4×5" added
By 1919: 10×5" and all 6pdr removed, 2×3"/50 AA added
Armour: Belt 4-16.5" (102-419mm), turrets 15-17" (381-432mm), 8" turrets 11" (279mm), bulkheads 10-12" (254-305mm), battery 5.5" (140mm), deck 4" (102mm), c/t 10" (254mm)
Complement: 554
Class notes: A new design which introduced superposed turrets with the secondary armament in turrets directly on top of the main turrets. Cagemasts replaced both military masts in 1912

'Illinois' Class (1896)

Pre-dreadnoughts: *Alabama* (BB-8), *Illinois* (BB-7) (see later photo), *Wisconsin* (BB-9) (see later photo)
Displacement: 11,565tons, 12,595f/l
Dimensions: 375'4(oa) 368(wl)×72'3×25 [114.4(oa) 112.2(wl)×22×7.6]; *BB-8:* 374 [114(oa)]
Machinery: 2 screws, VTE engines (builders), 8 cylindrical boilers (s/e); *BB-7, 1912:* 8 Mosher boilers
IHP 10,000 = 16knots
Endurance: 4,400/10
Armament: 4×13" (330mm)/35, 14×6" (152mm)/40, 16×6pdr, 4×18" (457mm) TT
1907: TT removed
1912: 4×3" added (removed 1917)
By 1918: 6×6" removed, 2×3"/50 AA added

Armour: Belt 4-16.5″ (102-419mm), turrets 14″ (355mm), barbettes 10-15″ (254-381mm), bulkheads 12″ (305mm), casemates 6″ (152mm), deck 4″ (102mm), c/t 10″ (254mm)
Complement: 681
Class notes: Similar to 'Kearsarge' class without superposed 8″ turrets and with two funnels abreast. Aft turret one deck lower than forward turret. Military foremast replaced by cagemast in 1909 and mainmast in *Wisconsin* replaced 1911 and in others in 1912

'Maine' Class (1898)

Pre-dreadnoughts: *Maine* (BB-10), *Missouri* (BB-11), *Ohio* (BB-12)
Displacement: 12,500tons, 13,500f/l
Dimensions: 393′10(oa) 388(wl)×72′3×26′8 [120(oa) 118.3(wl)×22×8.1]
Machinery: 2 screws, VTE engines (builders), 12 Thornycroft boilers (*BB-10*: 24 Niclausse); *BB-10, 1910:* 12 B&W boilers
IHP 16,000 = 18knots
Endurance: 4,900/10
Armament: 4×12″ (305mm)/40, 16×6″ (152mm)/50, 6×3″ (76mm)/50, 8×3pdr, 2×18″ (457mm) TT
By 1918: 6×6″ and 3″ removed, 2×3″/50 AA added
Armour: Belt 4-11″ (102-279mm), turrets 12″ (305mm), barbettes 8-12″ (203-305mm), battery 6″ (152mm), bulkhead 10″ (254mm), deck 3″ (76mm), c/t 10″ (254mm)
Complement: 799
Class notes: Improved 'Illinois' class with three tall funnels and electrically powered turrets. Military masts replaced by cagemasts 1909-11. First US battleships with submerged TT and watertube boilers

'Arkansas' Class (1898)

Monitors: *Arkansas* (BM-7), *Florida* (BM-9), *Nevada* (BM-8), *Wyoming* (BM-10) (see later photo)
Displacement: 3,225tons
Dimensions: 255′1(oa) 252(pp)×50×12′6 [77.8(oa) 76.8(pp)×15.2×3.8]
Machinery: 2 screws, VTE engines, 4 boilers (*BM-7:* Thornycroft; *BM-8:* Niclausse; *BM-9:* Mosher; *BM-10:* B&W)
IHP 2,400 = 12.5knots
Endurance: 1,680/10
Armament: 2×12″ (305mm)/40, 4×4″ (102mm)/50, 3×6pdr
1918: 2×3″ AA added
Armour: Belt 5-11″ (127-279mm), turret and barbette 11″ (279mm), deck 1.5″ (38mm), c/t 8″ (203mm)
Complement: 171
Class notes: Built for harbour defence, but of little value and used later as submarine depot ships

'Virginia' Class (1899-1900)

Pre-dreadnoughts: *Georgia* (BB-15), *Nebraska* (BB-14) (see later photo), *New Jersey* (BB-16), *Rhode Island* (BB-17), *Virginia* (BB-13) (see later photo)
Displacement: 14,948tons, 16,094f/l
Dimensions: 441′3(oa) 435(wl)×76′3×23′9 [134.5(oa) 132.6(wl)×23.2×7.2]
Machinery: 2 screws, VTE engines (builders), 12 B&W boilers (*BB-13* and *BB-15:* 24 Niclausse); *1916:* All had B&W boilers
IHP 19,000 = 19knots
Endurance: 4,920/10
Armament: 4×12″ (305mm)/40, 8×8″ (203mm)/45, 12×6″ (152mm)/50, 12×3″ (76mm)/50, 12×3pdr (*BB-16* and *BB-17*), 4×21″ (533mm) TT
By 1918: 6″ and 6×3″ removed, 2×3″/50 AA added
Armour: Belt 4-11″ (102-279mm), turrets 8-12″ (203-305mm), barbettes 7-10″ (178-254mm), deck 3″ (76mm), c/t 9″ (229mm)
Complement: 905
Class notes: Superposed 8″ turrets reintroduced, which caused excessive rolling. Two twin turrets fore and aft with twin turrets for secondary armament fore and aft and on each beam. Three funnels and two military masts. Torpedo tubes added after completion. Cagemasts installed 1910-11 and strengthened 1918. Casemate guns removed 1917

'Pennsylvania' Class (1899-1900)

Armoured Cruisers: *California* (CA-6) (see later photo), *Colorado* (CA-7), *Maryland* (CA-8), *Pennsylvania* (CA-4) (see also later photo), *South Dakota* (CA-9) (see later photo), *West Virginia* (CA-5)
Displacement: 13,680tons
Dimensions: 504(oa) 502(wl)×69′7×24′1 [153.6(oa) 153(wl)×21.2×7.3]
Machinery: 2 screws, VTE engines (builders), 16 B&W boilers (*CA-4* and *CA-7:* 20 Niclausse, replaced by B&W 1904)
IHP 23,000 = 22knots
Armament: 4×8″ (203mm)/45, 14×6″ (152mm)/50, 18×3″ (76mm)/50, 12×3pdr, 2×18″ (457mm) TT
By 1918: 10×6″ and 8×3″ removed, 2×3″/50 AA added
Armour: Belt 3.5-6″ (89-152mm), turrets 4-6.5″ (102-165mm), deck 4″ (102mm), casemates 6″ (162mm), c/t 9″ (229mm)
Complement: 829
Class notes: Armour and firepower sacrificed for slight increases in speed. Only two twin turrets fore and aft and secondary guns in casemates. Four funnels and two military masts. Military foremast replaced by cagemast 1918. *Pennsylvania* had forward funnel removed c1926

'Connecticut' Class (1902-1904)

Pre-dreadnoughts: *Connecticut* (BB-18) (see later photo), *Kansas* (BB-21) (see later photo), *Louisiana* (BB-19), *Minnesota* (BB-22), *New Hampshire* (BB-25) (see later photo), *Vermont* (BB-20) (see later photo)
Displacement: 16,000tons, 17,666f/l
Dimensions: 456′4(oa) 450(wl)×76′10×24′6 [139.1(oa) 137.2(wl)×23.4×7.5]
Machinery: 2 screws, VTE engines (builders), 12 B&W boilers
IHP 16,500 = 18knots
Endurance: 5,000/10
Armament: 4×12″ (305mm)/45, 8×8″ (203mm)/45, 12×7″ (178mm)/45, 20×3″ (76mm)/50, 12×3pdr (*BB-18:* 8; *BB-25:* none)
1909: 4×21″ (533mm) TT added
By 1918: 7″ and 8×3″ removed 2×3″/50 AA added
Armour: Belt 4-9″ (102-229mm) (*BB-18* and *BB-19:* 4-11″/102-279mm), turrets 8-12″ (203-305mm), barbettes 10″ (254mm), battery 7″ (178mm), deck 3″ (76mm), c/t 9″ (229mm)
Complement: 961
Class notes: Improved 'Virginia' class with 8″ guns in turrets amidships and not superposed. *Connecticut* and *Louisiana* differed in details of armour. Torpedo tubes added after completion; military masts replaced by cagemasts 1909-11. Casemate guns removed 1918

Above left:
Rochester* (CA-2) — Armoured cruiser, at Plymouth, May 1919, formerly *New York. *IWM*

Above:
***Monterey* (BM-6) — A monitor which crossed the Pacific in 1898.** *Marius Bar*

Far left:
***Brooklyn* (CA-3) — Armoured cruiser, as completed. Notice distinctive three tall funnels.** *IWM*

Left:
***Kearsarge* (BB-5) — Pre-dreadnought, with superimposed turrets. A drawback was that the turrets could not turn independently.** *Official US Navy*

Below left:
***Massachusetts* (BB-2) — Battleship of 'Indiana' class, after 1910, with cage mainmast added.** *Marius Bar*

Below:
***Iowa* (BB-4) — Battleship of 1892, after refit, with cage mainmast.** *Marius Bar*

Top, left to right:
***Alabama* (BB-8) — Pre-dreadnought, with two cagemasts, c1920.**

***Maine* (BB-10) — Pre-dreadnought of 1898, with military masts replaced by cagemasts.**

***New Jersey* (BB-16) — Pre-dreadnought of 'Virginia' class, as completed 1906.** *E. Muller*

Far left:
***Pennsylvania* (CA-4) — Armoured cruiser, fitting out prior to completion, 1904.** *E. Muller*

Left:
***Louisiana* (BB-19) — 'Connecticut' class battleship of 1902, c1912.**

Bottom left:
***Washington* (CA-11) — Armoured cruiser of 'Tennessee' class, 1910.**

Bottom right:
***Mississippi* (BB-23) — Pre-dreadnought of 'Mississippi' class, 1912, sold to Greece in 1914.** *E. Muller*

'Tennessee' Class (1902-1903)

Armoured Cruisers: *Montana* (CA-13) (see later photo), *North Carolina* (CA-12), *Tennessee* (CA-10), *Washington* (CA-11)
Displacement: 14,500tons
Dimensions: 504′6(oa) 502(wl)×72′11×27′2 [153.8(oa) 153(wl)×22.2×8.3]
Machinery: 2 screws, VTE engines (builders), 16 B&W boilers
IHP 23,000 = 22knots
Armament: 4×10″ (254mm)/40, 16×6″ (152mm)/50, 22×3″ (76mm)/50, 12×3pdr, 4×21″ (533mm) TT
By 1918: 12×6″ and 10×3″ removed, 2×3″/50 AA added
Armour: Belt 3-5″ (76-127mm), turrets 5-9″ (127-229mm), barbettes 7″ (178mm), deck 5″ (127mm), c/t 9″ (229mm)
Complement: 858
Class notes: Improved 'Pennsylvania' class with heavier armour and armament. Military foremast replaced by cagemast 1911. Casemate guns removed 1917-18

'Mississippi' Class (1903)

Pre-dreadnoughts: *Idaho* (BB-24), *Mississippi* (BB-23)
Displacement: 13,000tons, 14,465f/l
Dimensions: 382(oa) 375(wl)×77×24′8 [116.4(oa) 114.3(wl)×23.5×7.5]
Machinery: 2 screws, VTE engines (Cramp), 8 B&W boilers
IHP 10,000 = 17knots
Endurance: 5,775/10
Armament: 4×12″ (305mm)/45, 8×8″ (203mm)/45, 8×7″ (178mm)/45, 12×3″ (76mm)/50, 2×21″ (533mm) TT
Armour: Belt 4-9″ (102-229mm), turrets 8-12″ (203-305mm), barbettes 7.5-10″ (190-254mm), battery 7″ (178mm), deck 3″ (76mm) c/t 9″ (229mm)
Complement: 801
Class notes: Similar to 'Connecticut' class on a smaller hull, but too slow. Completed with one military mast but cage mainmast fitted 1908 and foremast 1911. Sold to Greece 1914

'South Carolina' Class (1905)

Dreadnoughts: *Michigan* (BB-27) (see also later photo), *South Carolina* (BB-26)
Displacement: 16,000tons, 17,617f/l
Dimensions: 452′9(oa) 450(wl)×80′3×24′6 [138(oa) 137.2(wl)×24.5×7.5]
Machinery: 2 screws VTE engines (GE), 12 B&W boilers
IHP 16,500 = 18.5knots
Endurance: 5,000/10
Armament: 8×12″ (305mm)/45, 22×3″ (76mm)/50, 2×21″ (533mm) TT
1918: 8×3″ replaced by 2×3″/50 AA
Armour: Belt 9-11″ (229-279mm), turrets 8-12″ (203-305mm), barbettes 8-10″ (203-254mm), bulkhead 10″ (254mm), deck 3″ (76mm), c/t 12″ (305mm)
Complement: 869
Class notes: First battleships designed with all big guns but laid down after *Dreadnought*. First battleships with all guns on the centreline, also had superfiring turrets, features copied by all other nations. Designed with military masts but completed with cagemasts. Original planned main armament was 4×12″ and 4×10″. An accident to *Michigan's* cagemast in 1918 led to strengthening of cagemasts in all ships

'Delaware' Class (1906-1907)

Dreadnoughts: *Delaware* (BB-28) (see also later photo), *North Dakota* (BB-29)
Displacement: *BB-28:* 20,380tons; *BB-29:* 20,000tons; 22,060f/l
Dimensions: 518′9(oa) 510(wl)×85′3×28′10 [158.1(oa) 155.4(wl)×26×8.8]
Machinery: 2 screws, *BB-28:* VTE engines (Newport News); *BB-29:* Curtis turbines (Fore River); 14 B&W boilers; *BB-29, 1917:* Parsons turbines
IHP/SHP 25,000 = 21knots
Endurance: 9,000/12
Armament: 10×12″ (305mm)/45, 14×5″ (127mm)/50, 2×3pdr, 2×21″ (533mm) TT
1918: 2×3″ AA added
1921: 6×3″ AA added
Armour: Belt 3-11″ (76-279mm), turrets 8-12″ (203-305mm), barbettes 10″ (254mm), deck —, c/t 12″ (305mm)
Complement: 945
Class notes: A very successful class with larger calibre secondary armament. *North Dakota* was first US battleship with turbines (which were unsatisfactory and were replaced in 1916). Five twin turrets with three aft, two funnels, the forward one between the two cage masts

'Florida' Class (1908)

Dreadnoughts: *Florida* (BB-30) (see also later photo), *Utah* (BB-31) (see later photo)
Displacement: 21,825tons, 23,033f/l
Dimensions: 521′6(oa) 518′9(wl) 510(pp)×88′3×30′4 [159(oa) 158.1(wl) 155.4(pp)×26.9×9.1]
1928: Beam 106 [32.3]
Machinery: 4 screws, Parsons turbines (builders), 12 B&W boilers; *1924:* Curtis geared turbines, 4 White-Forster boilers
SHP 28,000 = 20.75knots
Endurance: 6,720/10
Armament: 10×12″ (305mm)/45, 16×5″ (127mm)/51, 4×3pdr, 2×21″ (533mm) TT
1917: 4×5″ replaced by 2×3″/50 AA
1921: 4×5″ and 6×3″ AA added
1928: TT removed
Armour: Belt 3-11″ (76-279mm), turrets 8-12″ (203-305mm), barbettes 11″ (279mm), c/t 12″ (305mm)
Complement: 1,000
Class notes: Improved 'Delaware' class. Main battery of 8×14″ guns in four turrets was originally proposed, but they were completed with five twin turrets. First US battleships with four shafts. Two funnels now grouped between two cagemasts. Completion delayed by changes in design and failure to deliver turbine casings. Reconstructed in 1924, new engines, new boilers, single funnel fitted and cage mainmast replaced by pole mast

'Wyoming' Class (1909)

Dreadnoughts: *Arkansas* (BB-33) (see also later photo), *Wyoming* (BB-32)
Displacement: 26,000tons, 27,243f/l; *1925:* 29,000tons, 31,000f/l
Dimensions: 562(oa) 554(wl)×93′3×28′6 [171.3(oa) 168.9(wl)×28.4×8.7]
1926: Beam 106′3×32 [32.4×9.8]
Machinery: 4 screws, Parsons turbines (*BB-32:* Cramp; *BB-33:* Newport News), 12 B&W boilers; *1926:* Parsons geared turbines, 4 White-Forster boilers
SHP 26,000 = 20.5knots; *1926:* SHP 45,000 = 21knots
Endurance: 8,000/10
Armament: 12×12″ (305mm)/50, 21×5″ (127mm)/51, 2×21″ (533mm) TT
1918: 5×5″ removed, 2×3″/5C AA added
1926: 8×3″/23 AA, no TT

BB-33, 1945: 12×12″/50, 6×5″/51, 10×3″/50, 36×40mm
Armour: Belt 5-11″ (127-279mm), turrets 9-12″ (229-305mm), barbettes 11″ (279mm), bulkheads 9-11″ (229-279mm), battery 6.5″ (165mm), c/t 12″ (305mm)
Complement: 1,063; *1926:* 1,330
Class notes: Enlarged 'Florida' class with new 12″ guns and additional turret. Distinguished by elongated quarterdeck with four turrets aft. Originally designed with combined turbine and reciprocating machinery. Reconstructed 1925, new engines and boilers, cage mainmast replaced by small tripod further aft, single funnel replaced previous two, catapult fitted to 'P' turret, secondary battery raised one deck and bulges fitted. *Wyoming* demilitarised 1932, three turrets removed. *Arkansas* modernised 1941, cage foremast replaced by tripod, elevation of main battery increased, AA armament increased and casemate battery removed

'New York' Class (1910)

Dreadnoughts: *New York* (BB-34) (see also later photos), *Texas* (BB-35) (see later photo)
Displacement: 27,000tons, 28,367f/l; *1926:* 29,500tons, 32,000f/l; *1945:* 34,000f/l
Dimensions: 572′8(oa) 565(wl)×95′3×28′6 [174.6(oa) 172.2(wl)×29×8.7]
1926: Beam 106×32′3 [32.3×9.7]
Machinery: 2 screws, VTE engines (builders), 14 B&W boilers; *1926:* 6 Bureau-Express boilers
IHP 28,100 = 21knots
Endurance: 10,000/10
Armament: 10×14″ (355mm)/45, 21×5″ (127mm)/51, 4×21″ (533mm) TT
1917: 5×5″ removed, 2×3″ AA added
1926: 8×3″/25 AA added, TT removed
By 1945: 10×14″/45, 5×5″/51, 10×3″/50, 40×40mm AA
Armour: Belt 6-12″ (152-305mm, turrets 8-14″ (203-355mm), barbettes 12″ (305mm), bulkheads 10″ (254mm), battery 6″ (152mm), deck 2″ (52mm), c/t 12″ (305mm)
Complement: 1,040; *later:* 1,314
Class notes: First 'super-dreadnoughts'. Reverted to reciprocating engines as builders refused Navy Department standards for turbines. First battleships with 14″ guns, originally designed with 15×12″. Five twin turrets. Reconstructed 1926, new boilers, cagemasts replaced by tripods and mainmast resited further aft, single funnel replaced previous two, secondary battery raised one deck, catapult added on 'Q' turret and bulges added. Modernised 1941, elevation of main battery increased, secondary battery increased

'Nevada' Class (1911)

Dreadnoughts: *Nevada* (BB-36), *Oklahoma* (BB-37) (see also later photo)
Displacement: 27,500tons, 28,400f/l; *1929:* 29,000tons, 34,000f/l
Dimensions: 583(oa) 575(wl)×95′3×28′6 [177.7(oa) 175.3(wl)×29×8.7]
1929: Beam 107′11×33′6 [32.9×10.2]
Machinery: *BB-36:* 2 screws, Curtis turbines (New York), 12 B&W boilers
SHP 26,500 = 20.5knots
BB-37: 2 screws, VTE engines (builder), 12 Yarrow boilers
IHP 24,800 = 20.5knots
BB-36, 1929: Parsons geared turbines (Fore River)
Both, 1929: 6 Bureau-Express boilers
Endurance: 10,000/10
Armament: 10×14″ (356mm)/45, 21×5″ (127mm)/51, 4×21″ (533mm) TT
1918: 9×5″ removed; 4×3″ AA added
1929: 8×5″/25 AA added, TT removed
BB-36, by 1945: 10×14″/45, 16×5″/38, 32×40mm AA
Armour: Belt 8-13.5″ (203-343mm), turrets 9-18″ (229-457mm), barbettes 4-13.5″ (102-343mm), bulkheads 13.5″ (343mm), deck 3″ (76mm), c/t 16″ (406mm)
Complement: 1,049
Class notes: Second generation dreadnoughts with 'all-or-nothing' protection. First US battleships to burn only oil fuel and with triple turrets, having same number of guns as 'New York' class in fewer turrets. Single funnel and two cagemasts; two twin turrets superfiring over two triple turrets. Reconstructed 1927-30, new engines and boilers, cagemasts replaced by tripods, secondary battery raised one deck, catapults added on 'X' turret and stern, bulges added. *Nevada* reconstructed again 1942, mainmast removed, smaller foremast and funnel cap fitted, new secondary and AA armament

'Pennsylvania' Class (1912-1913)

Dreadnoughts: *Arizona* (BB-39) (see later photo), *Pennsylvania* (BB-38) (see also later photo)
Displacement: 31,400tons, 32,567f/l
BB-38, 1931: 33,100tons; *BB39, 1931:* 32,600tons; 36,500f/l
Dimensions: 608(oa) 600(wl)×97′1×28′10 [185.3(oa) 182.9(wl)×29.6×8.8]
1931: Beam 106′3×34 [32.4×10.4]; *BB-38, 1945:* 612′3 [186.6(oa)]
Machinery: 4 screws, Curtis (*BB-38*) and Parsons (*BB-39*) geared turbines, (*BB-38:* Westinghouse, *BB-39:* builder), 12 B&W boilers; *BB-38, 1931:* 5 Bureau-Express and 1 White-Forster boilers; *BB-39, 1931:* 6 Bureau-Express boilers
SHP 31,500 (*BB-39:* 34,000) = 21knots
Endurance: 10,000/10
Armament: 12×14″ (355mm)/45, 22×5″ (127mm)/51, 2×21″ (533mm) TT
1918: 8×5″ removed, 4×3″ AA added
1931: 8×5″/25 AA added, TT removed
BB-38, 1943: 12×14″, 16×5″/38, 40×40mm AA
Armour: Belt 8-13.5″ (203-343mm), turrets 9-18″ (229-457mm), barbettes 14″ (356mm), bulkheads 14″ (356mm), deck 4″ (102mm), c/t 16″ (406mm)
Complement: 915; *1931:* 1,358
Class notes: Improved 'Nevada' class with four triple turrets. Did not serve overseas in World War 1 because of shortage of tankers for oil fuel. Reconstructed 1920-33, new engines and boilers, cagemasts replaced by tripods, secondary battery raised one deck, catapults fitted on 'X' turret and stern, AA armament increased, bulges added.
Pennsylvania modernised 1942, tripod mainmast replaced by light pole post, heavy cranes and catapult removed from 'X' turret, new secondary and AA armament

'New Mexico' Class (1914)

Dreadnoughts: *Idaho* (BB-42) (see later photo), *Mississippi* (BB-41) (see later photo), *New Mexico* (BB-40)
Displacement: 32,000tons, 33,000f/l; *1933:* 33,400tons; *BB-41, 1933:* 33,000tons, 36,000f/l
Dimensions: 624(oa) 600(wl)×97′5×30 [190.2(oa) 182.9(wl)×29.7×9.1] *1933:* Beam 106′3×34′3 [32.4×10.4]
Machinery: 4 screws, Curtis (*BB-41*) and Parsons (*BB-42*) geared turbines, 9 B&W boilers
SHP 32,000 = 21knots
BB-40: Turbo-electric drive (Westinghouse), 9 B&W boilers
SHP 27,500 = 21knots

U.S.S DELAWARE

Top, left to right:
Michigan (BB-27) — Dreadnought, with strengthened cagemasts. *N. Moser*

Delaware (BB-28) — Dreadnought of 'Delaware' class, c1914.

Florida (BB-30) — Battleship, after 1924 reconstruction, with single funnel and pole mainmast. *IWM*

Above left:
Arkansas (BB-33) — Battleship, June 1934, as reconstructed with tripod mainmast and single funnel.

Above right:
New York (BB-34) — Battleship of 'New York' class, with the Grand Fleet 1918. *IWM*

Far left:
New York (BB-34) — Battleship, July 1938, as reconstructed, with tripod masts and single funnel.
Wright & Logan

Left:
Nevada (BB-36) — Battleship, June 1944, off Normandy, showing wartime reconstruction. *IWM*

Left, top to bottom:

***Nevada* (BB-36) — Battleship of 'Nevada' class, in the 1930s, after reconstruction. *Oklahoma* did not have topmost level on mainmast.**

***Oklahoma* (BB-37) — 'Nevada' class battleship, c1925.** *IWM*

***Pennsylvania* (BB-38) — Battleship of 'Pennsylvania' class, prior to reconstruction, c1921.**

Above, top to bottom:

***New Mexico* (BB-40) — Battleship of 'New Mexico' class, c1925, as fleet flagship.** *D. W. Waterman*

***Tennessee* (BB-43) — Battleship of 'Tennessee' class, as reconstructed 1943, at Capetown, November 1945.** *T. Rayner*

***West Virginia* (BB-48) — Battleship of 'Colorado' class, 1941.** *Ted Stone*

All, 1933: Westinghouse geared turbines, 6 Bureau-Express boilers; *BB-40, 1933:* 4 White-Forster boilers
SHP 40,000 = 22knots
Endurance: 10,000/10
Armament: 12×14" (356mm)/50, 14×5" (127mm)/51, 4×3" (76mm)/50, 2×21" (533mm) TT
1933: 2×5"/51 removed, 8×5"/25 AA added, TT removed
By 1945: 12×14"/50, 6×5"/51, 8×5"/25, 40×40mm
BB-42, by 1945: 12×14"/50, 10×5"/38, 40×40mm
Armour: Belt 8-13.5" (203-343mm), turrets 9-18" (229-457mm), barbettes 14" (356mm), deck 6" (152mm), c/t 16" (406mm)
Complement: 1,080
Class notes: Similar hull to 'Pennsylvania' class with clipper bow and improved compartmentation. *New Mexico* was first major vessel with turbo-electric drive for speed reduction between engines and shafts. Reconstructed 1930-34, cagemasts removed and replaced by increased superstructure, re-engined with new geared turbines, secondary armament raised one deck, catapults and bulges added. *New Mexico* received boilers from discarded *Florida*. All were to receive 16×5"/38 DP guns in twin turrets but only *Idaho* was so fitted in 1944

'Tennessee' Class (1915)

Dreadnoughts: *California* (BB-44) (see later photo), *Tennessee* (BB-43)
Displacement: 32,300tons, 33,190f/l; *1943:* 37,000tons, 40,300f/l
Dimensions: 624'6(oa) 600(wl)×97'4×30'3 [190.3(oa) 182.9(wl)×29.7×9.2]; *1943:* Beam 114×34 [34.7×10.4]
Machinery: 4 screws, turbo-electric drive (*BB-43:* Westinghouse; *BB-44:* GE), 8 B&W boilers (*BB-43),* 8 Bureau-Express boilers (*BB-44*)
SHP 26,800 (*BB-44:* 28,500) = 21knots
Endurance: 10,000/10
Armament: 12×14" (355mm)/50, 14×5" (127mm)/51, 4×3" (76mm)/50, 2×21" (533mm) TT
1922: 2×5" replaced by 4×3" AA
1928: 8×5"/25 AA replaced 3" AA
1935: TT removed
1943: 12×14", 16×5"/38, 40×40mm
Armour: Belt 8-13.5" (203-343mm), turrets 9-18" (229-457mm), barbettes 13" (330mm), deck 3.5" (89mm), c/t 16" (406mm)
Complement: 1,083; *later:* 1,480
Class notes: Repeat 'New Mexico' class with hull line clear of gunports and two thin funnels. Little changed prior to World War 2, reconstruction as 'New Mexico' class was planned for 1940s. *California* sunk at Pearl Harbour. *Tennessee* had cage mainmast replaced by small tower 1942. Both completely reconstructed 1943, tower foremast and massive single funnel fitted, new secondary and AA armament, blisters added to hull

'Colorado' Class (1916)

Dreadnoughts: *Colorado* (BB-45), *Maryland* (BB-46) (see later photo), *[Washington]* (BB-47), *West Virginia* (BB-48)
Displacement: 32,600tons, 33,590f/l; *BB-45, 1937:* 32,500tons; *BB-46, 1937:* 31,500tons; *BB-48, 1937:* 31,800tons, *BB-45* and *BB-46, 1943:* 34,000tons, 39,100f/l; *BB-48, 1943:* 37,800tons, 40,350f/l
Dimensions: 624(oa) 600(wl)×97'6×30'6 [190.2(oa) 182.9(wl)×29.7×9.3]; *BB-45* and *BB-46, 1943:* Beam 108'1×34'9 [32.9×10.6]; *BB-48, 1944:* Beam 114×34 [34.7×10.4]
Machinery: 4 screws, turbo-electric drive (*BB-45* and *BB-47:* Westinghouse; *BB-46* and *BB-48:* GE), 8 B&W boilers
SHP 28,900 = 21knots

***Lexington* (CC-1) — Official drawing of the final design of the battlecruisers, none of which was completed.**
Official US Navy

Endurance: 10,000/10
Armament: 8×16" (406mm)/45, 12×5" (127mm)/51, 8×3" (75mm)/50, 2×21" (533mm) TT
1930: 3" replaced by 8×5"/25 AA
1937: TT removed
BB-45 and *BB-46, 1943:* 8×16", 8×5"/38, 10×5"/51, 40×40mm
BB-48, 1944: 8×16", 16×5"/38, 40×40mm
Armour: Belt 8-13.5" (203-343mm),turrets 9-18" (229-457mm), barbettes 14-16" (355-406mm), bulkheads 14" (355mm), deck 3.5" (89mm), c/t 16" (406mm)
Complement: 1,407
Class notes: Built as a reply to Japanese new construction. Repeat *Tennessee* class with 16" guns in four twin turrets. *Washington* not completed to comply with Washington Treaty. Little changed prior to World War 2. AA armament increased 1935 and 1941. *West Virginia,* sunk at Pearl Harbour, completely reconstructed as 'Tennessee' class,1943-44. *Colorado* and *Maryland* had cage mainmast cut down 1942, completely removed and replaced by small tower 1943, when bulges and new AA armament added

'Lexington' Class (1916)

Battlecruisers: [*Constellation* (CC-2)], [*Constitution* (CC-5)], [*Lexington* (CC-1)], [*Ranger* (CC-4)], [*Saratoga* (CC-3)], [*United States* (CC-6)]
Displacement: 35,300tons, 43,500f/l
Dimensions: 874(oa) 850(wl)×105'5×31'3 [266.4(oa) 259.1(wl)×32.1×9.5]
Machinery: 4 screws, turbo-electric drive (GE; *CC-2* and *CC-4:* Westinghouse), 16 White-Forster boilers
SHP 180,000 = 33.25knots
Armament: 8×16" (406mm)/50, 16×6" (152mm)/53, 4×3" (76mm)/50 AA, 8×21" (533mm) TT
Armour: Belt 5-7.5" (127-190mm), turrets 5-11" (127-279mm), barbettes 9" (229mm), deck 2" (51mm), c/t 12" (305mm)
Complement: 1,315
Class notes: Original design included 10×14", 20×5" guns with displacement of 34,800tons. 12 of 24 boilers were placed above the waterline in an armoured box. After Jutland, number of boilers reduced so as to relocate all boilers below the armoured deck and number of funnels reduced from seven to five. 8×16" guns replaced 14" guns.
Final design (above) included improved underwater side

protection and fewer boilers, causing major modifications and increased beam. All cancelled 1922 to comply with Washington Treaty. *Lexington* and *Saratoga* completed as aircraft carriers

'South Dakota' Class (1917-1918)

Dreadnoughts: [*Indiana* (BB-50)], [*Iowa* (BB-53)], [*Massachusetts* (BB-54)], [*Montana* (BB-51)], [*North Carolina* BB-52)], [*South Dakota* (BB-49)]
Displacement: 43,200tons, 47,000f/l
Dimensions: 684(oa) 660(wl)×104′9×33 [208.5(oa) 201.2(wl)×31.9×10.1]
Machinery: 4 screws, turbo-electric drive (GE), 16 B&W boilers
SHP 60,000 = 23knots
Armament: 12×16″ (406mm)/50, 16×6″ (152mm)/53, 4×3″ (76mm)/50 AA, 2×21″ (533mm) TT
Armour: Belt 8-13.5″ (203-343mm), turrets 18″ (457mm), barbettes 13.5″ (343mm), deck 6-12″ (152-305mm), c/t 16″ (406mm)
Complement: 1,470

***Iowa* (BB-53) — Official drawing of the 'South Dakota' class cancelled in 1922. Notice the massive trunked funnel.** *Official US Navy*

Class notes: None completed. Designed with two cagemasts, massive quadruple-trunked funnel, double-decked secondary battery and four triple turrets. Cancelled to comply with Washington Treaty

'Langley' (1919)

Aircraft Carrier: *Langley* (CV-1)
Displacement: 12,700tons
Dimensions: 542(oa) 519(wl)×65′5×24 [165.2(oa) 158.2(wl)×19.9×7.3]
Machinery: 2 screws, turbo-electric drive (GE), 3 cylindrical boilers
SHP 7,200 = 15knots
Aircraft: 36
Armament: 4×5″ (127mm)/51
Complement: 411
Class notes: Built as a collier and converted in 1919. Superstructure removed and flightdeck erected the full length of the hull. Had no island and smoke was vented by a hinged funnel (later two) on port side. Conversion was considered a success

'Lexington' Class (1922)

Aircraft Carriers: *Lexington* (CV-2), *Saratoga* (CV-3) (see also later photo)

***Langley* (CV-1) — Aircraft carrier. Notice two hinged funnels.**

Displacement: *CV-2:* 35,689tons, *CV-3:* 35,544tons; 41,000f/l; *CV-3 1945:* 48,500f/l
Dimensions: 888(oa) 850(wl) 822(pp)×105'6×32 [270.7(oa) 259.1(wl) 250.5(pp)×32.2×9.8]; *CV-3, 1945:* 901'2(oa)×111'9(wl) 130(oa)×32'6 [274.7(oa)×34.1(wl) 39.6(oa)×9.9]
Machinery: 4 screws, turbo-electric drive (GE); *CV-2:* 16 Yarrow boilers; *CV-3:* 16 White-Forster
SHP 180,000 = 34knots
Endurance: 9,500/15
Aircraft: 90
Armament: 8×8" (203mm)/55, 12×5" (127mm)/25 AA, 4×6pdr
1941-42: 8" guns removed
CV-3, 1945: 16×5"/38, 96×40mm AA
Armour: Belt 7" (178mm), bulkheads 6" (152mm), deck 3" (76mm)
Complement: 2,122
Class notes: Laid down as battlecruiser and converted prior to launching, retaining original hull form and machinery and therefore high speed. Island very prominent with large funnel and tripod mast. Remained the largest carriers in the world until World War 2. *Saratoga* modernised 1942, superstructure and funnel cut down, AA armament increased. Modernised 1944, flightdeck enlarged and bulge added on port side to offset weight of island

'Ranger' (1930)

Aircraft Carrier: *Ranger* (CV-4)
Displacement: 14,500tons, 15,575f/l
Dimensions: 769(oa) 728(wl)×80'1×24'6 [234.4(oa) 221.9(wl)×24.4×7.5]
Machinery: 2 screws, Curtis and Parsons geared turbines (builder), 6 B&W boilers
SHP 53,500 = 29.5knots
Endurance: 11,500/15
Aircraft: 86
Armament: 8×5" (127mm)/25 AA
1942-45: 24×40mm AA added
Armour: Belt 2" (51mm), deck 1" (26mm)
Complement: 1,788
Class notes: First US carrier built as such from the keel up. Smoke was vented by three hinged funnels on each side of flightdeck. Speed sacrificed for other qualities, reducing its usefulness as a first-line unit. Too slow for use with Pacific carrier task forces and remained in Atlantic in World War 2. The arrangement of flightdeck and island built as superstructure and not part of the hull set the standard for later US carriers

'Yorktown' Class (1933)

Aircraft Carriers: *Enterprise* (CV-6), *Hornet* (CV-8), *Yorktown* (CV-5)
Displacement: 19,800tons, 22,900f/l
Dimensions: 809'6(oa) 761(wl)×83'11×21'8; 114 extreme beam [246.7(oa) 232(wl)×25.6×6.6; 34.5 extreme beam]; *CV-6:* 827'4(oa) 770(wl)×95'5×28 [252.2(oa) 234.7(wl)×29.1×8.5]
Machinery: 4 screws, Curtis & Parsons geared turbines, 9 B&W boilers
SHP 120,000 = 34knots
Endurance: 8,220/20
Aircraft: 85
Armament: 8×5" (127mm)/38 AA, 16×1.1" (28mm) AA
CV-6, 1945: 8×5"/38, 40×40mm AA
Armour: Belt and bulkheads 4" (102mm), deck 3" (76mm)
Complement: 2,919
Class notes: Development of 'Ranger' type. *Hornet* was modified type with slightly larger flightdeck and two catapults

***Saratoga* (CV-3) — Aircraft carrier, 1943. The 8" guns have been removed and tripod mast replaced by small tower.** *IWM*

'Wasp' (1934)

Aircraft Carrier: *Wasp* (CV-7)
Displacement: 14,700 tons, 21,000f/l
Dimensions: 741'4(oa) 688(wl)×80'9×28; 110 extreme beam [226(oa) 209.7(wl)×24.6×8.5; 33.5 extreme beam]
Machinery: 2 screws, Parsons geared turbines, 6 Yarrow boilers
SHP 75,000 = 29.5knots
Endurance: 8,000/20
Aircraft: 84
Armament: 8×5" (127mm)/38 AA, 16×1.1" (28mm) AA
Armour: Belt and bulkheads 4" (102mm), decks 1.5" (37mm), c/t 1.5" (37mm)
Complement: 1,889
Class notes: Size limited by naval treaties. Speed, protection and radius of action sacrificed for aircraft capacity. Small funnel and tripod on island, two aircraft elevators, one fitted at deck edge

'North Carolina' Class (1937)

Battleships: *North Carolina* (BB-55), *Washington* (BB-56) (see later photo)
Displacement: 35,000tons, 46,770f/l
Dimensions: 728'9(oa) 714'6(wl)×108'4×35'6 [222.2(oa) 217.8(wl)×33×10.8]
Machinery: 4 screws, GE geared turbines, 8 B&W boilers
SHP 121,000 = 27.6knots
Endurance: 17,450/15
Armament: 9×16" (406mm)/45, 20×5" (127mm)/38, 16×1.1" (28mm) AA
1943: 60×40mm AA
BB-55, 1945: 72×40mm AA
Armour: Belt 6.6-12" (168-305mm), turrets 9.8-16" (249-406mm), barbettes 11.6-17.3" (295-439mm), deck 5.3-6.3" (135-160mm), c/t 16" (406mm)
Complement: 1,890
Class notes: First US fast battleships, superior in speed, armament and protection to contemporary foreign ships except *Yamato*. Three triple turrets and tower foremast, secondary armament in twin turrets. Excellent design, armament and protection not sacrificed for speed. Light AA armament greatly increased during World War 2

***Ranger* (CV-4) — Aircraft carrier, as completed. The first purpose-built carrier. Funnels bent outwards for aircraft operation.**

'South Dakota' Class (1938)

Battleships: *Alabama* (BB-60), *Indiana* (BB-58), *Massachusetts* (BB-59), *South Dakota* (BB-57)
Displacement: 35,000tons, 46,200f/l
Dimensions: 680(oa) 666(wl)×108'2×36'4 [207.3(oa) 203(wl)×32.9×11.1]
Machinery: 4 screws, *BB-57* and *BB-59:* GE geared turbines, 8 B&W boilers; *BB-58* and *BB-60:* Westinghouse geared turbines, 8 Foster-Wheeler boilers
SHP 130,000 = 27knots
Endurance: 17,000/15
Armament: 9×16" (406mm)/45, 20×5" (127mm)/38 (*BB-57:* 16), 24×40mm AA (*BB-57:* 20×1.1" AA)
1945: 48×40mm AA (*BB-59:* 72; *BB-57:* 68)
Armour: Belt 12.2" (310mm), turrets 9.5-18" (241-457mm), barbettes 11.6-17.3" (295-439mm), deck 5-6" (127-152mm), c/t 16" (406mm)
Complement: 1,795
Class notes: Shorter version of 'North Carolina' class to obtain greater protection on same tonnage. Secondary battery mounted one deck higher and pyramidal superstructure with funnel faired into forward tower. *South Dakota* was fitted as fleet flagship

'Iowa' Class (1939-1940)

Battleships: *[Illinois]* (BB-65), *Iowa* (BB-61) (see later photo), *[Kentucky]* (BB-66), *Missouri* (BB-63), *New Jersey* (BB-62) (see later photo), *Wisconsin* (BB-64)
Displacement: 45,000tons, 55,250f/l
Dimensions: 887'3(oa) 861'3(wl)×108'2×37'9 [270.4(oa) 262.5(wl)×32.9×11.5]
Machinery: 4 screws, geared turbines (*BB-61, BB-63* and *BB-66:* GE; *BB-62, BB-64* and *BB-65:* Westinghouse), 8 B&W boilers
SHP 212,000 = 33knots
Endurance: 18,000/12
Armament: 9×16" (406mm)/50, 20×5" (127mm/38, 80×40mm AA
BB-61 and *BB-62, 1982:* 8×5" and all 40mm removed, 32 Tomahawk SSM (8 launchers) and 16 Harpoon SSM (4 launchers) added
Armour: Belt 12.2" (310mm), turrets 9.5-17" (241-432mm), bulkheads 11" (279mm), barbettes 11.6-17.3" (295-439mm), decks 1.5-5.5" (38-140mm), c/t 17.5" (445mm)

Top left:
***Yorktown* (CV-5) — Aircraft carrier, 1941.** *Ted Stone*

Top right:
***Wasp* (CV-7) — Aircraft carrier, 1942.** *IWM*

Centre:
***Massachusetts* (BB-59) — Battleship of 'South Dakota' class, at 15knots, July 1944.** *Official US Navy*

Bottom:
***New Jersey* (BB-62) — 'Iowa' class battleship, after modernisation, 1968. Notice modified tower foremast and lack of AA armament.** *US Navy*

Complement: 2,750
Class notes: Same armament as previous types but greater protection required greater length. Handsome vessels with two large funnels and tall tower foremast. Fastest battleships ever built with a high length to beam ratio, the armour belt was inside the hull. *Illinois* and *Kentucky* not completed. All were fitted with a light tripod mainmast after World War 2 and catapults were removed. In 1967 *New Jersey* was recommissioned with new radar fitted in wings on the forward tower. *New Jersey* and *Iowa* recommissioned 1982 and 1984; *Missouri* and *Wisconsin* scheduled to be reactivated 1987-88

'Alaska' Class (1940)

Battlecruisers: *Alaska* (CB-1), *Guam* (CB-2), *[Hawaii* (CB-3)], *[Philippines* (CB-4)], *[Puerto Rico* (CB-5)], *[Samoa* (CB-6)]
Displacement: 27,500tons, 34,250f/l
Dimensions: 809'3(oa) 791'6(wl)×91'1×32'4 [246.7(oa) 241.2(wl)×27.7×9.9]
Machinery: 4 screws, GE geared turbines, 8 B&W boilers SHP 150,000 = 33knots
Endurance: 12,000/15
Armament: 9×12" (305mm)/50, 12×5" (127mm)/38, 56×40mm AA
Armour: Belt 5-9" (127-229mm), turrets 5-12.75" (127-324mm), barbettes 11-13" (279-330mm), bulkheads 9" (229mm), deck 4" (102mm), c/t 10.6" (269mm)
Complement: 1,517
Class notes: Officially designated as cruisers they were between battleships and cruisers in size and power. Designed to counter a rumoured Japanese class developed from the German *Deutschland*. They were a sized-up version of the 'Baltimore' class with tower foremast, single tall funnel and amidships catapults. Only two were completed. Incomplete *Hawaii* was proposed for conversion to missile ship and later to a large tactical command ship but none of these plans was realised

'Montana' Class (1940)

Battleships: *[Louisiana* (BB-71)], *[Maine* (BB-69)], *[Montana* (BB-67)], *[New Hampshire* (BB-70)], *[Ohio* (BB-68)]
Displacement: 60,500tons, 70,500f/l
Dimensions: 921'3(oa) 890(wl)×121'2×36 [280.8(oa) 271.3(wl)×36.9×11]
Machinery: 4 screws, Westinghouse geared turbines, 8 B&W boilers
SHP 172,000 = 28knots
Endurance: 15,000/15
Armament: 12×16" (406mm)/50, 20×5" (127mm)/54, 32×40mm AA
Armour: Belt 10.2-16.1" (259-409mm), turrets 10-18" (254-457mm), barbettes 18-21.3" (457-541mm), deck 6" (152mm), c/t 18" (457mm)

Left, top to bottom:
***Alaska* (CB-1) — 'Alaska' class 'large cruiser' in dazzle camouflage.** *Official US Navy*

***Essex* (CVA-9) — Aircraft carrier, May 1957 after reconstruction, with angled flightdeck.** *Tom Molland Ltd*

***Intrepid* (CV-11) — Aircraft carrier of 'Essex' class, as completed, November 1943.**

Above:
***Antietam* (CV-36) — Aircraft carrier of 'Essex' class.**

Complement: 3,000
Class notes: Generally similar to 'Iowa' class with an extra 16" turret aft. First US warships designed too wide to pass through the Panama Canal. All were cancelled before construction started

'Essex' Class (1940-41)

Aircraft Carriers: *Bennington* (CV-20), *Bon Homme Richard* (CV-31), *Bunker Hill* (CV-17), *Essex* (CV-9), *Franklin* (CV-13), *Hornet* (CV-12), *Intrepid* (CV-11), *Lexington* (CV-16), *Wasp* (CV-18) (see later photos), *Yorktown* (CV-10)
Displacement: 27,100tons, 34,346f/l; *1958:* All but *CV-13, CV-17* and *CV-36:* 33,100tons, 43,600f/l; *CV-36, 1958:* 30,000tons, 38,000f/l
Dimensions: 872(oa) 820(wl)×93(wl) 147'6(oa)×28'7 [265.8(oa) 250(wl)×28.3(wl) 45(ao)×8.7]; *Modified vessels, 1958:* 899(oa)×102(wl) 192(oa)×31 [274(oa)×31.1(wl) 58.5(oa)×9.4]; *CV-39, 1958:* Beam 152 [46.3(oa)]
Machinery: 4 screws, Westinghouse geared turbines, 8 B&W boilers
SHP 150,000 = 33knots
Endurance: 16,900/15
Aircraft: 83
Armament: 18×5" (127mm)/38, 68×40mm AA
Armour: Belt 2-3" (51-76mm)
Complement: 3,448

Modified 'Essex' Class (1942-43)

Aircraft Carriers: *Antietam* (CV-36), *Boxer* (CV-21), *Hancock* (CV-19), *[Iwo Jima* (CV-46)], *Kearsarge* (CV-33), *Lake Champlain* (CV-39), *Leyte* (CV-32), *Oriskany* (CV-34), *Philippine Sea* (CV-47), *Princeton* (CV-37), *Randolph* (CV-15), *[Reprisal* (CV-35)], *Shangri-La* (CV-38), *Tarawa* (CV-40), *Ticonderoga* (CV-14), *Valley Forge* (CV-45) (see later photo); CV-50 to CV-55 unnamed
Details as 'Essex' class, except length: 888 [270.7(oa)]
Class notes: Six unnamed vessels (CV-50-55) cancelled March 27 1945. The largest class of carriers ever built they were an entirely new design unhampered by treaty limitations. Hangars and flightdeck were superstructure and unarmoured which contributed to damage sustained, but improved compartmentation limited spread of fire. These ships were the backbone of the fast carrier task forces in the Pacific war. The later vessels (modified 'Essex') have rounded bows. Altogether 24 ships were completed, although *Oriskany* did not enter service until 1950 — its modified design included a smaller island and heavier decks. Between 1949 and 1954, 11 units (*Bennington, Essex, Hancock, Hornet, Intrepid, Kearsarge, Lake Champlain, Randolph, Ticonderoga, Wasp* and *Yorktown*) were similarly modified and fitted with hydraulic catapults. *Antietam* received angled flightdeck in an experimental conversion 1952. *Oriskany* and those modified in 1949-54, except *Lake Champlain,* were similarly converted with angled flightdecks 1954-59, and *Bon Homme Richard, Lexington* and Shangri-La received the complete modification 1952-55. *Bunker Hill* and *Franklin* saw no further service after World War 2. *Leyte, Philippine Sea* and *Tarawa* were never modified; neither were *Boxer, Princeton* or *Valley Forge,* which were converted to amphibious assault ships 1961. *Lexington* became training carrier 1969. The converted vessels continued to serve for many years

'Independence' Class (1942)

Light Aircraft Carriers: *Bataan* (CVL-29), *Belleau Wood* (CVL-24), *Cabot* (CVL-28), *Cowpens* (CVL-26), *Independence* (CVL-22), *Langley* (CVL-27), *Monterey* (CVL-26), *Princeton* (CVL-23), *San Jacinto* (CVL-30)
Displacement: 11,000tons, 14,220f/l
Dimensions: 622'6(oa) 600(wl)×71'6(wl) 109'2(oa)×26 [189.7(oa) 182.9(wl)×21.8(wl) 33.3(oa)×7.9]
Machinery: 4 screws, GE geared turbines, 4 B&W boilers
SHP 100,000 = 31.6knots
Endurance: 6,500/15
Aircraft: 45
Armament: 1×5" (127mm)/38 (*Independence* only, later removed), 26×40mm AA
Armour: Belt 5" (127mm), deck 2" (51mm)
Complement: 1,569
Class notes: Laid down as 'Cleveland' class light cruisers, reordered as aircraft carriers 1942 when the need for aircraft

carriers was most urgent. To balance the built-up hangar and flightdeck on the hull, bulges were fitted on each side. They were completed with great speed and proved highly successful serving with the carrier task forces throughout the war, despite their small size and limited space. *Belleau Wood* and *Langley* transferred to France 1953. *Bataan* and *Cabot* were refitted as anti-submarine carriers 1950

'Saipan' Class (1942)

Light Aircraft Carriers: *Saipan* (CVL-48), *Wright* (CVL-49)
Displacement: 14,500tons, 17,800f/l
Machinery: 683'7(oa) 664(wl)×76'9)wl 108(oa)×25 [208.4(oa) 202.4(wl)×23.4(wl) 32.9(oa)×7.6]
Machinery: 4 screws, GE geared turbines, 4 B&W boilers SHP 120,000 = 33knots
Endurance: 8,000/15
Aircraft: 48
Armament: 40×40mm AA
Armour: Belt 4" (102mm), deck 3" (76mm)
Complement: 1,750
Class notes: Similar to 'Independence' class but designed from the start as carriers following hull and machinery of 'Baltimore' class heavy cruisers. Used mainly for training and experimental purposes. *Wright* was converted to command ship 1963, conversion of *Saipan* cancelled while underway and ship was completed as communications relay ship

Above:
***Belleau Wood* (CVL-24) — 'Independence' class light aircraft carrier, at sea in the South Pacific, December 22 1943. Notice the break in the hull below forward gun sponsons where hull was widened to balance built-up flightdeck and island.**

Right:
***Wright* (CVL-49) — 'Saipan' class light carrier, 1953.**
Marius Bar

Below:
***Coral Sea* (CVA-43) — 'Midway' class aircraft carrier, as modernised with angled flightdeck, launching aircraft.**
US Navy

'Midway' Class (1942-43)

Aircraft Carriers: *Coral Sea* (CVB-43), *Franklin D. Roosevelt* (CVB-42), *Midway* (CVB-41), CVB-44, CVB-56, CVB-57 (unnamed)
Displacement: 45,000tons, 60,000f/l; *1957:* 51,000tons, 62,000f/l; *CV-43, 1957:* 49,250tons, 63,383f/l; *CV-42, 1957:* 48,950tons, 62,674f/l
Dimensions: 968(oa) 933(wl) 852(pp)×113(wl) 136(oa)×32'9 [295(oa) 284.4(wl) 259.7(pp)×34.4(wl) 41.6 (oa)×10]; *1958:* 974(oa)×210(oa)×36 [296.6(oa)×64(oa)×11]; *1960:* 979(oa)×222(oa) [298.4(oa)×67.7(oa)]
Machinery: 4 screws, Westinghouse geared turbines (*CV-42:* GE), 12 B&W boilers
SHP 212,000 = 33knots
Endurance: 11,500/15
Aircraft: 137; *1970:* 70+
Armament: 18×5" (127mm)/54, 84×40mm
CV-43: 14×5", 76×40mm
CV-42, 1956: 10×5", 22×3"
CV-42, 1963: 4×5" only (removed 1978)
CV-41, 1984: 2 8-tube Sea Sparrow Mk 25 SAM
Armament: Belt 8" (203mm), deck 4" (102mm)
Complement: 4,085
Class notes: Three unnamed ships cancelled, CVB-44 on November 1 1943 and CVB-56 and CVB-57 on March 28 1945.
First US carriers with armoured flightdeck which, with additional armour protection, caused a great increase in size over previous vessels. They were unable to pass through the Panama Canal but could operate the new larger aircraft. Huge island with funnel and tripod mast, and gun armament mounted in single turrets below flightdeck level.
Roosevelt and *Midway* modernised 1954-56, armour belt removed, angled flightdeck and hydraulic catapults fitted. *Coral Sea* was similarly modernised in 1957-59 including new elevators and enclosed bow. *Midway* was rebuilt 1966-70 with new flightdeck and other improvements but conversion of *Roosevelt* was cancelled

49
43

'United States' (1948)

Aircraft Carriers: *[United States* (CVA-58)*]*
Displacement: 66,850tons, 78,500f/l
Dimensions: 1,090(oa) 1,030(wl)×130(wl) 190(oa)×34.5 [332.2(oa) 313.9(wl)×39.6(wl) 57.9(oa)×10.5]
Machinery: 4 screws, geared turbines, 8 boilers
SHP 280,000 = 33knots
Endurance: 12,000/20
Aircraft: 72
Armament: 8×5″/54, 12×3″/70
Armour: Deck 3″ (76mm)
Complement: 4,127
Class notes: Designed as an attack carrier operating long range bombers. Was to have a flush deck with no island and four catapults on flightdeck

Above:
***Independence* (CVA-62) — Aircraft carrier, 'Forrestal' class.** *INRO*

Right, top to bottom:
***John F. Kennedy* (CVA-67) — Aircraft carrier, October 1976.**

***Enterprise* (CVN-65) — The first nuclear-powered aircraft carrier. The superstructure was modified during 1980-81 refit.** *US Navy*

***Nimitz* (CVN-68) — Aircraft carrier. The enormous size of the ship is clearly seen here.** *US Navy*

'Forrestal' Class (1951-1954)

Aircraft Carriers: *Forrestal* (CVA-59), *Independence* (CVA-62), *Ranger* (CVA-61), *Saratoga* (CVA-60)
Displacement: 56,000tons, 78,700f/l; *CV-59:* 54,600tons, 76,000f/l
Dimensions: 1,039(oa) 990(wl)×129′6(oa)×37 [316.7(oa) 301.8(wl)×39.5(oa)×11.3]; *CV-62:* 1,046 [318.8(oa)]; *CV-59* and *CV-60, c1972:* 1,066(oa) [331(oa)]; *CV-61* and *CV62, c1972:* 1,071(oa) [326.4(oa)]
Machinery: 4 screws, GE geared turbines (*CV-59:* Westinghouse), 8 B&W boilers
SHP 280,000 = 34knots; *CV-59:* SHP 260,000 = 33knots
Endurance: 8,000/20
Aircraft: 90/100
Armament: 8×5″/54, 18×3″ AA
1967-74: 2 8-tube Sea Sparrow Mk 25 SAM
CV-61, 1982: Mk 29 SAM
Armour: Belt 2″ (51mm)
Complement: 4,132
Class notes: The first 'supercarriers', larger vessels able to handle larger aircraft with more spacious hangar deck, and angled flightdeck. *Forrestal* designed with axial flightdeck and converted during construction. Designed as attack carriers (CVA), later changed to multi-mission (CV) with addition of ASW aircraft. Guns removed in 1960s and replaced with missile systems

'Kitty Hawk' Class (1955-1964)

Aircraft Carriers: *America* (CVA-66), *Constellation* (CVA-64), *John F. Kennedy* (CVA-67) (see later photo), *Kitty Hawk* (CVA-63)
Displacement: 60,100tons, 80,800f/l; *CV-66:* 60,300tons; *CV-67:* 61,000tons
Dimensions: 1,047′6(oa) 990(wl)×129′6(oa)×37 [319.3(oa) 301.8(wl)×39.5(oa)×11.3]; *CV-63:* 1,062′6 [323.9(oa)]; *CV-64:* 1,072′6 [327(oa)]
Machinery: 4 screws, Westinghouse steam turbines (*CVA-67:* GE), 8 Foster-Wheeler boilers
SHP 280,000 = 34knots
Endurance: 8,200/20
Aircraft: 85+
Armament: 2 twin Terrier SAM
CV-67: 3 8-tube Sea Sparrow Mk 25 SAM
CV-63, 1980: Mk 29 Sea Sparrow
Armour: Belt 2″ (51mm)
Complement: 5,400
Class notes: Improved 'Forrestal' class. *Kennedy* officially a separate class, was delayed because of question whether ship should be nuclear-powered. As 'Forrestal' class, changed from attack carriers (CVA) to multi-mission (CV) in 1973-75. Designed with missile armament only. Four steam catapults and four deck edge elevators. Smokestack on *Kennedy* angled to starboard

'Enterprise' (1957)

Aircraft Carrier: *Enterprise* (CVAN-65) (see also later photo)
Displacement: 75,700tons, 89,600f/l
Dimensions: 1,123(oa) 1,040(wl)×133(wl)×35′9 [342.3(oa) 317(wl)×40.5(wl)×10.9]
Machinery: 4 screws, Westinghouse steam turbines, 8 water-cooled nuclear reactors
SHP 280,000 = 30+knots
Aircraft: 84+
Armament: *1967:* 2 8-tube Sea Sparrow Mk 25 SAM
Complement: 5,688
Class notes: First nuclear-powered carrier and second nuclear-powered surface warship. The largest warship in the world. Modified 'Kitty Hawk' design. Distinctive square superstructure modified 1980 and dome replaced by conventional island. Originally built without armament

68

'Nimitz' Class (1967-1974)

Aircraft Carriers: *Abraham Lincoln* (CVN-72), *Carl Vinson* (CVN-70), *Dwight D. Eisenhower* (CVAN-69) (see later photo), *George Washington* (CVN-73), *Nimitz* (CVAN-68) (see later photo), *Theodore Roosevelt* (CVN-71)
Displacement: 81,600tons, 96,350f/l
Dimensions: 1,092(oa) 1,040(wl)×134×37'8 [332.8(oa) 317(wl)×40.8×11.5]
Machinery: 4 screws, GE steam turbines, 2 water-cooled nuclear reactors
SHP 280,000 = 30+knots
Aircraft: 95+
Armament: 3 8-tube Sea Sparrow Mk 25 SAM
Armour: *CVN-70* and *CVN-71*: Mk 29
Complement: 6,288
Class notes: Completion long delayed by labour problems and slow delivery of some nuclear components. Similar to *Enterprise* with only two reactors. They have four steam catapults and four deck elevators. Similar to 'Kitty Hawk' class

Individual Ships

Abraham Lincoln (CVN-72)

Type: Aircraft Carrier
Class: 'Nimitz' (1967)
Nomenclature: Abraham Lincoln (1809-1865), President of the United States during the Civil War

History:
1983 Ordered from Newport News for completion in 1989

Agamenticus

Type: Monitor
Class: 'Miantonomoh' (1862)
Nomenclature: Mountain in Maine

History:
1862 Laid down at Portsmouth NYd
1863 March 19: Launched
1865 May 5: Completed
1865-70 Laid up at Boston
1869 June 15: Renamed ***Terror***
1872 June 10: Decommissioned
1874 Broken up

Ajax, see *Manayunk*

Nomenclature: Greek myth: a hero of the Trojan War

Alabama (BB-8)

Type: Pre-dreadnought
Class: 'Illinois' (1896)
Nomenclature: 22nd state of the Union, admitted 1819

History:
1896 December 1: Laid down by Cramp
1898 May 18: Launched
1900 October 16: Completed
1901-07 North Atlantic
1906 January 17: Damaged in collision with battleship *Kentucky* in New York Bay
1907-09 Great White Fleet

Above:
***Terror* — Monitor of 1862 with temporary pilot house on the forward turret, at Philadelphia between 1869 and 1874.**

Top right:
***Amphitrite* (BM-2) — Monitor, c1918 in New York Bay.**

Bottom right:
***Arizona* (BB-39) — Battleship of 'Pennsylvania' class, as reconstructed and as it appeared at the time of loss, 1941.** *Ted Stone*

1912 Refit, cagemasts installed
1914 Training ship
World War 1: Atlantic Fleet
1920 May 7: Decommissioned
1921 September 27: Sunk as target by army aircraft

Alabama (BB-60)

Type: Battleship
Class: 'South Dakota' (1938)

History:
1940 February 1: Laid down at Norfolk
1942 February 16: Launched
1942 August 16: Completed
World War 2: 1942 Arctic convoys, Gilbert Islands, Kwajalein, 1944 Raids on Truk and Palau; Saipan, Philippine Sea, Guam. Palau, 1944 Raids on Luzon and Taiwan; Okinawa, 1945 Raids on Japan

1945 June 5: Damaged in typhoon off Okinawa
1947 January 9: Decommissioned
1962 June 1: Stricken
—— Transferred to the State of Alabama and preserved as a memorial at Mobile

Alaska (CB-1)

Type: Battlecruiser
Class: 'Alaska' (1940)
Nomenclature: A territory of the US, purchased 1867, admitted 1959 as the 49th state

History:
1941 December 17: Laid down by New York Sbdg
1943 August 15: Launched
1944 June 17: Completed
World War 2: Iwo Jima, Okinawa, 1945 Raids on Japan
1947 February 17: Decommissioned
1960 June 1: Stricken
1961 June 30: Sold and broken up at Kearny

America (CVA-66)

Type: Aircraft Carrier
Class: 'Kitty Hawk' (1955)
Nomenclature: A reference to the US; 74-gun ship-of-the-line of 1782

History:
1961 January 9: Laid down by Newport News
1964 February 1: Launched
1965 January 23: Completed
1965-68 Atlantic Fleet
1968-70 Pacific Fleet, Vietnam
1971 Mediterranean
1972 Vietnam
1973—— Atlantic Fleet, Mediterranean
1975 June 30: Reclassified CV-66
1980 Refit

Amphitrite, see *Tonawanda*

Amphitrite (BM-2)

Type: Monitor
Class: 'Amphitrite' (1874)
Nomenclature: Greek myth: the goddess of the sea

History:
1875 Laid down by Harlan & Hollingsworth
1883 June 7: Launched
1895 April 23: Completed by Norfolk
1898 Operations off Cuba and Puerto Rico
1899-1901 Gunnery training ship, Boston
1910-17 Naval militia training ship
World War 1: Training ship, New York
1919 July 24: Stricken
1920 January 3: Sold; used as floating hotel in Florida
1942-45 Accommodation ship for war workers, Elizabeth City, NC
1952 Broken up

Antietam (CV-36)

Type: Aircraft Carrier
Class: Modified 'Essex' (1942)
Nomenclature: A battle of the Civil War near Sharpsburg, Md, September 1 1862

History:
1943 March 15: Laid down at Philadelphia
1944 August 20: Launched
1945 January 28: Completed
1945-49 Pacific Fleet
1946 November 19: Damaged by an explosion, at Hunters Point
1949 June 12: Decommissioned
1951 June 23: Recommissioned
1951-52 Korea
1952 Reconstructed at New York, angled flightdeck
1953-57 Atlantic Fleet and Mediterranean
1952 October 1: Reclassified CVA-36
1953 July 8: Reclassified CVS-36
1957-63 Training carrier
1963 August 5: Decommissioned
1973 May 1: Stricken
1973 December 19: Sold and broken up

Arizona (BB-39)

Type: Dreadnought
Class: 'Pennsylvania' (1912)
Nomenclature: 48th state of the Union, admitted 1912

History:
1914 March 16: Laid down at Brooklyn
1915 June 19: Launched
1916 October 17: Completed
1916-21 Atlantic Fleet
World War 1: US East coast
1919 Turkey and Aegean Sea
1921-41 Pacific Fleet
1929-31 Reconstructed at Norfolk, cagemasts replaced by tripods, secondary battery raised one deck, catapult added on stern, reboilered
1931 Carried President Hoover to the West Indies
1941 December 7: Hit by torpedo and eight bombs at Pearl Harbor, blew up and sank. Flagship of Rear-Adm Isaac C. Kidd who was killed (1,104 dead)
1945 Wreck preserved as a memorial at Pearl Harbor

Arkansas (BM-7)

Type: Monitor
Class: 'Arkansas' (1898)
Nomenclature: 25th state of the Union, admitted 1836

History:
1899 November 14: Laid down by Newport News

Above left:
***Arkansas* (BB-33) — As completed, 1912, with original tops to masts.**

Above right:
***Arkansas* (BB-33) — Dreadnought of 'Wyoming' class, c1921.**

1900 November 10: Launched
1902 October 28: Completed
1902-09 Atlantic
1909 March 2: Renamed ***Ozark***
1910-13 Naval militia training ship
1913 Refit, converted to submarine tender
1914 Mexico
World War 1: Gulf of Mexico and Panama Canal
1919 August 20: Decommissioned
1922 January 26: Sold and broken up

Arkansas (BB-33)

Type: Dreadnought
Class: 'Wyoming' (1909)

History:
1910 January 25: Laid down by New York Sbdg
1911 January 14: Launched
1912 September 17: Completed
1912 December: Carried President Taft to Panama
1913-18 Atlantic Fleet
1913 February 14: Went aground on coral reef
1914 Mexico
World War 1: Atlantic Fleet, 1918 Grand Fleet
1919-21 Pacific Fleet
1921-25 Atlantic Fleet, flagship Battle Force
1925-26 Reconstructed at Philadelphia; cage mainmast removed and replaced by small tripod mast further aft, catapult added to 'P' turret, single funnel replaced two, secondary battery raised one deck, reboilered
1926-32 Atlantic Fleet
1932-34 Pacific Fleet
1934-41 Atlantic Fleet
1942 Refit; cage foremast replaced by tripod, casemate battery removed, new AA guns fitted
World War 2: Atlantic convoys, Normandy, Southern France, Iwo Jima, Okinawa
1946 July: Target vessel, Bikini nuclear tests
1945 July 25: Sank as a result of second atomic explosion at Bikini

Atlas, see ***Nahant***

Nomenclature: Greek myth: a demigod who supported the sky on his shoulders

Bataan (CVL-29)

Type: Light Aircraft Carrier
Class: 'Independence' (1942)
Nomenclature: Scene of heroic resistance against Japanese invaders in the Philippines, 1942

History:
1940 Ordered as light cruiser ***Buffalo*** (CL-99)
1942 June 2: Reordered as light aircraft carrier ***Bataan***
1942 August 31: Laid down by New York Sbdg
1943 August 1: Launched
1943 November 17: Completed
World War 1: Hollandia, Saipan, Philippine Sea, Okinawa, 1945 Raids on Japan
1947 February 11: Decommissioned
1949 Converted for ASW, as CVL(K)
1950 May 13: Recommissioned
1951-53 Korea
1954 April 9: Decommissioned
1959 May 15: Reclassified AVT-4, aviation transport
1959 September 1: Stricken
1961 April 27: Sold and broken up

Belleau Wood (CVL-24)

Type: Light Aircraft Carrier
Class: 'Independence' (1942)
Nomenclature: Battle in France, World War 1, June 6 1918

History:
1941 August 11: Laid down by New York Sbdg as light cruiser ***New Haven*** (CL-76)
1942 February 16: Reordered as aircraft carrier, renamed ***Belleau Wood***
1942 December 6: Launched
1943 March 31: Completed
World War 2: Gilbert Islands, Kwajalein, 1944 Raids on Truk, Marianas and Palau; Hollandia, Morotai, Saipan, Philippine Sea, Guam, Palau, Leyte, 1944 Raids on Luzon, Taiwan and Okinawa; Iwo Jima, Okinawa, 1945 Raids on Japan
1944 October 30: Damaged by kamikaze off Leyte (92 dead)
1945 June 5: Damaged in typhoon in Philippine Sea
1947 January 13: Decommissioned
1953 September 5: Transferred to France, renamed ***Bois Belleau***
1960 September 12: Returned to US Navy
1960 November 21: Sold and broken up at Chester

Bennington (CV-20)

Type: Aircraft Carrier
Class: 'Essex' (1940)
Nomenclature: Battle of the American Revolution, August 16 1777

History:
1942 December 15: Laid down at Brooklyn
1944 February 26: Launched
1944 August 6: Completed
World War 2: Iwo Jima, Okinawa, 1945 Raids on Japan
1945 June 5: Damaged in typhoon in Philippine Sea
1946 November 8: Decommissioned
1951-52 Refit, hydraulic catapults fitted
1952 October 1: Reclassified CVA-20
1952 November 13: Recommissioned
1952-54 Atlantic Fleet
1953 April 27: Damaged by boiler explosion while off Guantanamo
1954 May 26: Damaged by catapult explosion off Narragansett Bay (103 dead)
1954-55 Reconstructed at New York, angled flightdeck
1955-70 Pacific Fleet
1963 FRAM II refit
1970 January 16: Decommissioned
1976 January 31: Stricken

Bon Homme Richard (CV-10), see ***Yorktown*** (CV-10)

Bon Homme Richard (CV-31)

Type: Aircraft Carrier
Class: 'Essex' (1940)
Nomenclature: 'Poor Richard' in honour of Benjamin Franklin; frigate of 1779 commanded by John Paul Jones

History:
1943 February 1: Laid down at Brooklyn
1944 April 29: Launched
1944 November 26: Completed
World War 2: 1945 Raids on Japan
1947 January 9: Decommissioned
1951 January 17: Recommissioned
1951-52 Korea
1952 October 1: Reclassified CVA-31
1953-55 Reconstructed at San Francisco; steam catapults and angled flightdeck
1956-71 Pacific Fleet
1971 July 2: Decommissioned

Boxer (CV-21)

Type: Aircraft Carrier
Class: Modified 'Essex' (1942)
Nomenclature: Prize taken 1814 by USS *Enterprise*

History:
1943 September 13: Laid down by Newport News
1944 December 14: Launched
1945 April 16: Completed
1945-59 Pacific Fleet
1950-53 Korea
1952 August 5: Damaged by fire in hangar deck, off Korea
1952 October 1: Reclassified CVA-21
1955 November 15: Reclassified CVS-21
1959 January 30: Reclassified LPH-4, amphibious assault ship
1959-69 Atlantic Fleet
1969 December 1: Stricken
1971 February: Sold and broken up at New York

Brooklyn (CA-3)

Type: Armoured Cruiser

Class: 'Brooklyn' (1892)
Nomenclature: City on Long Island, now part of New York City

History:
1893 August 2: Laid down at Brooklyn
1895 October 2: Launched
1896 December 1: Completed
1897-99 Atlantic Fleet
1898 Operations off Cuba, Santiago
1899-1902 Asiatic Squadron
1900 Boxer Rebellion
1903-07 Atlantic Fleet
1908-09 Refit; fire controls added, TT removed, two-stage hoists added to turrets
1915-21 Asiatic and Pacific, Siberia
1921 March 9: Decommissioned
1921 December 20: Stricken, broken up at San Francisco

Bunker Hill (CV-17)

Type: Aircraft Carrier
Class: 'Essex' (1940)
Nomenclature: Battle of the American Revolution in Charleston, Ma, June 17 1775

History:
1941 September 15: Laid down at Quincy
1942 December 7: Launched
1943 May 24: Completed
World War 2: Gilbert Islands, Kwajalein, 1944 Raids on Truk, Marianas and Palau; Hollandia, Saipan, Philippine Sea, Guam, Palau, 1944 Raids on Luzon and Okinawa; Iwo Jima, Okinawa
1944 June 19: Damaged by aircraft bomb near miss during Battle of the Philippine Sea
1945 May 11: Severely damaged by two kamikazes off Okinawa
1947 January 9: Decommissioned
1952 October 1: Reclassified CVA-17
1953 August 8: Reclassified CVS-17
1959 May 15: Reclassified AVT-9, aircraft transport
1966 November 1: Stricken, used as floating laboratory
1973 June 7: Sold
1973 July 25: Damaged in collision with freighter *Sidney Spiro* off Point Reyes, California, while under tow to breaking up at Portland

Cabot (CV-16), see *Lexington* (CV-16)

Cabot (CVL-28)

Type: Light Aircraft Carrier
Class: 'Independence' (1942)
Nomenclature: Brig of the Continental navy, 1775

History:
1942 March 16: Laid down by New York Sbdg as light cruiser ***Wilmington*** (CL-79)
1942 June 23: Reordered as aircraft carrier, renamed ***Cabot***
1943 April 4: Launched
1943 July 24: Completed
World War 2: Kwajalein, 1944 Raids on Truk and Palau; Saipan, Philippine Sea, Guam, Palau, Leyte, 1944 Raids on Luzon, Okinawa and Taiwan; 1945 Raids on Luzon, China coast and Taiwan; Iwo Jima, Okinawa
1944 November 25: Damaged by two kamikazes off Luzon (62 dead)
1944 December 18: Damaged in typhoon in Philippine Sea
1947 February 11: Decommissioned
1948 October 27: Recommissioned; converted for ASW as CVL(K)
1948-55 Atlantic Fleet
1955 January 21: Decommissioned
1959 May 15: Reclassified AVT-3, aircraft transport
1967 August 30: Transferred to Spain, renamed ***Dedalo***

California (CA-6)

Type: Armoured Cruiser
Class: 'Pennsylvania' (1899)
Nomenclature: 31st state of the Union, admitted 1850

History:
1902 May 7: Laid down by Union

Left:
***San Diego* (CA-6) — Armoured cruiser, formerly *California*.**

Above:
***California* (BB-44) — Battleship, 1940. The turrets are turned to port.**

1904 April 28: Launched
1907 August 1: Completed
1907-12 Pacific Fleet
1911 Refit, foremast replaced by cagemast
1912 Far East
1912-17 Pacific Fleet
1914 September 1: Renamed ***San Diego***
1915 January 21: Damaged by boiler explosion off La Paz, west coast of Mexico
World War 1: Atlantic convoys
1918 July 19: Sunk by mine off Fire Island, NY (six dead)

California (BB-40), see ***New Mexico*** (BB-40)

California (BB-44)

Type: Dreadnought
Class: 'Tennessee' (1915)

History:
1916 October 25: Laid down at Mare Island
1919 November 20: Launched
1921 August 10: Completed
1921-41 Pacific Fleet
1929-30 Refit; catapults added, AA armament increased
World War 2: Pearl Harbor, Saipan, Tinian, Guam, Leyte, Surigao Strait, Lingayen, Okinawa, 1945 Japan Raids
1941 December 7: Severely damaged by bombs at Pearl Harbor and sank on December 10 (98 dead)
1942 March 25: Refloated
1942 Reconstructed at Bremerton; funnels, superstructure and cagemasts replaced by single funnel and massive superstructure, new secondary armament
1944 January: Recommissioned
1944 June 14: Hit by shore batteries at Saipan
1944 August: Bow damaged in collision with battleship *Tennessee*
1945 January 6: Damaged by kamikaze off Lingayen (44 dead)
1947 February 14: Decommissioned
1959 July 17: Sold and broken up at Baltimore

Camanche

Type: Monitor
Class: 'Passaic' (1862)
Nomenclature: Nomadic Indian tribe of the Great Plains

History:
1863 Built by Secor, Jersey City for Donahue Ryan, San Francisco
—— Disassembled after completion and shipped in pieces to San Francisco aboard steamer *Aquila* which sank there at its pier, November 16 1863
1864 November 14: Launched by Union
1865 May 24: Completed
1895-97 Naval militia training ship
1899 February 15: Stricken
1899 March 22: Sold and broken up at Oakland, Ca

Canonicus

Type: Monitor
Class: 'Canonicus' (1862)
Nomenclature: A chief of the Narragansett Indians (1565-1647)

History:
1862 Laid down by Harrison Loring
1863 August 1: Launched
1864 April 16: Completed
Civil War: 1864 James River, 1864-65 N Atlantic BS, Fort Fisher
1865 January 13: Damaged by shore batteries at Fort Fisher
1865 June 30: Decommissioned
1869 June 15: Renamed ***Scylla***
1869 August 10: Renamed ***Canonicus***
1872-74 Reconstructed
1872-77 Recommissioned
1904 January 5: Stricken
1908 February 19: Sold and broken up

Carl Vinson (CVN-70)

Type: Aircraft Carrier
Class: 'Nimitz' (1967)
Nomenclature: Carl Vinson (1883-1981), congressman and chairman of the naval affairs committee

History:
1975 October 11: Laid down by Newport News
1980 March 15: Launched
1982 March 13: Commissioned
1982 Pacific Fleet

Castor, see ***Mahopac***

Nomenclature: Greek myth: one of the twin sons of Helen

Catawba

Type: Monitor
Class: 'Canonicus' (1862)
Nomenclature: River in North Carolina

History:
1862 Laid down by Swift Evans
1864 April 13: Launched
1865 June 10: Completed but never commissioned
1868 April 2: Sold to Peru, renamed ***Atahualpa***

Catskill

Type: Monitor
Class: 'Passaic' (1862)
Nomenclature: Mountain group in New York

History:
1862 Laid down by Continental
1862 December 6: Launched
1863 February 24: Completed
Civil War: 1863-65 S Atlantic BS, 1863 Attacks on Charleston
1865 July 26: Decommissioned
1869 June 15: Renamed ***Goliath***
1869 August 10: Renamed ***Catskill***
1873-77 Recommissioned
1874-75 Refit
1898 Coastal defence, New England
1901 October 21: Stricken
1901 December 4: Sold and broken up

Centaur, see ***Saugus***

Nomenclature: Greek myth: a monster, part man, part horse

Charlotte (CA-12), see ***North Carolina*** (CA-12)

Nomenclature: City in North Carolina

Cheyenne (BM-10), see ***Wyoming*** (BM-10)

Nomenclature: City in Wyoming

Colorado (CA-7)

Type: Armoured Cruiser
Class: 'Pennsylvania' (1899)
Nomenclature: 37th State of the Union, admitted 1876

History:
1901 April 25: Laid down by Cramp
1903 April 25: Launched
1905 June 19: Completed
1905-06 Atlantic Fleet
1906-07 Asiatic station
1907-11 Pacific Fleet
1911 Refit, foremast replaced by cagemast
1911-12 Asiatic Station
1913-16 Pacific Fleet
1916 November 9: Renamed ***Pueblo***
World War 1: South Atlantic
1919 Made six voyages as troop transport
1919 September 22: Decommissioned
1921-27 Receiving ship

Above:
***Camanche* — 'Passaic' class monitor, 1898. Transported to the Pacific coast in pieces 1863.** *US Navy*

Left:
***Colorado* (BB-45) — 'Colorado' class battleship, c1935.**

1930 February 21: Stricken
1931 September 14: Sold and broken up

Colorado (BB-45)

Type: Dreadnought
Class: 'Colorado' (1916)

History:
1919 May 29: Laid down by New York Sbdg
1921 March 22: Launched
1923 August 30: Completed
1924-41 Pacific Fleet
1930 June: Damaged by fire at sea, probably sabotage
1941-42 Refit at Bremerton
World War 2: 1942-43 Southwest Pacific, Gilbert Islands, Kwajalein, Eniwetok, Saipan, Tinian, Guam, Leyte, Lingayen, Okinawa
1942 Refit; cage mainmast cut down to stump, AA armament increased, catapult removed from 'X' turret
1944 Refit; mainmast stump replaced by tower, secondary armament replaced
1944 July 24: Damaged by shore batteries off Tinian
1944 November 27: Moderately damaged by two kamikazes in Leyte Gulf
1945 January 9: Hit by friendly gunfire at Lingayen
1945 April 20: Damaged by an explosion off Okinawa
1947 January 7: Decommissioned
1959 July 28: Sold and broken up at Seattle

Colossus, see *Kalamazoo*

Nomenclature: Giant statue at Rhodes, one of the seven wonders of the ancient world

Conestoga, see *Sangamon*

Nomenclature: Town in Pennsylvania

Connecticut (BM-8), see *Nevada* (BM-8)

Connecticut (BB-18)

Type: Pre-dreadnought
Class: 'Connecticut' (1902)
Nomenclature: One of the original 13 states

History:
1903 March 10: Laid down at Brooklyn
1904 September 29: Launched
1906 September 29: Completed
1906-07 Atlantic Fleet (flag)
1907-09 Great White Fleet (flagship)
1909-12 Atlantic Fleet
1911 Refit, cagemasts fitted
1914 Mexico
World War 1: Atlantic Fleet
1916 Fitted with AA guns
1919 Made four voyages as troop transport
1919-21 Atlantic Fleet
1921-22 Pacific Fleet
1923 March 1: Decommissioned
1923 November 1: Sold and broken up

***Connecticut* (BB-18) — Pre-dreadnought of 'Connecticut' class, c1912, after installation of cagemasts.**

Constellation (CC-2)

Type: Battlecruiser
Class: 'Lexington' (1916)
Nomenclature: Frigate of 1797

History:
1920 August 18: Laid down by Newport News
1922 August 22: Construction suspended when 22.7% complete
1923 August 17: Contract cancelled

Constellation (CVA-64)

Type: Aircraft Carrier
Class: 'Kitty Hawk' (1955)

History:
1957 September 14: Laid down at Brooklyn
1960 October 8: Launched
1960 December 19: Damaged by fire while fitting out at Brooklyn (50 dead)
1961 October 27: Completed
1961 Pacific Fleet
1975-76 Refit
1979 Refit, Terrier SAM replaced by Sea Sparrow
1980 June 25: In collision with merchant vessel *Banglar Joy* in Arabian Sea

Constitution (CC-1), see ***Lexington*** (CC-1)

Constitution (CC-5)

Type: Battlecruiser
Class: 'Lexington' (1916)
Nomenclature: Frigate of 1797 called 'Old Ironsides'

History:
1917 December 10: Renamed ***Constitution,*** having been ordered as ***Ranger***
1920 September 25: Laid down at Philadelphia
1922 August 2: Construction suspended when 13.4% complete
1923 August 17: Contract cancelled

Coral Sea (CVB-42), see ***Franklin D. Roosevelt***

Coral Sea (CVB-43)

Type: Aircraft Carrier
Class: 'Midway' (1942)
Nomenclature: Naval battle of World War 2, Southwest Pacific, May 4-8 1942

History:
1944 July 10: Laid down by Newport News
1946 April 2: Launched
1947 October 1: Completed
1947-57 Atlantic Fleet and Mediterranean
1952 October 1: Reclassified CVA-43
1957-60 Reconstructed at Bremerton; armour belt removed, angled flightdeck, enclosed bow, steam catapults
1975 July 1: Reclassified CV-43
1980 Indian Ocean

Cowpens (CVL-25)

Type: Light Aircraft Carrier
Class: 'Independence' (1942)
Nomenclature: Battle of the American Revolution in South Carolina, January 17 1781

History:
1941 November 17: Laid down by New York Sbdg as light cruiser ***Huntington*** (CL-77)
1942 March 27: Reordered as aircraft carrier, renamed ***Cowpens***
1943 January 17: Launched
1943 May 28: Completed
World War 2: Gilbert Islands, Kwajalein, 1944 Raids on Truk, Marianas and Palau; Morotai, Saipan, Philippine Sea, Hollandia, Palau, Leyte, 1944 Raids on Luzon, Taiwan and Okinawa; 1945 Raids on Luzon, China coast and Ryukyus; Iwo Jima, 1945 Raids on Japan
1947 January 13: Decommissioned
1959 May 15: Reclassified AVT-1, aircraft transport
1959 November 1: Stricken
1960 May 9: Sold
1962 Broken up at Portland, Or

Crown Point (CV-27), see ***Langley*** (CVL-27)

Crown Point (CV-32), see ***Leyte*** (CV-32)

Delaware (BB-28)

Type: Dreadnought
Class: 'Delaware' (1906)
Nomenclature: One of the original 13 states

History:
1907 November 11: Laid down by Newport News
1909 February 6: Launched
1910 April 4: Completed
1910-17 Atlantic Fleet
1911 January 17: Damaged by boiler explosion near Norfolk (eight dead)
1914 Mexico
World War 1: Atlantic Fleet, 1917-18 Grand Fleet
1919 Operations in Santo Domingo
1919-23 Atlantic Fleet
1923 November 10: Decommissioned
1924 February 5: Sold and broken up at Philadelphia

Dictator

Type: Monitor
Class: 'Dictator' (1862)
Nomenclature: A person exercising absolute power

History:
1862 August 16: Laid down by Delamater
1863 December 26: Launched
1864 November 11: Completed
Civil War: 1864-65 N Atlantic BS
1865 September 5: Decommissioned
1869-71 Recommissioned
1874-77 Recommissioned
1877 June 1: Decommissioned
1883 September 27: Sold and broken up

Top:
***Delaware* (BB-28) — Dreadnought of 'Delaware' class, at Rosyth while serving with Grand Fleet 1918.** *IWM*

Above:
***Dwight D. Eisenhower* (CVN-69) — The vast deck is completely empty of aircraft.**

Dunderberg

Type: Ironclad Ram
Class: 'Dunderberg' (1862)
Nomenclature: Thundering mountain

History:
1862 October 4: Laid down by Webb
1865 July 22: Launched
1866 September: Completed but not accepted by US Navy and returned to builder
1867 July: Sold to France, renamed ***Rochambeau***

Dwight D. Eisenhower (CVAN-69)

Type: Aircraft Carrier
Class: 'Nimitz' (1967)
Nomenclature: Dwight David Eisenhower (1890-1969), President of the US

History:
1970 Ordered as ***Eisenhower***
1970 May 25: Renamed ***Dwight D. Eisenhower***
1970 August 14: Laid down by Newport News
1975 June 30: Reclassified CVN-69
1975 October 11: Launched
1977 October 18: Completed
1977-79 Atlantic Fleet, Mediterrranean
1980 Indian Ocean

Eisenhower (CVAN-69), see *Dwight D. Eisenhower* (CVAN-69)

Enterprise (CV-6)

Type: Aircraft Carrier
Class: 'Yorktown' (1933)
Nomenclature: Schooner of 1799

History:
1934 July 16: Laid down by Newport News
1936 October 3: Launched
1938 May 12: Completed
1939-41 Pacific Fleet
World War 2: Pearl Harbor, 1942 Pacific raids, Midway, Guadalcanal-Tulagi, Eastern Solomons, Santa Cruz, Guadalcanal battle, Gilbert Islands, Kwajalein, Eniwetok, 1944 Truk raid, Hollandia, Saipan, Philippine Sea, Palau, Leyte, 1944 Raids on Luzon and Taiwan; 1944 Raids on Luzon and China coast; Iwo Jima, Okinawa
1942 April: Escorted carrier *Hornet* en route to Tokyo raid

***Enterprise* (CVN-65) — The world's largest warship.**
US Navy

1942 August 24: Hit by three bombs during Battle of Eastern Solomons (74 dead)
1942 October 26: Twice hit by bombs during Battle of Santa Cruz (44 dead)
1945 March 18: Slight damage from bomb hit, south of Japan
1945 April 11: Again damaged by kamikaze off Okinawa
1945 May 13: Severely damaged by kamikaze off Okinawa
1947 February 17: Decommissioned
1952 October 1: Reclassified CVA-6
1953 August 8: Reclassified CVS-6
1956 October 20: Stricken
1958 July 2: Sold and broken up at Kearny

Enterprise (CVAN-65)

Type: Aircraft Carrier
Class: 'Enterprise' (1957)

History:
1958 February 4: Laid down by Newport News
1960 September 24: Launched
1961 November 25: Completed
1961-65 Atlantic Fleet, Mediterranean
1965—— Pacific Fleet
1969 January 14: Damaged by fire and missile explosion off coast of Hawaii (27 dead)
1975 June 30: Reclassified CVN-65
1979-81 Reconstructed at Bremerton
1982 February: Recommissioned

Essex (CV-9)

Type: Aircraft Carrier
Class: 'Essex' (1940)
Nomenclature: Frigate of 1799

History:
1941 April 28: Laid down by Newport News
1942 July 31: Launched
1942 December 31: Completed
World War 2: 1943 Raids on Marcus and Wake Islands; Gilbert Islands, Kwajalein, 1944 Raids on Truk and Marianas; Saipan, Philippine Sea, Guam, Tinian, Palau, 1944 Raids on Luzon and Taiwan; Leyte, 1945 Raids on Luzon, China coast and Ryukus; Iwo Jima, Okinawa, 1945 Raids on Japan
1944 November 25: Damaged by kamikaze hit off Leyte

1945 April 11: Damaged by near miss of kamikaze off Okinawa
1947 January 9: Decommissioned
1949-51 Refit at Bremerton, hydraulic catapults added
1951 January 15: Recommissioned
1951-54 Korea
1951 September 16: Damaged by explosion caused by damaged aircraft crashing on landing off Korea
1952 October 1: Reclassified CVA-9
1955-56 Reconstructed at Bremerton, angled flightdeck
1957-69 Atlantic Fleet and Mediterranean
1960 March 8: Reclassified CVS-9
1962 FRAM II refit
1967 January 27: Went aground off Puerto Rico
1969 June 30: Decommissioned
1973 June 1: Stricken
1975 May: Sold and broken up

Florida (BM-9)

Type: Monitor
Class: 'Arkansas' (1898)
Nomenclature: 27th state of the Union, admitted 1845

History:
1899 January 23: Laid down by Lewis Nixon
1901 November 30: Launched
1903 June 18: Completed
1903-14 Atlantic
1908 June 20: Renamed ***Tallahassee***
1910 Experimental ordnance ship
1915 Submarine tender
World War 1: Canal Zone, Virgin Islands and Bermuda
1920-22 Reserve training ship
1921 July 1: Reclassified IX-16 (= unclassified ship)
1922 July 25: Sold and broken up

Florida (BB-30)

Type: Dreadnought
Class: 'Florida' (1908)

History:
1909 March 9: Laid down at Brooklyn
1910 May 12: Launched
1911 September 15: Completed
1912-31 Atlantic Fleet
1914 Mexico
World War1: 1917-19 Grand Fleet
1924 Refit; cage mainmast replaced by pole mast, re-engined, one funnel removed
1931 February 16: Decommissioned
1931 April 6: Stricken and broken up at Philadelphia

Forrestal (CVA-59)

Type: Aircraft Carrier
Class: 'Forrestal' (1951)
Nomenclature: James Vincent Forrestal (1892-1949), first Secretary of Defence

History:
1952 July 14: Laid down by Newport News
1954 December 11: Launched
1955 October 1: Completed
1956-65 Atlantic Fleet
1965-66 Refit
1967-68 Pacific Fleet, Vietnam
1967 July 29: Severely damaged by fire and explosion in Gulf of Tonkin (140 dead)
1968—— Atlantic Fleet
1975 June 30: Reclassified CV-59
1983-85 Refit

Franklin (CV-13)

Type: Aircraft Carrier
Class: 'Essex' (1940)
Nomenclature: Benjamin Franklin (1706-1790), statesman and scientist

***Florida* (BB-30) — Dreadnought, at Rosyth, with the Grand Fleet 1918.** *IWM*

History:
1942 December 7: Laid down by Newport News
1943 October 14: Launched
1944 January 31: Completed
World War 2: Guam, Palau, Leyte, 1944 Raids on Luzon, China coast and Taiwan; Okinawa
1944 October 13: Damaged when enemy plane crashlanded on flightdeck, east of the Philippines
1944 October 15: Again damaged by aircraft bomb
1944 October 30: Damaged by kamikaze, about 1,000 miles east of Samar
1945 March 19: Heavily damaged by bombs and fire about 50 miles south of Kyushu (724 dead)
1947 February 17: Decommissioned
1952 October 1: Reclassified CVA-13
1953 August 8: Reclassified CVS-13
1959 May 15: Reclassified AVT-8, aviation transport
1964 October 1: Stricken
1966 July 27: Sold and broken up at Newport News

Franklin D. Roosevelt (CVB-42)

Type: Aircraft Carrier
Class: 'Midway' (1942)
Nomenclature: Franklin Delano Roosevelt (1882-1945), President of the US during World War 2

History:
1943 December 1: Laid down by Brooklyn as ***Coral Sea***
1945 April 29: Launched
1945 May 8: Renamed ***Franklin D. Roosevelt***
1945 October 27: Completed
1946-47 Atlantic Fleet and Mediterranean
1947 Refit
1952 October 1: Reclassified CVA-42
1954-56 Reconstructed at Bremerton; armour belt removed, angled flightdeck, enclosed bow, steam catapults
1965 October 13: Damaged in collision with freighter *Charles Le Borgne* 100 miles southeast of Marseille
1966 November 5: Damaged by fire off Vietnam
1968 Second reconstruction cancelled
1975 July 1: Reclassified CV-42
1977 January 11: In collision with freighter *Oceanus* in Straits of Messina
1977 September 30: Stricken
1978 April 11: Sold and broken up at Kearny

Frederick (CA-8), see ***Maryland*** (CA-8)

Nomenclature: City in Maryland

George Washington (CVN-73)

Type: Aircraft Carrier
Class: 'Nimitz' (1967)
Nomenclature: George Washington (1732-1799), first President of the United States

History:
1983 Ordered from Newport News for completion in 1991

Georgia (BB-15)

Type: Pre-dreadnought
Class: 'Virginia' (1899)
Nomenclature: One of the original 13 states

History:
1901 August 31: Laid down by Bath
1904 October 11: Launched
1906 September 24: Completed
1906-07 Atlantic Fleet
1907 July 15: Damaged by powder explosion in 8" turret in Cape Cod Bay
1907-09 Great White Fleet
1909-14 Atlantic Fleet
1909 Refit, cagemasts fitted
1914 Mexico
World War 1: Atlantic Fleet
1919 Made five voyages as troop transport
1919-20 Pacific Fleet
1920 July 15: Decommissioned
1923 Sold and broken up at Oakland

Goliath, see ***Catskill***

Nomenclature: Biblical figure, Philistine king slain by David

Guam (CB-2)

Type: Battlecruiser
Class: 'Alaska' (1940)
Nomenclature: Island in the Marianas, a territory of the US since 1898

History:
1942 February 2: Laid down by New York Sbdg
1943 November 21: Launched
1944 September 17: Completed
World War 2: Okinawa. 1945 Raids on Japan
1947 February 17: Decommissioned
1960 June 1: Stricken
1961 May 24: Sold and broken up at Kearny

Hancock (CV-14), see ***Ticonderoga*** (CV-14)

Hancock (CV-19)

Type: Aircraft Carrier
Class: Modified 'Essex' (1940)
Nomenclature: A frigate of the Continental navy, 1776

History:
1943 January 26: Laid down by Quincy as ***Ticonderoga***
1943 May 1: Renamed ***Hancock***
1944 January 24: Launched
1944 April 15: Completed
World War 2: 1945 Raids on Luzon, China coast and Taiwan; Iwo Jima, 1945 Raids on Japan, 1944 Raids on Luzon and Taiwan; Okinawa
1944 October 14: Hit by bomb off Luzon
1944 November 25: Damaged by kamikaze off Luzon
1945 January 21: Damaged when aircraft crash landed on flightdeck (50 dead)
1945 April 7: Damaged by kamikaze off Okinawa (62 dead)
1946 April 29: Decommissioned
1952 October 1: Reclassified CVA-19
1952-54 Refit at Bremerton, steam catapults fitted
1954 February 15: Recommissioned
1954-56 Pacific Fleet
1956 Reconstructed at San Francisco, angled flightdeck
1956-75 Pacific Fleet
1975 July: Reclassified CV-19
1976 January 31: Stricken

Hawaii (CB-3)

Type: Battlecruiser
Class: 'Alaska' (1940)
Nomenclature: Island group in the Pacific annexed 1898, admitted 1959 as the 50th state

History:
1943 December 20: Laid down by New York Sbdg
1945 November 3: Launched
1947 February 17: Construction suspended when 82.4% complete
1952 February 26: Reclassified CBC-1, large command ship
1954 October 9: Conversion cancelled, reclassified CB-3
1955 June 9: Stricken
1959 April 15: Sold and broken up at Baltimore

Hecla, see ***Shackamaxon***

Nomenclature: Norse myth: a gateway to purgatory

Hercules, see ***Quinsigamond***

Nomenclature: Mythological hero renowned for his physical strength; son of Zeus

Hornet (CV-7)

Type: Aircraft Carrier
Class: 'Yorktown' (1933)
Nomenclature: A brig of 1805

History:
1939 September 25: Laid down by Newport News
1940 December 14: Launched
1941 October 20: Completed
World War 2: Midway, Guadalcanal, Santa Cruz
1942 April 18: Launched army B-25 bombers led by Colonel Doolittle for raid on Tokyo and other Japanese cities
1942 October 26: Damaged by aircraft torpedoes and bombs at Battle of Santa Cruz and sunk by Japanese destroyers after being abandoned (111 dead)

Hornet (CV-12)

Type: Aircraft Carrier
Class: 'Essex' (1940)

History:
1942 August 3: Laid down by Newport News as ***Kearsarge***
1943 January 24: Renamed ***Hornet***
1943 August 30: Launched
1943 November 29: Completed
World War 2: 1944 Raids on Palau and Truk; Hollandia, Saipan, Philippine Sea, Guam, Palau, Morotai, 1944 Raids on Luzon and Taiwan; 1945 Raids on Luzon, Taiwan and China coast; Iwo Jima, Okinawa
1945 June 5: Flightdeck damaged in typhoon in Philippine Sea
1947 January 15: Decommissioned
1952 October 1: Reclassified CVA-12
1952-53 Refit at New York
1953 September 11: Recommissioned
1954-70 Pacific Fleet
1955-56 Reconstructed at Bremerton; angled flightdeck
1958 June 27: Reclassified CVS-12
1962 Project 'Mercury' recovery ship
1965 Project 'Gemini' recovery ship
1965 FRAM II refit
1967-69 Vietnam
1970 June 26: Decommissioned
—— Stricken

Huntington (CA-5), see ***West Virginia*** (CA-5)

Nomenclature: City in West Virginia

Huron (CV-9), see ***South Dakota*** (CA-9)

Nomenclature: City in South Dakota

Idaho (BB-24)

Type: Pre dreadnought
Class: 'Mississippi' (1903)
Nomenclature: 43rd state of the Union, admitted 1890

History:
1904 May 12: Laid down by Cramp
1905 December 9: Launched
1908 April 1: Completed
1908-13 Atlantic Fleet
1908 Cage mainmast fitted
1912 Cage foremast fitted
1914 July 30: Sold to Greece, renamed ***Lemnos***

Idaho (BB-42)

Type: Dreadnought
Class: 'New Mexico' (1914)

History:
1915 January 20: Laid down by New York Sbdg
1917 June 30: Launched
1919 March 29: Completed

***Idaho* (BB-42) — 'New Mexico' class battleship. Aerial view at New York, May 1927.** *US Navy*

1919-41 Pacific Fleet
1931-34 Reconstructed at Norfolk; cagemasts removed, tower superstructures added, AA armament increase, bulges fitted, re-engined and reboilered
1941 Atlantic Fleet
World War 2: Attu, Gilbert Islands, Kwajalein, Saipan, Guam, Palau, Iwo Jima, Okinawa
1942 Refit, regunned
1944 Refit, new secondary armament
1945 June 13: Went aground off Okinawa
1946 July 3: Decommissioned
1947 November 24: Sold and broken up Newark

Illinois (BB-7)

Type: Pre-dreadnought
Class: 'Illinois' (1896)
Nomenclature: 21st state of the Union, admitted 1818

History:
1897 February 10: Laid down by Newport News
1898 October 4: Launched
1901 September 16: Completed
1902-03 European Squadron
1902 July 14: Went aground at Christiana, Norway
1903-07 North Atlantic
1904 March 1: Damaged in collision with battleship *Missouri* south of Cuba
1907-09 Great White Fleet
1912 Refit; cagemasts installed, reboilered
World War 1:
1921 Floating armoury, New York, reclassified IX-15
1941 January 23: Renamed ***Prairie State***
1956 March 26: Stricken
1956 May 18: Sold and broken up at Baltimore

Illinois (BB-65)

Type: Battleship
Class: 'Iowa' (1940)

History:
1945 January 15: Laid down at Philadelphia
1945 August 12: Construction cancelled when 22% complete

Independence (CVL-22)

Type: Light Aircraft Carrier
Class: 'Independence' (1942)
Nomenclature: First ship-of-the-line of the US Navy, 1814

History:
1941 May 1: Laid down by New York Sbdg as light cruiser ***Amsterdam*** (CL-59)
1942 January 10: Reordered as aircraft carrier, renamed ***Independence***
1942 August 22: Launched
1943 January 14: Completed
World War 2: 1943 Pacific raids, Gilbert Islands, Palau, Leyte, 1944 Raids on Luzon, Taiwan and Okinawa; 1945 Raids on Luzon, China coast and Ryukyus; 1945 Raids on Japan
1943 November 20: Severely damaged by aircraft torpedo off Tarawa
1946 July: Target vessel, Bikini nuclear tests
1946 August 28: Decommissioned
1951 January 29: Sunk as target off California

Above:
***Illinois* (BB-7) — Pre-dreadnought, in a British port, 1902.** *IWM*

Above right:
***Iowa* (BB-4) — Battleship, as completed, 1897.**

Right:
***Iowa* (BB-61) — 'Iowa' class battleship.**

Independence (CVA-62)

Type: Aircraft Carrier
Class: 'Forrestal' (1951)

History:
1955 July 1: Laid down at Brooklyn
1958 June 6: Launched
1959 January 10: Completed
1959-65 Atlantic Fleet
1965 Vietnam
1966—— Atlantic Fleet
1973 February 28: Reclassified CV-62

Indiana (BB-1)

Type: Pre-dreadnought
Class: 'Indiana' (1890)
Nomenclature: 19th state of the Union, admitted 1816

History:
1891 May 7: Laid down by Cramp
1893 February 28: Launched
1895 November 20: Completed
1895-1914 Atlantic
1898 Operations off Cuba and Puerto Rico, Santiago
1904 Reboilered
1908 6" guns and TT removed
World War 1: Training ship, New York
1919 January 31: Decommissioned
1920 November 1: Sunk as a target in explosive experiments off Tangier Island

Indiana (BB-50)

Type: Dreadnought
Class: 'South Dakota' (1917)

History:
1920 November 1: Laid down at Brooklyn
1922 February 8: Contract cancelled when 34.7% completed

Indiana (BB-58)

Type: Battleship
Class: 'South Dakota' (1938)

History:
1939 November 20: Laid down by Newport News
1941 November 21: Launched
1942 April 30: Completed
World War 2: Southwest Pacific, Gilbert Islands, Kwajalein, Philippine Sea, Saipan, Guam, Palau, Iwo Jima, 1945 Raids on Japan; Okinawa
1944 February 2: Damaged in collision with battleship *Washington* off Kwajalein
1944 June 19: Damaged by suicide plane off Saipan
1945 June 5: Damaged in typhoon off Okinawa
1947 September 11: Decommissioned
1962 June 1: Stricken
1963 September 6: Sold and broken up at Richmond, Ca

Intrepid (CV-11)

Type: Aircraft Carrier
Class: 'Essex' (1940)
Nomenclature: Ketch captured in 1803, used by Decatur to destroy the captured frigate *Philadelphia* in Tripoli harbour

History:
1941 December 1: Laid down by Newport News
1943 April 26: Launched
1943 August 16: Completed
World War 2: Kwajalein, 1944 Raid on Truk; Palau, 1944 Raids on Luzon, Taiwan, China coast and Ryukyus; Leyte, Okinawa
1944 February 17: Torpedoed by Japanese aircraft off Truk
1944 October 29: Damaged by kamikaze off Luzon

1944 November 25: Damaged by two kamikazes in Philippine Sea (65 dead)
1945 March 18: Lightly damaged by kamikaze and gunfire south of Kyushu
1945 April 16: Damaged by kamikaze off Okinawa
1947 March 22: Decommissioned
1952 October 1: Reclassified CVA-11
1952-54 Refit at Newport News, steam catapults fitted
1954 June 18: Recommissioned
1954-56 Atlantic Fleet and Mediterranean
1956-57 Reconstructed at New York, angled flightdeck
1961 April 25: Damaged by boiler explosion while off Virginia
1962 March 31: Reclassified CVS-11
1965 FRAM II refit
1966-67 Vietnam
1968-73 Atlantic Fleet and Mediterranean
1974 March 15: Decommissioned
1982 February 23: Stricken; preserved as museum at New York City

Iowa (BB-4)

Type: Pre-dreadnought
Class: 'Iowa' (1892)
Nomenclature: 29th state of the Union, admitted 1846

History:
1893 August 5: Laid down by Cramp
1896 March 28: Launched
1897 June 16: Completed
1897-98 Atlantic
1898 Operations off Cuba, Santiago
1899-1902 Pacific
1902-03 South Atlantic
1903 April 9: Damaged by turret explosion
1903 April 21: Damaged by burst steam pipe off Pensacola
1902 September 11: Went aground off southern Brazil
1904 February 4: Damaged by explosion in 8" turret
1903-07 North Atlantic
1908 Refit, cagemast fitted
World War 1: 1917 Receiving ship, Philadelphia; 1918 Training ship, Hampton Roads
1919 March 31: Decommissioned
1920 September 20: Reclassified IX-6; radio-controlled target ship
1923 March 23: Sunk by battleship *Mississippi* in Panama Bay

Iowa (BB-53)

Type: Dreadnought
Class: 'South Dakota' (1917)

History:
1920 May 17: Laid down by Newport News
1922 February 8: Contract cancelled when 31.8% complete

Iowa (BB-61)

Type: Battleship
Class: 'Iowa' (1939)

History:
1940 June 27: Laid down by Brooklyn
1942 August 27: Launched
1943 February 22: Completed
1943 July 16: Damaged by grounding off Maine
World War 2: Kwajalein, 1944 Raids on Truk and Palau; Hollandia, Saipan, Philippine Sea, Guam, Tinian, Palau, 1944 Raids on Luzon and Taiwan; Leyte, Okinawa, 1945 Raids on Japan
1943 October: Carried President Roosevelt to Casablanca Conference in Morocco
1944 March 18: Hit by shore batteries off Mili Island
1945-48 Pacific Fleet
1949 March 24: Decommissioned
1951 Refit, catapults removed, AA armament decreased
1951 August 25: Recommissioned
1952 Korea
1952-58 Atlantic Fleet
1958 February 24: Decommissioned
1984 April 28: Recommissioned

Iwo Jima (CV-46)

Type: Aircraft Carrier
Class: Modified 'Essex' (1940)
Nomenclature: Island south of Japan, scene of amphibious operation in World War 2, February 19 1945

History:
1945 January 29: Laid down by Newport News
1945 August 12: Contract cancelled

Jason, see *Sangamon*

Nomenclature: Greek myth: leader of the Argonauts

John F. Kennedy (CVA-67)

Type: Aircraft Carrier
Class: 'Kitty Hawk' (1955)
Nomenclature: John Fitzgerald Kennedy (1917-1963), President of the US

History:
1964 October 22: Laid down by Newport News
1967 May 27: Launched
1968 September 7: Completed
1968-—— Atlantic Fleet and Mediterranean
1974 December 1: Reclassified CV-67
1975 November 22: In collision with frigate *Belknap*, which was severely damaged, in the Ionian Sea
1979-80 Refit

Kalamazoo

Type: Monitor
Class: 'Kalamazoo' (1863)
Nomenclature: River in Michigan

History:
1863 Laid down at Brooklyn
1865 November 27: Construction suspended
1869 June 15: Renamed ***Colossus***
1884 Broken up on stocks

Kansas (BB-21)

Type: Pre-dreadnought
Class: 'Connecticut' (1902)
Nomenclature: 34th state of the Union, admitted 1861

History:
1904 February 10: Laid down by New York Sbdg
1905 August 12: Launched
1907 April 18: Completed

***John F. Kennedy* (CVA-67) — Aircraft carrier, March 1969, underway in the Atlantic.** *US Navy*

1907-09 Great White Fleet
1909-14 Atlantic Fleet
1911 Refit, cagemasts fitted
1914 Mexico
World War 1: Atlantic Fleet
1919 Made five voyages as troop transport
1921 December 16: Decommissioned
1923 October 9: Stricken
1924 January 23: Sold and broken up at Philadelphia

Kearsarge (BB-5)

Type: Pre-dreadnought
Class: 'Kearsarge' (1895)
Nomenclature: Mountain in New Hampshire

History:
1896 June 30: Laid down by Newport News
1898 March 24: Launched
1900 February 20: Completed
1900-07 North Atlantic
1906 April 13: Damaged by explosion in 13" turret off Cape Cruz, Cuba
1907-09 Great White Fleet
1912 Refit, cagemasts fitted, reboilered
1915-16 Mexico
World War 1: 1917-19 Engineering training ship
1920 May 10: Decommissioned for conversion to crane ship; converted at Philadelphia
1920 August 5: Reclassified AB-1
1941 November 6: Renamed ***Crane Ship No 1***
1955 June 22: Stricken
1955 September 8: Sold and broken up

Kearsarge (CV-12), see ***Hornet*** (CV-12)

Kearsarge (CV-33)

Type: Aircraft Carrier
Class: Modified 'Essex' (1940)

History:
1944 March 1: Laid down at Brooklyn
1945 May 5: Launched

***Kansas* (BB-21) — 'Connecticut' class pre-dreadnought, c1916.**

1946 March 2: Completed
1946-50 Atlantic Fleet and Mediterranean
1950 June 16: Decommissioned
1951-52 Refit, hydraulic catapults fitted
1952-53 Korea
1952 October 1: Reclassified CVA-33
1952-56 Pacific Fleet
1956-57 Reconstructed at Bremerton, angled flightdeck
1957-70 Pacific Fleet
1958 October 1: Reclassified CVS-33
1962 FRAM II refit
1967 December 23: Slightly damaged by fire, at Sasebo
1970 February 13: Decommissioned
1973 May 1: Stricken
1974 January 18: Sold and broken up

Kentucky (BB-6)

Type: Pre-dreadnought
Class: 'Kearsarge' (1895)
Nomenclature: 15th state of the Union, admitted 1792

History:
1896 June 30: Laid down by Newport News
1898 March 24: Launched
1900 May 15: Completed
1900-04 Far East
1904 April: Damaged by fire and explosion in ammunition handling room
1904-07 North Atlantic
1906 October 1: Landed marines at Havana
1906 January 17: Damaged in collision with battleship *Alabama* in New York Bay
1907-09 Great White Fleet
1912 Refit, cagemasts fitted, reboilered
1915-16 Mexico
World War 1: Training ship
1920 Conversion to crane ship (AB-2) cancelled
1920 May 29: Decommissioned
1923 March 24: Sold and broken up at Philadelphia

Kentucky (BB-66)

Type: Battleship
Class: 'Iowa' (1939)

History:
1944 December 6: Laid down at Norfolk
1947 February 17: Construction suspended when 69.2% complete; had been scheduled to commission September 23 1946
1950 January 20: Launched to clear slip
1954 October 15: Went aground in James River during hurricane
1956 Bow section used to repair damaged *Wisconsin*
1958 June 9: Stricken
1958 October 31: Sold and broken up at Baltimore

Kitty Hawk (CVA-63)

Type: Aircraft Carrier
Class: 'Kitty Hawk' (1955)
Nomenclature: Village in North Carolina where the Wright brothers made the first airplane flight, December 17 1903

History:
1956 December 27: Laid down by New York Sbdg
1960 May 21: Launched
1961 April 29: Completed
1961—— Pacific Fleet
1967 December 18: Slightly damaged by fire at Subic Bay
1973 December 11: Damaged by fire in machinery room 700 miles east of the Philippines
1973 April 29: Reclassified CV-63
1976-77 Refit, Terrier SAM replaced by Sea Sparrow
1980 Indian Ocean

Lake Champlain (CV-39)

Type: Aircraft Carrier
Class: Modified 'Essex' (1940)
Nomenclature: Naval battle of the War of 1812, September 11 1814

History:
1943 March 15: Laid down at Norfolk
1944 November 2: Launched
1945 June 3: Completed
1945-47 Atlantic Fleet
1945 November 26: Set Atlantic speed record which lasted until 1952 when broken by liner *United States*
1947 February 17: Decommissioned
1951-52 Refit at Newport News
1952 September 19: Recommissioned
1952 October 1: Reclassified CVA-39
1953 Korea
1954-66 Atlantic Fleet
1957 August 1: Reclassified CVS-39
1966 May 2: Decommissioned
1969 December 1: Stricken
1972 Sold and broken up at Kearny

Langley (CV-1)

Type: Aircraft Carrier
Class: 'Langley' (1919)
Nomenclature: Samuel Pierpont Langley (1834-1906), pioneer of aviation

History:
1911 October 18: Laid down at Mare Island as collier ***Jupiter*** (AC-3)
1912 August 24: Launched
1913 April 27 Completed
1919 July 11: Conversion to aircraft carrier authorised
1920 April 21: Renamed ***Langley*** (CV-1)
1922 March 20: Conversion by Norfolk completed
1924-36 Pacific Fleet
1937 Converted to seaplane tender at Mare Island
1937 January 14: Reclassified AV-3
1939-42 Far East
World War 2: East Indies
1942 February 27: Sunk by Japanese aircraft off Tjilatjap, Java (16 dead)

Langley (CVL-27)

Type: Light Aircraft Carrier
Class: 'Independence' (1942)

History:
1940 Ordered as light cruiser ***Fargo*** (CL-85)
1942 March 27: Reordered as aircraft carrier, renamed ***Crown Point***
1942 April 11: Laid down by New York Sbdg
1942 November 13: Renamed ***Langley***
1943 May 22: Launched
1943 August 31: Completed
World War 2: Kwajalein, Eniwetok, Hollandia, 1944 Raids on Palau and Truk; Saipan, Philippine Sea, Guam, Palau,

1944 Raids on Luzon, Taiwan and Okinawa; 1945 Raids on Luzon and China coast; Iwo Jima, Okinawa
1945 January 21: Damaged by bombs in South China Sea
1947 February 11: Decommissioned
1951 June 6: Transferred to France, renamed ***La Fayette***
1963 March 20: Returned to US Navy
1963 October: Sold and broken up at Baltimore

Lehigh

Type: Monitor
Class: 'Passaic' (1862)
Nomenclature: River in Pennsylvania

History:
1862 Laid down by Reaney
1863 January 17: Launched
1863 April 15: Completed
Civil War: 1863 N Atlantic BS, James River, S Atlantic BS, Attacks on Charleston, 1865 James River
1863 June 17: In action with Confederate ironclad *Atlanta*
1863 November 16: Went aground under fire off Sullivans Island
1865 June 9: Decommissioned
1875 Briefly recommissioned
1898 Coastal defence, New England
1904 April 16: Sold and broken up

Lexington (CC-1) (CV-2)

Type: 1) Battlecruiser, 2) Aircraft Carrier
Class: 1) 'Lexington' (1916), 2) 'Lexington' (1922)
Nomenclature: Battle of the American Revolution, 19 April 1776

History:
1917 Ordered as battlecruiser ***Constitution*** (CC-1)
1917 December 10: Renamed ***Lexington***
1921 January 8: Laid down by Fore River
1922 July 1: Reordered as aircraft carrier CV-2, when 33.8% complete
1925 October 3: Launched
1927 December 14: Completed
1928-41 Pacific Fleet
1929 December: Served as floating power plant for city of Tacoma, Washington
World War 2: 1942 Pacific raids, Coral Sea
1942 February: 8" guns removed
1942 May 8: Hit by two torpedoes and three bombs during Battle of Coral Sea and sank (216 dead)

Lexington (CC-4), see *Ranger* (CC-4)

Lexington (CV-16)

Type: Aircraft Carrier
Class: 'Essex' (1940)

History:
1941 July 15: Laid down at Quincy as ***Cabot***
1942 June 16: Renamed ***Lexington***
1942 September 26: Launched
1943 February 17: Completed
World War 2: 1943 Raids on Tarawa and Wake; Gilbert Islands, 1944 Raids on Palau and Truk; Hollandia, Saipan, Philippine Sea, Guam, Palau, Leyte, 1944 Raids on Luzon and Taiwan; 1945 Raids on Luzon, Taiwan, China coast and Ryukyus; Iwo Jima, 1945 Raids on Japan
1943 December 4: Torpedoed by Japanese aircraft off Wotje during raid on Kwajalein
1944 November 5: Damaged by kamikaze in Philippine Sea
1947 April 23: Decommissioned
1952 October 1: Reclassified CVA-16
1952-55 Reconstructed at Bremerton; steam catapults and angled flightdeck fitted
1955 August 15: Recommissioned
1955-62 Pacific Fleet
1962 October 10: Reclassified CVS-16
1969 January 16: Reclassified CVT-16, training carrier at Pensacola
1969 September 7: Damaged by boiler room fire while in drydock at Boston
1978 July 1: Reclassified AVT-16, pilot training ship

Leyte (CV-32)

Type: Aircraft Carrier
Class: Modified 'Essex' (1942)
Nomenclature: Naval battle in the Philippines, October 23-26 1944

History:
1944 February 21: Laid down by Newport News as ***Crown Point***
1945 May 8: Renamed ***Leyte***
1945 August 23: Launched
1946 April 11: Completed
1946-50 Atlantic Fleet and Mediterranean
1950-51 Korea
1951-59 Atlantic Fleet
1952 October 1: Reclassified CVA-32
1953 July 8: Reclassified CVS-32
1953 October 16: Damaged by explosion and fire while converting at Boston (37 dead)
1959 May 15: Decommissioned; reclassified AVT-10, aircraft transport
1969 June 1: Stricken
—— Sold and broken up

'Louisiana' (BB-19)

Type: Pre-dreadnought
Class: 'Connecticut' (1902)
Nomenclature: 18th state of the Union, admitted 1812

History:
1903 February 7: Laid down by Newport News
1904 August 27: Launched
1906 June 2: Completed
1906-07 Atlantic Fleet
1907-09 Great White Fleet
1909-14 Atlantic Fleet
1911 Refit, cagemasts fitted
1913 August 29: Went aground off Veracruz
1914 Mexico
World War 1: Atlantic Fleet
1919 Made four voyages as troop transport
1920 October 20: Decommissioned
1923 November 1: Sold and broken up at Baltimore

Louisiana (BB-71)

Type: Battleship
Class: 'Montana' (1940)

History:
1940 September 9: Ordered from Norfolk; never laid down
1943 July 21: Contract cancelled

Mahopac

Type: Monitor
Class: 'Canonicus' (1862)
Nomenclature: Lake in New York

History:
1862 Laid down by Secor
1864 May 17: Launched
1864 September 22: Completed
Civil War: 1864-65 S Atlantic BS, Fort Fisher, James River
1869 June 15: Renamed ***Castor***
1869 August 10: Renamed ***Mahopac***
1902 January 14: Stricken
1902 May 5: Sold and broken up

Maine

Type: Battleship
Class: 'Maine' (1886)
Nomenclature: 23rd state of the Union, admitted 1820

History:
1888 October 17: Laid down at Brooklyn
1890 November 18: Launched
1895 September 17: Completed
1895-98 North Atlantic
1898 February 15: Destroyed by coal gas explosion while in Havana harbour on visit to protect US interests (260 dead)
1912 February 13: Hulk refloated and sunk at sea

Maine (BB-10)

Type: Pre-dreadnought
Class: 'Maine' (1898)

History:
1899 February 15: Laid down by Cramp
1901 July 27: Launched
1902 December 29: Completed
1903-07 Atlantic Fleet
1907-08 Great White Fleet
1909-10 Refit, cagemasts fitted
World War 1: Training ship
1920 May 15: Decommissioned
1922 January 26: Sold and broken up at Philadelphia

Maine (BB-69)

Type: Battleship

***Mahopac* — Monitor, in the James River, 1864.**

Class: 'Montana' (1940)

History:
1940 September 9: Ordered from Brooklyn; never laid down
1943 July 21: Contract cancelled

Manayunk

Type: Monitor
Class: 'Canonicus' (1862)
Nomenclature: Town in Pennsylvania

History:
1862 Laid down by Snowden & Mason
1864 December 18: Launched
1865 September 27: Completed at Mound City, not commissioned
1867 Towed to New Orleans and laid up
1869 June 15: Renamed ***Ajax***
1871 January 1: First commissioned, but laid up
1874-76 Recommissioned
1895-98 Naval militia training ship
1899 July 8: Stricken
1899 October 10: Sold and broken up

Manhattan

Type: Monitor
Class: 'Canonicus' (1862)
Nomenclature: Island in New York Bay

History:
1862 Laid down by Secor
1863 October 14: Launched
1864 June 6: Completed
Civil War: Mobile Bay, 1864 Red River
1865 August: Laid up
1869 June 15: Renamed ***Neptune***
1869 August 10: Renamed ***Manhattan***
1872-73 Refit
1873-77 Recommissioned
1901 December 14: Stricken
1902 March 24: Sold and broken up

Maryland (CA-8)

Type: Armoured Cruiser
Class: 'Pennsylvania' (1899)
Nomenclature: One of the original 13 states

History:
1901 October 29: Laid down by Newport News
1903 September 12: Launched

1905 April 18: Completed
1905-06 Atlantic Fleet
1906-07 Asiatic Station
1907-17 Pacific Fleet
1911 Refit, foremast replaced by cagemast
1916 November 9: renamed ***Frederick***
World War 1: South Atlantic, Atlantic convoys
1919 Made six voyages as troop transport
1920-22 Pacific Fleet
1922 February 14: Decommissioned
1929 November 13: Stricken
1930 February 11: Sold and broken up

Maryland (BB-46)

Type: Dreadnought
Class: 'Colorado' (1916)

History:
1917 April 24: Laid down by Newport News
1920 March 20: Launched
1921 July 21: Completed
1922-41 Pacific Fleet
1928 Carried President Hoover to South America
1934 Refit; catapult added to 'X' turret, AA armament increased
World War 2: Pearl Harbor, Gilbert Islands, Kwajalein, Saipan, Palau, Leyte, Surigao Strait, Okinawa
1941 December 7: Damaged by two bombs during Japanese attack on Pearl Harbor
1942 Repaired at Bremerton; cage mainmast cut down to stump, AA armament increased, catapult removed from 'X' turret
1944 June 22: Damaged by aircraft torpedo hit in bow off Saipan
1944 November 29: Moderately damaged by kamikaze off Leyte (31 dead)
1944-45 Refit, mainmast stump replaced by tower, secondary armament replaced
1945 April 7: Damaged by kamikaze off Okinawa
1947 April 3: Decommissioned
1959 July 8: Sold and broken up at Oakland

Massachusetts, see ***Passaconaway***

Massachusetts (BB-2)

Type: Pre-dreadnought
Class: 'Indiana' (1890)
Nomenclature: One of the original 13 states

History:
1891 June 25: Laid down by Cramp
1893 June 10: Launched
1896 June 10: Completed
1896-1914 Atlantic
1898 Flying Squadron, operations off Cuba and Puerto Rico
1903 January 16: Damaged by 8" gun explosion off Culebra Island
1903 August 12: Went aground off Bar Harbor, Maine
1907-08 Refit; reboilered, rearmed
1910 Cage mainmast and 3" guns added
World War 1: Training ship
1919 March 31: Decommissioned
1920 November 22: Target ship for army aircraft
1921 January 6: Scuttled of Pensacola as target

Massachusetts (BB-54)

Type: Dreadnought
Class: 'South Dakota' (1917)

History:
1921 April 4: Laid down by Fore River
1922 February 8: Contract cancelled when 11% completed

Massachusetts (BB-59)

Type: Battleship
Class: 'South Dakota' (1938)

History:
1939 July 20: Laid down at Quincy
1941 September 23: Launched
1942 May 15: Completed

***Maine* — The first US battleship, completed in 1895.**

Right:
***Massachusetts* (BB-2) — 'Indiana' class battleship, as completed. Notice eagle between guns on forward turret.**

Far right:
***Michigan* (BB-27) — Dreadnought, c1911, first US battleship with superfiring turrets.** *IWM*

World War 2: North Africa, Gilbert Islands, Kwajalein, 1944 Raids on Truk and Palau, Hollandia, Palau, 1944 Raids on Luzon and Taiwan; Leyte, 1945 Raids on Luzon, Taiwan, China coast and Ryukyus; Iwo Jima, Okinawa, 1945 Raids on Japan
1942 November: Action at Casablanca with French battleship *Jean Bart* and destroyers
1945 June 5: Damaged in typhoon off Okinawa
1947 March 27: Decommissioned
1962 June 1: Stricken
1965 June 8: Transferred to the state of Massachusetts and preserved as a memorial at Fall River

Medusa, see ***Nantucket***

Nomenclature: Greek myth: a gorgon slain by Perseus

Memphis (CA-10), see ***Tennessee*** (CA-10)

Nomenclature: City in Tennessee

Miantonomoh

Type: Monitor
Class: 'Miantonomoh' (1862)
Nomenclature: Leader of the Narragansett Indians (d1643)

History:
1862 Laid down at Brooklyn
1863 August 15: Launched
1865 September 18: Completed
1866-67 Made Atlantic crossing to visit Europe
1867 July 26: Decommissioned
1869-70 Recommissioned
1874 Broken up at Chester, Pa

Miantonomah (BM-5)

Type: Monitor
Class: 'Amphitrite' (1874)

History:
1874 Laid down by John Roach
1876 December 5: Launched
1882 October 6: Commissioned incomplete and taken to Brooklyn for completion
1891 October 27: Completed
1898 Operations off Cuba
1906-15 Naval militia training ship
1915 December 15: Stricken; target hulk as target *C*
1922 January 30: Sold and broken up

Michigan (BB-27)

Type: Dreadnought
Class: 'South Carolina' (1905)
Nomenclature: 26th state of the Union, admitted 1837

History:
1906 December 17: Laid down by New York Sbdg
1908 May 26: Launched
1910 January 4: Completed
1910-16 Atlantic Fleet
—— Refit
1914 Mexico
World War 1: Atlantic Fleet
1918 January 15: Lost cage foremast in storm off Cape Hatteras
1919 Made two voyages as troop transport
1922 February 11: Decommissioned
1923 October 17: Stricken
1924 January 23: Sold and broken up at Philadelphia

Midway (CVB-41)

Type: Aircraft Carrier
Class: 'Midway' (1942)
Nomenclature: Naval battle in the Pacific, World War 2, June 3-6 1942

***Midway* (CVB-41) — Aircraft carrier, January 1954, modified but prior to reconstruction.**

History:
1943 October 27: Laid down by Newport News
1945 March 20: Launched
1945 September 10: Completed
1946-54 Atlantic Fleet and Mediterranean
1947 September: First firing of a guided missile from a carrier deck
1952 October 1: Reclassified CVA-41
1955 Pacific Fleet
1955-57 Reconstructed at Bremerton; armour belt removed, angled flightdeck, enclosed bow, steam catapults fitted
1957—— Pacific Fleet
1966-70 Reconstructed at San Francisco; new flightdeck and elevators
1975 July 1: Reclassified CV-41
1979-80 Indian Ocean
1980 July 29: Damaged in collision with merchant ship *Cactus* off Palawan Island

Minnesota (BB-22)

Type: Pre-dreadnought
Class: 'Connecticut' (1902)
Nomenclature: 32nd state of the Union, admitted 1858

History:
1903 October 27: Laid down by Newport News
1905 April 8: Launched
1907 March 9: Completed
1907-09 Great White Fleet
1909-16 Atlantic Fleet
1909 Refit, cage foremast fitted
1910 Cage mainmast fitted
World War 1: Atlantic Fleet
1918 September 29: Damaged by mine off Fenwick Light, De
1919 Made three voyages as troop transport
1921 December 1: Decommissioned
1923 October 9: Stricken
1924 January 23: Sold and broken up at Philadelphia

Mississippi (BB-23)

Type: Pre-dreadnought
Class: 'Mississippi' (1903)
Nomenclature: 20th state of the Union, admitted 1817

History:
1904 May 12: Laid down by Cramp
1905 September 30: Launched
1908 February 1: Completed
1908-14 Atlantic Fleet
1908 Cage mainmast fitted
1910 Cage foremast fitted

1914 January: Aeronautical station ship, Pensacola
1914 Floating seaplane base, Veracruz
1914 July 21: Transferred to Greece, renamed ***Kilkis***

Mississippi (BB-41)

Type: Dreadnought
Class: 'New Mexico' (1914)

History:
1915 April 5: Laid down by Newport News
1917 January 25: Launched
1917 December 18: Completed
1918-19 Atlantic Fleet
1919-41 Pacific Fleet
1924 June 12: Damaged by powder explosion in 14" turret off San Pedro (48 dead)
1931-33 Reconstructed at Norfolk; cagemasts removed, tower superstructures added, AA armament increased, bulges fitted, re-engined and reboilered
1941 Atlantic Fleet
World War 2: Pacific convoys, Attu, Gilbert Islands, Kwajalein, Palau, Leyte, Okinawa, Surigao Strait, Lingayen
1943 November 19: Damaged by 14" turret explosion off Makin Island (43 dead)
1945 January 9: Damaged by kamikaze off Lingayen
1945 June 5: Lightly damaged by kamikaze at Okinawa
1945 December 7: Reclassified AG-128, converted to training and experimental gunnery ship
1956 September 17: Decommissioned
1956 November 28: Sold and broken up at Baltimore

Missoula (CA-13), see ***Montana*** (CA-13)

see ***Montana*** (CA-13)

Nomenclature: City in Montana

Missouri (BB-11)

Type: Pre-dreadnought
Class: 'Maine' (1898)
Nomenclature: 24th state of the Union, admitted 1821

History:
1900 February 7: Laid down by Newport News
1901 December 28: Launched
1903 December 1: Completed
1904-07 Atlantic Fleet
1904 March 1: In collision with battleship *Illinois* south of Cuba
1904 April 13: Damaged by fire in after 12" turret off the Virginia Capes (30 dead)
1907-09 Great White Fleet
1909 Cage foremast fitted
1911 Cage mainmast fitted
World War 1: Atlantic Fleet

Above:
***Mississippi* (BB-41) — 'New Mexico' class battleship, October 1941, at Iceland as reconstructed.** *IWM*

Right:
***Monitor* — The original ship of this type in a view taken on board July 1862. Notice the dents in the turret from hits in action. No photographs of the complete vessel are known.**

1919 Made four voyages as troop transport
1919 September 8: Decommissioned
1922 January 26: Sold and broken up at Philadelphia

Missouri (BB-63)

Type: Battleship
Class: 'Iowa' (1939)

History:
1941 January 6: Laid down by Brooklyn
1944 January 29: Launched
1944 June 11: Completed
World War 2: Iwo Jima, 1945 Raids on Japan; Okinawa
1945 April 11 and 16: Lightly damaged by kamikazes off Okinawa
1945 June 5: Lightly damaged in typhoon off Okinawa
1945 September 2: Surrender of Japan signed on board in Tokyo Bay
1945-50 Atlantic Fleet
1950 January 17: Went aground on Thimble Shoal, Chesapeake Bay, refloated February 1
1951-51 Korea
1951-52 Atlantic Fleet
1952-53 Korea
1955 February 26: Decommissioned
1987 Scheduled to recommission

Monadnock

Type: Monitor
Class: 'Miantonomoh'(1862)
Nomenclature: Mountain in New Hampshire

History:
1862 Laid down at Boston
1864 March 23: Launched
1864 October 4: Completed
Civil War: 1865 N Atlantic BS, James River, Fort Fisher
1865-66 Sailed to San Francisco via Cape Horn
1866 June 30: Decommissioned
1882 Broken up at Mare Island

Monadnock (BM-3)

Type: Monitor
Class: 'Amphitrite' (1874)

History:
1875 January 15: Laid down by Continental, San Francisco
1883 September 18: Launched
1896 February 20: Completed by Mare Island
1898 Crossed the Pacific to Philippine Islands
1898-1909 Philippines and Far East
1912 Submarine tender, Cavite
1919 March 24: Decommissioned
1923 February 2: Stricken
1923 August 23: Sold at Manila

Monitor

Type: Monitor
Class: 'Monitor' (1861)
Nomenclature: One who keeps order

History:
1861 October 25: Laid down by Continental
1862 January 30: Launched
1862 February 25: Completed
Civil War; Hampton Roads, James River
1862 March 9: Fought celebrated action with Confederate ironclad *Virginia* in Hampton Roads
1862 December 31: Foundered off Cape Hatteras while in tow during rough weather (16 dead)

Montana (CA-13)

Type: Armoured Cruiser
Class: 'Tennessee' (1902)
Nomenclature: 41st state of the Union, admitted 1889

History:
1905 April 29: Laid down by Newport News
1906 December 15: Launched
1908 July 21: Completed
1908-17 Atlantic Fleet and Mediterranean
1912 Refit, foremast replaced by cagemast
World War 1: Atlantic convoys
1919 Made one voyage as troop transport
1920 June 7: Renamed ***Missoula***
1921 February 2: Decommissioned
1930 September 29: Sold and broken up

Montana (BB-51)

Type: Dreadnought
Class: 'South Dakota' (1917)

History:
1920 September 1: Laid down at Mare Island
1922 February 9: Contract cancelled when 27.6% complete

Montana (BB-67)

Type: Battleship

Class: 'Montana' (1940)

History:
1940 September 9: Ordered from Philadelphia; never laid down
1943 July 21: Contract cancelled

Montauk

Type: Monitor
Class: 'Passaic' (1862)
Nomenclature: Village on Long Island, New York

History:
1862 Laid down by Continental
1862 October 9: Launched
1862 December 17: Completed
Civil War: 1863-65 S Atlantic BS, Attacks on Charleston
1863 February 28: Damaged by a mine in Ogeechee River
1865 Decommissioned
1904 April 16: Sold and broken up

Monterey (BM-6)

Type: Monitor
Class: 'Monterey' (1889)
Nomenclature: Capital of the Spanish colony of California

History:
1889 December 20: Laid down by Union
1891 April 28: Launched
1893 February 13: Completed
1893-98 Pacific
1898 Crossed the Pacific to Philippine Islands
1900 Reboilered at Hong Kong
1900-04 Far East
1911-17 Philippines
1917 Towed to Hawaii; station ship, Pearl Harbor
1921 August 27: Decommissioned
1922 February 22: Sold and broken up at Oakland, Ca

Monterey (CVL-26)

Type: Light Aircraft Carrier
Class: 'Independence' (1942)

History:
1941 December 29: Laid down by New York Sbdg as light cruiser ***Dayton*** (CL-78)
1942 March 27: Reordered as aircraft carrier, renamed ***Monterey***
1943 February 28: Launched
1943 June 17: Completed
World War 2: Gilbert Islands, Kwajalein, 1944 Raids on Truk, Marianas and Palau; Hollandia, Morotai, Saipan, Philippine Sea, Guam, Palau, 1944 Raids on Luzon, Okinawa and Taiwan; Okinawa, 1945 Raids on Japan
1944 December 18: Damaged in typhoon in Philippine Sea
1947 February 11: Decommissioned
1950 September 15: Recommissioned; training ship at Pensacola
1956 January 16: Decommissioned
1959 May 15: Reclassified AVT-2, aircraft transport
1970 June 1: Stricken

Nahant

Type: Monitor
Class: 'Passaic' (1862)

Nomenclature: Town in Massachusetts

History:
1862 Laid down by Harrison Loring
1862 October 7: Launched
1862 December 29: Completed
Civil War: 1863-65 S Atlantic BS, 1863 Attacks on Charleston
1865 August 11: Decommissioned
1869 June 15: Renamed ***Atlas***
1869 August 10: Renamed ***Nahant***
1898 Harbour defence, New York
1904 April 16: Sold and broken up

Nantucket

Type: Monitor
Class: 'Passaic' (1862)
Nomenclature: Island off Cape Cod, Massachusetts

History:
1862 Laid down by Atlantic
1862 December 6: Launched
1863 February 26: Completed
Civil War: 1863-65 S Atlantic BS, 1863 Attacks on Charleston
1863 April 6: Damaged by shore batteries at Charleston
1865 June 24: Decommissioned
1869 June 15: Renamed ***Medusa***
1869 August 10: Renamed ***Nantucket***
1882 and 1884 Briefly recommissioned
1895-98 Naval militia training ship
1898 Harbour defence, Port Royal, SC
1900 March 30: Stricken
1900 November 14: Sold and broken up

Nebraska, see *Shackamaxon*

Nebraska (CA-4), see *Pennsylvania* (CA-4)

Above left:
***Montana* (CA-13) — Armoured cruiser, c1912, with new cagemasts, later renamed *Missoula*.**

Above right:
***Nebraska* (BB-14) — Pre-dreadnought of 'Virginia' class, c1914.**

Nebraska (BB-14)

Type: Pre-dreadnought
Class: 'Virgina' (1899)
Nomenclature: 37th state of the Union, admitted 1867

History:
1901 Ordered as ***Pennsylvania;*** renamed ***Nebraska***
1902 July 4: Laid down by Moran
1904 October 7: Launched
1907 July 1: Completed
1908-09 Great White Fleet
1909-16 Atlantic Fleet
1909 Cage foremast fitted
1911 Cage mainmast fitted
1914 Mexico
World War 1: Atlantic Fleet
1919 Made four voyages as troop transport
1919-20 Pacific Fleet
1920 July 2: Decommissioned
1923 November 30: Sold and broken up

Neptune, see ***Manhattan***

Nomenclature: Roman god of the sea

Nevada (BM-9)

Type: Monitor
Class: 'Arkansas' (1898)
Nomenclature: 36th state of the Union, admitted 1864

History:
1899 April 17: Laid down by Bath as ***Connecticut***
1900 November 24: Launched
1901 January: Renamed ***Nevada***
1903 March 5: Completed
1903-13 Atlantic
1909 March 2: Renamed ***Tonopah***
1913 Converted to submarine tender
World War 1: US east coast, Bermuda, Azores
1919 Decommissioned
1922 January 26: Sold and broken up

Nevada (BB-36)

Type: Dreadnought
Class: 'Nevada' (1911)

History:
1912 November 4: Laid down by Fore River
1914 July 11: Launched
1916 March 11: Completed
1916-24 Atlantic Fleet
World War 1: 1918 Ireland
1925-41 Pacific Fleet
1927-30 Reconstructed at Norfolk, cagemasts replaced by tripods, secondary armament raised one deck, catapults added on stern and 'X' turret, bulges fitted
1941 December 7: Beached at Pearl Harbor and severely damaged by torpedo and five bombs (50 dead)
1942 February 12: Refloated, reconstructed at Bremerton; mainmast removed, cap added to funnel, new secondary armament in turrets added, AA armament increased
World War 2: Pearl Harbor, Attu, Normandy, Southern France, Iwo Jima, 1945 Raids on Japan
1945 March 27: Damaged by kamikaze off Okinawa
1945 April 5: Hit by shore batteries at Okinawa
1946 July: Target vessel, Bikini nuclear tests
1946 August 29: Decommissioned
1948 July 31: Sunk as target by aircraft and gunfire off Hawaii

New Hampshire (BB-25)

Type: Pre-dreadnought

Left:
***New Hampshire* (BB-25) — 'Connecticut' class pre-dreadnought, c1910. The only one of its class with casings halfway up funnels.**

Below left:
***New Ironsides* — Broadside ship of 1861, seen in 1864.** *US Naval Historical Centre*

Below:
***New Jersey* (BB-62) — 'Iowa' class battleship, 1954.** *Real Photographs*

Bottom:
***New York* (CA-2) — Armoured cruiser, 1895, shortly after completion.** *IWM*

Class: 'Connecticut' (1902)
Nomenclature: One of the original 13 states

History:
1905 May 1: Laid down by New York Sbdg
1906 June 30: Launched
1908 March 19: Completed
1908-16 Atlantic Fleet
1910 Cage foremast fitted, mainmast fitted later same year
1914 Mexico
World War 1: Atlantic Fleet
1919 Made four voyages as troop transport
1921 May 21: Decommissioned
1923 November 1: Sold and broken up at Baltimore

New Hampshire (BB-70)

Type: Battleship
Class: 'Montana' (1940)

History:
1940 September 9: Ordered from Brooklyn
1943 July 21: Contract cancelled

New Ironsides

Type: Broadside Ship
Class: 'New Ironsides' (1861)
Nomenclature: A reference to 'Old Ironsides', sobriquet of the frigate *Constitution* of 1797

History:
1861 Laid down by Cramp
1862 May 10: Launched
1862 August 21: Completed
Civil War: 1862-64 S Atlantic BS, 1864 N Atlantic BS, Attacks on Charleston 1863, Fort Fisher
1863 September 8: Hit 50 times during attack on Fort Moultrie
1863 October 5: Hit by spar torpedo of Confederate torpedo boat *David* off Charleston, not damaged
1865 April 8: Decommissioned
1866 December 15: Burned and sank at League Island, Pa

New Jersey (BB-16)

Type: Pre-dreadnought
Class: 'Virginia' (1899)
Nomenclature: One of the original 13 states

History:
1902 April 2: Laid down by Fore River
1904 November 10: Launched
1906 May 12: Completed
1906-07 Atlantic Fleet
1907-09 Great White Fleet
1909 Refit, cagemasts fitted
1914 Mexico
World War 1: Training ship
1919 Made four voyages as troop transport
1920 August 6: Decommissioned
1922 July 12: Stricken
1923 September 5: Sunk as Army aircraft target off Diamond Shoals, NC

New Jersey (BB-62)

Type: Battleship
Class: 'Iowa' (1939)

History:
1940 September 16: Laid down at Philadelphia
1942 December 7: Launched
1943 May 23: Completed
World War 2: Kwajalein, Eniwetok, 1944 Raids on Truk and Palau; Hollandia, Saipan, Philippine Sea, Guam, Palau, 1944 Raids on Luzon and Taiwan; Leyte, 1945 Raids on Luzon, China coast and Taiwan; Iwo Jima, Okinawa
1946-48 Atlantic Fleet
1948 June 30: Decommissioned
1950 November 21: Recommissioned
1951-52 Korea
1952-57 Atlantic Fleet
1957 August 21: Decommissioned
1968 Refit; AA guns removed, helicopter landing pad fitted, tower foremast modified
1968 April 6: Recommissioned
1968-69 Vietnam
1969 December 17: Decommissioned
1981 August: Arrived at Long Beach for reactivation
1982 December 28: Recommissioned
1983 Lebanon

New Mexico (BB-40)

Type: Dreadnought
Class: 'New Mexico' (1914)
Nomenclature: 47th state of the Union, admitted 1912

History:
1915 October 14: Laid down at Brooklyn as ***California***
1916 March 22: Renamed ***New Mexico***
1917 April 23: Launched
1918 May 20: Completed
1919-41 Pacific Fleet
1931-33 Reconstructed at Philadelphia; cagemasts removed, tower structure added, AA armament increased, re-engined and reboilered, bulges fitted
1941 Atlantic Fleet
World War 2: Attu, Gilbert Islands, Kwajalein, Saipan, Guam, Leyte, Lingayen, Okinawa
1945 January 6: Damaged by kamikaze at Lingayen; British observer Lt Gen Herbert Lumsden killed (31 dead)
1945 May 12: Damaged by kamikaze and bomb off Okinawa (54 dead)
1946 July 19: Decommissioned
1947 February 25: Stricken
1947 November 9: Sold and broken up at Newark

New York (CA-2)

Type: Armoured Cruiser
Class: 'New York' (1888)
Nomenclature: One of the original 13 states

History:
1890 September 19: Laid down by Cramp
1891 December 2: Launched
1893 August 1: Completed
1894 South Atlantic
1895 Europe
1896-98 Atlantic Fleet
1898 Operations off Cuba
1901-03 Asiatic Squadron
1903-05 Pacific Squadron
1905 Reconstructed
1910-16 Asiatic Fleet
1911 February 16: Renamed ***Saratoga***
World War 1: Atlantic convoys
1917 December 1: Renamed ***Rochester***
1919 Made five voyages as troop transport
1923-31 Caribbean and Central America
1932 Reconstructed; one funnel and eight boilers removed
1932-33 Asiatic Fleet
1933 April 29: Decommissioned
1938 October 28: Stricken
1941 December 24: Hulk scuttled as a blockship in Subic Bay, Luzon to prevent capture by the Japanese

New York (BB-34)

Type: Dreadnought
Class: 'New York' (1910)

History:
1911 September 11: Laid down at Brooklyn
1912 October: 30: Launched
1914 April 15: Completed
1914 Mexico
1914-19 Atlantic Fleet
World War 1: 1917-18 Grand Fleet
1919-36 Pacific Fleet
1926 Reconstructed at Norfolk; cagemasts replaced by tripods
1936-41 Atlantic Fleet
1939 Carried first experimental shipborne radar
World War 2: Atlantic convoys, North Africa, Iwo Jima, Okinawa
1945 February 18: In collision with headquarters ship *Estes* off Iwo Jima
1945 April 14: Slightly damaged by kamikaze off Okinawa
1946 July: Target vessel, Bikini nuclear tests
1946 August 29: Decommissioned
1948 July 8: Sunk as target by aircraft off Hawaii

Nimitz (CVAN-68)

Type: Aircraft Carrier
Class: 'Nimitz' (1967)
Nomenclature: Chester William Nimitz (1885-1966), fleet admiral, commander of US forces in the Pacific during World War 2

History:
1968 June 22: Laid down by Newport News
1972 May 13: Launched
1975 May 3: Completed
1975 —— Atlantic Fleet
1975 June 30: Reclassified CVN-68
1980 Indian Ocean

North Carolina (CA-12)

Type: Armoured Cruiser
Class: 'Tennessee' (1902)
Nomenclature: One of the original 13 states

History:
1905 March 21: Laid down by Newport News

Top right:
New York **(BB-34) — Battleship, 1945, with wartime modifications.**

Centre right:
New York **(BB-34) — Direct overhead view, 1918.**

Bottom right:
Nimitz **(CVN-68) — Nuclear-powered aircraft carrier, c1978.** *Michael D. J. Lennon*

68

Oklahoma **(BB-37) — 'Nevada' class battleship, June 1936.** *Wright & Logan*

1906 October 6: Launched
1908 May 7: Completed
1908-15 Atlantic Fleet and Mediterranean
1912 Refit, foremast replaced by cagemast
1915 November 5: First ship to launch an airplane from catapult while underway
World War 1: Atlantic convoys
1919 Made six voyages as troop transport
1920-21 Pacific
1920 June 7: Renamed ***Charlotte***
1921 February 18: Decommissioned
1930 July 15: Stricken
1930 September 29: Sold and broken up

North Carolina (BB-52)

Type: Dreadnought
Class: 'South Dakota' (1917)

History:
1920 January 12: Laid down at Norfolk
1922 February 8: Contract cancelled when 36.5% complete

North Carolina (BB-55)

Type: Battleship
Class: 'North Carolina' (1937)

History:
1937 October 27: Laid down at Brooklyn
1940 June 13: Launched
1941 April 9: Completed
1941 Atlantic Fleet
World War 2: Guadalcanal-Tulagi, Eastern Solomons, Gilbert Islands, Kwajalein, 1944 Raids on Truk and Palau; Hollandia, Saipan, Philippine Sea, 1944 Raids on Luzon, Taiwan and China coast; 1945 Raids on Kyushu and Ryukyus; Iwo Jima, Okinawa, 1945 Raids on Japan
1942 September 15: Torpedoed by Japanese submarine *I19* near Espiritu Santo
1945 April 6: Hit by friendly gunfire off Okinawa
1947 June 27: Decommissioned
1960 June 1: Stricken
1961 September 6: Transferred to state of North Carolina and preserved as a memorial at Wilmington

North Dakota (BB-29)

Type: Dreadnought
Class: 'Delaware' (1906)

Nomenclature: 44th state of the Union, admitted 1889

History:
1907 December 16: Laid down by Fore River
1908 November 10: Launched
1910 April 11: Completed
1910-17 Atlantic Fleet
1914 Mexico
World War 1: Atlantic Fleet
1916-17 Re-engined
1917-18 Gunnery training ship
1919 Made two voyages as troop transport
1920 Refit
1923 November: Decommissioned
1924 May 28: Converted to mobile target ship
1931 January 7: Stricken
1931 March 16: Sold and broken up at Boston

Ohio (BB-12)

Type: Pre-dreadnought
Class: 'Maine' (1898)
Nomenclature: 17th state of the Union, admitted 1803

History:
1899 April 22: Laid down by Union
1901 May 18: Launched
1904 October 4: Completed
1905-07 Asiatic Fleet
1907-09 Great White Fleet
1909 Cage foremast fitted
1911 Cage mainmast fitted
1911-14 Atlantic Fleet
1914 Mexico
World War 1: Atlantic Fleet
1922 May 31: Decommissioned
1923 March 24: Sold and broken up

Ohio (BB-68)

Type: Battleship
Class: 'Montana' (1940)

History:
1940 September 9: Ordered from Philadelphia; never laid down
1943 July 21: Contract cancelled

Oklahoma (BB-37)

Type: Dreadnought
Class: 'Nevada' (1911)
Nomenclature: 46th state of the Union, admitted 1907

History:
1912 October 26: Laid down by New York Sbdg
1914 March 23: Launched
1915 July 19: Damaged by fire while fitting out at Camden
1916 May 2: Completed
1916-21 Atlantic Fleet
World War 1: 1918 Ireland
1921-41 Pacific Fleet
1927-29 Reconstructed at Philadelphia; cagemasts replaced by tripods, secondary armament raised one deck, catapults added on stern and 'X' turret, bulges fitted
1936 Rescued refugees from Civil War in Spain
1941 December 7: Hit by five torpedoes from Japanese aircraft at Pearl Harbor and capsized (415 dead)
1944 February 11: Refloated, not repaired
1944 November 22: Stricken
1946 December 5: Sold for breaking up
1947 May 17: Foundered in tow 540 miles east of Pearl Harbor

Oneota

Type: Monitor
Class: 'Canonicus' (1862)
Nomenclature: A tribe of Sioux Indians of present-day Nebraska

History:
1862 Laid down by Swift Evans
1864 May 21: Launched
1865 June 10: Completed but not commissioned
1868 April 2: Sold to Peru, renamed ***Manco Capac***

Onondaga

Type: Monitor
Class: 'Onondaga'(1862)
Nomenclature: Lake in New York

History:
1862 Laid down by Continental
1863 July 29: Launched
1864 March 24: Completed
Civil War: James River
1865 June 8: Decommissioned
1867 March 2: Sold to France

Oregon, see *Quinsigamond*

Oregon (BB-3)

Type: Pre-dreadnought
Class: 'Indiana' (1890)
Nomenclature: 33rd state of the Union, admitted 1859

History:
1891 November 19: Laid down by Union
1893 October 26: Launched
1896 July 15: Completed
1896-98 Pacific
1898 March 19: Sailed from San Francisco for historic voyage around Cape Horn to join the fleet of Cuba

***Onondaga* — Double turret monitor on the James River, 1864.**

1898 Operations off Cuba, Santiago
1899-1901 and 1903-06 Far East
1900 June 28: Went aground off China in Straits of Pechili, repaired at Kure
1910 Refit; cage mainmast fitted, 3" guns added
World War 1: West coast, Convoy escort to Vladivostok
1919 October 4: Decommissioned
1924 January 4: Disarmed, naval relic at Portland, Or (IX-22)
1942 November 2: Stricken
1942 December 7: Sold for breaking up, but retained by navy as ammunition hulk
1944 July: Towed to Guam
1948 November 14: Went adrift in typhoon; December 8 1948 located at sea 500 miles southeast of Guam and towed back
1956 March 15: Sold and broken up in Japan

Oriskany (CV-18), see ***Wasp*** (CV-18)

Oriskany (CV-34)

Type: Aircraft Carrier
Class: Modified 'Essex' (1942)
Nomenclature: Battle of American Revolution in New York, August 6 1777

History:
1944 May 1: Laid down by Brooklyn
1945 October 13: Launched
1947 August 12: Construction suspended
1950 September 25: Completed to modified design
1950-51 Atlantic Fleet and Mediterranean
1951 Refit, flightdeck modified
1952-53 Korea
1952 October 1: Reclassified CVA-34
1953-56 Pacific Fleet
1957-59 Reconstructed at San Francisco, angled flightdeck
1959-76 Pacific Fleet
1966 October 26: Severely damaged by fire in forward hangar deck off Vietnam (44 dead)
1975 July 1: Reclassified CV-34
1976 September 30: Decommissioned

Passaconaway

Type: Monitor
Class: 'Kalamazoo' (1863)
Nomenclature: Mountain in New Hampshire

History:
1863 November 18: Laid down at Portsmouth NYd
1865 November 27: Construction suspended
1869 June 15: Renamed ***Thunderer***
1869 August 10: Renamed ***Massachusetts***
1884 Broken up on stocks

Passaic

Type: Monitor
Class: 'Passaic' (1862)
Nomenclature: River in New Jersey

History:
1862 Laid down by Continental
1862 August 30: Launched
1862 November 25: Completed
Civil War: 1862-65 N Atlantic BS, 1863 Attacks on Charleston
1863 April 6: Damaged by shore batteries at Charleston
1863 August 22: Went around near Fort Wagner
1865 June 16: Decommissioned
1878-82 Receiving ship, Washington
1883-92 Receiving ship, Annapolis
1892-93 Receiving ship, Boston
1895-98 Naval militia training ship
1898 Coast defence, Key West and Pensacola
1899 July 25: Stricken
1899 October 10: Sold and broken up

Patapsco

Type: Monitor
Class: 'Passaic' (1862)
Nomenclature: River in Maryland

History:
1862 Laid down by Harlan & Hollingsworth
1862 September 27: Launched
1863 January 2: Completed
Civil War: 1863-65 N Atlantic BS, 1863 Attacks on Charleston
1865 January 16: Sunk by mine off Charleston (62 dead)

Pennsylvania (CA-4)

Type: Armoured Cruiser
Class: 'Pennsylvania' (1899)
Nomenclature: One of the original 13 states

History:
1901 July: Ordered as ***Nebraska,*** renamed ***Pennsylvania***
1901 August 7: Laid down by Cramp
1903 August 22: Launched
1905 March 9: Completed
1906-07 Asiatic station
1907-11 Pacific Fleet
1909 Refit, foremast replaced by cagemast
1911 January: First airplane landing and take-off on a ship
1912 August 27: Renamed ***Pittsburgh***
1914 Mexico
World War 1: South Atlantic
1919-20 Mediterranean
1922-26 Mediterranean
1926 Refit, one funnel and boilers removed
1927-31 Asiatic Fleet
1931 July 10: Decommissioned
1931 December 21: Sold and broken up at Baltimore

Pennsylvania (BB-14), see ***Nebraska*** (BB-14)

Pennsylvania (BB-38)

Type: Dreadnought
Class: 'Pennsylvania' (1912)

History:
1913 October 27: Laid down by Newport News
1915 March 16: Launched
1916 June 12: Completed
1916-21 Atlantic Fleet (flagship)
World War 1: US east coast
1922-41 Pacific Fleet (flagship)

Above:
***Pittsburgh* (CA-4) — Armoured cruiser, November 1919, formerly *Pennsylvania*.** *IWM*

Below:
***Pennsylvania* (BB-38) — Battleship, after reconstruction, c1935.**

1929-31 Reconstructed at Philadelphia; cagemasts replaced by tripods, secondary battery raised one deck, catapult added on stern, reboilered
World War 2: Pearl Harbor, Attu, Gilbert Islands, Kwajalein, Eniwetok, Saipan, Guam, Palau, Leyte, Surigao Strait, Lingayen
1941 December 7: Damaged by bombs while in drydock at Pearl Harbor
1942 Reconstructed, tripod mainmast removed, new secondary armament in turrets added, AA armament increased
1945 August 12: Severely damaged by Japanese aircraft torpedo in Buckner Bay, Okinawa. Only temporary repairs made following end of the war
1946 July: Target vessel, Bikini nuclear tests
1946 August 24: Decommissioned
1948 February 10: Sunk as target by aircraft off Kwajalein

Philippine Sea (CV-47)

Type: Aircraft Carrier
Class: Modified 'Essex' (1942)
Nomenclature: Naval battle of World War 2 in the Pacific, June 18-19 1944

History:
1944 August 19: Laid down at Quincy as ***Wright***
1945 February 12: Renamed ***Philippine Sea***
1945 September 5: Launched
1946 May 11: Completed
1946-50 Atlantic Fleet
1947 Antarctic
1950-58 Pacific Fleet
1950-53 Korea
1952 October 1: Reclassified CVA-47
1955 November 15: Reclassified CVS-47
1958 December 28: Decommissioned
1959 Reclassified AVT-11, aircraft transport
1969 December 1: Stricken
1970 August: Sold and broken up at Tacoma

Philippines (CB-4)

Type: Battlecruiser
Class: 'Alaska' (1940)
Nomenclature: An archipelago in Southwest Asia, a territory of the US from 1898, independent in 1946

History:
1940 Ordered from New York Sbdg; never laid down
1943 June 24: Contract cancelled

Pittsburgh (CA-4), see ***Pennsylvania*** (CA-4)

Nomenclature: City in Pennsylvania

Princeton (CVL-23)

Type: Light Aircraft Carrier
Class: 'Independence' (1942)
Nomenclature: Battle of the American Revolution in New Jersey, January 2-3 1777

History:
1941 June 2: Laid down by New York Sbdg as light cruiser ***Tallahassee*** (CL-61)
1942 February 16: Reordered as aircraft carrier, renamed ***Princeton***
1942 October 18: Launched
1943 February 25: Completed
World War 2: 1943 Pacific raids, Gilbert Islands, Kwajalein, Eniwetok, 1944 Raids on Palau and Truk; Hollandia, Saipan, Philippine Sea, Guam, Palau, Leyte, 1944 Raids on Luzon and Taiwan
1944 October 24: Sunk by fire and explosions after being damaged by aircraft bombs at Battle of Leyte Gulf

Princeton (CV-37)

Type: Aircraft Carrier
Class: Modified 'Essex' (1942)

History:
1943 September 14: Laid down at Philadelphia as ***Valley Forge***
1944 November 20: Renamed ***Princeton***
1945 July 8: Launched
1945 November 18: Completed
1945-46 Atlantic Fleet
1946-48 Pacific Fleet
1949 June 20: Decommissioned
1950 August 28: Recommissioned
1950-53 Korea
1952 October 1: Reclassified CVA-37
1953-59 Pacific Fleet
1954 January 1: Reclassified CVS-37
1959 March 2: Reclassified LPH-5, amphibious assault ship
1959-70 Pacific Fleet, Vietnam
1970 January 30: Stricken
1971 April 7: Sold and broken up at Portland, Oregon

Pueblo (CA-7), see ***Colorado*** (CA-7)

Nomenclature: City in Colorado

Puerto Rico (CB-5)

Type: Battlecruiser
Class: 'Alaska' (1940)
Nomenclature: Island in the West Indies, US territory acquired 1898

History:
1940 Ordered from New York Sbdg; never laid down
1943 June 24: Contract cancelled

Puritan

Type: Monitor
Class: 'Puritan' (1862)
Nomenclature: One of a group which founded Massachusetts

History:
1862 Laid down by Continental
1864 July 2: Launched
1865 Not completed because of delay in casting guns
1874 Broken up

Puritan (BM-1)

Type: Monitor
Class: 'Puritan' (1874)

History:
1875 Laid down by John Roach
1882 December 6: Launched
1896 December 10: Completed at Brooklyn
1898 Operations off Cuba
1904-08 Naval militia training ship
1905 June 14: Went aground off Point Lookout
1910 April 23: Decommissioned
1913 February 27: Stricken, target hulk as target 'B'
1922 January 26: Sold

Quinsigamond

Type: Monitor
Class: 'Kalamazoo' (1863)
Nomenclature: Lake in Massachusetts

History:
1864 April 15: Laid down at Boston
1865 November 27: Construction suspended
1869 June 15: Renamed ***Hercules***
1869 August 10: Renamed ***Oregon***
1884 Broken up on stocks

Randolph (CV-15)

Type: Aircraft Carrier
Class: Modified 'Essex' (1942)
Nomenclature: A frigate of the Continental navy, 1776; Peyton Randolph (1721-1775), first President of the Continental congress

History:
1943 May 10: Laid down by Newport News
1944 June 29: Launched
1944 October 9: Completed
World War 2: Iwo Jima, Okinawa, 1945 Raids on Japan
1945 March 11: Damaged by kamikaze at Ulithi
1948 February 25: Decommissioned
1952 October 1: Reclassified CVA-15
1952-53 Refit, hydraulic catapults fitted
1953 July 1: Recommissioned
1953-55 Mediterranean
1955-56 Reconstructed at Norfolk, angled flightdeck
1956-59 Mediterranean
1959 March 31: Reclassified CVS-15
1961 FRAM II refit
1959-69 Atlantic and Mediterranean
1969 February 13: Decommissioned
1973 June 1: Stricken
1975 May 14: Sold and broken up

Ranger (CC-4)

Type: Battlecruiser
Class: 'Lexington' (1916)
Nomenclature: A sloop of the Continental navy, 1777

History:
1917 Ordered as ***Lexington***
1917 December 10: Renamed ***Ranger***
1921 January 23: Laid down by Newport News
1922 August 2: Construction suspended when 4% complete
1923 August 17: Contract cancelled

Ranger (CC-5), see *Constitution* (CC-5)

Ranger (CV-4)

Type: Aircraft Carrier
Class: 'Ranger' (1930)

History:
1931 September 26: Laid down by Newport News
1933 February 25: Launched
1934 June 4: Completed
1935-39 Pacific Fleet
1939 July 12: Damaged by fire at Norfolk, Va
1939-41 Atlantic Fleet
World War 2: North Africa, 1943 Raid on Norway, Atlantic convoys
1944-45 Training operations, Hawaii
1946 October 18: Decommissioned
1947 January 3: Sold and broken up at Chester, Pa

Ranger (CVA-61)

Type: Aircraft Carrier
Class: 'Forrestal' (1951)

History:
1954 August 2: Laid down by Newport News
1956 September 29: Launched
1957 August 10: Completed
1957-58 Atlantic Fleet
1958-—— Pacific Fleet
1963 April 5: Damaged by boiler explosion off Japan
1972 Summer: Damaged by sabotage
1975 July 1: Reclassified CV-61
1979 April 5: In collision with Liberian tanker *Fortune* off Singapore

Reprisal (CV-30), see *San Jacinto* (CV-30)

Reprisal (CV-35)

Type: Aircraft Carrier
Class: Modified 'Essex' (1942)
Nomenclature: A brig of the Continental navy, 1776

History:
1944 July 1: Laid down at Brooklyn
1945 August 12: Construction cancelled when 52.3% complete
1945 Launched to clear slip
—— Hull used as experimental hulk and target
1949 August 2: Sold and broken up at Baltimore

Rhode Island (BB-17)

Type: Pre-dreadnought
Class: 'Virginia' (1899)
Nomenclature: One of the original 13 states

History:
1902 May 1: Laid down by Fore River
1904 May 17: Launched
1906 February 19: Completed
1906-07 Atlantic Fleet
1906 May 6: Went aground on York Spit
1907-09 Great White Fleet
1909-14 Atlantic Fleet
1909 Refit, cage foremast fitted

1911 Cage mainmast fitted
1914 Mexico
World War 1: Atlantic Fleet
1919 Made five voyages as troop transport
1919-20 Pacific Fleet
1920 June 30: Decommissioned
1923 November 1: Sold and broken up at Oakland

Roanoke

Type: Monitor
Class: 'Roanoke' (1862)
Nomenclature: A city in Virginia

History:
—— Laid down at Norfolk as a screw frigate
1855 December 13: Launched
1857 May 4: Completed
1862 March 25: Decommissioned for conversion to monitor
1862 December: Conversion commenced by Novelty Iron Works
1863 June 26: Completed
Civil War: Harbour defence, Hampton Roads
1865 June 25: Decommissioned
1874-75 Recommissioned
1883 September 24: Sold and broken up

Rochester (CA-2), see ***New York*** (CA-2)

Nomenclature: City in New York State

Saipan (CVL-48)

Type: Light Aircraft Carrier
Class: 'Saipan' (1942)
Nomenclature: Island in the Marianas Islands, scene of amphibious operation, June 15 1944

History:
1944 July 10: Laid down by New York Sbdg
1945 July 8: Launched
1946 July 14: Completed
1947-53 Atlantic Fleet
1953-57 Pacific Fleet
1957 October 3: Decommissioned
1959 May 15: Reclassified AVT-6, aircraft transport
1963-66 Converted to command ship
1964 Conversion cancelled, 65% complete
1964 January 1: Reclassified CC-3
1964 August 21: Reclassified AGMR-2
1964 September 1: Renamed ***Arlington***
1966 August 27: Recommissioned as communications relay ship
1966-70 Pacific Fleet, Vietnam
1970 January 14: Decommissioned
1975 August 15: Stricken

Samoa (CB-6)

Type: Battlecruiser
Class: 'Alaska' (1940)
Nomenclature: Islands in Southern Pacific, acquired 1899

History:
1940 Ordered from New York Sbdg, never laid down
1943 June 24: Contract cancelled

San Diego (CA-6), see ***California*** (CA-6)

Nomenclature: City in California

San Jacinto (CVL-30)

Type: Light Aircraft Carrier
Class: 'Independence' (1942)
Nomenclature: Battle in the Texan War for Independence, April 211836

History:
1940 Ordered as light cruiser ***Newark*** (CL-100)
1942 June 23: Reordered as aircraft carrier, renamed ***Reprisal***
1942 October 26: Laid down by New York Sbdg
1943 January 6: Renamed ***San Jacinto***
1943 September 26: Launched
1943 December 15: Completed
World War 2: Saipan, Philippine Sea, Guam, Palau, 1944 Raids on Luzon and Taiwan; 1945 Raids on Luzon, Taiwan and China coast; Iwo Jima, Okinawa, 1945 Raids on Japan
1944 December 18: Damaged in typhoon in Philippine Sea
1945 February 27: Damaged in collision with oiler *Merrimack* off Iwo Jima
1945 June 5: Damaged in typhoon in Philippine Sea
1947 March 1: Decommissioned
1959 May 15: Reclassified AVT-5, aircraft transport
1970 June 1: Stricken
1971 December 15: Sold and broken up at Terminal Island

Sangamon

Type: Monitor
Class: 'Passaic' (1942)
Nomenclature: River in Illinois

History:
1862 Laid down by Reaney as ***Conestoga***
1862 September 9: Renamed ***Sangamon***
1862 October 27: Launched
1863 February 9: Completed
Civil War: 1863-64 N Atlantic BS, 1864 S Atlantic BS, 1864-65 James River
1865 Decommissioned
1869 June 15: Renamed ***Jason***
1898 Harbour defence, Philadelphia
1904 April 16: Sold and broken up

Saratoga (CA-2), see ***New York*** (CA-2)

Saratoga (CC-3) (CV-3)

Type: 1) Battlecruiser, 2) Aircraft Carrier
Class: 1) 'Lexington' (1916), 2) 'Lexington' (1922)
Nomenclature: Battle of the American Revolution, in New York, October 17 1777

History:
1920 September 25: Laid down by New York Sbdg as battlecruiser
1922 July 1: Reordered as aircraft carrier CV-3, when 35.4% complete
1925 April 7: Launched

Saratoga (CV-3) — Aircraft carrier of 'Lexington' class. Note recognition stripe on funnel and 'SARA' on flightdeck aft.

1927 November 16: Completed
1928-41 Pacific Fleet
1941 Refit, flightdeck widened
World War 2: Guadalcanal-Tulagi, Eastern Solomons, 1943 Rabaul raids, Gilbert Islands, Kwajalein, Eniwetok, 1944 British Eastern Fleet (Indian Ocean), Sabang raid, Iwo Jima
1942 Refit, funnel cut down, 8" guns removed
1942 January 11: Torpedoed by Japanese submarine *I16* 500 miles southwest of Oahu
1942 August 31: Torpedoed by Japanese submarine *I26* southeast of Guadalcanal, towed to Tonga
1944 Refit, hull modified, bulge added to port side
1945 February 21: Severely damaged when hit by four kamikazes off Iwo Jima (123 dead)
1946 Target vessel, Bikini atomic tests
1946 July 25: Sunk as result of second atomic explosion

Saratoga (CVA-60)

Type: Aircraft Carrier
Class: 'Forrestal' (1951)

History:
1952 December 16: Laid down at Brooklyn
1955 October 8: Launched
1956 April 14: Completed
1957-72 Atlantic Fleet
1961 January 23: Damaged by fire in eastern Mediterranean
1968 Refit
1972 June 30: Reclassified CV-60
1972-73 Pacific Fleet
1972 October 29: Damaged by fire at Singapore
1973-80 Atlantic Fleet and Mediterranean
1973 September 22: Damaged by fire on hangar deck at Norfolk
1977 October 6: In collision with freighter *Ville d'Orient* in Straits of Messina
1980 October: Refit at Philadelphia
1983 February 1: Recommissioned

Saugus

Type: Monitor
Class: 'Canonicus' (1862)
Nomenclature: Town in Massachusetts

History:
1862 Laid down by Harlan & Hollingsworth
1863 December 16: Launched
1864 April 7: Completed
Civil War: 1864 James River, 1865 S Atlantic BS, Fort Fisher
1865 January 12: 15" gun exploded during operations at Fort Fisher
1865 June 13: Decommissioned
1869-77 Recommissioned
1869 June 15: Renamed ***Centaur***
1869 August 10: Renamed ***Saugus***
1871 Refit
1890 November 24: Stricken
1891 March 25: Sold and broken up

Scylla, see *Canonicus*

Nomenclature: Greek myth: a monster inhabiting a rock in the Straits of Messina

Seattle (CA-11), see *Washington* (CA-11)

Nomenclature: City in Washington

Shackamaxon

Type: Monitor
Class: 'Kalamazoo' (1863)
Nomenclature: Village of the Delaware Indians in Pennsylvania

History:

1863 Laid down at Philadelphia

1865 November 27: Construction suspended
1869 June 15: Renamed ***Hecla***
1869 August 10: Renamed ***Nebraska***
1874 Broken up on stocks

Shangri-La (CV-38)

Type: Aircraft Carrier
Class: Modified 'Essex' (1942)
Nomenclature: A fictitious kingdom in the Himalayas supposed to be the source of US bombers which attacked Tokyo, April 18 1942

History:
1943 January 15: Laid down at Norfolk
1944 February 24: Launched
1944 September 15: Completed
World War 2: Okinawa, 1945 Raids on Japan
1945-47 Pacific Fleet
1947 November 7: Decommissioned
1951 May 10: Recommissioned
1952 October 1: Reclassified CVA-38
1953-55 Reconstructed at Bremerton, steam catapults and angled flight deck fitted
1955-60 Pacific Fleet
1960-70 Atlantic Fleet and Mediterranean
1962 Refit
1969 June 30: Reclassified CVS-38
1970-71 Pacific Fleet, Vietnam
1971 July 30: Decommissioned
1981 July 15: Stricken

South Carolina (BB-26)

Type: Dreadnought
Class: 'South Carolina' (1905)
Nomenclature: One of the original 13 states

History:
1906 December 18: Laid down by Cramp
1908 July 11: Launched
1910 March 1: Completed
1910-17 Atlantic Fleet
1912 Refit
1914 January-April: Occupation of Haiti
1914 Mexico
1914-15 Refit
1916-17 Refit
World War 1: Atlantic Fleet
1917-18 Gunnery training ship
1919 Made four voyages as troop transport
1921 December 15: Decommissioned
1924 January 12: Stricken
1924 April 24: Sold and broken up at Philadelphia

South Dakota (CA-9)

Type: Armoured Cruiser
Class: 'Pennsylvania' (1899)
Nomenclature: 40th state of the Union, admitted 1889

History:
1902 September 20: Laid down by Union
1904 July 21: Launched
1908 January 27: Completed
1908-17 Pacific Fleet
1912 Refit, foremast replaced by cagemast
World War 1: South Atlantic
1919 Made two voyages as troop transport
1919-26 Asiatic station, Siberia
1920 June 7: Renamed ***Huron***
1927 June 17: Decommissioned
1929 November 13: Stricken
1930 February 11: Sold and broken up

South Dakota (BB-49)

Type: Dreadnought
Class: 'South Dakota' (1917)

History:
1920 March 15: Laid down at Brooklyn
1922 February 8: Construction cancelled when 38.5% complete

South Dakota (BB-57)

Type: Battleship
Class: 'South Dakota' (1938)

History:
1939 July 5: Laid down by New York Sbdg
1941 June 7: Launched
1942 March 20: Completed
World War 2: Santa Cruz, Guadalcanal battle, Gilbert Islands, Kwajalein, 1944 Raids on Truk and Palau; Hollandia, Saipan, Philippine Sea, Leyte, 1944 Raids on Luzon and Ryukyus; 1945 Raids on Luzon, China coast and Ryukyus; Iwo Jima, Okinawa, 1945 Raids on Japan
1942 September 6: Struck uncharted rock in Tonga Islands and damaged hull
1942 October 26: Hit by a bomb in 'A' turret at Battle of Santa Cruz
1942 October 30: Damaged in collision with destroyer *Mahan*
1942 November 15: Damaged by gunfire at Battle of Guadalcanal (38 dead)
1944 June 19: Hit by aircraft bomb off Saipan (27 dead)
1945 May 6: Damaged by powder explosion in turret
1947 January 31: Decommissioned
1962 October 24: Sold and broken up at Kearny

Tallahassee (BM-9), see ***Florida*** (BM-9)

Nomenclature: City in Florida

Tarawa (CV-40)

Type: Aircraft Carrier
Class: Modified 'Essex' (1942)
Nomenclature: Island in the Gilbert Islands, battle of World War 2, November 21-24 1943

History:
1944 March 1: Laid down at Norfolk
1945 May 12: Launched
1945 December 8: Completed
1946-49 Pacific
1949 June 30: Decommissioned
1951 February 3: Recommissioned
1952 October 1: Reclassified CVA-40
1952-54 Atlantic
1955 Refit, converted for ASW
1955 January 10: Reclassified CVS-40
1955-60 Atlantic
1960 May 1: Decommissioned
1961 May 1: Reclassified AVT-12, aircraft transport

***Huron* (CA-9) — Armoured cruiser of 'Pennsylvania' class, formerly *South Dakota*, March 1923, in the Far East.** *P. A. Vicary*

1967 June 1: Stricken
1968 October 3: Sold and broken up at Baltimore

Tecumseh

Type: Monitor
Class: 'Canonicus' (1862)
Nomenclature: Indian chief of the Shawnee tribe (1768-1813)

History:
1862 Laid down by Secor
1863 September 12: Launched
1864 April 19: Completed
Civil War: 1864 James River; Mobile Bay
1864 August 5: Sunk by mine during Battle of Mobile Bay (93 dead)

Tennessee (CA-10)

Type: Armoured Cruiser
Class: 'Tennessee' (1902)
Nomenclature: 16th state of the Union, admitted 1796

History:
1903 June 20: Laid down by Cramp
1904 December 3: Launched
1906 July 17: Completed
1907 European Squadron
1908-10 Pacific
1912 Refit, foremast replaced by cagemast
1912-13 Mediterranean
1916 Haiti
1916 May 25: Renamed ***Memphis***
1916 August 29: Driven ashore by tidal wave in Santo Domingo harbour (40 dead)
1922 January 17: Hulk sold
1937 Broken up

Tennessee (BB-43)

Type: Dreadnought
Class: 'Tennessee' (1915)

History:
1917 May 14: Laid down at Brooklyn
1919 April 30: Launched
1920 June 3: Completed
1920 October 30: Damaged by generator explosion at New York
1921-41 Pacific Fleet
1928 Refit, catapult added and new AA armament added
World War 2: Pearl Harbor, Gilbert Islands, Kwajalein, Eniwetok, Saipan, Guam, Palau, Tinian, Leyte, Surigao Strait, Iwo Jima, Okinawa
1941 December 7: Damaged by two bombs at Pearl Harbor
1942 January: Refit at Bremerton; after cagemast removed, AA armament increased
1942 September: Reconstructed at Bremerton
1943 May 7: Recommissioned
1944 June 15: Damaged by shore batteries at Saipan
1944 August: Damaged in collision with battleship *California*
1945 February 17: Hit by shore batteries at Iwo Jima
1945 April 12: Damaged by kamikaze off Okinawa (25 dead)
1947 February 14: Decommissioned
1959 July 10: Sold and broken up at Baltimore

Terror, see *Agamenticus*

Terror (BM-4)

Type: Monitor
Class: 'Amphitrite' (1874)

History:
1874 Laid down by Cramp
1883 March 24: Launched
1887 Delivered and towed to Brooklyn
1896 April 15: Completed
1898 Operations off Cuba and Puerto Rico
1901-05 Training ship
1906 May 8: Decommissioned
1915 December 15: Stricken and used as a target
1921 March 10: Sold after having sunk off Shooter's Island, NY

Texas

Type: Pre-dreadnought
Class: 'Texas' (1886)
Nomenclature: 28th state of the Union, admitted 1845

History:
1889 June 1: Laid down at Norfolk
1892 June 28: Launched
1895 August 15: Completed

***Texas* (BB-35) — Battleship, as reconstructed, 1941. *New York* lacked top level of foremast.** *Ted Stone*

1898 Operations off Cuba, Santiago
1902 November 29: Damaged by turret explosion
1908 Receiving ship, Charleston
1911 February 16: Renamed ***San Marcos,*** converted to target ship
1911 March 22: Sunk as target off Tangier Island, Md
1924 March: Hulk sold

Texas (BB-35)

Type: Dreadnought
Class: 'New York' (1910)

History:
1911 April 17: Laid down by Newport News
1912 May 18: Launched
1914 March 12: Completed
1914 Mexico
1914-19 Atlantic Fleet
World War 1: 1918 Grand Fleet
1917 September 27: Went aground on Block Island, NY
1919-24 Pacific Fleet
1925-26 Reconstructed at Norfolk; cagemasts replaced by tripods, mainmast resited further aft, single funnel replaced two, catapult added to 'Q' turret, casemate guns raised one deck, reboilered
1923 September 13: In collision with freighter *Steel Seafarer* off west coast of US
1927-44 Atlantic Fleet
1928 January: Carried President Hoover to Cuba
World War 2: Atlantic convoys, North Africa, Normandy, Southern France, Iwo Jima, Okinawa
1944 June 25: Damaged by shore batteries off Cherbourg
1948 April 21: Stricken; preserved as a memorial at Galveston, Tx

Theodore Roosevelt (CVN-71)

Type: Aircraft Carrier
Class: 'Nimitz' (1967)
Nomenclature: Theodore Roosevelt (1858-1919), President of the US

History:
1981 October 31: Laid down by Newport News

Thunderer, see *Passaconaway*

Nomenclature: A name for Zeus

Ticonderoga (CV-14)

Type: Aircraft Carrier
Class: Modified 'Essex' (1942)
Nomenclature: Fort near Lake Champlain captured 1775

History:
1943 February 1: Laid down by Newport News as ***Hancock***
1943 May 1: Renamed ***Ticonderoga***
1944 February 7: Launched

1944 May 8: Completed
World War 2: Palau, 1944 Raids on Philippines; Luzon; 1945 Raids on Formosa, Luzon and China; Okinawa, 1945 Raids on Japan
1945 January 21: Severely damaged by kamikazes in South China Sea
1947 January 9: Decommissioned
1952 October 1: Reclassified CVA-14
1952-54 Refit at Brooklyn; steam catapults fitted
1954 April: Recommissioned
1954-55 Atlantic Fleet and Mediterranean
1955-57 Reconstructed at Norfolk, angled flightdeck
1957 April: Recommissioned
1957-73 Pacific Fleet
1969 October 21: Reclassified CVS-14
1973 November 16: Stricken
1974 Sold and broken up at Portland, Or

Ticonderoga (CV-19), see ***Hancock*** (CV-19)

Tippecanoe

Type: Monitor
Class: 'Canonicus' (1862)
Nomenclature: River in Indiana

History:
1862 September 22: Laid down by Greenwood
1864 December 22: Launched
1866 February 15: Completed, not commissioned, laid up at New Orleans
1869 June 15: Renamed ***Vesuvius***
1869 August 10: Renamed ***Wyandotte***
1872-74 Rebuilt
1876 January 24: First commissioned
1885 Laid up
1898 April 30: Recommissioned
1898 December 6: Stricken
1899 January 17: Sold and broken up

Tonawanda

Type: Monitor
Class: 'Miantonomoh' (1862)
Nomenclature: Town in New York

History:
1863 Laid down at Philadelphia
1864 May 6: Launched
1865 October 12: Completed
1866-72 Training ship, Annapolis
1869 June 15: Renamed ***Amphitrite***
1874 Broken up at Wilmington, De

Tonopah (BM-8), see ***Nevada*** (BM-8)

Nomenclature: City in Nevada

United States (CC-6)

Type: Battlecruiser
Class: 'Lexington' (1916)
Nomenclature: Frigate of 1797

History:
1920 September 25: Laid down at Philadelphia
1922 August 2: Construction suspended when 12.1% complete
1923 August 25: Contract cancelled

United States (CVA-58)

Type: Aircraft Carrier
Class: 'United States' (1948)

History:
1949 April 18: Laid down by Newport News
1949 April 23: Contract cancelled

Utah (BB-31)

Type: Dreadnought
Class: 'Florida' (1908)
Nomenclature: 45th state of the Union, admitted 1896

History:
1909 March 15: Laid down by New York Sbdg
1909 December 23: Launched
1911 August 31: Completed
1911-31 Atlantic Fleet
1914 Mexico
World War 1: 1918 Ireland
1921 US Fleet, Europe (flag)
1926 Refit at Boston; cage mainmast replaced by pole, re-engined

1928 Carried President-elect Hoover to Brazil
1931 January 7: Reclassified AG-16, converted to target ship, armament removed
1941 December 7: Capsized after being torpedoed by Japanese aircraft at Pearl Harbor (58 dead)

Valley Forge (CV-37), see *Princeton* (CV-37)

Valley Forge (CV-45)

Type: Aircraft Carrier
Class: 'Modified Essex' (1940)
Nomenclature: Winter headquarters of Washington's army, 1777-78

History:
1944 September 7: Laid down at Philadelphia
1945 November 18: Launched
1946 November 3: Completed
1947 June 11: Damaged by explosion at Philadelphia following shakedown cruise
1947-53 Pacific Fleet
1950-53 Korea
1952 October 1: Reclassified CVA-45
1954 November 1: Reclassified CVS-45
1954-61 Atlantic Fleet and Mediterranean
1961 July 1: Reclassified LPH-8, amphibious assault ship
1964-69 Vietnam
1970 January 15: Stricken
1971 October 29: Sold and broken up

Vermont (BB-20)

Type: Pre-dreadnought
Class: 'Connecticut' (1902)
Nomenclature: 14th state of the Union, admitted 1790

History:
1904 May 21: Laid down by Fore River
1905 August 31: Launched

Above:
***Utah* (BB-31) — Dreadnought, as seen from the air, c1920.** *N. Moser*

Above right:
***Valley Forge* (CVS-45) — 'Essex' class aircraft carrier, c1958, virtually unchanged from original appearance.**

Right:
***Vermont* (BB-20) — 'Connecticut' class pre-dreadnought, at Auckland 1908.**

1907 March 4: Completed
1907 Atlantic Fleet
1907-09 Great White Fleet
1911 Refit, cagemasts fitted
1914 Mexico
World War 1: Training ship
1919 Made four voyages as troop transport
1920-21 Pacific Fleet
1923 November 9: Stricken
1923 November 30: Sold and broken up

Vesuvius, see *Tippecanoe*

Nomenclature: Volcano in the Bay of Naples

Virgina (BB-13)

Type: Pre-dreadnought
Class: 'Virginia' (1899)
Nomenclature: One of the original 13 states

History:
1902 May 21: Laid down by Newport News
1904 April 5: Launched
1906 May 7: Completed
1906 November 3: In collision with merchant ship *Monroe* in Hampton Roads
1907-09 Great White Fleet
1909 Cage foremast fitted
1911 Refit, cage mainmast fitted

1914 Mexico
1916 Reboilered
World War 1: Training and convoy escort
1919 Made five voyages as troop transport
1920 August 13: Decommissioned
1923 September 5: Sunk as target by army aircraft off Diamond Shoals, NC

Washington (CA-11)

Type: Armoured Cruiser
Class: 'Tennessee' (1902)
Nomenclature: 42nd state of the Union, admitted 1889

History:
1903 September 23: Laid down by New York Sbdg
1905 March 18: Launched
1906 August 7: Completed
1906-07 Atlantic Fleet
1907-10 Pacific Fleet
1912 Refit, foremast replaced by cagemast
1911-13 Atlantic Fleet
1914 Mexico
1916 November 9: Renamed ***Seattle***
World War 1: Atlantic convoys
1919 Made six voyages as troop transport
1922 Fitted as administrative flagship
1923-27 Flagship US Fleet
1927-41 Receiving ship, New York
1931 July 1: Reclassified IX-39
1946 July 19: Stricken
1946 December 3: Sold and broken up at Baltimore

Washington (BB-47)

Type: Dreadnought

***Virginia* (BB-13) — Pre-dreadnought of 'Virginia' class, 1919.**

Class: 'Colorado' (1916)

History:
1919 June 30: Laid down by New York Sbdg
1921 September 1: Launched
1922 February 8: Construction suspended when 75.9% completed
1924 November 25: Incomplete hull sunk as a target

Washington (BB-56)

Type: Battleship
Class: 'North Carolina' (1937)

***Washington* (BB-56) — 'North Carolina' class battleship, North Atlantic, April 1942.** *IWM*

History:
1938 June 14: Laid down at Philadelphia
1940 June 1: Launched
1941 May 15: Completed
World War 2: 1942 Arctic convoys, Guadalcanal, Guadalcanal battle, Gilbert Islands, Kwajalein, Saipan, Philippine Sea, Guam, 1944 Raids on Palau, Philippines and Formosa; Palau, Leyte, 1945 Raids on Formosa, Luzon, China coast, Kyushu and Japan; Iwo Jima, Okinawa
1942 March 27: Rear-Adm John W. Wilcox lost overboard in North Atlantic
1944 February 2: Damaged in collision with battleship *Indiana* off Kwajalein
1947 June 27: Decommissioned
1960 June 1: Stricken
1961 May 24: Sold and broken up at Newark

Wasp (CV-7)

Type: Aircraft Carrier
Class: 'Wasp' (1934)

Nomenclature: Ship captured and commissioned 1806

History:
1936 April 1: Laid down at Quincy
1939 April 4: Launched
1940 April 25: Completed
1940-41 Atlantic Fleet
World War 2: 1942 Malta, Guadalcanal
1942 April and May: Made two trips ferrying aircraft to Malta
1942 March 17: Rammed destroyer *Stack* in collision in North Atlantic
1942 September 15: Torpedoed and sunk by Japanese submarine *I19* south of Guadalcanal (193 dead)

Wasp (CV-18)

Type: Aircraft Carrier
Class: 'Essex' (1940)

History:
1942 March 18: Laid down at Quincy as ***Oriskany***
1942 November 13: Renamed ***Wasp***
1943 August 17: Launched
1943 November 24: Completed
World War 2: Morotai, Saipan, Philippine Sea, Guam, Palau, 1944 Raids on Philippines; 1945 Raids on Formosa, Luzon, China coast and Japan; Iwo Jima, Okinawa, 1945 Raids on Honshu
1944 June 19: Slightly damaged by aircraft bomb during Battle of the Philippine Sea
1945 March 19: Damaged by aircraft bomb south of Kyushu
1947 February 17: Decommissioned
1949-51 Refit
1951 September 10: Recommissioned

***Wasp* (CVA-18) — 'Essex' class aircraft carrier, after first modernisation.**

1952 April 26: Sank destroyer-minesweeper *Hobson* in collision in North Atlantic
1952 October 1: Reclassified CVA-18
1952-53 Atlantic
1953-55 Pacific
1955 Reconstructed at San Francisco; angled flightdeck fitted
1955-56 Pacific
1956 November 1: Reclassified CVS-18
1957-70 Atlantic and Mediterranean
1967 March 24: Damaged in collision with oiler *Salamonia* off San Juan
1972 July 1: Stricken
1973 May 21: Sold and broken up at Kearny, NJ

Weehawken

Type: Monitor
Class: 'Passaic' (1862)
Nomenclature: Town in New Jersey

History:
1862 June 17: Laid down by Secor
1862 November 5: Launched
1863 January 18: Completed
Civil War: 1863 S Atlantic BS, Attacks on Charleston
1863 June 17: Fought action with Confederate ironclad *Atlanta* which surrendered
1863 September 8: Went aground during reconnaissance of Charleston harbour

***Wasp* (CVA-18) — 'Essex' class aircraft carrier, May 1969, after modernisation, with angled flightdeck.**
G. A. Osbon

1863 December 6: Damaged by shore batteries and foundered off Morris Island in Charleston harbour (31 dead)

West Virginia (CA-5)

Type: Armoured Cruiser
Class: 'Pennsylvania' (1899)
Nomenclature: 35th state of the Union, admitted 1863

History:
1901 September 16: Laid down by Newport News
1903 April 18: Launched
1905 February 23: Completed
1906-08 Asiatic Squadron
1908-14 Pacific Fleet
1911 Foremast replaced by cagemast
1914 Mexico
1916 November 11: Renamed ***Huntington***
1917 Catapult installed for experimental purposes
World War 1: Atlantic convoys
1919 Made six voyages as troop transport
1920 September 1: Decommissioned
1930 August 13: Sold and broken up

West Virginia (BB-48)

Type: Dreadnought
Class: 'Colorado' (1916)

History:
1920 April 12: Laid down by Newport News
1921 November 19: Launched
1923 December 1: Completed
1924 January 16: Went aground in Hampton Roads
1924-41 Pacific Fleet
1930 Refit, catapult added to 'X' turret, AA armament increased
1937 Refit
World War 2: Pearl Harbor, Leyte, Surigao Strait, Lingayen, Iwo Jima, Okinawa
1941 December 7: Sank at moorings after being torpedoed by Japanese aircraft at Pearl Harbor (105 dead)
1942 May: Refloated
1942-44 Reconstructed at Puget Sound NYd; funnels, superstructure and cagemasts replaced by single funnel and massive superstructure, new secondary armament
1944 September: Recommissioned
1945 April 1: Damaged by kamikaze off Okinawa
1947 January 9: Decommissioned
1959 July 23: Sold and broken up at Seattle

Wisconsin (BB-9)

Type: Pre-dreadnought
Class: 'Illinois' (1896)
Nomenclature: 30th state of the Union, admitted 1848

History:
1897 February 9: Laid down by Union
1898 November 26: Launched
1901 February 4: Completed
1901-07 Pacific and Asiatic Fleets
1907-09 Great White Fleet
1909 Refit, cage foremast fitted
1911 Cage mainmast installed
World War 1: Training ship
1920 May 15: Decommissioned
1922 January 26: Sold and broken up

Wisconsin (BB-64)

Type: Battleship
Class: 'Iowa' (1939)

History:
1941 January 25: Laid down at Philadelphia
1943 December 7: Launched
1944 April 16: Completed

World War 2: 1944 Raids on Luzon; 1945 Raids on Luzon, China coast and Taiwan; Iwo Jima, Okinawa, 1945 Raids on Japan
1946-48 Atlantic
1948 July 1: Decommissioned
1951 March 3: Recommissioned
1951-52 Korea
1952 March 15: Hit by shell from shore batteries off Korea
1952-58 Atlantic Fleet
1958 May 7: In collision with destroyer *Eaton* off the Virginia Capes; repaired with bow section of incomplete *Kentucky*
1958 March 8: Decommissioned
1988 Scheduled to recommission

Wright (CV-47), see ***Philippine Sea*** (CV-47)

Wright (CVL-49)

Type: Light Aircraft Carrier
Class: 'Saipan' (1942)
Nomenclature: Wilbur Wright (1867-1912) and Orville Wright (1871-1948), made first successful powered flight 1903

History:
1944 August 21: Laid down by New York Sbdg
1945 September 1: Launched
1947 February 9: Completed
1947-54 Atlantic Fleet
1954-56 Pacific Fleet
1956 March 15: Decommissioned
1959 May 15: Reclassified AVT-7, aircraft transport
1962 September 1: Reclassified CC-2, command ship; converted at Bremerton
1963 May 11: Recommissioned
1970 May 27: Decommissioned
1977 December 1: Stricken

Wyandotte, see ***Tippecanoe***

Nomenclature: Indian tribe of Michigan

Wyoming (BM-10)

Type: Monitor
Class: 'Arkansas' (1898)
Nomenclature: 44th state of the Union, admitted 1890

History:
1899 April 11: Laid down by Union
1900 September 8: Launched
1902 December 8: Completed
1902-10 Pacific
1908 First ship in US Navy converted to oil fuel
1909 January 1: Renamed ***Cheyenne***
1910-13 Naval militia training ship
1913 August: Converted to submarine tender at Bremerton
World War 1: Atlantic Fleet
1919 Mexico
1920-26 Reserve training ship, Baltimore
1921 July 1: Reclassified IX-4 (Unclassified)
1926 June 1: Decommissioned
1937 January 25: Stricken
1939 April 20: Sold and broken up

Wyoming (BB-32)

Type: Dreadnought
Class: 'Wyoming' (1909)

***Wisconsin* (BB-9) — Pre-dreadnought of 'Illinois' class, with cage foremast only, c1910.**

History:
1910 February 9: Laid down by Cramp
1911 May 25: Launched
1912 September 25: Completed
1912-17 Atlantic Fleet
1914 Mexico
World War 1: 1917-18 Grand Fleet
1919-21 Pacific Fleet
1921-31 Atlantic Fleet
1926-27 Reconstructed, cage mainmast removed and replaced by small tripod mast further aft, catapult added to 'P' turret, single funnel replaced two, secondary battery raised one deck, reboilered
1932 April 25: Reclassified AG-17, converted to training ship, three turrets and armour belt removed
1941 November: Gunnery training ship
1944 Remaining turrets removed
1947 August 1: Decommissioned
1947 September 16: Stricken
1947 December 5: Sold and broken up at Newark

Yorktown (CV-5)

Type: Aircraft Carrier
Class: 'Yorktown' (1933)
Nomenclature: Battle of the American Revolution in Virginia, 1781

History:
1934 May 21: Laid down by Newport News
1936 April 4: Launched
1937 September 30: Completed
1939-41 Pacific Fleet
1941 Atlantic Fleet
World War 2: 1942 Pacific raids, Coral Sea, Midway
1942 May 8: Damaged by bombs at Battle of the Coral Sea
1942 June 5: Damaged by bombs at Battle of Midway and torpedoed and sunk two days later by submarine *I-168*

Yorktown (CV-10)

Type: Aircraft Carrier
Class: 'Essex' (1940)

History:
1941 December 1: Laid down by Newport News as ***Bon Homme Richard***
1942 September 26: Renamed ***Yorktown***
1943 January 21: Launched
1943 April 15: Completed
World War 2: 1943 Raids on Marcus and Wake Islands; Gilbert Islands, Kwajalein, 1944 Raids on Truk, Marianas and Palau; Hollandia, Saipan, Philippine Sea, Guam, 1944 Raids on Luzon; 1945 Raids on Luzon, Taiwan, China coast and Ryukyus; Iwo Jima, Okinawa, 1945 Raids on Japan
1945 March 18: Damaged by aircraft bomb off Kyushu
1947 January 9: Decommissioned
1952 October 1: Reclassified CVA-10
1952-53 Refit at Bremerton
1953 February 20: Recommissioned
1953-68 Pacific Fleet
1953 Korea
1955 Reconstructed at Bremerton, angled flightdeck
1957 September 1: Reclassified CVS-10
1966 FRAM II refit
1966-68 Vietnam
1969-70 Atlantic Fleet
1970 June 27: Decommissioned
1973 June 1: Stricken
1975 June 9: Transferred to State of South Carolina for preservation as a memorial

***Wyoming* (BM-10) — Monitor, as completed, later renamed *Cheyenne*.**

Index

Page numbers in italics refer to photographs.

Addenda

'Charles de Gaulle' (France)

Aircraft Carrier: *Charles de Gaulle*
Displacement: 36,000tons
Dimensions: 853(oa) 780′9(wl)×104′4×23 [260(oa) 238wl×31.8×7]
Machinery: Nuclear-powered turbines
SHP = 28knots
Armament: 1 Sadral SAM launcher, 2 Crotale SAM launchers
Class notes: *Charles de Gaulle* to be built at Brest.A second unit, as yet unnamed, is projected. The two units are planned to replace *Foch* and *Clemenceau* in the 1990s.

'Principe de Asturias' (Spain)

Aircraft Carrier: *Principe de Asturias*
Displacement: 14,500tons
Dimensions: 640(oa)×80×22 [195.1(oa)×24.4×6.7]
Machinery: 1 screw, gas turbines
SHP 46,450 = 24knots
Endurance: 7,500/20
Aircraft: 17
Complement: 780
Class notes: Laid down by Bazan, Ferrol 8 October 1979; launched May 1982

'Kiev' class aircraft carrier *Kharkov* in fact named ***Baku*** (see p371 and p377)

New additional unit of Russian 'Kirov' class is named ***Maksim Gorki***